Starting & Running a Business
ALL-IN-ONE

FOR DUMMIES®
2ND EDITION

By Liz Barclay, Colin Barrow, Paul Barrow, Greg Brooks, Ben Carter, Frank Catalano, Peter Economy, Lita Epstein, Kim Gilmour, Alex Hiam, Greg Holden, Jane Kelly, Sarah Laing, Dan Matthews, Ruth Mortimer, Bob Nelson, Steven Peterson, Richard Pettinger, Bud Smith, Craig Smith, Paul Tiffany and John A. Tracy

Edited by Colin Barrow

WILEY

A John Wiley and Sons, Ltd, Publication

Starting & Running a Business All-in-One For Dummies,® 2nd Edition

Published by
John Wiley & Sons, Ltd
The Atrium
Southern Gate
Chichester
West Sussex
PO19 8SQ
England

E-mail (for orders and customer service enquires): cs-books@wiley.co.uk

Visit our Home Page on www.wiley.com

For general information on our other products and services, please contact our Customer Care Department within the U.S. at 877-762-2974, outside the U.S. at 317-572-3993, or fax 317-572-4002.

For technical support, please visit www.wiley.com/techsupport.

Wiley also publishes its books in a variety of electronic formats and by print-on-demand. Some content that appears in standard print versions of this book may not be available in other formats. For more information about Wiley products, visit us at www.wiley.com.

British Library Cataloguing in Publication Data: A catalogue record for this book is available from the British Library

ISBN: 978-1-119-97527-4 (paperback), 978-1-119-97564-9 (ebook), 978-1-119-97565-6 (ebook), 978-1-119-97566-3 (ebook)

Printed and bound in Great Britain by TJ International, Padstow, Cornwall

10 9 8 7 6 5 4 3

WILEY

About the Authors

Liz Barclay has worked as an adviser, trainer, and manager with the Citizens Advice Bureau and still advises small businesses and sole traders on relationship management with staff and customers. Liz is well connected within the media; she presents *You and Yours*, a factual radio programme on Radio 4, and has worked on a wide range of business and finance programmes for the BBC both on TV and radio. As a writer, Liz specialises in personal finance. She has written for the *News Of The World*, *The Express*, *Moneywise*, *Family Circle*, *Save Money* and the *Mail On Sunday* personal finance magazine.

Colin Barrow was, until recently, Head of the Enterprise Group at Cranfield School of Management, where he taught entrepreneurship on the MBA and other programmes. He is also a visiting professor at business schools in the US, Asia, France, and Austria. His books on entrepreneurship and small business have been translated into twenty languages including Russian and Chinese. He worked with Microsoft to incorporate the business planning model used in his teaching programmes into the software program, Microsoft Business Planner. He is a regular contributor to newspapers, periodicals and academic journals such as the *Financial Times*, *The Guardian*, *Management Today*, and the *International Small Business Journal*.

Thousands of students have passed through Colin's start-up and business growth programmes, going on to run successful and thriving enterprises, and raising millions in new capital. He is on the board of several small businesses, is a University Academic Governor, and has served on the boards of public companies, venture capital funds, and on Government Task Forces.

Paul Barrow trained and qualified as a Chartered Accountant with Deloitte & Touche before obtaining his MBA at Bradford University. As a senior consultant with Ernst & Young he was responsible for managing and delivering quality consulting assignments. During the mid-1980s, he was Investment Review Director for a UK venture capital business.

In 1998, as Group Finance Director of Adval Group plc, he was part of the team which took their software company on to the Alternative Investment Market. Adval specialises in providing multimedia training – both bespoke and generic. Paul has also been a director of several owner-managed businesses, and has started up and sold other businesses. He currently works with businesses as diverse as software, turkey farming, and food retailing.

Paul is a Visiting Fellow at Cranfield University where he teaches on the Business Growth Programme. This programme is designed specifically for owner managers who want to grow and improve their businesses. He also teaches at Warwick University and Oxford Brookes on similar programmes.

Paul has written several business books: *The Business Plan Workbook* and *Raising Finance* (both Kogan Page/Sunday Times); *The Best Laid Business Plans* and *The Bottom Line* (both Virgin Books). All these books are aimed at owner managers trying to grow and improve their businesses.

Greg Brooks is Content Strategy Director at C Squared, publisher of *M&M* magazine, creative media website www.creamglobal.com and producer of the Festival of Media. He is also a freelance journalist and digital media consultant with ten years experience covering the global digital industry. He has been a regular contributor to UK national titles such as *Marketing*, *New Media Age*, *Brand Strategy*, *Broadcast*, *Future Media*, *The Guardian* and Channel 4's *4Talent* online portal. He is also co-author of *Digital Marketing for Dummies*. In a consultancy he role he has worked with Sky, McDonald's, News International, BT, Red Bull, Camelot (UK Lottery operator), EnergyWatch, Visit Britain and OfCOM (UK communications regulator), advising on the future strategic use of digital media.

Ben Carter runs his own digital agency helping famous and not-so-famous brands launch marketing initiatives to capitalise on the changing media landscape and ever-changing consumer behaviour.

Clients of Ben Carter & Associates include npower and AOL. The company has also provided consultancy services for several major UK-based blue-chip companies. Before setting up BCA, Ben worked as a business journalist for eight years, covering the UK's media and marketing sectors and most recently was News Editor of *Marketing* magazine. He has also freelanced for a number of national newspapers including *The Times* and *The Guardian* and is used regularly as a commentator on the digital economy by different media, including the BBC, *The Independent* and CNN.

Frank Catalano is a veteran marketing consultant and analyst. He's the principal of Catalano Consulting, a strategic marketing firm advising Internet and technology companies. His consulting assignments include stints as Managing Director for PC Data's Internet Monitoring Division, VP Marketing for McGraw-Hill Home Interactive, VP Marketing for iCopyright, and VP Marketing for Apex Computer. He also was a marketing manager for Egghead Software and for the Apple Programmers and Developers Association. When not consulting, Frank provides tech industry analysis and commentary for KCPQ-TV Fox Seattle and is the author of the long-running Byte Me columns for *Seattle Weekly* and others. His essays and short fiction about technology have appeared in a wide variety of print and broadcast media, including ClickZ, Omni, Inside Multimedia, and Analog.

Peter Economy, MBA is associate editor of *Leader to Leader*, the award-winning magazine of the Peter F. Drucker Foundation for Nonprofit Leadership, and author of numerous books. Peter combines his writing expertise with more than 15 years of management experience to provide his readers with solid, hands-on information and advice. He received his bachelor's degree (with majors in economics and human biology) from Stanford University and his MBA at the Edinburgh Business School. Visit Peter at his website: www.petereconomy.com.

Lita Epstein, who earned her MBA from Emory University's Goizueta Business School, enjoys helping people develop good financial, investing, and tax planning skills.

While getting her MBS, Lita worked as a teaching assistant for the financial accounting department and ran the accounting lab. After completing her MBA, she managed finances for a small nonprofit organization and for the facilities management section of a large medical clinic.

She designs and teaches online courses on topics such as investing for retirement, getting ready for tax time, and finance and investing for women. She's written more than ten books, including *Streetwise Retirement Planning* and *Trading For Dummies*.

Lita was the content director for a financial services website, MostChoice.com, and managed the website Investing for Women. As a Congressional press secretary, Lita gained firsthand knowledge about how to work within and around the Federal bureaucracy, which gives her great insight into how government programmes work. In the past, Lita has been a daily newspaper reporter, magazine editor, and fundraiser for the international activities of former US President Jimmy Carter through The Carter Center.

Kim Gilmour is a freelance journalist and author with more than 13 years of experience demystifying the world of technology for small businesses and consumers. As senior researcher/writer at *Which? Computing*, the UK's biggest computing magazine, she conducted high-profile news investigations, product reviews and tutorials, and is still a regular contributor. She was also features editor at *Internet Magazine*, one of the first publications to help businesses get online and guide them through the rise and subsequent fall of the dotcom boom. Prior to this, Kim was assistant editor at an Australian business technology title.

Kim's articles have appeared in *Web User, PC Pro* and *Computer Shopper*, amongst others. She is the author of *Digital Photography for the Older and Wiser* and *Spotify For Dummies* (October 2011), and is co-author of *eBay.co.uk Business All-in-One For Dummies* and *Starting and Running an Online Business For Dummies* (October 2011). All books are published by Wiley.

Alex Hiam is a consultant, corporate trainer, and public speaker with 20 years of experience in marketing, sales, and corporate communications. He is the director of Insights, which includes a division called Insights for Marketing that offers a wide range of services for supporting and training in sales, customer service, planning, and management. His firm is also active in developing the next generation of leaders in the workplace through its Insights for Training & Development. Alex has an MBA in marketing and strategic planning from the Haas School at U.C. Berkeley and an undergraduate degree from Harvard. He has worked as marketing manager for both smaller high-tech firms and a *Fortune* 100 company, and did a stint as a professor of marketing at the business school at U. Mass. Amherst.

Alex is the co-author of the best-seller, *The Portable MBA in Marketing* (Wiley) as well as *The Vest-Pocket CEO* and numerous other books and training programmes. He has consulted to a wide range of companies and not-for-profit and government agencies, from General Motors and Volvo to HeathEast and the U.S. Army (a fuller list of clients is posted at www. insightsformarketing.com).

Alex is also the author of a companion volume to this book, the *Marketing Kit For Dummies* (Wiley), which includes more detailed coverage of many hands-on topics involved in creating great advertising, direct mail letters, websites, publicity campaigns, and marketing plans. On the CD that comes with the *Marketing Kit For Dummies*, you'll find forms, checklists, and templates that may be of use to you. Also, Alex maintains an extensive website of resources that he organised to support each of the chapters in the book.

Greg Holden started a small business called Stylus Media, which is a group of editorial, design, and computer professionals who produce both print and electronic publications. The company gets its name from a recording stylus that reads the traces left on a disk by voices or instruments and translates those signals into electronic data that can be amplified and enjoyed by many. He has been self-employed for the past ten years. He is an avid user of eBay, both as a buyer and seller, and he recently started his own blog.

One of the ways Greg enjoys communicating is through explaining technical subjects in nontechnical language. The first edition of *Starting an Online Business For Dummies* was the ninth of his more than 30 computer books. He also authored *eBay PowerUser's Bible* for Wiley Publishing. Over the years, Greg has been a contributing editor of *Computer Currents* magazine, where he writes a monthly column. He also contributes to *PC World* and the University of Illinois at Chicago alumni magazine. Other projects have included preparing documentation for an electronics catalog company in Chicago and creating online courses on Windows 2000 and Microsoft Word 2000.

Greg balances his technical expertise and his entrepreneurial experience with his love of literature. He received an M.A. in English from the University of Illinois at Chicago and also writes general interest books, short stories, and poetry. Among his editing assignments is the monthly newsletter for his daughters' grade school.

After graduating from college, Greg became a reporter for his hometown newspaper. Working at the publications office at the University of Chicago was his next job, and it was there that he started to use computers. He discovered, as the technology became available, that he loved desktop publishing (with the Macintosh and LaserWriter) and, later on, the World Wide Web.

Greg loves to travel, but since his two daughters were born, he hasn't been able to get around much. He was able to translate his experiences into a book called *Karma Kids: Answering Everyday Parenting Questions with Buddhist Wisdom*. However, through the Web, he enjoys traveling vicariously and meeting people online. He lives with his family in an old house in Chicago that he has been rehabbing for – well, for many years now. He is a collector of objects such as pens, cameras, radios, and hats. He is always looking for things to take apart so that he can see how they work and fix them up. Many of the same skills prove useful in creating and maintaining Web pages. He is an active member of Jewel Heart, a Tibetan Buddhist meditation and study group based in Ann Arbor, Michigan.

Jane Kelly is a qualified Chartered Management Accountant currently living and working in the Peak District. She has used Sage software for a number of years and has taught Bookkeeping to further education students, as well as edited and co-authored *Bookkeeping For Dummies*. Her first book Sage *50 Accounts For Dummies* is currently selling well and is now into it's second edition. Jane can be contacted via her blog which offers hints and tips for Sage 50 users. Please go to www.sagemadesimple.co.uk.

Sarah Laing is a Chartered Tax Adviser and a member of the Chartered Institute of Taxation. She has been writing professionally since joining CCH Editions in 1998, as a senior technical editor, where she contributed to a range of highly regarded tax publications. She became Publishing Manager for the tax and accounting portfolio in 2001 and later went on to help run CCH's conferences and courses business. She originally worked for the Inland Revenue in the Newbury and Swindon tax offices before moving out into practice in 1991. She has worked for both small and 'Big 5' firms, and now works as a freelance author providing technical writing services for the tax and accountancy profession. Sarah is the News Editor and a director of TaxationWeb Limited (www.taxationweb.co.uk) which provides free information and resources on UK taxes to taxpayers and professionals.

Dan Matthews is Group Online Editor of Caspian Publishing, which produces magazines, websites and events for an audience of UK entrepreneurs. Primarily working on realbusiness.co.uk, Dan writes about stellar business success stories as well as up-and-coming start-ups.

He was previously Group Online Editor of Crimson Business Publishing, with responsibility for sites such as startups.co.uk and growingbusiness.co.uk. He has contributed to a range of business magazines, including being contributing editor of *Real Business Magazine* and *Growing Business Magazine*, and is the co-author of *Starting a Business on eBay.co.uk For Dummies*.

Ruth Mortimer is associate editor for *Marketing Week* magazine. In charge of a team of dedicated features writers at the publication, she appears regularly in national press such as *The Independent* and the *Daily Express* discussing issues relating to business, marketing and branding. She also appears on TV and radio as an expert commentator in this field for multiple programmes, including those on the BBC and Sky.

Previous to joining *Marketing Week*, Ruth was editor of global business title *Brand Strategy*, as well as writing for Channel 4's '4talent' service to let young people know about new talents in music, design, arts and digital techniques. At *Brand Strategy*, she took the magazine through a full redesign and repositioning, introducing a new range of supplements and a conference programme, while contributing articles to sister titles *Design Week* and *New Media Age*. Before writing about marketing for a living, Ruth was an archaeologist, working mainly in the Middle East.

Bob Nelson, PhD is founder and president of Nelson Motivation, Inc., a management training and products firm headquartered in San Diego, California. As a practising manager, researcher, and best-selling author, Bob is an internationally recognised expert in the areas of employee motivation, recognition and rewards, productivity and performance improvement, and leadership.

Bob has published 20 books and sold more than 2.5 million books on management, which have been translated in some 20 languages. He earned his BA in communications from Macalester College, his MBA in organisational behavior from UC Berkeley, and his PhD in management from the Peter F. Drucker Graduate Management Center of the Claremont Graduate University.

Visit his website at www.nelson-motivation.com or contact Bob directly at BobRewards@aol.com.

Steven Peterson is a senior partner and founder of Home Planet Technologies, a management training company specializing in hands-on software tools designed to enhance business strategy, business planning, and general management skills. He is the creator and designer of The Protean Strategist, a state of the art computer-based business simulation. The simulation creates a dynamic business environment where participants run companies and compete against each other in a fast-changing marketplace. Each management team in the simulation is responsible for developing its own strategy, business plan, and program to make the plan work.

Steven has used The Protean Strategist to add excitement, hands-on experience, teamwork, and a competitive challenge to corporate training programs around the world. He has worked with both large and small companies on products and services in industries ranging from telecommunications to financial services and from high technology to consumer goods and industrial equipment. He can be reached by e-mail at `peterson@ HomePlanetTech.com`.

When he's not planning his own business, Steven is planning to remodel his 80-year old house or to redesign the garden. And he confesses that of the three, the garden proves to be the most difficult. Steven holds advanced degrees in mathematics and physics, receiving his doctorate from Cornell University. He teaches part-time at the Haas School of Business, University of California at Berkeley, and lives in the Bay Area with his long-time companion, Peter, and their long-lived canine, Jake.

Richard Pettinger, MBA has taught since 1989 at University College London, where he is principal teaching fellow (reader) in management education and director of the Information Management for Business courses – part of a UK national initiative to bring about the required quality of management and technology education demanded for the future. Richard teaches general, strategic and operational management, change and organisational behaviour to a wide variety of domestic and international students on undergraduate, postgraduate and executive programmes.

Since 2005, Richard has been visiting professor at the Jagiellonian University Business School in Krakow, Poland, developing a wide range of teaching, learning and research initiatives.

Richard is the author of over forty books on all aspects of business and management. He also produces professional, conference and study papers.

Bud Smith's experience is split between the technical and marketing sides of the computer and Internet industries. Bud was a short-order cook before starting in the computer industry at age 21. He was a data entry supervisor, programmer, and technical writer before working as a competitive analyst and QuickTime marketing manager at Apple Computer. He has been a full-time writer and has joined Frank in several consulting projects. Bud is currently Director of Marketing at AllPublish, a venture-funded Silicon Valley startup. Bud's writing experience is all on the nonfiction side and includes computer and medical articles as well as a dozen computer books.

Craig Smith is the former editor of *Marketing*, the UK's highest circulation weekly magazine, and PPA Weekly Business Magazine of the Year, serving the marketing and advertising industries. He has worked as a business journalist for many years and is a regular commentator on marketing issues to the national press and broadcast media.

Craig works closely with industry trade bodies the Association of Publishing Agencies and Business in the Community to promote best practice in the areas of customer magazines and cause related marketing.

Paul Tiffany is the managing director of Paul Tiffany & Associates, a Santa Rosa, California-based firm that has offered management training and consulting services to organizations throughout the world for the past fifteen years. In addition, he has taught business planning courses at some of the top business schools in the country, including Stanford, Wharton, and The Haas School of Business at the University of California, Berkeley, where he currently serves as adjunct professor. He holds an MBA from Harvard University and a Ph.D. from Berkeley. He can be reached by e-mail at tiffany@haas.berkeley.edu.

John A. Tracy is Professor of Accounting, Emeritus, in the College of Business and Administration at the University of Colorado in Boulder. Before his 35-year tenure at Boulder he was on the business faculty for four years at the University of California in Berkeley. He has served as staff accountant at Ernst & Young and is the author of several books on accounting, including *The Fast Forward MBA in Finance* and *How To Read a Financial Report*. Dr Tracy received his MBA and PhD degrees from the University of Wisconsin and is a CPA in Colorado.

Publisher's Acknowledgements

We're proud of this book; please send us your comments through our Dummies online registration form located at www.dummies.com/register/.

Some of the people who helped bring this book to market include the following:

Commissioning, Editorial, and Media Development

Project Editor: Steve Edwards

Commissioning Editor: Claire Ruston

Assistant Editor: Ben Kemble

Proofreader: David Price

Production Manager: Daniel Mersey

Cover Photos: ©iStock/Andrew Lilley

Cartoons: Ed McLachlan

Composition Services

Project Coordinator: Kristie Rees

Layout and Graphics: Samantha K. Cherolis, Corrie Socolovitch

Proofreader: Lindsay Amones

Indexer: Rebecca R. Plunkett

Publishing and Editorial for Consumer Dummies

Kathleen Nebenhaus, Vice President and Executive Publisher

Kristin Ferguson-Wagstaffe, Product Development Director

Ensley Eikenburg, Associate Publisher, Travel

Kelly Regan, Editorial Director, Travel

Publishing for Technology Dummies

Andy Cummings, Vice President and Publisher

Composition Services

Debbie Stailey, Director of Composition Services

Contents at a Glance

Table of Contents

Introduction

● ●

*W*elcome to this latest edition of *Starting & Running a Business All-in-One For Dummies*, your launch pad to understanding the fundamentals of setting up, establishing, running and growing a successful small business. In today's challenging environment, with the world still reeling from the credit crunch, it has never been more important to be well informed on every aspect of business.

This book draws together information on the key areas of successful business – planning, funding, staying on the right side of the law, employing staff, bookkeeping, accounting and tax, marketing and promotion, e-commerce and planning for growth – all in one bumper guide.

With help from this book, you can make even better business decisions and transform a simple idea into your very own business empire.

About This Book

This book is the ultimate business adviser, providing expert guidance for businesses at every stage of the start-up process.

This second edition of *Starting & Running a Business All-in-One For Dummies* draws on advice from several other For Dummies books, which you may wish to check out for more in-depth coverage of certain topics (all published by Wiley):

- ✔ *Bookkeeping For Dummies,* 2nd Edition (Jane Kelly, Paul Barrow and Lita Epstein)
- ✔ *Business Plans For Dummies,* 2nd Edition (Paul Tiffany, Steven D. Peterson and Colin Barrow)
- ✔ *Digital Marketing For Dummies* (Ben Carter, Gregory Brooks, Frank Catalano, Bud Smith)
- ✔ *Management For Dummies,* 2nd Edition (Richard Pettinger, Bob Nelson and Peter Economy)
- ✔ *Marketing For Dummies,* 2nd Edition (Ruth Mortimer, Greg Brooks, Craig Smith and Alexander Hiam)
- ✔ *Tax 2010/2011 For Dummies* (Sarah Laing)
- ✔ *Small Business Employment Law For Dummies* (Liz Barclay)
- ✔ *Starting a Business For Dummies,* 3rd Edition (Colin Barrow)

> ✔ *Starting & Running An Online Business For Dummies* (Kim Gilmour, Dan Matthews and Greg Holden)
>
> ✔ *UK Law and Your Rights For Dummies* (Liz Barclay)
>
> ✔ *Understanding Business Accounting For Dummies,* 2nd Edition (John A. Tracy and Colin Barrow)

Conventions Used in This Book

To make your reading experience easier and to alert you to key words or points, we use certain conventions in this book:

> ✔ *Italics* introduces new terms, and explains what they mean.
>
> ✔ **Bold** text is used to show the action part of bulleted and numbered lists.
>
> ✔ `Monofont` is used to highlight web addresses, showing you exactly what to type into your computer.

Foolish Assumptions

This book brings together the elements of knowledge that are essential for understanding the world of small business. As a consequence, to keep the book down to a reasonable number of pages, we've made a few assumptions about you (we hope you don't mind!). Maybe you're:

> ✔ An entrepreneur looking for a start-up bible
>
> ✔ A small business owner-manager seeking a comprehensive reference guide
>
> ✔ A business owner with aspirations to grow

How This Book Is Organised

We've divided *Starting & Running a Business All-in-One For Dummies* into six separate books. This section explains what you'll find out about in each one of these books. Each book is broken into chapters tackling key aspects of that part of the business world.

Book 1: Planning Your Business

This book is the one to turn to first if you're thinking about starting up a new business. It runs through all of your main considerations during the initial planning phase, and offers all sorts of advice and information to get you off to a flying start.

Book II: Sorting Out Your Finances

You may not be running your business to get rich (on the other hand, you actually may be running your business for exactly that reason!), but without mastering the basis of finance, you won't stay in business for long. This book walks you through the basic money matters you'll need to know and stay on top of.

Book III: Finding and Managing Staff

Unless you're intending to run your business all by yourself, you need to master the essentials of recruiting and retaining staff, and employing them safely and legally. This book tackles the 'people management' section of business, regardless of whether you employ one or 100 members of staff.

Book IV: Keeping on Top of the Books

Tax, financial records, profit and loss, and balance sheets. With HM Revenue and Customs on the warpath looking for ways to top up the government's tax receipts, you need to know the facts and figures outlined in this book. And even if you are an accountant, this book tackles the business side of figures.

Book V: Marketing and Advertising Your Wares

One of the keys to successful business is bringing in customers. This book looks at the many and varied ways of doing just this, from humble beginnings for a new start-up to grander ideas for an expanding venture.

Book VI: Growing and Improving Your Business

If you've already made a success of your business – or if you've followed the advice in the other books to their most profitable conclusion – this is the book you need to read! Showing you how to expand your business into an even greater one, this book considers factors as diverse as being a great manager to undertaking a TV advertising campaign.

Icons Used in This Book

When you flick through this book, you'll notice some snazzy little icons in the margin. These pick out key aspects of starting and running a business, and present you with important nuggets of information:

Want to get ahead in business? Check out the text highlighted by this icon to pick up some sage advice.

They say elephants never forget and nor should good business owners. This icon focuses on key information you should never be without.

Running a business isn't without it's dangers – be they financial or legal – and the text beside this icon points out common pitfalls to avoid.

Sometimes we give you information that is interesting but not absolutely essential to starting or growing your own business. If you see this icon next to a paragraph, you have our permission to skip by if it's not of immediate interest to you – doing so won't harm your chances in business.

This icon gives real-life specifics on how to perform a specific task.

Where to Go from Here

Starting & Running a Business All-in-One For Dummies, 2nd Edition, can help you succeed no matter what kind of business expertise you're looking for. If you have a great and proven business idea, you may want to plug straight into finding out how to raise finance (head over to Book II). If you need more than just yourself to get your great business idea off the ground, then you may want to know how to find great employees (check out Book III). If you're planning to take care of your own bookkeeping and finances then you may want to find out how to successfully balance the books and take care of tax (flick through to Book IV). Or perhaps you've already started out and you're looking for advice on how to take your business to the next level (Book VI gives some great advice). This book is set up so that you can dip in and out of it in a number of ways depending on your situation.

Book I
Planning Your Business

'OK – Here's the business plan. Nigel takes charge of marketing, Tristram sales, Keith accounts and Psycho makes sure clients pay on time.'

In this book . . .

If you're contemplating starting up a new business – or even if you just want to check that your current business is running smoothly – you've come to the right place! In this book we address the basic issues to consider when you're setting out on your career in business.

Here are the contents of Book I at a glance:

Chapter 1: Preparing for Business

Chapter 2: Being Your Own Boss

Chapter 3: Can You Do the Business?

Chapter 4: Starting Your Business Plan

Chapter 5: Establishing Your Starting Position

Chapter 6: Researching Your Customers, Competitors and Industry

Chapter 1

Preparing for Business

. . . .

. . . .

*W*hen you're starting a business, particularly your first business, you need to carry out the same level of preparation as you would for crossing the Gobi Desert or exploring the jungles of South America. You're entering hostile territory.

Your business idea may be good, it may even be great, but such ideas are two a penny. The patent office is stuffed full of great inventions that have never returned tuppence to the inventors who spent so much time and money filing them. It's how you plan, how you prepare and how you implement your plan that makes the difference between success and failure. And failure is pretty much a norm for business start-ups. Tens of thousands of small firms fail, some disastrously, every year. Most are perfectly ordinary enterprises – catastrophe isn't confined to brash Internet whiz kids entering markets a decade or so ahead of the game.

This chapter sets the scene to make sure that you're well prepared for the journey ahead.

Getting in Shape to Start Up

You need to be in great shape to start a business. You don't have to diet or exercise, at least not in the conventional sense of those words, but you do have to be sure that you have the skills and knowledge you need for the business you have in mind, or know how to tap into sources of such expertise.

The following sections help you through a pre-opening check-up so that you can be absolutely certain that your abilities and interests are closely aligned to those that the business you have in mind requires. The sections also help you to check that a profitable market exists for your products or services. You can use these sections as a vehicle for sifting through your business ideas to see whether they're worth the devotion of time and energy that you need to start up a business.

You may well not have all the expertise you need to do everything yourself. In this book you can find information on the zillions of agencies and advisers who can fill in the gaps in your expertise.

Assessing your abilities

Business lore claims that for every ten people who want to start their own business, only one finally does. It follows that an awful lot of dreamers exist who, while liking the idea of starting their own business, never get around to taking action. Book I Chapter 3 looks in detail at how you can assess whether you're a dreamer or a doer when it comes to entrepreneurship. For now, see whether you fit into one of the following entrepreneurial categories:

- ✔ **Nature:** If one of your parents or siblings runs their own business, successfully or otherwise, you're highly likely to start up your own business. No big surprise here, as the rules and experiences of business are being discussed every day and some of it's bound to rub off. It also helps if you're a risk taker who's comfortable with uncertainty.

- ✔ **Nurture:** For every entrepreneur whose parents or siblings have a business there are two who don't. If you can find a business idea that excites you and has the prospect of providing personal satisfaction and wealth, then you can assemble all the skills and resources needed to succeed in your own business. You need to acquire good planning and organisational skills (Book I Chapter 4 covers all aspects of writing a business plan) and either develop a well-rounded knowledge of basic finance, people management, operational systems, business law, marketing and selling, or get help and advice from people who have that knowledge.

- ✔ **Risk taker:** If you crave certainty in everything you do, then running your own business may be something of a culture shock. By the time the demand for a product or service is an absolutely sure-fire thing, there may already be too many other businesses in the market to leave much room for you. Don't confuse risk taking with a pure gamble. You need to be able to weigh matters up and make your risk a calculated one.

- ✔ **Jack-of-all-trades:** You need to be prepared to do any business task at any time. The buck definitely stops with you when you run your own business. You can't tell a customer that his delivery is late just because a driver fails to show up. You just have to put in a few more hours and do the job yourself.

Discovering a real need

You may be a great potential entrepreneur, but you still need to spell out exactly what it is you plan to do, who needs it and how it can make money. A good starting point is to look around and see whether anyone is dissatisfied with their present suppliers. Unhappy customers are fertile ground for new businesses to work in.

One dissatisfied customer isn't enough to start a business for. Make sure that unhappiness is reasonably widespread, because that gives you a feel for how many customers may be prepared to defect. After you have an idea of the size of the potential market, you can quickly see whether your business idea is a money-making proposition.

Aside from asking around, one way to get a handle on dissatisfaction levels is to check out websites that allow consumers to register their feelings, such as www.complaints.com, www.grumbletext.co.uk and www.blagger. com. Then scour blogs (short for weblogs), where irate people can complain their hearts out. Check out websites such as www.technorati.com, www. totalblogdirectory.com and www.bloghub.com, which all operate blog-indexing services that can help you filter through the 70 million plus blogs and reach the few dozen that serve the sector you're interested in.

The easiest way to fill a need that people are going to pay to have satisfied is to tap into one or more of these triggers:

- ✔ **Cost reduction and economy:** Anything that saves customers money is always an attractive proposition. Lastminute.com's appeal is that it acts as a 'warehouse' for unsold hotel rooms and airline tickets that you can have at a heavy discount.

- ✔ **Fear and security:** Products that protect customers from any danger, however obscure, are enduringly appealing. When Long-Term Capital Management (LTCM), one of America's largest hedge funds, collapsed and had to be rescued by the Federal Reserve at a cost of $2 billion, it nearly brought down the American financial system single-handedly. Two months later Ian and Susan Jenkins launched the first issue of their magazine, *EuroHedge*. At the time 35 hedge funds existed in Europe, but investors knew little about them and were rightly fearful for their investments. *EuroHedge* provided information and protection to a nervous market and five years after its launch the Jenkinses sold the magazine for £16.5 million.

- ✔ **Greed:** Anything that offers the prospect of making exceptional returns is always a winner. *Competitors' Companion* (www.competitors companion.com), a magazine aimed at helping anyone become a regular competition winner, was an immediate success. The proposition was simple: subscribe and you get your money back if you don't win a competition prize worth at least your subscription. The magazine provided details of every competition being run that week, details of how to enter, the factual answers to all the questions and pointers on how to answer any tie-breakers. It also provided the inspiration to ensure success with this sentence: 'You have to enter competitions in order to have a chance of winning them.'

✔ **Niche markets:** Big markets are usually the habitat of big business – encroach on their territory at your peril. New businesses thrive in markets that are too small even to be an appetite whetter to established firms. These market niches are often easy prey to new entrants because businesses have usually neglected, ignored or served them badly in the past.

Checking the fit of the business

Having a great business idea and possessing the attributes and skills you require to start your own business successfully are two vital elements to get right before you launch. The final ingredient is to be sure that the business you plan to start is right for you.

Before you go too far, make an inventory of the key things that you're looking for in a business. These may include working hours that suit your lifestyle; the opportunity to meet new people; minimal paperwork; a chance to travel. Then match those up with the proposition you're considering. (Book I Chapter 3 talks more about finding a good business fit.)

Confirming Viability

An idea, however exciting, unique, revolutionary and necessary, isn't a business. It's a great starting point, and an essential one, but you have to do a good deal more work before you can sidle up to your boss and tell him exactly what you think of him.

The following sections explore the steps you need to take so that you don't have to go back to your boss in six months and plead for your old job back (and possibly eat a large piece of humble pie at the same time).

Researching the market

However passionate you are about your business idea, you're unlikely already to have the answers to all the important questions concerning your marketplace. Before you can develop a successful business strategy, you have to understand as much as possible about your market and the competitors you're likely to face.

The main way to get to understand new business areas, or areas that are new to you at any rate, is to conduct market research. The purpose of that research is to ensure that you have sufficient information on customers, competitors and markets so that your market entry strategy or expansion plan is at least on target, if not on the bull's eye itself. In other words, you need to explore whether enough people are attracted to buy what you want to sell at a price that gives you a viable business. If you miss the target altogether, which you may well do without research, you may not have the necessary resources for a second shot.

Book I

**Planning
Your
Business**

The areas to research include:

✔ **Your customers:** Who may buy more of your existing goods and services and who may buy your new goods and services? How many such customers exist? What particular customer needs do you meet?

✔ **Your competitors:** Who are you competing with in your product/market areas? What are those firms' strengths and weaknesses?

✔ **Your product or service:** How can you tailor your product or service to meet customer needs and give you an edge in the market?

✔ **The price:** What do customers see as giving value for money, so encouraging both loyalty and referral?

✔ **The advertising and promotional material:** What newspapers, journals and so forth do your potential customers read and what websites do they visit? Unglamorous as it is, analysing data on what messages actually influence people to buy, rather than just to click, holds the key to identifying where and how to promote your products and service.

✔ **Channels of distribution:** How can you get to your customers and who do you need to distribute your products or services? You may need to use retailers, wholesalers, mail order or the Internet. All have different costs and if you use one or more, each wants a slice of your margin.

✔ **Your location:** Where do you need to be to reach your customers most easily at minimum cost? Sometimes you don't actually need to be anywhere near your market, particularly if you anticipate most of your sales coming from the Internet. If this is the case you need to have a strategy to make sure that potential customers can find your website.

Try to spend your advertising money wisely. Nationwide advertisements or blanketing the market with free CD-ROMs may create huge short-term growth, but little evidence exists that indiscriminate blunderbuss advertising works well in retaining customers. Certainly, few people using such techniques make any money.

Doing the numbers

Your big idea looks as though it has a market. You've evaluated your skills and inclinations and you believe that you can run this business. The next crucial question is – can it make you money?

You absolutely must establish the financial viability of your idea before you invest money in it or approach outsiders for backing. You need to carry out a thorough appraisal of the business's financial requirements. If the numbers come out as unworkable, you can then rethink your business proposition without losing anything. If the figures look good, then you can go ahead and prepare cash flow projections, a profit and loss account and a balance sheet, and put together the all-important business plan. (Chapters 2, 3 and 4 in Book II cover these procedures.)

You need to establish for your business:

- ✔ Day-to-day operating costs
- ✔ How long it will take to reach break-even
- ✔ How much start-up capital you need
- ✔ The likely sales volume
- ✔ The profit level you require for the business not just to survive, but also to thrive
- ✔ The selling price of your product or service

Many businesses have difficulty raising start-up capital. To compound this, one of the main reasons small businesses fail in the early stages is that they use too much start-up capital to buy fixed assets. Although some equipment is clearly essential at the start, you can postpone other purchases. You may be better off borrowing or hiring 'desirable' and labour-saving devices for a specific period. This obviously isn't as nice as having them to hand all the time, but remember that you have to maintain and perhaps update every photocopier, printer, computer and delivery van you buy and they become part of your fixed costs. The higher your fixed costs, the longer it usually takes to reach break-even point and profitability. And time isn't usually on the side of the small, new business: it has to become profitable relatively quickly or it simply runs out of money and dies.

Raising the money

Two fundamentally different types of money that a business can tap into are debt and equity.

✔ **Debt** is money borrowed, usually from a bank, and that you have to repay. While you're making use of borrowed money you also have to pay interest on the loan.

✔ **Equity** is the money that shareholders, including the proprietor, put in and money left in the business by way of retained profit. You don't have to give the shareholders their money back, but shareholders do expect the directors to increase the value of their shares, and if you go public they'll probably expect a stream of dividends too.

If you don't meet the shareholders' expectations, they won't be there when you need more money – or, if they're powerful enough, they'll take steps to change the membership of the board.

Alternative financing methods include raising money from family and friends, applying for grants and awards, and entering business competitions. Check out Book II Chapter 1 for a review of all these sources of financing.

The Financial Services Authority, a City watchdog, ordered all banks to publish statistics on complaints on their website from 31 August 2010. Lloyds had received 288,717 complaints in the first six months of the year, Santander 244,978, Barclays 195,956 and HSBC had just 65,236. If your bank is high on this name-and-shame list get straight on to Book II Chapter 1 where we cover all aspects of raising money.

Writing up the business plan

A *business plan* is a selling document that conveys the excitement and promise of your business to potential backers and stakeholders. These potential backers can include bankers, venture capital firms, family, friends and others who may help you launch your business if they only know what you want to do. (Book II Chapter 1 considers how to find and approach sources of finance.)

Getting money is expensive, time-consuming and hard work, but you can get a quick decision. One recent start-up succeeded in raising £3 million in eight days, after the founder turned down an earlier offer of £1 million made just 40 minutes after he presented his business plan. Your business plan needs to cover what you expect to achieve over the next three years. (Book I Chapter 4 gives full details on how to write a winning business plan.)

Most business plans are dull, badly written and frequently read only by the most junior of people in the financing organisations they're presented to. One venture capital firm in the United States went on record to say that in one year it received 25,000 business plans asking for finance and invested in only 40. Follow these tips to make your business plan stand out from the crowd:

✔ **Hit them with the benefits.** You need to spell out exactly what you do, for whom and why that matters. One such statement that has the ring of practical authority is: 'Our website makes ordering gardening products simple. It saves the average customer two hours a week browsing catalogues and £250 a year through discounts not otherwise available from garden centres. We have surveyed 200 home gardeners, who rate efficient purchasing as a key priority.'

✔ **Make your projections believable.** Sales projections always look like a hockey stick – a straight line curving rapidly upwards towards the end. You have to explain what drives growth, how you capture sales and what the link between activity and results is. The profit margins are key numbers in your projections, alongside sales forecasts. Financiers tend to probe these figures in depth, so show the build-up in detail.

✔ **Say how big the market is.** Financiers feel safer backing people in big markets. Capturing a fraction of a percentage of a massive market may be hard to achieve – but if you get it at least the effort is worth it. Going for 10 per cent of a market measured in millions rather than billions may come to the same number, but the result isn't as interesting.

✔ **Introduce yourself and your team.** You need to sound like winners with a track record of great accomplishments.

✔ **Include non-executive directors.** Sometimes a heavyweight outsider can lend extra credibility to a business proposition. If you know or have access to someone with a successful track record in your area of business who has time on his hands, you can invite him to help. If you plan to trade as a limited company (Book I Chapter 2 has details on legal structures) you can ask him to be a director, without specific executive responsibilities beyond being on hand to offer advice. But non-executive directors do need to have relevant experience or be able to open doors and do deals. Check out organisations such as Venture Investment Partners (www.ventureip.co.uk) and First Flight Placement's non-exec search site (www.nonexecutivedirector.co.uk) for information on tracking down the right non-executive director for your business.

✔ **Provide financial forecasts.** You need projected cash flows, profit and loss accounts and balance sheets for at least three years ahead. No one believes them after Year 1, but the thinking behind them is important.

✔ **Demonstrate the product or service.** Financiers need to see what the customer is going to get. A mock-up is okay or, failing that, a picture or diagram. For a service, show how customers can gain from using it – that it can help with improved production scheduling and so reduce stock holding, for example.

✔ **Spell out the benefits to your potential investors.** Tell them that you can repay their money within x years, even on your most cautious projections. Or if you're speaking to an equity investor, tell him what return he may get on his investment when you sell the business in three or five years' time.

Going for Growth

Growth is as natural a feature of business life as it is of biological life. People, animals and plants all grow to a set size range and then stop. A few very small and very large specimens come to fruition, but the vast majority fit within a fairly narrow size band.

Businesses follow a similar formula: most successful new businesses, those that survive that is, reach a plateau within five to seven years. At that stage the business employs 5 to 20 people and has annual sales of between £250,000 and £1 million. Of the 4.4 million private businesses operating in the United Kingdom, fewer than 120,000 have a turnover in excess of £1 million a year. That doesn't represent a bad result. Viewed from the position of a one-man-band start-up, having a couple of hundred thousand pounds in sales each year is an admirable (and unusual) success.

The following sections demonstrate the great benefits of growth. (Books V and VI contain more advice on how to make your business grow.)

Gaining economies of scale

After a business starts to grow, you can spread overhead costs over a wider base. You can buy materials and services in larger quantities, which usually means better terms and lower costs. These factors generally lead to a higher profit margin, which in turn provides funds to improve the business, which in turn can lead to even lower costs. This *virtuous circle* can make a growing firm more cost-competitive than one that's cautiously marking time.

Securing a competitive advantage

A new business can steal a march on its competitors by doing something vital that established businesses can't easily imitate. For example, a new hair-dressing shop can locate where customers are, but an existing shop has to content itself with its current location, at least until its lease expires.

A growing firm can gain advantages over its slower competitors. For example, launching new products or services gives a firm more goods to sell to its existing customer base. This puts smaller competitors at a disadvantage, because they're perceived as having less to offer than the existing supplier. This type of growth strategy can, if coupled with high quality standards, lead to improved customer retention and this too can lead to higher profits – a further push on the momentum of the virtuous circle.

Retaining key staff

The surest way to ensure that a business fails is to have a continual churn of employees coming and going. You have to invest valuable time and money in every new employee before he becomes productive, so the more staff you lose the more growth you sacrifice. Most employers believe that their staff work for money and their key staff work for more money. The facts don't really support this hypothesis. All the evidence is that employees want to have an interesting job and recognition and praise for their achievements. In Book III Chapter 6 you can find out how to get the best out of your staff.

By growing the business you can let key managers realise their potential. In a bigger business you can train and promote your staff, moving them up the ladder into more challenging jobs, earning higher salaries on merit, while they stay with you rather than leaving for pastures new. And if employees are good at their jobs, the longer they stay with you, the more valuable they become. You save time and money on recruitment and you don't have to finance new managers' mistakes while they learn how to work in your business.

Gaining critical business mass

Bigger isn't always better, but a growing business has a greater presence in its market and that's rarely a bad strategy. Large businesses are also more stable, tending to survive better in turbulent times. Bigger businesses do sometimes go bust, but smaller, 'doing nicely' businesses are far more likely to go bump.

A small company often relies on a handful of customers and just one or two products or services for most or all of its profits. If its main product or service comes under competitive pressure or if a principal customer goes bust, changes supplier, or spreads orders around more thinly, the small company is in trouble. Expanding the number of customers so that you break out of the 80/20 cycle, in which 80 per cent of the business comes from 20 per cent of customers, is a sensible way to make the business safer and more predictable.

One-product businesses are the natural medium of the inventor, but are very vulnerable to competition, changes in fashion and technological obsolescence. Having only one product can limit the growth potential of the enterprise. A question mark hangs over such ventures until they can broaden their product base. Adding successful new products or services helps a business to grow and become a safer and more secure venture. This process is much like buying a unit trust rather than investing in a couple of shares. The individual shares are inevitably more volatile, but the spread over dozens of shares smoothes the growth path and reduces the chances of disaster significantly.

Chapter 2

Being Your Own Boss

*A*t some time or another, most people have thought about how good it would be to be their own boss – no more being at the beck and call of someone else or working hard just to put money into an employer's pocket! Every year, almost 300,000 people take the plunge. If you've got a big idea for your own business, this year may be the one to make it happen.

But running your own operation isn't always a bed of roses, and the more help and advice you get on the various aspects of it, the better prepared you are to deal with the problems as they arise – or, even better, to take steps to avoid them arising in the first place. Working for yourself can be very isolating, as well as extremely time-consuming. You and those around you need to be aware of just how much effort it takes to become successful and that your loved ones are willing to offer their support.

Going into Business

About 300 businesses failed every week in the UK in 2011, and around a third of all start-ups don't make it past their first birthday. The ones that fall by the wayside usually do so because they've been set up on a wing and a prayer without all the necessary preparation. Of course, sectors do vary widely: in 2011 only the hotel and catering sector saw an increase in failures.

Just because you've got a good idea doesn't mean that it will fly without a lot of research and planning. If you really want to work for yourself, talk to one of the organisations, such as the Government's small business advisory service Business Link, that can help you work out whether a sustainable market exists for your products or services or whether the competition has it sewn up already. You need also to discuss how to set up your business, if you do decide it's worth a try.

The first step to setting up your business it to call *Business Link,* England's local business advice office. (If you're in Scotland, Wales or Northern Ireland, the equivalent services have slightly different names; to keep it simple, we refer to the service as Business Link throughout this book.) Business Link, the national business advice service, offers free advice and support and runs all sorts of useful courses for people starting up their own enterprises.

After you decide to take the plunge into entrepreneurship, you need to consider how you're going to trade. You can choose to go it alone as a *sole trader,* form a *partnership* with someone else, or set up a *limited company.* These entities differ in terms of the administration involved, whether you're prepared to risk your own personal assets, and how you want to be viewed for tax purposes. You can talk to a solicitor or an accountant about the legal form your business should take, but an adviser at Business Link is also able to help. The Law Society has a list of lawyers who offer small firms a free initial legal consultation; contact 020-7405-9075 or go to www.lawsociety. org.uk/choosingandusing/helpyourbusiness/foryourbusiness. law. You can find a chartered accountant through the Institute of Chartered Accountants (www.icaew.co.uk).

Working as a sole trader

Are you going to go it alone? You can establish yourself as a sole trader very easily. You don't have to fill out a lot of forms, and you've got only yourself to answer to.

Most people who work on a freelance basis are sole traders, doing what they know best for a range of clients, as and when those clients need their services – say, a photographer who wants to work for herself rather than an employer. You can leave your job, make up a portfolio of your work or a brochure advertising your particular skills, and market your services to anyone you think may pay for them.

As a sole trader, you make your own business decisions; you answer only to clients, and the profits (and any losses) you make are yours. If you do make losses and run up debts, you're personally responsible for those debts. If things go badly wrong, you may ultimately have to sell some possessions, perhaps even your home, to pay off your debts. Basically, as a sole trader, you're running your business on your own. If you expand, you may decide to take on other people to work for you – as employees or as freelancers on short-term contracts – but the business is yours.

Most sole traders are self-employed and are taxed as such by Her Majesty's Revenue and Customs (HMRC). You need to register with HMRC within three months of starting up. You can find more information on the HMRC website at www.hmrc.gov.uk or from your local tax office, which is listed in the phone book.

You have to be careful because if you're a sole trader and you do most of your work for just one client, HMRC may not accept that you're self-employed. It may decide that you're an employee of that client. Talk your situation through with HMRC if you're in any doubt.

Someone who is genuinely self-employed works under a contract for service rather than a contract of employment. You're contracted to provide services. For more on how the tax office views self-employed people, see the section 'Minding Money Matters', later in this chapter.

Forming a partnership

If you're planning to set up your business with someone else or more than one other person, you can form a *partnership*. You run the business together and share all the management decisions, risks, costs, losses and, hopefully, the profits. In any venture where you're working with other people, you need to be clear from the outset what your goals and priorities are. A partnership may be the answer if you don't have enough money to get up and running, and you know someone who has some money to invest.

You may think that you know your prospective partner or partners very well and will have no difficulty working together, but it's often said that you don't really know anyone until you live or work with her. Many a business falls apart because partners disagree on the basic aims of their venture and find that they can't work together.

Making it formal

If you simply form an informal partnership, nothing stops one partner from making decisions and going ahead without the consent of the others. One partner can take on binding contracts without the others having their say. As a result, it's a good idea to have a solicitor draw up a partnership agreement between you, setting out how the business will be run. (Another option is to use a Business Link adviser.)

You want to address issues such as how the profits are to be split, who puts in what in terms of finance, who is responsible for what aspects of the operation, and to what extent decisions can be made by individuals and which decisions must be made jointly. This partnership agreement helps everyone know where they stand from the beginning so that you can avoid disputes further down the line. If you do set out to draw up such an agreement, any differences of opinion are likely to surface before your commit yourself.

Partners are often taxed as self-employed, but as with sole traders, this setup isn't always the case, so talk it over with HM Revenue and Customs. Like a sole trader, you need to register with HMRC within three months of starting up.

Limiting the liability of the partnership

Members of a partnership are all liable for any debts their venture incurs. Partners are each personally liable, so that means that they could end up selling personal possessions, perhaps even their homes, to clear their debts. If one partner can't pay her share of those debts or simply disappears owing money, the other partner or partners are left holding the bills.

You can, however, limit the personal responsibility of the partners for business debts by setting up a *limited liability partnership* (unless you're in Northern Ireland, where these partnerships don't exist). Basically, your liability as a partner in a limited liability partnership is limited to the amount of money you invested at the outset and to any personal guarantees you gave if you were borrowing money for the business. A limited liability partnership is a more complicated and expensive way to form a partnership, and you need the help of a solicitor or an agent who forms companies. The local Business Link can give you advice and information and help you decide whether this partnership is the right option for you.

Opting for a limited company

The other option when setting up a business is to become a *limited company*. A limited company is a private business set up in such a way that, legally, the liability of the owners for any debts it incurs is limited to their shares in the company. Their personal assets are safeguarded if the business gets into financial trouble. Limited companies have 'Limited' after their names and some people like the status that gives and feel that customers will be more impressed or confident in the organisation they're dealing with. But many limited companies are no more than a one-person organisation run from the spare room in the same way as sole traders operate.

Basically, if you set up a limited company, you and your business partners are directors of the company. You can buy a company that's already registered with Companies House 'off the shelf' with an existing name, but you may want to start from scratch and come up with your own name. Companies House is the official Government register of UK companies, and you can find more information on its website at www.companieshouse.gov.uk or call 0870-333-3636. Becoming a limited company is a fairly straightforward process and costs just a few hundred pounds.

The advantage for the directors is that you have a limited liability for any debts the company runs up so that you don't usually risk losing personal assets, such as your home. Your personal risk is limited to the amount of money you invest in the first place and to any financial guarantees you give to an organisation, such as the bank or individual investors when you're borrowing money to put into the business. You can raise money by allowing other people, businesses, or employees to buy shares in your business. If the company does well, your buyers make a return on their investment because they're entitled to a share of those profits – depending on how many shares they bought in the first place.

You don't usually risk losing personal assets if you form a limited company, but you do have duties as a company director. If the company goes down the pan because you haven't carried out those duties, you may become liable, personally, for company debts or be disqualified from being a director of another company.

You have to draw up a *Memorandum of Association* and *Articles of Association* to get started. These documents cover the details of how you run the business, where it will be based, and what it will do. You have to send this paperwork, along with registration forms, to Companies House before you start trading. Your solicitor or an agent who specialises in forming companies can help you through the process. An adviser at Business Link can also give you all the information you need and discuss the process with you before you make your decision about going down this path.

If you do become a limited company, you pay a *corporation tax* on your company profits and send yearly returns to Companies House with details of directors, shareholders and finances. Your company account is audited if your turnover is big enough, but most small businesses don't make enough and are exempt.

Becoming a franchisee

A lot of the chains on the high street are franchises. The person who comes up with the original idea sets up the business – usually in the form of a limited company and then sells off licences to people who want to operate branches of that business. The franchisee buys the right to use the company name and logo, sell the company products or offer the company services. The franchisor – the originator of the business – sets out in the contract various details of how the business is to be run, gives advice on running the operation and takes a share of the proceeds. You may find it easier to run a business this way because someone else has put all the effort into working out what will make it successful but you may eventually find it limiting because there won't be so much scope for using you own initiative or putting your own stamp on the business. You can get more information from Business Link or from the British Franchise Association at www.british-franchise.org or on 01491-578-050.

What's in a name?

Many people opt for a limited company because they like having a business name that includes the word 'Limited'. They feel that clients will think they're better established and that it sounds more professional. It's all part of the image.

So, too, is the business name. As a sole trader or a partnership, you can operate under your own name – such as R. U. Reliable. If you decide to call yourself something else, such as Reliable Services, you have to put that name on all your letterheads, contracts and invoices. You have to register the name of your Limited Liability Partnership or Limited company with Companies House. You can buy a company from the shelf of Companies House if one is already registered with a name that you want to use but isn't in use.

If you want to have a website for your company, it's a good idea to check out whether the name you're using is available as a domain name or already in use by someone else. You can check through Nominet UK at www.nic.uk or Netnames at www.netnames.co.uk. You can't register a company name that is already used by a company in operation and registered at Companies House. You can contact Companies House (0870-333-3636 or www.companieshouse.gov.uk) for more information on the do's and don'ts of company names.

Taking on Employees

One of the most important decisions for any business owner – whether he's a sole trader, in a partnership, or operating as a limited company – is when to take on employees. One minute everything is ticking along nicely, and then suddenly you have too much work to cope with and you need help. If you take a look at the chapters in Book III you can see what employees can expect from their employers and of their rights. You have to make sure that you don't do anything to contravene those rights, or you may find that your employees can make a claim against you at an employment tribunal. If the tribunal finds in favour of your employee, you can then face a bill for compensation.

Right from the moment you decide to take on a staff member, you have to stay on the right side of the law. *Employment Law For Small Businesses For Dummies* (Wiley) covers the legalities in detail. If you need to talk things over with someone before taking the first steps, an adviser at Business Link is a good place to start.

Minding Money Matters

When it comes to money and your business, there are two sides to the coin. You may want to raise finance to get your business started or to help you run it and develop it. On the other hand, you must first consider the money you have to pay out, such as tax and national insurance.

Getting money to run the business

You may not need any capital to get going simply because the business you're starting up depends on little more than your own skills. You may simply turn your spare room into the place you work from, advertise your services, and wait for the jobs to roll in.

However, few businesses need no money to get off the ground. You probably need to pay for phone calls, website setup, advertising literature, and equipment. Many people start up by doing freelance work while keeping their day jobs, use their savings, or get help from family and friends.

When the venture is a bit bigger, though, finding the money you need can be harder. Banks are often not interested in dealing with a small venture. They're looking for something more profitable to invest in. Business people often say that borrowing ten million pounds is much easier than borrowing £100,000. That's not to say that approaching the banks isn't worth it. If you're looking to borrow money at the lower end of the scale, you may be able to arrange a small business loan. Other than that possibility, you can raise cash through other methods, including grants and loans. (Business Link can advise you about possible financial help from enterprise and development agencies.) Accountants are also an important source of business advice and support and many will give free advice on the phone. You can find a chartered accountant through the Institute of Chartered Accountants' website at www.icaew.co.uk.

In addition, venture capital companies and individual investors are looking for good business ideas to invest in. (Check with the Business Venture Capital Association at 020-7025-2950 or www.bvca.co.uk.) Business Angels are investors who have been in business themselves and have retired, but want to put something back in the form of financial backing and business expertise. National Business Angels attempts to match business ventures with angel investors – contact 0207-329-2929 or www.bestmatch.co.uk.

If you go to anyone to raise cash, whether it's a bank for a loan or an investor, they'll want to see detailed business plans. These documents set out your ideas and aims clearly and your projections for how the business will grow. You need to do your research to show that you know that a good, sustainable market exists for your goods or services and that the market has enough room for you. No matter how good a hairdresser you are, no one will be interested in investing in yet another hairdresser in a location that already has several hairdressers. The business plan needs to reflect your market research, your marketing plans, and your ideal location for your venture.

People need to be convinced that investing in your business is worth their while in terms of a fair return. Your business plan is your most important document, so get help to draft it. Business Link run courses and have advisers who can help with business planning or point you in the direction of funding sources.

Most people or organisations willing to give you business funding will want personal guarantees from you about how much money you're putting up yourself. Even if you're planning to trade as a limited company with limited liability for business debts, investors may expect you to give additional guarantees that you'll put in more than just your original investment in certain circumstances. You may have to adjust your ambitions to fit the amount of funding you're able to raise. Don't leave yourself in the position where you may lose your home and leave your partner and dependents without a roof over their heads. If you're going to take that kind of risk, everyone involved has to be convinced that the gamble is worth taking.

Paying out

After you're trading and getting paid for your work, you have to start paying out. How you're taxed depends on how you set up your business and how you run it. If you're set up as a sole trader or a partnership, whether you're taxed as self-employed or as an employee depends on how your work is organised. You're likely to be classed as self-employed if you:

- ✔ Can send someone else along in your place to do the work
- ✔ Can work for more than one business at the same time
- ✔ Can work as and when you're required
- ✔ Provide your own tools or equipment to do the job
- ✔ Pay your own support staff if you need any
- ✔ Are responsible for your own profits and loss

You may be classed as self-employed for one job that you do but as an employee for the next job, in which case the employer is expected to deduct the correct income tax from your wages before handing them to you. You must sort out your status with HMRC within three months of starting up (although it's best to sort it out before you start trading) to be sure that you're taxed properly. At the same time, you must sort out your National Insurance, either as a self-employed person or as an employee. You can contact the local HMRC office – you can find details in the phone book, or you can find more information and contacts on the website at www.hmrc.gov.uk.

If you set up a limited company, you're considered a director of the company and are taxed as a company employee. The company also pays Corporation Tax on its profits. Again, HMRC, an accountant, or the local Business Link can help you put all the necessary processes in place to pay your tax.

If you take on employees, you or the company need to deduct the correct tax and national insurance from their wages and pay that amount to the HMRC.

You must also consider *Value Added Tax* (VAT). You don't pay VAT on profits, but on the sale of goods and services. Basically, as a business, you collect VAT on behalf of the Government. No matter how your business is set up, if you have a turnover in your business of circa £70,000 a year or more, you have to register for VAT with HMRC. Go to the HMRC website at www.hmrc.gov.uk to get information or get help from your local Business Link.

You also need to consider business rates and capital gains tax. All in all, a lot of financial issues are involved in setting up and running a business. While you can deal with these issues yourself, having an accountant or financial adviser on hand to give advice and support is helpful until you're completely confident.

Getting paid on time

If you're selling goods or services as a sole trader, in a partnership, or as a limited company, you can keep afloat only as long as you're getting paid for what you do. A large proportion of the businesses that go under cite cash flow problems as the main reason for their demise. For that reason, you need good processes in place to deal with preparing invoices and chasing money that's due.

Stipulate on your contracts the terms for payment. Even if your terms and conditions of invoices don't say it, you should receive your money within 30 days; if not, the law allows you to charge interest – of the Bank of England base rate plus 8 per cent – on the overdue amount. You can also claim compensation of £40 on debts of less than £1,000, £70 on debts of £1,000 up to £9,999, and £100 on debts of £10,000 or more.

If you pay late, other companies can take the same steps against you. Don't treat your creditors as a bank.

You don't want to be in the position where you have to charge interest or chase it up because you run the risk of losing your customers. You certainly don't want to go to the time and expense of chasing your debts through the courts. You may be throwing good money after bad. The best way is to have very clear payment terms from the minute you start up. If you do a good job, give your customers that little bit of extra care and attention and form a good relationship with each of them, they're more likely to stick to those payment terms for fear that you won't be available next time they need your services.

Planning for your retirement

Many business owners forget about saving into a pension fund to provide an income for their own retirement. If your business is worth a lot of money when you retire, you may be able to sell it to provide you with a retirement income. However, if you sell your business, you may be liable for Capital Gains Tax (see www.hmrc.gov.uk/cgt/index.htm for the latest rules in this area). Seek advice from an accountant if you're planning to sell.

On the other hand, you may find that your business is worth very little without you in it. In that case, you need to plan ahead by paying into a pension or saving money in some other type of investment. If you have five or more employees, you can offer them access to some type of pension, even if it's just a stakeholder pension.

You don't have to make contributions to any pension you make available, but prospective employees may view pension contributions as a more important perk than a higher salary, enabling you to recruit the best people.

Talk to an accountant or financial adviser about pensions for yourself and your employees.

Safeguarding Your Business Assets

When you think of your business assets, you probably think first and foremost of your equipment or machinery, company cars and so on. It's important to make sure that all those assets are looked after and insured, as well as protected by alarms and locks to cut down the risk of damage or loss. However, if you're in the business of inventing things or coming up with new ideas or you have logos or symbols that are a vital part of your business brand or image, those intangibles can be valuable assets. You can take care of most material assets, such as premises and computers, with insurance, but assets that fall under the heading of *intellectual property* are a lot harder to protect but even more damaging to lose.

Protecting your name

A rose by any other name may smell as sweet, but would your business be as successful if it was called something else? If you've worked hard to build a good reputation and your customers keep returning and sending referrals, your name is vitally important. For that reason, you don't want anyone else using it and perhaps tarnishing it by selling inferior goods or services to the ones you provide. If someone is in competition with you and tries to use the same or a similar name as yours, you can take her to court and claim that she's passing off her products as yours.

Of course, the last thing you want is to get involved in costly court proceedings, and you have to be sure that you have a good case. For example, the other company may not realise that another company with the same or similar name is doing a similar line of business. Try to negotiate before taking

court action, but don't wait too long before taking action or your good reputation may be lost. Take legal advice as soon as you recognise a potential
conflict with another firm.

Guarding your logos and trademarks

Often when you buy goods, you see a *registered trademark* – a symbol or logo
that has been registered by that company as its own trademark. If you think
about your favourite brands, you can conjure up in your mind their various
logos and symbols. These items help customers recognise your products.
People are searching for brands well known for quality, so logos and trademarks are important marketing tools.

If you register your trademarks, you can go to court to stop anyone else
from using them, and you may even be able to claim damages as well. If you
haven't registered your trademarks, you can still take legal action to stop
another business from using them, but you have to prove the following:

✔ The trademark or symbol represents your good reputation.

✔ If someone else uses your trademark or symbol, customers will be
confused.

✔ Your business has been damaged as a result of someone using your
trademark or logo.

Register your trademarks at the Patent Office (www.patent.gov.uk or
08459-500-505). You can initially register them for ten years and then renew
them every ten years for as long as you're trading.

Copyrighting your creations

You can't register *copyright* in the same way as you can trademarks. (See the
preceding section for more information on trademarks.) Copyright is the
exclusive legal right to print, publish, perform, film or record literary, artistic
or musical material and to authorise other people to do the same. If you've
created a piece of music or written a book, you're the owner of the copyright.
The copyright exists automatically when the material becomes a physical
entity – for example, when it's put onto paper. You can't copyright an idea,
only the embodiment of the idea – the musical score as written on paper, for
example, but you have to prove that you own the copyright.

Copyright gives you say over how your material is used, – for example,
whether it can be copied, performed or broadcast – and covers music, plays,
books, stories, paintings, computer programs, sound recordings, films,
videos and so on.

You can sell or transfer ownership of your copyright to someone else, and you can give someone else licence to use it – as composers of music or songs do. Each time someone else uses your copyrighted material, you receive *royalties* – an agreed sum of money that's paid each time a book sells or each time your music is performed in public. Copyright terms range from 50 years for broadcasts and sound recordings to 70 years after the death of the creator of books, plays and music.

If you do come up with something that is eligible for copyright, keep records of when it was written or produced. You may even want to keep a dated and sealed copy in a bank box or safe or lodged with your solicitor. That way, if copyright is ever an issue, you can prove that you were the original creator, and the copyright belongs to you.

If you employ someone to come up with this kind of material as part of her job, you're the owner of the copyright unless you've agreed otherwise. You may employ someone to design computer software, for example, and you own the copyright of that software.

If you hire someone to do a particular job – on a contract specifically for that job – and it involves a piece of artistic work, such as taking photographs or designing a website, that person is likely to own the copyright unless you state otherwise in the contract. Make the situation clear when the contract is being drawn up.

Protecting your designs

If your creation is some type of design, you have protection similar to copyright. *Design right* is automatic after the design exists, and you can use it to stop other people from making, using or selling your designs or similar ones. Design right applies to a product's outward shape.

If you want stronger protection, consider a *registered design,* which covers design features like the shape or patterns on a piece of pottery. You need to apply to the Patent Office for a registered design, which lasts for 5 years and can be extended for up to 25 years. You can get more information from the Patent Office (08459-500-505 or www.patent.gov.uk).

Patenting your inventions

When you buy certain goods, you may see a patent number on them or the words *patent pending,* which means that a patent has been applied for.

Patents are meant to stop someone else from making, selling or using something you've invented without your permission. If you invent a machine for making beds, for example, the patent covers the technical elements of the invention and how it works. You can patent the following items:

✔ Something that's completely new

✔ Something that's an improvement on something that already exists

✔ Something already existing that has a new use

People often worry that if they do apply for a patent at some point in the process, their idea will become known to other people and stolen. But without a patent, you can't stop someone else from using your product or process for their own good. Patents protect your invention for 20 years. You can go to court to enforce it and apply for compensation if someone else has damaged your business. In that time, you benefit because no one else can make and sell your product so you can charge whatever the market will pay without competition bringing down the price. You can also sell the patent or license it out to other people to use while paying you royalties.

You can get more information about patents and how to apply for one from the Patent Office (08459-500-505 or `www.patent.gov.uk`) or from patent attorneys who are members of the Chartered Institute of Patent Agents (020-7405-9450 or `www.cipa.org.uk`).

Closing Down Your Business

Even if your business becomes very successful, you may decide that you've had enough and want to call it a day. If you have many willing buyers, you can sell to whomever you choose.

You need to take advice because the rules over transferring your business, and in particular your staff and their contracts and rights, to a new owner are complicated. As with anything to do with your business, Business Link can help, but you need a solicitor to draw up all the necessary paperwork.

If the business is really all about you and won't continue without you, you may have no choice but to simply close it down. Even then, you're faced with the problem of having to make your employees redundant.

However, most businesses close down because they run into problems. You can be very successful for years and then go into a decline simply because the market has changed and you've failed to keep that necessary one step ahead of the game. Then the contracts dry up, and the customers move on to something new and more exciting elsewhere.

Laying off staff and cutting hours

If you're facing a shortage of orders but you haven't yet decided to make redundancies, you can consider laying off employees or putting them on short-time working – where they have less than half a normal week's work and pay. Be careful, though. If nothing in their contracts allows you to lay them off or put them on short time, you'll be in breach of contract. If you cut their wages, they can claim for unauthorised deductions from wages.

If their contracts do allow you to lay them off or cut their hours, those employees who have worked for you for at least one month are entitled to a guaranteed payment for up to five days in the three-month period following the first day they were sent home because no work was available. If the staff contract, Written Statement of Employment Particulars, or the staff handbook says that employees will be paid their usual pay if they're laid off, then you must pay them that amount. If not, then you must pay the legal minimum.

Employees who have been laid off or put on short time may leave and may be entitled to claim redundancy payments if the lay-off or short-time working lasts for:

- Four consecutive weeks or longer
- A series of six weeks or more – of which not more than three were consecutive – within a 13-week period.

Making people redundant

Redundancy means that jobs are going, and therefore the people who are doing those jobs are being dismissed by reason of redundancy. Redundancy isn't the same as sacking them for disciplinary reasons. It's fair to dismiss people because of redundancy, but, as with any dismissal, you have to go the right way about it.

You have to be fair in who you decide to make redundant and go through all the necessary procedures in the correct way; otherwise, your employees can claim that they were unfairly selected for redundancy and take a claim against you at an employment tribunal. Even if you're not selecting people for redundancy but closing down your whole operation and making everyone redundant, you have to do it properly. Talk to a business adviser as soon as you think redundancies may be in the pipeline so that you know how to tackle the process.

Before you issue a redundancy notice, you must consult with your employees, even if you believe you have nothing to discuss with them. If 20 to 100 jobs are to go, you have to have at least 30 days in which to consult with unions and staff. If more than 100 jobs are to go, the consultation period has to be at least 90 days. The purpose of consultation is to see whether you can find ways to save jobs. The staff may have ideas or perhaps even want to come up with some sort of proposal to buy the business and carry on.

If you're making 20 people or more redundant, you have to notify the Secretary of State through the Department of Trade and Industry. If you don't, you can be fined up to £5,000.

People are entitled to notice that their employment is ending. Most employees are entitled to a redundancy payment. How much they're entitled to depends on how long they've worked for you, how much they earn, and what age they are. The Advisory, Conciliation and Arbitration Service (ACAS) produces a ready reckoner, which shows how many weeks' payment your employees are entitled to. You can find it on the website at ACAS at www.acas.org.uk or by contacting the helpline on 08457-47-47-47.

If you don't give employees the right notice or money in lieu of notice or don't give them written details of the calculations of their redundancy payments, they can make claims against you at an employment tribunal.

Paying what you owe

Closing down your business can be an expensive process if you have quite a few employees, and you've been in operation for some time. Add up the final payments – redundancy payments, payments in lieu of notice, and wages owed (including any bonuses and overtime to be paid and any holiday pay due).

If you can't pay your employees what you owe them, they become creditors of your business and as such are entitled to what's owed to them if enough money is left in the pot after the business is sold. Your employees become preferred creditors and should receive their money after your secured creditors, who have security such as a mortgage. You need to keep employees informed of what's going on and make sure that they know how to claim from the state through the National Insurance Fund if you don't have enough money to go around. Your employees can contact the Redundancy Payments Helpline at 0845-1450-0034 for help. See the Department for Business, Innovation and Skills website at www.bis.gov.uk.

Getting Help

If you want to work for yourself as a self-employed sole trader or are thinking much bigger and want to set up a company that grows and grows, take all the good advice you can get from the vast wealth of information out there.

Most big banks provide useful brochures, packs, and leaflets on all aspects of running a business. Your solicitor and accountant, if you have them, will be helpful, but don't take petty problems to them; you have to pay for their time, and you may have more cost-effective ways of getting help and support. If you do decide to turn to your solicitor or accountant, make sure that they are experienced in dealing with businesses the size of yours. Big businesses are quite different animals from small ones.

The government runs Business Link in England and the equivalent in Scotland, Wales and Northern Ireland, with offices in most big towns and cities, as well as advisers with a whole range of business expertise. This free service provides advice, guidance and support on everything to do with setting up and running a business. Business Link also has a very comprehensive website at www.businesslink.gov.uk, which gives you most of the information you need.

Of course, websites can't always give you the necessary support. You can get details about the nearest office to you on the website or in the local telephone directory or call 0845-600-9006. In Scotland, the organisation is Business Gateway (0845-609-6611 or www.bgateway.com). In Wales, contact Business Eye (0845-796-9798 or www.businesseye.org.uk). In Northern Ireland, contact Invest Northern Ireland (0289-023-9090 or www.investni.com).

ACAS (08457-47-47-47 or www.acas.org.uk) is an invaluable source of help for businesses.

The Federation of Small Businesses has 185,000 members with 1.25 million employees between them. For an annual subscription of between £100 and £750, depending on how many employees you have, you get various services, including access to the legal helpline where you can talk to an adviser about any legal problems you have. Call 01253-336-000 or check out the website at www.fsb.org.uk.

The Equality and Human Rights Commission (www.equalityhumanrights.com) can help on disability issues. Other organisations you may find useful include

- ✔ **British Chambers of Commerce** (www.chamberonline.co.uk) provides a range of business services locally.

- ✔ **Institute of Directors** (0207-839-1233 or www.iod.com) represents individual company directors.

- ✔ **The Prince's Trust** (0800-842-842 or www.princes-trust.org.uk) offers advice and financial support for young people starting up.

- ✔ **Shell LiveWIRE** (0845-757-3252 or www.shell-livewire.org) provides advice and support for people under 30 in business.

- ✔ **Inside UK Enterprise** (0870-458-4155 or www.iuke.co.uk) brings together established firms with start-ups for advice.

- ✔ **Disabled Entrepreneurs Network** (www.disabled-entrepreneurs.net) provides help for business owners with disabilities.

- ✔ **Trade associations** (020-7395-8283 or www.taforum.org) can provide assistance.

Chapter 3

Can You Do the Business?

In This Chapter

▶ Understanding whether being your own boss is right for you

▶ Checking out various ventures

▶ Figuring out your profit motive

▶ Taking a skills inventory to identify any gaps

Governments are keen to foster entrepreneurship: new businesses create jobs for individuals and increased prosperity for nations, which are both primary goals for any government. If those new firms don't throw people out of work when recessions start to bite, supporting them becomes doubly attractive.

But people – you included – don't start businesses or grow existing ones simply to please politicians or to give their neighbours employment. They have many reasons for considering self-employment. The idea of escaping the daily grind of working for someone else and being in charge of their own destiny attracts most people. But despite the many potential benefits, they face real challenges and problems, and self-employment isn't a realistic option for everyone.

The questions you need to ask yourself are: Can I do it? Am I really the entrepreneurial type? What are my motivations and aims? How do I find the right business for me? This chapter can help you discover the answers.

Deciding What You Want from a Business

See whether you relate to any of the most common reasons people give for starting up in business:

- Being able to make your own decisions
- Having a business to leave to your children
- Creating employment for the family
- Being able to capitalise on specialist skills
- Earning your own money when you want
- Having flexible working hours
- Wanting to take a calculated risk
- Reducing stress and worry
- Having the satisfaction of creating something truly your own
- Being your own boss
- Working without having to rely on other people

The two central themes connecting all these reasons seem to revolve around gaining personal satisfaction – making work as much fun as any other aspect of life – and creating wealth – essential if an enterprise is going to last any length of time. Even when your personality fits and your goals are realistic, however, you have to make sure that the business you're starting is a good fit for your abilities. The following sections explore these reasons in more detail.

Gaining personal satisfaction (or, entrepreneurs just wanna have fun)

No one particularly enjoys being told what to do and where and when to do it. Working for someone else's organisation brings all those disadvantages. When you work for yourself, the only person to blame if your job is boring, repetitive or takes up time that you should perhaps spend with family and friends is yourself.

Another source of personal satisfaction comes from the ability to 'do things my way'. Employees are constantly puzzled and often irritated by the decisions their bosses impose on them. All too often managers in big firms say that they'd never spend their own money in the way the powers that be encourage or instruct them to do. Managers and subordinates alike feel constrained by company policy, which seems to set out arbitrary standards for dealing with customers and employees in the same way.

The high failure rate for new businesses suggests that the glamour of starting up on their own seduces some people who may be more successful and more contented in some other line of endeavour.

Running your own firm allows you to do things in a way that you think the market, and your employees, believe to be right at the time.

Making money

Apart from winning the lottery, starting your own business is the only possible way to achieve full financial independence. But it isn't risk-free. In truth, most people who work for themselves don't become mega-rich. However, many do and many more become far wealthier than they would probably have become working for someone else. You can also earn money working at your own pace when you want to and even help your family to make some money too.

Running your own business means taking more risks than you do if you're working for someone else. If the business fails, you stand to lose far more than your job. If, like most owner-managers, you opt for *sole trader status* – someone working usually on his own without forming a limited company (find more on business categories in Book I Chapter 2) – you can end up personally liable for any business debts you incur. This can mean having to sell your home and other assets to meet your obligations. In these circumstances, not only will all your hard work have been to no avail, but you can end up worse off than when you started. Also, winding up a business is far from fun or personally satisfying.

We don't want to discourage you, just to apply a reality check. The truth is that running your own business is hard work that often doesn't pay well at first. You have to be okay with those facts to have a chance of success.

Saving the planet

Not everyone has making money as his sole aim when setting up in business. According to the government's figures, around 20,000 'social entrepreneurs' run businesses aiming to achieve sustainable social change, and trade with a social or environmental purpose. They contribute almost £25 billion to the national economy and assist local communities by creating jobs, providing ethical products and services using sustainable resources, and reinvesting a share of the profits back into society.

Ethical businesses have some unique advantages. For example, according to those running such firms they can relatively easily attract and retain intelligent people. Over 70 per cent of students say that a potential employer's track record is an important factor in job choice. Customers also like ethical firms. According to a recent European Union survey on sustainable consumption, 86 per cent of those polled in the United Kingdom, Spain, Germany, Greece and Italy said that they felt very strongly about wanting things to be produced and marketed responsibly. They also blamed brands for not providing more environmentally and socially friendly products.

If you want to explore the prospects for starting a social enterprise, contact the School for Social Entrepreneurs (website: www.sse.org.uk; tel: 020-8981-0300), which can help with specific and tailored support. If you need funds to start a social enterprise, contact Bridges Community Ventures (website: www.bridgesventures.com; tel: 020-7262-5566), a venture capital firm with a social mission. Its founding principle is that all the funds it invests go to businesses with a clear social purpose as well as aiming to achieve financial returns for investors.

Exploring Different Types of Business

At one level all businesses are the same – they sell something to people who want to buy from them, while trying to make a profit. At another level many very different types of business and ways of doing business exist, even within what superficially can appear to be very similar fields.

Selling to other businesses

Business-to-business (B2B) enterprises, such as those selling market research, database management, corporate clothing, management consultancy, telemarketing or graphic design, involve one businessperson selling to another. The attractions are that you're dealing with other people who have a definite need and usually buy in relative large quantities and at regular intervals. For example, an individual may buy envelopes in packs of a dozen a few times a year, but a business buys scores, perhaps even thousands, and puts in an order every month. Corporate customers are harder to win, but are often worth more when you have them. And unlike private individuals, businesses like to forge relationships that endure over time.

Some downsides exist too. Business customers expect credit, perhaps taking between 60 and 90 days to pay up. If they go bust they may owe money and take suppliers down with them. You may have to attend exhibitions to make your presence known, a costly and time-consuming process, or advertise in trade directories. Check out these websites to find out more about these topics: www.idealbusinessshow.co.uk and www.b2bindex.co.uk.

Opening all hours

Conventional shops, restaurants and the like have long opening hours and have to meet the expectations of increasingly savvy consumers, whose access to the Internet has made them aware of competitive prices as well as high specifications and standards of service. The upside of any form of retailing is that you're almost always paid up front. But just because you get the cash in your hand doesn't mean that you don't have to meet exacting standards. Customers are protected in their dealings in a myriad of ways and if you fall short of their legal entitlement you can end up with a bigger bill than a simple cash refund. (We cover legal issues in Book V Chapter 2, 'Marketing Your Wares'.) In conventional retailing you also have to rent premises and stock them with products. Both factors can add significantly to the business risk.

Increasingly, new retail business start-ups are Internet-based. The website is in effect the shop window and the stock of products being sold may even be in a warehouse owned by a third party. This keeps up-front costs down but means keeping abreast of fast-changing technologies – the Internet, servers and computer hardware and software. (We look at these in more depth in Book V Chapter 8.)

Making products

One of the attractions of manufacturing is that you have a greater degree of control over the quality, cost and specification of the end product than a retailer or wholesaler might. But with those advantages come some hefty penalties. Factories, equipment, stocks of raw materials and employees are costly overheads. You have to incur these expenses well before you're certain of any orders – an unlikely way into business for someone without previous manufacturing experience and a deep wallet. Such owners also bear some significant risks towards their employees. The UK manufacturing sector reports over 32,000 work-related accidents to the Health and Safety Executive each year. This figure includes over 6,200 major injuries such as fractures and amputations as well as around 40 fatalities.

A more likely route to manufacturing for a new business is subcontracting, where you work for a manufacturer on part of a product. The most common examples of subcontractors are plumbers, electricians and carpenters in building work, metal and plastic casing production and the like in civil engineering and a range of activities in the information technology sector.

Servicing customers

Service industries now dominate the British economy and account for around 70 per cent of gross domestic product (the value of the goods and services that the country produces). Services include financial intermediaries, hairdressing, real estate, computer services, research and development, education, health and social work, refuse disposal, recreational, cultural and sporting activities, and an extensive range of other activities where no physical goods play a major part in any transaction. In truth, however, most manufactured goods include a service element, though the business functions are often separated. For example, manufacturing businesses produce cars but are quite separate from the garage chains that repair those vehicles. But some manufacturers go further – Dell manufactures computers and also carries out delivery and many other service functions.

Service businesses require a high degree of personal involvement and as such call for founders who see their people skills as pivotal. In a nutshell, if you don't enjoy understanding the intimate details of what makes customers tick and then going out of your way to meet their needs, running a service business may be of little appeal.

Assessing Yourself

Business isn't just about ideas and market opportunities. Business is about people too, and at the outset it's mostly about *you*. You need to make sure that you have the temperament to run your own business and the expertise and understanding required for the type of business you have in mind.

The test at the end of this section requires no revision or preparation. You may find out the truth about yourself and whether or not running a business is a great career option or a potential disaster for you.

Discovering your entrepreneurial attributes

Business founders are frequently characterised as people who are bursting with new ideas, highly enthusiastic, hyperactive and insatiably curious. But the more you try to create a clear picture of the typical small business founder, the fuzzier that picture becomes. In reality, the most reliable indicator that a person is likely to start a business is that he has a parent or sibling who runs a business – such people are highly likely to start businesses themselves. That being said, commentators generally accept some fairly broad characteristics as desirable, if not mandatory. Check whether you recognise yourself in the following list of entrepreneurial traits.

- ✔ **Accepting of uncertainty:** An essential characteristic of someone starting a business is a willingness to make decisions and to take risks. This doesn't mean gambling on hunches. It means carefully calculating the odds and deciding which risks to take and when to take them.

- ✔ Managers in big business tend to seek to minimise risk by delaying decisions until they know every possible fact. They feel that working without all the facts isn't prudent or desirable. Entrepreneurs, on the other hand, know that by the time the fog of uncertainty has completely lifted, too many people are able to spot the opportunity clearly. In fact, an entrepreneur is usually only interested in decisions that involve accepting a degree of uncertainty.

✔ **Driven to succeed:** Business founders need to be results-oriented. Successful people set themselves goals and get pleasure out of trying to achieve them as quickly as possible and then move on to the next goal. This restlessness is very characteristic.

✔ **Hardworking:** Don't confuse hard work with long hours. At times an owner-manager has to put in 18-hour days, but that shouldn't be the norm. Even if you do work long hours, as long as you enjoy them, that's fine. Enthusiasts can be very productive. Workaholics, on the other hand, have a negative, addictive, driven quality where outputs (results) are less important than inputs. This type of hard work is counterproductive. Real hard work means sticking at a task, however difficult, until you complete it. It means hitting deadlines even when you're dead-beat. It means doing some things you don't much enjoy so you can work your way through to the activities that you enjoy most.

✔ **Healthy:** Apart from being able to put in long days, successful small business owners need to be on the spot to manage the firm every day. Owners are the essential lubricant that keeps the wheels of small business turning. They have to plug any gaps when other people are ill or because they can't afford to employ anyone else for that particular job. They can't afford the luxury of sick leave. Even a week or so's holiday is something of a luxury in the early years of a business's life.

✔ **Innovative:** Most people recognise innovation as the most distinctive trait of business founders. They tend to tackle the unknown; they do things in new and difficult ways; they weave old ideas into new patterns. But they go beyond innovation itself and carry their concept to market rather than remain in an ivory tower.

✔ **Self-disciplined:** Owner-managers need strong personal discipline to keep themselves and the business on the schedule the plan calls for. This is the drumbeat that sets the timing for everything in the company. Get that wrong and you send incorrect signals to every part of the business, both inside and out.

A common pitfall for novice businesspeople is failing to recognise the difference between cash and profit. Cash can make people feel wealthy and if it results in a relaxed attitude to corporate status symbols such as cars and luxury office fittings, then failure is just around the corner.

✔ **Totally committed:** You must have complete faith in your business idea. That's the only way in which you can convince all the doubters you're bound to meet along the route. But blind faith isn't enough. You have to back your commitment up with a sound business strategy.

✔ **Well rounded:** Small business founders are rarely geniuses. Some people in their business nearly always have more competence in one field than they can ever aspire to. But the founders have a wide range of ability and a willingness to turn their hand to anything that has to be done to make the venture succeed. They can usually make the product, market it and count the money, but above all they have the self-confidence that lets them move comfortably through uncharted waters.

Working out a business idea that's right for you

Take some time to do a simple exercise that can help you decide what type of business is a good match with your abilities. Take a sheet of paper and draw up two columns. In the left-hand column, list all your hobbies, interests and skills. In the right-hand column, translate those interests into possible business ideas. Table 3-1 shows an example of such a list.

Table 3-1	Matching a Business Idea to Your Skills
Interest/Skills	*Business Ideas*
Cars	Car dealer; repair garage; home tuning service; valet and cleaning/taxi
Cooking	Restaurant; home catering service; providing produce for home freezers
Gardening	Supplying produce to flower or vegetable shops; running a nursery or garden centre; landscape design; running a gardening service
Using a computer	Typing authors' manuscripts from home; typing back-up service for busy local companies; running a secretarial agency; web design; bookkeeping service; selling online

Having done this exercise, balance the possibilities against the criteria that are important to you in starting a business.

Figuring out what you're willing to invest

We're not just talking about money here. How much are you willing to invest of your time, your interest and your education, as well as your (and your investors') money?

Spending time

How much time are you willing to devote to your business? That may sound a basic enough question, but different businesses done in different ways can have quite different time profiles. One business starter we know started a French bakery in London. He was determined to make his own croissants and did so for the first three months. But making his own bread meant starting work at 4 a.m. Because he didn't close until city workers passed his door on their way home, by the time he had cleaned up and taken stock, he was working a 15-hour day. But he still had the books to do, orders to place and plans to prepare. He eventually settled for a 10-hour day, which meant that he had to buy in ready-baked croissants.

Furthering your education

You may have identified a market opportunity that requires skills over and above those that you currently have. There may, for example, be a gap in the market for Teaching English as a Foreign Language (TEFL), but to do so requires a month of intensive study plus a £1,000 course fee. Doing the TEFL certificate may involve you in more skill upgrading than you want to commit to, at the outset at least. So either you need to find customers who don't require you to have that qualification, or you need to think about a less educationally challenging business.

Keeping things interesting

If you want to start a restaurant and have never worked in catering, get a job in one. That's the best way to find out whether you like a particular type of work. You may find that a restaurant looks very different from behind the chair as opposed to on it. Some businesses are inherently repetitive, with activities that follow a predictable pattern. If that suits you, fine, but if not, then perhaps you need to consider a business venture with a range of tasks.

Weighting your preferences

After you have an idea of some of the businesses you may want to start, you can rank those businesses according to how closely they match what you want from starting a business. Go through the standards you want your business to meet and assign a weight between 1 and 5 to each, on a range from 'not important at all' to 'absolutely must have'. Next, list your possible business opportunities and measure them against the graded criteria.

Table 3-2 shows a sample ranking for Jane Clark, an imaginary ex-secretary with school-aged children who needs work because her husband has been made redundant and is looking for another job. Jane isn't in a position to raise much capital, and wants her working hours to coincide with her children's school day. She wants to run her own show and to enjoy what she does.

Book I

Planning Your Business

Table 3-2	Weighing Up the Factors
Criteria	*Weighting Factor*
Minimal capital required	5
Possibility to work hours that suit lifestyle	5
No need to learn new skills	4
Minimal paperwork	3
Work satisfaction	2
Opportunity to meet interesting people	1

Because minimal capital was an important criterion for Jane she gave it a weight of 5, whereas meeting interesting people, being less important to her, was only weighted 1. Jane gave each of her three business ideas a rating in points (out of five) against these criteria. A secretarial agency needed capital to start, so she gave it only 1 point. Back-up typing needed hardly any money and she allocated 5 points to it. Her worked-out chart is shown in Table 3-3.

Table 3-3		Scoring Alternatives					
		Secretarial agency		*Back-up typing*		*Authors' manuscripts*	
	Weighting Factor	*Points*	*Score*	*Points*	*Score*	*Points*	*Score*
Criteria							
Minimal capital	5 ×	1	5	5	25	4	20
Flexible hours	5 ×	1	5	3	15	5	25
No new skills	4 ×	2	8	5	20	5	20
Work satisfaction	3 ×	4	12	1	3	3	9
Minimal paperwork	2 ×	0	0	4	8	5	10
Meeting people	1 ×	4	4	3	3	4	4
Total score			34		74		88

The weighting factor and the rating point multiplied together give a score for each business idea. The highest score indicates the business that best meets Jane's criteria. In this case, typing authors' manuscripts scored over back-up typing, because Jane could do it exactly when it suited her.

Chapter 4

Starting Your Business Plan

· ·

In This Chapter

▶ Getting the most out of your plan

▶ Using your plan as a record of the past and a guide to the future

▶ Making your plan function as your company description

▶ Figuring out who makes the plan and who can help

▶ Checking out what the written plan looks like

· ·

Most of us go through life thinking ahead. We plan to paint the house, plan to go back to university, plan to take a holiday and plan for retirement – we always have a plan or two in the works. Why do we plan so much? We certainly can't predict what's going to happen, so why bother? Certainly, none of us knows the future. But each of us knows that tomorrow will be different from today, and today isn't the same as yesterday. Planning for those differences is one way to move forward and face things that are unfamiliar and uncertain. Planning is a strategy for survival.

Companies make business plans for many of the same reasons. Planning is a strategy to improve the odds of success in a business world that's constantly changing. Business plans aren't a guarantee, of course. Business planning isn't a science that offers you right and wrong answers about the future. But business planning is a process that gets you ready for what's to come. And making a plan increases the likelihood that down the road, your company will be in the right place at the right time.

In this chapter, we explore what planning is all about, how you can use your business plan and why having a plan is so important. We talk about your business plan as a guide to your company's future, as well as a record of where you've been and how you've done. Because your plan is a ready-made description of your company, we also talk about the kinds of people who may be interested in seeing your business plan. Then we help you get a handle on who should be involved in putting your plan together, depending on how big your company is. Finally, we show you what your business plan should look like on paper.

Getting the Most Out of Your Plan

A *plan* originally meant only one thing: a flat view of a building, viewed from above. If you've ever had a house built or remodelled, you know that this kind of plan is still around (and still expensive). Over the centuries, however, the meaning of the word *plan* has expanded to include time as well as space. A *plan* in the modern sense also refers to a view of the future, seen from the present. You make plans for a birthday party next week or a business trip next month.

A *business plan* is a particular view of your company's future, describing the following things:

- ✔ What your industry will look like
- ✔ What markets you'll compete in
- ✔ What competition you'll be up against
- ✔ What products and services you'll offer
- ✔ What value you'll provide customers
- ✔ What long-term advantages you'll have
- ✔ How big and profitable your company will become

To create a detailed view of the future, you have to make a lot of predictions about what's going to happen down the road. If your company manufactures crystal balls, of course, you're in luck. If not, you have to find other ways to make some basic business assumptions about the future, which we share with you throughout this book.

In the end, your business plan is only as good as all the assumptions you put into it. To make sure that your assumptions make sense, much of your planning should involve trying to understand your surroundings today – what's going on right now in your own industry and marketplace. By making these assumptions, you can better predict your business and its future. Will your predictions actually come true? Only time will tell. Fortunately, the planning process makes you better prepared for whatever lies ahead.

Looking to the future

A business plan provides a view of the future. Whether your company is large or small, whether you're just starting a business or are part of a seasoned company, you still need some sort of planning process to point you in the right direction and guide you along the way.

✔ A brand-new company makes a business plan to get its bearings and often uses the plan to get funding.

✔ An up-and-running company uses a plan to be better prepared.

✔ A large company needs a plan so that everybody sees the same view ahead.

✔ A small company makes a plan if it wants to make sure that it survives those crucial first two years.

In fact, a small company needs a business plan most of all. If you own or manage a small business, you already know that you're the jack-or-jill-of-all-trades. You hardly have enough time to get your daily business tasks done, much less plan for next week, next month or next year. But because you run a small business, you simply can't afford *not* to plan.

When a giant company stumbles, it usually has the financial reserves to break the fall and get back on its feet. If your resources are limited, however, a single mistake – such as exaggerating the demand for your products or underestimating how long you have to wait to get paid – can spell the end of everything you've invested in and worked so hard to achieve. A business plan points out many dangers, alerting you to the hazards and obstacles that lie ahead, so that you can avoid such pitfalls. Remember: two thirds of all new businesses cease trading within their first two or three years.

Accounting for your history

A business plan paints a picture of where your company has been and how it has changed over the years. By reviewing past performance, particularly from your accounts and sales reports, you can use your plan to figure out what worked and what didn't. In effect, your business plan offers you an opportunity to keep score, allowing you to set goals for your company and then keep track of your achievements. For example

✔ Your plan creates a view of the future. In years to come, you can use old copies of your plan to look back and determine just how good you are at seeing what lies ahead.

✔ Your plan maps out a direction to go in and the route to take. You can use it to gauge how skilful you are at accomplishing what you set out to do.

✔ Your plan forecasts where you want to be. You can use it to check out how close you have come to your targets for the industry, your market and your finances.

Your history, as described in your business plan, teaches you important lessons about the business you're in – so you aren't doomed to make the same mistakes over and over again. If you can't remember exactly where your company has been, you probably won't see where it's heading.

Anticipating your audience

You can use your business plan to tell the world (or at least anyone out there who's interested) all about your company. No matter who you're dealing with or why, your plan has a ready-made description to back up the claims you make. Your plan comes in handy when you're dealing with the following people:

- ✔ Suppliers who you're asking to extend you credit and offer you terms
- ✔ Distributors that want to add your product or service to their line-ups
- ✔ Big customers that hope to establish long-term business relationships with you
- ✔ The board of directors or other advisers who want to offer support
- ✔ Outside consultants you bring in to help out with specific issues
- ✔ Bankers who decide on whether or not to lend you money
- ✔ Investors who are interested in taking a stake in your company

All these people have their own special reasons for wanting more information about you, and each probably is interested in a different part of your plan. A well-written business plan satisfies all these groups and makes your company stronger in the process.

- ✔ A business plan improves your company's chances of success.
- ✔ A business plan shows you where your company has been and how it has changed.
- ✔ A business plan provides a blueprint for the future.
- ✔ Business planning is an ongoing process.

Naming Your Planners

Okay, a business plan is essential. Who's supposed to put the wretched thing together? In some sense, the answer depends on how big your company is.

- ✔ **Small businesses:** If your business is really just you – or maybe you and a couple of other people – you already know exactly who's responsible for making a plan for the company. That's not such a bad thing, when you think about it. Who better to create a view of the future and set business goals and objectives than the people who are also responsible for reaching the goals and making the future happen?

- ✔ **Medium-sized companies:** If your company is a bit bigger, you probably don't want to go it alone when it comes to putting together your business plan. First of all, putting together a plan is a big job. But more than that, involving all the key people in the planning process has a certain advantage: everyone involved in the plan has a stake in making sure that your company succeeds.

- ✔ **Large companies:** If you're part of a big company, you may need serious help to make a business plan that's complete and always up-to-date. To get all the work done, you may have to hire people who have nothing to do but tend to your company's business plan full time. Unfortunately, creating a planning staff involves a real danger: Your plan can take on a life of its own and get completely divorced from what's really happening with your business.

- ✔ You have to make sure that your planners don't create plans all by themselves. To be of any use in the long run, the planning staff must support the managers who actually have to carry out the business plan.

Using business planning software

Software programs allow you to assemble automatically all the components of a business plan, turning them into a polished, ready-to-print document. The best programs also make easier work of the financial parts of business planning – creating income statements and cash-flow statements, for example, or making financial projections (see Chapters 3 and 4 in Book II). Most software programs also allow you to add graphics, such as tables and charts, to your plan, providing an easy way for your audience to see at a glance what you're describing in the written document.

To review the latest software offerings, enter Business Plan Software into the window of a search engine, and then browse through the offerings of leading software providers. You can often find sample business plans that you can review to get a sense of the product you can produce with each software tool.

Business-planning software programs can make the job of business planning seem a bit too easy. With all the software bells and whistles, newcomers can inadvertently skip the serious (that is, difficult) work of creating and writing an effective plan. Remember, the best software-planning tools guide you through the important aspects of business planning and then keep track of your words, sentences and paragraphs – but they don't think for you. You still have to do the serious mental work yourself.

Investors and bankers who make a living reviewing and funding business plans are all too familiar with the look and feel of the most popular software-generated business-planning documents. When using one of these programs, customise your plan to make it unique. The last thing you want is for your business plan to look exactly like the others that cross a venture capitalist's desk.

Bplans.com (`www.bplans.co.uk`) created by Palo Alto Software, offers thousands of pages of free sample plans, planning tools and expert advice to help you start and run your business. Their site has 60 free sample business plans on it and their software package, Business Plan Pro, has these plans plus a further 140. The sample business plans are tailored for every type of business from Aircraft Rental to a Yoga Centre.

Getting help with the plan

No one knows the ins and outs of planning and running a business better than someone who has done it before. If you have questions you can't answer, or if you run out of ideas on ways to get your plan off the ground, turn to someone with tried-and-tested expertise for advice.

The first place to look for expert advice is in your address book. You'll probably have an easier time getting a 'yes' from someone you know on a personal or professional basis. If that tactic doesn't pan out, ask friends and colleagues for suggestions. Other good places to look for help are the chamber of commerce and the business section of your local newspaper. You may end up paying for some of this advice, but when you really need help, it's worth the investment.

When looking for an expert who can guide you, you want to choose someone with experience in a company that's similar to the one you're planning. When you've identified such a person, decide exactly what kind of assistance you need. After all, you can't ask someone to plan your whole business for you, but you can ask for help fine-tuning your marketing strategy, for example, or reviewing and critiquing your financial projections.

Putting Your Plan on Paper

When you put together a business plan, your efforts take you in many directions. You face all sorts of issues related to the business that you're in. For example, you need to answer immediately basic questions about your company and what you want it to be in the future. Then you have to decide what targets to aim for as you look ahead and set business goals and objectives.

A large part of creating a business plan requires only a dose of good common sense on your part. But if you want to make sure that your business plan succeeds, you also have to take the time to do the following:

- ✔ Look closely at your industry
- ✔ Get to know your customers
- ✔ Check out your competitors
- ✔ List all your company's resources
- ✔ Note what makes your company unique
- ✔ List your company's advantages
- ✔ Figure out your basic financial condition
- ✔ Put together a financial forecast and a budget

In addition, you have to be prepared for everything to change down the road. So you also need to think about other options and alternatives and be on the lookout for new ways to make your company prosper.

You don't want to scare people – yourself included – with a written plan that's too long. The longer your plan is, in fact, the less likely people are to read it. Ideally, for a small or medium-sized company, your written plan needs to be 15 or 20 pages maximum. Remember that you can always support the main text with all the exhibits, appendixes and references that you think it needs. If you want to glance at a sample business plan, take a look at *Business Plans For Dummies* (Wiley) or check out Bplans.com (www.bplans.co.uk) who have hundreds of free sample plans on their website.

To remind yourself (and other people) that your written plan is forever a work in progress, we suggest that you keep it in a ring binder, or its electronic equivalent. That way, you can add or delete pages and replace entire sections as your business plan changes – and we're certain that it *will* change. Fortunately, however, the format you use – all the major sections of a business plan – will stay the same.

Before you get your business plan under way, take a moment to review the following sections.

Executive summary

Your executive summary touches on everything that's important in your business plan. It's more than just a simple introduction: it's the whole plan, only shorter. In many cases, the people who read your plan won't need to go any further than the executive summary; if they do, the summary points them to the right place.

The executive summary isn't much longer than a page or two, so wait until the rest of the business plan is complete before you write it. That way, all you have to do is review the plan to identify the key ideas you want to convey.

If you want to make sure that people remember what you tell them, you have to say what you're going to say, say it, and then say what you've said. The executive summary is where you say what you're going to say.

Company overview

The company overview provides a place to make important observations about the nature of your business. In the overview, you discuss your industry, your customers and the products and services you offer or plan to develop. Although you try to touch on your company's business history and major activities in the overview, you can leave many of the details for the later sections.

To put together this kind of general company overview, you draw on several key planning documents, including the following:

- ✔ **Mission statement:** A statement of your company's purpose, establishing what it is and what it does.

- ✔ **Goals and objectives:** A list of all the major goals that you set for your company, along with the objectives that you have to meet to achieve those goals.

- ✔ **Values statement:** The set of beliefs and principles that guide your company's actions and activities.

- ✔ **Vision statement:** A phrase or two that announces where your company wants to go or paints a broad picture of what you want your company to become.

Business environment

The section of your business plan that deals with your business environment covers all the major aspects of your company's situation that are beyond your immediate control, including the nature of your industry, the direction of the marketplace and the intensity of your competition. You need to look at each of these areas in detail to come up with lists of both the opportunities that your business environment offers and the threats that your company faces. Based on your observations, you can then describe what it takes to be a successful company.

Pay special attention to how your industry operates. Describe the primary business forces that you see out there, as well as the key industry relationships that really determine how business gets done. Next, you need to talk about your marketplace and your customers in more detail, perhaps even dividing the market into segments that represent the kinds of customers you serve. Finally, spend some time on the competition, describing what those companies are, what they're like, how they work and what they're likely to be up to in the future.

Company description

In the company description, you go into much more detail about what your company has to offer. The description includes some information about your management, the organisation, new technology, your products and services, company operations, your marketing potential – in short, anything special that you bring to your industry.

In particular, you need to look carefully and objectively at the long list of your company's capabilities and resources. Separate the capabilities that represent strengths from those that are weaknesses. In the process, try to point out where you have real advantages over your competitors.

Examining your company through your customers' eyes helps. With this viewpoint, you sometimes can discover customer value that you didn't know you were providing, and as a result, you can come up with additional long-term ways to compete in the market.

Business strategy

The section on company strategy brings together everything that you know about your business environment and your own company so as to come up with your projections for the future.

You want to take time in this section to map out your basic strategies for dealing with the major parts of your business, including the industry, your markets and the competition. Talk about why the strategy is the right one, given your business situation. Describe how the strategy will play out in the future. Finally, point out specifically what your company needs to do to ensure that the strategy succeeds.

Everybody knows that the future is uncertain, so you also need to talk about ways in which your business world may be different in the future from how it is today. List alternative possibilities, and in each case, describe what your company is doing to anticipate the changes and take advantage of new opportunities.

Financial review

Your financial review covers both where you stand today and where you expect to be in the future.

Here you describe your current financial situation by using several standard financial statements. True, these statements don't make for the liveliest reading, but the people who are interested in this part of your business plan expect to see them. The basic financial statements include:

- ✔ **Profit and loss account:** A list of numbers that adds up all the revenue that your company brings in over a month, a quarter or a year and then subtracts the total costs involved in running your business. What's left is your *bottom line* – the profit that you make during the period.

- ✔ **Balance sheet:** A snapshot of your financial condition at a particular moment, showing exactly what things your company owns, what money it owes and what your company is really worth.

- ✔ **Cash-flow statement:** A record that traces the flow of cash in and out of your company over a given period, tracking where the money comes from and where it ends up. The cash-flow statement only tracks money when you actually receive it or spend it.

Your projections about your future financial situation use exactly the same kind of financial statements. But for projections, you estimate all the numbers in the statements, based on your understanding of what's going to happen. Because nothing is certain, make sure to include all the assumptions you made to come up with your estimates in the first place.

Action plan

Your action plan lays out how you intend to carry out your business plan. This section points out proposed changes in management or the organisation itself, for example, as well as new policies or procedures that you expect to put in place. You also include any additional skills that you, your managers and your employees may need to make the plan work. Finally, you want to talk a bit about how you're going to generate excitement for your business plan inside your company, so as to create a culture that supports what you're trying to accomplish. Only then can you have real confidence that your business plan is going to succeed.

✔ The executive summary touches on all the important parts of your plan.

✔ The company overview describes the nature of your business, using your mission, values and vision statements.

✔ Your business plan analyses your business environment.

✔ The company description identifies your company's specific capabilities and resources.

✔ The plan discusses your current business strategy.

✔ A financial review includes a profit and loss account, balance sheet and cash-flow statement.

Book I

**Planning
Your
Business**

Chapter 5

Establishing Your Starting Position

*W*hen you look into a mirror, you expect to see an image of yourself. When you listen to your voice on an answering machine, you expect to hear yourself. When you look at photos or home videos, you expect to recognise yourself. But how many times have you said

> That doesn't look like me.

or

> Is that what I really sound like?

An honest self-portrait – whether it's seeing and hearing yourself clearly or making objective statements about your own strengths and weaknesses – is tough to put together. Strengths and weaknesses have to be measured relative to the situations at hand, and a strength in one circumstance may prove to be a weakness in another. Leadership and snap decision making, for example, may serve you extremely well in an emergency. But the same temperament may be a liability when you're part of a team that's involved in delicate give-and-take negotiations.

You're going to face similar problems in seeing clearly and objectively when you take on the task of measuring your company's internal strengths and weaknesses. You may be surprised by how many businesses fail miserably at the job of objective self-analysis – companies that cling to a distorted image of the resources that they command and the capabilities that they bring to the marketplace.

In this chapter, we help you get a handle on your company's strengths and weaknesses in relation to the opportunities and threats that you face. First, we look at ways that you can spot potential strengths and weaknesses by making a list of your capabilities and resources. Next, we show you how the critical success factors in your industry come into play to determine which of those capabilities and resources are strengths and which aren't. Then we help you pull all the pieces of the puzzle together – your company's strengths, weaknesses, opportunities and threats – to create a complete picture. We also create a strategic balance sheet that helps you keep track of where you stand, what you need to do and when to do it.

Analysing Your Situation

We examine your company's situation by using a tried-and-tested approach known as SWOT – an acronym for *strengths, weaknesses, opportunities* and *threats*.

Your company's strengths and weaknesses can't be measured in a vacuum, of course. Your situation depends not only on your own capabilities and resources, but also on the opportunities and threats that arise from things beyond your control. Check out Chapter 6 in this Book to review opportunities and threats. Depending on the situations that you face, opportunities and threats appear, disappear and change all the time, and your company's strengths and weaknesses change with them.

A thorough SWOT analysis is something that you complete more than once. In fact, you'll probably carry out a SWOT review on a regular basis, depending on how fast your business environment, the industry and your own company change.

Identifying Strengths and Weaknesses

Your company's *strengths* are the capabilities, resources and skills that you can draw upon to carry out strategies, implement plans and achieve the goals that you've set for yourself. Your company's *weaknesses* are any lack of skills or a deficiency in your capabilities and resources relative to the competition that may stop you from acting on strategies and plans or accomplishing your goals.

When a strength becomes a weakness

For 30 years, Marks and Spencer hired its managers and supervisors from a talent pool that consisted almost exclusively of young men and women under 26 years of age who had graduated from its own Management Training Programme. M & S saw this hiring policy as being a major corporate strength, creating a remarkable sense of unity and consistency in its outlook and its internal culture. The company didn't need seminars and workshops to develop a common sense of values and vision; M & S values were built in from the beginning.

But that apparent strength was challenged in the late 1980s, when M & S's dominance and the stability of the entire retail sector were thrown up for grabs. Big food companies – Tesco, Sainsbury's and the others – encroached on M & S's traditional advantage in the quality pre-prepared market sector, and no one at M & S seemed to have the slightest idea

what that was going to mean. Many forward-thinking, out-of-the-mould managers had already been driven out of the straitjacket management line-up. Everyone in the organisation came from the same background and thought in much the same way. Nobody understood the speed or magnitude of the competitive threat – or the changes that were about to engulf the company.

What started as an important company strength turned into a serious weakness as Marks and Spencer faced a battle for survival. The company began an aggressive campaign to hire managers with different backgrounds and diverse experience. It also moved to recruit its very top management from outside of the founding family members and time-serving employees in an all-out effort to prepare for a future in which fast-moving change and fierce competition became the name of the game.

To capture your own first impressions of your company, complete the Company Strengths and Weaknesses Questionnaire (see Figure 5-1). On the right side of the questionnaire, assess your capabilities and resources in each area. On the left side, rate the importance of these elements to your industry.

Frames of reference

Once you've completed the questionnaire shown in Figure 5-1, you'll have an initial list of your company's strengths and weaknesses. In order to be objective, however, you need to go beyond first impressions and look at your business assets from more than one point of view. Different frames of reference offer the advantage of smoothing out biases that are bound to creep into a single viewpoint. They also offer the best chance of making your list as complete as it can be.

Company Strengths and Weaknesses Questionnaire							
Importance to Industry			**Business Area**	**Your Capabilities and Resources**			
Low	*Moderate*	*High*		*Poor*	*Fair*	*Good*	*Excellent*
❏	❏	❏	Management	❏	❏	❏	❏
❏	❏	❏	Organisation	❏	❏	❏	❏
❏	❏	❏	Customer base	❏	❏	❏	❏
❏	❏	❏	Research & development	❏	❏	❏	❏
❏	❏	❏	Operations	❏	❏	❏	❏
❏	❏	❏	Marketing & sales	❏	❏	❏	❏
❏	❏	❏	Distribution & delivery	❏	❏	❏	❏
❏	❏	❏	Financial condition	❏	❏	❏	❏

Figure 5-1:
Company
Strengths
and Weak-
nesses
Question-
naire.

✔ **Internal view.** Draw on the management experience inside your company (use your own experience, or that of your friends and former co-workers if you're self-employed) to come up with a consensus on your business strengths and weaknesses. You may want to use the same people to get a sense of what's happened in the recent past as well. A little corporate history can show you how your company's strengths and weaknesses have changed over time – and how easily the organisation shifts gears.

✔ **External view.** Beware of becoming too self-absorbed in this analysis. It's important to step back and look around, using your competitors as yardsticks, if you can. All of your competitors do business in the same industry and marketplace that you do, and they're strong or weak in all the key areas that you're interested in. If your list is going to mean anything when the time comes to apply it to your own business situation, your strengths and weaknesses have to be measured against those of your competitors. (Flip to Chapter 6 in this Book for more information on the competition.)

✔ **Outside view.** Perhaps you identify company strengths that are assets only because your competitors haven't reacted yet, or maybe you ignore real weaknesses because everybody else has them, too. Every once in a while, you need an objective outside assessment of what's happening in your business. That's where consultants can actually be of some use. If you can't afford that kind of advice, make sure that you at least monitor the business press to get an outside view of what the experts are saying about your industry's key players. Business Link in England (and equivalents in Scotland and Wales) can generally help firms to set up an objective appraisal of the strengths and weaknesses of a business.

If you don't have a management team that can conduct a situation analysis, bring together one of the informal groups that you rely on for some of your other planning tasks. Ask the group members to spend a little time analysing strengths and weaknesses. Make sure that the group looks at your company's situation from various perspectives, using the different frames of reference in the preceding list.

Capabilities and resources

In putting together a list of your company's capabilities and resources, cast your net as widely as possible. Look at your capabilities and resources in a systematic way, reviewing all the business areas introduced in the Company Strengths and Weaknesses Questionnaire (refer to Figure 5-1 earlier in this chapter). In each area, try to identify as many capabilities and resources as possible by using different frames of reference. At the same time, assess how relevant each capability or resource is in helping you to carry out your plans and to achieve your business goals. You're going to use this master list as raw material when the time comes to identify your company's strengths and weaknesses.

Management: Setting direction from the top

Your company's management team brings together skills, talent and commitment. You want team members to find their direction from your company's mission, vision and values statements, as well as from the business goals and objectives that you plan to achieve. Top-notch managers and owners are particularly important in industries that face increasing competition or fast-changing technologies. It's hard to think of an industry that doesn't fit into one of these two categories.

Management is there to determine what your company's going to do. Senior managers are officially charged with setting the direction and strategy for your company, but all managers indirectly set a tone that encourages certain activities and discourages others. Office products leader 3M, for example, gives its managers the freedom to be entrepreneurs in their own right, allowing the company to recognise and invest in new business opportunities with the speed and flexibility of much smaller rivals. The Body Shop, on the other hand, is recognised for its environmentally aware management. The company attracts highly qualified men and women who want to work in a business environment that values both personal and corporate social responsibility.

Following are some key questions to ask about the management and/or ownership of your company:

✔ How long have managers been around at various levels in your company? (Alternatively, what variety of experiences do you have as an owner?)

✔ Does your company plan to hire from the outside or promote from within?

✔ What's the general tone set by you or your company's management?

✔ Do you have a management development programme in place? (Alternatively, how do you plan to develop your own skills, if you're a sole proprietor?)

✔ What backgrounds do you or your managers have?

✔ How is management performance measured in your company?

✔ How would you rate the general quality of your own skills or those of your management team?

Organisation: Bringing people together

The people who make up your company and its work force represent a key resource, both in terms of who they are and how they are organised. Although human resources are important to all companies, they're especially critical to companies in service industries, in which people are a big part of the product. (We take a closer look at your organisation in Chapter 4 in this Book when we talk about making your business plan work.)

Your organisation starts with who your employees are, and that depends first on how well you select and train them. Beyond that, the work environment and your company's incentive systems determine who goes on to become a dedicated, hard-working employee and who gets frustrated and finally gives up. The set-up of your organisation (how it's structured and how it adapts) can be just as important as your employees are when it comes to creating a company team – even a small one – that performs at the highest levels, year in and year out.

Pharmaceutical companies, for example, hire hundreds of new sales people annually. Are these companies really growing that fast? Of course not. But the industry routinely loses up to 60 per cent of new employees by the end of the third year, after investing heavily in their training. Why? The industry discovered one problem was in their selection process: too many of their new sales people were unsuited to the stresses and strains of hitting challenging sales goals and making upwards of 20 field calls a day, with hundreds of miles of driving thrown in. After all, the typical industry sales new person was a young university graduate. So the industry revised its hiring practices – candidate advertising, interviewing and psychometric testing – and has already started to see major improvements in both sales performance and longevity.

Following are some key questions about your organisation to consider:

- ✔ What words best describe the overall structure of your organisation?

- ✔ How many reporting levels do you have between a front-line employee and your CEO?

- ✔ How often does your company reorganise?

- ✔ What are your employees' general attitudes to their jobs and responsibilities?

- ✔ How long does the average employee stay with your company?

- ✔ How does your absenteeism level compare with industry benchmarks?

- ✔ Does your company have ways to measure and track employees' attitudes and morale?

- ✔ What does your company do to maintain morale and positive job performance?

Customer base: Pleasing the crowds

Your company's business depends, to a great extent, on the satisfaction and loyalty of your customers. In Chapter 6 in this Book and Chapter 1 in Book V, you discover who those customers are and how you can find out as much as you can about them, because understanding your customers and satisfying their wants and needs are critical to the future of your company.

Nordstrom, for example, is an American department-store chain that appeals to upmarket shoppers. The company bases its reputation on the simple idea that the customer is always right. And the company means it. As the story goes, a disgruntled customer once stormed into the back loading dock of a Nordstrom store, demanding satisfaction and the immediate replacement of defective tyres that he'd recently purchased. The store managers were extremely polite. They quickly discovered that the man was indeed one of their best customers, and they arranged an immediate reimbursement for the full price of the tyres. In a better mood, the customer decided that he'd rather just have a new set installed. When he asked where he should take the car, he was informed that Nordstrom doesn't sell tyres. Obviously, this man became a satisfied customer – and a Nordstrom advocate for life.

Following are some key questions to consider when you study your own customer base:

- ✔ What does your company do to create loyal customers?

- ✔ How much effort do you put into tracking customers' attitudes, satisfaction and loyalty?

- ✔ What do you offer customers that keeps them coming back?

- ✔ How easy and economical is it for your company to acquire new customers?

- ✔ How many years does a typical customer stay with you?

- ✔ How many markets does your company serve?

- ✔ Are you either number one or number two in the markets in which you compete?

Research and development: Inventing the future

Research and development (R&D) often plays an important role in the long-term success of a company, and R&D is particularly critical in industries in which new and better products are coming along. But research and product development must balance the other forces that are at work in your marketplace. R&D is one business area in which even an A-1 team effort doesn't automatically pay off.

Consider the cosmetics industry. Estée Lauder or Revlon could easily spend millions of additional pounds on research and development. These companies could fund any number of studies to learn more about everything from the properties of skin to humans' sense of smell. They could construct state-of-the-art laboratories, hire teams of dedicated dermatologists and top-notch chemists, and in the process become unchallenged leaders in basic cosmetics research. But would the funds invested in these additional capabilities translate into enduring company strengths? Probably not. These companies don't want their products to be turned into drugs that have to be regulated by government departments. Most cosmetics products live or die on the strength of their images and on the resources invested in advertising and promoting them. Customers tend to buy the hype behind beauty aids – not the ingredients inside them.

On the other hand, the makers of integrated circuits and microprocessors – the brains of computers – have little choice but to commit themselves to aggressive R&D efforts. Intel and Motorola have world-class R&D organisations because their industry is driven by continuous product innovation. These companies continually push for greater processing speed and power in ever-smaller packages. Failure to maintain leadership in research could result in catastrophe for either company.

The following key questions help you examine the role of R&D in your company:

✔ To what extent is your industry driven by technology?

✔ Can you get enough results for your money to bother with R&D?

✔ Does your company have a consistent, long-term commitment to R&D?

✔ How many pounds do you spend on basic research as opposed to applied research?

✔ How long have the key people on your research staff been with you?

✔ Does your company protect what it owns with copyrights and patents?

✔ Have you set up partnerships with universities or outside research labs?

✔ Do you have technology agreements with other companies in your industry?

✔ Are you aware of the favourable UK tax treatment of R&D expenditure?

✔ Are you aware of possible UK government grant aid for R&D projects?

Operations: Making things work

The operations side of your business is obviously critical if you happen to be a manufacturing company. The products that you make (and the way that they work, how long they last and what they cost) depend entirely on the capabilities and resources of your production facilities and work force – so much so that you can easily forget that operations are equally important to companies in the service sector. Customers demand value in all markets today, and they're simply unwilling to pay for inefficiencies in any business. Whether you make cars or carpets, produce cereal boxes or serial ports, run a bank or manage a hotel, operations are at the heart of your enterprise.

Operations in your own company are probably driven, to some extent, by costs on one side and product or service quality on the other. The tension between controlling costs and improving quality has led many companies to explore ways to reduce costs and increase quality at the same time. One way for you to do that is to involve outside suppliers in certain aspects of your operations, if those suppliers have resources that you can't match. Another way to achieve both goals is to streamline parts of your operations (through automation, for example).

Automation can also be a source of growth and may even create new business opportunities for your company. The airline industry is as big as it is today because of the computer revolution; computers enable airlines to track millions of passenger reservations and itineraries at the same time. Imagine the queues at airports if airlines were still issuing tickets by hand and completing passenger flight lists by using carbon paper.

When American Airlines developed its computer-based SABRE reservation system, however, it couldn't predict that *yield management* – the capability to monitor demand for flights and continuously adjust prices to fill seats – would become as important as on-time arrivals. The company has increased its profit margins because yield-management software ensures that each American flight generates as much revenue as possible. The software is so sophisticated and successful that Robert Crandall, American Airlines' chairman, spun off SABRE as a separate company. SABRE's expertise can now be used to benefit industries such as the hotel business, in which yield-management software can automatically adjust room rates and make sure that as many beds as possible are filled each night.

Following are some questions on the operations side of your business to mull over:

- Does your company have programmes for controlling cost and improving quality?
- Has your company taken full advantage of new technologies?
- Are your production costs in line with those of the rest of the industry?
- How quickly can you boost production or expand services to meet new demand?
- Does your company use outside suppliers?
- Is your operations workforce flexible, well trained and prepared for change?
- Can you apply your operations expertise to other parts of the business?

Sales and marketing: Telling a good story

The best product or service in the world isn't going to take your company far if it's not successfully marketed and sold to all those potential customers out there. Your sales and marketing people (or you, if you're operating your own small business) are your eyes and ears, giving you feedback on what customers think about and look for. Your sales and marketing people are also your voice. They tell your company's story and put your products in context, offering solutions, satisfying needs and fulfilling wants in the marketplace.

What could a marketing department possibly do, for example, to package and promote a boring old bulk chemical such as sodium bicarbonate? It turns out that such a department can do quite a bit, if it's connected with Arm & Hammer, which sells sodium bicarbonate (baking soda) toothpaste. The 'Wow' adverts, showing people smiling with gleaming white teeth, as if 'they had been cleaned by the dentist', ensured Arm and Hammer gained 4 per cent of the toothpaste market in Britain, just over a year after being launched. All this from a common, readily available chemical salt.

Following are a few key questions to ask about the marketing of your product line:

✔ How broad is your company's product or service line?

✔ Do consumers identify with your company's brand names?

✔ Do you have special processes or technologies that your competitors can't take advantage of?

✔ Are you investing in market research and receiving continuous customer feedback?

✔ Are you using all the marketing resources that are at your disposal?

✔ Is your company's sales force knowledgeable, energetic and persuasive?

Distribution and delivery: Completing the cycle

Distribution and delivery means that your products and services are actually getting to their final destinations and into your customers' hands. No matter how good you think your products are, your customers have to be able to get their hands on them when and where they want them. How customers shop is often just as important as what they buy, so it's not surprising that when a different way to deliver products and services comes along (over the Internet, for example), the new system revolutionises a marketplace or even an entire economy. The Internet promises a future in which companies can reach out to their customers more directly, increasing company clout and at the same time lowering distribution costs.

Right now, your company probably distributes its products and services through *traditional channels* – time-tested ways in which you and your competitors reach customers – and your distribution and delivery costs may represent a significant part of your total expenses. The standard costs often include warehouse operations, transportation and product returns. If you're in a retail business, you can end up paying for expensive shelf space as well. Supermarkets now routinely ask for money upfront before they stock a new item, and you pay more for the best locations. After all, supermarkets control what customers see – and buy – as harried shoppers troop down the aisles, children and trollies in tow.

Many innovative products and companies succeeded in the past because of their novel approaches to the costs and other hurdles associated with traditional distribution networks. When Amazon decided to enter the book market, for example, Jeff Bezos, Amazon.com's founder faced established competition and a stodgy distribution system dominated by traditional retail outlets.

Rather than tackle all these problems head-on, the company set off in a new direction. Bezos realised that no single bookshop could carry a comprehensive inventory of the books in print. The distributors who carried thousands of titles acted as the warehouse for most shops, particularly smaller book-sellers. When customers asked a shop for a book it didn't have in stock, they filled the customer's order through one of the handful of large distributors. These companies' inventory lists were digitised in the late 1980s. The online inventory lists would enable Bezos to offer books online through the company he planned to create.

The naming of Amazon.com was based on the importance of its relative size. Bezos reasoned that the River Amazon was ten times as large as the next largest river, which was the Mississippi, in terms of volume of water, and Amazon.com had six times as many titles as the world's largest physical bookstore. Amazon has revolutionised traditional bookselling and buying, and has spawned many imitators.

Following are some questions about the distribution and delivery of your product or service:

- ✔ What are the costs associated with your company's inventory system?
- ✔ Can you reduce inventories by changing the way that orders are processed?
- ✔ How much time does it take for a customer order to get filled, and can the time be reduced?
- ✔ How many distribution channels does your company use?
- ✔ What are the relative costs in various channels, and which are most effective?
- ✔ How much control over your company do distributors have?
- ✔ Can you use any new channels to reach your customers more directly?

Financial condition: Keeping track of money

The long-term financial health of your company determines the health of your company, full stop. You simply can't survive in business for long without having your financial house in order. Come to think of it, the things that you have to track when it comes to company finances aren't all that different from the issues that you face in running your own household. If you're just starting in business, for example, how much money your company can get its hands on upfront (your *initial capital*) is a key to survival. (Does this sound like trying to buy and furnish your first house?) When your company's up and running, it's important to make sure that more money comes in than goes out (a *positive cash flow*), so that you can pay all your bills. (Remember those times when the mortgage and utility bills were due, and it wasn't payday yet?)

Figuring out how to keep your company financially fit is critical to planning your business. When you take the time to look over your important financial statements periodically, you give your company the benefit of a regular financial checkup. The checkup is usually routine, but every once in a while you uncover an early-warning symptom – profits that are too low, for example, or a promotional expense that's too large. That's when all your financial vigilance is worth it.

Following is a list of oh-so-painful questions to ask about your company's financial health.

- ✔ Are your revenue and profits growing?

- ✔ Are you carefully monitoring your company's cash flow?

- ✔ Does your company have ready access to cash reserves?

- ✔ Does your company – and every business unit or area – have a budget for the coming year?

- ✔ Do you consistently track key financial ratios for the company?

- ✔ How does your company's financial picture compare with that of the competition?

Critical success factors

It's important to decide whether your capabilities and resources represent company strengths that you can leverage or weaknesses that you must correct as you plan for the future. To do that, you have to be clear about exactly what's important to your industry and the marketplace. The *critical success factors* (CSFs) are those capabilities and resources that absolutely have to be in place if you want your company to succeed over the long haul.

You may have already prepared a list of CSFs. (If you haven't, take a look at *Business Plans For Dummies*, published by John Wiley.) Along with a CSF list, you need a set of your company's capabilities and resources. You can use the two lists to construct a grid, which in turn allows you to compare your capabilities and resources with those that your industry thinks are important. In a perfect world, the lists would be identical, but that's seldom the case. The completed grid helps you identify your company's current strengths and weaknesses (see Figure 5-2).

Figure 5-2:
Compare
your capa-
bilities and
resources
with those
that are
thought to
be critical
success
factors in
your
industry.

Company Strengths and Weaknesses

Importance to Industry

Capabilities and Resources

Critical Success Factors

Strengths

Weaknesses

Excellent

Good

Fair

Poor

Must Have   Nice to Have   Not Necessary

To complete a grid similar to the one in Figure 5-2, remember the following:

✔ The capabilities and resources that you place up and down the left side of the grid are in your industry's 'must have' category. They represent critical success factors.

✔ The capabilities and resources that you place in the top-left corner of the grid are critical success factors in which your company is good or excellent. They represent your company's strengths.

✔ The capabilities and resources that you place in the bottom-left corner of the grid are critical success factors in which your company is only fair or even poor. They represent your company's weaknesses.

It's easy to find some value in the capabilities that your company already excels in, and it's just as easy to underestimate the importance of things that your company doesn't do as well. Try to be as objective as you can here. It's hard to admit that you're devoting valuable resources to things that don't really matter, and it's equally hard to admit that you may be neglecting key business areas.

✔ Different people have different ideas about what your company's strengths and weaknesses really are.

✔ By combining different viewpoints, both inside and outside your company, you get a more balanced picture.

✔ Be sure to assess your capabilities and resources in every area, from management to marketing to R&D to delivery.

✔ Strengths are strengths only if your capabilities and resources line up with the critical success factors in your industry.

Analysing Your Situation in 3-D

You must be prepared to take advantage of your company's strengths and minimise your weaknesses, which means that you have to know how to recognise opportunities when they arise and prepare for threats before they overtake you. Timing is everything here, and it represents a third major dimension that you have to think about.

Book I Chapter 6 discusses where major opportunities and serious threats come from. These dragons can come from almost any source and from all directions. They often change the rules of the game and can even alter critical success factors that you assumed would always be part of your industry. Many opportunities and threats are the direct result of change; others come directly from your competitors and the uncertainty that they introduce.

A glance at competitors

It's a good idea to create strengths-and-weaknesses grids for two or three of your most intense competitors. (Turn to Chapter 6 in this Book for a look at exactly who your competitors are and what information you have about them.) You won't know as much about your competitors as you know about yourself, of course, so the grids aren't going to be as complete as they may be about your own company. But what you *do* know is going to tell you a great deal.

Comparing the strengths and weaknesses of competitors with your own can help you see where competitive opportunities and threats to your business may come from. Opportunities often arise when your company has a strength that you can exploit in a critical area in which your competition is weak. And you can sometimes anticipate a threat when the situation is reversed – when a competitor takes advantage of a key strength by making a move in an area where you're not as strong. Because the competitive landscape is always changing, plan to monitor these grids on a regular basis.

Completing your SWOT analysis

A SWOT analysis (an analysis of your strengths, weaknesses, opportunities and threats) allows you to construct a strategic balance sheet for your company. In the analysis, you bring together all the internal factors, including your company's strengths and weaknesses. You then weigh these factors against the external forces that you've identified, such as the opportunities and threats that your company faces due to competitive forces or trends in your business environment. How these factors balance out determines what your company needs to do and when to do it. Follow these steps to complete the SWOT analysis grid:

1. **Divide all the strengths that you've identified into two groups, based on whether they're associated with potential opportunities in your industry or with latent threats.**

2. **Divide all the weaknesses the same way – one group associated with opportunities, the other with threats.**

3. **Construct a grid with four quadrants.**

4. **Place your company's strengths and weaknesses, paired with industry opportunities or threats, in one of the four boxes (see Figure 5-3).**

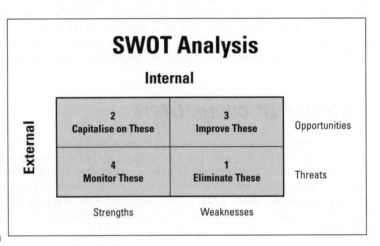

Figure 5-3: The SWOT grid balances your company's internal strengths and weaknesses against external opportunities and threats.

The SWOT analysis provides a bit of useful strategic guidance. Most of it is common sense. First, fix what's broken. Next, make the most of the business opportunities that you see out there. Only then do you have the luxury of tending to other business issues and areas. Be sure to address each of the following steps in your business plan:

1. **Eliminate any company weaknesses that you identify in areas in which you face serious threats from your competitors or unfavourable trends in a changing business environment.**

2. **Capitalise on any business opportunities that you discover where your company has real strengths.**

3. **Work on improving any weaknesses that you identify in areas that may contain potential business opportunities.**

4. **Monitor business areas in which you're strong today so that you won't be surprised by any latent threats that may appear.**

Change is the only constant in your business, your industry and your market-place. Constant change means that you can't complete your SWOT analysis only once; you have to revise the grid regularly as your company grows and as the environment around you changes. Think of your SWOT analysis as being a continuous process – something that you do repeatedly as an important part of your business-planning cycle.

✔ To identify potential opportunities and threats, take a close look at the strengths and weaknesses of your competitors.

✔ A SWOT grid places your strengths and weaknesses in the context of opportunities and threats, and thereby tells you what to do.

✔ The SWOT strategy is to eliminate weaknesses in areas where threats loom and also to capitalise on strengths in areas where you see opportunities.

Measuring Market Share

In any competitive market there will typically be a market leader, a couple of market followers and a host of businesses trailing in their wake. The slice each competitor has of a market is its *market share*. You'll find that marketing people are fixated on market share, perhaps even more so than on absolute sales. That may appear little more than a rational desire to beat the 'enemy' and appear higher in rankings, but it has a much more deep-seated and profound logic. The old saying 'success breeds success' applies here and winning the battle for market share gives a business a very important leg up.

Back in the 1960s a firm of American management consultants observed a consistent relationship between the cost of producing an item (or delivering a service) and the total quantity produced over the life of the product concerned. They noticed that total unit costs (labour and materials) fell by between 20 per cent and 30 per cent for every doubling of the cumulative quantity produced.

So any company capturing a sizeable market share will have an implied cost advantage over any competitor with a smaller market share. That cost advantage can then be used to make more profit, lower prices and compete for an even greater share of the market, or to invest in making the product better and so stealing a march on competitors.

A glance at Figure 5-4 provides a clue as to how Tesco can stay competitive, outgrow other players in the market and make a good return for shareholders.

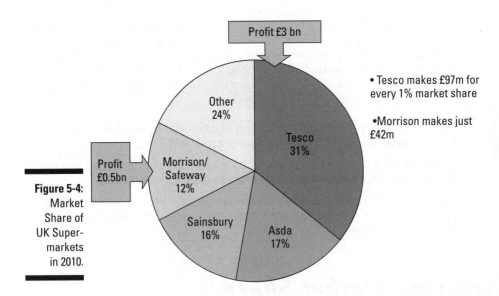

Figure 5-4:
Market
Share of
UK Super-
markets
in 2010.

• Tesco makes £97m for every 1% market share

•Morrison makes just £42m

Profit £3 bn

Profit £0.5bn

Other
24%

Tesco
31%

Morrison/
Safeway
12%

Sainsbury
16%

Asda
17%

Chapter 6

Researching Your Customers, Competitors and Industry

* *

* *

*W*hat makes your product or service better or worse than that of your competitors? That question, and more like it, can help you tighten up your strategy, make more accurate sales projections and decide what to emphasise (visually or verbally) in your marketing communications. A little research can go a long way towards improving the effectiveness of your marketing.

One per cent of companies do 90 per cent of all market research. Big businesses hire research firms to do extensive customer surveys and to run discussion groups with customers. The marketers then sit down to 50-page reports filled with tables and charts before making any decisions. We don't recommend this expensive approach, which can lead to analysis paralysis. In other words, marketers spend more time poring over the mountains of data in front of them than actually acting upon them.

Instead, in this chapter, we want to help you adopt an inquisitive approach by sharing relatively simple and efficient ways of learning about customers, competitors and the environment. As a marketer, you need to challenge assumptions by asking the questions that lead to useful answers – something you can do on any budget. In the end, not only will you know what you need to know about your customers and competitors, you'll also better understand your own business.

Understanding Why Research Matters – and Knowing What to Focus On

Many large companies do research, in part, to cover the marketer's you-know-what if the resulting campaign subsequently fails – 'Well, it's not our fault, this is what the research told us to do!' – and more than half of all market research expenditure just builds the case for pursuing strategies the marketers always planned to do anyway. These marketers use research in the same way a drunk uses a lamppost – for support rather than illumination. Other businesspeople refuse to research anything at all because they know the answers already – or think they do. Gut instinct will only get you so far before the ideas, customers or both run out.

Many companies use focus groups for research. A *focus group* is a group of potential or actual customers who sit behind a one-way mirror discussing your product while a trained moderator guides their conversation and hidden video cameras immortalise their every gesture and phrase. Of course, you don't have to be so formal with your research techniques. You can always just ask your customers what they think of your product or service directly; the resulting information's not as impartial, but it may tell you everything you need to know without having to pay professional researchers.

So, what are good reasons to do research? Doing research to cover your backside or to bolster your already-decided-upon plans is a waste of time and money. Basically, if you can get a better idea or make a better decision after conducting market research, then research is worth your while. You need to embrace research because it's the first step to making your company customer-oriented rather than product-oriented. In other words, asking what your customers want from your business is a better starting point than merely trying to sell them what you've already got. It makes for a more profitable business. If you can find out where your customers are, what they want and how best to reach them, then you're on the right path to doing better business.

Research for better ideas

Information can stimulate the imagination, suggest fresh strategies or help you recognise great business opportunities. So always keep one ear open for interesting, surprising or inspiring facts. Don't spend much money on this kind of research. You don't need to buy in an expensive trendwatching service to keep a businesslike eye on new consumer developments that may affect your market. Instead, take subscriptions for a diverse range of publications, read free blogs on the Internet such as Trendwatching (www.trendwatching.com) and make a point of talking to people of all sorts, both in your industry and beyond it, to keep you in the flow of new ideas and facts. Also, ask other people for their ideas and interests.

Every marketer should carry an ideas notebook with her wherever she goes and make a point of collecting a few contributions from people every day. This habit gets you asking salespeople, employees, customers and complete strangers for their ideas and observations. You never know when a suggestion may prove valuable.

Research for better decisions

Do you have any situations that you want more information about before making a decision? Then take a moment to define the situation clearly and list the options you think are feasible. Choosing the most effective advertising medium, making a more accurate sales projection or working out what new services your customers want are all examples of important decisions that research can help you make.

Suppose, for example, that you want to choose between print ads in industry magazines and email advertisements to purchased lists. Figure 6-1 shows what your notes may look like.

Research for your strengths and weaknesses

Perception is everything. What customers think of your product or service is ultimately what determines the success of your business, which is why you need to make a habit of asking them, on a regular basis, what they love and what they hate about it.

So how do you find out what customers think? By asking customers to rank you on a list of descriptors for your business/product/service. The scale ranges from 1 to 10 (to get a good spread), with the following labels:

1	2	3	4	5	6	7	8	9	10
Very bad		Bad		Average		Good		Very good	

Decision	Information Needs	Possible Sources	Findings
Choose between print ads in industry magazines and email advertisements to purchased lists	How many actual prospects can print ads reach?	Magazines' ad salespeople can tell us.	Three leading magazines in our industry reach 90 per cent of good customers, but half of these are not in our geographic region. May not be worth it?
	What are the comparable costs per prospect reached through these different methods?	Just need to get the budget numbers and number of people reached and divide available money by number of people.	Email is a third of the price in our market.
	Can we find out what the average response rates are for both magazine ads and emails?	Nobody is willing to tell us, or they don't know. May try calling a friend in a big ad agency; they may have done a study or something.	Friend says response rates vary wildly, and she thinks the most important thing is how relevant the customer finds the ad, not the medium used.
	Have any of our competitors switched from print to email successfully?	Can probably get distributors to tell us this. Will call several and quiz them.	No, but some companies in similar industries have done this successfully.

Conclusions?

Seems like we'll spend less and be more targeted if we design special emails and send them only to prospects in our region. Don't buy magazine ad space for now; we can experiment with email, instead. But we need to make sure the ads we send are relevant and seem important, or people just delete them without reading them.

Figure 6-1:
Analysing the information needs of a decision.

If you collect a rating of all the descriptive features of your product from customers, many of those ratings will prove quite ordinary. Consider the type of responses you'd get for a bank branch. The list of items to rate in a bank may include: current accounts, savings accounts, speed of service and the friendliness of banking staff, along with many other things you'd need to put on the list in order to describe the bank in detail. You're likely to discover that some items, like current accounts and savings accounts, get average ratings. The reason is that every bank offers those and, in general, each one handles such accounts in the same way. But a few of the features of a particular bank may be exceptional – for better or for worse.

Notable negatives, such as long queues at lunchtime when people rush out to do their banking, stand out in customers' minds. They remember those queues and tell others about them. Long queues at lunchtime may lead customers to switch banks and drive away other potential customers through bad word of mouth. Similarly, notably good customer service sticks in customers' minds, too. If that same branch has very friendly staff and express queues for simple transactions during busy periods, this warmth and efficiency can build loyalty and encourage current customers to recruit new customers through word of mouth.

With this information, you know what things your customers think you do brilliantly and what features you need to do some work on. Now improve on the worst-on-the-list features to make them average, at least, and emphasise the high-rated items by talking them up in marketing, and investing even more in them to maximise their attractiveness.

Here are a few tips to keep in mind as you gather customer ratings:

✔ Draw a graph of all the features of your product, rated from negative to neutral to positive. A graph gives you a visual image of how your customers perceive your business's strengths and weaknesses. Most features cluster in the middle of the resulting bell curve, failing to differentiate you from the competition. A few features stick out on the left as notably negative, other features, hopefully, stand out on the right as notably positive.

✔ Offer customers a reward for filling in a survey sheet (that's how important survey sheets are). You can offer a free prize draw for the returned survey sheets, a reduction on current fees or a discount on future products. Whichever option you choose, let your customers know that their views matter to you; that alone can improve your customer-service scores.

✔ If you want to get fancy, you can also ask some customers to rate the importance to them, personally, of each item on the list. If you're lucky, your brilliant areas are important to them and your bad areas aren't.

Bright spark

Research can help you discover weaknesses and turn them into strengths. Comet, the chain of electrical stores, had been losing sales for several years to supermarkets and general retailers as they entered the market. It decided that some flashy destination stores would fix the problem and set about overhauling the layout, product ranges and signage to differentiate them from Comet's new competitors.

The size and design of the stores wasn't the main solution to the problem, though. A simple and, at £20,000, inexpensive research programme discovered that Comet's customers felt that its greatest weakness was the quality of its staff. This was a twofold problem as they also felt that the most important aspect of customer satisfaction was, you guessed it, the quality of the staff. Comet accepted the truth and acted on it by changing its criteria for customer satisfaction. Soon after, it achieved a record trading performance.

Planning Your Research

Start research with a careful analysis of the decisions you must make. For example, say you're in charge of a two-year-old software product that small businesses use to manage their invoicing. As the product manager, what key decisions do you need to make? The following are the most likely:

- ✔ Should we launch an upgrade or keep selling the current version?
- ✔ Is our current marketing plan sufficiently effective, or should we redesign it?
- ✔ Is the product positioned properly, or do we need to change its image?

So before you do any research, you need to think hard about those decisions. Specifically, you need to:

- ✔ Decide what realistic options you have for each decision.
- ✔ Assess your level of uncertainty and risk for each decision.

Then, for any uncertain or risky decisions, you need to pose questions whose answers can help you reduce the risk and uncertainty. And now, with these questions in hand, you're ready to begin your research!

When you work through this thinking process, you often find that you don't actually need research. For example, maybe your boss has already decided to invest in an upgrade of the software product you manage, so researching the decision is pointless. Right or wrong, you can't realistically change that decision. But some questions do make it through the screening process and turn out to be good candidates for research. For these research points, you need to pose a series of questions that have the potential to reduce your decision-making uncertainty or to reveal new and exciting options for you as a decision maker.

Take the question, 'Is the product positioned properly, or do we need to change its image?' To find out whether repositioning your product makes sense, you may ask how people currently perceive the product's quality and performance, how they view the product compared with the leading competitor's and what the product's personality is. If you know the answers to all these questions, you're far better able to make a good decision.

You need to start by defining your marketing decisions very carefully. Until you know what decisions you must make, market research has little point. See Figure 6-2 for a flowchart of the research process.

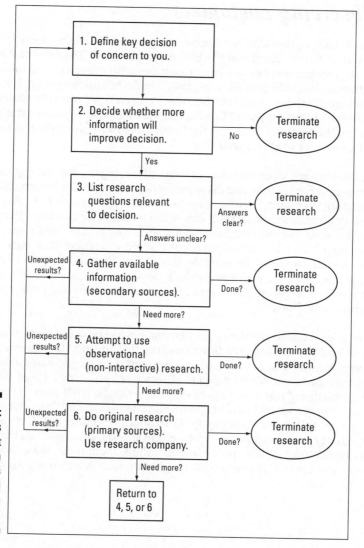

Figure 6-2:
Follow this
market
research
process
to avoid
common
errors.

Carrying Out Primary Research

Primary research gathers data from people by observing them to see how they behave or by asking them for verbal or written answers to questions. You can, and should, ask your customers all the time whether they are happy with the service they get from your company, but taking some time out to question your assumptions about how customers view your product or service can yield some valuable insights.

Observing customers

Going 'back to the floor' has become something of a phenomenon of modern business, to the extent that the BBC made a popular TV series of the same name. The experiences of a senior manager who's thrown back into the thick of things alongside general workers can make hilarious viewing. But how and why did these executives become so disengaged from the basics of their business in the first place? Getting and staying close to your customers, as well as the front-line staff who deal with them every day, is one of the most valuable ways to spend your time.

Consumers are all around you – shopping for, buying and using products. Observing consumers, and discovering new and valuable information by doing so, isn't hard. Even *business-to-business (B2B) marketers* (who sell to other businesses instead of individual consumers) can find plenty of evidence about their customers at a glance. The number and direction of a company's lorries on various roads can tell you where their business is heaviest and lightest, for example. Despite all the opportunities to observe, most marketers are guilty of Sherlock Holmes's accusation that 'you have not observed, and yet you have seen'. Observation is the most underrated of all research methods.

Find a way to observe one of your customers as she uses one of your products. Professional research firms can provide a location for customers to come and use your products or can even put their people into the homes of willing customers. We want you to observe, not just watch. Bring along a pad and pencil, and take care to notice the little things. What does the customer do, in what order and how long does she spend doing it? What does she say, if anything? Does she look happy? Frustrated? Disinterested? Does anything go wrong? Does anything go right – is she surprised by how well the product performs? Take detailed notes and then think about them. We guarantee that you'll end up gaining at least one insight into how to improve your product.

Asking questions

Survey research methods are the bread and butter of the market research industry, and for a good reason. You can often gain something of value just by asking people what they think. If your product makes customers happy, those customers come back. If not, goodbye. Because recruiting new customers costs on average ten times as much as retaining existing ones, you can't afford to lose any. You need to measure and set goals for customer satisfaction.

The survey methods do have their shortcomings. Customers don't always know what they think or how they behave – and even when they do, getting them to tell you can be quite costly. Nonetheless, every marketer finds good uses for survey research on occasion.

Measuring customer satisfaction

Try to design a customer satisfaction measure that portrays your company or product in a realistic light. You can measure customer satisfaction with survey questionnaires or with the rate of customer complaints; measures combining multiple sources of data into an overall index are the best.

Your customer satisfaction has to be high, relative to both customer expectations and competitors' ratings, before it has much of an effect on customer retention rates. So make sure that you ask tough questions to find out whether you're below or above customers' current standards. To gauge customer satisfaction, ask your customers revealing questions, similar to the following list:

1. **Which company (or product) is the best at present?**

   (Provide a long list, with instructions to circle one, and give a final choice, labelled 'Other', where respondents can write in their own answer.)

2. **Rate [your product] compared with its competitors:**

Far worse		Same			Far better	
1	2	3	4	5	6	7

3. **Rate [your product] compared with your expectations for it:**

Far worse		Same			Far better	
1	2	3	4	5	6	7

You can get helpful customer responses by breaking down customer satisfaction into its contributing elements. (Focus groups or informal chats with customers can help you come up with your list of contributing elements.) For example, you can ask the following questions about a courier company:

1. **Rate Flash Deliveries compared with its competitors on speed of delivery:**

Far worse		Same			Far better	
1	2	3	4	5	6	7

2. **Rate Flash Deliveries compared with its competitors on reliability:**

Far worse		Same			Far better	
1	2	3	4	5	6	7

3. **Rate Flash Deliveries compared with its competitors on ease of use:**

Far worse		Same			Far better	
1	2	3	4	5	6	7

4. **Rate Flash Deliveries compared with its competitors on friendliness:**

Far worse		Same			Far better	
1	2	3	4	5	6	7

You can find useful guidelines on how to design a questionnaire on the website of the Market Research Society (`www.mrs.org.uk`), under 'Guidance', within the Frequently Asked Questions section. The site also includes advice on how to select a research agency and lists sources of free statistical and demographic information.

Customer satisfaction changes with each new interaction between person and product. Keeping up with customer opinion is a never-ending race and you need to make sure that you're measuring where you stand relative to those shifting customer expectations and competitor performances.

Avoiding the traps

As you conduct a customer survey, avoid these all-too-common traps which can render your research practically useless:

- ✔ **Make sure your survey (or surveyor, for that matter) doesn't puff up customer satisfaction to conceal problems.** In bigger companies, we sometimes see people pressurising customers to give them good ratings because it helps their own prospects. One of the authors recently bought car insurance over the phone from an enthusiastic salesperson who unashamedly asked him to give her a high rating on a survey so that she could win the monthly customer service bonus. You can award her ten out of ten for effort, but this was probably not what the company had in mind when it set up the survey. Design your customer service measure to find areas of the business you can improve, which means asking questions that expose any weak spots. The more 'honest' your questions are, the more meaningful the responses will be.

✔ **Watch out for over-general questions or ratings.** Any measure based on a survey that asks customers to 'rate your overall satisfaction with our company on a 1-to-10 scale' isn't much use. What does an average score of 8.76 mean? This number seems high, but are customers satisfied? You didn't really ask customers this question. Even worse, you didn't ask them if they're more satisfied with you than they used to be or if they're less satisfied with competitors than with you. Ask a series of more specific questions, such as: 'Was doing business with us convenient and easy?'

✔ **Don't lose sight of the end goal – customer satisfaction.** You may need to find out about a lot of other issues in order to design your marketing plan or diagnose a problem. None of what you find out matters, however, unless it boils down to increased customer satisfaction in the long run. Whatever else you decide to research, make sure you keep one eye on customer satisfaction: it's the ultimate test of whether your marketing's working!

Using the answers

When you've gathered the data, make sure that it gets put to good use, rather than becoming a pile of questionnaires gathering dust in the corner. So which parts of the information you've amassed do you include as action points in your next marketing plan?

Even the most rudimentary piece of research can throw up a range of different, and sometimes contradictory, findings. One customer may think the most important thing is for you to lower your prices; another may be prepared to pay more for greater staff expertise. You probably can't achieve both of these goals simultaneously. Here are a few strategies that can help you focus your response:

✔ **Allow your own instinct to sort the good research results from the bad.** This doesn't mean ignoring what you don't want to hear, but it does mean you shouldn't unquestioningly react to everything the research tells you. When Sony asked people whether they'd like a portable device so they could listen to music on the move, the company found no demand existed. People didn't know that they wanted music on the move because it wasn't available to them yet. Sony went ahead and launched the Walkman anyway, because the company felt it had a great product innovation. You needn't always believe the expression 'the customer's always right' but one that you can heed when doing any research is 'they don't know what they don't know'.

✔ **Concentrate on just one of the strengths and one of the weaknesses.** If your product or service has a quality that's unique in your market, you need to exploit it to the full. If you have a real problem that may drive valuable customers away, you need to put it right fast.

> ✔ **Pay attention to your most valuable customers.** You can't please all
> of the people all of the time, so don't try. One of the hidden benefits of
> observing and asking questions of customers is that doing so can help
> distinguish your most valuable customers from those you'd be better off
> without (yes, they really do exist). By looking at survey responses, you're
> soon able to spot ideas and customers that generate additional value and
> those that simply want more for less. Surveys help you to establish priori-
> ties for your business that will keep profitable customers loyal.

The life cycle of any piece of research should last no longer than your next
marketing plan – any longer and the market or competition will have moved
anyway.

Introducing a Dozen Ideas for Low-Cost Research

You don't have to spend thousands of pounds researching ideas for a new
ad campaign (or anything else). Instead, focus on ways of gaining insight or
checking your assumptions using free and inexpensive research methods.
But how can you do useful research without a lot of time, money and staff to
waste? This section shares ideas to get you off on the right foot.

Watching what your competitors do

When you compare your marketing approach to your competitors', you
easily find out what customers like best. Make a list of the things that your
competitors do differently to you. Does one of them price higher? Does
another one give away free samples? Do some of them offer money-back guarantees? How and where do they advertise? Make a list of at least five points
of difference. Now ask ten of your best customers to review this list and tell
you what they prefer – your way or one of the alternatives. Keep a tally. You
may find that all your customers vote in favour of doing something different
to the way you do it now. Don't discount something just because your rivals
have been doing it; if your customers want that service or feature, simply find
a way of doing it differently and better.

Creating a customer profile

Take photographs of people you think of as your typical customers. Post
these pictures on a noticeboard and add any facts or information you can
think of to create profiles of your 'virtual' customers. Whenever you aren't
sure what to do about a certain marketing decision, you can sit down in front

of the noticeboard. Use it to help you tune into your customers and what they do and don't like. For example, make sure the artwork and wording you use in a letter or ad is appropriate for the customers on your noticeboard. Will these customers like it, or is the style wrong for them?

Entertaining customers to get their input

Invite good customers to a lunch or dinner, or hold a 'customer appreciation' event. Entertaining your customers puts you in contact with them in a relaxed setting where they're happy to chat and share their views. Use these occasions to ask them for suggestions and reactions. Bounce a new product idea off of these customers or find out what features they'd most like to see improved. Your customers can provide an expert panel for your informal research, and you just have to provide the food! They may even become more vocal advocates of your products to friends and family because they feel their advice is taken seriously.

Using email for single-question surveys

If you market to businesses, you probably have email addresses for many of your customers. Try emailing 20 or more of these customers for a quick opinion on a question. Result? Instant survey! If a clear majority of these customers say they prefer using a corporate credit card because the card is more convenient than being invoiced, well, you've just gained a useful research result that may help you revise your approach.

Don't email customers with questions unless they're happy to be approached. You don't want to be treated as an email spammer!

Watching people use your product

Be nosy. Find ways to observe people as they shop for and consume your product or service. What do they do? What do they like? What, if anything, goes wrong? What do they dislike? You can gain insight into what your consumers care about, how they feel, and what they like by observing them in action. Being a marketing Peeping Tom provides you with a useful and interesting way to do research, all at no charge. If you're in a retail business, be (or ask someone else to be) a *secret shopper* by going in and acting like an ordinary customer to see how you're treated.

If you have an online business, you can take part in usability testing that will do everything from tracking where consumers click and get stuck on your website to monitoring where their eyes move to across a screen and how their heart rate and electrical impulses change when they encounter your online marketing or use your online product. This information, gathered by companies such as Bunnyfoot (`www.bunnyfoot.com`), the Usability Company (`www.theusabilitycompany.com`) and Webcredible (`www.webcredible.co.uk`), can be hugely revealing.

Establishing a trend report

Email salespeople, distributors, customer service staff, repair staff or willing customers once a month, asking them for a quick list of any important trends they see in the market. You flatter people by letting them know that you value their opinion and email makes giving that opinion relatively easy for them. A trend report gives you a quick indication of a change in buying patterns, a new competitive move or threat, and any other changes that your marketing may need to respond to. Print out and file these reports from the field and go back over them every now and then for a long-term view of the effectiveness of your marketing strategies.

Researching your strengths

Perhaps the most important element of any marketing plan or strategy is clearly recognising what makes you especially good and appealing to customers (we talk more about identifying your strengths in Chapter 5 in Book 1). To research the strengths that set you apart from the competition, find the simplest way to ask ten good customers this simple but powerful question: 'What's the best thing about our [fill in the name of your product or service] from your perspective?' (Or you can undertake the more detailed survey we describe in the 'Research for your strengths and weaknesses' section earlier in this chapter.)

The answers to this question usually focus on one or, at most, a few features or aspects of your business. Finding out how your customers identify your strengths proves a great help to your marketing strategy. When you know what you do best, you can focus on telling the story about that best attribute whenever you advertise, create publicity or communicate with your market in any way. Investing in your strengths (versus your competitors' strengths or your weaknesses) tends to grow your sales and profits most quickly and efficiently.

Analysing customer records

Most marketers fail to mine their own databases for all the useful information they may contain. Studying your own customers with the goal of identifying three common traits that make them different or special is a good way to tap into this free data – because you already own it!

A computer shop we frequent went through its records and realised that its buyers are:

✔ More likely to be self-employed or entrepreneurs than the average person.

✔ More sophisticated users of computers than most people.

✔ Big spenders who care more about quality and service than the absolute cheapest price.

This shop revised its marketing goal to find more people who share these three qualities. What qualities do your customers possess that make them special and what would constitute a good profile for you to use in pursuing more customers like them?

Surveying your own customers

You can gather input from your own customers in a variety of easy ways because your customers interact with your employees or firm. You can put a stamped postcard in shipments, statements, product packages or other communications with your customers. Include three or fewer simple, non-biased survey questions, such as, 'Are you satisfied with this purchase? no = 1 2 3 4 5 = yes.' Also, leave a few lines for comments, in case the customers have something they want to tell you. You generally get low response rates with any such effort, but that doesn't matter. If someone has something to tell you, they let you hear about it, particularly when it's negative. But even a 5 per cent response gives you a steady stream of input you wouldn't otherwise have.

Testing your marketing materials

Whether you're looking at a letter, web page, press release or ad, you can improve that material's effectiveness by asking for reviews from a few customers, distributors or others with knowledge of your business. Do they like the material? Do they like it a lot? If the responses are only lukewarm, then you know you need to edit or improve the material before spending money on publishing and distributing it. Customer reviewers can tell you quickly whether your marketing communications have a real attention-generating, wow factor.

Big companies do elaborate, expensive tests of ads' readability and pulling power, but you can get a pretty good idea for much less money. Just ask a handful of people to review a new marketing material while it's still in draft form.

Interviewing defectors

You can find out far more from an angry customer than you can from ten happy ones. If you have a customer on the phone who wants to complain, look on her as an opportunity, not a call to be avoided. If you can find out what went wrong and fix it, that customer may well become one of your greatest advocates.

You can easily overlook another gold mine: company records of past customers. Work out what types of customer defect, when and why. If you can't pinpoint why a customer abandoned ship, try to make contact and ask her directly.

Tracking these lost customers down and getting them on the phone or setting up an appointment may prove difficult. Don't give up! Your lost customers hold the key to a valuable piece of information: what you do wrong that can drive customers away. Talk to enough of these lost customers and you may see a pattern emerge. Probably three quarters of them left you for the same reason (which may be pricing, poor service, inconvenient hours and so on – that's for you to find out).

Plug that hole and you lose fewer customers down it. Keeping those customers means you don't have to waste valuable marketing resources replacing them. You can keep the old customers and grow every time you add a new one.

Asking your kids

Seriously, consider this tactic! Get your children – or any kids on hand – to think about your market for a few minutes; they'll probably have a unique and more contemporary view than you. Ask them simple questions such as, 'What's going to be the next big thing in [name your product or service here]?' 'What's cool and what's not this year?' Kids know, and you don't. In any consumer marketing, you need to make sure that you're cool and your competitors aren't. Since kids lead the trends in modern society, why not ask them what those trends are? Even in B2B and industrial markets, kids and their sense of what's happening in society can be helpful. They may offer you early indicators of shifts in demand or new technologies that could have an impact all the way up the line, from consumers to the businesses that ultimately serve them.

Finding Free Data

Whatever aspect of marketing you're looking at, further information's available to you – and it won't cost a penny. Some of that data can give you just what you need to get started on your research project. So before you buy a report or hire a research firm, dig around for some free (or at least cheap) stuff.

A world of free data exists out there, if you know where to look. Also keep in mind that free data generally falls into a category known as *secondary data* – meaning the information's already been collected or published by someone else – so you get it second hand. While this data's useful stuff, remember that it isn't specific to your company and your competitors can easily access it too.

Getting info from the web

Throughout this book, we include numerous websites, as these are the quickest and easiest places to find free information. For instance, the Internet Advertising Bureau (IAB) and the Interactive Media in Retail Group (IMRG) have more data on how many customers are connected to the Internet and who shop online than we can possibly include here or even in Book V Chapter 9 on e-marketing. Look out for these website references, but more importantly remember that Internet search engines, such as Google, make finding free data simple – and the more you use them, the easier it is to filter out all the sites you're not interested in.

Say you want to set up a website where customers can buy your products directly. You want to know how many people have access to the Internet in the UK and how many are prepared to use their credit card details to buy things. You may also want to find a website developer who can create a secure and fully transactional site for you. Already you have three questions that need answers and you haven't even started your search.

Go to the Google search engine (www.google.co.uk), type in the key words 'internet access', and you get a list of 199 million sites, most of them trying to sell you something. You can narrow the information down by being more specific. The phrase 'online shoppers' will return just over 46.7 million sites; this number is better, but still too many. Type in 'online shoppers market size', however, and you get just 300,000 suggestions, which is better again. Explore these results but if you don't find the information you need, the IAB or IMRG have the answers to all three questions. You only need a bit of practice to be able to find relevant information on the Web quickly and easily.

Hooking up with a librarian

If you don't want to do the search yourself, you can get a professional to search for you, and it'll hardly cost you a penny (well, maybe a few pounds). Libraries are an undervalued national treasure and librarians are trained to archive information as well as know how to access it. Your local library is a good starting place, but you can also get a wealth of market information from university libraries and specialist business libraries.

You can find a lot of what you may need, including industry guides, through the British Library (www.bl.uk). You can make enquiries by phone: 020-7412-7454, or by email: business-information@bl.uk.

Tapping into government resources

Often, the best source of free information is national and local government. Many governments collect copious data on economic activity, population size, and trends within their borders. In Britain, the UK Statistics Authority, now an independent, non-ministerial body accountable directly to Parliament, and its executive arm, the Office for National Statistics (ONS), are the best general sources of data on a wide range of demographic and economic topics.

We're always amazed at the sheer range and quantity of information available on the UK Statistics Authority site, and you probably will be too. Of course, we don't know whether you need to know crime statistics in a certain London borough, but if you do, this is the right place! Described as the 'home of official UK statistics', you can access the ONS at www.ons.gov.uk.

Much of the data on the UK population is based on the Census. Although the Census only takes place every ten years, the information's very detailed and, usefully, can be broken down by neighbourhood. The statistics on inflation and prices, consumer spending, business investment – in fact, anything financial – are more up to date, usually to the last full quarter.

Getting media data

If you're doing any advertising, ask the magazine, newspaper, website or radio station you buy advertising space from to give you information about their customer base – snippets about the people exposed to your ads. This information can help you make sure you reach an appropriate audience. You can also use the exposure numbers to calculate the effectiveness of your advertising.

If you've yet to decide where to advertise, or even in which media, some useful media websites can give you the numbers on how many and what kind of consumers each title or station will deliver. You can trust these sources because in most cases they were set up and are supported by the media owners operating in that area to provide an independent verification of sales and audience profiles so that advertisers can see what they're getting – and hopefully buy more. For this reason, most of the data, for occasional users like you, is free.

The Audit Bureau of Circulations (ABC; www.abc.org.uk) has data on magazines, national and local newspapers, and exhibition visitors. You can find out how many people are reading the titles, where they live and what type of consumers they are; for B2B magazines, you can find out what sector they work in and what their job titles are. For data about online readers, visit the specific ABC site for electronic media (www.abce.org.uk). Most of the different media have organisations providing this sort of data: for TV, see BARB (www.barb.co.uk); for radio, see RAJAR (www.rajar.co.uk); and for outdoor media such as posters, see POSTAR (www.postar.co.uk).

Book II
Sorting Out Your Finances

'It used to be called "The Economic Miracle" in the boom days.'

Book II

Sorting Out Your

Finances

In this book . . .

Getting a solid financial footing is important to any business. Without this, you'll never really be sure how well (or badly) you're doing. This book looks at the most straightforward ways of running the money side of your business – and don't worry, you won't need to be a mathematical wizard to make sense of the chapters we include here.

Here are the contents of Book II at a glance:

Chapter 1

Finding the Money

● ●

In This Chapter

▶ Working out how much outside money you need

▶ Looking at the different types of money available to you

▶ Choosing the best source of money for you

▶ Finding money to work with

● ●

*B*usinesses need a continuous flow of customers, products or services to sell, and space to work from or store unsold goods. But they need money to make all these things happen. The more the business actually does, the more money it needs.

Even during the recent world Credit Crunch, small businesses needed and, despite some anecdotal evidence to the contrary, accessed money. The latest British Banking Association (BBA; www.bba.org.uk) statistics published on 30 July 2010 showed that on a daily average basis banks were making available around £27 million of new term lending to small businesses each working day. Over the preceding 12 months, banks – the major but by no means the only source of money for new and small businesses – had lent out £54.5 billion in long and short-term loans, just a squeak ahead of the £51.8 billion they'd put up three years ago.

Starting a business on the road to success involves ensuring that you have sufficient money to survive until the point where income continually exceeds expenditure. You need a steady flow of money from many different sources along the way. Data from a recent survey by Warwick Business School of small and medium enterprises (SMEs; businesses with up to 250 employees) shows that over a three-year period about 55 per cent make use of a personal or business credit card; 53 per cent use an overdraft; 24 per cent use a term loan; 6 per cent have access to a grant; 3 per cent use invoice discounting; and 3 per cent use equity finance. Karan Bilimoria, founder of Cobra Beer, raised money from almost every source imaginable in the decade or so it took to get his business from start-up to £100 million annual turnover. (Check out the Entrepreneurs section of www.startups.co.uk for his story.)

This chapter helps you to find the right type of money for your business and avoid common pitfalls.

Assessing How Much Money You Need

Work out from the outset how much money you need to get your business off the ground. If your proposed venture needs more cash than you feel comfortable either putting up yourself or raising from others, then the sooner you know the better. Then you can start to revise your plans. The steps that lead to an accurate estimate of your financial requirements start with the sales forecast, along with advice on estimating costs for initial expenditure such as retail or production space, equipment, staff and so on.

Forecasting cash flow is the most reliable way to estimate the amount of money a business needs on a day-to-day basis.

Do's and don'ts for creating a cash-flow forecast:

- ✔ Do ensure that your projections are believable. This means you need to show how you're going to achieve your sales.

- ✔ Do base projections on facts not conjecture.

- ✔ Do describe the main assumptions that underpin your projections.

- ✔ Do explain what the effect of these assumptions not happening to plan may be. For example, if your projections are based on recruiting three salespeople by month three, what would happen if you could only find two suitable people by that date?

- ✔ Do for all forecasting come up with best and worst outcomes as well as the most likely outcomes.

- ✔ Do make sure that you include things like job losses and losses of confidence in the markets that you serve. After all, even if your products and services are excellent, if people have lost confidence because of the bad actions of one of your competitors, you may suffer also.

- ✔ Don't use data to support projections without saying where it came from.

- ✔ Don't forget to allow for seasonal factors. At certain times of the year most businesses are influenced by regular events. Sales of ice cream are lower in winter than in summer, sales of toys peak in the lead-up to Christmas and business-to-business sales dip in the summer and Christmas holiday periods. So rather than taking your projected annual sales figure and dividing by 12 to get a monthly figure, you need to consider what effect seasonal factors may have.

✔ Don't ignore economic factors such as an expanding (or shrinking) economy, rising (or falling) interest rates and an unemployment rate that is so low that it may influence your ability to recruit at the wage rate you want to pay.

✔ Don't make projections without showing the specific actions that can get those results.

✔ Don't forget to get someone else to check your figures – you may be blind to your own mistakes, but someone else is more likely to spot the flaws in your projections.

Projecting receipts

Receipts from sales come in different ways, depending on the range of products and services on offer. And aside from money coming in from paying customers, business owners may, and in many cases almost certainly will, put in cash of their own. However, not all the money necessarily goes in at the outset. For example, you can budget so that £10,000 goes in at the start, followed by sums of £5,000 in months four, seven and ten respectively.

You may be drawing on other sources of outside finance, say from a bank or investor, but these are best left out at this stage. In fact, the point of the cash-flow projection, as well as showing how much money the business needs, is to reveal the likely shortfall after you, the owner, have put what you can into the business and the customers have paid up.

Be sure to have contingency approaches in place, in case people are late in paying you.

Total up the projected receipts for each month and for the year as a whole. You're well advised to carry out this process using a spreadsheet program, which saves you from any problems caused by faulty maths.

A sale made in one month may not result in any cash coming into the business bank account until the following month, if you're reasonably lucky, or much later if you're not. Make sure you know the ways in which people pay their bills in the sectors in which you're working.

Estimating expenses

Some expenses, such as rent, rates and equipment leases, you pay monthly. Other bills, such as telephone, utilities and bank charges, come in quarterly.

If you haven't yet had to pay utilities, for example, put into your forecast your best guesstimate of how much you're going to spend and when. Marketing, promotion, travel, subsistence and stationery are good examples of expenses you may have to estimate. You know you face costs in these areas, but they may not be all that accurate as projections.

After you've been trading for a while, you can get a much better handle on the true costs you're likely to incur.

Total up the payments for each month and for the year as a whole.

The accounting convention is to show payments out and negative sums in brackets, rather than with minus signs in front.

Working out the closing cash balances

This is crunch time, when the real sums reveal the amount of money your great new business needs to get it off the ground. Working through the cash-flow projections allows you to see exactly how much cash you have in hand, or in the bank, at the end of each month, or how much you need to raise. This is the closing cash balance for the month. It's also the opening cash balance for the following month, because that's the position you're carrying forward.

Testing your assumptions

Little disturbs a financier more than a firm that has to go back cap in hand for more finance too soon after raising money, especially if you should've seen and allowed for the additional requirement at the outset.

So in making projections you have to be ready for likely pitfalls and the unexpected events that knock your cash flow off target. Forecasts and projections rarely go to plan, but you can anticipate the most common pitfalls and to some extent allow for them.

You can't really protect yourself against freak disasters or unforeseen delays, which can hit large and small businesses alike. But some events are more likely than others to affect your cash flow.

In particular watch out for sales taking longer to come in than you thought. Customers take time to make decisions, particularly if they already have a satisfactory alternative supplier. Also make sure they'll pay on time. Costs are also a difficult area to predict, as not all are easy to anticipate. Finding out, for example, that your motor insurance will be much higher as a consequence of using a car for your business is one cost missed from projections.

Even if you haven't anticipated events you can allow for them when estimating financing needs. Analysis using a cash-flow spreadsheet enables you to identify worst-case scenarios that can knock you off-course. After this you end up with a realistic estimate of the financing requirements of the business or project.

You can check out potential customers by using a credit reference agency such as Snoop4 Companies (www.snoop4companies.co.uk) for businesses or Experian (www.experian.co.uk) for private individuals. Basic credit reports cost between around £3 and £35 and may save you time and money if you have any reservations about a potential customer's ability to pay.

During periods of economic downturn, recessions to you and me, unsurprisingly customers take longer to settle their bills. Big firms, though perhaps a safer bet and more likely to survive, are rarely sympathetic to a small firm's plight. Expect them to go to the wire when it comes to settling up.

Research by Bacs Payment Schemes Limited (www.bacs.co.uk), the organisation behind Direct Debit and Bacs Direct Credit, published in March 2010 shows that since the Credit Crunch struck British small and medium enterprises (SMEs) are having to wait an average of 41 days longer than their original agreed payment terms before invoices are paid. That's an increase of 9.5 days compared to before the Crunch.

Reviewing Your Financing Options

Knowing how much money you need to get your business successfully started is an important first step, but it's only that – a first step. Many sources of funds are available to small firms. However, not all are equally appropriate to all firms at all times. These different sources of finance carry very different obligations, responsibilities and opportunities. You have to understand the differences to allow an informed choice.

Most small firms confine their financial strategy to long-term or short-term bank loans, viewing other financing methods as either too complex or too risky. In many respects the reverse is true. Almost every finance source other than banks shares some of the risks of doing business with you to a greater or lesser extent.

Deciding between debt capital and equity capital

At one end of the financing spectrum lie shareholders – either individual *business angels* who put their own money into a business, or corporate organisations such as *venture capital providers* (also known as venture capitalists or VCs), who provide equity capital that buys a stake in a business. These investors share all the risks and vagaries of the business alongside you and expect a proportionate share in the rewards if things go well. They're less concerned with a stream of dividends – which is just as well because few small companies ever pay them – and instead hope for a radical increase in the value of their investment. They expect to realise this value from other investors who want to take their place for the next stage in the firm's growth, rather than from any repayment by the founder. Investors in new or small businesses don't look for the security of buildings or other assets to underpin their investment. Rather, they look to the founder's vision and the core management team's ability to deliver results.

At the other end of the financing spectrum are debt financiers – banks that try hard to take no risk and expect some return on their money irrespective of your business's performance. They want interest payments on money lent, usually from day one. They too hope that the management is competent, but they're more interested in making sure that either you or the business has some type of asset such as a house that they can grab if things go wrong. At the end of the day, and that day can be sooner than the borrower expects, a bank wants all its money back, with interest. Think of bankers as people who help you turn part of an illiquid asset such as property into a more liquid asset such as cash – for a price.

Understanding the differences between lenders, who provide debt capital, and investors, who provide equity or share capital, is central to a sound grasp of financial management.

In between the extremes of shareholders and the banks lie a myriad of other financing vehicles, which have a mixture of lending or investing criteria. You need to keep your business finances under constant review, choosing the most appropriate mix of funds for the risks you plan to take and the economic climate ahead. The more risky and volatile the road ahead, the more likely taking a higher proportion of equity capital is to be appropriate. In times of stability and low interest, higher borrowings may be more acceptable.

As a rule of thumb, you use debt and equity in equal amounts to finance a business. If the road ahead looks more risky than usual, go for £2 of equity to every £1 of debt.

Table 1-1 illustrates some of the differences between risk-averse lenders and risk-taking investors.

Table 1-1	Comparing Benefits of Lenders and Investors	
Category	*Lenders*	*Investors*
Interest	Paid on outstanding loan	None, though dividends sometimes paid if profits warrant it
Capital	Repaid at end of term or sooner if lender has concerns	Returned with substantial growth through new shareholders
Security	Either from assets or personal guarantees	From belief in founders and their business vision

If your business sector is viewed as very risky, and perhaps the most reliable measure of that risk is the proportion of firms that go bust, then financing the business almost exclusively with borrowings is tantamount to gambling.

Debt has to be serviced whatever your business performance, so in any risky, volatile marketplace, you stand a good chance of being caught out one day.

If your business risks are low, profits are probably relatively low too. High profits and low risks always attract a flood of competitors, reducing your profits to levels that ultimately reflect the riskiness of your business sector. Because venture capitalists and shareholders generally look for better returns than they can get by lending the money, they'll be disappointed in an investment in a low-risk, low-return business. So if they're wise they don't get involved in the first place, or if they do they don't put any more money in later.

Examining your own finances

Obviously, the first place to start looking for money to finance your business is in your own pockets. You may not have much in ready cash, but you may have assets that you can turn into cash or use to support borrowing.

Start by totalling your assets and liabilities. The chances are that your most valuable *assets* are your house, your car and any life assurance or pension policies you may have. Your *liabilities* are the debts you owe. The difference between your assets and your liabilities, assuming that you have more of the former than the latter, is your *net worth*. That, in effect, is the maximum security you can offer anyone outside the business from whom you want to raise money.

The big questions are, what is your appetite for risk and how certain are you that your business will be successful? The more of your own money you can put into your business at the outset, the more you're truly running your own business in your own way. The more outside money you have to raise, the more power and perhaps value you have to share with others.

Now you have a simple piece of arithmetic to do. How much money do you need to finance your business start-up, as shown in your worst-case scenario cash-flow forecast? How much of your own money are you willing and able to put into your business? The difference is the sum you're looking to outside financiers to back you with.

If that sum is more than your net worth, then you're looking for investors. If it's less, then bankers may be the right people to approach.

If you do have free cash or assets that you could but won't put into your business, then you need to ask yourself whether the proposition is worth pursuing. You can be absolutely certain that any outsider you approach for money will ask you to put up or shut up.

Another factor to consider in reviewing your own finances is your ongoing expenses. You have to live while getting your business up and running. So food, heat and a roof over your head are essential expenses. But perhaps a two-week long-haul summer holiday, a second car and membership of a health club aren't essentials – great while you were a hired hand and had a salary cheque each month, but an expendable luxury when you're working for yourself.

Determining the Best Source of Finance for You

Choosing which external source of finance to use is to some extent a matter of personal preference. One of your tasks in managing your business's financial affairs is to keep good lines of communication open with as many sources as possible. The other key task is to consider which is the most appropriate source for your particular requirement at any one time. We explore the main issues you need to consider in the following sections.

Considering the costs

Clearly, if a large proportion of the funds you need to start your business is going to be consumed in actually raising the money itself, then your set-up costs are going to be very high. Raising capital, especially if the amounts are relatively small (under £500,000), is generally quite expensive. You have to pay your lawyers and accountants, and those of your investor or lender, to prepare the agreements and to conduct the due diligence examination (the business appraisal). Spending between 10 and 15 per cent of the first £500,000 you raise on set-up costs isn't unusual.

An overdraft or factoring agreement is relatively cheap to set up, usually a couple of per cent or so. However, long-term loans, leasing and hire-purchase agreements can involve some legal costs.

Sharing ownership and control

The source of your money helps determine how much ownership and control you have to give up in return. Venture capitalists generally want a large share of stock and often a large say in how the business is run. At the other end of the spectrum are providers of long-term loans, who generally leave you alone so long as you service the interest and repay the capital as agreed. You have to strike the balance that works best for you and your business.

If you don't want to share the ownership of your business with outsiders, then clearly raising equity capital isn't a good idea. Even if you recognise that owning 100 per cent of a small venture isn't as attractive as owning 40 per cent of a business ten times as large, it may not be the right moment to sell any of your shares; particularly if, in common with many business founders, long-term capital gain is one of your principal goals. If you hold on to your shares until profits are reasonably high, you realise more gain for every share sold than if you sell out in the early years or while profits are low.

Parting with shares inevitably involves some loss of control. Letting 5 per cent go may be merely a mild irritation from time to time. However, after 25 per cent has gone, outsiders can have a fair amount of say in how you run things. At that point, even relatively small groups of shareholders can find it easy to call an Extraordinary General Meeting and vote to remove you from the board. Nevertheless, while you have over 51 per cent you're in control, if only just. When you're past the 51 per cent things can get a little dangerous. Theoretically, you can be outvoted at any stage.

Some capital providers take a hands-on approach and have a view on how you should run the business.

Beating the clock

Overdrafts can be arranged in days; raising venture capital can take months. You need very different amounts of scarce management time, dependent on the financing route you take. So if speed matters, your funding options may be limited.

Venture capital providers have been known to string out negotiations long enough to see whether the bullish forecasts made in the business plan come to pass. After all, venture capital is there to help businesses grow faster than they might otherwise do, not just to keep them afloat. Don't expect a decision from a venture capital firm in under three months, whatever their brochure says. Four to six months is a more realistic timescale and nine months isn't too unusual.

Business angels can usually make investment decisions much more quickly than venture capitalists; after all, they're risking their own money. Weeks rather than months is the timescale here.

Obtaining bank finance is usually a fairly speedy process. Even large loans of £100,000 and upwards can be arranged in a few weeks. But the speed depends more on how much collateral you have to give the bank manager comfort that the bank's money is safe.

Staying flexible

As your plans change, the amount of money you need may alter during negotiations. Some sources of funds such as leasing, hire-purchase agreements and long-term loans dictate the amount that has to be agreed at the outset. If you sell shares in the company you have some fluidity during negotiations, and if you arrange an overdraft you can draw down only what you need at any one time, with the upper limit usually negotiated each year.

After you've investigated and used a source of funds, you may want to be able to use that source again as your plans unfold. Loans and hire-purchase/leasing agreements are for a specific sum and it can be difficult and expensive going back to the same source for more.

Gaining security and certainty

For most sources of money, if you comply with the agreed terms, the future is reasonably predictable – in so far as that money is concerned. The exception to this rule is an overdraft. An overdraft is technically, and often actually, repayable on demand. Overdrafts are sometimes called in at the moment you need them most.

Limiting personal liability

As a general rule, most providers of long-term loans and overdrafts look to you and other owners to provide additional security if the business assets are in any way inadequate. You may be asked to provide a personal guarantee – an asset such as your house. Only when you raise new share capital, by selling more stock in your company, do you escape increasing your personal liability. Even with the new share capital, you may be asked to provide warranties to assure new investors that you've declared everything in the company's history.

Going for Debt

You can explore borrowing from a number of possible sources in your search for outside finance. It's worth giving them all the once-over, but most people start and stop at a bank. The other major first source of money is family and friends, but many business starters feel nervous about putting family money at risk, and prefer to deal with professional financiers. *Credit unions* and *mezzanine finance* are fairly unusual sources of finance for a start-up, but finding money to start a business is a tough task, so don't completely overlook any source.

Borrowing from banks

Book II

Sorting Out Your Finances

Banks are the principal, and frequently the only, source of finance for nine out of every ten new and small businesses.

Banks are usually a good starting point for almost any type of debt financing. They're also able to provide many other cash-flow and asset-backed financing products, although they're often not the only or the most appropriate provider. As well as the main clearing banks, a number of the former building societies and smaller regional banks are competing hard for small firm lending.

Hippychick

When new mother Julie Minchin discovered the Hipseat, she knew she'd found a helpful product. Anything that makes carrying a baby around all day without ending up with excruciating backache has got to be a benefit. It was only later that she realised that selling the product for the German company that made the Hipseat could launch her into business. At first Julie acted as their UK distributor but later she wanted to make some major improvements to the product. That meant finding a manufacturer to make the product especially for her business. China was the logical place to find a company flexible enough to make small quantities as well as being able to help her keep the cost of the end product competitive.

Julie funded the business, Hippychick, with a small family loan, an overdraft facility and a variety of grants secured with the help of Business Link. Now in its tenth year the company has a turnover of £3 million a year and sells 14 new and unique products aimed at the baby market. Hippychick supplies national chains such as Boots, Mothercare and Blooming Marvellous, as well as independents. It also sells via a catalogue and website, and is in the process of building a network of distributors for the branded products.

Keeping the money men happy

Most owner-managers don't give much thought to how to deal with their bank, factoring company or venture capitalist. They just jump right into their business and don't think about how they should treat these people, what their bankers can do for them and what their bankers in turn look for in a client. But with a little thought and effort, you can ensure that you get the most from your banking relationships.

Your banker, or any other source of finance, has the ability to influence the success of your business radically. Developing long-term, personal relationships with the banker is important – if you do that, when you hit the inevitable bumps in the road the banker will be there to help you.

Keep in mind when you meet your banker for the first time that you want to develop a long-term relationship with this person. The meeting should be a two-way interview. You need to ask yourself: 'Is this person genuinely interested in me? Is this person trying to understand my business? Does this person understand my objectives?' If the answer to any of these is no, then find another banker.

You often hire your lawyer and accountant by the hour or job, but your banker is another matter – your banker makes money off the fees that your business generates. Your banker is usually happy to help you, and can therefore be a source of free consulting, though you do need to be a little more careful today because bankers are beginning to get wise to the idea of charging for services.

Shop around for the best-buy bank just as you do for any other product or service. Check out Money Facts (http://moneyfacts.co.uk/compare/banking) or Which 4 U (www.which4u.co.uk/bank-accounts) to see who's offering the best deals.

If you import raw materials, your bank can provide you with Letters of Credit, which guarantee your suppliers payment from the bank when they present proof of satisfactory delivery. If you have a number of overseas suppliers who prefer settlement in their own currency for which you need foreign currency, cheque facilities or to buy money at a fixed exchange rate before you need it, banks can make the necessary arrangements.

Running an overdraft

The principal form of short-term bank funding is an *overdraft*. An overdraft is permission for you to use some of the bank's money when you don't have enough of your own. The permission is usually agreed annually, but can be withdrawn at any time. A little over a quarter of all bank finance for small firms is in the form of an overdraft. The overdraft was originally designed to cover the time between having to pay for raw materials to manufacture finished goods and selling those goods. The size of an overdraft is usually limited to a modest proportion of the amount of money that your customers owe you and the value of your finished goods stock. The bank sees those items as assets, which in the last resort it can use to get its money back.

Starting out in a cleaning business, for example, you need sufficient funds initially to buy the mop and bucket. Three months into the contract you've paid for these and so getting a five-year bank loan to cover this expenditure is pointless, because within a year you'll have cash in the bank.

However, if your overdraft doesn't get out of the red at any stage during the year, you need to re-examine your financing. All too often companies utilise an overdraft to acquire long-term assets, and that overdraft never seems to disappear, eventually constraining the business.

The attraction of overdrafts is that they're very easy to arrange, except in the most unusual of circumstances such as during a global credit crunch. Also they take little time to set up. But their inherent weakness is that the keywords in the arrangement document are 'repayable on demand', which leaves the bank free to make and change the rules as it sees fit. (This term is under review and some banks may remove the term from the arrangement.) With other forms of borrowing, as long as you stick to the terms and conditions, the loan is yours for the duration; not so with overdrafts.

Seeing the five Cs

Bankers like to speak of the five Cs of credit analysis, factors they look at when they evaluate a loan request. When applying to a bank for a loan, prepare to address the following points:

- **Capacity:** This is a prediction of the borrower's ability to repay the loan. For a new business, bankers look at the business plan. For an existing business, bankers consider financial statements and industry trends.

- **Capital:** Bankers scrutinise a borrower's net worth, the amount by which assets exceed debts.

- **Character:** Bankers lend money to borrowers who appear honest and who have a good credit history. Before you apply for a loan, it makes sense to obtain a copy of your credit report and clean up any problems.

- **Collateral:** Bankers generally want a borrower to pledge an asset that can be sold to pay off the loan if the borrower lacks funds.

- **Conditions**: Whether bankers give a loan can be influenced by the current economic climate as well as by the amount requested.

Banks also use CAMPARI, which stands for Character, Ability, Means, Purpose, Amount, Repayment, Insurance. You can find out more about this alternative system on this website: `www.bytestart.co.uk/content/finance/funding/business-bank-loan.shtml`.

Taking on a term loan

If you're starting up a manufacturing business, you'll be buying machinery to last probably five years, designing your logo and buying stationery, paying the deposit on leasehold premises, buying a vehicle and investing funds in winning a long-term contract. Because you expect the profits on this to flow over a number of years, they need to be financed over a similarly long period, either through a bank loan or by inviting someone to invest in shares in the company – in other words, a long-term commitment.

Term loans, as these long-term borrowings are generally known, are funds provided by a bank for a number of years. The interest can be either variable – changing with general interest rates – or fixed for a number of years ahead. In some cases you may be able to move between having a fixed interest rate and a variable one at certain intervals. You may even be able to have a moratorium (break) on interest payments for a short period, to give the business some breathing space. Provided that you meet the conditions of the loan in such matters as repayment, interest and security cover, the money is available for the period of the loan. Unlike having an overdraft, the bank can't pull the rug from under you if your circumstances (or the local manager) change.

Going with a loan guarantee

Banks operate loan guarantees at the instigation of governments in the UK, and in Australia, the US and elsewhere. These schemes guarantee loans from banks and other financial institutions for small businesses with viable business proposals that have tried and failed to obtain a conventional loan because of a lack of security.

Currently called the Enterprise Finance Guarantee Scheme, these government-backed loans are available for periods of between two and ten years on sums from £5,000 to £2.5 million. The government guarantees 70–90 per cent of the loan. In return for the guarantee, the borrower pays a premium of 1–2 per cent per year on the outstanding amount of the loan. The commercial aspects of the loan are matters between the borrower and the lender.

You can find out more about the details of the scheme on the Business Link website (www.businesslink.gov.uk; go to Finance and Grants; Finance Options; Borrowing; Loans and Overdrafts; and then Enterprise Finance Guarantee).

Cashflow Acceleration, an independent finance broker and a member of the Federation of Small Businesses, provides a free independent quotation search service for customers looking for commercial finance. At www.cash flow-acceleration.co.uk (go to Services and then Enterprise Finance Guarantee) you can see whether a bank may be prepared to lend under the scheme to your business.

Destination London

Rachel Lowe, a 29-year-old single mother with two children, came up with her winning business idea while working part-time as a taxi driver in Portsmouth. She invented a game involving players throwing a dice to move taxi pieces around a board collecting fares to travel to famous destinations while aiming to get back to the taxi rank before they ran out of fuel. Being able to run the business from home meant Rachel could spend more time with her children and still be a breadwinner.

But despite having a business plan written up when she entered a local business competition, she had serious hurdles to cross before she could get started. With a deal from Hamleys, the London toyshop, in the bag and a manufacturer and distributor lined up, all that was missing was a modest amount of additional funding

to help with marketing and stock. She pitched her proposal to the BBC's *Dragons' Den* and was given a thorough roasting. To say the dragons weren't enthusiastic would be a serious understatement. They reckoned Monopoly would wipe the floor with her. Bowed but far from beaten Rachel then turned to South Coast Money Line, a Community Development Finance Institution and part of the Portsmouth Area Regeneration Trust Group (www.part. org.uk). With a loan from them she propelled her game – Destination London – into the top ten best-selling games, even beating Monopoly! A deal with Debenhams to stock regional versions of the game and signing up to produce Harry Potter and Disney versions left her with a business worth £2 million, at a conservative estimate.

Grabbing some cash locally

Many communities, particularly those operating in rundown areas in need of regeneration, have a facility to lend or even invest in businesses that could bring employment to the area. The nearby sidebar 'Destination London' offers one such example. Funding from these sources could be for anything from start-up, right through to expansion, or in some cases even rescue finance, to help prevent a business from folding, shedding a large number of jobs or relocating to a more benign business environment.

Financing cash flow

When your business is trading, two other sources of finance open up that can smooth out cash-flow troughs when dealing with business customers. Factoring and invoice discounting are both methods of funding sales after you've submitted an invoice.

Factors provide three related services:

✔ Immediate finance of up to 80 per cent of invoiced sales, with the balance (minus administration and finance charges) payable after a set period or when the invoice is paid

✔ Managing the sales ledger, including sending out invoices and ensuring they're paid

✔ Advising on credit risk and insuring clients against bad debts

This type of finance is provided against the security of trade debts (the amount of money customers owe you). Normally, when you raise an invoice you send a copy to the factor, who then funds up to 85 per cent against the invoice in advance of the customer paying. The remainder becomes payable either on a maturity date or when the customer pays. Because the invoice is assigned to the factor, payment by the customer is direct to the factor.

Invoice discounting operates in a similar way, except the seller retains control of its debtors and is responsible for collecting the money.

These forms of finance are directly related to sales levels and can be particularly helpful during growth spurts.

The Factors and Discounters Association (www.thefda.org.uk/public/membersList.asp) provides a list of over 40 members on its website, which has a search facility to help you define which organisations are best placed to meet your individual business requirements.

Getting physical

You can usually finance assets such as vehicles, computers, office equipment and the like either by leasing them or buying them on hire purchase, leaving your other funds free to cover less tangible expenses such as advertising or living expenses. You can use a lease to take the risk out of purchasing an asset that becomes obsolete or for taking account of repairs and maintenance costs. In return for this 'certainty' you pay a fee that's added to the monthly or quarterly charge. However, knowing the exact cost of purchasing and using an asset can be attractive and worth paying for. Hire purchase differs from leasing in that you have the option eventually to become the owner of the asset after a series of payments. Important tax implications apply to using these types of finance and you need to discuss them with your accountant.

The Finance and Leasing Association website (www.fla.org.uk/asset/members) gives more information on the different products on offer to finance assets and has a directory of members and their contact details. You can also use the calculator at www.leasing.co.uk/leasecalculator to get some idea of the monthly repayments for different types of assets (such as software, furniture or cars) over different time periods.

Uniting with a credit union

If you don't like the terms on offer from the *high-street banks*, as the major banks are often known, you may consider forming your own bank. The idea isn't as crazy as it sounds. Credit unions formed by groups of small businesspeople, both in business and aspiring to start up, have been around for decades in the UK, US and elsewhere. They're an attractive option for people on low incomes, and provide a cheap and convenient alternative to banks. Some self-employed people such as taxi drivers have also formed credit unions. They can then apply for loans to meet unexpected capital expenditure either for repairs, refurbishments or technical upgrading.

Established credit unions usually require you to have a particular trade, have paid money in for a number of months or years and have a maximum loan amount limited to the types of assets people in your trade are likely to need.

Credit union usage in the UK has more than doubled in the past five years. Some 40,258 credit unions operate in 79 countries, enabling 118 million members to access affordable financial services. The Association of British Credit Unions (`www.abcul.org`) offers information and a directory of providers.

Book II

Sorting Out Your Finances

Borrowing from family and friends

Those close to you are often willing to lend you money or invest in your business. This helps you avoid the problem of pleading your case to outsiders and enduring extra paperwork and bureaucratic delays. Help from friends, relatives and business associates can be especially valuable if you've been through bankruptcy or had other credit problems that make borrowing from a commercial lender difficult or impossible.

Involving friends and family in your business brings a range of extra potential benefits – but also costs and risks that aren't a feature of most other types of finance. You need to decide whether these are acceptable.

Some advantages of borrowing money from people you know well are that they may charge you a lower interest rate, you may be able to delay paying back money until you're more established, and you may have more flexibility if you get into a jam. But after you agree to the loan terms, you have the same legal obligations as with a bank or any other source of finance.

Borrowing money from relatives and friends can have a major disadvantage. If your business does poorly and those close to you end up losing money, you may damage your personal relationships. So in dealing with friends, relatives and business associates be careful to establish clearly the terms of the deal and put them in writing, and also to make an extra effort to explain the risks. In short, your job is to make sure that your helpful friend or relative doesn't suffer true hardship if you're unable to meet your financial commitments.

When raising money from family and friends, follow these guidelines.

- ✔ Do agree proper terms for the loan or investment.
- ✔ Do put the agreement in writing and if it involves a limited partnership, share transaction or guarantee, have a legal agreement drawn up.
- ✔ Do make an extra effort to explain the risks of the business and the possible downside implications for their money.
- ✔ Do make sure when raising money from parents that other siblings are compensated in some way, perhaps via a will.
- ✔ Do make sure you want to run a family business before raising money from them. It's not the same as running your own business.
- ✔ Don't borrow from people on fixed incomes.
- ✔ Don't borrow from people who can't afford to lose their investment.
- ✔ Don't make the possible rewards sound more attractive than you would, say, to a bank.
- ✔ Don't offer jobs in your business to anyone providing money unless the person is best for the job.
- ✔ Don't change the normal pattern of social contact with family and friends after they've put up the money.

Sharing Out the Spoils

If your business is particularly risky, requires a lot of up-front finance or involves new technology, then you usually have to consider selling a proportion of your business's shares to outside investors.

However, if your business plan doesn't show profit returns in excess of 30 per cent per annum for the next three to five years and you aren't prepared to part with upwards of 15 per cent of your business, then equity finance probably isn't for you.

A number of different types of investor may be prepared to put up the funds if the returns are good enough. We talk about each type in the following sections.

Benefiting by business angels

One source of equity or risk capital is private individuals, with their own funds and perhaps some knowledge of your type of business, who are willing to invest in your company in return for a share in the business.

Such investors have been christened *business angels*, a term first coined to describe private wealthy individuals who backed theatrical productions, usually a play on Broadway or in London's West End.

By their very nature such investments are highly speculative. The angel typically has a personal interest in the venture and may want to play some role in the company – often an angel is determined to have some involvement beyond merely signing a cheque.

Business angels are informal suppliers of risk capital to new and growing businesses, often taking a hand at a stage when no one else is prepared to take the chance; a sort of investor of last resort. But although they often lose their shirts, business angels sometimes make serious money. The angel who backed software company Sage with £10,000 in its first round of £250,000 financing saw his stake rise to £40 million, and Ian McGlinn, the former garage owner who advanced Anita Roddick the £4,000 she needed to open a second shop in return for about 25 per cent of her company's shares, eventually wound up with a couple of hundred million pounds from his stake in The Body Shop.

Book II

Sorting Out Your Finances

In the UK and the US hundreds of networks operate with tens of thousands of business angels who are prepared to put several billion pounds each year into new or small businesses. One estimate is that the UK has approximately 18,000 business angels and that they annually invest in the region of £500 million.

Two organisations that can put you in contact with a business angel are:

- The British Business Angels Association (BBAA; website: www.bbaa. org.uk).

- Angel Investment Network (www.angelinvestmentnetwork.co.uk), which operates a service matching entrepreneurs to angels. Its website also has a number of useful tools to help you get investor-ready.

Alternatively, you can apply to appear on the BBC's business reality show *Dragons' Den* (www.bbc.co.uk/dragonsden) and put your proposition face to face to five angels and five million television viewers.

Going for venture capital

Venture capital is a means of financing the start-up, development, expansion or the purchase of a company. The venture capitalist acquires a share of the company in return for providing the requisite funding. Venture capital firms often work in conjunction with other providers of finance in putting together a total funding package for a business.

Venture capital providers invest other people's money, often from pension funds. They're likely to be interested in investing a large sum of money for a large stake in a company.

Venture capital is a medium- to long-term investment of not just money but of time and effort. The venture capital firm's aim is to enable growth companies to develop into the major businesses of tomorrow. Before investing, a venture capital provider goes through *due diligence*, a process that involves a thorough examination of both the business and its owners. Accountants and lawyers subject you and your business plan to detailed scrutiny. You and your directors are required to warrant that you've provided *all* relevant information, under pain of financial penalties.

In general venture capitalists expect their investment to pay off within seven years. But they're hardened realists. Two in every ten investments they make are total write-offs, and six perform averagely well at best. So the one star in every ten investments they make has to cover a lot of duds. Venture capitalists have a target rate of return of 30 per cent plus, to cover this poor success rate.

Raising venture capital isn't a cheap option. The arrangement costs almost always run to six figures. The cost of the due diligence process is borne by the firm raising the money, but is paid out of the money raised, if that's any consolation. Raising venture capital isn't quick either. Six months isn't unusual and over a year has been known. Every venture capitalist has a deal done in six weeks in his portfolio, but that truly is the exception.

Venture capital providers want to exit from their investment at some stage. Their preferred route is via a public offering, taking your company onto the stock market, but a trade sale to another, usually larger, business in a related line of work is more usual.

New venture capital funds are coming on stream all the time and they too are looking for a gap in the market.

The British Venture Capital Association (www.bvca.co.uk) and the European Venture Capital Association (www.evca.com) both have online directories giving details of hundreds of venture capital providers. VFinance (www.vfinance.com), a global financial services company specialising in high-growth opportunities, has a directory of 1,541 venture capital firms and over 23,000 business angels. Its website also contains a useful business plan template. (See Chapter 4 in Book I for more on business planning.)

Karen Darby left school at 16 with just one GCSE. While working in a call centre in 2002 she hit on the idea of helping people find the cheapest gas, electricity and telephone companies and providing a user-friendly way to switch suppliers for free. She pitched her business proposition to Bridges Community Ventures, a venture capital firm, and raised £300,000. Three years down the road she sold her company, SimplySwitch, to Daily Mail and General Trust, leaving Karen £6 million richer.

Looking to corporate venturing

Alongside the venture capital firms are 200 or so other businesses that have a hand in the risk capital business, without it necessarily being their main line of business. For the most part these are firms with an interest in the Internet or high technology that want an inside track to new developments. Their own research and development operations have slowed down and become less and less entrepreneurial as they've grown bigger. So they need to look outside for new inspiration.

Even successful firms invest hundreds of millions of dollars each year in scores of other small businesses. Sometimes, if the company looks a particularly good fit, they buy the whole business. Apple, for example, while keeping its management team focused on the core business, has a $12 million stake in Akamai Technologies, whose software tries to keep the Web running smoothly even under unusual traffic demands.

Book II

Sorting Out Your Finances

Not only high-tech firms go in for corporate venturing. Any firm whose arteries are hardening a bit is on the look-out for new blood. McDonald's, for example – hardly a business in the forefront of the technological revolution – has stakes in over a dozen ventures. It once had a 35 per cent stake in Pret a Manger, but when it decided that the Pret model didn't fit well with the McDonald's business it offloaded its stake to Bridgepoint for £345 million – four times its initial stake; a good result for both parties.

When Alex Cassie was casting around for cash to get his new business started making parts for car companies such as Aston Martin, he was steered to an apparently unlikely source, Michelin, the French tyre firm. Since 2003 Michelin has operated a scheme pledged to put £3 million into small firms near its British plants. Michelin put £20,000 into Cassie's business, which within four years employed 68 people with an annual turnover of £5 million.

Understanding due diligence

Usually, after a private equity firm signs a letter of intent to provide capital and you accept, they conduct a *due diligence* investigation of both the management and the company. During this period the private equity firm has access to all financial and other records, facilities and employees to investigate before finalising the deal. The material the firm examines includes copies of all leases, contracts and loan agreements in addition to copious financial records and statements. The firm wants to see any management reports, such as sales reports, inventory records, detailed lists of assets, facility maintenance records, aged receivables and payables reports, employee organisation charts, payroll and benefits records, customer records and marketing materials. They want to know about any pending litigation, tax audits or insurance disputes. Depending on the nature of the business, they may also consider getting an environmental audit and an insurance check-up.

Innocent

In the summer of 1998, when Richard Reed, Adam Balon and Jon Wright had developed their first smoothie recipes but were still nervous about giving up their jobs, they bought £500 worth of fruit, turned it into smoothies and sold them from a stall at a London music festival. They put up a sign saying 'Do you think we should give up our jobs to make these smoothies?' next to bins saying 'YES' and 'NO', inviting people to put the empty bottle in the appropriate bin. At the end of the weekend the 'YES' bin was full, so they went to work the next day and resigned. The rest, as they say, is history. Virtually a household name, Innocent Drinks has experienced a decade of rapid growth.

But the business stalled in 2008, with sales slipping back and their European expansion soaking up cash at a rapid rate. The founders, average age 28, decided that they needed some heavy-weight advice and talked to Charles Dunstone, Carphone Warehouse founder, and Mervyn Davies, chairman of Standard Chartered. The strong advice was to get an investor with deep pockets and ideally something else to bring to the party to augment the youthful enthusiasm of the founders. They launched their search for an investor the day that Lehman Brothers filed for bankruptcy. In April 2009 the Innocent team accepted Coca-Cola as a minority investor in their business, paying £30 million for a stake of 10–20 per cent. They chose Coca-Cola because as well as providing the funds, the company can help get Innocent products out to more people in more places. They'll also be able to learn a lot from Coca-Cola, who have been in business for over 120 years.

The sting in the due diligence tail is that the current owners of the business are required to personally warrant that everything they've said or revealed is both true and complete. In the event that it proves not to be so, owners will be personally liable to the extent of any loss incurred by those buying the shares.

Finding Free Money

Sometimes, if you're very lucky or very smart, you can get some of the money you need for free. The following sections tell you how to cash in on government grants and how winning a contest can earn you lots of lovely loot.

Getting a grant

Unlike debt, which you have to repay, or equity, which has to earn a return for the investors, grants and awards from the government or the European Union are often not refundable. So, although they're frequently hard to get, grants can be particularly valuable. Almost every country has incentives to encourage entrepreneurs to invest in particular locations or industries. The US, for example, has an allowance of Green Cards (work and residence permits) for up to several hundred immigrants each year who are prepared to put up sufficient funds to start up a substantial business in the country.

In the UK, if you're involved in the development of a new technology you may be eligible for a grant for research and development. Under the scheme you can claim 60 per cent of eligible project costs up to a maximum grant of £75,000 on research projects; 35 per cent of costs up to £200,000 on development projects; 35 per cent of costs up to £500,000 on exceptional development projects; and 50 per cent of costs up to a maximum grant of £20,000 on micro projects. Business Link (www.businesslink.gov.uk) can give full details of the grants.

Book II

Sorting Out Your Finances

Support for business comes in a very wide variety of forms. The most obvious is the direct (cash) grant, but other forms of assistance are also available including free or subsidised consultancy, which may help you with market research, staff development or identifying business opportunities, or with access to valuable resources such as research facilities.

Grants often come with strings attached including you needing to locate in a specific area, take on employees or find matching funding from another source.

Though several grant schemes operate across the whole of the UK and are available to all businesses that satisfy the outline criteria, myriad schemes exist that are administered locally. Thus the location of your business can be absolutely crucial, and funding may strongly depend on the area into which you intend to grow or develop. Additionally, extra grants may well be available to a business investing in an area of social deprivation, particularly if it involves sustainable job creation.

Keep yourself informed about which grants are available. Grants are constantly being introduced and withdrawn, but no system lets you know about them automatically. The Business Link (www.businesslink.gov.uk; go to Finance and Grants) and Grants Online (www.grantsonline.org.uk) websites can help you find out about grants.

Winning money

If you enjoy publicity and like a challenge then you can look out for a business competition to enter. Like government grants, business competitions are ubiquitous and, like national lotteries, they're something of a hit-or-miss affair. But one thing is certain: if you don't enter you can't win.

More than 100 annual awards take place in the UK alone, aimed at new or small businesses, and are mostly sponsored by banks, major accountancy bodies, chambers of commerce, local or national newspapers, business magazines and the trade press. Government departments may also have competitions for promoting their initiatives for exporting, innovation, job creation and so forth. The nature and amount of the awards change from year to year, as do the sponsors. But looking in the national and local press, particularly the small business sections of *The Times*, *Daily Telegraph*, *Daily Mail* and *The Guardian*, and on the Internet, should put you in touch with a competition organiser. Money awards constitute 40 per cent of the main competition prizes. For the most part, these cash sums are less than £5,000. However, a few do exceed £10,000 and one British award is for £50,000.

Business Match (www.businessmatch.org.uk/576.asp), the Design Council (www.designcouncil.org.uk/our-work/investment), the National Business Awards (www.nationalbusinessawards.co.uk) and the Growing Business Awards (http://gba.realbusiness.co.uk) are all websites that can help you find out about competitions.

Business Link has a Business Awards Finder (http://online.business link.gov.uk/bdotg/action/bafSearch). Just put in your postcode and business sector and the site provides details of any award you may be eligible to apply for. The website warns that not all the awards it flags up involve cash, but the free publicity should be more than worthwhile.

Chapter 2

Figuring Out Financials

. . . .

In This Chapter

▶ Understanding a profit and loss account

▶ Interpreting the balance sheet

▶ Examining cash flow

▶ Evaluating financial ratios

. . . .

*N*umbers. Some people love them; others are bored by them; still others begin to stammer, shake and exhibit other physical signs of distress around them. But almost everyone agrees that, love 'em or hate 'em, numbers are the way that we keep track of things – football, cholesterol, the stock market and our latest business venture. There's a lot more to numbers than simply the score at the end of the game or the final Footsie closing, however. When they're put together in the right ways, numbers paint detailed pictures and tell stories about everything from the career of a football player to the state of the global economy.

You're probably familiar with the numerical snapshots that a bank requires when you want to borrow money for a new car, a bigger house, or the caravan in Devon that you've always wanted. Those snapshots always include a profit and loss account, as well as some sort of balance sheet. The profit and loss account tells the bank where you get your money and where you spend it. The balance sheet lists the value of all the things that you own and balances it against the money that you owe, including your car loans, mortgages, credit cards and even personal IOUs.

Financial statements tell the bank a great deal about you, and the bank learns even more by taking numbers from the statements and calculating a load of ratios. The bank totals your monthly loan payments and divides that number by your monthly income, for example, and then compares this ratio with the average for other borrowers. The result gives the bank a relatively good measure of your ability to repay the loan. Taken together, the statements and ratios create a financial portrait that the bank uses to get to know you better. And the better the bank knows you, the more reliable its decision is.

In this chapter, we introduce the basic financial statements and ratios that are widely used in business planning – which really are the same ones that paint a picture of your personal finances. First, we show you how a profit and loss account and a balance sheet are put together. Next, we explain cash-flow statements, which do pretty much what the name implies. Finally, we explore simple financial ratios that you can use to evaluate your business.

Understanding a Profit and Loss Account

A *profit and loss account* presents the proverbial bottom line. By adding all the revenue that you receive from selling goods or services and then subtracting the total cost of operating your company, the profit and loss account shows *net profit* – how much money the company has made or lost over a given period. Here's how to think of net profit:

Net profit = Revenue – Cost

The important thing to remember is the fact that the profit and loss account captures a simple idea. No matter what your accountants call it – a profit and loss account, earnings report, or statement of profit and loss – or how complicated accounting types make it look, it still uses the same basic principle of subtracting cost from revenue to come up with profit.

Your profit and loss account needs to cover a period that makes the most sense for your business planning: monthly, quarterly or yearly. (The tax people, of course, are always interested in seeing your profit and loss account once a year.) You get a better financial picture of your company and where it's going if you look at profit and loss accounts over several periods and even over several years. Look at the various parts of a profit and loss account for Global Gizmos Company (see Figure 2-1). Notice that Global Gizmos includes a two-year comparison to show how revenue, costs and profits have changed over time. Global Gizmos is a small company; if you want to make it a big company, add three zeros after all the numbers. In either case, the profit and loss account works exactly the same way.

Revenue

Revenue refers to all the money that a company receives as a result of being in business. The most important source of revenue (usually, the sale of goods or services) always appears as the first item in the income statement – in the case of Global Gizmos, gross revenue on sales. In this context, *gross* doesn't mean anything unpleasant; it indicates that the revenue is a total, without costs subtracted. Revenue from sources other than sales usually shows up a bit later in the profit and loss account.

Figure 2-1:
The profit
and loss
account
starts
with gross
revenue
and then
subtracts
the costs
of various
business
activities
to arrive at
different
kinds of
profit.

Profit and Loss at a Glance

Global Gizmos Company

PROFIT AND LOSS ACCOUNT AS OF DECEMBER 31	This Year	Last Year
Gross Revenue on Sales	£ 810,000	£ 750,000
Cost of goods sold	-560,000	-520,000
Gross Profit	250,000	230,000
Sales, general, and administration	-140,000	-140,000
Depreciation expense	-30,000	- 25,000
Operating Profit	80,000	65,000
Dividend and interest income	+ 3,000	+ 2,000
Interest expense	- 13,000	- 14,000
Profit Before Taxes	70,000	53,000
Taxes	- 20,000	- 18,000
NET PROFIT FOR YEAR	**£ 50,000**	**£ 35,000**

(markers 1, 2, 3, 4, 5 appear alongside the rows)

Gross revenue on sales

Gross revenue on sales is based on the number of units actually sold during
a particular period multiplied by the prices actually paid. Global Gizmos sold
32,400 widgets at a price of £25 each, for a gross revenue of £810,000. Things
can be a little more complicated than this example, of course; your company
may have several products or kinds of service, or your prices may change
over time. Maybe you have to make an allowance for items that are returned.
All these considerations contribute to your own calculation of gross revenue
on sales.

Dividend and interest income

Your company may have sources of revenue besides sales – the income
from savings accounts and other securities, for example. Because you must
have money to operate the company anyway, you probably want that money
to make money while it's sitting around. You need to keep this investment
income separate from your revenue on sales, however, so that you always
know how much money the company itself is generating. In your profit and
loss account your dividends and interest income appear separately from
your other revenue.

Costs

Unfortunately, you have to spend money to make money. The cost of doing business is usually divided into general categories that reflect the separate activities that a company is involved in and the different kinds of expenses that it incurs. Major cost categories include cost of goods sold, sales and administrative expenses, depreciation, interest expense – and don't forget taxes. Each item deserves its own entry in the profit and loss account.

Cost of goods sold

The *cost of goods sold* (COGS) combines all the direct costs of putting together your product or service. Raw materials, supplies and the labour involved in assembling a product are all part of the COGS; so are the electricity, water and gas used in manufacturing, as well as the costs of maintaining production facilities. If you offer dog-walking for pet owners, for example, the costs associated with delivering that service – leads and pooper scoopers – go into the COGS.

You may have to make a judgement call here and there about what is or isn't part of the COGS. Just remember to be consistent over time.

Sales, general and administration

Sales, general and administration expenses (SG&A) combine all the costs associated with supporting your product or service. If the company is just you, a telephone and a tiny rented office above the hardware shop, the costs won't amount to much. But for larger companies, these costs seem to go on and on. SG&A includes salaries and overheads for the sales staff as well as the receptionist, secretary and the boss. SG&A also includes advertising and promotion, travel, telephone calls, accounting fees, office supplies, dues and subscriptions and everyone's favourite, miscellaneous expenses.

SG&A costs are tracked separately because they're not tied directly to revenue and can easily get out of hand. Make sure that you keep an eye on this particular entry.

Depreciation expense

Depreciation expense is a standard way to spread both the cost and the usefulness of expensive items out over time. Whether it's a building, a truck, or a computer, almost any durable item that your company buys slowly declines in value, because of simple wear and tear or because new technology makes the item obsolete. Bean-counters have come up with various ways to calculate that depreciation. All the methods allow you to allocate a portion of the purchase price as a business expense each year, to reflect a decrease in value. (Land, by the way, isn't included in depreciation expenses and can't be depreciated.)

Interest expense

Interest expense includes all the money that you pay out to the parties that loaned you funds to operate the company. You don't want to overlook this cost. You may have entered into agreements with banks or other investors, for example, and are obliged to pay back interest on a fixed schedule. An interest expense (often called a *fixed charge*) is isolated in the profit and loss account because it absolutely, positively has to be paid year after year.

Taxes

Even Albert Einstein stopped short of trying to figure out his own taxes. But taxes are a fact of life and represent another cost of doing business. You can minimise your company's taxes by making sure that you keep careful track of all your other expenses.

Profit

Profit is the Holy Grail. When you do things right, the total costs flowing out of your business are less than all the revenue coming in. Your profit, of course, represents the difference. But it's useful to talk about different kinds of profit at various stages along the way. In particular, you can keep track of gross profit, operating profit and profit before taxes, as well as your overall net profit. Comparing profit at different stages gives you a clearer picture of where your company is most efficient and where you can do better.

Gross profit

Gross profit measures how much money your company still has after you subtract all the direct costs of putting together your product or service (COGS) from the total revenue generated by sales. This profit doesn't include the many indirect expenses that you have in running the company or any revenue sources other than sales.

Operating profit

Operating profit accounts for all those additional sales, general and administration (SG&A) costs that you incur as part of operating your business; it also subtracts the depreciation expense of your costly purchases. Operating profit reflects the money that you make from your overall business operations.

Profit before taxes

Profit before taxes takes everything else into account, including any financial transactions that you make. Your income from other sources (such as investment dividends and interest) is included here, as well as your interest payments to creditors.

Net profit

Net profit, of course, is the bottom line after the company's tax bite is subtracted. Global Gizmos made money in its most recent period.

- ✔ A profit and loss account begins with your revenue and subtracts all your costs to come up with net profit, usually for a year.
- ✔ Revenue includes all the money that you take in from sales, as well as income that you receive from dividends and interest.
- ✔ Your costs include the cost of goods sold; sales, general and administrative expenses; depreciation; interest expense; and taxes.
- ✔ By calculating profit at various stages – gross profit, operating profit and profit before taxes – you can see precisely where the money comes from and where it goes.

Margins matter

Profit is the way you keep the score in the business game, so clearly a high figure is better than a lower one. But that begs the question what exactly is high? One way to keep track is to measure the profit relative to the level of business activity. So for example if the gross profits are £10 and the sales turnover is £100 the gross profit margin is 10 per cent per cent (10/100 × 100). If last year the gross profit was £5 and the sales turnover was £50 the gross profit margin was 10 per cent per cent also, meaning that whilst the amount of profit has doubled so has the activity required to make it. That doesn't mean the profit growth isn't worth having, just that it would have been even better if we had, say, only had to have a turnover of £80 to make that £10 gross profit. Had we done so our gross profit margin would have been 12.5 per cent per cent (10/80 × 100), a much better result than 10 per cent per cent.

You can do the same sum for operating profit, and for profit before and after tax. Measuring margins in this way is particularly useful as it allows you to compare profit performance in a meaningful way irrespective of the size of the organisation. We look at this in more detail, and at some other useful financial relationships, later in this chapter in the section 'Evaluating Financial Ratios'.

Interpreting the Balance Sheet

Whereas a profit and loss account captures the financial results of your operations for a given period, a *balance sheet* is more like a snapshot of your financial condition at a particular moment. The profit and loss account lists your revenue, your costs and the profit that you make. The balance sheet, on the other hand, addresses what your company owns, what it owes and what it's worth at a given moment. Ideally, the balance sheet tells you just how much money you'd have left over if you sold absolutely everything and then paid every last one of your debts.

The things that your company owns are called *assets* by the same people who look forward to audits and dream about accounting standards. The amounts that you owe make up your *liabilities*. The difference between the two represents the *equity* in your business. Think of equity in terms of the following equation:

> Equity = assets – liabilities

You have to admit that the equation is simple. Unfortunately, our accounting friends have dreamed up another, less straightforward way of looking at this equation:

> Assets = liabilities + equity

Go work that out. Anyway, the US balance sheet is based on this second equation.

A US balance sheet is always divided into two parts. One part deals with all the company's assets; the other part lists liabilities and equity. Because of the second equation, the two parts are always in balance, adding up to exactly the same amount. Although the two totals always match, the entries along the way say a great deal about the overall financial health of the company.

Just as the profit and loss account usually covers a full year, the balance sheet is often compiled for the last day of the year. Figure 2-2 shows Global Gizmos' balance sheet. In this case, figures are provided for two years, so that the reader (you or the accountant) can make a comparison between those years.

Assets

Your company's *assets* include anything and everything you own that has any monetary value. When you think about your assets in terms of the balance sheet, all that you're concerned about is how much each asset is worth and how quickly it can be sold. So assets are separated into categories, depending on how *liquid* they are – how fast and easy it is to liquidate them, turning them into cold, hard cash. *Current assets* are those that you can dispose of within a year, if you have to, whereas *fixed assets* often take much longer to get rid of. *Intangibles* may never be converted to cash.

Balance Sheet at a Glance

Global Gizmos Company

BALANCE SHEET ON DECEMBER 31		
ASSETS	**This Year**	**Last Year**
Current Assets		
Cash	30,000	15,000
Investment portfolio	35,000	20,000
Debtors	135,000	150,000
Stock	115,000	120,000
Prepaid expenses	5,000	5,000
Total Current Assets	£ 320,000	£ 310,000
Fixed Assets		
Land	60,000	60,000
Buildings, equipment, machinery	355,000	315,000
Minus accumulated depreciation	-125,000	-95,000
Total Net Fixed Assets	£ 290,000	£ 280,000
Intangibles (goodwill, patents)	£ 5,000	£ 5,000
TOTAL ASSETS	**£ 615,000**	**£ 595,000**
LIABILITIES & OWNERS' EQUITY	**This Year**	**Last Year**
Current Liabilities		
Creditors	60,000	70,000
Accrued expenses payable	80,000	90,000
Total Current Liabilities	£ 140,000	£ 160,000
Long-term Liabilities	£ 90,000	£ 100,000
Owners' Equity		
Share capital	155,000	150,000
Reserves	230,000	185,000
Total Owners' Equity	£ 385,000	£ 335,000
TOTAL LIABILITIES & OWNERS' EQUITY	**£ 615,000**	**£ 595,000**

Figure 2-2:
The US
balance
sheet.

Current assets

Current assets represent your company's readily available reserves. As such, they're the assets that you draw on to fund your day-to-day business operations, as well as the assets that you may have to turn to in a financial emergency. Current assets include the following:

- ✔ **Cash.** You can't get any more liquid than cash, which is just what you expect it to be: notes and coins in the till, the petty-cash fund and money on deposit in the bank.

- ✔ **Investment portfolio.** Investments are also usually liquid assets. Your investment portfolio includes savings accounts, short-term government bonds and other safe securities that you invest in to watch your cash earn a bit of money while you wait to use it.

- ✔ **Debtors.** *Debtors* represent the money that customers owe you for goods and services that you've already delivered. Maybe you give customers 30, 60 or 90 days to pay. You want to keep tabs on this particular asset. You may end up reducing it by some percentage if you run into deadbeat customers who just won't pay up.

- ✔ **Stock.** The cash value of your stocks can be a bit tricky to calculate, but it reflects the costs of the raw materials and supplies that you have on hand, as well as the value of partially finished products and products that are ready to be shipped.

- ✔ **Prepaid expenses.** If you pay any of your business expenses ahead of time, treat them as current assets. These expenses may include paid-up insurance premiums or retainers for unused accounting or advertising services.

Fixed assets

Fixed assets are fixed in the sense that they can't be readily converted to cash. These assets are the items that usually cost a great deal of money up front and are meant to last for several years – things like buildings, trucks, machines and computers.

In the balance sheet, the value of a fixed asset is based on its original cost minus its accumulated depreciation over time, so the figure doesn't necessarily reflect the true market value of the asset or how much it may actually cost to replace it. Fixed assets can include the following:

- ✔ **Land.** The land that your company owns is listed separately in the balance sheet, because it doesn't depreciate over time; its value on the books remains the same from year to year.

- ✔ **Buildings, equipment, machinery.** This asset represents the original cost of all the expensive items that you've invested in to operate your company. The entry includes anything you purchase that's expected to last more than a year.

✔ **Minus accumulated depreciation.** Depreciation measures the decline in the useful value of an expensive item over time, so the original cost of all your fixed assets (excluding any land) is reduced by an amount equal to the total depreciation accumulated over the years. Notice that Global Gizmos shows accumulated depreciation increasing by £30,000 in its most recent year. Because its fixed assets are now worth £30,000 less on paper, Global Gizmos also takes a £30,000 depreciation expense in its profit and loss account (refer to number three in Figure 2-1).

Intangibles

Even though you can't polish any of these assets, intangibles can be extremely important to your company. *Intangibles* include such things as your rights to a manufacturing patent, a long-term contract, or an exclusive service franchise. Intangibles also cover something called goodwill. Although it's not at all obvious from the name, *goodwill* represents the extra money that you may spend for an asset above and beyond its fair market value – maybe because it's worth more to your company than to anybody else.

By definition, intangibles are hard to describe and difficult to put a real value on. Some companies don't even try. Instead, they place a nominal value of £1 on all their intangibles to indicate that although these assets exist, there's no way to measure what they're actually worth.

Liabilities and owners' equity

Your company's *liabilities* cover all the debts and obligations that you enter into while you run your company. In the same way that assets are divided up, your liabilities are separated into categories, based on how soon they are due. *Current liabilities* are those that have to be paid off within a year; *long-term liabilities* may stay on the books much longer. When these liabilities are subtracted from total assets, you're left with *owners' equity*, which is a measure of how much the company is actually worth.

Current liabilities

Current liabilities are the debts that your company has agreed to pay in the short term (say, within a year), so you have to be able to cover them from your current assets. What's left over (the difference between your current assets and current liabilities) is so important that it has a name: *working capital,* which is the chunk of money that you actually have to work with. Here are some standard liabilities:

✔ **Creditors.** *Creditors* represent the amounts that you owe your regular business creditors as part of your ongoing operations. At any given time, you may have accounts payable to all sorts of outside suppliers and service people, including the merchants, professionals and even utility companies that you deal with every day.

🖊 **Accrued expenses payable.** On any given day, your company also owes salaries and wages to its employees, interest on bank loans and maybe insurance premiums – not to mention the taxes that you haven't sent in. To the extent that any of the obligations are unpaid on the date of the balance sheet, these liabilities are totalled as *accrued expenses payable*.

Long-term liabilities

Long-term liabilities usually represent large chunks of money that you're scheduled to pay back over several years. These liabilities are often at the centre of your company's financing. You may have issued bonds or a 'Director's Loan' to investors, for example, or you may have gone directly to the bank and secured a loan against your company's assets. In any case, you're probably using the money to invest in long-term growth of the company – acquiring new equipment, building a new manufacturing facility, developing additional products, or expanding into new markets.

Owners' equity

A company's owners come in various shapes and sizes. Their investments and equity in the company are arranged and distributed in all sorts of ways and can become incredibly complicated, especially if the company is a traded public limited company (plc). But don't be confused. All this complexity boils down to two major sources of equity: money and resources that flow in from outside the company, and profits that the owners keep and pump back into the company. Owners' equity can be any of the following:

🖊 **Share capital.** The money that's invested in your company can take various forms, from the direct infusion of cash by inside owners who manage the business to the buying and selling of shares that represent small chunks of the company owned by outside investors. Share capital represents the total of all this money, no matter where it comes from or how it's described.

🖊 **Retained earnings.** Your company makes a profit each year (at least, we hope it does), and you choose what to do with that excess cash. You can distribute it to the owners (that arrangement is where dividends come from) or keep part of it to reinvest in the company. If you put profits back into the company, it can grow. And if the company grows, you can increase the company's net worth and owners' equity (at least, we hope you do). *Retained earnings*, also known as reserves, represent the profits that you plough back into the company year after year.

Keep the following in mind when interpreting the balance sheet:

🖊 A balance sheet is a snapshot of your financial condition at a particular moment – usually, the end of the year.

🖊 Your assets include everything that has monetary value, ranging from cash and investments to buildings and stocks.

> ✔ Liabilities include all the debts and financial obligations that you incur in running your company.
>
> ✔ Subtract liabilities from assets to calculate your equity in the business.

Growing Up

Unless you're working in the United States, where the balance sheet is always set out in the straightforward and logical way we have used so far, you have to enter the 'grown-up' world of UK accountancy. Here, instead of keeping assets and liabilities apart, we jumble them up all over the place. Actually once you get used to the UK method its logic is appealing and it certainly makes analysing accounting data rather easier.

So far we have kept to this system as it is much simpler to explain, but we always had to make that leap, so here goes.

Figure 2-3 sets out the same data as in Figure 2-2, for one year only, but follows the layout of the UK balance sheet. The conventions, concepts, rules, regulations, resulting ratios, in fact the whole thing, is exactly the same, its just that things are in a different order.

In this layout we start with the *fixed assets*, rather than liquid assets such as cash, and work our way down. After the fixed asset sum has been calculated we arrive at the residual unwritten-down 'value' of those assets, tangible (land, buildings and so on) and intangible: in this case £295,000. We then work our way down the current assets in the reverse order of their ability to be turned into cash. Don't ask why it's done this way, it just is. Actually, it doesn't really matter a jot which order things come in as long as they are slotted into the right section of the balance sheet. The total of the current assets comes to £320,000.

Next we get the *current liabilities*, which come to a total of £140,000, and take that away from the current asset total to come to a figure of £180,000.

The sum left over after deducting the current liabilities from the current assets is the *net current assets*. This is often referred to as the *working capital*, as it represents the money circulating through the business day to day.

By adding the *net current assets* (working capital) of £180,000 to the total fixed assets of £295,000 – bingo: we can see we have £475,000 tied up in net total assets. Deduct the money we owe long-term, the creditors due over one year – a fancy way of describing bank and other debt other than overdraft, and we arrive at the net total assets. Net, by the way, is accountant-speak for deduction of one number from another, often adding a four-figure sum to the bill for doing so.

Fixed assests	*£s*	*£s*	*£s*
Land	60,000		
Buildings, equipment, machinery	355,000		
Less accumulative depreciation	125,000		
Net book value		290,000	
Intangible (goodwill, patents)		5,000	
Total fixed assets			295,000
Current assets			
Pre-paid expenses	5,000		
Stock	115,000		
Debtors	135,000		
Investments	35,000		
Cash	30,000		
Total current assets		320,000	
Less current liabilities			
Creditors	60,000		
Accrued expenses payable	80,000		
Total current liabilities		140,000	
Net current assets			180,000
Total assets			475,000
Less creditors, amounts falling due in over one year			90,000
Net Total Assets			385,000
Financed by			
Share capital	155,000		
Reserves (retained earnings)	230,000		
Total owner's equity			385,000

Figure 2-3: The UK balance sheet.

The net total assets figure of £385,000 bears an uncanny similarity to the total of the money put in by the owners of the business when they started out, £155,000, and the sum they have left in by way of profits undistributed over the years, £230,000. So the balance sheet balances, but at a very different total to that of the US balance sheet.

The UK balance figure is Shareholders Equity (= Assets – Liabilities)

The US balance figure is Assets (= Liabilities + Equity)

You need to recognise both the UK and the US balance sheets, as chances are that some of the companies you compete with, buy from, won shares in, or perhaps plan to buy will be reporting using US balance sheets. Now you can see that the accounting processes, like the language, have much in common, but still have some pitfalls for the unwary.

Examining the Cash-Flow Statement

If you know what your company is worth and how much it makes every year, can't you just relax and assume that your financial plan is in reasonably good order? After all, what else do you need to know?

As it turns out, you've got to keep close track of one other absolutely indispensable resource: cash. No matter how good things look on paper – no matter how bright the balance sheet and how rosy the income statement, you still need cash on hand to pay the bills. The fact that you've got assets and profits doesn't automatically mean that you have money in the bank. Cash can turn out to be much more important than income, profits, assets and liabilities put together, especially in the early stages of your company.

The *cash-flow statement* monitors changes in your cash position over a set period. The top half of the statement tracks the flow of cash in and out of your company; the bottom half reports where the funds end up. Just like the balance sheet, the top and bottom halves of a cash-flow statement match. Given the importance of ready cash, you want to look at cash-flow statements on a regular basis – quarterly, monthly or maybe even weekly.

Figure 2-4 shows a cash-flow statement for Global Gizmos Company. The cash-flow statement contains many of the same elements as a profit and loss account, but with a few critical adjustments.

Cash Flow at a Glance

Global Gizmos Company

CASH FLOW AS OF DECEMBER 31		
INFLOW AND OUTFLOW	**This Year**	**Last Year**
Funds Provided By:		
Gross receipts on sales	825,000	760,000
Dividend and interest income	3,000	2,000
Share capital	5,000	10,000
Total Funds In	£ 833,000	£ 772,000
Funds Used For:		
Cost of goods produced	555,000	515,000
Sales, general, and administration	160,000	150,000
Interest expense	13,000	14,000
Taxes	20,000	18,000
Buildings, equipment, machinery	40,000	50,000
Long-term debt reduction	10,000	5,000
Dividend distribution to owners	5,000	5,000
Total Funds Out	£ 803,000	£ 757,000
NET CHANGE IN CASH POSITION	**£ 30,000**	**£ 15,000**
CHANGES BY ACCOUNT	**This Year**	**Last Year**
Changes In Liquid Assets		
Cash	15,000	5,000
Investment portfolio	15,000	10,000
Total Changes	£ 30,000	£ 15,000
NET CHANGE IN CASH POSITION	**£ 30,000**	**£ 15,000**

1 ▷
2 ▷
3 ▷
4 ▷

Figure 2-4:
A cash-flow statement monitors changes in the company's cash position over time.

Cash in and cash out

The top half of the cash-flow statement deals with the inflow and outflow of cash, tracking where your company gets funds and what you use those funds for. Cash flow is a little more honest than a profit and loss account, because the cash-flow statement shows money coming in only when you actually deposit it and money going out only when you actually write a cheque.

Funds provided by

Where does all that money originate? Because the cash-flow statement reflects the actual receipt of cash, no matter where it comes from, the entries are a bit different from the revenue shown in a company's profit and loss account. These funds are usually made up of the following:

- **Gross receipts on sales.** This entry represents the total money that you take in on sales during the period. Gross receipts are based on your gross revenue, of course, but they also take into account when you actually receive payment. Global Gizmos, for example, received all of its £810,000 in gross revenue this year, plus £15,000 in debtors that the company was owed from last year, for a total of £825,000.

- **Dividend and interest income.** Your income from savings accounts and other securities is also reported in your profit and loss account. The amounts should be the same, as long as you actually receive the money during the period covered by the cash-flow statement.

- **Share capital.** The money invested in your company shows up as part of the owners' equity in your balance sheet. Invested capital doesn't represent revenue from your business operations, of course, so it never appears in the profit and loss account, but it can be a source of cash for the company. As Figure 2-4 shows, Global Gizmos received an additional £5,000 in invested capital this year.

Funds used for

Where does all the money go? The cash-flow statement keeps track of the costs and expenses that you incur for anything and everything. Some of the expenses appear in the profit and loss account; others don't, because they don't directly relate to your costs of doing business. These funds usually consist of the following:

- **Cost of goods produced.** This entry represents the total cost of producing your product or service during the period. The cost of goods produced often differs from the cost of goods sold shown in your profit and loss account, because the cost of goods sold also includes sales out of stock (items that your company has already produced and paid for) and doesn't include the cost of products that you add to stock. Global Gizmos, for example, reduced its overall inventory by £5,000 this period, so the company's cost of goods produced was £5,000 less than its cost of goods sold from the profit and loss account.

- ✔ **Sales, general and administration (SG&A).** These expenses are the same SG&A expenses that appear in a profit and loss account, except that paying off bills that you owe or postponing payments may change the amount. Global Gizmos paid down £10,000 in both its accounts payable and expenses payable this year, increasing its SG&A cash outflow by £20,000, for a total of £160,000.

- ✔ **Interest expense.** Interest expense shows up in the profit and loss account as well. The number reflects the amount that you actually pay out during the period.

- ✔ **Taxes.** Taxes also appear in the profit and loss account. But in the cash-flow statement, taxes are the ones that you actually pay out during the period.

- ✔ **Buildings, equipment, machinery.** When your company buys an expensive item, it doesn't appear in your profit and loss account as an expense, because you're really just trading cash for another asset. Instead, you take a depreciation expense each year to reflect the spread of that cost over the asset's useful life. When you buy the building, lorry, or whatever, however, you've got to pay for it. The cash-flow statement reflects those costs. Global Gizmos, for example, shelled out £40,000 this year for new equipment.

- ✔ **Long-term debt reduction.** It costs you money to reduce any long-term debt that your company may have, and that expense doesn't appear in the profit and loss account. Global Gizmos reduced its long-term debt by £5,000 last year and £10,000 this year.

- ✔ **Dividend distribution to owners.** The portion of your company's profits that you decide to give back to the owners comes directly out of your cash box. Again, this entry isn't a business expense in the profit and loss account, but it costs you nonetheless. Global Gizmos distributed £5,000 to its owners this year.

Book II

Sorting Out Your Finances

What's left over

The flow of cash in and out of your business is like water flowing in and out of a reservoir. If more water comes in than goes out, the water level goes up, and vice versa. When your company's cash reserves rise, however, the money flows into one or more of your liquid-asset accounts. The bottom half of your cash-flow statement keeps track of what's happening to those accounts.

Changes in liquid assets

With cash flowing in and out of the company, your liquid assets are going to change during the period covered by the cash-flow statement. The items listed in this portion of the cash-flow statement are the same ones that appear in the balance sheet. This year, for example, Global Gizmos improved its cash reserves and investment portfolio by £15,000 each.

Net change in cash position

Raising the level of your liquid-asset accounts has the happy effect of strengthening your cash position. Global Gizmos increased its liquid assets and cash position by £30,000 this year. Not coincidentally, this £30,000 is also the difference between the £833,000 that Global Gizmos took in during the year (Total Funds In) and the £803,000 that it spent (Total Funds Out).

- A cash-flow statement tracks the movement of cash in and out of your company.

- Cash in represents money that you deposit; cash out, the cheques that you write.

- Cash flow can be more important than income, assets and profits combined, especially for a new business.

Evaluating Financial Ratios

Armed with a profit and loss account, a balance sheet and a cash-flow statement, you have a relatively complete financial picture of your company in front of you. But when you look everything over, what does that financial picture actually tell you? Is it good news or bad news? What things should you plan to do differently as you go forward?

Your financial picture may tell you that you pay your bills on time, keep a cash cushion and make some money. But can your company do a better job down the road? It would be nice if you could look at the picture year after year and compare it against a competitor, several competitors, or even your entire industry. But companies come in all shapes and sizes, and it's hard to compare numbers from any two companies and make sense of them.

As a result, companies use *financial ratios*. When you divide one number by another, thereby creating a ratio, you eliminate many of the problems of comparing things on different scales.

Take your personal finances as an example. You're looking for help on investments. One friend boasts that she made £5,000 on the stock market last month; another made only £1,000. Who do you ask for advice? It depends. If the first friend has £500,000 invested and the second friend has only £20,000, who's the savvy investor?

A ratio gives you the answer. The first friend saw a return of only 1 per cent (5,000 ÷ 500,000), whereas the second friend realised a better return of 5 per cent (1,000 ÷ 20,000).

Comparing two companies of different sizes works just the same way. If you want to compare your company's financial ratios with those of major competitors or with an industry average, you need to get your hands on some outside data. You can always start by asking your banker, accountant or investment adviser, because financial institutions keep close track of standard ratios across industries. But also check out financial-data services such as Standard and Poor's, Value-Line, and Moody's. Also, Dun & Bradstreet offers a publication called *Industry Norms and Key Business Ratios*.

With all these data in hand, you can see how your company measures up, because you can bet that your investors, creditors and competitors are going to, even if you don't.

Financial ratios fall into three categories. The first two categories take your company's vital signs to see whether you're going to make it (remain solvent). One set of ratios measures the company's capability to meet its obligations in the short term; the other looks at the long term. The final set of ratios indicates just how strong and vigorous your company really is, measuring its relative profitability from several points of view.

Book II

Sorting Out Your Finances

Short-term obligations

The overriding importance of being able to pay your bills every month is the major reason why current assets and current liabilities are separated in the company's balance sheet. The difference between the two – your working capital – represents a safety net that protects you from almost certain financial catastrophe.

How much working capital do you need to ensure survival? Having the liquid assets available when you absolutely need them to meet short-term obligations is called *liquidity*. You can use several financial ratios to test your company's liquidity. You can monitor the following ratios year by year and measure them against your competitors' ratios and the industry averages.

Current ratio = current assets ÷ current liabilities

You determine your company's current ratio by looking at the balance sheet and dividing total current assets by total current liabilities. Global Gizmos Company, for example, has a current ratio of £320,000 ÷ £140,000, or 2.3 (refer to Figure 2-2). You can also express this ratio as 2.3 to 1 or 2.3:1.

Like most financial ratios, the current ratio isn't an especially precise measurement, so there's no point in calculating it to more than one or two decimal places.

What's the magic number to aim for? If your company falls below a current ratio of 1.0, you're in serious financial danger. In most cases, you want the number to stay above 2.0, meaning that you have more than twice the current assets that you need to cover current liabilities. But again, the answer depends on your industry. Companies that move stocks quickly can often operate with somewhat lower current ratios, because the stocks themselves are a little more liquid. You don't want your current ratio to get too high, either. Then you could be sitting on excess cash that should really be put to work and invested back in the company.

Quick ratio = (cash + investments + debtors) ÷ current liabilities

The quick ratio sometimes is called the *acid test,* because it's more stringent than the current ratio. The quick ratio doesn't allow you to count stock and prepaid expenses as part of your current assets, because it's sometimes hard to turn them back into cash quickly, especially in an emergency. This situation is particularly true in industries in which products go out of fashion rapidly or are quickly outdated by new technology.

Global Gizmos has a quick ratio of £200,000 ÷ £140,000, or 1.4, this year (refer to Figure 2-2). You want to keep your own company's quick ratio above 1.0 by a comfortable margin that is in line with your industry.

Stock turnover = cost of goods sold ÷ stock

Stock turnover tells you something about how liquid your stocks really are. This ratio divides the cost of goods sold, as shown in your yearly profit and loss account, by the average value of your stock. If you don't know the average, you can estimate it by using the stock figure as listed in the balance sheet at the end of the year.

Global Gizmos has a stock turnover of £560,000 ÷ £115,000, or 4.9. (Refer to Figures 2-1 and 2-2 for the company's profit and loss account and balance sheet, respectively.) This ratio means that Global Gizmos turns over its stock almost five times each year. Expressed in days, Global Gizmos carries a 75-day (365 ÷ 4.9) supply of stock.

Is a 75-day inventory good or bad? It depends on the industry and even on the time of year. A car dealer who has a 75-day supply of cars at the height of the season may be in a strong stock position, but the same stock position at the end of the season could be a real weakness. As automation, computers and information systems make business operations more efficient across all industries, stock turnover is on the rise, and the average number of days that stock of any kind hangs around continues to shrink.

Debtor turnover = sales on credit ÷ debtors

Debtor turnover tells you something about liquidity by dividing the sales that you make on credit by the average debtors. If an average isn't available, you can use the debtors from a balance sheet.

If Global Gizmos makes 80 per cent of its sales on credit, its debtor turnover is ($810,000 × 0.8) ÷ $135,000, or 4.8. (Refer to Figures 2-1 and 2-2 for Global Gizmos' profit and loss account and balance sheet.) In other words, the company turns over its debtors 4.8 times per year, or once every 76 days, on average. That's not so good if Global Gizmos' payment terms are 30 or 60 days. Unlike fine wine, debtors don't improve with age.

Long-term responsibilities

Your company's liquidity keeps you solvent from day to day and month to month, but what about your ability to pay back long-term debt year after year? Two financial ratios indicate what kind of shape you're in over the long haul. The first ratio gauges how easy it is for your company to continue making interest payments on the debt; the second tries to determine whether the principal amount of your debt is in any danger.

If you've read this chapter from the beginning, you may be getting really bored with financial ratios by now, but your lenders – bankers and bondholders, if you have them – find these long-term ratios to be incredibly fascinating, for obvious reasons.

Times interest earned = earnings before interest and taxes ÷ interest expense

Don't get confused – earnings before any interest expense and taxes are paid (EBIT) really is just the profit that you have available to make those interest payments in the first place. Global Gizmos, for example, has an EBIT of $57,000 and an interest expense of $13,000 this year for a times-interest-earned ratio of 4.4. (Refer to Figure 2-1 for the company's income statement.) In other words, Global Gizmos can meet its interest expense 4.4 times over.

You may also hear the same number called an *interest coverage*. Lenders get mightily nervous if this ratio ever gets anywhere close to 1.0, because at that point, every last penny of profits goes for interest payments on the long-term debt.

Debt-to-equity ratio = long-term liabilities ÷ owners' equity

The debt-to-equity ratio says a great deal about the general financial structure of your company. After all, you can raise money to support your company in only two ways: borrow it and promise to pay it back with interest, or sell pieces of the company and promise to share all the rewards of ownership. The first method is debt; the second, equity.

Global Gizmos has a debt-to-equity ratio of $90,000 ÷ $385,000, or .23. (Refer to Figure 2-2 for Global Gizmos' balance sheet.) This ratio means that the company has more than four times as much equity financing as it does long-term debt.

Lenders love to see lots of equity supporting a company's debt, because they know that the money they loan out is safer. If something goes wrong with the company, they can go after the owners' money. Equity investors, on the other hand, actually want to take on some risk. They like to see relatively high debt-to-equity ratios, because that situation increases their leverage and (as the following section points out) can substantially boost their profits. So the debt-to-equity ratio that's just right for your company depends not only on your industry and how stable it is, but also on who you ask.

Relative profitability

If profit is the bottom line for your business, profitability is the finishing line. Profitability tells you how well you measure up when it comes to creating financial value out of your company. Profitability ratios allow you to keep track of your own performance year by year. They also allow you to compare that performance against that of other competitors, other industries and even other ways of investing resources.

You can easily invest the money that flows into your company in other businesses, for example, or in bank accounts, property, or government bonds. Each of these investments involves a certain level of risk. By comparing profitability ratios, you begin to see whether your own company measures up, generating the kinds of financial rewards that justify the risks involved.

Profitability ratios come in three flavours. The first type of ratio examines profit relative to your company sales. The second type examines profit relative to total assets. The final type examines profit relative to owners' equity. Each of the ratios reflects how attractive your company is to an investor.

Net profit margin = net profit ÷ gross revenue on sales

The net profit margin is your net profit divided by your gross revenue. The ratio really says more about your costs in relation to the prices that you charge, however. If your net profit margin is low compared with that of other companies in your industry, your prices are generally lower or your costs are too high. Lower margins are quite acceptable if they lead to greater sales, larger market share and bigger profits down the road, but you want to monitor the ratio carefully. On the other hand, no one's going to quibble with net profit margins that are on the high side, although they're an awfully good way to attract new competitors.

Global Gizmos Company has a net profit margin of £50,000 ÷ £810,000, or 6.2 per cent, this year. (To examine Global Gizmos' profit and loss account, refer to Figure 2-1.) That result is a substantial increase from the 4.6 per cent for the year before. The company didn't grow just in terms of revenue, but also became more profitable.

When you calculate your own net profit margin, you also need to think about calculating margins based on your operating profit and gross profit. Together, these ratios give you a better idea of where your company's profitability really comes from.

Return on investment = net profit ÷ total assets

Net profit divided by total assets gives you the overall return that you're able to make on your company's assets – referred to as *return on assets* (ROA). Because these assets are equal to all your debt and equity combined, the ratio also measures an average return on the total investment in your company. What does the ratio mean? It's similar to the yield on Grandma's savings bonds or the return on that hot new mutual fund that you've discovered. *Return on investment* (ROI) is widely used as a test of company profitability, because you can compare it to other types of investments that an investor can put money into.

Book II

Sorting Out Your Finances

Watch out for one thing, though: The value of the total assets used in the calculation of ROI usually is taken from a company's balance sheet and can be misleading. If the assets have been around for a while, the numbers on the page may not reflect real replacement costs, and if the assets are undervalued, the ROI is bound to be a bit exaggerated.

Global Gizmos has an ROI of £50,000 ÷ £475,000, or 10.5 per cent, this year. (Refer to Figures 2-1 and 2-2 for the company's profit and loss account and balance sheet.) That figure is up from 7.1 per cent the year before, and the increase certainly is good news.

Whether your own company's ROI is where it should be depends to a large extent on your industry, as well as on what the economy is doing at the moment.

Return on equity = net profit ÷ owners' equity

Net profit divided by the owners' equity in your company gives you the return on just the equity portion of the investment (ROE). Keep in mind that you've already taken care of all your bankers and bondholders first by paying their return – the interest expense on your debt – out of your profits. Whatever is left over goes to the owners and represents their return on equity.

Your creditors always get paid first, and they get paid a fixed amount; everything else goes to the owners. That's where *leverage* comes in. The more you finance your company by using debt, the more leveraged you are, and the more leveraged you are, the more you're using other people's money to make money. Leverage works beautifully as long as you're good at putting that money to work – creating returns that are higher than your interest costs. Otherwise, those other people may end up owning your company.

Global Gizmos, for example, has an ROE of £50,000 ÷ £385,000, or 13.0 per cent. (The profit and loss account and balance sheet shown in Figures 2-1 and 2-2, earlier in this chapter, shed some light on where these figures come from.) Without any leverage, that ROE would be the same as the company's ROI, or only 10.5 per cent. More leverage probably would raise the ROE even higher, upping the risk at the same time. In short, leverage makes the good years better for the owners and the bad years much worse.

  ✔ Financial ratios allow you to compare your performance with that of other companies, especially your competitors.

  ✔ One set of ratios examines your company's vital signs to see if your company is going to remain solvent.

  ✔ Another set of ratios examines your company's financial health by measuring profit in terms of sales, assets and equity.

Understanding Break-Even

At the start of this chapter, when costs were introduced, we implied that all of them were broadly similar, in that they were expenses to deduct from sales income in order to arrive at a figure for the profit being made. However, you need to grasp that two fundamentally different types of cost exist. *Fixed costs* are those that don't vary with the volume of output. So the rent on a retail outlet, for example, remains 'fixed' irrespective of the amount of sales actually achieved. Of course the cost itself isn't necessarily fixed, as the landlord could change the rent. *Variable costs* are those that do change with sales levels. So a retailer needs to buy in stock to meet rising demand, and a manufacturer needs more raw materials and more workers' hours.

The break-even equation is:

Break-even point (in units) = Fixed costs/(Selling price – Unit variable cost)

So if the fixed costs are £10,000, the selling price is £5 and the cost of buying in the only product we sell is £3, then the break-even point is 5,000 units. If your goal was to make £10,000 profit then by adding that to the fixed costs you can see that sales then need to reach 10,000 units.

There are a number of online spreadsheets and tutorials that will take you through the process. biz/ed (`www.bized.co.uk`) has a simulation that lets you see the effect of changing variables on a fairly complex break-even calculation. Score (`www.score.org/template_gallery.html`) provides a break-even analysis template and BizPep (`www.bizpeponline.com/PricingBreakeven.html`) sell a software program that calculates your break-even for prices plus or minus 50 per cent of your proposed selling price. You can tweak costs to see how to optimise your selling price and so hit your profit goal.

Margin of safety is the term bandied around by accountants to describe a business's capacity for making profit. For example, a business's production line is able to produce 7,000 units, and no more. If these units were all sold at £5 each the maximum sales revenue would be £35,000. The break-even level is calculated as being when 5,000 units are sold at £5 each, generating £25,000. So the business's capacity for making profit is the 2,000 units the factory could make over and above the 5,000 required to break-even. This is usually expressed as a percentage – 2,000 / 7,000 × 100 = 29 per cent. A low percentage, below 25 and 30 per cent, say, means that a business must sell a high proportion of its capacity in order to break even and vice versa. The higher the margin of safety the sooner break-even can be reached and the greater the potential to make more profit.

Book II

Sorting Out Your Finances

Chapter 3

Cash Flows and the Cash Flow Statement

- -

In This Chapter

▶ Separating the three types of cash flow

▶ Figuring out how much actual cash increase was generated by profit

▶ Looking at a business's other sources and uses of cash

▶ Being careful about free cash flow

▶ Evaluating managers' decisions by scrutinising the cash flow statement

- -

*T*his chapter talks about *cash flows* – which in general refers to cash inflows and outflows over a period of time. Suppose you tell us that last year you had total cash inflows of £145,000 and total cash outflows of £140,000. We know that your cash balance increased by £5,000. But we don't know where your £145,000 cash inflows came from. Did you earn this much in salary? Did you receive an inheritance from your rich uncle? Likewise, we don't know what you used your £140,000 cash outflow for. Did you make large payments on your credit cards? Did you lose a lot of money at the races? In short, cash flows have to be sorted into different sources and uses to make much sense.

The Three Types of Cash Flow

Accountants categorise the cash flows of a business into three types:

▸ Cash inflows from making sales and cash outflows for expenses; sales and expense transactions are called the *operating activities* of a business (although they could be called profit activities just as well, because their purpose is to make profit).

✔ Cash outflows for making investments in new assets (buildings, machinery, tools, and so on), and cash inflows from liquidating old investments (assets no longer needed that are sold off); these transactions are called *investment activities.*

✔ Cash inflows from borrowing money and from the additional investment of money in the business by its owners, and cash outflows for paying off debt, returning capital that the business no longer needs to owners and making cash distributions of profit to its owners; these transactions are called *financing activities.*

The cash flow statement (or *statement of cash flows*) summarises the cash flows of a business for a period according to this three-way classification. Generally accepted accounting principles (GAAP) require that whenever a business reports its income statement, it must also report its cash flow statement for the same period – a business shouldn't report one without the other. A good reason exists for this dual financial statement requirement.

The income statement is based on the *accrual basis of accounting* that records sales when made, whether or not cash is received at that time, and records expenses when incurred, whether or not the expenses are paid at that time. (Book IV Chapter 3 explains accrual basis accounting.) Because accrual basis accounting is used to record profit, you can't equate bottom-line profit with an increase in cash. Suppose a business's annual income statement reports that it earned £1.6 million net income for the year. This doesn't mean that its cash balance increased by £1.6 million during the period. You have to look in the cash flow statement to find out how much its cash balance increased (or, possibly, decreased!) from its operating activities (sales revenue and expenses) during the period.

In the chapter, we refer to the net increase (or decrease) in the business's cash balance that results from collecting sales revenue and paying expenses as *cash flow from profit*, as the alternative term for *cash flow from operating activities.* Cash flow from profit seems more user-friendly than cash flow from operating activities, and in fact the term is used widely. In any case, don't confuse cash flow from profit with the other two types of cash flow – from the business's investing activities and financing activities during the period.

Before moving on, here's a short problem for you to solve. Using the three-way classification of cash flows explained earlier, below is a summary of the business's net cash flows (in thousands) for the year just ended, with one amount missing:

(1) From profit (operating activities)	?
(2) From investing activities	− £1,275
(3) From financing activities	+ £160
Decrease in cash balance during year	− £15

Note that the business's cash balance from all sources and uses decreased £15,000 during the year. The amounts of net cash flows from the company's investing and financing activities are given. So you can determine that the net cash flow from profit was £1,100,000 for the year. Understanding cash flows from investing activities and financing activities is fairly straightforward. Understanding the net cash flow from profit, in contrast, is more challenging – but business managers and investors should have a good grip on this very important number.

Book II

Sorting Out Your Finances

Setting the Stage: Changes in Balance Sheet Accounts

The first step in understanding the amounts reported by a business in its cash flow statement is to focus on the *changes* in the business's assets, liabilities and owners' equity accounts during the period – the increases or decreases of each account from the start of the period to the end of the period. These changes are found in the comparative two-year balance sheet reported by a business. Figure 3-1 presents the increases and decreases during the year in the assets, liabilities, and owners' equity accounts for a business example. Figure 3-1 isn't a balance sheet but only a summary of *changes* in account balances. We don't want to burden you with an entire balance sheet, which has much more detail than is needed here.

Take a moment to scan Figure 3-1. Note that the business's cash balance decreased £15,000 during the year. (An increase is not necessarily a good thing, and a decrease is not necessarily a bad thing; it depends on the overall financial situation of the business.) One purpose of reporting the cash flow statement is to summarise the main reasons for the change in cash – according to the three-way classification of cash flows explained earlier. One question on everyone's mind is this: How much cash did the profit for the year generate for the business? The cash flow statement begins by answering this question.

Assets	
Cash	(15)
Debtors	800
Stock	975
Prepaid Expenses	145
Fixed Assets	1,275
Accumulated Depreciation*	(1,200)
Total	1,980
Liabilities & Owners' Equity	
Creditors	80
Accrued Expenses Payable	1,20
Income Tax Payable	20
Overdraft	200
Long-term Loans	300
Owners' Invested Capital	60
Retained Earnings	1,200
Total	1,980

Figure 3-1: Changes in balance sheet assets and operating liabilities that affect cash flow from profit.

* Accumulated Depreciation is a negative asset account which is deducted from Fixed Assets. The negative £1,200 change increases the negative balance of the account.

Getting at the Cash Increase from Profit

Although all amounts reported on the cash flow statement are important, the one that usually gets the most attention is *cash flow from operating activities*, or *cash flow from profit* as we prefer to call it. This is the increase in cash generated by a business's profit-making operations during the year, exclusive of its other sources of cash during the year (such as borrowed money, sold-off fixed assets, and additional owners' investments in the business). *Cash flow from profit* indicates a business's ability to turn profit into available cash – cash in the bank that can be used for the needs of the business. Cash flow from profit gets just as much attention as net income (the bottom-line profit number in the income statement).

Before presenting the cash flow statement – which is a rather formidable, three-part accounting report – in all its glory, in the following sections we build on the summary of changes in the business's assets, liabilities and owners' equities shown in Figure 3-1 to explain the components of the £1,100,000 increase in cash from the business's profit activities during the year. (The £1,100,000 amount of cash flow from profit was determined earlier in the chapter by solving the unknown factor.)

The business in the example experienced a rather strong growth year. Its accounts receivable and stock increased by relatively large amounts. In fact, all the relevant accounts increased; their ending balances are larger than their beginning balances (which are the amounts carried forward from the end of the preceding year). At this point, we need to provide some additional information. The £1.2 million increase in retained earnings is the net difference of two quite different things.

The £1.6 million net income earned by the business increased retained earnings by this amount. As you see in Figure 3-1, the account increased only by £1.2 million. Thus there must have been a £400,000 decrease in retained earnings during the year. The business paid £400,000 cash dividends from profit to its owners (the shareholders) during the year, which is recorded as a decrease in retained earnings. The amount of cash dividends is reported in the *financing activities* section of the cash flow statement. The entire amount of net income is reported in the *operating activities* section of the cash flow statement.

Book II

Sorting Out Your Finances

Computing cash flow from profit

Here's how to compute cash flow from profit based on the changes in the company's balance sheet accounts presented in Figure 3-1:

Computation of Cash Flow from Profit (in thousands of pounds)

	Negative Cash Flow Effects	Positive Cash Flow Effects
Net income for the year		£1,600
Debtors increase	£800	
Stock increase	£975	
Prepaid expenses increase	£145	
Depreciation expense		£1,200
Creditors increase		£80
Accrued expenses payable increase		£120
Income tax payable increase		£20
Totals	£1,920	£3,020
Cash flow from profit (£3,020 positive increases minus £1,920 negative increases)	£1,100	

Note that net income (profit) for the year – which is the correct amount of profit based on the accrual basis of accounting – is listed in the positive cash flow column. This is only the starting point. Think of this the following way: if the business had collected all its sales revenue for the year in cash, and if it had made cash payments for its expenses exactly equal to the amounts recorded for the expenses, then the net income amount would equal the increase in cash. These two conditions are virtually never true, and they aren't true in this example. So the net income figure is just the jumping-off point for determining the amount of cash generated by the business's profit activities during the year.

We'll let you in on a little secret here. The analysis of cash flow from profit asks what amount of profit would have been recorded if the business had been on the cash basis of accounting instead of the accrual basis. This can be confusing and exasperating, because it seems that two different profit measures are provided in a business's financial report – the true economic profit number, which is the bottom line in the income statement (usually called *net income*), and a second profit number called *cash flow from operating activities* in the cash flow statement.

When the cash flow statement was made mandatory, many accountants worried about this problem, but the majority opinion was that the amount of cash increase (or decrease) generated from the profit activities of a business is very important to disclose in financial reports. In reading the income statement, you have to wear your accrual basis accounting lenses, and in the cash flow statement you have to put on your cash basis lenses. Who says accountants can't see two sides of something?

The following sections explain the effects on cash flow that each balance sheet account change causes (refer to Figure 3-1).

Getting specific about changes in assets and liabilities

As a business manager, you need to keep a close watch on each of your assets and liabilities and understand the cash flow effects of increases (or decreases) caused by these changes. Investors should focus on the business's ability to generate a healthy cash flow from profit, so investors should be equally concerned about these changes.

Debtors increase

Remember that the debtors asset shows how much money customers who bought products on credit still owe the business; this asset is a promise of cash that the business will receive. Basically, debtors is the amount of uncollected sales revenue at the end of the period. Cash doesn't increase until the business collects money from its customers.

But the amount in debtors *is* included in the total sales revenue of the period – after all, you did make the sales, even if you haven't been paid yet. Obviously, then, you can't look at sales revenue as being equal to the amount of cash that the business received during the period.

To calculate the actual cash flow from sales, you need to subtract from sales revenue the amount of credit sales that you didn't collect in cash over the period – but you add in the amount of cash that you collected during the period just ended for credit sales that you made in the *preceding* period. Take a look at the following equation for the business example:

£25 million sales revenue – £0.8 million increase in debtors = £24.2 million cash collected from customers during the year

The business started the year with £1.7 million in debtors and ended the year with £2.5 million in debtors. The beginning balance was collected during the year but at the end of the year the ending balance hadn't been collected. Thus the *net* effect is a shortfall in cash inflow of £800,000, which is why it's called a negative cash flow factor. The key point is that you need to keep an eye on the increase or decrease in debtors from the beginning of the period to the end of the period.

- ✔ If the amount of credit sales you made during the period is greater than the amount collected from customers during the same period, your debtors *increased* over the period. Therefore you need to *subtract* from sales revenue that difference between start-of-period debtors and end-of-period debtors. In short, an increase in debtors hurts cash flow by the amount of the increase.

- ✔ If the amount you collected from customers during the period is greater than the credit sales you made during the period, your debtors *decreased* over the period. In this case you need to *add* to sales revenue that difference between start-of-period debtors and end-of-period debtors. In short, a decrease in debtors helps cash flow by the amount of the decrease.

In the example we've been using, debtors increased by £800,000. Cash collections from sales were £800,000 less than sales revenue. Ouch! The business increased its sales substantially over last period, so you shouldn't be surprised that its debtors increased. The higher sales revenue was good for profit but bad for cash flow from profit.

An occasional hiccup in cash flow is the price of growth – managers and investors need to understand this point. Increasing sales without increasing debtors is a happy situation for cash flow, but in the real world you can't have one increase without the other (except in very unusual circumstances).

Stock increase

Stock is the next asset in Figure 3-1 – and usually the largest short-term, or *current,* asset for businesses that sell products. If the stock account is greater at the end of the period than at the start of the period – because either unit costs increased or the quantity of products increased – what the business actually paid out in cash for stock purchases (or manufacturing products) is more than the business recorded as its cost-of-goods-sold expense in the period. Therefore, you need to deduct the stock increase from net income when determining cash flow from profit.

In the example, stock increased £975,000 from start-of-period to end-of-period. In other words, this business replaced the products that it sold during the period *and* increased its stock by £975,000. The easiest way to understand the effect of this increase on cash flow is to pretend that the business paid for all its stock purchases in cash immediately upon receiving them. The stock on hand at the start of the period had already been paid for *last* period, so that cost doesn't affect this period's cash flow. Those products were sold during the period and involved no further cash payment by the business. But the business did pay cash *this* period for the products that were in stock at the end of the period.

In other words, if the business had bought just enough new stock (at the same cost that it paid out last period) to replace the stock that it sold during the period, the actual cash outlay for its purchases would equal the cost-of-goods-sold expense reported in its income statement. Ending stock would equal the beginning stock; the two stock costs would cancel each other out and thus would have a zero effect on cash flow. But this hypothetical scenario doesn't fit the example because the company increased its sales substantially over the last period.

To support the higher sales level, the business needed to increase its stock level. So the business bought £975,000 more in products than it sold during the period – and it had to come up with the cash to pay for this stock increase. Basically, the business wrote cheques amounting to £975,000 more than its cost-of-goods-sold expense for the period. This step-up in its stock level was necessary to support the higher sales level, which increased profit – even though cash flow took a hit.

It's that accrual basis accounting thing again: the cost that a business pays *this* period for *next* period's stock is reflected in this period's cash flow but isn't recorded until next period's income statement (when the products are actually sold). So if a business paid more *this* period for *next* period's stock than it paid *last* period for *this* period's stock, you can see how the additional expense would adversely affect cash flow but would not be reflected in the bottom-line net income figure. This cash flow analysis stuff gets a little complicated, we know, but hang in there. The cash flow statement, presented later in the chapter, makes a lot more sense after going through this background briefing.

Prepaid expenses increase

The next asset, after stock, is prepaid expenses (refer to Figure 3-1). A change in this account works the same way as a change in stock and debtors, although changes in prepaid expenses are usually much smaller than changes in those other two asset accounts.

Again, the beginning balance of prepaid expenses is recorded as an expense this period but the cash was actually paid out last period, not this period. This period, a business pays cash for next period's prepaid expenses – which affects this period's cash flow but doesn't affect net income until next period. So the £145,000 increase in prepaid expenses from start-of-period to end-of-period in this business example has a negative cash flow effect.

As it grows, a business needs to increase its prepaid expenses for such things as fire insurance (premiums have to be paid in advance of the insurance coverage) and its stocks of office and data processing supplies. Increases in debtors, stock and prepaid expenses are the price a business has to pay for growth. Rarely do you find a business that can increase its sales revenue without increasing these assets.

The simple but troublesome depreciation factor

Depreciation expense recorded in the period is both the simplest cash flow effect to understand and, at the same time, one of the most misunderstood elements in calculating cash flow from profit. To start with, depreciation isn't a cash outlay during the period. The amount of depreciation expense recorded in the period is simply a fraction of the original cost of the business's fixed assets that were bought and paid for years ago. (Well, if you want to nit-pick here, some of the fixed assets may have been bought during this period, and their cost is reported in the investing activities section of the cash flow statement.) Because the depreciation expense isn't a cash outlay this period, the amount is added back to net income in the calculation of cash flow from profit – so far so good.

When measuring profit on the accrual basis of accounting you count depreciation as an expense. The fixed assets of a business are on an irreversible journey to the junk heap. Fixed assets have a limited, finite life of usefulness to a business (except for land); depreciation is the accounting method that allocates the total cost of fixed assets to each year of their use in helping the business generate sales revenue. Part of the total sales revenue of a business constitutes *recovery of cost invested in its fixed assets*. In a real sense, a business 'sells' some of its fixed assets each period to its customers – it factors the cost of fixed assets into the sales prices that it charges its customers. For example, when you go to a supermarket, a very small slice of the price you pay for that box of cereal goes towards the cost of the building, the shelves, the refrigeration equipment and so on. (No wonder they charge so much for a box of cornflakes!)

Net income + depreciation expense doesn't equal cash flow from profit!

The business in our example earned £1.6 million in net income for the year, plus it received £1.2 million cash flow because of the depreciation expense built into its sales revenue for the year. The sum of these is £2.8 million. Is £2.8 million the amount of cash flow from profit for the period? The knee-jerk answer of many investors and managers is 'yes'. But if net income + depreciation truly equals cash flow, then *both* factors in the brackets – both net income and depreciation – must be fully realised in cash. Depreciation is, but the net income amount isn't fully realised in cash because the company's debtors, stock and prepaid expenses increased during the year, and these increases have negative impacts on cash flow.

Each period, a business recoups part of the cost invested in its fixed assets. In other words, £1.2 million of sales revenue (in the example) went towards reimbursing the business for the use of its fixed assets during the year. The problem regarding depreciation in cash flow analysis is that many people simply add back depreciation for the year to bottom-line profit and then stop, as if this is the proper number for cash flow from profit. It ain't so. The changes in other assets as well as the changes in liabilities also affect cash flow from profit. You need to factor in *all* the changes that determine cash flow from profit, as explained in the following section.

Adding net income and depreciation to determine cash flow from profit is mixing apples and oranges. The business didn't realise £1,600,000 cash increase from its £1,600,000 net income. The total of the increases of its debtors, stock and prepaid expenses is £1,920,000 (refer to Figure 3-1), which wipes out the net income amount and leaves the business with a cash balance hole of £320,000. This cash deficit is offset by the £220,000 increase in liabilities (explained later), leaving a £100,000 net income *deficit* as far as cash flow is concerned. Depreciation recovery increased cash flow by £1.2 million. So the final cash flow from profit equals £1.1 million. But you'd never know this if you simply added depreciation expense to net income for the period.

The managers didn't have to go outside the business for the £1.1 million cash increase generated from its profit for the year. Cash flow from profit is an *internal* source of money generated by the business itself, in contrast to *external* money that the business raises from lenders and owners. A business doesn't have to 'go begging' for external money if its internal cash flow from profit is sufficient to provide for its growth.

In passing, we should mention that a business could have a negative cash flow from profit for a year – meaning that despite posting a net income for the period, the changes in the company's assets and liabilities caused its cash balance to decrease. In reverse, a business could report a bottom-line *loss* in its income statement, yet have a *positive* cash flow from its operating activities: the positive contribution from depreciation expense plus decreases in its debtors and stock could amount to more than the amount of loss. More realistically, a loss often leads to negative cash flow or very little positive cash flow.

Operating liabilities increases

The business in the example, like almost all businesses, has three basic liabilities that are inextricably intertwined with its expenses: creditors, accrued expenses payable and income tax payable. When the beginning balance of one of these liability accounts is the same as the ending balance of the same account (not too likely, of course), the business breaks even on cash flow for that account. When the end-of-period balance is higher than the start-of-period balance, the business didn't pay out as much money as was actually recorded as an expense on the period's income statement.

In the example we've been using, the business disbursed £720,000 to pay off last period's creditors balance. (This £720,000 was reported as the creditors balance on last period's ending balance sheet.) Its cash flow this period decreased by £720,000 because of these payments. But this period's ending balance sheet shows the amount of creditors that the business will need to pay next period – £800,000. The business actually paid off £720,000 and recorded £800,000 of expenses to the year, so this time, cash flow is *richer* than what's reflected in the business's net income figure by £80,000 – in other words, the increase in creditors has a positive cash flow effect. The increases in accrued expenses payable and income tax payable work the same way.

Therefore, liability increases are favourable to cash flow – in a sense the business borrowed more than it paid off. Such an increase means that the business delayed paying cash for certain things until next year. So you need to add the increases in the three liabilities to net income to determine cash flow from profit, following the same logic as adding back depreciation to net income. The business didn't have cash outlays to the extent of increases in these three liabilities.

The analysis of the changes in assets and liabilities of the business that affect cash flow from profit is complete for the business example. The bottom line (oops, we shouldn't use that term when referring to a cash flow amount) is that the company's cash balance increased by £1.1 million from profit. You could argue that cash should have increased by £2.8 million – £1.6 million net income plus £1.2 million depreciation that was recovered during the year – so the business is £1.7 million behind in turning its profit into cash flow (£2.8 million less the £1.1 million cash flow from profit). This £1.7 million lag in converting profit into cash flow is caused by the £1,920,000 increase in assets less the £220,000 increase in liabilities, as shown in Figure 3-1.

Presenting the Cash Flow Statement

The cash flow statement is one of the three primary financial statements that a business must report to the outside world, according to generally accepted accounting principles (GAAP). To be technical, the rule says that whenever a business reports a profit and loss account, it should also report a cash flow statement. The *profit and loss account* summarises sales revenue and expenses and ends with the bottom-line profit for the period. The *balance sheet* summarises a business's financial condition by reporting its assets, liabilities and owners' equity. You can probably guess what the *cash flow statement* does by its name alone: this statement tells you where a business got its cash and what the business did with its cash during the period. We prefer the name given in the old days in the US to the predecessor of the cash flow statement, the *Where Got, Where Gone* statement. This nickname goes straight to the purpose of the cash flow statement: asking where the business got its money and what it did with the money.

To give you a rough idea of what a cash flow statement reports, we repeat some of the questions we asked at the start of the chapter: How much money did you earn last year? Did you get all your income in cash (did some of your wages go straight into a pension plan or did you collect a couple of IOUs)? Where did you get other money (did you take out a loan, win the lottery or receive a gift from a rich uncle)? What did you do with your money (did you buy a house, support your out-of-control Internet addiction or lose it playing bingo)?

Getting a little too personal for you? That's exactly why the cash flow statement is so important: It bares a business's financial soul to its lenders and owners. Sometimes the cash flow statement reveals questionable judgement calls that the business's managers made. At the very least, the cash flow statement reveals how well a business handles the cash increase from its profit.

Understanding the cash flow statement

As explained at the start of the chapter, the cash flow statement is divided into three sections according to the three-fold classification of cash flows for a business:

- ✔ Cash flow from **operating activities** (which we also call *cash flow from profit* in this chapter): The activities by which a business makes profit and turns the profit into cash flow (includes depreciation and changes in operating assets and liabilities).

- ✔ Cash flow from **investing activities**: Investing in long-term assets needed for a business's operations; also includes money taken out of these assets from time to time (such as when a business disposes of some of its long-term assets).

✔ Cash flow from **financing activities:** Raising capital from debt and owners' equity, returning capital to these capital sources and distributing profit to owners.

The cash flow statement reports a business's net cash increase or decrease based on these three groupings of the cash flow statement. Figure 3-2 shows what a cash flow statement typically looks like – in this example, for a *growing* business (which means that its assets, liabilities and owners' equity increase during the period).

Cash Flow Statement for Year (in thousands of pounds)		
Cash Flows from Operating Activities		
Net Income		£ 1,600
Debtors	£ (800)	
Stock Increase	£ (975)	
Prepaid Expenses Increase	£ (145)	
Depreciation Expense	£ 1,200	
Creditors Increase	£ 80	
Accrued Expense Increase	£ 120	
Income Tax Payable Increase	£ 20	£ (500)
Cash Flow from Operating Activities		£ 1,100
Cash Flows from Investing Activities		
Purchases of Property, Plant & Equipment		£ (1,275)
Cash Flows from Financing Activities		
Short-term Debt Borrowing Increase	£ 200	
Long-term Debt Borrowing Increase	£ 300	
Share Issue	£ 60	
Dividends Paid Stockholders	£ (400)	£ 160
Increase (Decrease) In Cash During Year		£ (15)
Beginning Cash Balance		£ 2,015
Ending Cash Balance		£ 2,000

Figure 3-2: Cash flow statement for the business in the example.

The trick to understanding cash flow from profit is to link the sales revenue and expenses of the business with the changes in the business's assets and liabilities that are directly connected with its profit-making activities. Using this approach earlier in the chapter, we determined that the cash flow from profit is £1.1 million for the year for the sample business. This is the number you see in Figure 3-2 for cash flow from operating activities. In our experience, many business managers, lenders and investors don't fully understand these links, but the savvy ones know to keep a close eye on the relevant balance sheet changes.

What do the figures in the first section of the cash flow statement (refer to Figure 3-2) reveal about this business over the past period? Recall that the business experienced rapid sales growth over the last period. However, the downside of sales growth is that operating assets and liabilities also grow – the business needs more stock at the higher sales level and also has higher debtors.

The business's prepaid expenses and liabilities also increased, although not nearly as much as debtors and stock. The rapid growth of the business yielded higher profit but also caused quite a surge in its operating assets and liabilities, the result being that cash flow from profit is only £1.1 million compared with £1.6 million in net income – a £500,000 shortfall. Still, the business had £1.1 million at its disposal after allowing for the increases in assets and liabilities. What did the business do with this £1.1 million of available cash? You have to look to the remainder of the cash flow statement to answer this key question.

A very quick read through the rest of the cash flow statement (refer to Figure 3-2) goes something like this: The company used £1,275,000 to buy new fixed assets, borrowed £500,000 and distributed £400,000 of the profit to its owners. The bottom line (should we use that term here?) is that cash decreased by £15,000 during the year.

A better alternative for reporting cash flow from profit?

We call your attention, again, to the first section of the cash flow statement in Figure 3-2. You start with net income for the period. Next, changes in assets and liabilities are deducted or added to net income to arrive at cash flow from operating activities (the cash flow from profit) for the year. This format is called the *indirect method*. The alternative format for this section of the cash flow statement is called the *direct method* and is presented like this (using the same business example, with pound amounts in millions):

Cash inflow from sales	£24.2	
Less cash outflow for expenses	£23.1	
Cash flow from operating activities		£1.1

You may remember from the earlier discussion that sales revenue for the year is £25 million, but that the company's debtors increased £800,000 during the year, so cash flow from sales is £24.2 million. Likewise, the expenses for the year can be put on a cash flow basis. But we 'cheated' here – we have already determined that cash flow from profit is £1.1 million for the year, so we plugged the figure for cash outflow for expenses. We would take more time to explain the direct approach, except for one major reason.

Although the Accounting Standards Board (ASB) expresses a definite preference for the direct method, this august rule-making body does permit the indirect method to be used in external financial reports – and, in fact, the overwhelming majority of businesses use the indirect method. Unless you're an accountant, we don't think you need to know much more about the direct method.

Sailing through the Rest of the Cash Flow Statement

Once you get past the first section, the rest of the cash flow statement is a breeze. The last two sections of the statement explain what the business did with its cash and where cash that didn't come from profit came from.

Investing activities

The second section of the cash flow statement reports the investment actions that a business's managers took during the year. Investments are like tea leaves which serve as indicators regarding what the future may hold for the company. Major new investments are the sure signs of expanding or modernising the production and distribution facilities and capacity of the business. Major disposals of long-term assets and the shedding of a major part of the business could be good news or bad news for the business, depending on many factors. Different investors may interpret this information differently, but all would agree that the information in this section of the cash flow statement is very important.

Certain long-lived operating assets are required for doing business – for example, Federal Express wouldn't be terribly successful if it didn't have aeroplanes and vans for delivering packages, and computers for tracking deliveries. When those assets wear out, the business needs to replace them. Also, to remain competitive, a business may need to upgrade its equipment to take advantage of the latest technology or provide for growth. These investments in long-lived, tangible, productive assets, which we call *fixed assets* in this book, are critical to the future of the business and are called *capital expenditures* to stress that capital is being invested for the long haul.

One of the first claims on cash flow from profit is capital expenditure. Notice in Figure 3-2 that the business spent £1,275,000 for new fixed assets, which are referred to as *property, plant and equipment* in the cash flow statement (to keep the terminology consistent with account titles used in the balance sheet, because the term *fixed assets* is rather informal).

Cash flow statements generally don't go into much detail regarding exactly what specific types of fixed assets a business purchased – how many additional square feet of space the business acquired, how many new drill presses it bought, and so on. (Some businesses do leave a clearer trail of their investments, though. For example, airlines describe how many new aircraft of each kind were purchased to replace old equipment or expand their fleets.)

Note: Typically, every year a business disposes of some of its fixed assets that have reached the end of their useful lives and will no longer be used. These fixed assets are sent to the junkyard, traded in on new fixed assets, or sold for relatively small amounts of money. The value of a fixed asset at the end of its useful life is called its *salvage value.* The disposal proceeds from selling fixed assets are reported as a source of cash in the investments section of the cash flow statement. Usually, these amounts are fairly small. In contrast, a business may sell off fixed assets because it's downsizing or abandoning a major segment of its business. These cash proceeds can be fairly large.

Financing activities

Note that in the annual cash flow statement (refer to Figure 3-2) of the business example we've been using, the positive cash flow from profit is £1,100,000 and the negative cash flow from investing activities is £1,275,000. The result to this point, therefore, is a net cash outflow of £175,000 – which would have decreased the company's cash balance this much if the business didn't go to outside sources of capital for additional money during the year. In fact, the business increased its short-term and long-term debt during the year, and its owners invested additional money in the business. The third section of the cash flow statement summarises these financing activities of the business over the period.

The term *financing* generally refers to a business raising capital from debt and equity sources – from borrowing money from banks and other sources willing to loan money to the business and from its owners putting additional money in the business. The term also includes the flip side; that is, making payments on debt and returning capital to owners. The term *financing* also includes cash distributions (if any) from profit by the business to its owners.

Most businesses borrow money for a short term (generally defined as less than one year), as well as for longer terms (generally defined as more than one year). In other words, a typical business has both short-term and long-term debt. The business in our example has both short-term and long-term debt. Although not a hard-and-fast rule, most cash flow statements report just the *net* increase or decrease in short-term debt, not the total amount borrowed and the total payments on short-term debt during the period. In contrast, both the total amount borrowed from and the total amount paid on long-term debt during the year are reported in the cash flow statement.

For the business we've been using as an example, no long-term debt was paid down during the year but short-term debt was paid off during the year and replaced with new short-term notes payable. However, only the net increase ($200,000) is reported in the cash flow statement. The business also increased its long-term debt by $300,000 (refer to Figure 3-2).

The financing section of the cash flow statement also reports on the flow of cash between the business and its owners (who are the stockholders of a corporation). Owners can be both a *source* of a business's cash (capital invested by owners) and a *use* of a business's cash (profit distributed to owners). This section of the cash flow statement reports capital raised from its owners, if any, as well as any capital returned to the owners. In the cash flow statement (Figure 3-2), note that the business did issue additional stock shares for $60,000 during the year and it paid a total of $400,000 cash dividends (distributions) from profit to its owners.

Free Cash Flow: What on Earth Does That Mean?

A new term has emerged in the lexicon of accounting and finance – *free cash flow*. This piece of language is not – we repeat, *not* – an officially defined term by any authoritative accounting rule-making body. Furthermore, the term does *not* appear in the cash flow statements reported by businesses. Rather, free cash flow is street language, or slang, even though the term appears often in *The Financial Times* and *The Economist*. Securities brokers and investment analysts use the term freely (pun intended). Like most new words being tossed around for the first time, this one hasn't settled down into one universal meaning although the most common usage of the term pivots on cash flow from profit.

The term *free cash flow* is used to mean any of the following:

- ✔ Net income plus depreciation (plus any other expense recorded during the period that doesn't involve the outlay of cash but rather the allocation of the cost of a long-term asset other than property, plant and equipment – such as the intangible assets of a business)

- ✔ Cash flow from operating activities (as reported in the cash flow statement)

- ✔ Cash flow from operating activities minus some or all of the capital expenditures made during the year (such as purchases or construction of new, long-lived operating assets such as property, plant and equipment)

- ✔ Cash flow from operating activities plus interest, and depreciation, and income tax expenses, or, in other words, cash flow before these expenses are deducted

In the strongest possible terms, we advise you to be very clear on which definition of *free cash flow* the speaker or writer is using. Unfortunately, you can't always determine what the term means in any given context. The reporter or investment professional should define the term.

One definition of free cash flow, in our view, is quite useful: cash flow from profit minus capital expenditures for the year. The idea is that a business needs to make capital expenditures in order to stay in business and thrive. And to make capital expenditures, the business needs cash. Only after paying for its capital expenditures does a business have 'free' cash flow that it can use as it likes. In our example, the free cash flow is, in fact, negative – £1,100,000 cash flow from profit minus £1,275,000 capital expenditures for new fixed assets equals a *negative* £175,000.

This is a key point. In many cases, cash flow from profit falls short of the money needed for capital expenditures. So the business has to borrow more money, persuade its owners to invest more money in the business, or dip into its cash reserve. Should a business in this situation distribute some of its profit to owners? After all, it has a cash *deficit* after paying for capital expenditures. But many companies like the business in our example do, in fact, make cash distributions from profit to their owners.

Scrutinising the Cash Flow Statement

Analysing a business's cash flow statement inevitably raises certain questions: What would I have done differently if I were running this business? Would I have borrowed more money? Would I have raised more money from the owners? Would I have distributed so much of the profit to the owners? Would I have let my cash balance drop by even such a small amount?

One purpose of the cash flow statement is to show readers what judgement calls and financial decisions the business's managers made during the period. Of course, management decisions are always subject to second-guessing and criticising, and passing judgement based on a financial statement isn't totally fair because it doesn't reveal the pressures the managers faced during the period. Maybe they made the best possible decisions given the circumstances. Maybe not.

The business in our example (refer to Figure 3-2) distributed £400,000 cash from profit to its owners – a 25 per cent *pay-out ratio* (which is the £400,000 distribution divided by £1.6 million net income). In analysing whether the pay-out ratio is too high, too low or just about right, you need to look at the broader context of the business's sources of, and needs for, cash.

First look at cash flow from profit: £1.1 million, which isn't enough to cover the business's £1,275,000 capital expenditures during the year. The business increased its total debt by £500,000. Given these circumstances, maybe the business should have hoarded its cash and not paid so much in cash distributions to its owners.

So does this business have enough cash to operate with? You can't answer that question just by examining the cash flow statement – or any financial statement for that matter. Every business needs a buffer of cash to protect against unexpected developments and to take advantage of unexpected opportunities. This particular business has a £2 million cash balance compared with £25 million annual sales revenue for the period just ended, which probably is enough. If you were the boss of this business how much working cash balance would you want? Not an easy question to answer! Don't forget that you need to look at all three primary financial statements – the profit and loss account and the balance sheet as well as the cash flow statement – to get the big picture of a business's financial health.

You probably didn't count the number of lines of information in Figure 3-2, the cash flow statement for the business example. Anyway, the financial statement has 17 lines of information. Would you like to hazard a guess regarding the average number of lines in cash flow statements of publicly owned companies? Typically, their cash flow statements have 30 to 40 lines of information by our reckoning. So it takes quite a while to read the cash flow statement – more time than the average investor probably has to read this financial statement. (Professional stock analysts and investment managers are paid to take the time to read this financial statement meticulously.) Quite frankly, we find that many cash flow statements are not only rather long but also difficult to understand – even for an accountant. We won't get on a soapbox here but we definitely think businesses could do a better job of reporting their cash flow statements by reducing the number of lines in their financial statements and making each line clearer.

You can download an Excel spreadsheet from the SCORE website (go to www. score.org and click on 'Business Tools', 'Template Gallery', and 'Cash Flow Statement') that enables you to tailor a cash flow statement to your own needs. The spreadsheet has scope for three categories of cash in, thirty categories of cash out, and space at the bottom of the spreadsheet for non-cash flow operating data such as depreciation, sales volume, bad debts and stock. A very useful tool!

Chapter 4

Forecasting and Budgeting

- -

In This Chapter

▶ Constructing your financial forecast

▶ Putting together a pro-forma profit and loss account

▶ Estimating a balance sheet

▶ Projecting your cash flow

▶ Exploring financial alternatives

▶ Preparing your company's budget

- -

*H*ow many times have you sat around the table with your family (or maybe just your dog) and talked about the importance of putting the household on a budget? Everybody knows what a budget is, of course: it's a way of figuring out how much you're going to spend on essentials (the things that you need) and incidentals (all the frills). By its very nature, a budget is something that looks ahead, combining a forecast and a set of guidelines for spending money.

As you probably know from experience, it's a lot easier to put together a budget if you have some basic financial information to work with. It's nice to know how much money's going to come in, for example, and when you expect it to arrive. It's also important to keep track of the expenses that absolutely have to be taken care of, such as the mortgage and the car payment. Only then can you begin to get a handle on what you have left over, which is called your *working capital.*

For your company, this kind of basic financial information resides in its financial statements. (For more information on financial statements, refer to Chapter2 in this Book.) These financial statements – profit and loss accounts, balance sheets, cash flow – are fairly straightforward, because they're based on how your company performed last year or the year before. Unfortunately, financial information isn't quite as easy to put together and use when you have to plan for next year, three years from now or even five years from now.

Why go to all the trouble of putting financial information together in the first place? The answer is simple: although the numbers and financials aren't your business plan by themselves, they help you to fulfil your business plan. Without them, you're in real danger of allowing your financial condition – money (or the lack of it) – to take control of, or even replace, your business plan.

In this chapter, we help you construct a financial forecast for your company, including a pro-forma profit and loss account, an estimated balance sheet, and a projected cash-flow statement. Because nothing in the future is certain, we also introduce scenario planning and what-if analysis as ways to consider several financial alternatives. Finally, we talk about how you can use the financial information to create a budget, explaining what goes into a budget and how to go about making one.

Constructing a Financial Forecast

Every philosopher-wannabe has spoken profound words about the future and about whether we should try to predict it. But we can't avoid the future. It's there, it's uncertain, and we're going to spend the rest of our lives in it.

All of us make decisions every day based on our own personal view of what's ahead. Although things often end up surprising us, our assumptions about the future at least give us a basic framework to plan our lives around. Our expectations, no matter how far off the mark they are, encourage us to set objectives, to move forward and to achieve our goals somewhere down the road.

You can think about the future of your company in much the same way. Assumptions about your own industry and marketplace – that you'll have no new competitors, that a new technology will catch on, or that customers will remain loyal, for example – provide a framework to plan around. Your expectations of what lies ahead influence your business objectives and the long-term goals that you set for the company.

You want to be clear about what your business assumptions are and where they come from, because your assumptions are as important as the numbers themselves when it comes to making a prediction. If you are convinced that no new competitors will enter the market, say why. If you see a period of rapid technological change ahead, explain your reasons. Don't try to hide your business assumptions in a footnote somewhere; place them in a prominent position. That way, you make your financial forecast as honest, adaptable, and useful as it can be. If all your assumptions are out in the open, nobody can possibly miss them.

- ✔ Everybody who looks at your forecast knows exactly what's behind it.

- ✔ You know exactly where to go when your assumptions need to be changed.

As you may have guessed, coming up with predictions that you really believe in isn't always easy. You may trust some of the numbers (next year's sales figures) more than you do others (the size of a brand-new market). Some of your financial predictions are based on your best estimate. You may arrive at others by using sophisticated number-crunching techniques. When you get the hang of it, though, you begin to see what a broad and powerful planning tool a financial forecast can be. You'll find yourself turning to it to help answer all sorts of important questions, such as the following:

- ✔ What cash demands does your company face in the coming year?
- ✔ Can your company cover its debt obligations over the next three years?
- ✔ Does your company plan to make a profit next year?
- ✔ Is your company meeting its overall financial objectives?
- ✔ Do investors find your company to be an attractive business proposition?

With so many important questions at stake, a financial forecast is worth all the time and effort that you can spend on it. Because, if you're not careful, a forecast can turn out to be way off the mark. Did you ever hear the old computer programmer's expression 'Rubbish in, rubbish out'? The same is true of financial forecasts. Your financial forecast is only as good as the numbers that go into it. If the numbers are off the mark, it's usually for one of the following reasons:

- ✔ Expectations were unrealistic.
- ✔ Assumptions weren't objective.
- ✔ Predictions weren't checked and rechecked.

The following sections examine the financial statements that make up a financial forecast. After we've explained how to put these statements together, we point out which of the numbers are most important and which are the most sensitive to changes in your assumptions and expectations about the future.

Pro-forma profit and loss account

Pro forma refers to something that you describe or estimate in advance. (It can also mean something that is merely a formality and can be ignored – but don't get your hopes up; we're talking about a serious part of a business plan.) When you construct your financial forecast, try to include *pro-forma profit and loss accounts* – documents that show where you plan to get your money and how you'll spend it – for at least three years and for as long as five years in the future, depending on the nature of your business. Subdivide the first two years into quarterly profit projections. After two years, when your profit projections are much less certain, annual projections are fine. (For a look at a profit and loss account, flip to Book IV Chapter 5.)

Your company's pro-forma profit and loss accounts predict what sort of profit you expect to make in the future by asking you to project your total business revenue and then to subtract all your anticipated costs. The following should help you get ready:

- ✔ If you're already in business and have a financial history to work with, get all your past financial statements out right away. You can use them to help you figure out what's likely to happen next.

- ✔ If you have a new company on your hands and don't have a history to fall back on, you have to find other ways to get the information that you need. Talk to people in similar businesses, sit down with your banker and your accountant, visit a trade association, and read industry magazines and newspapers.

The pro-forma profit and loss account has two parts – projected revenue and anticipated costs.

Projected revenue

Your company's projected revenue is based primarily on your sales forecast – exactly how much of your product or service you plan to sell. You have to think about two things: how much you expect to sell, naturally, and how much you're going to charge. Unfortunately, you can't completely separate the two things, because any change in price usually affects the level of your sales.

Your sales forecast is likely to be the single most important business prediction that you'll ever make. If you get it wrong, the error can lead to mountains of unsold stock or a sea of unhappy, dissatisfied customers – a financial disaster in the making. A souvenir-T-shirt company that *over*estimates how many Cup Final T-shirts customers will buy, for example, is going to be left with an awful lot of worthless merchandise. By the same token, the corner toy shop that *under*estimates how many kids will want the latest Bratz will have to answer to many frustrated parents and unhappy children – and will suffer lost sales.

How do you get the sales forecast right? Start by looking at its formula:

Sales forecast = market size × growth rate × market-share target

- ✔ Market size estimates the current number of potential customers.
- ✔ Growth rate estimates how fast the market will grow.
- ✔ Market-share target estimates the percentage of the market that you plan to capture.

Because your sales forecast has such a tremendous impact on the rest of your financial forecast – not to mention on the company itself – try to support the estimates that you make with as much hard data as you can get your hands on. Depending on your situation, you can also rely on the following guides:

✔ **Company experience.** If you already have experience and a track record in the market, you can use your own sales history to make a sales prediction. But remember that your sales are a combination of the size of the market and your own share of the market. You may still need other sources of data (listed in the following paragraphs) to help you estimate how the market and your share of it are likely to change in the future.

✔ Using data from outside your company also ensures that you're taking full advantage of all the growth opportunities that are available. All too often, companies use last year's sales as a shortcut to estimating next year's sales, without taking the time to look at how their markets are changing. Because a sales forecast can be self-fulfilling, those companies may never know what they missed!

✔ **Industry data.** Industry data on market size and estimates of future growth come from all quarters, including trade associations, investment companies, and market-research firms (covered more extensively in Chapter 6 in Book I). You can also get practical and timely information from industry suppliers and distributors.

✔ **Outside trends.** In certain markets, sales levels are closely tied to trends in other markets, social trends or economic trends. Car sales, for example, tend to move with the general economy. So when car dealers track what's happening with the Gross Domestic Product (GDP), they get an estimate of where car sales are headed.

Book II

Sorting Out Your Finances

Even if a product is brand-new, you can sometimes find a substitute market to track as a reference. When frozen yogurt first appeared on the scene, for example, frozen-yogurt makers turned to the sales history of ice cream to help support their own sales forecasts.

Speaking of ice cream, don't forget to factor sales cycles into your forecast; in most of the UK, ice cream sales freeze over in January and February. Other markets may have other cycles.

Next, multiply your sales forecast by the average price that you expect to charge. The result is your projected revenue and it looks like this:

Projected revenue = sales forecast × average price

Where does the average price come from? Your average price is based on what you think your customers are willing to pay and what your competitors are charging. Use the information that you pack away on your industry and the marketplace. The price should also take into account your own costs and your company's overall financial situation.

Now put all the numbers together and see how they work. We'll use a company called Global Gizmos as an example. Sally Smart, widgets product manager, is putting together a three-year revenue projection. Using industry and market data along with the company's own sales history, Sally estimates that the entire market for widgets will grow by about 10 per cent a year and that Global Gizmos' market share will increase by roughly 2 per cent a year, with projected price increases of approximately £1 to £2. She puts the numbers together in a table so that she can easily refer to the underlying estimates and the assumptions that support them (see Table 4-1).

Table 4-1	Widget Revenue Projection for Global Gizmos Company		
Revenue projection	*Year 1*	*Year 2*	*Year 3*
Projected market size (units)	210,000	231,000	254,100
Projected market share (per cent)	20	22	24
Sales forecast (units)	42,000	50,820	60,980
Average price	£26	£27	£29
Projected revenue	£1,092,000	£1,372,140	£1,768,420

Anticipated costs

When you've completed your revenue projection, you're still not quite finished. You still have to look at anticipated costs – the price tag of doing business over the next several years. To make life a little easier, you can break anticipated costs down into the major categories that appear in a pro-forma profit and loss account: projected cost of goods sold, projected sales, general and administration expenses, projected interest expenses, and projected taxes and depreciation. The following list defines these categories.

- **Projected cost of goods sold (COGS).** COGS, which combines all the direct costs associated with putting together your product or delivering your service, is likely to be your single largest expense. If you have a track record in the industry, you have a useful starting point for estimating your company's future COGS.

  Even though the following formula may look ugly, it's actually a simple way to calculate your projected COGS. Based on the assumption that the ratio of your costs to your revenue will stay the same:

  Projected COGS = (current COGS ÷ current revenue on sales) × projected revenue

  If you haven't been in business long or if you're just starting a company, you won't have access to this kind of information. But you can still estimate your projected COGS by substituting industry averages or by using data that you find on other companies that have similar products or services.

Although this ratio approach has the advantage of being simple, you can get into trouble if you don't confirm the COGS that you come up with. At the very least, you need to sum up the estimates of the major costs looming ahead (materials, labour, utilities, facilities and so on) to make sure that the projected COGS makes sense. This method is tougher, but it gives you a chance to make separate assumptions and projections for each of the underlying costs. You may be pleasantly surprised; you may discover that as your company gets bigger and you're in business longer, your projected revenue goes up faster than your costs do. The effect is called the experience curve (explained thoroughly in Chapter 1 of Book VI), and it means that your COGS-to-revenue ratio will actually get smaller in the coming years.

✔ **Sales, general and administration (SG&A).** SG&A represents your company's overheads: sales expenses, advertising, travel, accounting, telephones and all the other costs associated with supporting your business. If your company is brand-new, try to get a feel for what your support costs may be by asking people in similar businesses, cornering your accountant, or checking with a trade association for average support costs in your industry. Also come up with ballpark numbers of your own, including estimates for all the major overhead expenses that you can think of.

If you've been in business for a while, you can estimate a range for your SG&A expenses using two calculations. The first method projects a constant spending level, even if your company's sales are growing. In effect, you assume that your support activities will all get more efficient and will accommodate your additional growth without getting bigger themselves. The other method projects a constant SG&A-to-revenue ratio. In this case, you assume that support costs will grow as fast as your revenue and that you won't see any increase in efficiency. An accurate SG&A forecast probably lies somewhere in between. Given what you know about your company's operations, come up with your own estimate, and include the assumptions that you make.

✔ **Interest expense.** Your interest expense is largely the result of decisions that you make about your company's long-term financing. Those decisions, in turn, are influenced by your ability to pay your interest costs out of profits. Think about what sort of financing you'll need and what interest rates you may be able to lock in, then estimate your interest expense as best you can.

✔ **Taxes and depreciation.** Taxes certainly affect your bottom line, and you want to include your projections and assumptions in your anticipated costs. It's usually pretty simple to estimate their general impact in the future by looking at their impact on your company now. If you're starting a new business, do a bit of research on tax rates.

Depreciation, on the other hand, is an accountant's way of accounting for the value that your asset purchases lose over the time in which you're using them. As such, it's an expense that doesn't really come out of your pocket every year. You can estimate the numbers, but don't get too carried away. In the future, your depreciation expense will include a portion of those expensive items that you have to buy to keep the business healthy and growing (computers, cars, forklifts and so on).

When you plug the numbers into your pro-forma profit and loss account and calculate your net profit, be prepared for a shock. You may discover that the profit you were expecting in the first year or two has turned into a projected loss. But don't panic. New business ventures often lose money for some time, until their products catch on and some of the startup costs begin to get paid off. Whatever you do, don't try to turn a projected loss into a profit by fiddling with the numbers. The point isn't to make money on paper; the point is to use the pro-forma profit and loss account as a tool that can tell you what sort of resources and reserves you need to survive until losses turn into predicted profits.

Even if your projection shows a healthy profit, ensure you also complete a Cash Flow Projection (see below) to make sure you can afford to trade at the projected level. Making a profit doesn't always mean that you have *cash* on hand to buy raw materials, pay staff and pay taxes.

Estimated balance sheet

Another part of your financial forecast is the *estimated balance sheet,* which, like a regular balance sheet, is a snapshot of what your company looks like at a particular moment – what it owns, what it owes and what it's worth. Over the years, these snapshots (estimated balance sheets) fill a photo album of sorts, recording how your company changes over time. Your estimated balance sheets describe what you want your company to become and how you plan to get it there. The estimated balance sheets that you put together as part of your financial forecast should start with the present and extend out three to five years in a series of year-end projections. (For much more information on balance sheets, check out Chapter 2 of this Book.)

While the pro-forma profit and loss accounts in your financial forecast project future revenue, costs and profits, your estimated balance sheets lay out exactly how your company will grow so that it can meet those projections. First, you want to look at what sorts of things (*assets*) you'll need to support the planned size and scale of your business. Then you have to make some decisions about how you're going to pay for those assets. You have to consider how you'll finance your company – how much debt you plan to take on (*liabilities*) and how much of the company's own money (*equity*) you plan to use.

Assets

Your company's projected assets at the end of each year include everything from the money that you expect to have in the petty-cash drawer to the buildings and machines that you plan to own. Some of these assets will be current assets, meaning that you can easily turn them into cash; others will be fixed assets. Don't be confused by the word *current;* we're still talking about the future.

> ✔ **Current assets.** The cash on hand and your investment portfolio, as well as debtors and stocks, add up to your current assets. How much should you plan for? That depends on the list of current liabilities (debts) you expect to have, for one thing, because you'll have to pay short-term debts out of your current assets. What's left over is your working capital. The amount of working capital that you'll need depends on your future cash-flow situation.
>
> Your estimates of future debtors (money that customers will owe you) depend on the payment terms that you offer and on the sales that you expect to make on credit.
>
> Projected stocks (the amount of stuff in your warehouse) depend on how fast your company can put together products or services and get them to customers. The longer it takes to build products, the bigger the stock cushion you may need.
>
> ✔ **Fixed assets.** Land, buildings, equipment, machinery and all the other things that aren't easy to dispose of make up your company's fixed assets. Your estimated balance sheets should account for the expensive items that you expect to purchase or get rid of. Your capital purchases (such as additional buildings, more equipment and newer machines) can play a major role in company growth, increasing both your revenue and the scale of your business operations.

Book II

Sorting Out Your Finances

Keep an eye on how each machine or piece of equipment will help your bottom line. If you plan to buy something big, make a quick calculation of its *payback period* (how long it will take to pay back the initial cost of the equipment out of the extra profit that you'll make). Is the payback period going to be months, years or decades? As you plan for the future, you also want to keep track of your overall expected *return on assets* (ROA), which is your net profits divided by your total assets. This figure monitors how well you expect all your assets to perform in the future. Compare your estimated ROA with industry averages and even with other types of investments.

Extruding better returns

A small, up-and-coming West Country company (we'll call it Klever Kitchens) has made a big name for itself in the kitchen-accessories business. Klever Kitchens produces all sorts of newfangled gadgets and utensils for the gourmet chef – everything from pasta hooks to melon scoops. Because many of the company's products are made of plastic, the owners face a decision about the purchase of a second plastic-extruding machine. They know that the investment is sound, because the new £20,000 machine will allow the company to grow, and they expect it to generate an additional £4,000 a year in profit, resulting in an estimated pay-back period of about five years (£20,000 divided by £4,000). The question is whether to pay for the extruder by borrowing the funds or by using some of the company's equity reserves.

The owners understand that using debt is a way to leverage the company. The bank has already agreed to loan Klever Kitchens 75 per cent of the £20,000 investment at a fixed 8 per cent interest rate. But what do the numbers say?

Return on equity (ROE) really measures how much money Klever Kitchens makes on the money that it invests (ROE = (added profit – interest expense) ÷ equity). By taking on debt, the owners expect to earn an additional £2,800 on their investment of £5,000 in the new extruder, for an ROE of 56 per cent. That figure is almost three times the return that they would receive by putting up the funds themselves.

Acting like a financial crowbar, leverage allows Klever Kitchens to use other people's money to generate profits for itself. The risks are also a bit higher, of course, because the owners have to make added interest payments or face losing the extruder and maybe the entire company. In this case, Klever Kitchens should borrow the funds, deciding that the rewards are well worth the risks.

Additional plastic extruder	No leverage	Leverage
Liability	£0	£15,000
Equity	£20,000	£5,000
Added net profit	£4,000	£4,000
Added interest expense	£0	£1,200
Added profit minus interest expense	£4,000	£2,800
Return on equity (ROE)	20 per cent	56 per cent

Liabilities and owners' equity

Estimated balance sheets have to balance, of course, and your projected assets at the end of each future year have to be offset by all the liabilities that you intend to take on, plus your projected equity in the company. Think about how *leveraged* you intend to be (how much of your total assets you expect to pay for out of money that you borrow). Your use of leverage in the future says a great deal about your company. It shows how confident you are about future profits; it also says, loud and clear, how willing you are to take risks for future gain.

- ✔ **Current liabilities.** This category consists of all the money that you expect to owe on a short-term basis. That's why these debts are called *current liabilities,* although we're still talking about the future. Current liabilities include the amounts that you expect to owe other companies as part of your planned business operations, as well as payments that you expect to send to the tax people. You have to plan your future current assets so that they not only cover these estimated liabilities, but also leave you some extra capital to work with.

- ✔ **Long-term liabilities.** The long-term debt that you plan to take on represents the piece of your company that you intend to finance. Don't be surprised, however, if potential creditors put a strict limit on how much they'll loan you, especially if you're just starting out. It's hard to buy a house without a down payment, and it's almost impossible to start a company without one. The down payment is your equity contribution. In general, bankers and other lenders alike want to see enough equity put into your business to make them feel that you're all in the same boat, risk-wise. Equity reassures them that you and other equity investors have a real financial stake in the company, as well as tangible reasons to make it succeed.

How much are lenders willing to loan you, and how much of a down payment do you need to come up with to satisfy them? The answer depends on several things. If you're already in business, the answer depends on how much debt your company already has, how long your company's been around, how you've done up to now, and what the prospects are in your industry. If your company is new, financing depends on your track record in other businesses or on how well you do your homework and put together a convincing business plan.

Before you take on a new loan, find out what kind of debt-to-equity ratios similar companies have. (For help, turn to Chapter 6 in Book I.) Make sure that yours will fall somewhere in the same range. As an additional test, run some numbers to make sure that you can afford the debt and the interest payments that come along with it.

- ✔ **Owners' equity.** The pieces of your company that you, your friends, relatives, acquaintances and often total strangers lay claim to are all lumped together as *owners' equity.* Although the details of ownership can become ridiculously complex, the result of the process is fairly straightforward. All owners own part of your company, and everybody sinks or swims, depending on how well the company does.

In general, you can estimate how well the company is likely to do for its owners by projecting the return that you expect to make on the owners' investment (refer to Chapter 2 in this Book for the details). Then you can compare that return with what investors in other companies, or even other industries, are earning.

In the initial stages of your company, equity capital is likely to come from the owners themselves, either as cash straight out of the wallet or from the sale of shares to other investors. The equity at this stage is crucial, because if you want to borrow money later, you're going to have to show your bankers that you have enough invested in your business to make your company a sound financial risk. When the company is up and running, of course, you can take some of your profits and (rather than buy the little sports car that you've always wanted) give them back to the company, creating additional equity.

Unfortunately, profit has another side, and the down side is definitely in the red. Although you probably don't want to think about it, your company may lose money some years (especially during the early years). Losses don't generate equity; on the contrary, they eat equity up. So you have to plan to have enough equity available to cover any anticipated losses that you project in your pro-forma profit and loss accounts (refer to the section 'Pro-forma profit and loss account' earlier in this chapter).

Projected cash flow

The flow of cash through a business is much like the flow of oil through an engine: it supports and sustains everything that you do and keeps the various parts of your company functioning smoothly. We all know what happens when a car's oil runs dry: the car belches blue smoke and dies. Running out of cash can be just as catastrophic for your company. If you survive the experience, it may take months or even years for your company to recover.

Cash-flow statements keep track of the cash that comes in and the cash that goes out of your company, as well as where the money ends up. These statements are crucial. Projected cash-flow statements ensure that you never find the cash drawer empty at the end of the month when you have a load of bills left to pay.

Cash-flow statements should project three to five years into the future, and for the first two years, they should include monthly cash-flow estimates. Monthly estimates are particularly important if your company is subject to seasonal cycles or to big swings in sales or expenses. (If you're not sure what a cash-flow statement looks like and how it's different from a profit and loss account, flip to Chapter 3 in this Book.)

You get a bonus from all this work: the effort that you put into creating cash-flow statements for the company gives you a head start when the time comes to create a budget for your business (see 'Making a Budget' later in this chapter).

✔ Your financial forecast should include a pro-forma profit and loss account, an estimated balance sheet and a projected cash-flow statement.

✔ The business assumptions behind your forecast are as important as the numbers themselves.

✔ Your company's pro-forma profit and loss account predicts the profit that you expect to make in future years.

✔ Your estimated balance sheet lays out how you expect your company to grow in the future.

✔ Your company's projected cash-flow statement tracks your expected cash position in coming years.

Book II

Sorting Out Your Finances

Exploring Alternatives

Wouldn't it be nice if you could lay out a financial forecast – create your pro-forma profit and loss accounts, estimated balance sheets and projected cash-flow statements – and then just be done with it? Unfortunately the uncertain future that makes your financial forecast necessary in the first place is unpredictable enough to require constant attention. To keep up, you have to do the following things:

✔ Monitor your financial situation and revise the parts of your forecast that change when circumstances – and your own financial objectives – shift.

✔ Update the entire financial forecast regularly, keeping track of when past predictions were on target or off, and extending your projections another month, quarter or year.

✔ Consider financial assumptions that are more optimistic and more pessimistic than your own best predictions, paying special attention to the estimates that you're the least certain about.

Why take the time to look at different financial assumptions? For one thing, they show you just how far off your forecast can be if things happen to turn out a bit differently from what you expect. Also, the differences that you come up with are an important reminder that your forecasts are only that. You have to be prepared for alternatives.

The DuPont formula

If you really want to get a feel for what's going to happen when you change any of the estimates that make up your company's financial forecast, you have to understand a little bit about how the numbers relate to one other.

The DuPont company came up with a formula that turned out to be so useful that other companies have been using a similar one ever since.

The idea behind the *DuPont formula* is simple. The recipe describes all the ingredients that play a role in determining your return on equity (ROE) – a number that captures the overall profitability of your company. ROE is your company's overall net profit divided by the owners' equity. But knowing that your ROE is 13 per cent, for example, is a lot like getting B+ on a test. You think that you did relatively well, but why did you get that particular mark? Why didn't you get an A? You want to know what's behind the mark so that you can do better next time.

By learning what's behind your company's ROE, you have a way to measure the impact of your financial predictions on your profitability. The DuPont chart shown in Figure 4-1 turns the formula into a pyramid, with the ROE at the top. Each level of the pyramid breaks the ratio into more basic financial ingredients.

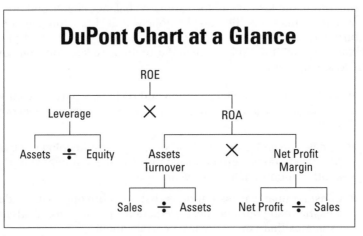

Figure 4-1:
The DuPont chart turns the DuPont formula into a pyramid, with return on equity (ROE) at the top.

First level

ROE = ROA × leverage

You can increase your company's return on equity by increasing the overall return on your company assets or by increasing your leverage (the ratio of your total company assets to equity).

Second level

Leverage = assets ÷ equity

As your debt increases relative to equity, so does your company's leverage.

ROA = asset turnover × net profit margin

You can increase your return on company assets by turning those assets into more sales or by increasing the amount of money that you make on each sale.

Third level

Asset turnover = sales ÷ assets

Asset turnover is the amount of money that you take in on sales relative to your company's assets. The bigger your asset turnover, the more efficient you are at turning assets into sales.

Net profit margin = net profit ÷ sales

Net profit margin is the profit that you make after subtracting expenses divided by the amount of money you take in on sales. The larger your profit margin, the lower your overall costs relative to the prices that you charge.

Book II

Sorting Out Your Finances

What-if analysis

Now you've seen how the DuPont formula is put together, you can start exploring different assumptions and what happens when you change the financial forecast. With the DuPont formula, you can look at how those changes are likely to affect your projected profitability, measured by your return on equity. The DuPont formula makes answering questions like the following much easier:

- ✔ What if you cut prices by 3 per cent?
- ✔ What if you increase sales volume by 10 per cent?
- ✔ What if cost of goods sold goes up by 8 per cent?
- ✔ What if you reduce your leverage by 25 per cent?

If you get your computer and a spreadsheet program involved in the analysis (see your local computer guru for help, if necessary), you can ask ten what-if questions and get the answers before you have time to think of the next ten.

The better you understand where your revenue and profits come from, the better prepared you are to meet financial challenges. For more help on preparing for change, check out Chapter 6 in Book VI.

- ✔ Looking at different financial assumptions allows you to cover your bets in an uncertain future.
- ✔ The DuPont formula describes exactly what goes into your return on equity, which is a measure of your overall profitability.
- ✔ Using the DuPont formula, you can ask what-if questions to gauge the effects of changing your financial assumptions.

Making a Budget

The pieces of your financial forecast – the pro-forma profit and loss accounts, estimated balance sheets and projected cash-flow statements – are meant to create a moving picture of your financial situation tomorrow, next month, next year and three or even five years out. Your financial picture is likely to be much clearer in the near term, of course, and much cloudier the farther out you try to look. Fortunately, you can use the best of your forecasts to make near-term decisions about where, when and how much money to spend on your company in the future.

Making a budget for your company is one of the most important steps that you'll take as you prepare your business plan. Your budget, in effect, consists of a series of bets that you're willing to place, based on what you expect to happen in your industry and in the marketplace in general. Your budget spells out exactly where your company's resources will come from and where they're going to go, and helps ensure that you make the right financial decisions.

A budget is more than a collection of numbers, though. Your budget is also a business tool that helps you communicate, organise, monitor and control what's going on in your business. Your company's budget does the following things:

- ✔ Requires managers to communicate with one another so that they can agree on specific financial objectives, including revenue levels and spending targets.

- ✔ Establishes roles and responsibilities for managers, based on how much money they're in charge of bringing in and how much they're allowed to spend.

- ✔ Creates a standard way of measuring and monitoring management performance by keeping track of how well the revenue targets and spending limits are met.

- ✔ Promotes the efficient and effective use of your financial resources by making sure that all your resources point towards a common set of business goals.

What's in the budget

The rough outlines of your company's budget look a lot like your projected cash-flow statement. In fact, the cash-flow statement is the perfect place to start. Projected cash flow is a forecast of where you think the company's money will come from and where it's going to go in the future. Your budget fills in all the details, turning your financial forecast into a specific plan for taking in money and doling it out.

The *master budget* that you create is meant to account for everything that your company plans to do over the next year or two. Although you spend your company's money in all sorts of ways, all those ways can be divided into short-term and long-term spending. In the short term, you use money to keep the business up and running every day, covering the costs and expenses of putting together and selling products and services. Over the longer term, you use money to invest in things that will make your company bigger, better or more profitable.

If your company is small and you have only a few employees, a single master budget should be all that you need to keep your day-to-day finances on track as well as to make decisions in the future. When your company gets a little bigger, however, you may want to think about your company's finances in terms of more than one budget, each of which covers a different aspect of your business. You may want to create the following budgets:

- ✔ **Operating.** This budget deals with all the costs that are directly associated with putting your product or service together, such as materials, supplies, labour, utilities, services and facilities.

- ✔ **Administrative.** This budget deals with the expenses that are involved in supporting your products and services, sales and advertising, administrative salaries, phone and fax lines, and travel expenses.

- ✔ **Financial.** This budget deals with the overhead expenses involved in managing your assets, including keeping your books, doing your taxes, controlling your product stock, and keeping track of your debtors (the money that customers owe you).

- ✔ **Capital.** This budget deals with funds that are earmarked for the purchase of expensive items, such as new equipment, computers, a company car and additional office space.

- ✔ **Development.** This budget deals with money that is set aside for developing new products, opening branches in other cities, or marketing to brand-new groups of customers.

When you need several budgets, like those in the preceding list, you use a master budget to pull all the separate budgets together and make sure that they meet your company's larger goals and financial objectives.

Global Gizmos Company put together a budget for the next two years based on a financial forecast and its projected cash flow (see Figure 4-2). The company's master budget looks a great deal like one of its cash-flow statements (flip to Chapter 3 in this Book for a comparison). But the budget goes into more detail in dividing the broad financial objectives into actual revenue and expense targets for specific company activities. The cost of goods produced, for example, is broken down into the cost of raw materials and supplies, labour, and utilities and facilities.

Master Budget

Global Gizmos Company

REVENUE AND EXPENSES	Next Year	Year After
Budgeted Revenue:		
Gross receipts on sales	£895,000	£970,000
Dividend and interest income	4,000	5,000
Total Revenue Available	**£ 899,000**	**£ 975,000**
Budgeted Expenses:		
Cost of goods produced	£ 600,000	£ 650,000
Raw materials and supplies	250,000	275,000
Labor costs	300,000	325,000
Utilities and facilities	50,000	50,000
Sales, general, and administration	£ 165,000	£ 170,000
Sales and distribution	90,000	95,000
Advertising and promotion	30,000	30,000
Product service	15,000	20,000
Accounting and office support	30,000	30,000
Interest expense	12,500	12,000
Taxes	22,000	24,000
Buildings, equipment, machinery	40,000	£100,000
Equipment and computers	35,000	25,000
Expanded warehouse	5,000	75,000
Development projects	10,000	15,000
New product development	8,000	5,000
New market development	2,000	10,000
Long-term debt reduction	2,500	2,000
Dividend distribution to owners	6,000	7,000
Total Expenses Out	**£ 858,000**	**£ 980,000**
NET CHANGE IN CASH POSITION	**£ 41,000**	**£ -5,000**

Figure 4-2: The master budget looks a lot like the company's projected cash-flow statement.

Capital budgets

Big ticket expenditure – say on a new production line or buying out a competitor – involves spending a large lump sum now in order to get a stream of profits in future years. This activity is known as *capital budgeting* and is carried out separately from the general budgeting activity, before being consolidated into the master budget.

The reason for keeping capital budgeting separate is because some special financial tools are needed to decide whether or not the proposed investment makes sound commercial sense. It's not just a matter of seeing that, say, for an outlay of £100,000 you'll make £150,000 of profit, but when that profit is likely to occur. If most of it is coming in five years' time, it's obviously not worth as much to you as money coming in earlier. The subject of *investment appraisal*, as this area is known, is riddled with terms such as 'discounted cash flow', 'net present value' and 'internal rate of return'. Check out *Understanding Business Accounting For Dummies*, Second Edition, by John A. Tracy and Colin Barrow (Wiley) to get a handle on this subject.

Book II

Sorting Out Your Finances

How budgets are made

Somehow, it's never the right time to sit down and make a budget, because you always have something much more important to do. This situation seems to hold true for household and company budgets alike. Why doesn't anybody like to do them? Often, there doesn't seem to be enough financial information around to make a budget that's of any real use. If you complete a financial forecast first, however, your company's budget is much easier to complete.

So when do you get started? If you're just starting your company, there's no time like the present. If you're already up and running, when you create a budget depends on the company's size. For really big companies, the yearly budget process may begin six to nine months in advance. No wonder that the job can feel a bit like never-ending drudgery! Most companies, however, can count on spending some serious time with their budgets three or four months before the next year gets under way.

Established companies can use their track records and financial histories as starting points for next year's budget. But be careful. When you're a veteran, it's easy to get a bad case of budgetary laziness, using last year's numbers as a shortcut to next year's numbers. Unfortunately, you can veer off financial course before you know it. A good compass for this situation is something called *zero-based budgeting*. When you insist on zero-based budgeting, you ask everybody – including yourself – to go back and start from the bottom in preparing a budget. Rather than use last year's budget numbers, you make full use of your financial forecast, building up a new set of numbers from scratch. The process takes a bit longer but is almost always worthwhile.

The process of making a budget often gets a bad name in the business world. Rather than see budgeting as a helpful business tool, business owners often rank budgeting among the greatest evils on earth, and managers often talk about it in unprintable ways. So what gives? When the budgeting process falls apart in a company, at least one of the following things probably happened:

- ✔ The budget was handed down from above and used to control the company's managers, taking away their ability to influence the business decisions that they were ultimately responsible for carrying out.

- ✔ The budget was based on short-term thinking, ignoring the company's longer-term plans and strategic goals.

- ✔ The budgeted revenue and expense targets had nothing to do with the company's larger financial objectives or its real financial situation.

To make sure that your own company's budget doesn't suffer these fatal flaws, take a close look at two ways to put together a budget.

Top-down budgeting approach

The top-down approach to making your budget is the simplest way to work through your company's financial plans. The process pretty much begins and ends with the people who are in charge. If your company is small, you may want to invite some outside people to join you – people whom you trust, such as your banker, accountant or maybe a close business associate. The process goes something like this:

1. **Put the finishing touches on your company's financial forecast, including pro-forma profit and loss accounts, expected balance sheets, and projected cash-flow statements.**

   If certain pieces are missing or incomplete, try to get the information that you need, or make a note that the document you need is unavailable.

2. **Meet with the company's decision-makers (or your trusted group, if you're self-employed) to review the financial forecast.**

   Take time to discuss general expectations about the future. Talk about the business assumptions that go into the forecast and the key predictions and estimates that come out of it.

3. **Meet again to explore possible financial alternatives.**

   Look at different sets of business assumptions and weigh up their potential effects on the forecast. Continue to meet until the group either agrees or agrees to disagree about the future.

4. **Come up with revenue and expense targets for each of your company's major business activities or functional areas (whichever is more appropriate to your company).**

5. **Meet one last time after the budget is in place to review the numbers and get it approved.**

   Produce a written summary to go with the numbers so that everyone knows what the budget is, where it comes from and what it means.

Top-down budgeting does a fairly good job when you know all the people in your company by their first names, but the approach has some disadvantages when your company gets bigger. By including only the managers at the top, you run the risk of leaving out large chunks of the organisation and losing track of your real business situation when it's time to plug in the numbers.

Bottom-up budgeting approach

The bottom-up approach to creating your budget is an expanded version of the top-down process, taking into account the demands of a bigger company and of more people who have something to say. You still want to begin putting together your budget by getting a group of senior managers together to spend time reaching a general understanding of, and agreement on, your company's financial forecast, along with the business assumptions and expectations for the future that go with it. But rather than forcing a budget from the top, this approach allows you to build the budget up from the bottom.

Don't ask the group of senior managers to go on and dictate the company's budget. At this point in the budget process, the bottom-up approach means that it's time to get managers and supervisors at all levels of the company involved. The process goes like this:

1. **Meet with senior managers and ask them to review the company's broad financial objectives for each of the major business areas.**

   Try to come up with guidelines that set the tone and direction for budget discussions and negotiations throughout the company.

2. **Ask managers to meet with their managers and supervisors at all levels in the organisation.**

   Meetings can start with a recap of the budget guidelines, but discussions should focus on setting revenue and expense targets. After all, these managers are the ones who actually have to achieve the numbers and stay within the spending limits.

3. **Summarise the results of the budget negotiations.**

   If necessary, get the senior group members together again to discuss revisions in the financial objectives, based on the insights, perceptions, and wisdom of the company's entire management team.

4. **Go through the process again, if you have to, so that everyone at every level of the organisation is on board (or at least understands the reasoning behind the budget and its numbers).**

Book II

Sorting Out Your Finances

5. Approve the budget at the top.

Ensure that everybody understands what the budget means, applying the budget to financial objectives and larger business goals.

- Your budget spells out exactly where your company's resources will come from and where they'll go.

- Your budget is based on your projected cash-flow statements.

- Top-down budgeting is done by the top people – owners or senior managers – and works best in small companies.

- Bottom-up budgeting involves all management levels, which can mean more realistic revenue targets and spending limits.

Using ratios to improve your budget

You can use the ratios we looked at in Chapter 2 in this Book to deduce any unknown future costs. Suppose you want to get an idea of what your business phone bill will be in the year for which you are budgeting. If last year the bill represented 1 per cent of sales, you can use that ratio to get a first fix on that item of expense. You can use the same technique across most areas of the budget. So if you know that you usually keep 20 days' stock of your product in the warehouse, just scale up your stock to match the budgeted sales level.

At the template gallery (www.score.org/template_gallery.html) on the SCORE website you can find a downloadable Excel spreadsheet from which you can plan future sales and use ratios to compare performance with previous years.

Analysing variances

Any performance needs to be carefully monitored and compared against the budget as the year proceeds, and you need to take corrective action if you have to, to keep the two consistent. This has to be done on a monthly basis (or using shorter time intervals if required), showing both the company's performance during the month in question and throughout the year so far.

Look at Figure 4-3. You can see at a glance that the business is behind on sales for this month, but ahead on the yearly target. The convention is to put unfavourable variations in brackets. Hence, a higher-than-budgeted sales figure doesn't have brackets, whilst a higher materials cost does. We can see that, whilst profit is running ahead of budget, the profit margin is just behind (–0.30 per cent). This is partly because other direct costs, such as labour and distribution in this example, are running well ahead of budgeting variances.

Figure 4-3:
A fixed budget. Figures are in thousands of pounds. Note that figures rounded up and down to the nearest thousand may affect percentages.

Book II

Sorting Out Your Finances

Heading	Month			Year to date		
	Budget	Actual	Variance	Budget	Actual	Variance
Sales	805*	753	(52)	6,358	7,314	956
Materials	627	567	60	4,942	5,704	(762)
Materials margin	178	186	8	1,416	1,610	194
Direct costs	74	79	(5)	595	689	(94)
Gross profit	104	107	3	820	921	101
Percentage	**12.92**	**14.21**	**1.29**	**12.90**	**12.60**	**(0.30)**

Flexing your budget

A budget is based on a set of sales goals, few of which are likely to be exactly met in practice. Figure 4-3 shows that the business has used £762,000 worth more of materials than budgeted. As more finished product has been sold, this is unsurprising. The way to manage this situation is to flex the budget to show what would be expected to happen to expenses, given the sales that actually occurred. You do this by applying the budget ratios to the data. For example, materials were planned to be 22.11 per cent of sales in the budget. Apply that to the actual month's sales, you arrive at a materials cost of £587,000.

Looking at the flexed budget in Figure 4-4 you can see that the business has spent £19,000 more than expected on the material given the level of sales actually achieved, rather than the £762,000 overspend shown in the fixed budget. The same principle holds for other direct costs, which appear to be running £94,000 over budget for the year. When we take into account the extra sales shown in the flexed budget, we can see that the company has actually spent £4,000 over budget on direct costs. Whilst this is serious, it's not as serious as the fixed budget suggests. The flexed budget allows you to concentrate your efforts on dealing with true variances in performance.

Figure 4-4:
A flexed budget. Figures are in thousands of pounds – note that figures rounded up and down to the nearest thousand may affect percentages.

Heading	Month			Year to date		
	Budget	Actual	Variance	Budget	Actual	Variance
Sales	753*	753	–	7,314	7,314	–
Materials	587	567	20	5,685	5,704	(19)
Materials margin	166	186	20	1,629	1,610	(19)
Direct costs	69	79	(10)	685	689	(4)
Gross profit	97	107	10	944	921	(23)
Percentage	**12.92**	**14.21**	**1.29**	**12.90**	**12.60**	**(0.30)**

Book III
Finding and Managing Staff

'Being a pretty boy, being able to peel grapes and being a good talker with flying experience would have made you the perfect cabin steward but it would have saved us <u>both</u> a lot of time if you'd sent in a photograph, Mr Joseph.'

Book III

Finding and

In this book . . .

Finding and keeping the best people is a challenge for any business, but this book gets you off to a flying start. As well as keeping your staff happy, you need to treat them fairly and abide by employment law, and this book navigates you through the basics. In addition to this vital information, we offer tips on developing your staff within their roles and inspiring them to greater achievements in the workplace.

Here are the contents of Book III at a glance:

Chapter 1

Staying on the Right Side of the Law

As a small business employer or in the management level of a small company, you may feel that staying on top of the law is just too much hassle. As long as you don't do anything blatantly illegal, everyone should be content. After all, you've got a business to run and you have to make a living. While that's true, if you get on the wrong side of the law the results can be devastating. You can end up seriously out of pocket because a tribunal or court finds in favour of a disgruntled, or even worse a seriously injured, employee and awards large amounts of compensation against you. Tribunals can award anything from a very basic amount up to a maximum of £56,800 in unfair dismissal cases. But if they decide that you've discriminated against someone when you've dismissed him or made him redundant there's no cap on the amount of compensation they can award. If they find that you didn't follow, to the letter, all the new dismissal and disciplinary procedures that came into force in October 2004 they can increase the compensation they order you to pay and there's no upper limit in the case of a workplace accident or illness claim. Many small businesses can't recover from that kind of a blow.

But it isn't only the financial penalties that can be seriously damaging. When a dispute or an accident occurs in the workplace it affects everyone, not merely the employee directly involved. People lose trust in an employer if they see that things aren't run properly and safely, or if the employer has no real respect for workers' rights.

Employers frequently struggle to find suitable employees or have to train applicants from scratch. You can't afford to lose employees because they have no confidence in the way your business is run. It costs a lot of money to recruit staff and train them. The more often people leave, the more time you spend fire-fighting instead of improving performance and increasing productivity.

Small business owners are always worried about the amount of legislation that applies to them. There are a lot of laws, regulations and codes of best practice out there, and staying on the right side of the law can be a tough job. Knowing what the law says before setting up a business or before employing your first member of staff is important, and if you start out with all the information you need, it's not as difficult or expensive to apply the law as you go along – and take it into consideration each time you make a business decision. Changing your habits later on can be much trickier.

Good employment practices encourage good employee–boss relationships. In turn that breeds loyalty and staff stay. People who are loyal work better. They have the interests of your business at heart because you have their interests at heart. Everyone's a winner.

Cutting Through the Red Tape

'Red tape' is a term that conjures up images of bad regulations, strangling your business and making your life more difficult. Commentators sometimes blame the employment laws in the United Kingdom for putting too heavy a burden on business owners, but they're really intended to protect employees from bad employers, not from good ones. These laws also help employers protect themselves.

The law isn't a burden to good employers who want to do right by their employees; it's a source of clear guidance that helps you to keep employees instead of losing them to better employers. When hard workers with the skills you need seem hard to find, your business's success depends on your reputation as a desirable employer; rather than seeing the law as just so much red tape, think of it as a guide to becoming that kind of desirable employer.

Business people most often cite the National Minimum Wage and family friendly legislation about maternity, paternity and parental leave as causing them difficulties. Yet motivated employees who feel fairly paid and who know they can take the time needed to take care of family matters can increase your company's productivity, so it's well worth your investment in sound policies.

Perhaps the biggest problem is that the legislation relating to small businesses is scattered around so many acts and regulations that keeping a grip on them can be difficult. Some acts, like the Data Protection Act or the Regulation of Investigatory Powers Act 2000, have such a wide scope that it's easy to forget that they can apply to small businesses and their employees. The headache isn't always so much the red tape as pulling it all together and knowing exactly what it means for your business.

Working Out What the Law Expects from You

Working out what the law expects from you can sometimes be quite demanding. Most employers wait until something has gone wrong or an employee has taken legal advice and made a claim against them before checking out where they stand legally. But forewarned is forearmed when it comes to small businesses and the law. If you're setting up a business or about to take on your first employee, this is the time to get advice on your legal position. If you already employ people and you haven't put a lot of thought into the legalities of your situation, take the time now to find out what your obligations and responsibilities are as an employer. It makes good business sense and will stop you making costly mistakes in the future.

Employees, whether full-time or part-time – apart from those who are exempt and as long as they've been employed by you for the relevant qualifying period – have employment rights including the following:

- ✔ National Minimum Wage
- ✔ Maximum weekly working hours (with breaks)
- ✔ Equal pay for equal work
- ✔ Four weeks' paid holiday (at least)
- ✔ Protection from discrimination
- ✔ A safe working environment
- ✔ Notice that their employment is ending (after one month)
- ✔ Written Statement of Employment Particulars (within the first eight weeks)
- ✔ Statutory sick pay and statutory maternity, paternity and adoption pay
- ✔ Maternity, paternity and adoption leave

✔ Parental leave and time off for family emergencies

✔ To request flexible working arrangements

✔ Protection from unfair dismissal (after one year)

✔ Redundancy pay (after two years)

Phew, that's quite a list – but this book covers all these aspects.

If employees are unfairly treated and denied their employment rights, they can make a claim against you at an Employment Tribunal or in some cases in the civil courts. If you break the law, you can face prosecution in the criminal courts by an enforcing body such as the Health and Safety Executive.

In most cases the legislation is reasonably clear, but some areas of employment law are governed by common law. *Common law* is the body of law that builds up as cases are heard in court and judges make their decisions, as opposed to *statutory law* which is passed by parliament.

Going the Extra Distance

Whatever the law says is just the start. You can go further and offer your workers better terms and conditions than the law demands. You can follow various codes of practice which will help you to not merely to comply with the law but to go further. For example, the code on monitoring employees at work will not only help you comply with the Data Protection Act but following it will also help you to gain your employees' trust. ACAS – the Advisory, Conciliation and Arbitration Service – produces useful codes of practice on issues such as the dismissal and disciplinary procedures which came into force in October 2004. You absolutely must comply with these if you're disciplining, dismissing or making someone redundant. Contact ACAS on 08457-474747 or through the website – acas.org.uk. Business Link will also point you in the right direction – their website www.businesslink.gov.uk has links to other organisations and departments which produce useful codes of practice.

Putting company policies in place dealing with workplace issues that don't come under the scope of legislation is a good idea. For example, you may decide to add a policy on the use of email and the Internet. That's not a legal requirement but that way everyone knows up front whether employees can use company facilities for personal reasons.

None of this preparation costs much in terms of cash outlay, but planning, writing and distributing policies does take time. However once you've brought yourself up to date with the law, implemented the codes of practice and drawn up your policies, all employees know where they stand, and staying on the right side of the law becomes second nature to your company's culture.

Deciding Who Has Rights

The people who work for you may not all have the same employment rights. Employees have different rights to people who work for you on a self-employed basis. Some rights are acquired by working for you for a particular length of time. Some are automatic no matter how long a person has worked for you and if you try to deny him those rights you'll automatically be in the wrong. Some people who do particular types of work are excluded from rights that other people working in different jobs automatically have. Other rights apply to everyone who works in your workplace regardless of their status. Even people who don't work for you yet but have applied for jobs have some rights (see Chapter 2 in this Book on recruiting employees).

Potentially confusing? This section provides some definitions to help you navigate your way as your read through this book.

Employees

Employees work for you under a contract of employment. They include apprentices. It's all fairly clear-cut where a written document exists labelled 'contract of employment' or *Written Statement of Employment Particulars* (see Chapter 3). Problems arise when nothing is in writing and the worker argues that he's an employee and the employer argues that he's self-employed.

Employees start off from day one of your employment with some employment rights. Some of those rights are set out by law (known as *statutory rights*) and others are rights you give your employees through their contract terms and conditions (known as *contractual rights*). A contract exists as soon as you make an offer of employment and the employee accepts it, so anything in that contract stands and can't be changed without his agreement or you may be in breach of contract.

An employee has statutory rights from day one, such as the right to be paid at least the National Minimum Wage, the right not to be discriminated against, and the right to a healthy and safe environment to work in. The right to paid holidays starts to build up from day one and the regulations on working hours and breaks apply. Employees have to be given a Written Statement of Employment Particulars by the time they've been with you for eight weeks If you try to deny an employee his statutory rights and sack him for asking for them, you've dismissed him unfairly in the eyes of the law.

You also give your employees rights through their contracts. You can give people better terms and conditions than the law allows – longer holidays, better rights to sickness pay, better redundancy payments – but you can't give them less than the law says. If you do offer better terms in the contract, you have to deliver or you're in breach of contract and the employee can make a claim against you.

Book III

Finding and Managing Staff

If a contract is for a particular length of time – for example for three months – the employee has all the same rights as any other employee for those three months, but doesn't acquire the other rights that build up over time (such as maternity or paternity leave or redundancy payments).

Be careful if you go on extending someone's employment on short-term contracts: continuous employment for a year, or for two years, may allow an employee to argue at a tribunal that he has acquired rights, such as those to claim unfair dismissal (one year) and redundancy pay (two years) over that period of time.

Full time

A *full-time employee* is someone who works the normal working hours for your business. *Small Business Employment Law For Dummies* (Wiley) details the rules about the maximum number of hours someone can be expected to work in a week and the breaks you must give him, but all your full-time employees are entitled to all the statutory employment rights unless you work in certain employment sectors (see the section 'Exemptions', later in this chapter).

Part-time

Anyone who works fewer than the normal number of full-time hours in your business is a *part-time employee*. Part-time employees have all the same statutory rights as full-timers and they can't be treated less favourably just because they don't work the same number of hours. Some employers try to give part-time employees less favourable conditions through their contracts – perhaps a lower hourly rate of pay – but you have to be careful not to discriminate.

You must pay part-time workers on a pro-rata basis. *Pro-rata pay* means that if they work half the hours of a full-time person you need to pay them the same amount per hour for half the hours. You need to give them equal rates of pay, overtime pay, holiday pay, and the same rights in their contracts to training, career breaks, sick pay, maternity pay and paternity pay. Similarly, if you offer full-time employees the right to join a company pension scheme and refuse your part time employees this scheme, you can be judged to be discriminating.

Self-employed

Someone who works for you on a self-employed basis isn't an employee and doesn't enjoy the same rights as an employee. However, not everyone who works for you on what you may consider to be a self-employed basis is in reality self-employed. Some employers hire people on a self-employed basis in order to avoid giving them employment rights, but if a dispute arises and the worker takes a case to a tribunal, the tribunal may find that he has been an employee all along.

Someone who is genuinely self-employed works under a contract for service rather than a contract of employment. You're contracting that person to provide services. He is genuinely self-employed if some or all of the following apply; if he:

✔ Can send someone else along in his place to do the work

✔ Can work for more than one business at the same time

✔ Can work as and when he's required

✔ Provides his own tools or equipment to do the job

✔ Pays his own support staff if he needs any

✔ Is responsible for his own profits and loss

Employers sometimes see proof of self-employed status in the fact that workers pay their own tax, National Insurance and VAT, don't get sickness pay, paid holiday or regular wages, and don't come under the firm's disciplinary procedures. Those factors do count, but if those are the only factors that can be used to prove self-employment, a tribunal may decide that the relationship is really one of employer and employee and that you're just trying to avoid employment legislation.

Book III

Finding and Managing Staff

People who are brought in as genuinely self-employed to do some work for you may not qualify for the same employment rights as your employees, but if they are working on your premises they have the right to a healthy and safe working environment (see *Small Business Employment Law For Dummies* (Wiley) for more on this) and they have the right to have information about them treated properly and fairly under the Data Protection Act.

Consultants

Consultants working in your workplace are usually either self-employed or employees of other companies. If you take them on under a contract of employment on a temporary basis, they become employees. If their firms send them to deliver consultancy services under a contract for services, their employers should take steps to ensure that yours is a healthy and safe environment for them to work in, but you have the same obligations as for other self-employed workers.

Agency workers

Companies often employ temporary workers through agencies. This saves you having to go through lengthy recruitment procedures to employ someone for a short time. These workers have a contract with the agency and the agency has a contract with you. In this case, the agency pays the worker direct and you pay the agency for delivering the service. The contract you have with the agency isn't an employment contract, so the worker isn't your employee.

However, it's not quite that straightforward. Over a period of time it's possible for a relationship to develop where something like a contract of employment exists between you and the agency temp, even if only in implied terms. If you insist that the agency can't send someone else along instead, if the person can't work for anyone else, if you supply all the tools and equipment, include the temp at your staff meetings, more or less treat him like one of your employees, and most importantly have control of the worker on the day-to-day supervision of his work, a tribunal can decide that he is in reality an employee. A recent Court of Appeal case decided that once an agency worker has more than one year's service with a single 'end-user' employer they are almost bound to be the employer of the worker and other cases have followed suit. If you need to keep him on for longer than originally anticipated, offering him a job as an employee is a good idea.

A whole range of EU regulations giving workers protection have effectively given agency workers rights to paid holidays, rest breaks, minimum wages, maximum working hours and protection from being treated less favourably if they are part time. The Secretary of State can extend individual employment rights to groups of people who aren't covered by current employment law, so it's likely that all workers, other than the ones who are genuinely self-employed, will eventually have the same protection as employees.

Home workers

If people work in their own homes they'll be employees unless they're genuinely self-employed. If you have an obligation to provide them with work, they can't pass that work on to someone else, you supply the tools and equipment, and they can't work under more than one contract for different employers at the same time, they are likely to be considered employees.

Exemptions

There are exceptions to every rule and some employees aren't entitled to all employment rights. Police, share fishermen and merchant seamen employed wholly outside the UK and who aren't ordinarily resident in the UK have no right to claim unfair dismissal or statutory redundancy pay. People who work for government departments can't claim statutory redundancy pay or minimum periods of notice. Members of the armed forces have no statutory employment rights other than the right not to be discriminated against. Temporary and casual workers won't usually be able to claim unfair dismissal or redundancy pay because they won't work for an employer long enough to acquire those rights.

The law doesn't protect people working under illegal contracts. If someone is, for example, paid cash in hand to avoid paying income tax and National Insurance, he has no employment rights. Anyone who is employed to do something illegal won't be protected either. The principle is that a wrong-doer mustn't benefit from his wrong-doing.

New age discrimination laws came into effect in October 2006, so the best advice is to be very careful about treating your older workers less favourably than your younger ones. Of course you won't be able to discriminate against younger workers either.

Young people

From the age of 18, workers are entitled to the National Minimum Wage of £4.10 an hour (£4.25 from October 2005), which goes up to £4.85 an hour (£5.05 from October 2005) when they're 22. And you have to pay 16- and 17-year-olds a National Minimum Wage of £3 per hour, although apprentices under 19 are exempt. Anyone aged 16 and 17 may be entitled to time off with pay to study and you may be expected to help with those costs. You can take on someone under the age of 24 on an apprenticeship scheme. The Learning and Skills Council website has the details – www.lsc.gov.uk.

You can't employ a child under 13. The only exception is for child actors. Strict rules govern the hours that 13- to 16-year-olds are allowed to work: they can't work, paid or unpaid, before 7 a.m. and after 7 p.m. They can't work more than two hours on a school day or a Sunday and they can't work more than 12 hours a week during term time. In the school holidays 13- and 14-year-olds can work up to 25 hours a week and over-15s can do 35 hours. Rules also exist about breaks and time off. Some local authorities have other rules about school-age children working, so check with them before you take any young people onto your books.

Once they are over school leaving age and up to the age of 18, the Children and Young Persons Act still protects young people and they can't work more than 8 hours a day or 40 hours a week. Their breaks are clearly set out too.

Book III

Finding and Managing Staff

Deciding What to Put in the Contract

Employees have statutory rights and you can't do anything that takes away those rights. When it comes to the contract you can offer more generous terms and conditions of employment, but you can't write in clauses that take away the statutory rights.

Employees are entitled to a *Written Statement of Employment Particulars* within eight weeks of starting work. That should include all the main terms and conditions of their employment or refer employees to other relevant written documents.

Drawing Up Other Employment Policies

Your policies on pay, working hours, holidays, sickness absence, maternity, paternity and adoption leave should all be covered in the Written Statement of Employment Particulars. Apart from those and the terms that form part of the contract whether in writing or not, there are also policies for running your business that the law says you have to have and there may be others that would help everyone be clear about where they stand.

Some working parents have the legal right to request flexible working patterns and you may want to extend these to your whole work force.

You must have written policies on disciplinary procedures, grievance procedures, health and safety, and discrimination including dealing with bullying, harassment and victimisation (see *Small Business Employment Law For Dummies* for more details on all of these matters).

You may also want to consider drawing up policies on the use of alcohol and drugs, telephone, email and the Internet, smoking and even dress codes.

Your policies should all be in writing and you should make sure all your employees are aware of them and can have access to them at any time. They set the standards for everyone to aspire to and everyone knows exactly where they are from the start.

Managing Without an HR Department

Big firms usually have special departments employing human resources specialists to ensure they stay on the right side of the law, respond to all the government's latest demands on flexibility, and draw up policies that make everyone aware of how the workplace should operate. Most small businesses don't, but that doesn't prevent good small business bosses getting it right. Many of the small businesses that do get it right are no bigger than yours and have no more facilities, no bigger turnover, and no more profit. They have the systems in place right from the start to help them make sure they are complying with the law and good practice has become part of the culture. Each time a change in the law comes along that can pile on the pressure, little change is required because they're most of the way there already.

You don't need an HR or personnel department if everyone in the workplace knows exactly where they stand and everyone knows who is in charge of what. The person who pays the staff knows the legislation on pay and making deductions from pay, and deals with sick and maternity or paternity pay. Someone else looks after the workplace, making sure that you don't break the health and safety regulations. It gets harder when it's just you who has to know everything about everything and make sure you don't break the law. However, it's still a question of putting the systems in place right from the start and building the business around them, instead of grafting on the means of complying with each piece of legislation as you find out about it.

Getting Help and Advice

You need good sources of information and some way of keeping up to date with changes as they come along the pipeline.

Most big banks provide very useful information on all aspects of running a business. Your solicitor and accountant, if you have them, will be helpful, but don't take petty problems to them as you have to pay for their time and there may be more cost-effective ways of getting help and support. Make sure any solicitor and accountant you use are experienced in dealing with small businesses. Big businesses are quite different animals and experience of working with big firms doesn't qualify people to work with small ones.

The government runs Business Links around the country, with offices in most big towns and cities and advisers with a whole range of business expertise. The service is free and can give you advice, guidance and support on everything to do with setting up and running a business, including how to deal with all aspects of employees' rights. Business Link also has a very comprehensive website where you can get most of the information you need (www.businesslink.gov.uk). Nevertheless, websites can't always give you the necessary support. You can get details of the nearest office to you on the website or in the local telephone directory or call 0845-6009006.

The Department for Business, Innovation and Skills (BIS) website also has lots of useful information for employers: www.bis.gov.uk

ACAS (the Advisory, Conciliation and Arbitration Service) is an invaluable source of help to business. Its helpline number is 0845-7474747 and the website is www.acas.org.uk.

The Federation of Small Businesses is a group you may want to join. It has 185,000 members with 1.25 million employees between them. For an annual subscription of between £100 and £750 depending on how many employees you have, you get various services, including access to the legal helpline where you can talk to an adviser about any legal problems you have, including all aspects of employment law. The organisation lobbies government on issues of concern to small businesses, so as well as helping you stay on the right side of the law, the Federation can give you a voice. Call 01253-336000 or check out the website at www.fsb.org.uk.

Chapter 2

Finding Person Friday – Advertising and Interviewing

As a small business manager, situations arise requiring you to find new members of staff. Whether you're looking to take on your first ever assistant, hoping to replace a worker who's left the business, or are expanding and need an extra pair of hands, you need to get the recruitment process correct. Good recruitment practice should bring in good candidates, and ultimately benefits your business.

But first things first! Do you really need to take on a new member of staff? It costs time and money to employ someone new, so take a careful look at how you staff your business at the moment. Be sure that you really need another person, or to replace someone who's left, before you start advertising. Also make sure that the person you advertise for is really the employee you need – if you're replacing someone who has left, think about why she left and the skills she had that you need to replace.

Before heading down an external advertising route, consider promoting current employees, or find out if any of your part-time workers would like full-time jobs, or if anyone would appreciate the chance to do some overtime. Something as simple as changing working hours – allowing some people to start earlier and others to finish later – may be enough to get the work done without recruiting. It has the added benefit of giving your existing employees flexible working patterns.

Filling the Gap

Work out the skills that your new recruit should have and what her job will really involve. Think about whether you need someone permanent or someone to see you through a temporary period of increased workload. Maybe you don't really need another full-time person. Can a part-timer do the job? For many small businesses, part-timers are the answer when it comes to filling the gaps. They have all the same rights as full-time employees, but being part-time allows many people to work and still fulfil their family or caring obligations when working full-time isn't an option. That gives you a wider pool of experienced and skilled people to recruit from.

If the job you have to offer is full-time, think about job sharing. As the name suggests, job sharing means that two (or more) people in effect share one job. They may split the week, work alternate weeks or alternate days, or some of their hours may overlap, but they do one job between them and share the pay and benefits of a full-time job. It can cost you a bit more in terms of training and admin, but job sharing can benefit you in a number of ways. Job sharing:

✔ Enables you to keep on experienced people who can't continue working full-time but who still want to be employed.

✔ Gives you more flexibility if you have peaks and troughs in demand.

✔ Means one job sharer is around when the other is on holiday or off sick, and because they have more control over their hours, job sharers usually have less time off sick and suffer less from stress.

You need to choose people to job share who get on well together, which is never an exact science! They should have complementary skills and experience. Make sure that they divide the work fairly, that they have a way of communicating if they rarely see each other, and that each doesn't end up doing less or more than the hours you're paying them for.

Other methods of employment can be useful to know about. You can consider having people who work for you in term time and don't work during the school holidays. Or you can employ people on contracts where they're available as and when you need them and you pay them for the work they do (called *zero-hours contracts* because you don't specify any particular number of hours). Or you can recruit people temporarily as and when you need them to see you over periods of increased production.

You also have to think carefully about how much you can afford to pay any new employees. Pay has a bearing on whether or not you can afford to look for someone better qualified than a person who has left, or whether you can afford to entice someone from outside the area (which can be expensive in terms of relocation expenses).

Don't forget the obvious factors like space and desks. If you're replacing someone and can use her old workspace that's fine, but adding an extra employee to the workforce means you need somewhere for her to work without leaving everyone else squashed and being in danger of breaching health and safety regulations.

Getting It Right from the Start

Getting your recruitment procedure right is crucial for the success of any business. If you hire the wrong person – someone with the wrong skills, someone who can't do the job, or someone who isn't competent and puts your other employees under stress or at risk – your whole operation is in danger of falling apart. At best working relationships become strained and at worst you start losing good employees or good customers or both. Don't waste time and money taking on the wrong person. And don't forget that certain aspects of employment law such as the laws on discrimination (see Chapter 3 of this Book) apply to people during the recruitment process, before they ever work for you.

Deciding on full- or part-timers

One important decision you need to make early on is whether you need to hire a full-time person. Some very good reasons may exist for not doing so. If, for example, the demand for your products is highly seasonal and has major peaks and troughs, keeping people on during slack periods may make no sense. This may be the case if you're selling heating oil, where you can expect demand to peak in the autumn and tail off in the late spring because of variations in the weather. Other examples of seasonal fluctuations are increased sales of garden furniture and barbeques in summer, and toys and luxury items before Christmas.

Using part-timers can open up whole new markets of job applicants, sometimes of a higher quality than you may expect on the general job market. Highly skilled and experienced retired workers, or women who've given up successful careers to have a family, can be tempted back into temporary or part-time work. You may sometimes be able to have two members of staff sharing one job, each working part-time. You can also use this tactic to retain key staff members who want to leave full-time employment. This makes for continuity in the work, allows people to fit in their job around their personal circumstances and brings to the business talents that it may lose if it insists on full-time work.

Part-time work is more prevalent than many people think. Up to a third of all those in employment in some countries are working part-time and most of those are working in small firms whose flexibility in this area can often be a key strength over larger firms when it comes to recruiting and retaining employees.

You can find part-time staff using the same methods as for full-time employees, which I discuss in the next sections.

Coming up with the job description

Having put a lot of thought into the kind of job or person you need, write a job description. No law says you have to have one, but it's a valuable exercise that helps you to define very clearly the job you want done. When you send the job description to potential applicants they can see exactly what they are applying for. A *job description* should:

- ✔ Give the job title
- ✔ Explain where the job fits into the overall structure – who the applicant will report to and who she will be responsible for
- ✔ Say where she will be expected to work
- ✔ Give all the duties she will be expected to carry out and the objectives of the job

As well as putting the details of the job on paper you can draw up a *person specification* of the kind of applicant you're looking for. You need to be careful when you're doing this: it's against the law even at this stage to discriminate against certain people (see *Small Business Employment Law For Dummies* for more details about discrimination). If specific skills, qualifications, and experience are required in order to do the job, you can list those. You can then list the qualities that you'd like the applicant to have that aren't essential for the job, but make it clear what's essential and what isn't.

When writing a person specification, don't put down things that exclude a whole set of people from applying if that quality isn't essential. For example, if you don't need someone with 10 years' experience, by putting it in the specification you rule out all those who can do the job but have less experience. Don't discriminate, but equally don't reduce the pool of people you receive applications from or you may not get the best candidates.

Advertising – what you can and can't say

Writing a job description and a person specification makes writing an ad easier. You can say anything in your ad as long as it isn't discriminatory.

If you say in a job ad that you want a man for the job, but in reality it's not absolutely essential, you're discriminating against women. But if you really do need a man (or woman) because it is a 'genuine occupational requirement', you're not discriminating. If, for instance, you run a shop selling women's clothes and you need someone who can help women in the changing-room, being female will be a requirement of the job.

Don't use words like waitress or manageress. Even if you'll take on a man or a woman, it looks as if you intend to take just women and therefore discriminate against men. Use words that apply to both sexes or make it clear in the ad that the job is open to both sexes.

You can't discriminate against anyone on the grounds of age, race, sex, religion or other beliefs, sexual orientation, or disability. You can find out more about the code on The Department for Work and Pensions website (www.dwp.gov.uk/age-positive/). You also can't refuse to appoint someone because they belong to a union or won't join a union.

In certain instances, you can advertise for someone solely from a particular sex or race. If in the last year, for example, few men or black people have been working in your particular field and you want to get a better representation in your workforce, you can encourage them to apply through your ads. But because the discrimination laws are a minefield, it's advisable to take advice from an organisation like the Equality and Human Rights Commission at www.equalityhumanrights.com or 0845-604-6610.

Placing your ads

Your ad needs to be to the point, but give enough information to allow people to decide whether or not to apply. Good job ads list:

- Essential skills required
- Relevant experience desired
- Necessary qualifications
- Application processes – where to send a CV or who to contact for an application form
- The job title and an outline of the tasks involved
- The closing date for applications

Where you decide to advertise depends on the audience you want to reach. If you're just looking for someone who lives locally, try the local papers (including any free ones that get put through letterboxes), local radio, schools or universities, and your local newsagent's noticeboard. If you know that you're likely to have to go further afield to get the skills you need, think about the national papers.

Don't forget the trade press and magazines that people who work in your industry read. More employers are now using the Internet to reach a wider audience quickly. If you go into a search engine and type in 'job vacancies' you can see that there are many websites that carry job ads: www.jobsearch. co.uk; www.jobsin.co.uk or www.fish4jobs.co.uk to name just three. Some websites like www.reed.co.uk will carry job ads for free. If you want to attract people with disabilities, Jobcentre Plus offices are useful, but other options such as the Talking Newspaper Association are also available. You can contact them on 01435-866102 or at www.tnauk.org.uk. Think about making job descriptions available in large print or on tape for people with visual impairments or in different languages for applicants whose first language isn't English.

The wider you advertise, the more applications, CVs, phone calls and emails you're likely to get. Make sure that someone's available to deal with enquiries, send out forms and collate all the applications.

Using an agency

Employment agencies can advertise on your behalf and can provide lists of possible candidates for you to look at. You have to pay a fee for an agency's services, so find out what they charge before you decide which agency to use.

Many agencies specialise in particular areas of work. These types of agencies can save you a lot of time, but they can also be very expensive.

You can recruit people through an agency on a temporary basis, meaning that the agency employs them rather than you – so the agency looks after their pay, tax and National Insurance. This system enables you to try people out on a temporary basis before deciding whether to employ them yourself permanently. Using an agency also means that your business name doesn't have to be included in the advertising if you'd rather it didn't. Of course, if the agency can't find you anyone suitable you're back to square one and have lost valuable time, but you don't usually have to pay a fee in these circumstances. Just be aware that if you take on agency workers for more than a year, an Employment Tribunal may decide you've become their employer even if they're described as being self-employed by the agency or by themselves. For more on agency workers see Chapter 1 in this Book.

Alternatively you can employ a firm of recruitment consultants to take you through the whole recruitment process from deciding on your person specification, to interviewing, to making a final choice. A recruitment consultancy differs from an employment agency in that the agency offers you the pick of people registered on its books and a recruitment consultancy charges a fee to do the job of recruiting for you. If the job is a very important one within your organisation you can use a firm of *headhunters* who actively look for the very best person on your behalf. They tend to be very specialised and because they know a lot about their industry, they know where to look for people already working at the level you require.

Recruiting over the Internet

The fastest-growing route to finding new job applicants is via the Internet. The number of websites offering employment opportunities has exploded in recent years. The advantages of Internet recruitment to both candidates and clients are obvious. Internet recruitment offers a fast, immediate and cheap service compared to more traditional methods of recruitment. A number of recruitment sites have established formidable reputations in Europe and the US. These include:

- ✔ **Futurestep** (www.futurestep.com), which covers all job functions and industry sectors.

- ✔ **Monster** (www.monster.co.uk), which attracts approximately 100,000 visits per month and contains over a million curricula vitae. Its vacancies cover every industry sector and regional area.

- ✔ **Web Recruit** (www.webrecruit.co.uk), which offers to fill your vacancy through its online service for £6595, or give you your money back.

Another option is to have a job-listing section on your own website. This is absolutely free, although you're certain to be trawling in a very small pool. This may not matter if the right sort of people are already visiting your site. At least they know something about your products and services before they apply.

Using the Jobcentre

You get a similar service from Jobcentre Plus as from an employment agency (see the previous section 'Using an agency') but it doesn't cost you anything. You can advertise your job and get help from one of the vacancy managers. Advertising in the Jobcentre Plus can be a quick way to find new employees and you can arrange to take someone on, on a trial basis, before you offer them a permanent job. The people who use the Jobcentre are actively looking for work and often ready to start work straight away. If you employ someone through Jobcentre Plus you employ them and pay their salary direct to them, whereas if you recruit through an agency the person you take on may not be your employee, but paid by the agency (see the section 'Agency Workers' in Chapter 1 of this Book).

Another advantage of using Jobcentre Plus is the advice the centre offers not only on recruitment but on just about every other aspect of employment, including help with employing people with disabilities.

The centres also run the *New Deal* scheme. Through New Deal you can get financial help if you take on a new employee and train them. Employers have been put off in the past because they felt that it was only people who were unemployed and therefore unemployable who went to Jobcentres to look for work, but as unemployment rates have fallen the people who use them are more often already employed and looking for better opportunities. You can find information on the New Deal and details of your local office at www.job centreplus.gov.uk or in the telephone directory.

Following up recommendations – and remembering to be fair!

Finding someone suitable to fill your vacancy can be as simple as asking around! Talk to your existing employees and colleagues, other people working in the area or industry, friends, family, or local business people and organisations. How successful this method is usually depends on the level of expertise you're looking for. You may find someone if you're looking for a receptionist, but you may not if you're looking for a highly experienced financial director. It's certainly well worth thinking about as part of your recruitment plan, but you may be seen as trying to poach other people's employees. Also, if you rely on word of mouth alone you're limiting the pool of potential applicants to people who know people you know.

Considering Diversity

More and more businesses are realising the advantages of having members of staff of different racial and cultural backgrounds, ages, genders, sexual orientation or religious beliefs, and those with disabilities. Customers and suppliers appreciate being able to do business with a diverse workforce that reflects the community around it and it may improve your reputation. If you spread your net more widely when recruiting you're likely to have more applicants to choose from, with different experiences, knowledge and skills, and your employees from varied backgrounds can help you understand your customers better. Some customers, for example, may prefer to deal with older people because they feel that older staff are more experienced and understand their needs better. If you only have young people on your staff, those customers may well take their custom elsewhere.

Think carefully about having an equal opportunities policy. If you do face a claim for discrimination, an Employment Tribunal will ask to see that policy. Use these guidelines to help prevent discrimination:

- Make sure that you don't exclude any one group when you write your job ad and job descriptions.

- Think about where you advertise. You may have to advertise in a wider range of publications than you've done in the past in order to get to all the people you'd like to reach.

- Make sure that people with disabilities who apply for jobs with you are able to get to interviews, and have access to your premises – otherwise you risk falling foul of the Disability Discrimination Act and the Equality Act 2010 that has substantially replaced it (see www.equalities.gov. uk/equality_act_2010.aspx).

Sorting the Wheat from the Chaff – CVs and Application Forms

You need to decide how to extract the information from your candidates' applications in order to decide which ones to interview. Application forms and CVs both have their advantages and disadvantages, outlined in Table 2-1 for application forms and Table 2-2 for CVs.

Book III

Finding and Managing Staff

Table 2-1	The Pros and Cons of Application Forms
Pros	**Cons**
You can decide exactly what you want to find out from your applicants, and can design the form yourself or buy ones from stationery suppliers.	You need to put a lot of thought into how the forms are designed and they need to be easy to fill in, or some people will be put off applying.
Every applicant fills in the same form so it's easy to compare skills, experience and qualifications.	You have all the effort and cost of producing them and sending them out.
Some people feel happier about filling in a form as it gives them a guide as to what information is needed.	You have to be careful not to ask discriminatory questions.

Table 2-2	The Pros and Cons of CVs
Pros	*Cons*
The way a CV and covering letter are laid out will tell you something about the applicant's abilities.	You have no control over the information that's included in an individual's CV.
You don't have any of the costs of production, design or sending them out.	All CVs have different information and layouts, so they're harder to compare.
People are more likely to apply if they don't have to fill in a form.	Applicants can easily hide work gaps.

Some employers prefer to use application forms that allow them to remove the personal information. This takes away the temptation not to see anyone over a certain age or who is of a particular sex or ethnic background. They then use just the parts of the forms that refer to skills, experience and qualification when deciding who to interview, preventing bias or discrimination against a candidate when drawing up their shortlist. That's harder to do with CVs.

Whichever you decide to use, you're likely to get a better response in terms of the information people give you if you send them a copy of the job description and the person specification. Doing so gives applicants a much clearer idea than an ad can of what the job entails and of whether they've got a chance of getting it.

If people lie on CVs or application forms about their qualifications or experience and you offer them a job, you can later withdraw the offer or dismiss them if you rumble them. Make it clear that you'll check all their claims.

Under the Data Protection Act the personal information you collect about individuals has to be used for the recruitment process only. Only those people involved in the recruitment process should have access to it: you can't pass it on to anyone else without the applicant's consent and it should be kept confidential and in a secure place so it doesn't fall into the wrong hands.

Drawing up your shortlist

After you've got all the applications in, you need to decide who to interview. Decide how many people you have time to interview (allowing 45 minutes to an hour is about right), and come up with a shortlist of that number. Five or six candidates is usually enough.

Whittle the applications down to the number on your shortlist by using this process:

1. **List all the candidates and work out how well they fit your person specification and the job description.** Some applicants probably won't have the qualifications you need so you can reject them straight away.

2. **Give the rest a tick or a number of points for how well they meet each of the essential requirements to do the job.** If you do use a points system, make sure that you apply it equally fairly to all the applicants.

3. **Check to see if you now have the right number for your shortlist.** If you still have too many people in the running, look at how well each one of those who have the essentials match the other qualities you'd like your new employee to have.

If you take personal information into consideration, be very careful. Having more than one person involved in the shortlisting process is a smart move because it helps avoid any personal bias on your part. For example, many employers still fall into the trap of thinking that men who have children won't want to ask for time off to look after them but that women will, and make biased decisions on that basis. One employer was sued after a candidate submitted the same CV twice – once using an Indian name, the other time using an English name. The application with the English name was shortlisted for interview and the one with the Indian name wasn't. Be fair.

Dealing with the ones that don't make the shortlist

Book III

Finding and Managing Staff

Write to the applicants you don't want to interview so that they aren't kept hanging on, hoping. Thank them for their interest. If any of them do contact you to ask why they didn't get an interview, simply explain that other applicants were better suited to the job because they had more relevant qualifications, skills or experience. Don't go down the route of saying that people were too old or too young or that they didn't have skills that you didn't specifically ask for in the job description or person specification.

Handling the Practicalities of Interviews

After deciding who's on your shortlist, invite them for an interview. However you contact the shortlisted candidates, it's wise to confirm the details in writing.

Include the following information with your invitation:

- ✔ Where the interview takes place
- ✔ When the interview takes place
- ✔ How long the interview will be

✔ Whether any tests or presentations are required and whether the person will complete them at the time of the interview or during a separate appointment

✔ Details of anything the candidates need to bring with them

✔ Details of who will be on the interview panel

✔ Who to ask for when they arrive

✔ How to get to the interview (with a map)

✔ Details of travel expenses

Also give the candidates a person to contact with any questions before the interview if they have problems getting there at the time you've given them or if they have any information they'd like you to know in advance (such as needing a car parking space close to the building because of a disability).

Making flexible appointments

The fun starts when everyone on your shortlist phones up to ask for a different date or time to the one you've allotted. Remember that you do need to hire someone suitable – these few candidates are your best chance so try to be as flexible as possible. Think before you allocate the times: if you're interviewing in Glasgow and someone is coming from Glossop, either allow time for her to get there and back in a day for an interview at a reasonable hour, or offer to put her up overnight in Glasgow. Similarly, there may be people on the list who have caring responsibilities first thing in the morning. In fact, some people may have applied and not told their current employer that they have an interview, so be prepared to start or finish later or earlier, to fit them in before or after work. Don't let a request for a later start immediately set alarm bells ringing about bad timekeeping. Keep an open mind.

Making sure everyone can get into the building

When you invite people for interview, ask them to let you know if they have any special needs. Someone may be a wheelchair-user, for example. You aren't expected to take out walls or build ramps, but be prepared to make reasonable adjustments so that the interview can take place without the candidate being in any way embarrassed or discriminated against. That can be something as simple as making sure someone gives up their car parking space for a few hours so that the candidate can park close to the main entrance. It may mean moving the interview from a room on the first floor to one on the ground floor, or making arrangements to use a room somewhere away from your work premises.

If you do have to move the venue for one interviewee, move the venue for them all in order to avoid any embarrassment or confusion.

Paying for expenses

You don't have to pay for travel expenses. If your applicants are all from your local area, the issue probably won't arise. If they're coming from further afield and you don't cover expenses, you run the risk that your best applicants may not be able to afford the journey. After you've selected your shortlist, look at where people are in the country. If you decide that you probably do need to cover some people's costs, it's better to offer to pay everyone's expenses.

Planning the Interviews

Employers often give little thought to either the process building up to the interview or how to conduct the interview itself. You're spending time and money to recruit someone, so preparing for the interview is well worth doing so that you can be sure to get the best out of it.

You'll be gaining first impressions of the people you interview, but they'll also be gaining first impressions of you. If you don't seem very well organised they may decide there and then that they don't want to work for you.

Work out who, apart from yourself, should be on the interviewing panel. As a small business owner or manager you may decide to do the interviewing yourself, but it usually helps to have at least one other person's opinion. Two heads are normally better than one. Consider involving some of the following people on your interview panel:

- ✔ If you have business partners or management colleagues, see if one of them is available to help.
- ✔ If the new employee will report directly to someone other than you, consider involving that manager.
- ✔ If you have a human resources or personnel department, enlist their help.
- ✔ If you've used a recruitment agency to help find candidates, try to involve the agency in the interviews.
- ✔ If the job requires a particular skill, invite a relevant member of staff onto the panel, to assess the level of that skill for each candidate.

It really helps if everyone involved in the interview knows the candidates' application forms or CVs reasonably well and has them available at the interview. You can use this information to come up with the list of questions you want to ask. If there are any unexplained mysteries about gaps in employment, you may want to ask the candidate about those.

Decide how long you realistically need for each interview and leave some time afterwards to discuss each candidate with the other people on your interview panel. The length of the interview is important for the candidates as well as for you. You need time to extract the information you want and the interviewees need to feel they've had time to get their points across. So 45 minutes to an hour is usually enough, although you may want to set aside extra time for specific tests.

Working out what to ask

The essential skills, qualifications and expertise to do the job are the most important issues to concentrate on at an interview. Asking good questions should get you good answers in return. Prepare the kinds of questions that don't invite a 'yes' or 'no' answer. Other questions will arise as the interview goes on, depending on what the candidate has to say.

Start by introducing everyone on the panel, explaining a little bit about your business and its structure and where the job fits into that. Outline how the interview will be conducted. That allows time for the interviewees to get settled. Give each interviewee a chance to ask you any questions they have at the end and explain what happens next.

Be very wary of asking personal questions. You can't ask women about their child-care arrangements and not ask men the same questions – unless you want to end up being sued for discrimination. Only ask questions that are relevant to the job: asking about whether someone is married or not or has children may be used against you later. Questions about disability have to be carefully worded too. You have to discuss how you can help someone with a disability to do the job you're offering rather than talk about why it would stop them doing the job. You can't use a disability as a reason not to employ someone unless it's justified. A person who is seriously visually impaired may not be able to drive your forklift truck, but if the job you're trying to fill is an office job, her visual impairment may not rule her out. If she can do the job as long as you make reasonable adjustments around your workplace, then you have to ignore the disability.

Don't make any rash promises during an interview – if you offer an interviewee the job there and then with a package that includes all sorts of benefits (such as a company car) and she accepts your offer, you can't then change the offer later if you realise you can't afford it.

Setting tests

If a job requires a very particular skill you may want to conduct some kind of test of that skill as part of the interview process – for example a typing or shorthand test or a forklift driving test. *Psychometric tests* (measuring intelligence, decision-making and problem-solving skills, aptitude and personality) are popular, especially when it's difficult to compare every candidate's skills and experience. If you do decide to include any tests, they must be relevant to the job and not discriminatory.

Tests can be done during, after or before the interview, but you need to use them as part of the selection process rather than as the one and only method of choosing the best person for the job.

Taking notes

After each interview, write notes of key information, otherwise you may mix up important points. Only record what was said in the interview. Stick to the facts.

To make accurate notes as soon as possible, build into the interviewing time breaks where you can discuss the candidates and compare notes with fellow interviewers. Otherwise, by the end of a day, remembering which candidate said what can become tricky!

After the interviews are finished, you may want to add notes that explain the criteria you used to select the eventual winner. The candidates have the right to see interview notes and may ask to see them if you don't offer them the job and they plan to bring a case against you at a tribunal for discrimination.

After the interviewing is over, only keep personal information if it's relevant to the selection process, and keep the notes and personal information somewhere safe where they can't fall into other people's hands.

Checking Up on Your Chosen One

After going through the selection process and picking your best candidate, you can carry out a few checks before making the job offer, or you can make the job offer conditional on all your checks being satisfactory. Some checks are essential, others are your choice, as explained in this section.

When making your checks on the candidate:

- ✔ Only do checks that are necessary and for specific purposes.
- ✔ Do checks only for the candidates you want to appoint.
- ✔ Let people know you're going to do checks beforehand and whom you're checking with.
- ✔ Don't use information that doesn't come from reliable sources.
- ✔ If the checks throw up something negative, give the person the chance to explain.
- ✔ Make sure that the information you get is kept confidential and secure.

Following up references

You can take up references at any point during the recruitment process, but don't forget that most candidates will probably prefer you not to contact their current employers unless you're making them a firm job offer. You can't contact referees without a candidate's agreement, and previous employers don't have to give references unless they work in the financial services sector.

Despite the fact that many employers complain that they've had good references for employees who later turned out to be a disaster, most bosses do still use referees to check out a candidate's details.

You can insist on referees' details being given and make a job offer conditional on getting satisfactory references but an outside chance remains that if the references aren't satisfactory, or someone refuses to give one, and you do withdraw the job offer, you can still be sued for breach of contract.

When asking for references, you're using personal information supplied to you on application forms and CVs. Under the Data Protection Act you have to keep that information confidential. Get the applicant's permission before you follow up references. You can have a section on the application form that you ask applicants to sign to give their consent and that makes it clear you'll be using the information they've given you.

Employers have to tell it as it is. If they do agree to give a reference it has to be truthful. If you later find that someone exaggerated an applicant's skills and you lose out because of that, you can sue the referee. Similarly, employees can make claims against employers who give them references that they feel unfairly damage their careers. The upshot is that many big organisations will now only give references confirming the very basic facts such as length of employment and job title. If you don't get the references you want, think about offering the job on a trial basis.

Proving that potential staff are entitled to work in the UK

All your employees have to be entitled to work in the UK and you have to check that they are. It's a criminal offence to employ anyone 16 or over who doesn't have permission to work in the UK or to do the type of work you're employing them for. You can be fined up to £5,000. The rules are very complicated, so check up with the UK Border Agency on its website (www.ukba.homeoffice.gov.uk/employers/).

Check and keep a record of the documents you used to confirm that someone is entitled to work before employing her. If you've made your checks and kept copies of the documents used, and done all you can to make sure that the person who showed you the documents was the person they rightfully belonged to, you'll have a good defence if it later turns out that she wasn't telling the truth.

Checking convictions

If the job you're offering involves working with children or adults who are vulnerable – disabled or elderly, you must check convictions with The Criminal Records Bureau (CRB) (www.crb.homeoffice.gov.uk). Only make these checks if you've decided to offer someone the job, and make the offer conditional on getting a satisfactory result. Some legal and financial jobs require these checks too.

Book III

Finding and Managing Staff

Two types of conviction checks may be made:

- ✔ **A standard disclosure.** This tells you whether the candidate has any cautions, warnings, or reprimands and any spent or unspent convictions.

- ✔ **An enhanced disclosure.** This tells you all the same information plus information from local police forces such as regarding acquittals.

If the job involves child care you can also ask on the Criminal Records Bureau application form whether someone is on the Government's lists of people considered unsuitable for that kind of work.

Convictions are *spent* if someone was convicted of a crime and had no further convictions during her rehabilitation period. Treat someone with spent convictions as if those convictions had never happened. If the person was in prison for more than 30 months because of a conviction, it can never be spent.

Checking health

Some employers insist on a potential employee having a medical examination before starting the job. If that's the case, make it clear when you make the job offer that you want a satisfactory medical report to show that the candidate is fit to do the job and that if she refuses or the results aren't satisfactory the job offer won't stand. Other employers ask for a health questionnaire to be filled in, which, if it does throw up problems, can be followed up with a medical.

Only insist on health checks if you're sure that you want to take someone on. Don't insist that someone with a disability has a medical if you wouldn't insist on someone else having the same checks, or you'll be guilty of discriminating. Checks should really only be necessary if there's a legal requirement, such as an eye test for someone doing a driving job.

Some employers worry that candidates may be drug users and insist on health checks for that reason. If the employee may be at risk if her judgement is impaired due to drug use or she may put other employees at risk, tests can be justified. Make it clear when you make the job offer that drug use would rule the candidate out as being unfit to do the job and that relevant tests would be part of the medical.

Candidates have the right to refuse a health check; you have to have their written consent before you ask a doctor to do a medical report. If her own doctor does the examination, a potential employee has a right to see the report and can refuse to let you see it even though you have to pay the doctor's fee. Of course, you have the ultimate sanction in that if you insist on a satisfactory medical report and don't get it, you can decide not to take the person on.

Checking qualifications

If a qualification is essential for the job, check it! You can make a job offer that's conditional on that check being positive. You can ask for certificates, or check with colleges, universities or any other professional organisations or examining boards.

Experian offers a service for checking out degrees (www.uk.experian. com), the Qualifications and Curriculum Authority has a database of vocational qualifications (www.qca.org.uk), the Learning and Skills Council can help you check on National Vocational Qualifications (www.lsc.gov.uk), and the National Academic Recognition Information Centre can check overseas qualifications (www.naric.org.uk).

Offering a Job to Your Dream Candidate

As soon as you make an offer – whether it's over the phone, by email, or by letter – and the candidate has accepted it, a contract exists between you and your new employee.

In theory you don't have to put anything in writing at this stage. The law says that an employee has to be given a Written Statement of Particulars of Employment not later than eight weeks after she starts employment with you.

If you don't really want to appoint any of the candidates or you don't feel any are right, don't appoint anyone. Get a temp in to tide you over and start looking again. Better this than giving the job to the wrong person.

Making an offer that can't be refused

After finding the right candidate, you have to discuss money. You may have mentioned ball-park figures during the interview, but now it's time to make an offer and negotiate a deal that suits both you and the employee.

Think about the whole package you're prepared to offer. You may have already thought this through when you were considering employing someone in the first place. You can attract good employees with contributions to an occupational pension scheme, use of a company car, or better holiday and sick pay than most employers. Sometimes it's not just money that matters to employees. Your chosen candidate may be happy to settle for the money you're offering as long as she has a few extra days of holiday or flexible hours of work. Discuss and negotiate and come up with a package she can't refuse. Don't forget that if she's moving from a job outside the area she may have the costs of selling a home and buying another, plus the costs of moving.

After an agreement has been reached, put the whole deal in a follow-up letter with the main terms and conditions of employment. It makes things easier for everybody and allows no cause for dispute.

Setting the start date

You may want your new employee to start straight away, but unless she's already out of work that's not likely to be possible. Most people have to give their bosses at least a week's notice and many have contracts that stipulate much longer notice periods. She isn't likely to be willing to hand in her notice

Book III

Finding and Managing Staff

while there are conditions to the offer and she may well want an unconditional offer, with all the main terms and conditions, in writing, before she takes that final step. She may be able to negotiate that her current boss lets her go sooner than the contract allows, but think about how you'd feel if one of your employees wanted to go without working out her notice.

Withdrawing a job offer

After the job offer has been made and accepted, a contract exists. If you made it conditional on getting satisfactory checks and the results weren't what you'd hoped for, you can withdraw your offer. However, if you made the offer conditional on satisfactory references and you don't get them and withdraw the offer, you can be sued for breach of contract.

If you just change your mind after making an offer or you made promises of terms and conditions that you later find you can't deliver, the employee can sue you for breach of contract and damages. Someone who has been unemployed would find it difficult to claim damages, but someone who gives up a good job and starts to make arrangements to move homes can run up quite a lot of expenses and have quite a sizeable claim.

You can offer the job on a trial basis for a particular period of time – long enough to find out if the chosen candidate is really up to the job. If you then decide to withdraw the job offer at the end of that time, you have to give the employee the correct period of notice or extend the trial period and provide some training. If you withdraw the job offer after a trial period but you don't come up with the training you promised at the outset, the employee can sue for breach of contract.

Dealing with requests for feedback

At some stage, you're going to disappoint someone by your decision not to appoint her and she may want to talk to you about why. Tell her what it was that gave the winning candidate the edge and discuss anything the rejected candidate can do better next time. Stick to the facts, such as that the person you've appointed had more experience or better qualifications. Suggest training courses that may make the person you've turned down more suitable next time. And be impressed that she's keen, really wanted the job, and felt that feedback from you can help her progress in her career. She may be exactly the right person for the job next time!

Chapter 3

Employing People Successfully

In This Chapter

▶ Deciding on motivations and rewards

▶ Keeping on the right side of employment law

*U*nless you intend working on your own, when running a business you're involved in employing and motivating others to do what you want them to do. Even if you don't employ people full-time, or if you out-source some portion of your work to others, you have to choose who to give those tasks to, how to get the best out of people and how to reward their achievements.

Motivating and Rewarding Employees

After you've recruited the staff you want, you need to manage them in the most suitable way for your business. Management is the art and science of getting people to do what you want them to do because *they* want to do it. This is easier said than done.

Most entrepreneurs believe that their employees work for money and their key staff work for more money. Pay them enough and they'll jump through any hoop. In contrast, most research ranks pay as third or even fourth in the reasons for people coming to work.

If they don't necessarily work for money, why do people work in a particular organisation? We help provide some of the answers in the following sections.

Getting the best out of employees

The best advice for getting the best out of your employees is: get to know everyone. This may sound insane in a small firm – after all, you almost certainly recruited them all in the first place. By observing and listening to your employees you can motivate them by making them feel special.

The starting point in getting people to give of their best is to assess them as individuals and to recognise their specific needs and motivations. A person's age, gender or job influences these differences, as does the individual's personality. You need to tailor your actions to each person to get the best results.

Some practical tools and techniques can help you get the most out of your employees.

- **Show an interest in people's work.** This has nothing to do with monitoring performance and more to do with managing by walking about, seeing everyone and talking with them as often as possible.

 If you employ fewer than five people you need to spend some time with each of them every day; if up to ten people, spend time with them every week. After that, you need to have managers doing much the same thing, but you still need to get around as often as possible.

- **Give praise as often as you can.** The rule is simple: minimise your reaction to bad results and maximise your appreciation of good results. Autocratic employers continually criticise and complain, finding only poor performance wherever they look. Criticism reinforces poor behaviour. Everyone wants to be recognised and strangely enough people often prefer to be shouted at than ignored. So if doing things wrong is the only way to get noticed in your company, that's what may well happen.

 If you do need to criticise, keep it constructive and lighten it with some favourable comment. For example, if an employee is making some progress but is short of being satisfactory, saying something like, 'This is certainly an improvement, but we still have a way to go. Let's spend a little time together and I'll see whether we can't get to the bottom of what's holding you back', may produce a better level of motivation than just shouting out your criticism.

- **Create a no-blame culture.** Everything in business is a risk. To a greater or lesser extent, you delegate some of the responsibility for taking risks to your employees. But how should you react when the inevitable happens and things go wrong? If you jump up and down with rage, then no one will ever take a risk again. They'll leave all the decisions to you and you'll become even more overworked. Good people will get highly demotivated and leave. If you take a sympathetic and constructive attitude to failure, you motivate and encourage employees to try again.

You need to make it clear that tolerance of mistakes has its limits and that repetition of the same mistake won't receive an equally tolerant reaction.

✔ **Reduce demotivation.** Very often the problem isn't so much motivating people, but avoiding demotivating them! If you can keep off employees' backs they're more likely to motivate themselves. After all, most people want the same things – a sense of achievement or challenge, recognition of their efforts, an interesting and varied job, opportunities for responsibility, advancement and job growth.

Dealing with difficult or demotivated employees

Difficult or demotivated people need prompt and effective managing. Dissatisfaction can spread quickly and lower other people's motivation levels. The first step is to identify the causes of the problem – is it to do with the employee or with the job itself? The problem may be brought about by illness, stress or a personality clash between people working together.

Whatever the cause, the initiative for remotivating an employee has to come from you. However, the only reason for going through this effort is that either the employee has delivered satisfactory results in the past or you believe he has the potential to do so, if you can only find the key.

Book III

Finding and Managing Staff

Keeping motivation in the family

Over 80 per cent of small businesses are family businesses in which one or more relatives work in the organisation. Family businesses have both strengths and weaknesses when it comes to motivation. By being aware of them you can exploit the former and do your best to overcome the latter to give your business a better chance of prospering.

The factors that motivate or demotivate family members can be different to those affecting non-family members.

The overwhelming strength of a family business is its different atmosphere and feel. A sense of belonging and common purpose usually leads to good motivation and performance. Another advantage is that a family firm has greater flexibility, because the unity of management and shareholders provides the opportunity to make quick decisions and to implement rapid change if necessary. On the downside, several weaknesses exist. Although these weaknesses aren't unique to family businesses, family firms are particularly prone to them.

✔ **Unwillingness to change is the single most common cause of low motivation in family firms.** Family firms often do things the way they've always done them just because that's the way they've always done them. This can lead to stagnation in the marketplace and failing confidence in investors. Resistance to change is exacerbated by diminishing vitality, as the founders grow old.

✔ **Family goals and commercial goals can come into conflict.** Unlike other businesses, family firms have additional objectives to their financial performance targets, such as building family reputation and status in the community; providing employment for the family; protecting family wealth; ensuring independence; and a dynastic wish to pass on a position, in addition to wealth, to the next generation. However, superimposing these family values on the business can lead to difficulties. For example, nepotism may lead to employment of family members at a level beyond their competence, or a salary above their worth. This can lead to discontent and be demotivational for non-family members.

✔ **Conflict may exist between growth and ownership.** Families prefer majority ownership of a small company to minority holdings in a big company where they're answerable to outside shareholders. A dilemma that all family managers face is either growing the company, keeping purely commercial goals in mind at whatever risk to family control, or subordinating the firm's welfare to family constraints. This affects all areas of the business, from recruitment through to management.

✔ **The impact and career prospects of non-family employees may be limited.** At management level family pride sometimes doesn't allow a situation where its members are subordinate to an outsider – even if the outsider is a better person for the job. Also, reliance on family management to the exclusion of input from outsiders may starve a growing firm of new ideas. A family firm may become inward-looking, insensitive to the messages of the marketplace, unreceptive to outside ideas and unwilling to recruit competent outside managers. None of these factors is likely to be motivational to others in the business.

A family firm must address these problems to avoid all the effort it puts into motivating employees being seen as a cynical deception. Having a clear statement of family policy on the employment of family members, succession and ownership can be helpful. Then non-family members can either buy into this policy or not join the company in the first place.

Rewarding achievements

Different types of work have different measurable outcomes. You need to identify the outcomes you want and arrive at a scale showing the base rate of pay and payment above that base for achieving particular objectives. Different types of 'payment by results' schemes are in common use and to make sure you pick the right mix of goals and rewards, examine carefully the conditions that most favour these types of pay.

Setting pay scales

People don't come to work just for money, but they certainly won't come if you don't pay them, and they won't stay and be motivated to give of their best if you don't give them the right pay. But how much is the right amount? Get it too low and you impair your ability to attract and retain productive and reliable people capable of growing as your business grows. But pay too much and your overheads rise so high that you become uncompetitive. Small firms face the very real danger of a wage bill that represents their largest single business expense.

The ground rules for pay aren't very complicated but they are important:

- ✔ Pay only what you can afford. Don't sink the company with a wage bill that it can't meet.

- ✔ Make sure that pay is fair and equitable and that everyone sees it as such.

- ✔ Make sure that people know how you arrive at your pay scales.

- ✔ See that pay scales for different jobs reflect the relative importance of the job and the skills required.

- ✔ Ensure that your pay scales are in line with the law on minimum wage requirements. The UK has a *statutory minimum wage*, the amount of which is governed by the age of the employee and whether an employee is undergoing training. The hourly rate changes over time, so you need to keep abreast of the latest rates (www.hmrc.gov.uk/nmw has information on current rules in this area).

- ✔ Ensure that your pay scales are competitive with those of other employers in your region or industry. PayScale (www.payscale.com/hr/default) is a site where you can get accurate real-time information on pay scales.

Ways to find out the going rate for a job include:

- ✔ Reading articles on pay, as well as job advertisements on the Internet, in local papers and in the relevant trade journals. You may have to correct some pay rates to allow for variations. For example, pay rates for similar jobs are often much higher in or near major cities than they are in rural areas.

- ✔ Talking to your chamber of commerce or trade association, some of which publish salary surveys, and to other local employers and business owners in your network.

✔ Contacting employment agencies, including those run by the Government. They're usually a bit ahead of the rest of the market in terms of pay information. Other employers know only what they're paying their present staff. Recruitment agencies know what you have to pay to get your next employee.

Deciding the pay rates of people who work for you arbitrarily may appear to be one of the perks of working for yourself. But inconsistent pay rates quickly upset people and staff members tend to jump ship at the first opportunity.

Matching pay to performance

You may want to add to people's salaries by rewarding them with money or benefits for the level of performance they achieve. We discuss various reward approaches in this section, which all follow the same ground rules for matching pay to performance:

✔ Make the rules clear so that everyone knows how the reward system works.

✔ Make the goals to be achieved specific and if possible quantifiable.

✔ Make the reward visible so that everyone knows what each person or team receives.

✔ Make the reward matter. It has to be worthwhile and commensurate with the effort involved.

✔ Make the reward fair, so that people believe it's correctly calculated.

✔ Make the goals realistic, because if you set the target too high no one will try to achieve it.

✔ Make the reward happen quickly.

Paying a commission

This is perhaps the easiest reward system, but it really only works for those directly involved in selling. A *commission* is a payment based in some way on the value of sales that the individual or team concerned has secured.

You have to make sure that the order is actually delivered or executed before you pay any commission and you may even want to make sure that the customer has paid up. However, as with all rewards, you must keep the timescale between doing the work and getting the reward as short as practicably possible, otherwise people forget what the money is for.

Base the commission on your gross profit (the value of sales less the cost of generating those sales) rather than your sales turnover – otherwise you can end up rewarding salespeople for generating unprofitable business.

Awarding bonuses

A *bonus* is a reward for successful performance, usually paid in a lump sum related as closely as possible to the results that an individual, team or the business as a whole has obtained. In general, bonuses are tied to results, so how an individual contributed directly to the result achieved is less obvious. For example, a company bonus may be paid to everyone if the firm as a whole achieves a certain level of output. Keeping everyone informed about how the firm is performing towards achieving that goal may well be motivational, but the exact role that, say, a cleaner or office worker has in helping to attain that goal isn't easy to assess – not as easy as it is to calculate a salesperson's commission.

You can pay bonuses periodically or as a one-off payment for a specific achievement.

Sharing profits

Profit-sharing involves giving a specific share of the company's profit to its employees. The share of the profits can be different for different jobs, length of service or seniority.

This type of reward has the great merit of focusing everyone's attention on the firm's primary economic goal – to make money. One or more employees can be performing well while others drag down the overall performance. In theory, in such circumstances the high-performing staff put pressure on the others to come up to the mark.

If profits go up, people get more; but profits can also go down, which can be less attractive. Also, the business can miss profit targets for reasons outside of employees' direct control. If your company depends on customers or supplies from overseas, for example, and the exchange rate moves against you, profits, and hence profit-related pay, can dip sharply. However unfair this may seem to a receptionist who's been hoping for extra cash to pay for a holiday, this is the hard reality of business. If you think your employees are adult enough to take that fact on board, then profit sharing can be a useful way to reward staff.

Sharing ownership

Share option schemes give employees the chance to share in the increase in value of a company's shares as it grows and prospers.

The attraction of turning employees into shareholders is that doing so gives them a long-term stake in the business, hopefully makes them look beyond short-term issues and ensures their long-term loyalty. Of course, unwelcome side effects can occur if the value of the business goes down rather than up. Share schemes also have some important tax implications that you need to take into account. You can find out all about these on the HM Revenue and Customs website (www.hmrc.gov.uk/shareschemes).

Giving skill and competence awards

You can give a skill or competence award when an employee reaches a certain level of ability. These awards aren't directly tied to an output such as improved performance, but you must believe that raising the skill or competence in question ultimately leads to better business results.

The award itself can be cash, gift certificates, extra days of holiday, a trip to a show or sports event, or whatever else your employees may appreciate. Bottles of wine always seem to be well received!

Creating a menu of benefits

A *benefit* is defined as any form of compensation that's not part of an employee's basic pay and isn't tied directly to his performance in his job. Non-salary benefits such as a pension or changes in working conditions can also play a part in keeping people on your side.

A wide range of other perks is on offer to employees, ranging from being allowed to wear casual dress to on-site child care. Other benefits available in some organisations include personal development training, company product discounts, flexible hours, telecommuting and fitness facilities.

It's now obligatory to consider flexible working if an employee requests it and has sufficient reason, and setting up some form of pension scheme looks set to become compulsory for most businesses soon.

Staying on the Right Side of Employment Law

All businesses operate within a legal framework, whose elements the owner-manager must be aware of. The areas we cover in the following sections summarise only a few of the key legal issues. Different types of business may have to consider different legal issues and employment law itself is dynamic and subject to revision and change.

The Advisory, Conciliation and Arbitration Service (ACAS; www.acas.org.uk) and the British Safety Council (www.britishsafetycouncil.org) are useful organisations that can help with aspects of employment issues. Emplaw (www.emplaw.co.uk) is a website covering basic British employment law information and can direct you to a lawyer in your area who specialises in the aspect of employment law you're concerned with.

Keeping employment records

You need to keep records about your employees, both individually and collectively. Keeping proper records makes the process of employing people run more smoothly. Some of the data you need to keep is a legal requirement, such as information on accidents. Some of the information is also invaluable in any dispute with an employee, for example in a case of unfair dismissal.

The individual employee information you retain should include:

✔ Application form

✔ Interview record and results of any selection tests used

✔ Job history, including details of promotions and assignments

✔ Current and past job descriptions

✔ Current pay and bonus details and a record of the amount and date of any changes

✔ Details of skills and competences

✔ Education and training records, with details of courses attended

✔ Details of performance assessments and appraisals

✔ Absence, lateness, accident, medical and disciplinary records, together with details of any formal warnings and suspensions

✔ Holiday entitlement

✔ Pension contribution data

✔ Termination record, giving date, details of exit interview and suitability for re-engagement

✔ Copies of any correspondence between you and the employee

Collective information should include:

✔ Numbers of staff, grades and job titles

✔ Absenteeism, staff turnover and lateness statistics

✔ Accident rates

✔ Records on age and length of service

✔ Wage and salary structures

✔ Employee costs

✔ Overtime statistics showing hours worked and costs

Book III

Finding and Managing Staff

- ✔ Records of grievances and disputes
- ✔ Training records showing how many person-days have been devoted to training and how much that's cost
- ✔ Gender, ethnic and disability profiles

Employees have three basic rights over the information an employer keeps in their employment records:

- ✔ To be able to obtain access to their personal data
- ✔ To be able to claim damages for losses caused by the use of inaccurate data or the unauthorised use of data, or by the loss or destruction of data
- ✔ To apply to the courts if necessary for rectification or erasure of inaccurate data

This means that an employee is entitled to gain access to his personal data at reasonable intervals and without undue delay or expense. This request must legally be put in writing, although you may choose not to insist on this, and you must provide the information within 40 days of the request.

Preparing contracts of employment

You have to give an employee a written statement of certain terms and conditions of his employment within two months of his starting working for you.

The list of terms that form part of this statement include the following:

- ✔ The employee's full name
- ✔ When the employee started working for you
- ✔ How and how much you pay your employee
- ✔ Whether pay is weekly or monthly
- ✔ The hours you expect the employee to work
- ✔ The number of days' holiday the employee is allowed, including public holidays, and how that holiday is accumulated
- ✔ The employee's job title or a brief description of his work
- ✔ Where you expect the employee to work and what conditions apply if you expect him to work elsewhere
- ✔ Whether you intend the employment to be permanent or, if it's for a fixed term, when it starts and finishes
- ✔ Details of who manages the employee and whom he can talk to if he has any dispute with that person

✔ Any terms and conditions relating to sickness or injury, including any provision for sick pay

✔ Any terms and conditions relating to pensions and pension schemes

✔ Any disciplinary rules applicable to the employee

✔ The period of notice required, which increases with length of service; a legal minimum of one week's notice per year of service is required up to a maximum of 12 weeks (express terms in the contract may override this)

The job description forms the cornerstone of the contract of employment that exists between employer and employee. However, the contract is rarely a single document and may not even be completely documented. A contract comes into existence as soon as someone accepts an offer of paid employment, even if both offer and acceptance are only verbal. In practice, the most important contractual document may be the letter offering the person the job, and detailing the salary and other basic employment conditions. Many employers don't document the contractual relationship with employees properly and end up with disputes. A contract of employment consists of four sets of terms:

✔ **Express terms:** Terms specifically agreed to between employer and employee, whether in writing or not.

✔ **Implied terms:** Terms considered to be so obvious that they don't need spelling out. These include such matters as the employee complying with reasonable instructions and taking care of business property and equipment. For the employer these can include taking reasonable care of the employee and paying him for work done.

✔ **Incorporated terms:** Terms from outside sources, most commonly from trade union agreements, which are included in the contract.

✔ **Statutory terms:** These include any work requirements laid down by law – safety regulations, for example.

Book III

Finding and Managing Staff

The Business Link website has information on everything you need to meet your obligations as an employer when it comes to taking on staff (www. businesslink.gov.uk; go to Employment and Skills, then Becoming an Employer, and then Taking on a New Employee).

Working legal hours

Although the owner of a business may be content to work all hours, the law strictly governs the amount of time employees can be asked to put in. The Working Time Regulations apply to any staff over the minimum school-leaving age. This includes temporary workers, home workers and people working for you overseas.

As an employer, you must keep records that show you comply with the working-time limits and that you've given night workers the opportunity for a health assessment.

The Directgov website has information on everything you need regarding working hours (www.direct.gov.uk; click on Employment, then Employment Terms and Conditions, and then Working Hours).

Granting leave

Occasions are bound to arise when you're obliged to give your staff time off work other than their usual holidays or when they're unwell. You have to meet statutory obligations of course. Otherwise you may not have to pay them when these occasions occur, but you do have to respect their right to be absent for compassionate or sickness reasons. And if they are off sick, always meet up with them when they return, just to make sure that all is well and that there are not any underlying problems.

Protecting parents

Employees who become parents either naturally or by adopting a child are entitled to paid time off and other benefits, including Statutory Maternity, Paternity and Adoption Pay. The employee may also be entitled to have his job back at some later date.

Work Smart, a Trade Union Council-run website, has a full description of the latest rules and regulations on these ever-changing topics. (Go to www.worksmart.org.uk, click on Your Rights and then Working Life and Family-friendly Policies.)

Recognising emergency leave

Employees have the right to reasonable unpaid leave where their *dependants* – spouses, children, parents, other people living in an employee's house (except lodgers) and others who rely on an employee in emergencies, such as elderly neighbours – are affected by:

- Illness, injury, assault or childbirth
- Breakdown in child-care/other care arrangements
- The consequences of a death
- A serious incident at school or during school hours

To take this leave, your employee should give notice as soon as reasonably practical, giving the reason for, and likely duration of, his absence. The legislation doesn't define *reasonable* time off, but usually one or two days should suffice.

Avoiding discrimination

By and large business owners can employ whoever they want. However, when setting the criteria for a particular job or promotion, discriminating on the grounds of sex, race, age, marital status, religious beliefs, sexual orientation or union membership is usually illegal. Regulations also prevent part-time employees from being treated less favourably than comparable full-time employees – that is, someone doing broadly similar work and with a similar level of skills and qualifications. The Emplaw website (www.emplaw.co.uk) has a free area covering the current regulations in British employment law, and also details on how you can find a lawyer in your area who specialises in the aspect of employment law you're concerned with.

Discrimination starts right from when vacancies are advertised – you can't include such phrases as 'women required' or 'young person sought', or 'no blacks' or 'no whites'. It extends to the pay, training and promotion of those who work for you.

Victimising someone who's complained about being discriminated against is illegal. Sexual harassment is also a form of discrimination, defined as the 'unwanted conduct of a sexual nature or other conduct based on sex affecting the dignity of men and women at work'. This can include unwelcome physical, verbal or non-verbal conduct. Finally, it's unfair to include in your reason for dismissing an employee that he's a member of a particular minority group protected by law.

To avoid discriminating in your employment, you need to ensure that all your policies and procedures meet the following criteria:

- ✔ They're applied equally to all who work for you irrespective of sex, race and so forth.

- ✔ They don't limit the proportion of one group who comply compared with another.

- ✔ They don't disadvantage any individual.

- ✔ They can be objectively justified. For example, no argument exists when being a man or a woman is a genuine occupational qualification – for example, for the purpose of a particular photographic modelling assignment or an acting role. The same is true when you have a part-time vacancy so have no need of a full-time employee.

To make sure that you're not discriminating at work, follow this six-point checklist:

- ✔ Ensure that your business has an equal opportunities policy.

- ✔ Train staff in equal opportunities policies.

- ✔ Keep records of interviews showing why you rejected candidates.

> ✔ Ensure that you take complaints about discrimination seriously, fully investigate them and address any problems that emerge.
>
> ✔ Conduct staff surveys to help determine where discrimination may exist within your business.
>
> ✔ Examine the payroll – pay should reflect employees' job titles, not their gender.

Keeping the work environment healthy and safe

By law you have to provide a reasonably safe and healthy environment for your employees, visitors and members of the general public who may be affected by what you do. This applies to both the premises you work from and the work itself. An inspector has the right to enter your premises to examine it and enforce legal requirements if your standards fall short in any way.

When you have employees you must take some or all of the following measures, depending on the number of people you employ. However, a prudent employer should take all these measures whether or not the law requires them. Doing so sets a standard of behaviour that's common in the very best firms.

> ✔ Inform the organisation responsible for health and safety at work for your business of where you are and what you do. For most small businesses this is the Environmental Health Department of your local authority (you can find contact details in your local telephone directory). The Health and Safety Executive website (www.hse.gov.uk) has a section devoted to small firms, covering both regulations and advice on making your work environment safer.
>
> ✔ Get employer's liability insurance to cover you for any physical injury or disease your employees may suffer as a result of their work. The amount of coverage must be at least £2 million and the insurance certificate must be displayed at all your places of work.

You, as an employer, can in turn expect your employees:

> ✔ To take reasonable care of their own health, safety at work and of other people who may be affected by their acts or omissions.
>
> ✔ To co-operate with the employer in ensuring that the requirements imposed by the relevant statutory provisions are complied with.

Chapter 4

Disciplining and Dismissing Staff

. . . .

In This Chapter

▶ Implementing a disciplinary procedure

▶ Getting rid of employees – the correct way

▶ Avoiding wrongful or constructive dismissal

▶ Understanding what happens if you do get dismissals wrong

. . . .

*S*acking people isn't a nice job, but sometimes you're left with no other choice. If the job an employee has been doing no longer needs to be done and you have no other job that's suitable, you can make that member of staff redundant but if you want to dismiss an employee for another reason and her job still exists, you have to be sure of your standing and tread very carefully through the legal minefield of dismissal.

The Dispute Resolution Regulations that came into force in October 2004 substantially changed the way employers have to deal with disputes and disciplinary and grievance procedures. An employer who dismisses someone and gets those procedures wrong can have a case brought against them at an Employment Tribunal. They'll be found to have unfairly dismissed the employee, and as a result they can be ordered to pay greatly increased compensation. Don't think you can ignore the rules and procedures. More and more cases are being brought against employers who simply don't know the law has changed.

Most importantly, the reason for the dismissal has to be fair; the way you dismiss also has to be fair and you have to follow all the right procedures. This chapter helps you to work out what's fair and what's not, and begins by taking a look at your disciplinary options *before* deciding to sack a member of staff.

Resolving Disputes

Firing an employee really should be the very last option you consider. If a member of staff's performance is causing you or other employees concern, your first step is to follow your company's disciplinary procedure (see the section 'Following a disciplinary procedure'). The statutory dismissal and disciplinary procedures that came into force in October 2004 apply and your company procedures must at least comply with those minimum standards. The ACAS website at www.acas.org.uk has information on the current rules about this and related subjects.

Pretty much every story has two sides to it, so if you go into a meeting or begin an investigation with the idea of resolving the problem, rather than being determined to get rid of the thorn in your side, it's better all round. A disciplinary meeting is an opportunity to find a solution to a problem rather than just to mete out discipline and punishment.

Morale around the workplace can plummet when an employee is sacked. Unless the person has been a complete pain, colleagues may feel you've just been looking for an excuse and weren't listening to the employee's views. Resolving a dispute and making things work can have a very positive effect on the rest of the workers and ultimately your business will benefit.

Following a disciplinary procedure . . . right through to dismissal

All employers are legally required to have a disciplinary procedure. Some bosses have separate procedures dealing with conduct and underperformance; some use the same procedure for both. When employees join your firm you have to let them know how the disciplinary procedure operates and the kind of behaviour that gets employees fired. If this information isn't spelled out in detail in the Written Statement of Employment Particulars it has to be in a company handbook or in some other written document that your employees have easy access to (see Chapter 3 in this Book).

ACAS (the Advisory, Conciliation and Arbitration Service) produces a code of practice on disciplinary procedures with details on how to draw up and operate a disciplinary procedure. The code is used as the yardstick to judge how reasonable an employer has been if an employee brings a claim for unfair dismissal to an Employment Tribunal, so get a copy and incorporate it into your own procedures. You can contact ACAS at 0845-7474747 or through the website at www.acas.org.uk.

The minimum the law says you have to implement in your disciplinary procedure is the following:

1. **Get all the facts straight, and decide whether or not any further action must be taken.** Investigate the situation fully by talking to the employee concerned and any other employees who may be able to throw some light on events. Gather any evidence you can find – emails, letters and so on. Interview any witnesses and take signed written statements from them.

2. **Start informal discussions, coaching, or counselling for the employee involved.** Make it clear to her that this isn't part of a formal disciplinary procedure – you're trying to help her and to avert more problems.

3. **If the problematic situation doesn't change, let the employee know in writing what she's doing wrong.** Be sure to include any evidence you have, and explain to her why the situation cannot continue, what you expect her to do to remedy the situation and by when.

4. **Hold a disciplinary hearing to discuss the situation.** The employee can bring along a work companion or a union representative. Before the hearing you must set out in writing the concerns which have led you to hold the meeting and the employee must have a copy of that statement. At the hearing explain your complaint and your evidence and give the employee the chance to state her case, ask questions, give evidence, and call her own witnesses.

5. **Let the employee know what you've decided in light of the hearing.** If you decide on disciplinary action rather than the sack, give her a written warning spelling out what the misconduct is, what has to be done about it, and by when. And explain the consequences if things don't change – perhaps a final written warning and then the sack.

6. **Allow the employee the right to appeal.** If she does, hold an appeal meeting. If your business is big enough, try to have a different manager hear the appeal to the one who made the decision to dismiss. Once the appeal is over you have to let the employee know your final decision.

The list shows the basic statutory requirements – your own disciplinary procedure may allow for more warnings and more meetings and other courses of action such as demotion or suspension.

If you don't follow this basic procedure and you've employed the member of staff for more than a year, she can claim automatic unfair dismissal and the resulting tribunal can increase the compensation it orders you to pay.

Calling in the arbitrators

If you can't resolve a disciplinary problem inside your organisation, think about calling in an outsider as an arbitrator. If your organisation recognises a union, that union may be able to send someone in to arbitrate. ACAS may also be able to help – the contact details are earlier in this chapter.

Dismissing Staff – the Right Way

Most things in life can be done in a right way and a wrong way, and dismissing staff is definitely one of those areas where you have to get it right. The law protects most employees from being unfairly dismissed or from being forced to quit because of their boss's unreasonable behaviour. And that means that if an employee thinks she has been unfairly dismissed, she can take a case against you at an Employment Tribunal.

If you need any incentive to stop and reflect before you wield the axe, just remember that a tribunal can order you to pay compensation if it decides you've got it wrong. That can be anything from a basic award worked out based on a weekly wage figure of £280 and the number of years the employee has worked for you, up to a maximum compensatory award of £56,800 (a maximum that is index-linked and increases annually). It wouldn't take too many payments like that to bring many small businesses to their knees. If the tribunal also decides that the dismissal was discriminatory the compensation is uncapped!

Having fair grounds to sack an employee

For a dismissal to be fair you have to have an acceptable reason for getting rid of your employee.

It's fair to dismiss a member of staff when:

- ✔ Her job no longer exists. But remember it's the job that's redundant, never the person.

- ✔ She turns out not to be capable of doing the job or is not qualified (including lying about qualifications in a job application).

- ✔ She's guilty of some misdemeanour (constantly being late, absent, careless or having a bad attitude, for example).

- ✔ She does something so bad that it amounts to gross misconduct (such as stealing something, hitting someone, committing fraud or sexually harassing other staff). See the later section 'Dismissing for gross misconduct'.

> ✔ You can't let the employee go on doing her job because to do so would be breaking the law (such as a job that involves driving when the employee has been banned from driving).

If none of those reasons apply to the employee you want to sack, one more category may give you a get-out clause. You may be able to fire someone for 'some other substantial reason'. Isn't the law wonderfully clear? Basically, this other reason has to be one that you can defend in a tribunal hearing. One of the most common reasons is that you have to restructure your business for financial reasons and that means jobs aren't redundant but are changing and so your contract with your employee has to change too. If an employee refuses to accept these contractual changes it can then be fair to dismiss her.

Although employees past retirement age haven't been protected against unfair dismissal in the past, some recent legal cases cast doubt on this. If you haven't set a normal retirement age for your workplace, employees over 65 generally count as being of an age to retire. Starting in 2006, new legislation regarding age discrimination kicked in that may well prevent you firing old-timers (regardless of whether they're past retirement age). Although the details haven't been worked out yet the government may give older employees the same rights to claim unfair dismissal and compensation as their younger colleagues.

Applying your decision

If you've got good grounds for dismissing an employee, the next step is to go about the dismissal fairly. That means first giving the employee a fair hearing by going through all the necessary disciplinary procedures explained in the section 'Following a disciplinary procedure . . . right through to dismissal' earlier in this chapter.

Even if you have no choice but to sack someone because it would be breaking the law for her to carry on in her job, you still have to be fair in how you go about it. You have to discuss, investigate and consider the possibility of keeping the person on in another capacity if other jobs are available. If you end up having to explain yourself to a tribunal panel they'll want to know that you gave the employee a fair hearing; that you investigated the whole situation fully; and that you were being reasonable when you decided that the reason was substantial enough to merit the sack. A dismissal has to be fair all round.

Keep detailed records of all the procedures you go through – copies of letters, warnings, records of meetings, and the evidence you gather. If the case does come to a tribunal, you'll need to be able to prove that you did everything fairly and squarely.

Book III

Finding and Managing Staff

Giving written reasons for dismissal

If you've investigated, warned, followed the procedure, and finally decided you have good reason to dismiss someone, you've got to let the employee know what your reasons are. If you've followed the correct disciplinary procedure outlined in the section 'Following a disciplinary procedure . . . right through to dismissal', this shouldn't come as a surprise to the employee and she should be fully aware of all the reasons already – but you still have to put the reasons for dismissal in writing.

Giving notice of dismissal

Except in cases of gross misconduct, you have to give the appropriate period of notice for any dismissal. Details of an employee's notice entitlement should be outlined in her contract.

The law says that someone who has worked for at least a month but less than a year is entitled to one weeks notice. Someone who has worked for two full years is entitled to two weeks' notice, three full years means three weeks' notice, and so on up to a maximum of 12 weeks' notice. You may offer more generous terms in your employees' contracts. You can increase the amount of notice employees are entitled to depending on how long they've worked for you, and your more senior employees – such as managers – may have longer notice periods.

Don't forget that an employee who is retiring is in reality being dismissed (because of retirement) and so is entitled to be given notice of dismissal in the same way as anyone else or to be paid money in lieu of notice.

If you don't want the employee around the workplace after you've given her notice, you can let her go immediately but you have to pay her in place of the notice period anyway. So if she's entitled to six weeks' notice, you have to give her six weeks' pay. She also has to be paid for any other fringe benefits she may be entitled to under the contract, such as the use of a company car.

Dismissing for gross misconduct

Examples of misconduct can be constantly being late or not turning up at all, making careless mistakes, or not really caring how their work goes! Misconduct is irritating in the extreme and possibly a reason to sack someone. While ordinary misconduct may be annoying, beyond that it becomes gross misconduct.

Gross misconduct is something so serious that it brings the contract between you and the guilty party to an end immediately. Examples of acts at work that may constitute gross misconduct include:

- ✔ Theft
- ✔ Dishonesty
- ✔ Fraud
- ✔ Violence
- ✔ Deliberately damaging company property
- ✔ Sexual harassment
- ✔ Bullying
- ✔ Downloading pornographic material from the Internet
- ✔ Inciting racial hatred
- ✔ Gross insubordination

If you sack someone for gross misconduct, without notice, you have to be able to justify that action. What you're actually saying is that the employee has done something that has damaged the relationship of trust and confidence between you, destroyed her working contract, and made it impossible to carry on as boss and employee. If you can't prove that, the employee may make a claim for wrongful dismissal at a tribunal.

In such cases, the tribunal will want to know:

- ✔ Whether any of your other staff ever acted in the same way and whether you took that case seriously enough to fire them without notice.
- ✔ If whatever has happened really has broken down the trust and confidence between you and your employee.

This means that you have to have fully investigated the incident and given the employee a fair hearing before you come to your decision. The principles of fairness apply just the same to cases of gross misconduct as they do to ordinary cases of misconduct or poor performance (read the section on 'Avoiding wrongful dismissal', later in this chapter). Employees should already know what kind of gross misconduct will get them fired on the spot – this should be in your staff handbook.

 Be very careful about summarily dismissing someone for what you see as gross misconduct. If she brings a case against you at an Employment Tribunal and the tribunal decides the conduct didn't amount to gross misconduct, you can end up having to pay greatly increased compensation. You must follow all the basic dismissal and disciplinary procedures outlined earlier in this chapter.

If employees are guilty of actions outside the workplace that would constitute gross misconduct at work you may be able to fairly dismiss them. If that happens take your solicitor's advice.

Plain old ordinary misconduct is handled differently. Ordinary misconduct doesn't bring the contract to an immediate end, and you must follow a fair disciplinary procedure with all the necessary warnings.

Dismissing for underperformance

We all have days when we go home without having done much. But you can't sack an employee for the occasional lazy day unless it happens week in, week out.

If an employee is seriously underperforming – her work isn't up to scratch, she just isn't capable of doing the job, or she's always off sick or late so that the job isn't getting done properly, or she hasn't got the qualifications she needs – you can have a reason for firing her fairly on the grounds of lack of capability or qualifications.

The minimum procedures you have to go through are the same as for other disciplinary procedures (see the section 'Following a disciplinary procedure . . . right through to dismissal' earlier in this chapter) or follow your company's own disciplinary procedure.

Give people the chance to improve before dismissing them, and be reasonable about the timescale you set for seeing their work improve. You can allow any amount of time between a few weeks and several months. A tribunal considers how long the employee has been with you, how bad the performance was, what warnings you had given that things had to improve, the effect on your business, and the size of the workforce. If you have other people who can 'carry' underperforming employees while they are trying to improve, you can afford to give them a bit longer than if you're dependent on that one person.

Be objective about deciding whether or not an employee has made an improvement. Getting exasperated and being determined not to see any improvement isn't your best way forward. Taking a second opinion from another manager or a colleague is a good idea.

Annual appraisals are a good way of assessing how people are performing and they give you a legitimate reason to discuss any problems. It's good to talk.

Dismissing Staff – the Wrong Way

If you just snap and fire a member of staff without a full investigation, without giving her the chance to put her case across or to improve, and without going through all the correct procedures, your sacked employee will most likely feel very aggrieved and seek legal advice. And a solicitor is likely to tell her that she has a case for unfair dismissal if she has at least one years' service. The next thing you know, your former employee has filed a claim, and you have to prepare your case for the defence.

Avoiding wrongful dismissal

Wrongful dismissal is when you decide to end a member of staff's contract by dismissing her without notice or by giving her a period of notice less than what she's entitled to. Doing so means you're in breach of contract and the aggrieved party can file a claim against you at a tribunal within three months of the event or within six years in the courts.

You must give the notice period set out in the employee's contract unless you're firing her for gross misconduct (refer to the section 'Dismissing for gross misconduct' earlier in this chapter). If you haven't put a notice period into the employee's contract, the statutory minimum applies. See 'Giving notice of dismissal'.

You have to give notice or pay in lieu of notice. If the employee can show that she didn't get the right notice and that she has suffered financially as a result, she can claim at an Employment Tribunal or in the County Court for amounts up to £25,000. For sums over £25,000 the employee can apply to the High Court.

If you haven't made clear in the contract how much notice an employee gets and you fire her using the statutory minimum, in some cases she can also ask a court or tribunal to rule that the period of notice, although perfectly legal, was unreasonably short. The more skilled, well-paid and senior an employee is, the more likely the tribunal is to agree.

Steering clear of constructive dismissal

If you behave in such a way that employees feel they have no choice but to quit, that's *constructive dismissal* (to use the full title, constructive unfair dismissal). Once the employee has gone, providing she has one year's service, she can make a claim against you for unfair dismissal and possibly wrongful dismissal too if you haven't got the notice period or pay right.

If as an employer you just keep forgetting to buy the teabags and coffee or are merely an irritable pain, no one can quit and claim constructive dismissal. You have to have done something seriously wrong – such as changing the job she does without any discussion. The trust and confidence that exist in the employee's contract, whether in writing or not, have to be broken.

If you do something serious, such as reduce an employee's pay without her agreement, the longer she stays on after the event, the more she would be seen to have accepted the change and the less likely she would be to win a constructive dismissal claim. If, however, the employee works 'under protest', making it clear that she doesn't accept the changes, it's possible for her to resign some time after the breach of contract and successfully sue you. If she left because she had a better job offer, she would have a hard time proving that your behaviour was the catalyst pushing her into going.

Automatic unfair dismissal

You can't dismiss an employee for being pregnant or because she has dared to ask for something that she's entitled to by law (such as written terms and conditions of employment or parental leave). A situation where you sack an employee for asking for something she had the right to ask for is known as *automatic unfair dismissal*. In cases of automatic unfair dismissal, the tribunal will automatically come down on the side of the employee. The tribunal has no choice – because you've broken the law – and this is costly for the employer. For example, the minimum basic award where you dismiss someone because of her union membership or activities, or for being a health and safety representative or occupational pension scheme trustee is £3,800.

As we said earlier in this chapter, if you dismiss someone without following all the right procedures that will also be automatic unfair dismissal and you can be penalised by being ordered to pay increased compensation.

Tying Up the Loose Ends

Even when all the procedures have been gone through and a leaving date is settled, that's not the end of the matter. You aren't under any obligation to offer an exit interview to an employee who is leaving, but it can be useful for you as well as the employee. She may have comments to make about the way your business operates that would be useful to consider – as well as letting her get it off her chest! It can help to clear the air.

Don't forget the paperwork. Just as you have to do when an employee hands in her notice and chooses to leave, there are loose ends that need to be tidied up.

Handing over paperwork to a new employer

Paperwork is always involved when an employee leaves. Tax forms need to go to HMRC (HM Revenue and Customs) as well as to a new employer. Here's a summary of the paperwork that you need to sort out before your dismissed employee leaves:

- ✔ **A P45.** This form is the most important piece of paperwork, because it details where you're up to with deducting tax and national insurance for the year so far. The P45 can be passed on directly to a new employer, but if the employee doesn't have a job to go to you need to give it to her. She will need it to claim Job Seeker's allowance until she gets back into work.

- ✔ **A P60.** If the redundancy happens near the end of the tax year, the employee should get a P60, detailing all of her tax deductions for the year.

- ✔ **A P11B.** This form shows all the benefits in kind that the employee has received so far during the year. The HMRC's website (www.hmrc.gov.uk) has details of all the forms you need and provides downloadable forms too.

You must also give new employers details of all the entitlements employees have taken so far in the current year of employment – maternity leave, paternity leave or parental leave, for example.

Give the dismissed employee a copy of all her tax and benefits details plus any certificates she may have gained while she's been employed by you (such as qualifications or safety certificates or courses related to her job).

Book III

Finding and Managing Staff

Sorting out outstanding payments

Check that the dismissed employee has been paid everything she's owed. She may not have taken her full holiday entitlement up to and including her last day.

If this is the case she may be entitled to be paid for that accrued holiday under the terms of her contract or under the working time regulations. You can agree that she takes her remaining holiday during her notice period, but if you want her to do that, make sure that you give her enough notice to do so. You also need to check that a dismissed employee has been fully paid for any overtime, extra hours she's put in, expenses she's due, or for anything else that she would normally expect to have been paid for while in your employment, such as bonuses and commissions.

If you decide to take a company car away from an employee during her notice period, you have to work out how much she should be paid to compensate for that loss.

You need to check if the employee is entitled to any tax rebates through the PAYE (Pay As You Earn) scheme. The member of staff who works out wages should be able to sort this out with the help of the Inland Revenue – now HM Revenue and Customs. Chapter 5 in Book III gives more details on paying wages.

Any overpayments are returned in the employee's final pay cheque. All the money due to them should be detailed in the final pay slip.

Paying instead of allowing staff to work their notice

If you want your employee to go this minute and never darken your door again, you have to pay her money for the period she would otherwise have had to work – money in place of the notice that her contract or the law says she's entitled to. Not only that, but she has to be in the same financial position as she would have been in if you had let her work through the notice period. That may mean paying out more than just a few weeks' pay. For example, if the employee had the use of a company car, she can have expected to use that during the notice period so you'll have to compensate her for the loss of that too.

The right to pay in lieu of notice is always an option open to an employer, whether or not it says so in the employee's contract, and the employee doesn't have the right to demand to work out her notice.

The other thing you can do is to send the employee on garden leave. *Garden leave* means that your dismissed employee spends the period of her notice still employed by you but at home and with no work to do while still being paid. You may decide to do that if you're worried about what damage she could do to your business if she worked out her notice in the office – maybe by stealing all your best customers or contacts.

Dealing with pensions

When employees leave a job and start a new one, they have to decide what to do about the money they've paid into your company pension, if you provided one. The same goes for employees you dismiss.

Restricting what employees can do after leaving

In certain cases, the new business activities of a recently dismissed employee can harm your company. For example, if you're a hairdresser and a former employee sets up her own salon in close proximity and takes her customers away, you'll lose out.

You have the option of taking steps to protect your business by putting into your employees' contracts terms that limit what they can do when they leave you. These are known as *restrictive covenants*. You can say that former employees are not to set up in competition with you for a period of three months after leaving your firm or restrict them to setting up their business outside a particular geographical area.

You have to be reasonable about any restrictive covenants you put in a contract if you're not likely to be able to enforce them if the employee ignores them. If you try to sue for breach of contract the courts can find your restrictive covenants too restrictive and you'll lose – and be out of pocket for the legal fees. Take advice from a good lawyer before you draw up contracts with these kinds of restrictions.

Giving references

You don't have to give any employee a reference, whether she's resigned or been dismissed, but if you do agree to, the reference has to say what you believe to be accurate and fair and you have to give it without malice.

If you give an unfair, malicious or negligent reference and the employee loses out as a result, she can sue you. On the other hand, you have to be truthful for the sake of any prospective employers as well. If they lose out as a result of a negligent reference, they can sue you too!

If you've dismissed an employee you may not be too bothered about how quickly she gets back to work, but be objective about this. She may have been in the wrong job and may be rather good in a different company with a job that suits her better.

Be truthful in your reference, but don't be tempted to exaggerate an employee's negative points. Employees will have the right to see what you've written about them in references once they've started work with their new employer, so make sure that what's in the reference is what has already been discussed in the course of the fair dismissal procedure and can be proved to be true. Don't add little extras out of spite.

Make sure you don't give a discriminatory reference to someone because of her sex, race, disability, religion or religious beliefs, or sexual orientation, and be careful too about age!

Don't be tempted to try to smooth things over with an employee you're dismissing over a dispute by offering a glowing reference. This can backfire on you. The employee can use your reference to prove that she wasn't guilty of misconduct or incompetence after all.

Facing Tribunals – Something to Be Avoided

Tabloid writers love a good story about an unfairly dismissed employee managing to win thousands of pounds from her employer. Some very high-profile cases take place, for example where employees of big financial firms win huge sums at Employment Tribunals for discrimination or in court for breaches of contract. They should act as a warning that you can't afford to be unfair.

If you do unfairly dismiss, wrongfully dismiss, or constructively unfairly dismiss an employee, she can take a claim against you at an Employment Tribunal. Sometimes, even when you're in the right, vexed employees feel you've acted unfairly and want their day in court. If you really do have good reason to dismiss and scrupulously follow the correct dismissal procedures (explained in the earlier section 'Following a disciplinary procedure . . . right through to dismissal') you'll be able to convince a tribunal should it come to that. But avoid this scenario if at all possible!

If an ex-employee brings a claim of unfair dismissal against you and wins, the tribunal can instruct you to:

✔ Pay compensation ranging from a basic award up to the top compensatory award of £56,800 depending on the details of the case (the maximum amount is index-linked and increases each year).

✔ Reinstate the employee in her former job.

✔ Re-engage the employee in a different job.

The employee is less likely to want reinstatement or re-engagement because it isn't likely that the two of you will be able to work together again comfortably. For a small business, even sums of far less than the maximum compensation figure can be crippling. So you really do want to make sure that you're on a very solid footing before you decide to sack someone. It pays to be fair.

Chapter 5

Paper Money, Money Paper – Payslips and Deductions

. . . .

In This Chapter

▶ Wading through wage slips

▶ Understanding tax and National Insurance wage deductions

▶ Being aware of other possible wage deductions

. . . .

*W*hatever, however and whenever you decide to pay your employees, a lot of calculations and paperwork are involved. Not only giving with one hand, you have to take back quite a bit with the other and hand it over to the taxman. People working for you on a freelance or self-employed basis usually send you an invoice at the end of the job or at intervals you've agreed and you pay them in full, leaving them to work out and hand over their own income tax and National Insurance payments to HM Revenue & Customs – the new name for the Inland Revenue, but you have a responsibility to collect tax and insurance from your own employees. On top of that you have to comply with the law on the National Minimum Wage, Statutory Sick Pay, maternity, paternity and adoption pay, and holiday pay. Phew – is it any wonder that one of the first jobs many bosses farm out is the payroll?

Setting Everything Out on the Payslip

Employees have a legal right to a written pay statement – a *payslip* or *wage slip* – that itemises their pay and anything deducted from their pay. One of the main reasons for these written statements is that they notify employees of the deductions made from their pay. You have to give out these itemised statements each time (or just before) you pay your employees.

An employee's payslip must include:

- The *gross amount* of his wages (his salary before any deductions).

- The *net amount* he earns (what's left after you've made any deductions).

- Any amounts that you've deducted and why (some of these are fixed deductions made every pay-day and some are variable from pay period to pay period).

- The breakdown of different payment methods, if you pay your employees in this way (for example, what amounts are paid by cheque and what are paid in cash).

If you don't provide wage slips or don't include the correct details on them, your employees can complain to an Employment Tribunal. The Tribunal can make you pay back any unnotified deductions you made in the 13-week period before the employee complained, even if you were entitled to make them.

Gross pay

Gross pay is the amount of pay your employee earns before you make any deductions. Gross pay comprises the basic wage and any other elements of pay due in the pay period, and may include elements such as:

- Bonuses
- Commission
- Holiday pay
- Statutory Sick Pay
- Maternity pay
- Overtime

The gross pay is the top line – earnings go downhill from there. Gross pay doesn't include items such as loans or advances in wages, expenses or redundancy payments.

Deductions

Employees are entitled to know in advance what deductions you'll be making from their gross pay and why. Most deductions are regulated by the Employment Rights Act 1996 and are legal only when your employees' contracts clearly explain in what circumstances you'll make such deductions, or when your employees give you written consent to make them. But some deductions are exempt from regulation by the Employment Rights Act (more details are given later in this chapter):

- ✔ Deductions for previous overpayment of wages.

- ✔ Deductions under statutory provisions such as tax and National Insurance.

- ✔ Deductions that you make by law and hand over to a third party, such as an attachment of earnings order.

- ✔ Deductions that you pay to a third party where the employee consents in writing, such as payments to a pension company.

- ✔ Deductions relating to strike action.

- ✔ Deductions to satisfy a ruling by a court or tribunal that an employee has to pay you a certain amount.

If you're intending to make any deductions not shown on this list, you need prior written consent from your employee (you must have the consent in writing before the event that gives rise to the deduction). If you get consent *after* you've deducted the money, that deduction is considered unlawful. That's because you've changed an employee's pay without his consent and were in breach of contract. In other words, the contract needs to include a provision (agreed to by the employee) that in the particular circumstances you can take money out of his wages.

If you're making exactly the same fixed deductions each pay period, you can give out *standing statements* notifying employees of these deductions in advance; standing statements may be valid for up to a year (so you'll have to issue them annually at least). Any variable or additional deductions still have to appear on the monthly or weekly payslips, and any changes to the fixed deductions must be notified in writing or through an amended standing statement of fixed deductions.

Book III

Finding and Managing Staff

Net pay

Net pay is what your employee's left with after the taxman and anyone else entitled to a cut has had their share; net pay amounts to gross pay minus any deductions. Net pay is the bottom line, and it's what your employee is left to play with to reward him for all his hard work!

Carrying Out Your Tax-Collecting Duties

Small business owners often complain that life would be a lot simpler if – on top of running the business – they didn't have to act as unpaid collectors of taxes. But unfortunately, you do have to fulfil certain duties on behalf of the Inland Revenue. You must:

- ✔ Work out how much tax and National Insurance your employees should be paying (along with any contributions you, as boss of the outfit, have to make to the Exchequer yourself).

- ✔ Collect these payments and get them to the right government department by the correct date.

Rather than doing this complicated task yourself and tackling the payroll on your own, you may wish to call in expert accountants. Not all employers can afford to do this, of course, and even if you can, it's still a good idea to read the following sections to understand what deductions you must make from your employees' payslips.

You must send the most recent amounts that you deduct from employees' pay to HM Revenue & Customs by the 19th of each month. If you make your payments electronically you have until the 22nd of every month to pay.

Deducting income tax

PAYE (or Pay As You Earn) is HM Revenue & Customs' system for collecting income tax from employees. As an employer, you're responsible for the administration of your employees' PAYE deductions.

All the help you need in calculating income tax is available from HM Revenue & Customs in the form of tables, forms, advice and software. The Inland Revenue (now HM Revenue & Customs) used to have a reputation for being less than helpful, but that really isn't true any more. It runs helplines for just about every aspect of tax that you'll ever have to deal with. Two phone helplines are specifically for employers:

- ✔ 0845-6070143 for new employers.

- ✔ 0845-7143143 for established employers.

- ✔ The HM Revenue and Customs website holds lots more information covering all aspects of tax in the UK: www.hmrc.gov.uk.

Employees normally have to pay income tax on just about every payment you give them:

- ✔ Wages

- ✔ Overtime and shift pay

- ✔ Tips

- ✔ Bonuses and commissions

✔ Statutory sick pay, maternity pay, paternity pay and adoption pay

✔ Lump sums (such as redundancy payments) over and above any tax-free amount

✔ Some cash expense allowances

Tax and allowances change every year, usually in the March budget. Consider the figures that follow as indicative only; they could be substantially different when you come to use them. Income tax and National Insurance are the subject of a review with a view to merging them into one tax structure. The HMRC website (www.hmrc.gov.uk) has all the current tax rules and rates.

Not all of the money an employee earns is taxable. Certain sums known as a *personal allowance* must be earned before a person starts to pay tax. The personal allowance for a person under 65 is currently £7,475, which means that the first £7,475 an employee earns in any tax year isn't taxable.

When an employee earns more than his tax-free amount the employer deducts tax from his pay at different rates. Table 5 -1 shows how this would be calculated. And rather than paying an employee his full tax-free earnings in the first part of the tax year, you give him a proportion of these earnings in every wage packet throughout the tax year, adding up to his full tax-free earnings by the end of the year, but taxing him that little increment less throughout the year.

Book III

Finding and Managing Staff

Table 5-1	Taxable Pay Breakdown
Taxable pay	*Rate taxed at*
Applies only to some savings	10%
£0 to £35,000	20%
£35,000 - £150,000	40%
Beyond £150,000	50%

Each employee's circumstances dictate how much income tax he has to pay. HM Revenue and Customs (formerly the Inland Revenue) gives each of your employees a tax code each year showing how much tax-free earnings they're entitled to before you need to start deducting their tax contributions. When a new employee joins your staff his P45 shows you his current tax code.

Special PAYE situations

All sorts of reasons may occur allowing an employee to earn more than his personal allowance before starting to pay tax, or where he has to pay tax on some of the first £7,475 he earns. He may be entitled to some tax relief or have paid too much tax last year and so the figure will be higher. He may have paid too little tax last year and the figure will be lower. Any benefits that he gets on which he has to pay tax will affect that tax-free amount. Benefits in kind, such as company cars and medical insurance, are subject to tax – but only at the end of your tax year, rather than through the PAYE system. If you pay your employees with shares or vouchers, the Inland Revenue taxes these on their cash value under the PAYE system.

Help with child-care costs is an exception. If you give an employee child care or child-care vouchers up to the value of £55 a week, this won't be taxed as long as:

- ✔ The child-care scheme is registered child care or approved home child care.
- ✔ The child-care scheme is available to all your employees.

If a new employee turns up without a P45 (perhaps because his previous employer hasn't handed over all the necessary paperwork), you won't immediately have the correct tax code for him. He needs to fill in a form P46, available from the HMRC website or your local office, which you must send off to HMRC (formerly the Inland Revenue); doing so eventually results in a new P45 and tax code being issued. In the meantime you have to deduct tax from any wages he gets using an emergency code, meaning that you may deduct more tax than necessary (but that can be refunded in future wage packets when you've received your employee's correct tax code).

Keeping PAYE records

Because PAYE is such a complicated system covering all sorts of individual situations, you need to maintain your tax deduction records in good order. Using HMRC (Inland Revenue) forms is the easiest way to do this – you can get your local tax office to send them to you or download them from the HMRC website www.hmrc.gov.uk.

You need to keep the following for your own records:

- ✔ Records showing all wage and salary payments you've made in whatever form, including benefits in kind.
- ✔ Wage slips showing how you've calculated each employee's wages along with his tax deductions.
- ✔ P45s for each employee, showing his tax codes. (And when an employee leaves, you give him a P45 to pass on to his new employer.)
- ✔ P60s for each employee, showing the total amount of tax that you've deducted for the whole tax year.

At the end of the tax year, send HMRC (the Inland Revenue) the following:

✔ Details of each employee's pay and deductions.

✔ Details of all employee expenses and benefits.

✔ Details of National Insurance contributions (see 'Deducting National Insurance' for more details about this).

At the end of the tax year, you must also give each employee:

✔ His P60.

✔ A copy of the information you've sent the Inland Revenue about his expenses and benefits.

Deducting National Insurance

National Insurance Contributions (NICs) fund future benefits for the contributor, such as state pensions and Job Seeker's Allowance. NICs fall into different classes, and the class of contributions paid affects the contributor's entitlements in future.

Most people who work have to pay NICs and as an employer you also have to pay NICs on most of your workers. HM Revenue and Customs (formerly The Inland Revenue) collects National Insurance and again you get to play the role of unpaid collector. You don't have to pay NICs for people who are self-employed – they take care of their own NICs.

As with the PAYE scheme, it's up to you to calculate, deduct and pay HM Revenue and Customs (the Inland Revenue). Once you've registered as an employer with the HMRC (Inland Revenue) you'll get payment slips to fill in and return with your NICs.

Book III

Finding and Managing Staff

NICs for employees

Different classes of NICs exist. Some classes are paid at a flat rate and some depend on earnings. Self-employed people pay their own contributions, so you don't have to deduct them from any money you pay out to people working for you on a self-employed basis. All other employees pay Class 1 contributions, and some employees may also pay Class 3 contributions. Here's how you know who pays what:

✔ **Employees pay Class 1 contributions on earnings over the *Earnings Threshold* (ET).** The ET usually changes at the beginning of each tax year. The 2011 rate was £102 a week. An employee pays 11 per cent of his gross earnings over the ET into National Insurance up to the *Upper Earnings Limit* (£770 per week in 2011). If he earns more than the Upper Earnings Limit, he just pays 1 per cent on any earnings above that rate.

✔ **People who haven't paid enough National Insurance in the past to qualify for certain benefits like a full state pension pay Class 3 contributions at a flat rate.** Usually that's because the person's been taking time out of work or he's been abroad. You usually pay Class 3 contributions direct to HM Revenue and Customs (the Inland Revenue).

Keeping NIC records

All sorts of records need to be kept showing how you arrived at the calculations and what payments you've made. You need to keep the following records relating to NICs:

✔ Payroll records for all staff including payslips, deductions, salary details and NICs deducted.

✔ Evidence of how you calculated the NICs.

✔ Records of NIC payment to the Inland Revenue.

✔ Copies of P60s given to employees each year showing NICs for the year.

✔ Copies of P11D forms for each employee showing the benefits in kind and the NICs due on them.

✔ Evidence of calculations and payments of any additional NICs over the year.

You need to keep these records for the current year and for at least the previous three tax years.

Counting Up Any Other Deductions

Your employees' wage deductions don't necessarily stop with tax and National Insurance. Depending on your employees' circumstances, you may need to deduct other amounts too.

Most students won't get through university without taking on a student loan and they have to pay this money back as soon as they are earning enough. HM Revenue and Customs is responsible for collecting repayments on loans taken out after August 1998 meaning that you end up with the job of collecting them on HMRC's (the Revenue's) behalf. When you take on a new employee, look on his P45 form for a box marked 'Continue Student Loans Deduction'. If there's a 'Y' for yes in that box you need to make deductions. Alternatively the Inland Revenue may send you a *Start Notice* (form SL1) relating to one of your employees; in this case you must start making deductions. Special student loan deduction tables are available to help you work out what to deduct and pay to HM Revenue & Customs.

Include details of student loan deductions on the employee's payslips; if he leaves you have to put details of the deductions on his P45 so that the next employer knows the score.

You can get help administering student loan repayments from HM Revenue and Customs' telephone helpline: 0845-7646646 or by looking at their website: www.hmrc.gov.uk.

Deducting pension contributions

Employers generally must offer their employees the chance to belong to a pension scheme. This can be an occupational scheme, a group personal pension, or at the very least a stakeholder scheme. If an employee is a member of a scheme you need his permission in writing to take his pension contributions out of his wages. It's your job to:

✔ Pass contributions to the pension scheme.

✔ Keep records of these payments.

✔ Pay the contributions by the date they're due or by the 19th of the following month.

Making child support payments

You can find yourself having to make deductions from an employee's pay to cover child support payments. The Child Support Agency sometimes has difficulties getting non-resident parents to pay towards their child's upbringing and has the right to ask the court to order that the employer takes the payments directly from an employee's wages. If that happens you're the one who'll have to deduct the money and hand it over to the agency. This is known as a *Deductions from Earning Order*. 'Handling Attachment of Earnings Orders' later in this chapter deals with these sorts of deductions.

Child support payments must be handed over to the Child Support Agency by the 19th of the month following the deduction from pay and it's an offence not to comply with one of these orders.

The Child Support Enquiry Line can provide assistance to you; the telephone number is 0845-7133133 and the website address is www.csa.gov.uk.

Giving to charity

Enabling staff to make regular charitable donations directly from their wages (known as a *payroll-giving scheme*) is an extra option you may want

Book III

Finding and Managing Staff

to provide. It's very little effort for many good causes; it makes it easier and more worthwhile for employees to give to charity; and it boosts your image as a caring, socially responsible employer. Employees don't pay tax on the amounts they give to charity and most of the paperwork is done by Payroll-Giving Agencies approved by HM Revenue and Customs. If you set up a contract with one of these agencies, you need to keep the following records:

✔ A copy of your contract with the Payroll-Giving Agency

✔ Forms filled in by your employees authorising you to take their contributions

✔ Details of the deductions from pay

✔ Receipts from the agency

Dishing out union dues

Members of a union have to pay their regular union subscriptions, and if you have a recognised union in your workplace these subs will usually come directly out of pay – which you deduct and hand over to the union. You need written consent from employees to make the deductions and need either to show the deduction on each payslip or (as the deduction's likely to be a fixed deduction each month) give employees a standing statement of what the deductions will be for the next year.

Handling Attachment of Earnings Orders

You may sometimes have to take deductions from an employee's wages due to a court order. That is, a court may order that a certain amount of money must be taken directly from your employee's wages in order to pay someone he owes money to. This is called an *Attachment of Earnings Order* (or in some cases a *Deduction from Earnings Order*).

The order instructs you (the employer) to pay a certain sum of money at a regular interval – probably monthly – directly to the court office. You must take that sum of money directly from the employee's wages before you pay him. The main reasons a court will issue an Attachment Of Earnings Order are when someone:

✔ Owes child support.

✔ Owes maintenance to an ex-partner.

✔ Has a court judgement against him for debts of more than £50.

✔ Has to make payments under an *administration order* (an order for a single regular payment to cover a series of debts owed to various creditors).

✔ Has to pay fines having been convicted in a criminal court.

✔ Has to make contributions towards the repayment of Legal Aid.

Under an Attachment of Earnings Order you have a legal obligation to make the deduction and send it on to the court. For the purposes of an order, 'earnings' means:

✔ Wages

✔ Bonuses

✔ Commission

✔ Overtime

✔ Pension payments

These are called *attachable earnings*. But limits as to what can be deducted are in place – your employee can't be left with nothing to live on. The court has to assess what the employee needs to live on for his basic needs, and that amount is known as *protected earnings*. The court can't order deductions that will leave your employee with less than the protected earnings amount. The courts can make more than one Attachment of Earnings Order against an employee at any one time and these take priority in chronological order.

You're within your rights to charge your employee a small amount to cover any extra administration costs that you run up as a result of an Attachment of Earnings Order. You can deduct that amount from his wages too, but you have to give him notice in writing.

Be fair. If you can absorb the costs and forget about them it will be better for your working relationship. If you do charge him, don't charge more than your actual costs – such as postage and stationery. He can already be struggling to survive on what the court has left him to live on.

If you're faced with an Attachment of Earnings Order you have no choice but to do the court's bidding or you'll be in the dock yourself. If you don't make the deductions and pass the money on to the court office, you can be convicted and fined.

Dealing with Overpayments

If you've overpaid an employee you're usually legally entitled to have that money paid back to you. You can deduct it from future wages. In this situation, you don't have to have an employee's written consent to make the 'payback' deductions but you need his agreement in writing before you begin to make the deductions.

The employee may plead that he's already spent the money but that doesn't mean that he doesn't have to pay up. Take into consideration that he may have genuinely been unaware that he'd been overpaid – maybe through a clerical error. If the error has been made for a few months in a row it's possible he owes you quite a lot of money. It will be unreasonable to ask him to pay it back all in one lump sum. Be prepared to negotiate a deal whereby he pays back – or you deduct out of his wages – a certain manageable amount each pay-day. This is the kind of scenario where you'd certainly want his consent to the deal in writing.

The odd occasion may arise when an employee argues that (in good faith) as a result of the extra money he changed his financial standing and ran up bills that he wouldn't otherwise have run up. If you take him to court to get the money back or he takes you to an Employment Tribunal because he feels you were unlawfully deducting money from his wages to recover the overpayment and he can convince the court he spent the money in good faith, you won't get it back. The *good faith* element of this defence is crucial, implying that he didn't know and can't reasonably have known that he was being overpaid.

Make sure that your pay system is very transparent so that your employees know what to expect in their pay packets and there's no chance of a member of staff getting extra pay without realising that it's a mistake.

Taking Money to Make Up for Shortfalls

If you work in the retail industry the till may sometimes be short, or unexplained gaps in your stock may occur; if so, you can make deductions from wages to recover those. But you can only do so as long as this is covered in the employee's contract and:

- ✔ You tell the employee in writing what the total shortfall amounts to.
- ✔ You make a written demand for payment on the pay-day you're making the deduction from.

You have to make the deduction within 12 months of discovering that there was a shortfall and you can't take any more than one tenth of an employee's gross wages out of any wage packet (unless it's a final wage). Investigate fully and make sure the employee is the one responsible for the shortfall – otherwise the employee may make a claim against you for an unlawful deduction of wages. He may even feel that your actions had left him unable to go on working for you; that he had no choice but to quit and claim constructive unfair dismissal.

Chapter 6

Inspiring Employees to Better Performance

*T*he question of how to motivate employees has loomed large over managers ever since management was first invented. Most of management comes down to mastering skills and techniques for motivating people – to make them better, more productive employees who love their jobs more than anything else in the world. Well, perhaps not quite that much; but you do want them to turn up and be as happy, effective and productive as possible.

You have two ways to motivate employees – rewards and punishments. If employees do what you want them to do, reward them with incentives that they desire – awards, recognition, important titles, money and so on. We often call these *positive consequences*. Alternatively, if employees don't do what you want, punish them with what they don't desire – warnings, reprimands, demotions, firings and so on – often known as *negative consequences*. By nature, employees are drawn towards positive consequences and shy away from negative consequences.

Increasingly, however, with today's employees, to be an effective manager you have to work harder at providing a greater number of positive consequences on an ongoing basis when employees perform well (they expect it). And you have to be *much* more selective as to when and how you use negative consequences. Firing people is much harder than in previous times, and wrongful and unfair dismissals get you into trouble with the law.

This chapter deals with the positive side of employee motivation – positive consequences, especially recognition and rewards. A hundred years of research in behavioural science and continuing extensive studies at all of the world's major business schools show that you have a much greater impact on getting the performance you want from your employees when you use positive consequences rather than negative ones.

We aren't saying that negative consequences don't have a place; sometimes you have no choice but to punish, reprimand or even dismiss employees. However, first give your employees the benefit of the doubt that they do want to do a good job and acknowledge them when they do so. Make every effort to use positive recognition, praise and rewards to encourage the behaviours you seek, and catch people doing things right. If you follow this approach, your employees are more motivated to want to excel in their jobs, performance and morale improve, and employees consider your company a much better place to work.

By leading with positive reinforcements, not only can you inspire your employees to do what you want, but you can also develop happier, more productive employees in the process – and that combination is tough to beat.

Introducing the Greatest Management Principle in the World

We're about to let you in on the Greatest Management Principle in the World. This simple rule can save you countless hours of frustration and extra work, and it can save your company many thousands or perhaps even millions of pounds. Sounds pretty awe-inspiring, doesn't it? Are you ready? Okay, the statement is:

You get what you reward.

Don't let the seeming simplicity of the statement fool you – read on to explore it.

Recognition isn't as simple as it looks

You may think that you're rewarding your employees to do what you want them to do, but are you really?

Consider the following example. You have two employees: Employee A is incredibly talented and Employee B is a marginal performer. You give similar assignments to both employees. Employee A completes the assignment before the due date and hands it in with no errors. Because Employee A is already done, you give her two additional assignments. Meanwhile, Employee B is not only late, but when she finally hands in the report you requested, it's full of errors. Because you're now under a time crunch, you accept Employee B's report and then correct it yourself.

What's wrong with this picture? Who's actually being rewarded: Employee A or Employee B?

If you answered Employee B, you're right. This employee has discovered that submitting work that's substandard and late is okay. Furthermore, she also sees that you personally fix her mistakes. That's quite a nice reward for an employee who clearly doesn't deserve one. (Another way to put it is that Employee B certainly has you well trained!)

On the other hand, by giving Employee A more work for being a diligent, out-standing worker, you're actually punishing her. Even though you may think nothing of assigning more work to Employee A, she knows the score. When Employee A sees that all she gets for being an outstanding performer is more work (while you let Employee B get away with doing less work), she's not going to like it one little bit. And if you end up giving both employees basi-cally the same pay rise (and don't think that they won't find out), you make the problem even worse. You lose Employee A, either literally, because she takes another job, or in spirit, because she stops working so hard.

If you let the situation continue, all your top performers eventually realise that doing their best work isn't in their best interest. As a result, they leave their position to find an organisation that values their contribution, or they simply sit back and forget about doing their best work. Why bother? No one (that means you, the manager) seems to care anyway.

Biscuit motivation

Giving everyone the same incentive – the same salary increase, equal rec-ognition or even equal amounts of your time – we call *biscuit motivation*. Although this treatment may initially sound fair, it isn't.

Nothing is as unfair at work as the equal treatment of unequal performers. You need to assess the performance of everyone. You then make clear to all people why they've received rewards and bonuses, or why they haven't. You must evenly and honestly distribute these rewards. And if everyone meets the standards demanded, then reward them all as you've promised.

If people aren't performing to standard, then take the particular individuals aside and tell them why. Tell them what they need to do to make the grade, and how they can go about it. Doing so is much better than letting people go about things without your active involvement and interest. You want everyone working as well as possible, and your job is to sort out those who aren't up to scratch.

Thinking through your rewards

A City of London branch of an international bank that was having problems with sickness absence. Staff were phoning in sick for all kinds of reasons, and collective absenteeism was in the order of 7 per cent (it was taking 107 people to do the work of 100 at any given time).

Being a concerned employer, the bank decided to reward positive behaviour rather than punishing bad or negative behaviour. Consequently, a note went round to all staff informing them that anyone who hadn't taken any self-certificated sickness absence was entitled to an extra week's holiday the following year.

Needless to say, the plan misfired. Genuine hardworking employees who'd had a day or two off as the result of real illnesses and injuries now found themselves slighted – tarred with the same brush as malingerers. Having had a day or two off with genuine ailments, good staff now used holiday entitlement rather than sickness days so as not to miss out on the additional week's holiday that everyone else was getting.

The bank's human resources department met to review the policy. Acknowledging the weakness of the plan, another note informed staff that they would still get their extra week's holiday provided that all absences were covered by a doctor's certificate. In no time at all, HR became swamped with doctors' certificates, and had to take on another member of staff just to deal with them. Those with genuine illnesses and injuries complained about having to visit a doctor and often paying for a certificate – to prove that their condition was real. For the malingerers, payment for a doctor's certificate simply validated a false position.

The bank reviewed the policy again. The suggestion was raised (seriously) that all those who'd had fewer than five days self-certificated absence should be entitled to an extra two weeks' holiday the following year. Only at this point did the HR director take matters into her own hands; at last, she cancelled the policy and concentrated efforts on the malingerers rather than the genuine, committed and hardworking staff.

Don't forget the Greatest Management Principle in the World – you get what you reward.

Before you set up a system to reward your employees, make sure that you know exactly what behaviours you want to reward and then align the rewards with those behaviours.

After you've put your employee reward system in place, check periodically to see that the system is getting the results that you want. Check with those you're trying to motivate and see whether the programme is still working. If it isn't, change it!

Discovering What Employees Want

In today's tight, stressful, changing times, what things are most important to employees? Bob conducted a survey of about 1,500 employees from across seven industries to answer that question. We list the top ten items that employees said were most important, along with some thoughts on how you can better provide each of these elements for your own employees:

- ✔ **A learning activity (No. 1) and choice of assignment (No. 9):** Today's employees most value opportunities in which they gain skills that can enhance their worth and marketability in their current job as well as future positions. Discover what your employees want to find out, how they want to grow and develop, and where they want to be in five years. Give them opportunities as they arise and the ability to choose work assignments whenever possible. When you give employees the choice, more often than not they rise to meet or exceed your expectations.

- ✔ **Flexible working hours (No. 2) and time off from work (No. 7):** Today's employees value their time – and their time off. Be sensitive to their needs outside work, whether they involve family or friends, charity or church, education or hobbies. Provide flexibility whenever you can so that employees can meet their obligations. Time off may range from an occasional afternoon to attend a child's play at school or the ability to start the work day an hour early so the employee can leave an hour early. By allowing work to fit best with employees' life schedules, you increase the chances that they're motivated to work harder while they're at work, and do their best to make their schedules work. And from a managerial standpoint, as long as the job gets done, what difference does it make what hours someone works? Bear in mind that employees now have a legal right to request flexible working hours, and you have a legal obligation to consider their request.

- ✔ **Personal praise – verbal (No. 3), public (No. 8) or written (No. 10):** Although you can thank someone in 10 to 15 seconds, most employees report that they're never thanked for the job they do – especially not by their manager. Systematically start to thank your employees when they do good work, in person, in the hallway, in a group meeting, on voice-mail, in a written thank-you note, in an email or at the end of each day at work. Better yet, go out of your way to act on and share and amplify good news when it occurs – even if it means interrupting someone to thank her for a great job she's done. By taking the time to say you noticed and appreciate her efforts, you help those efforts – and results – to continue. And bring her efforts to your manager's attention; doing so reinforces your own integrity as well as ensures full credit goes where it's due.

- ✔ **Increased autonomy (No. 5) and authority (No. 4) in their job:** The ultimate form of recognition for many employees is to have increased autonomy and authority to get their job done, including the ability to spend or allocate resources, make decisions or manage others. Greater autonomy and authority says, 'I trust you to act in the best interests of the company, to do so independently and without the approval of myself or others.' Award employees with increased autonomy and authority as a form of recognition for their past results. Autonomy and authority are privileges, not rights, which you should grant to those employees who've most earned them, based on past performance, and not based on tenure or seniority.

Book III

Finding and Managing Staff

✔ **Time with their manager (No. 6):** In today's fast-paced world of work in which everyone is expected to get more done faster, personal time with your manager is in itself also a form of recognition. Because managers are busier, taking time with employees is even more important. The action says, 'Of all the things I have to do, one of the most important is to take time to be with you, the person or people I most depend on for us to be successful.' Especially for younger employees, time spent with a manager is a valued form of validation and inspiration, as well as serving a practical purpose of learning, communicating, answering questions, discussing possibilities or just listening to an employee's ideas, concerns and opinions.

By the way, you may wonder where money ranked in importance in this survey. A 'cash reward' ranked 13th in importance to employees. (We say more about the topic of money as a motivator later in this chapter.) Everyone needs money to live, but work today involves more than what anyone gets paid.

Employees report that the most important aspects at work today are primarily the intangible aspects of the job that any manager can easily provide – if she makes it a priority to do so. Now we're going to tell you a big secret. This secret is the key to motivating your employees. You don't need to attend an all-day seminar or join the management-DVD-of-the-week club to discover this secret: we're letting you in on it right here and right now at no extra charge:

Ask your employees what they want.

This statement may sound silly, but you can take a lot of the guesswork out of your job by simply being clear about what your employees most value in their jobs. It may be one or more of the items we mention earlier in this section, or it may be something entirely different. The simplest way to find out how to motivate your employees is to ask them. Often managers assume that their employees want only money. These same managers are surprised when their employees tell them that other things – such as being recognised for doing a good job, being allowed greater autonomy in decision making or having a more flexible work schedule – may be much more motivating than cash. Regardless of what preferences your employees have, you're much better off knowing those preferences explicitly rather than guessing or ignoring them. So:

✔ **Plan to provide employees with more of what they value.** Look for opportunities to recognise employees for having done good work and act on those opportunities as they arise, realising that what motivates some employees doesn't motivate others.

✔ **Stick with it over time.** Motivation is a moving target and you need to constantly be looking to meet your employees' needs in order to keep them motivated to help you meet your needs.

Consider the following as you begin setting the stage for your efforts:

1. **Create a supportive environment for your employees by first finding out what they most value.**

2. **Design ways to implement recognition to thank and acknowledge employees when they do good work.**

3. **Be prepared to make changes to your plan, based on what works and what doesn't.**

Creating a supportive environment

Today's new business realities bring a need to find different ways to motivate employees. Motivation is no longer an absolute proposition. The incredible acceleration of change in business and technology is coupled with greatly expanded global competitive forces. With these forces pressing in from all sides, managers can have difficulty keeping up with what employees need to do, much less figure out what to tell them to do. In fact, a growing trend is for managers to manage individuals who are doing work that the managers themselves have never done. (Fortunately, given a little time and a little trust, most employees can work out what needs to be done by themselves.)

Inspiring managers must embrace these changing business forces and management trends. Instead of using the power of their position to motivate workers, managers must use the power of their ideas. Instead of using threats and intimidation to get things done, managers must create environments that support their employees and allow creativity to flourish.

You, as a manager, can create a supportive workplace in the following ways:

Book III

Finding and Managing Staff

- ✔ **Build and maintain trust and respect.** Employees whose managers trust and respect them are motivated to perform at their best. By including employees in the decision-making process, today's managers get better ideas (that are easier to implement), and at the same time they improve employees' morale, loyalty and commitment.

- ✔ **Remove the barriers to getting to work.** If you ask your employees what are the biggest hurdles they face in coming to work, you get a huge range of answers – rush-hour traffic, getting the kids to school, having to use public transport and so on. By allowing them to choose their hours of work, you give your staff the opportunity to work around these barriers. You're also entitled to expect that, having chosen their hours of work, they then show up and do a good job. You can't do this for every eventuality, and crises always happen. However, as long as the employee is prepared to give you a reasonable and regular pattern of hours, you need to at least consider being flexible.

✔ **Open the channels of communication.** The ability of all your employees to communicate openly and honestly with one another is critical to the ultimate success of your organisation and plays a major role in employee motivation. Today, quick and efficient communication of information throughout your organisation can be what differentiates you from your competition. Encourage your employees to speak up, to make suggestions and to break down the organisational barriers – the rampant departmentalisation, turf protection and similar roadblocks – that separate them from one another, where and whenever they find them.

✔ **Make your employees feel safe.** Are your employees as comfortable telling you the bad news as they are telling you the good news? If the answer is no, you haven't created a safe environment for your employees. Everyone makes mistakes; people discover valuable lessons from their mistakes. If you want employees who are motivated, make it safe for them to take chances and to let you know the bad along with the good. And use mistakes and errors as opportunities for growth and development; never punish mistakes and errors except those generated as the result of negligence or incompetence.

✔ **Develop your greatest asset – your employees.** By meeting your employees' needs, you also respond to your organisation's needs. Challenge your employees to improve their skills and knowledge and provide them with the support and training that they need to do so. Concentrate on the positive progress they make and recognise and reward such success whenever possible.

Having a good game plan

Motivated employees don't happen by accident. You need a plan to reinforce the behaviour you want. In general, employees are more strongly motivated by the potential to earn rewards than they are by the fear of punishment, so a well-thought-out and planned motivation, incentive and rewards system is important to creating a committed, effective workforce. Here are some simple guidelines for setting up a system of low-cost rewards in your organisation:

✔ **Link rewards to organisational goals.** To be effective, rewards need to reinforce the behaviour that leads to achieving an organisation's goals. Use rewards to increase the frequency of desired behaviour and decrease the frequency of undesired behaviour.

✔ **Define parameters and mechanics.** After you've identified the behaviours you want to reinforce, develop the specifics of your reward system. Create rules that are clear and easily understood by all employees. Make sure that goals are attainable and that all employees have a chance to obtain rewards, whatever their job and occupation.

✔ **Obtain commitment and support.** Of course, communicate your new rewards programme to your employees. Many organisations publicise their programmes at group meetings. They present the programmes as positive and fun activities that benefit both the employees and the company. To get the best results, plan and implement your rewards programme with your employees' direct involvement.

✔ **Monitor effectiveness.** Is your rewards system getting the results you want? If not, take another look at the behaviours you want to reinforce and make sure that your rewards are closely linked to them. Even the most successful reward programmes tend to lose their effectiveness over time as employees begin to take them for granted. Keep your programme fresh by discontinuing rewards that have lost their lustre and bringing in new ones from time to time.

Deciding What to Reward

Most organisations and managers reward the wrong things, if they reward their employees at all. This tendency has led to a crisis of epic proportions in the traditional system of incentives and motivation in business. For example:

✔ A major London commodity market gave bonuses of 6 per cent of salary to outstanding employees and 3 per cent of salary to everyone else. Average and adequate performers were therefore receiving exactly the same reward.

✔ A top professional footballer on many thousands of pounds a week joined one of the very top football clubs, only to find himself playing in the reserve team at exactly the time when he was trying to develop his career and reputation through playing regularly. He was therefore receiving a very good reward, but not the one that he wanted.

✔ A council employee rated 'exceptional' was told by her manager that she had to be downgraded to 'average' because her department had no money to pay her bonus.

Book III

Finding and Managing Staff

If workers aren't being rewarded for doing outstanding work, what are they being rewarded for? As we point out in the 'Biscuit motivation' section, organisations often reward employees just for showing up for work.

For an incentive programme to have meaningful and lasting effects, it must focus on performance – nothing less and nothing more.

'But wait a second,' you may say, 'that isn't fair to the employees who aren't as talented as my top performers.' If that's what you think, we can straighten out that particular misunderstanding right now. Everyone, regardless of how smart, talented or productive they are, has the potential to be a top performer.

Suppose that Employee A produces 100 widgets an hour and stays at that level of performance day in and day out. On the other hand, Employee B produces 75 widgets an hour but improves output to 85 widgets an hour. Who should you reward? Employee B! This example embodies what you want to reward: the efforts that your employees make to improve their performance, not just to maintain a certain level (no matter how good that level is).

The following are examples of *performance-based measures* that any manager must recognise and reward. Consider what measures you should be monitoring, measuring and rewarding in your organisation. Don't forget, just showing up for work doesn't count.

- Defects decrease from 25 per 1,000 to 10 per 1,000.
- Annual sales increase by 20 per cent.
- The department records system is reorganised and colour-coded to make filing and retrieval more efficient.
- Administrative expenses are held to 90 per cent of the authorised budget.
- Mail is distributed in 1 hour instead of 1½ hours.

Some managers break incentives into two categories – *results measures*, where measures are linked to the bottom line, and *process measures*, where the link to the bottom line isn't as clear. You need to recognise achievement in both categories.

Starting with the Positive

You're more likely to lead employees to great results by focusing on their positive accomplishments rather than by finding fault with and punishing their negative outcomes. Despite this fact, many managers' primary mode of operation is correcting their employees' mistakes instead of complimenting their successes.

In a recent study, 58 per cent of employees reported that they seldom received a personal thank-you from their manager for doing a good job even though they ranked such recognition as their most motivating incentive. They ranked a written thank-you for doing a good job as motivating incentive No. 2, but 76 per cent said that they seldom received thanks from their managers. Perhaps these statistics show why a lack of praise and recognition is one of the leading reasons people leave their jobs.

Praising guidelines

A basic foundation for a positive relationship is the ability to praise well. To offer effective praise, one option is to use a system called 'ASAP-cubed', which means:

✔ **As soon:** Timing is very important when using positive reinforcement. Give praise as soon as the person displays the desired behaviour.

✔ **As sincere:** Words can fall flat if you're not sincere in why you're praising someone. Praise someone because you're truly appreciative and excited about the other person's success. Otherwise, the praise may come across as a manipulative tactic or simply patronising.

✔ **As specific:** Avoid generalities in favour of details of the achievement. For example, 'You really turned that angry customer around by focusing on what you could do for her, not on what you couldn't do for her.'

✔ **As personal:** A key to conveying your message is praising in person, face to face. This shows that the activity is important enough to you to put aside everything else you have to do and just focus on the other person.

✔ **As positive:** Too many managers undercut praise with a concluding note of criticism. When you say something like 'You did a great job on this report, but you made quite a few typos', the *but* becomes a verbal erasure of all that came before.

✔ **As proactive:** Lead with praise and catch people doing things right. Otherwise, you tend to be reactive – typically about mistakes – in your interactions with others.

You can give praise directly to the employee, in front of another person (in public) or when the person isn't around (via letter, email, voice-mail and so forth). Praising employees only takes a moment, but the benefits to your employees and to your organisation last for years.

Years of psychological research clearly show that positive reinforcement works better than negative reinforcement for several reasons. Without getting too technical, the reasons are that positive reinforcement:

✔ Increases the frequency of the desired behaviour

✔ Creates good feelings within employees

On the other hand, negative reinforcement may decrease the frequency of undesired behaviour, but doesn't necessarily result in the expression of desired behaviour. Instead of being motivated to do better, employees who receive only criticism from their managers eventually come to avoid their managers whenever possible. Furthermore, negative reinforcement (particularly when manifested in ways that degrade employees and their sense of self-worth) can create tremendously bad feelings in employees. And employees who are unhappy with their employers have a much more difficult time doing a good job than employees who are happy with their employers.

The following ideas can help you seek out the positive in your employees and reinforce the behaviours you want:

- ✔ **Have high expectations for your employees' abilities.** If you believe that your employees can be outstanding, soon they believe it too.

- ✔ **Recognise that your employees are doing their best.** If a shortfall in performance occurs, then support and encourage; punishing people for things that they can't do is pointless.

- ✔ **Give your employees the benefit of the doubt.** Do you really think that your employees want to do a bad job? No one wants to do a bad job; so your job is to work out everything you can do to help employees do a good job. Additional training, encouragement and support should be among your first choices – not reprimands and punishment.

- ✔ **Catch your employees doing things right.** Most employees do a good job in most of their work, so instead of catching your employees doing things wrong, catch them doing things right. Not only can you reinforce the behaviours that you want, but you can also make your employees feel good about working for you and for your organisation.

Making a Big Deal about Something Little

Okay, here's a question for you: should you reward your employees for their little day-to-day successes, or should you save up rewards for when they accomplish something really major? The answer to this question lies in the way that most people get their work done on a daily basis.

For most people in business, work isn't a string of dazzling successes that come one after another without fail. Instead, most work consists of routine, daily activities; employees perform most of these duties quietly and with little fanfare. A manager's typical workday, for example, may consist of an hour or two reading memos and emails, listening to voice-mail messages and talking to people on the phone. The manager spends another few hours in meetings and perhaps another hour having one-to-one discussions with staff members and colleagues, much of which involves dealing with problems as they occur. With additional time spent on preparing reports or completing forms, the manager actually devotes precious little time to decision making – the activity that has the greatest impact on an organisation.

For a line worker, this dearth of opportunities for dazzling success is even more pronounced. If the employee's job is assembling lawnmower engines all day (and she does a good, steady job), when does she have an opportunity to be outstanding in the eyes of her supervisor?

Saga recognises – everyone!

Saga, a specialist holiday, travel and financial services company for the over-fifties, had just completed its best ever year. Profits rose by 25 per cent; turnover by 40 per cent. The company was set to be listed on the London Stock Exchange. Sydney De Haan, the company's founder, considered how best to reward everyone involved in this success. He instituted a scheme of annual bonuses, based on both individual and collective performance. At the end of the bumper year, he also paid for a holiday for all staff and their families.

We've taken the long way around to say that major accomplishments are usually few and far between, regardless of your place in the organisational chart. Work is a series of small accomplishments that eventually add up to big ones. If you wait to reward your employees for their big successes, you may be waiting a long time.

Reward your employees for their small successes as well as their big ones. You may set a lofty goal for your employees to achieve – one that stretches their abilities and tests their resolve – but remember that praising your employees' progress towards the goal is perhaps even more important than praising them when they finally reach it.

Book III

Finding and Managing Staff

Considering Money and Motivation

You may think that money is the ultimate incentive for your employees. After all, who isn't excited when they receive a cash bonus or pay rise? *As visions of riches beyond her wildest dreams danced through her head, she pledged her eternal devotion to the firm.* The problem is that money really isn't the top motivator for employees – at least not in the way that most managers think. And money can be a huge demotivator if you manage it badly.

Compensating with wages and salaries

Money is important to your employees, to pay bills, buy food and clothes, put petrol in their cars and afford other necessities. Most employees consider the money they receive to be a fair exchange for the work they put in. Payment for work carried out is a legal right. Recognition, though, is a gift. Using recognition, however, helps you get the best effort from each employee.

Realising when incentives become entitlements

In particular, employees who receive annual bonuses and other periodic, money-based rewards quickly come to consider them part of their basic pay. The problem arises when achieving bonuses and incentives is easy or straightforward. Productivity and output begin to flatten out and the incentive effect of the payments themselves begins to diminish. People work on the basis that the incentives and bonuses are forthcoming anyway.

Incentives work best when they're related to goals or targets and short-term performance. In particular, incentives don't make a bad or boring job more interesting – they make it more bearable, and only in the short term.

So the issue becomes again: what are you rewarding? You need to work out what the goals are, what rewards people expect for achieving them and the best way to deliver these rewards. Consolidating incentives into standard pay and reward packages just puts up payroll costs without any tangible returns.

The ineffectiveness of money as a motivator for employees is a good news/ bad news kind of thing. We start with the bad news. Many managers have thrown lots of money into cash-reward programmes, and for the most part these programmes haven't really had the positive effect on motivation that the managers expected. Although we don't want to say that you waste your money on these programmes, you can use it more effectively.

Now you get the good news: because you know that money isn't the most effective motivation tool, you can focus on using tools that are more effective – and the best forms of recognition cost little or no money!

Working out what motivates your staff

If you're a busy manager, cash rewards are convenient because you simply fill out a single request to take care of all your motivation for the year. By contrast, the manager-initiated, based-on-performance stuff seems like a lot of work. To be frank, running an effective rewards programme does take more work on your part than running a simple but ineffective one. But as we show you, the best rewards can be quite simple. When you get the hang of using them, you can easily integrate these rewards into your daily routine.

To achieve the best results:

- ✔ Concentrate on what the employees need, want and expect. The only way to be absolutely sure is to ask them.

- ✔ Concentrate rewards on the things you really want done. And keep in mind that what gets rewarded gets done.

Don't save up recognition for special occasions only – and don't just use them with the top performers. You need to recognise all employees when they do good work in their job. Your employees are doing good things – things that you want them to do – every day. Catch them doing something right and recognise their successes regularly and often.

The following incentives are simple to execute, take little time and are the most motivating for employees:

- Personal or written congratulations from you for a job well done
- Public recognition, given visibly by you for good job performance
- Morale-building meetings to celebrate successes
- Time off or flexibility in working hours
- Asking employees their opinions and involving them in decision making

Ten ways to motivate employees

Here are some easy, no-cost things you can do to create a motivating workplace:

- Personally thank employees for doing a good job – one-to-one, in writing or both. Do it timely, often and sincerely.

- Take the time to meet with and listen to employees – as much as they need or want.

- Provide employees with specific and frequent feedback about their performance. Support them in improving performance.

- Recognise, reward and promote high performers; deal with low and marginal performers so that they improve.

- Provide information on how the company makes and loses money, upcoming products and services, and strategies for competing. Explain the employee's role in the overall plan.

- Involve employees in decisions, especially those that affect them. Involvement equals commitment.

- Give employees a chance to grow and develop new skills; encourage them to be their best. Show them how you can help them meet their goals while achieving the organisation's goals. Create a partnership with each employee.

- Provide employees with a sense of ownership in their work and their work environment. This ownership can be symbolic (for example, business cards for all employees, whether they need them to do their jobs or not).

- Strive to create a work environment that's open, trusting and fun. Encourage new ideas, suggestions and initiative. Learn from, rather than punish for, mistakes.

- Celebrate successes – of the company, of the department and of individuals. Take time for team- and morale-building meetings and activities. Be creative and fresh.

Book III

Finding and Managing Staff

Realising that you hold the key to your employees' motivation

In our experience, most managers believe that their employees determine how motivated they choose to be. Managers tend to think that some employees naturally have good attitudes, that others naturally have bad attitudes and that managers can't do much to change these attitudes. 'If only we could unleash the same passion and energy people have for their families and hobbies,' these managers think, 'then we could really get something done around here.'

As convenient as blaming your employees for their bad attitudes may be, looking in a mirror may be a more honest approach. Managers need to

✔ Recognise their employees for doing a good job

✔ Provide a pleasant and supportive working environment

✔ Create a sense of joint mission and teamwork in the organisation

✔ Treat their employees as equals

✔ Avoid favouritism

✔ Make time to listen when employees need to talk

For the most part, you determine how motivated (and demotivated) your employees are. Managers create a motivating environment that makes it easier for employees to be motivated. When the time comes, recognise and reward them fairly and equitably for the work they do well.

When giving rewards, remember that employees don't want handouts, and they hate favouritism. Provide rewards for performance that helps you be mutually successful. Don't give recognition when none is warranted. Don't give it just to be nice, or with the hope that people will like you better. Doing so cheapens the value of the incentive for the employee who received it and loses you credibility your other employees' eyes. Trust and credibility are two of the most important qualities that you can build in your relationship with your employees; if you lose these qualities, you risk losing the employee.

Chapter 7

Coaching and Development

· ·

In This Chapter

▶ Understanding what a coach is

▶ Developing basic coaching skills

▶ Recognising the development needs of your employees

▶ Creating the conditions for successful and enduring development

· ·

*T*he best managers are *coaches* – that is, individuals who guide, talk with and encourage others on their journey. With the help of coaches, employees can achieve outstanding results, organisations can perform better than ever and you can sleep well at night, knowing that everything is just fine.

 Coaching plays a critical part in the learning process for employees who are developing their skills, knowledge and self-confidence. Your employees don't learn effectively when you simply tell them what to do. In fact, they usually don't learn at all.

 As the maxim goes:

> Tell me . . . I forget.
>
> Show me . . . I remember.
>
> Involve me . . . I learn.

Nor do your employees learn effectively when you throw a new task at them with no instruction or support whatsoever. Of course, good employees can, and do, eventually work things out for themselves, but they waste a lot of time and energy in the process. 'What on earth am I supposed to be doing? Let's have a go anyway and see what happens!'

Between these two extremes – being told what to do and being given no support whatsoever – is a happy medium where employees can thrive and the organisation can prosper. This is the happy land where everyone lives in peace, harmony, prosperity and achievement – and this happy medium starts and finishes with coaching.

Playing a Coach's Role

Even if you have a pretty good sense of what it means to be a manager, do you really know what it means to be a coach? A coach is a colleague, counsellor and cheerleader, all rolled into one. Based on that definition, are you a coach? How about your boss? Or your boss's boss? Why or why not?

We bet that you're familiar with the role of coaches in other non-business activities. A drama coach, for example, is almost always an accomplished actor. The drama coach's job is to conduct auditions for parts, assign roles, schedule rehearsals, train and direct cast members throughout rehearsals and support and encourage the actors during the final stage production. These roles aren't all that different from the roles that managers perform in a business, are they?

Coaching a team of individuals isn't easy, and certain characteristics make some coaches better than others. Fortunately, as with most other business skills, you can discover, practise and improve your grasp of the traits of good coaches. You can always find room for improvement, a fact that good coaches are the first to admit. The following list highlights some important characteristics of coaching:

- ✔ **Coaches set goals.** Whether an organisation's vision is to become the leading provider of global positioning systems in the world, to increase revenues by 20 per cent a year or simply to get the staffroom walls painted this year, coaches work with their employees to set goals and deadlines for completion. Coaches then withdraw, to allow their employees time to work out how to achieve the goals.

- ✔ **Coaches support and encourage.** Employees – even the best and most experienced – can easily become discouraged from time to time. When employees are learning new tasks, when a long-term account is lost or when business is down, coaches are there, ready to step in and help the team members through the worst of it. 'That's okay, Kim. You've learned from your mistake, and I know that you can get it right next time!'

- ✔ **Coaches emphasise both team success and individual success.** The team's overall performance, not the stellar abilities of a particular team member, is the most important concern. Of course, you need everyone's contribution; but coaches know that no one person can carry an entire team to success. Winning takes the combined efforts of everyone. The development of teamwork skills is a vital step in an employee's progress in an organisation.

- ✔ **Coaches can quickly assess the talents and shortfalls of team members.** The most successful coaches can quickly determine their team members' strengths and weaknesses and, as a result, tailor their approach accordingly. For example, if one team member has strong analytical skills but poor presentation skills, a coach can concentrate on providing support to help the employee develop better presentation skills. 'You know, Mark, I want to spend some time with you to work on making your sales presentations more effective.'

✔ **Coaches inspire their team members.** Through their support and guidance, coaches are skilled at inspiring their team members to the highest levels of human performance. Teams of inspired individuals are willing to do whatever it takes to achieve their organisation's goals.

✔ **Coaches create environments that allow individuals to be successful.** Great coaches ensure that their workplaces are structured to let team members take risks and stretch their limits without fear of retribution if they fail.

✔ **Coaches provide feedback.** Communication and feedback between coach and employee form a critical element of the coaching process. Employees must know where they stand in the organisation – what they're doing right, and what they're doing wrong. Equally important, employees must let their coaches know when they need help or assistance. And this must be a continuous process for both parties. Otherwise problems get raised only at performance reviews and appraisals, or, worse still, get lost altogether.

Coaches are available to advise their employees or just to listen to their problems if need be, whether the issue is work-related or personal.

Firing someone doesn't constitute effective feedback. Unless an employee has engaged in some sort of intolerable offence (such as physical violence, theft or intoxication on the job), a manager needs to give the employee plenty of verbal and written feedback before even considering termination. With employees who simply can't see what they're doing wrong, your coaching either makes or breaks. If you simply fire someone, you never know whether the problem was his – or yours.

Book III

Finding and Managing Staff

Coaching: A Rough Guide

Besides the obvious coaching roles of supporting and encouraging employees in their quest to achieve an organisation's goals, coaches also teach their employees *how* to achieve those goals. Drawing from their experience, coaches lead their workers step by step through work processes or procedures. When the workers discover how to perform a task, the coach delegates full authority and responsibility for its performance to them.

For the transfer of specific skills, you can find no better way of teaching – and learning – than the *show-and-tell* method. If you need to get people up to speed on workplace skills, knowledge and understanding, then do it on the job. There's simply no better place. And – if you need to – you can get people working fully productively very quickly.

Show-and-tell or on-the-job coaching has three steps:

1. *You do, you say.* **Sit down with your employees and explain the procedure in general terms while you perform the task.** All businesses now use computers as a critical tool for getting work done. If you're coaching a new employee in the use of an obscure word processing or spreadsheet program, the first thing you need to do is to explain the technique to the employee while you demonstrate it. 'I click my left mouse button on the Insert command on the toolbar and pull down the menu. Then I point the arrow to Symbol and click again. I choose the symbol I want from the menu, point my arrow to it and click to select it. I then point my arrow to Insert and click to place the symbol in the document; then I point my arrow to Close and click again to finish the job.'

2. *They do, you say.* **Next get the employee to do the same procedure as you explain each step.** 'Click your left mouse button on the Insert command on the toolbar and pull down the menu. Okay, good. Now point your arrow to Symbol and click again. Excellent! Choose the symbol you want from the menu and point your arrow to it. Now click to select it. All right – point your arrow to Insert and click to place the symbol in the document. Okay, you're almost done now. Point your arrow to Close and click again to finish the job. There you are!'

3. *They do, they say.* **Finally, as you observe, get your employee to perform the task again as he explains to you what he's doing.** 'Okay, Miles, now it's your turn. I want you to insert a symbol in your document and tell me what you're doing.'

   'All right, Senti. First, I click my left mouse button on the Insert command on the toolbar and pull down the menu. Then I point the arrow to Symbol and click again. I decide the symbol I want from the menu, point my arrow to it and click to select it. Next, I point the arrow to Insert and click to place the symbol in the document. Finally, I point my arrow to Close and click again to finish the job. I did it!'

Get employees to create a 'crib sheet' of the new steps to refer to until they become habit.

Coaching Metaphors for Success in Business

In business, when it comes to coaching and teamwork, the metaphor of a company as a winning sports team is often applied. In many organisations chief executives hire professional athletes and coaches to lecture their employees on the importance of team play and winning. Managers are labelled *coaches* or *team leaders*, and workers are labelled *players* or *team members*.

This being the case, ignoring the obvious parallels between coaching in sport and in business is difficult. So we're going to get this out of our system once and for all and refrain from linking coaching in sport and business anywhere else in this book after the following list of examples:

- Terry Venables, legendary football coach, on his appointment to Barcelona FC: 'The first thing that I had to do was to get this group of highly talented individuals playing as a team.'

- Clive Woodward, World Cup-winning England rugby coach: 'To build a team, you have to coach people as a team. Of course, you work on individual strengths and weaknesses; in the end, however, it is how they perform together, not how they perform individually, that determines your success.'

- Arsène Wenger, manager and head coach at Arsenal FC: 'One of the most important things that I have to do is to maintain the players' belief in themselves. This is easy when you are winning – sometimes you have to rein them in. But when you are losing – this is the most important part of the job. And if you simply shout at people or threaten them – you will always fail.'

- José Mourinho, legendary (some would say controversial) football coach who's produced winning teams in three different countries and cultures already: 'If the players do not want to do things my way, I do not want them. Good players who will work as team members will always do better than brilliant individuals working in isolation.'

- Alf Ramsey, World Cup-winning England football manager and coach: 'The best teams are not necessarily made up of the best individuals. When one player thanked me for picking him, I replied: "I don't pick individuals, I pick teams."'

One last point: in sport, as in business, *everybody* needs a coach. Who's the greatest tennis player of all time? Pete Sampras? Probably. But most people don't realise that all the time he was playing, even Pete Sampras had a coach to help him stay sharp and to improve.

Tapping into the Coach's Expertise

Coaching isn't a one-dimensional activity. Because every person is different, the best coaches tailor their approach to their team members' specific, individualised needs. If one team member is independent and needs only occasional guidance, recognise where the employee stands and provide that level of support. This support may consist of an occasional, informal progress check while making the rounds of the office. If, on the other hand, another team member is insecure and needs more guidance, the coach recognises this employee's position and assists as required. In this case, support may consist of frequent, formal meetings with the employee to assess progress and to provide advice and direction as needed.

Although every coach has an individual style, the best coaches employ certain techniques to elicit the greatest performance from their team members:

- **Meet and make time for team members.** Managing is primarily a people job. Part of being a good manager and coach is being available to your employees when they need your help. If you're not available, your employees may seek out other avenues to meet their needs – or simply stop trying to work with you. Always keep your door open to your employees and remember that they're your Number 1 priority. Manage by walking around. Regularly get out of your office and visit your employees at their workstations. 'Do I have a minute, Elaine? Of course, I always have time for you and the other members of my staff.'

- **Provide context and vision.** Instead of simply telling employees what to do, effective coaches explain *why*. Coaches provide their employees with context and a big-picture perspective. Instead of spouting long lists of do's and don'ts, they explain how a system or procedure works and then define their employees' parts in the scheme of things. 'Sanjeev, you have a very important part in the financial health and vitality of our company. By ensuring that our customers pay their invoices within 30 days after we ship their products, we're able to keep our cash flow on the plus side, and we can meet our obligations such as rent, electricity and your salary on time.'

- **Transfer knowledge and perspective.** A great benefit of having a good coach is the opportunity to discover information and know-how from someone who has more experience than you do. In response to the unique needs of each team member, coaches transfer their personal knowledge and perspective. 'We faced the exact situation about five years ago, Hayden. I'm going to tell you what we did then, and I want you to tell me whether you think that it still makes sense today or if you have a better idea that we could try.'

- **Be a sounding board.** Coaches talk through new ideas and approaches to solving problems with their employees. Coaches and employees can consider the implications of different approaches to solving a problem and role-play customer or client reactions before trying them out for real. By using active listening skills, coaches can often help their employees work through issues and come up with the best solutions themselves. 'Okay, David, you've told me that you don't think your customer will buy from us if we put the prices up by 20 per cent. What options do we have with price increases, and are some better than others?'

- **Obtain necessary resources.** Sometimes coaches can help their employees make the jump from marginal to outstanding performance simply by providing the resources that their employees need. These resources can take many forms – money, time, staff, equipment or other tangible assets. 'So, Kathleen, you're confident that we can improve our cash flow if we put two more staff on to invoicing? Okay, let's give it a try.'

> ✔ **Offer a helping hand.** For an employee who's learning a new job and is still responsible for performing her current job, the total workload can be overwhelming. Coaches can help workers through this transitional phase by reassigning current duties to other employees, authorising overtime or taking other measures to relieve the pressure. 'Jill, while you're learning how to debug the new software, I'm going to assign the rest of your workload to Rachel. We can get back together at the end of the week to see how you're doing.'

Developing and Mentoring Employees

Developing your employees is the other side of coaching. You have to have employees who can and are willing to be developed. Taking people on in isolation from what you expect of them is useless; they must always be prepared to do things your way, making their expertise work for the good of everyone.

So, it's time for a quick look in the mirror. What kind of manager are you? Do you take on new employees and then just let them go on their merry way? Or do you stay actively involved in the progress and development of your employees, helping to guide them along the way? If you're a manager-to-be, do you know what having a mentor is like, someone who takes a personal interest in your career development? Mentoring is vitally important because as well as needing to make your own mistakes (and you will!), you also need someone to guide you, act as a sounding board, strengthen and test your determination, and indicate areas where you could improve.

Book III

Finding and Managing Staff

Employee development is the process by which you make everyone (including yourself) better at their jobs and improve their willingness to carry them out to the best of their abilities. Employee development is also concerned with the development of skills, knowledge, attitudes and behaviour, building experience and achievements into expertise. Employee development concentrates on the key areas of workplace development, professional and occupational priorities, and personal choices, so that everyone benefits and individuals take active responsibility for their own future.

The best employee development is continuous and requires that you support and encourage your employees' initiative. Recognise, however, that all development is self-development; you can really only develop yourself. You can't force your employees to develop; they have to want to for themselves. You can, however, help create an environment that makes it more likely that they want to develop, grow and succeed.

Explaining How Employee Development Helps

Development boils down to one important point: as a manager, you're in the best position to provide your employees with the support they need to advance in your organisation. Not only can you provide them with the time and money required for training, you can also offer unique on-the-job learning opportunities and assignments, mentoring, team participation and more. Besides, someone's got to be there to take your place when you get promoted. Employee development involves a lot more than just going to a training class or two. In fact, approximately 90 per cent of development occurs on the job.

Training, learning and development are all different aspects of the same process:

- **Training** is the most straightforward – you tell people how to do something that's either more or less standard; or you take a step-by-step approach to something more complex.

- **Learning** requires you to create the conditions, environment and context – and employee confidence – in which development is most effective.

- **Development** is what goes on with everyone in all aspects of their lives, including work. From a manager's point of view, you need to see employee development as a combination of personal, professional, occupational and career advancement and enhancement; and the improvement of knowledge, attitudes, behaviour and experience, as well as skills and expertise.

Now, have you ever wondered why your employees continue to mess up assignments that you know they can perform? In case you don't have any inkling whatsoever why developing your employees is a good idea, the following list provides the full justification:

- Development ensures that your employees have the knowledge they need.

- Employees who work effectively are better employees.

- Someone has to be prepared to step into your shoes; for example, when you go on holiday, or in case you yourself move on.

The reason that many managers don't have to call their offices when they're on holiday is because they make it a point to help develop their employees to take over when they're gone. You can do the same thing too; the future of your organisation depends on it. Really.

> ✔ Your employee wins, and so does your organisation; and most important, you prepare your employees to fulfil the roles that your organisation needs them to fulfil in the future.

Your employees are worth your time and money. And if this sounds almost too obvious to state at all, remember that employees take anything up to three-quarters of the fixed costs of any organisation. So make sure that you make them as capable and as willing to work for you as you possibly can. Constantly offer new challenges and opportunities for all your employees; and make sure that they respond by stretching themselves to the limit.

Creating Career Development Plans

The career development plan is the heart and soul of your efforts to develop your employees. Unfortunately, many managers don't take the time to create development plans with their employees, instead trusting that when a need arises, they can find training to accommodate that need. This kind of reactive thinking ensures that you're always playing catch up to the challenges that your organisation faces.

Why wait for the future to arrive before you prepare to deal with it? Are you really so busy that you can't spend a little of your precious time planting the seeds that your organisation can harvest years from now? No! Although you do have to take care of the seemingly endless crises that arise in the here and now, you also have to prepare yourself and your employees to meet the challenges of the future. To do otherwise is an incredibly short-sighted and ineffective way to run your organisation.

All career development plans must contain as a minimum the following key elements:

- ✔ **Specific learning goals, supported by milestones along the way:** Each and every employee in your organisation benefits from having learning goals; and you need to set individual goals for each person. For example, say that your employee's career path starts at the position of junior buyer and works up to manager of purchasing. The key learning goals for this employee may be learning the stocks and supplies, training how to plan for stock replacement, spreadsheet analyses, and introduction to management.

- ✔ **Resources required to achieve the designated learning goals:** Make sure you can resource everything that's needed.

- ✔ **Employee responsibilities and resources:** Career development is the joint responsibility of an employee and his manager. A business can and does pay for things, but so can employees. A good career development plan should include what the employee is doing in his own time.

Book III

Finding and Managing Staff

✔ **Required dates of completion for each learning goal:** Make sure that employees stick to these dates, or else that they can give a clear explanation for failure to meet the dates for completion.

✔ **Standards for measuring the accomplishment of learning goals:** Assess these at each milestone.

Helping Employees to Develop

Employee development takes the deliberate and continuous efforts of employees with the support of their managers. If employees or managers lose heart, commitment or faith, then employees don't develop, and the organisation suffers the consequences of not having the employees it needs to meet the challenges it faces. This outcome definitely isn't good. As a manager, you want your organisation to be ready for the future, not always trying to catch up with it.

The employee's role is to identify the areas where development can help to make him a better and more productive worker, and then to relay this information to his manager. When the employee identifies further development opportunities, the manager and employee work together to schedule and implement them.

As a manager, your role is to be alert to the development needs of your employees and to keep an eye out for potential development opportunities. Managers in smaller organisations may be assigned to determine where the organisation will be in the next few years. Armed with that information, you're responsible for finding ways to ensure that employees are available to meet the needs of the future organisation. Your job is then to provide the resources and support required to develop employees so that they're able to fulfil the organisation's needs.

To develop your employees to meet the coming challenges within your organisation, follow these steps:

1. **Meet each employee to discuss his career.**

   Meet individuals to discuss where you see them in the organisation and also to find out where in the organisation they want to go.

   This effort has to be a joint one! Having elaborate plans for an employee to rise up the company ladder in sales management isn't going to do you any good if your employee hates the idea of leaving actual sales to become a manager of other salespeople.

2. **Discuss your employee's strengths and weaknesses.**

   Have a frank discussion regarding the employee's strengths and areas for development. Your main goal here is to identify the areas that the employee is interested in and good at – that is, strengths that your employee can develop to allow his continued progress in the organisation and to meet the future challenges that your business faces. Focus the majority of your development efforts and resources on these opportunities.

Spend time developing strengths as well as improving weaknesses. Improving and enhancing a skill that your employee finds easy and enjoyable is more valuable for you and your organisation than forcing the employee to be merely adequate at things others excel in. However, everyone needs to be proficient in essential tasks, even if they don't like them.

3. **Assess where the employee is now.**

   Determine the current state of your employee's skills and talents. Doing an assessment provides you with an overall road map to guide your development efforts.

4. **Create a career development plan.**

   A *career development plan* is an agreement between you and your employee that spells out exactly what formal support (tuition, time off, travel expenses and so on) your employee may receive to develop his skills, and when he may receive it. Career development plans have review and evaluation points, assessments of progress and agreements on the next step.

5. **Follow through on your agreements, and make sure that the employee follows through on his.**

   Don't break the development plan agreement. Make sure that you provide the support that you agreed to provide. Make sure that your employee upholds his end of the bargain too! Check on his progress regularly. If he misses schedules because of other priorities, reassign his work as necessary to ensure that he has time to focus on his career development plans.

So when is the best time to sit down with your employees to discuss career planning and development? The sooner the better! Conducting a career development discussion twice a year with each of your employees isn't too often. Quarterly is even better; and a brief chat once a month is best of all. And make sure that you commit to the discussion – it represents time, money and effort well spent! Include a brief assessment in each discussion of the employee's development needs. Ask your employee what he can do to fulfil these needs. If he requires additional support, determine what form of support the employee needs and when to schedule the support. Adjust career development plans and redirect resources as necessary.

Top ten ways to develop employees

The basics for developing employees are:

- Provide employees with opportunities to learn and grow.
- Be a mentor to an employee.
- Let an employee fill in for you at staff meetings.
- Give employees secondment and project work opportunities.
- Allow employees to pursue and develop any ideas they have.
- Provide employees with a choice of assignments.
- Send an employee to a seminar on a new topic.
- Take an employee along with you when you call on customers.
- Introduce your employees to top managers in your organisation and arrange to have them perform special assignments for senior people.
- Allow an employee to shadow you during your workday.

Chapter 8

Being an Expert at Performance Appraisal and Management

Setting goals – for individuals, for teams and for the overall organisation – is extremely important. (Chapter 6 in this Book addresses the whys and wherefores of setting goals.) However, ensuring that the organisation is making progress towards the successful completion of its goals (in the manner and time frames agreed to) is equally important. The organisation's performance depends on each individual who works within it. Achieving goals is what this chapter is all about.

Measuring and monitoring the performance of individuals in your organisation is like walking a tightrope: you don't want to over-measure or over-monitor your employees. Doing so only leads to needless bureaucracy and red tape, which can negatively affect your employees' ability to perform their tasks. Neither do you want to under-measure or under-monitor your employees. Such a lack of watchfulness can lead to nasty surprises when a task is completed late, over budget or not at all. 'What? The customer database conversion isn't completed yet? I promised the sales director that we'd have that job done two weeks ago!'

Please keep in mind that, as a manager, your primary goal in measuring and monitoring your employees' performance isn't to punish them for making a mistake or missing a milestone. Instead, you help your employees stay on track and find out whether they need additional assistance or resources to do so. Few employees like to admit that they need help getting an assignment done – whatever the reason. Because of their reluctance, you must systemati-cally check on the progress of your employees and regularly give them feed-back on how they're doing.

If you don't monitor desired performance, you won't achieve desired perfor-mance. Don't leave achieving your goals to chance; develop systems to moni-tor progress and ensure that employees achieve your goals. And you can't measure anything except against what you set out to achieve.

Taking the First Steps

The first step in checking your employees' progress is to determine the key indi-cators of a goal's success. Set goals with your employees that are few in number and *SMART* (specific, measurable, attainable, relevant and time-bound).

When you quantify a goal in precise numerical terms, your employees have no confusion over how their performance is measured and when their job performance is adequate (or less than adequate). For example, if the goal is to produce 100 sprockets per hour, with a reject rate of 1 or lower, your employees clearly understand that producing only 75 sprockets per hour with 10 rejects is unacceptable performance. You leave nothing to the imagi-nation, and the goals aren't subject to individual interpretation or to the whims of individual supervisors or managers.

How you measure and monitor the progress of your employees towards com-pletion of their goals depends on the nature of the goals. You can measure goals in terms of time, units of production or delivery of a particular work product (such as a report or a sales proposal), for example.

Table 8-1 offers examples of different goals and ways to measure them.

Table 8-1	Sample Goals and Measurements
Goal	*Measurement*
Plan and implement a company news-letter before the end of the second quarter of the current fiscal year	The specific date (for example 30 June) that the newsletter is sent out (*time*)
Increase the number of mountain bike frames produced by each employee from 20 to 25 per day	The exact number of mountain bike frames produced by the employee each day (*quantity*)
Increase profit on the project by 20 per cent in financial year 2012	The total percentage increase in profit in the year to 31 December 2012 (*per-centage increase*)

Although noting when your employees attain their goals is obviously important, recognising your employees' *incremental* progress towards attaining their goals is just as important. For example:

✔ The goal for your drivers is to maintain an accident-free record. This goal is continuous – no deadline exists. To encourage drivers in their efforts, you can prominently post a huge banner in the middle of the garage that reads '153 Accident-Free Days'. Increase the number for each day of accident-free driving.

✔ The goal of your accounts clerks is to increase the average number of transactions from 150 per day to 175 per day. To track their progress, you can publicly post a summary of the daily production count at the end of each week. As production increases, praise the progress of your employees towards the final goal.

✔ The goal set for your production staff is to turn customer orders around within 24 hours, without errors. You can publicly post the results for all to see; and in this case, when orders are either not turned around within 24 hours or when errors occur, you have a very quick, public and agreed point for investigation.

The secret to performance measuring and monitoring is the power of positive feedback. When you give positive feedback (increased number of units produced, percentage increase in sales and so on), you encourage the behaviour that you want. However, when you give negative feedback (number of errors, number of work days lost and so on), you aren't encouraging the behaviour you want; you're only discouraging the behaviour that you don't want. Consider the following examples:

✔ **Instead of measuring this:** Number of defective cartridges

✔ **Measure this:** Number of correctly assembled cartridges

✔ **Instead of measuring this:** Number of days late

✔ **Measure this:** Number of days on time

✔ **Instead of measuring this:** Quantity of late transactions

✔ **Measure this:** Quantity of completed transactions

From our experience as managers, we find that you're much more likely to get the results you want when you put group performance measures (total revenues, average days sick and so on) out in the open for everyone to see, but keep individual performance measures (sales performance by employee, absence rankings by employee and so on) private. The intention is to get a team to work *together* to improve its performance – tracking and publicising group measures and then rewarding improvement in them can lead to dramatic advances in the performance you seek. What you do *not* want to do is embarrass your employees or subject them to ridicule by other employees when their individual performance isn't up to par. Instead, deal with these employees privately, and coach them (and provide additional training and support, as necessary) to improve performance.

Developing a System for Providing Immediate Performance Feedback

You can measure an infinite number of behaviours or performance characteristics. What you measure and the values you measure against are up to you and your employees. Keep certain points in mind when you design a system for measuring and monitoring. Build your system on the *MARS – milestones, actions, relationships* and *schedules* – system. We describe each element of the MARS system in the following sections.

Application of each characteristic – milestones, actions, relationships and schedules – results in goals that you can measure and monitor. If you can't measure and monitor goals, chances are that your employees never achieve them and you don't know the difference.

Setting your checkpoints: The milestones

Every goal needs a starting point, an ending point and points in between to measure progress along the way. *Milestones* are the checkpoints, events and markers that tell you and your employees how far along you are on the road to reaching the goals you've set together.

For example, suppose that you establish a goal of finalising corporate budgets in three months' time. The third milestone along the way to your ultimate goal is that draft department budgets are submitted to division managers no later than 1 June. If you check with the division managers on 1 June and your employees haven't submitted the draft budgets, you quickly and unambiguously know that the project is behind schedule. If, however, all the budgets are in on 15 May, you know that the project is ahead of schedule and that you may reach the final goal of completing the corporate budgets sooner than you originally estimated.

Reaching your checkpoints: The actions

Actions are the individual activities your employees perform to get from one milestone to the next. To reach the third milestone in your budgeting project – submitting draft department budgets to division managers by 1 June – your employees must undertake and complete several actions after they reach the second milestone in the project. In this example, these actions may include the following:

- Review prior-year expenditure reports and determine the relationship, if any, to current activities.

- Review current-year expenditure reports and project and forecast final results.

- Meet department staff to determine their training, travel and capital equipment requirements for the new financial year.

- Review the possibilities of new staff, lay-offs, redundancies and pay rises to determine the impact on payroll costs.

- Put everything onto a computerised draft budget spreadsheet using the figures from the actions already taken.

- Print off the draft budget and double-check the results, correcting them if necessary.

- Submit the draft budget to your own manager before forwarding it to the division manager.

Each action gets your employees a little farther along the way towards reaching the third milestone in the project and is therefore a critical element in their performance.

When developing a plan for completion of any activity or project, note each action in writing. By taking notes, you make concentration easier for your employees because they know exactly what they must do to reach a milestone, how far they've gone and how much farther they have to go. And each time they do reach a milestone, record it.

Acting in sequence: The relationships

Relationships are how milestones and actions interact with one another. Relationships shape the proper sequencing of activities that lead you to the successful, effective accomplishment of your goals. Although sequences don't always matter, it's often more effective to perform certain actions before others and to attain certain milestones before others.

For example, in the list of actions needed to achieve the third project milestone, covered in the preceding section, trying to perform the fifth action before the first, second, third or fourth isn't going to work! If you don't work out the right numbers to put into your spreadsheet before you fill in the blanks, your results are meaningless.

Keep in mind that you may have more than one way to reach a milestone and give your employees the scope to find their own ways to reach their goals. Doing so empowers your employees to take responsibility for their work and to benefit from both their mistakes and their successes. The results are successful performance and happy, productive employees.

Establishing a timeframe: The schedules

How do you determine how far apart your milestones should be and how long project completion should take? You can plan better by estimating the *schedule* of each individual action in your project plan.

Using your experience and training to develop schedules that are realistic and useful is important. For example, if you give someone a deadline of two years' time, she won't take any notice of it until two or three months before the actual date. If you do need to set long-term deadlines, then make sure that you break the activities up into milestones and points of reference that you can realistically measure along the way.

Reducing shrinkage

Shrinkage refers to the amount of products, equipment and supplies lost through wastage, theft, damage or breakage. Shrinkage is therefore a euphemism for sloppiness, lack of attention and, above all, an inability to set standards of performance that stick.

Measuring instead of counting

According to management guru Peter Drucker, most business people spend too much time counting and too little time measuring the performance of their organisations. Drucker likens counting to a doctor using an X-ray machine to diagnose an ill patient. Although some ailments – broken bones, pneumonia and so on – do show up on an X-ray, other, more life-threatening illnesses such as leukaemia, hypertension and AIDS don't. Similarly, most managers use accounting systems to X-ray their organisation's financial performance. However, accounting systems don't measure a catastrophic loss of market share or a failure to innovate until the problem has already gone on too long, and the 'patient' is damaged – perhaps irretrievably.

Many organisations are complacent about shrinkage. According to Lawrence King, managing director of the ORIS Group, a consultancy that monitors the efficiency and effectiveness of resource utilisation for its customers,

> *Some retailers especially do not even know what their shrinkage numbers are. I know of two major businesses, one in pharmaceuticals and the other in fashion, neither of which want to know how bad the problem is, because they know that they would have to do something about it if they did know. They have therefore put this problem into the 'too hard to cope with' basket. The trouble is, it does cost money to find out what the losses are. And then once you know what the losses are, you clearly have to do something about it.*

In the past, organisations thought that shoplifting and petty pilfering were the only real sources and causes of shrinkage, and so considered they had little to worry about. Shrinkage, however, occurs through staff dishonesty and information systems failure as well as through theft by customers. Part of the problem is a result of changing patterns of employment. King states:

> *Not that long ago, most retail staff were full-time. It was a career, and they worked until they drew their pensions. Now, retailers have cut their costs, there are far more part-time staff, so the manager in a typical retail outlet may be the only full-time member of staff. That may not be quite true in bigger stores of course; but the general trend is the same. There is consequently a lot less loyalty and a lot less commitment than there used to be. In addition, the pay is almost invariably lower. Retail has never been the best pay in the world, so maybe people feel that there is an opportunity to supplement low rates of pay by helping themselves a bit.*

Creating programmes based on desired behaviours

Any organisation faced with a serious shrinkage problem has to be able to establish absolute standards – standards below which it doesn't slip, or allow employees to slip. You can only address shrinkage problems under the following conditions:

- ✔ **Recognising the issue at all levels.** Recognition must be underpinned by a determination at board level to deal fully and effectively with the problem.

- ✔ **Enforcing zero tolerance for theft or fraud among staff.** No matter how senior, experienced or valued the colleague is, she must be dismissed if she's caught stealing from the business. This is the *only* way to deal with pilfering.

- ✔ **Making shrinkage culturally unacceptable.** Make it clear that shrinkage is an enemy of the business. Relate shrinkage rates to turnover and profitability in all staff briefings.

Book III

Finding and Managing Staff

✔ **Rewarding the desired behaviour.** The desired behaviour is established through a combination of policies and practice. The policies very clearly state both what's required and how people are to behave and not behave. In particular, you need to focus on the conduct of everyone from the point of view of ensuring that

- Everyone knows and understands that stealing, lying and cheating are an affront to everyone.

- You monitor all aspects of shrinkage that concern you, and make sure that you also involve all the staff.

- Shrinkage is treated from the point of view that, by stealing or lying, individuals affect not just themselves but also everyone else.

Making sure that you reward honest employees adequately for their work, so that you remove their temptation to steal, is the key to this problem. An open and honest culture needs to underpin the organisation; ensuring that employees are honest is impossible if those further up the organisation aren't. Paying attention to matters such as punctuality, commitment and enthusiasm helps to generate loyalty and engagement; and the more loyal and engaged employees are, the less likely they are to steal from their employer.

Reading the Results

You establish your goals, you set performance measures and you obtain pages of data for each of your employees and activities. Now what? Now you determine whether your employees achieved the expected results, as follows:

✔ **Compare results to expectations.** Did your employees achieve the expected goal? Suppose that the goal is to complete the budget by 1 June. When did your employees complete the budget? It was completed on 17 May – well ahead of the deadline. Brilliant! The employees accomplished the mission with time to spare.

✔ **Record the results.** Make note of the results – perhaps put them in the files that you maintain for each employee or print them out on your computer and post them in the work area.

✔ **Praise, coach or counsel your employees.** If they did the job right, on time and within budget, congratulate your employees for a job well done and reward them appropriately: a written note of appreciation, a day off with pay, a formal awards presentation – whatever you decide.

However, if employees didn't achieve the expected results, find out why and what you can do to ensure that they are successful next time. If employees need only additional support or encouragement, coach them for a better performance. Listen to your employees, clarify their difficulties and then formulate a response; consider referring them to other employees for advice or providing your own personal examples that may be applicable to their situation. If the poor results stem from a more serious shortcoming, then retrain, or discipline, your employees. (See Chapter 4 in this Book for the lowdown on disciplining staff.)

Appraising Performance: Why It Matters

You can find many good reasons for conducting regular formal performance appraisals with your employees and of your activities. Formal performance appraisals are just one part of an organisation's system of delegation, goal setting, coaching, motivating and ongoing informal and formal feedback on employee performance. If you don't believe us, try a few of these positive elements of performance appraisals on for size:

✔ **A chance to meet regularly:** Meeting regularly means that you know what your employees are doing and they know you're available for support. When you establish regular informal meetings, you also have a much better basis for effective regular formal reviews when they happen.

✔ **A chance to summarise past performance and establish new performance goals:** All employees want to know whether they're doing a good job. Formal performance appraisals force managers to communicate performance results – both good and bad – to their employees and to set new goals. In many organisations, the annual performance appraisal is the only occasion when supervisors and managers speak to their employees about performance expectations and the results of employee efforts for the preceding appraisal period.

✔ **An opportunity for clarification and communication:** You need to continually compare expectations. Try this exercise with your manager. List your ten most important activities. Then ask your manager to list what she considers to be your ten most important activities. The chances are that your lists are quite different. On average, businesspeople who do this exercise find that their lists overlap by only 40 per cent at best. Performance appraisals help the employer and employee to compare notes and make sure that assignments and priorities are in sync.

✔ **A forum for learning goals and career development:** In many organisations, career development takes place as a part of the formal performance appraisal process. Managers and employees are all very busy and often have difficulty setting aside the time to sit down and chart out the steps that they must take to progress in an organisation or career. Although career development discussions should generally take place in a forum separate from the performance appraisal process, combining the activities does afford the opportunity to kill both birds with the same stone . . . or something like that.

Book III

Finding and Managing Staff

✔ **Formal documentation to promote advancement or dismissal:** Most employees get plenty of informal performance feedback, at least of the negative kind along the lines of: 'You did what? Are you nuts?' Most informal feedback is verbal and undocumented. If you're trying to build a case to give your employee a promotion, you can support it more easily if you have plenty of written documentation (including formal performance appraisals) to justify your decision. And if you're coming to the conclusion that you need to dismiss someone for poor performance, then you must have written evidence, including performance appraisals, that you've tried to address this performance before.

So, the preceding list gives very important reasons for conducting regular, formal performance appraisals. However, consider this statement: many companies have paid a lot of money to employees and former employees who've successfully sued them for wrongful or unfair dismissal, or for other biased and prejudicial employment decisions. Imagine how lonely you'd feel on the witness stand in the following scene, a scene that's replayed for real in courts of law and employment tribunals the length and breadth of the country:

Lawyer: So, Manager-on-the-spot, would you please tell the court exactly why you terminated Employee X?

Manager-on-the-spot: Certainly, I'll be glad to. Employee X was a very poor performer – clearly the worst in my department.

Lawyer: During the five years that my client was with your firm, did you ever conduct formal performance appraisals with her?

Manager-on-the-spot: Er . . . well, no. I meant to, but I'm a very busy person. I was never quite able to get around to it.

Lawyer: Manager-on-the-spot, do you mean to say that, in all the time with your firm, Employee X never received a formal performance appraisal? Exactly how was my client supposed to correct the alleged poor performance when you failed to provide her with the feedback needed to do so?

Manager-on-the-spot: Hmmm . . .

Spelling Out the Performance Appraisal Process

One of the most important things you can do as a manager is to conduct accurate and timely performance appraisals of your employees. Many managers, however, tend to see the performance appraisal process in narrow terms: how can I get this thing done as quickly as possible so I can get back to my real job? (Whatever their 'real' job is as managers.) In their haste to get the appraisal done and behind them, many managers merely consider a few examples of recent performance and base their entire appraisal on them. And because few managers give their employees the kind of meaningful, ongoing performance feedback that they need to do their jobs better, the performance appraisal can become a dreaded event – full of surprises and dismay. Or it can be so sugar-coated that it becomes a meaningless exercise in management. Neither scenario is the right way to evaluate your employees.

Have separate discussions for each of the following:

- ✔ Pay rises and bonuses
- ✔ Promotions
- ✔ Career development
- ✔ Ways to improve present performance and develop future performance
- ✔ Poor performance

Of course, in practice you can't possibly keep each of the topics totally separate from the rest. But you can prioritise; and you need to spell out to the employee the specific purpose of the present discussion.

The performance appraisal process begins on the day that your employees are hired, continues each and every day that they report to you and doesn't end until, through transfer, promotion, dismissal or resignation, they move out of your sphere of responsibility.

The performance appraisal process is much broader than just the formal, written part of it. The following steps help you encompass the broader scope of the process. Follow them when you evaluate your employees' performance:

1. **Set goals, expectations and standards – together.**

   Before your employees can achieve your goals, or perform to your expectations, you have to set goals and expectations with them and develop standards to measure their performance. After you've done all this, you have to communicate the goals and expectations *before* you evaluate your employees, not after. In fact, the performance review really starts on the first day of work. Tell your employees immediately how you evaluate them, show them the forms to be used and explain the process.

   Ensure that job descriptions, tasks and priorities are unambiguous and clear, and that you and your employees understand and agree to the standards set for them. In this two-way process, ensure that employees have a voice in setting their goals and standards and that you have their agreement. Refer to Chapter 6 in this Book for more on setting goals.

2. **Give continuous and specific feedback.**

   Catch your employees doing things right – every day of the week – and tell them about it then and there. And if you catch them doing wrong (nobody's perfect!), let them know about that too. Feedback is much

Book III

Finding and Managing Staff

more effective when you give it regularly and often than when you save it up for a special occasion (which can become victimisation if the feedback is constantly negative). The best formal performance appraisals contain the fewest surprises.

Constantly bombarding your employees with negative feedback has little to do with getting the performance that you want from them and costs you their respect.

3. **Prepare a formal, written performance appraisal with your employee.**

Every organisation has different requirements for the formal performance appraisal. Some appraisals are simple, one-page forms that require you to tick a few boxes; others are multi-page extravaganzas that require extensive narrative support. The form often varies by organisation, and by the level of the employee being evaluated. Regardless of your organisation's requirements, the formal performance appraisal should be a summary of the goals and expectations for the appraisal period – events that you've discussed previously (and frequently) with your employees. Support your words with examples and make appraisals meaningful to your employees by keeping your discussion relevant to the goals, expectations and standards that you developed in Step 1.

As a collaborative process, have the employee complete her own performance appraisal. Then compare your (the manager's) comments with the employee's comments; the differences that you find become topics of discussion and mutual goal setting.

4. **Meet employees personally to discuss the performance appraisal.**

Most employees appreciate the personal touch when you give the appraisal. Set aside some quality time to meet them to discuss their performance appraisal. This doesn't mean five or ten minutes, but at least an hour or maybe more. When you plan performance appraisal meetings, less is definitely not more. Pick a place that's comfortable and free from distractions. Make the meeting positive and upbeat. Even when you have to discuss performance problems, centre discussions on ways that you and your employees can work together to solve them.

The tone of performance appraisals and discussions can often become defensive as you raise negative elements and the employee starts to feel that she'll get a small, or no, pay rise. Start with letting the employee share how her job is going, what's working – and what's not – then share your assessment, starting with the positive.

5. **Set new goals, expectations and standards.**

The performance appraisal meeting gives you and your employee the opportunity to step back from daily issues for a moment and take a look at the big picture. You both have an opportunity to review and discuss the things that worked well and those that, perhaps, didn't work so well. Based on this assessment, you can then set new goals, expectations and standards for the next review period. The last step of the performance appraisal process becomes the first step, and you start all over again.

The entire performance appraisal process consists of setting goals with your employees, monitoring their performance, coaching them, supporting them, counselling and guiding them, and providing continuous feedback on their performance – both good and bad. If you do these things before you sit down for your annual or semi-annual performance appraisal sessions with your employees, reviews will be a pleasant and positive experience, looking at past accomplishments, instead of a disappointment for both you and them.

When it comes to conducting performance appraisals, managers have plenty of things to remember. Here are a few more:

✔ Communication with employees should be frequent so that no surprises occur (okay, *fewer* surprises). Give your employees informal feedback on their performance early and often.

✔ The primary focus of performance appraisals should be on going forward – setting new goals, improving future performance – rather than on looking back.

✔ Learning and development should always be included as a part of the performance appraisal process (although sometimes a discussion about pay rises can be separate).

✔ You need to make performance appraisal a priority yourself – a part of your 'real' job – you are, after all, dependent on the performance of your employees for your own success and effectiveness.

Preparing for the No-Surprises Appraisal

If you're doing your job as a manager, the appraisal holds no surprises for your employees. Follow the lead of the best managers: keep in touch with your employees and give them continuous feedback on their progress. Then, when you do sit down with them for their formal performance appraisal, the session is a recap of the things that you've already discussed during the appraisal period, instead of an ambush. Keeping up a continuous dialogue lets you use the formal appraisal to focus on the positive things that you and your employees can work on together to get the best possible performance.

Above all, be *prepared* for your appraisals!

Like interviews, many managers leave their preparation for performance appraisal meetings to the last possible minute – often just before the employee is scheduled to meet them. 'Oh, no. Cathy is going to be here in five minutes. Now, what did I do with her file? I know it's here somewhere!' The average manager spends about one hour preparing for an employee review covering a whole year of performance.

Turning the tables

Recently a new kind of performance appraisal has emerged. Instead of the typical downward appraisal where managers review their workers' performance, the *upward appraisal process* requires workers to evaluate their managers' performance. If you think that getting a performance appraisal from your manager is uncomfortable, you haven't seen anything yet. Nothing's quite like the feeling you get when a group of your employees appraise you, giving you direct and honest feedback about the things you do that make it hard for them to do a good job. Ouch!

However, despite the discomfort that you may feel, upward appraisal is invaluable – who better to assess your impact on the organisation than your employees? The system works so well that companies such as Federal Express have institutionalised the upward appraisal and made it part of their corporate culture. Surveys show that many of the world's top companies are using some form of the upward performance appraisal to assess the performance of their managers.

Also popular is the 360-degree evaluation. The *360-degree evaluation process* is when you're appraised from all sides – superiors, subordinates, colleagues and anyone from other departments with whom you happen to be working at the time. Levi Strauss & Co, for example, dictates that all employees are evaluated by their supervisors and by their underlings and peers.

The results can be a surprise to the manager who's the subject of the appraisal, who may find that other employees see her as less caring and visionary than she thought. A study by Charles Handy many years ago found that 70 per cent of managers and supervisors who rated themselves as caring and concerned were rated in turn as autocratic and distant by employees.

To avoid this unprofessional and unproductive situation, follow these tips:

- ✔ Set time aside, make an appointment with the employee and stick to it.
- ✔ Make a clear statement to the employee: 'The purpose of this performance appraisal is as follows . . .' and stick to it.

Performance appraisal is a year-round job. Whenever you recognise a problem with your employees' performance, mention it to them, make a note of it and drop it in their files. And do the same whenever your employees do something great. Then, when you're ready to do your employees' periodic performance appraisals, you can pull out their files and have plenty of documentation on which to base them. This practice makes the process easier for you, and makes the appraisal more meaningful and productive for your employees.

Book IV
Keeping on Top of the Books

'The taxmen never give up, do they?'

In this book . . .

Smoothly negotiating your way through tax and book-keeping helps keep your head above the financial high tide. You can, of course, employ specialists to do this work for you, but having a firm grasp of the basics means you can keep things in check through the financial year, or even manage your books yourself. We also look at keeping tabs on profit and loss.

Here are the contents of Book IV at a glance:

Chapter 1

Satisfying the Tax Inspector

In This Chapter

▶ Reporting on self-employment and partnership tax

▶ Filing taxes for limited companies

*P*aying taxes and reporting income for your business are very important jobs, and the way in which you complete these tasks properly depends on your business's legal structure. From sole traders (self-employment) to limited companies and everything in between, this chapter briefly reviews business types and explains how taxes are handled for each type.

Tax Reporting for Sole Traders

HM Revenue & Customs doesn't consider sole traders and partnerships to be individual legal entities, so they're not taxed as such. Instead, sole proprietors report any business earnings on their annual tax returns – that's the only financial reporting they must do. In effect, sole traders and partnerships pay income tax on their business profits. To be technical, they pay their income tax on their business profit under what is called *trading income*. A sole trader may well have another job as well, on which he pays tax under the normal PAYE system. All these (and other sources of income) are pulled together on his tax return to assess the overall income tax liability.

The basic tax return covers everything that a person in paid employment needs to tell HM Revenue & Customs to get his tax assessed correctly. The numerous pages of questions cover every aspect of tax related to normal tax life – working, receiving dividends, earning interest, paying and receiving pensions, making small capital gains – as we said, everything.

As the bookkeeper for a sole trader, you're probably responsible for pulling together the sales, Cost of Goods Sold and expense information needed for the forms. In most cases, you then hand this information to the business's accountant to fill out all the required forms.

Ultimately, because sole traders pay income tax on all their earnings, you need to note the current rates of tax for sole traders (and other unincorporated bodies) based on their taxable profits. Table 1-1 gives this information. (The tax rates used in this chapter are illustrations only as the actual rates vary each year in the Budget. In the uncertain economic climate brought about after the credit crunch, all matters relating to tax are subject to even more frequent changes. HM Revenue and Customs has the current rules and rates on its website www.hmrc.gov.uk.)

Table 1-1	2010/11 Tax Rates
Tax Rate	*2010/11 Taxable Profits*
Basic rate: 20%	£0–£37,400
Higher rate: 40%	£37,401–£150,000
Additional rate: 50%	Over £150,000

Fortunately most people have simple tax affairs. Because employment is usually taxed under the PAYE system (the employer acts as the unpaid tax collector) and most other sources of income have the basic rate of tax deducted at source, you don't need to complete a tax return each year. The tax return is needed to pull all the earnings together only where an individual may have a liability to higher rate tax, for example other earnings that haven't had tax deducted at source that pushes his taxable earnings above the basic tax rate.

Expanding to the supplementary pages

To deal with liability at a higher tax rate or areas too complex for the standard annual tax return, you need supplementary pages. The supplementary pages cover:

- ✔ **Employment:** To cover more complicated employment situations, for example, an employee who has more than one job.

- ✔ **Share schemes:** To cover an employee who receives shares under an employee share ownership scheme.

- ✔ **Self-employment:** These pages cover business profits for the sole trader. We look at this more closely in the next section.

- ✔ **Partnerships:** To declare your share of any partnership profits.

- ✔ **Land and property:** For example, where any rental income is received from any property.

- ✔ **Foreign:** To cover any overseas sources of income.

- ✔ **Trusts:** To cover any income received by means of a distribution from any trust set up for you.

- ✔ **Capital gains:** To cover any gains made from the disposal of assets rather than trading income.

- ✔ **Non-residence:** To cover any income received by non-residents in the UK and thus liable to UK tax.

HM Revenue & Customs sends supplementary pages only if you ask for them or have received them before. As a taxpayer, you are responsible for asking for a tax return and completing one every year.

Filling out the self-employment supplementary pages

This section concentrates on the supplementary pages that relate to running a business. If you want to know more about filling in the rest of your tax return and saving tax, you may find *Paying Less Tax For Dummies* useful – if only such a title existed.

Depending on your turnover, you use one of two different self-employment supplementary pages. If your turnover is less than £68,000, you can complete the shortened version, which is only two pages long. (See Figures 1-1 and 1-2.) Double-check that you are eligible to use the shortened form by referring to the guide to completing the self-employment supplementary pages. You can find it on the HMRC website, www.hmrc.gov.uk.

On the first page, SES1, shown in Figure 1-1, you put down details of the business name and address and when it began or ceased trading. You also use this page to enter your business income and allowable business expenses. You put your total business expenses in box 19 if your turnover is less than £68,000. On the second page, SES 2 (shown in Figure 1-2), you summarise the capital allowances that the business is claiming for any of its assets. You then calculate your taxable profits and read page SESN9 of the notes to see if you need to make any adjustments.

Losses, Class 4 NICs and CIS deductions are entered in the final section. (Make sure you read page SESN10 of the notes to help you complete this section correctly.)

Book IV

Keeping On Top of the Books

HM Revenue & Customs

Self-employment (short)

Tax year 6 April 2009 to 5 April 2010

Your name	Your unique taxpayer reference (UTR)

Read page SESN 1 of the *notes* to check if you should use this page or the *Self-employment (full)* page.

Business details

1 Description of business

2 Postcode of your business address

3 If your business name, description, address or postcode have changed in the last 12 months, put 'X' in the box and give details in the 'Any other information' box of your tax return

4 If you are a foster carer or adult placement carer, put 'X' in the box – *read page SESN 2 of the notes*

5 If your business started after 5 April 2009, enter the start date *DD MM YYYY*

6 If your business ceased before 6 April 2010, enter the final date of trading

7 Date your books or accounts are made up to – *read page SESN 2 of the notes*

Business income – if your annual business turnover was below £68,000

8 Your turnover – *the takings, fees, sales or money earned by your business*

£ . 0 0

9 Any other business income not included in box 8 – *excluding Business Start-up Allowance*

£ . 0 0

Allowable business expenses

If your annual turnover was below £68,000 you may just put your total expenses in box 19, rather than filling in the whole section.

10 Costs of goods bought for resale or goods used

£ . 0 0

11 Car, van and travel expenses – *after private use proportion*

£ . 0 0

12 Wages, salaries and other staff costs

£ . 0 0

13 Rent, rates, power and insurance costs

£ . 0 0

14 Repairs and renewals of property and equipment

£ . 0 0

15 Accountancy, legal and other professional fees

£ . 0 0

16 Interest and bank and credit card etc. financial charges

£ . 0 0

17 Phone, fax, stationery and other office costs

£ . 0 0

18 Other allowable business expenses – *client entertaining costs are not an allowable expense*

£ . 0 0

19 Total allowable expenses – *total of boxes 10 to 18*

£ . 0 0

Figure 1-1: Page SES1 of the self-employment supplementary pages shows business details, capital allowances and income and expenditure for annual turnover below £68,000.

SA103S 2010   Tax return: Self-employment (short): Page SES 1   HMRC 12/09 net

Net profit or loss

20 Net profit – *if your business income is more than your expenses (if box 8 + box 9 minus box 19 is positive)*

£ [   ] • 0 0

21 Or, net loss – *if your expenses exceed your business income (if box 19 minus (box 8 + box 9) is positive)*

£ [   ] • 0 0

Tax allowances for vehicles and equipment (capital allowances)

There are 'capital' tax allowances for vehicles and equipment used in your business (you should not have included the cost of these in your business expenses). Read pages SESN 4 to SESN 8 of the *notes* and use the example and Working Sheets to work out your capital allowances.

22 Annual Investment Allowance

£ [   ] • 0 0

24 Other capital allowances

£ [   ] • 0 0

23 Allowance for small balance of unrelieved expenditure

£ [   ] • 0 0

25 Total balancing charges – where you have disposed of items for more than their value

£ [   ] • 0 0

Calculating your taxable profits

Your taxable profit may not be the same as your net profit. Read page SESN 9 of the *notes* to see if you need to make any adjustments and fill in the boxes which apply to arrive at your taxable profit for the year.

26 Goods or services for your own use – *read page SESN 9 of the notes*

£ [   ] • 0 0

28 Loss brought forward from earlier years set off against this year's profits – *up to the amount in box 27*

£ [   ] • 0 0

27 Net business profit for tax purposes (*if box 20 + box 25 + box 26 minus (boxes 21 to 24) is positive*)

£ [   ] • 0 0

29 Any other business income not included in boxes 8 or 9 – *for example, Business Start-up Allowance*

£ [   ] • 0 0

Total taxable profits or net business loss

30 Total taxable profits from this business (*if box 27 + box 29 minus box 28 is positive*)

£ [   ] • 0 0

31 Net business loss for tax purposes (*if boxes 21 to 24 minus (box 20 + box 25 + box 26) is positive*)

£ [   ] • 0 0

Losses, Class 4 NICs and CIS deductions

If you have made a loss for tax purposes (box 31), read page SESN 10 of the *notes* and fill in boxes 32 to 34 as appropriate

32 Loss from this tax year set off against other income for 2009–10

£ [   ] • 0 0

35 If you are exempt from paying Class 4 NICs, put 'X' in the box – *read page SESN 10 of the notes*

[   ]

33 Loss to be carried back to previous year(s) and set off against income (or capital gains)

£ [   ] • 0 0

36 If you have been given a 2009–10 Class 4 NICs deferment certificate, put 'X' in the box – *read page SESN 10 of the notes*

[   ]

34 Total loss to carry forward after all other set-offs – *including unused losses brought forward*

£ [   ] • 0 0

37 Deductions on payment and deduction statements from contractors – *construction industry subcontractors only*

£ [   ] • 0 0

SA103S 2010

Tax return: Self-employment (short): Page SES 2

Figure 1-2: Page SES2 of the self-employment supplementary pages shows details of capital allowances, taxable profits, losses and Class 4 NICs.

Book IV

Keeping On Top of the Books

Filing Tax Forms for Partnerships

If your business is structured as a partnership (meaning it has more than one owner) and isn't a limited liability company, your business doesn't pay taxes. Instead, all money earned by the business is split up among the partners and they pay the tax due between them very much as if they were sole traders. However, a partnership is required to complete a partnership tax return to aid the assessment of the members of the partnership. Essentially, the partnership tax return is sent out to the nominated partner and he completes the partnership tax return in a manner similar to the sole trader tax return explained in the preceding sections. That partner states what profit share is attributable to each partner, and each partner is responsible for showing this profit figure in his own personal tax return.

Don't be tempted to forget to include partnership profits (or any other source of income for that matter), because HM Revenue & Customs knows from the partnership tax return what you earned in that tax year.

Paying Taxes for Limited Companies

Limited companies are more complex than sole traders and partnerships. Although many aspects of their accounting and taxation are similar, their accounts are open to public scrutiny because each year a limited company must file its accounts at Companies House, the UK government organisation responsible for tracking information about all UK limited companies. This means that although only HM Revenue & Customs knows the full details of a sole trader or partnership, the whole world has access (for a fee) to a limited company's accounts.

Companies make a separate tax return, known as a CT600, to HM Revenue & Customs, in which they detail their financial affairs. As a result, the limited company pays corporation tax on its earnings (profit) as well as tax on any dividends paid out to its shareholders. This means that its shareholders receive dividends net of basic rate of income tax because the company has already paid it for them.

Two forms of CT600 exist: a short version, only four pages, is sufficient for companies with straightforward tax affairs, but more complicated companies, as designated by HM Revenue & Customs, must complete the eight-page return. The following (among others) must file the eight-page return:

✔ Any company that owns 25 per cent of another non-UK company

✔ Any insurance company (or friendly society) having business treated as overseas life assurance business

✔ Any company liable to pay its corporation tax in instalments (profit in excess of £1.5m)

For full details, please refer to the *CT600 Guide (2010)*, which can be obtained from the HMRC website at www.hmrc.gov.uk.

Corporation tax rates vary according to how much taxable profit the company makes. Although starting rates are low for a limited company, they soon escalate to the higher (main) rate. Current corporation tax rates on profits are shown in Table 1-2.

Table 1-2	Corporation Tax Rates	
Tax Rate	*2010/11 Taxable Profits*	*2011/12 Taxable Profits*
Small profits rate:	21%	20%
Small profits rate can be claimed by qualifying companies with profits not exceeding:	£300,000	N/A
Marginal relief: lower limit	£300,000	N/A
Marginal relief: upper limit	£1,500,000	N/A
Main rate:	28%	27%

Check with your accountant to determine whether incorporating your business makes sense for you. A strong argument exists in favour of some smaller businesses incorporating, because they pay less corporation tax than income tax at some levels. But tax savings isn't the only issue you have to think about; operating a limited company also increases administrative, legal and accounting costs. Make sure that you understand all the costs before incorporating.

Book IV

Keeping On Top of the Books

Chapter 2

Completing Year-End
Payroll and Reports

In This Chapter

▶ Mastering employee reporting

▶ Taking care of annual statutory returns

*R*unning your own business means not only that you have to keep the business's books and tax position straight, you also need to submit forms for each of your employees as well as some summary reports. End-of-the-year HM Revenue & Customs paperwork takes some time, so to help make the process as painless as possible, this chapter reviews the forms you need to complete, the information you need for each form and the process for filing your business's payroll information with HM Revenue & Customs.

Reporting on Employees

Although you keep individual records for deduction of PAYE tax and National Insurance for each employee, and make payments to HM Revenue & Customs throughout the year, at the end of the tax year on 5 April, HM Revenue & Customs wants more information to be sure that you haven't missed on any PAYE tax and National Insurance Contributions (NICs). We cover the forms you need to submit in detail in the following sections in the order in which they need to be submitted – so you know when to panic!

HM Revenue & Customs publishes an *Employer Helpbook E10* each year that covers finishing the tax year, available at its website, www.hmrc.gov.uk.

Form P14

The P14 form, shown in Figure 2-1, is pretty straightforward.

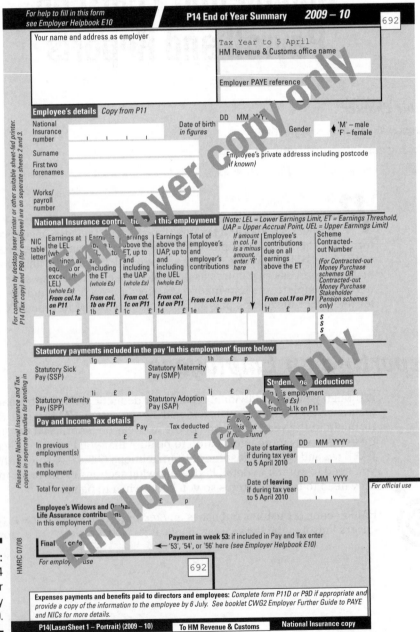

Figure 2-1:
Sample P14
End of Year
Summary
for 2009/10.

In essence the P14 is a summary of each employee's P11 that you've been working with all tax year, and you don't need any more information than what you already have on the employee's P11. Remember that if you don't send a P14 to HM Revenue & Customs for every employee each tax year, they won't have a record of that person's PAYE, NICs and other deductions. Also, if you have more than one employee please ensure that you send these to HM Revenue & Customs in alphabetical order. Table 2-1 tells you what to put in each section.

The P14 is due mid-May; check with HM Revenue & Customs for the exact date for the current year.

With this form, and all the end-of-the-year employee-related forms, the key word is accuracy – take care and complete the form slowly. Make sure that you pick up the correct tax year details.

Table 2-1	Sections of Form P14
Section	*What to Do*
Employer's name and address	Show your address. Include the postcode.
Inland Revenue office name and Employer's PAYE reference	Enter your Inland Revenue office name and Employer's PAYE reference from the front of form P35. You can also find this on your payslip booklet.
Tax year to 5 April 2010	Usually pre-printed on the form. Take care to submit the correct year's figures!
Employee's details National Insurance number	Copy this from the front of form P11.
Date of birth	Enter the day and month as well as all four numbers of the year.
Surname and first two forenames	If you don't know all the employee's forenames, put initials. Don't put titles (Mr, Mrs, Miss and so on).
National Insurance contributions in this employment NIC (National Insurance Contribution) Table letter	Copy from the End of Year Summary section on the back of form P11.

(continued)

Book IV

Keeping On
Top of the
Books

Table 2-1 *(continued)*

Section	What to Do
Columns 1a to 1c	Copy these amounts from the End of Year Summary of form P11. Make entries in whole pounds and right-justify the figures. If an entry exists in column 1a, you must still send in form P14 even though no NICs may be payable.
Columns 1d to 1f	Copy these amounts from the End of Year Summary of form P11. Make entries in pounds and pence. Where you operate a contracted-out pension scheme and the column 1d total to be carried forward from the P11 is a minus figure, enter 'R' in the corresponding box immediately to the right of the column 1d total boxes on the P14.
Statutory payments in this employment Box 1g	Insert the total amount of Statutory Sick Pay (SSP) paid in those months for which an amount has been recovered under the Percentage Threshold Scheme.
Boxes 1h to 1j	Copy these amounts from the corresponding columns on form P11.
Scheme Contracted-Out number	Complete this only if the employee is a member of a Contracted-Out Money Purchase (COMP) scheme, COMP Stakeholder Pension (COMPSHP) scheme, or the COMP part of the Contracted-Out Mixed Benefit (COMB) scheme you operate. Members of these schemes only receive their Age Related Rebate (ARR) if this part is entered correctly.
Student loan deductions	Copy this amount from the totals box at the bottom of column 1k on form P11. Enter whole pounds only.

Section	What to Do
Date of starting and date of leaving	Make entries if an employee starts and/or leaves your employment during the tax year (2009/10 in this example).
	Enter date as figures: 09 05 2010, for example.
Pay and income tax details In previous employment(s)	Copy these amounts from the End of Year Summary of form P11.
In this employment	Copy these amounts from the End of Year Summary of form P11.
Total for year	Copy these amounts from the End of Year Summary of form P11.
	Fill in these boxes only if the employee was still working for you at 5 April.
Employee's Widows and Orphans/ Life Assurance contributions in this employment	Applies where an employee is legally obliged to pay contributions that qualify for tax relief but aren't authorised under 'net pay arrangements' for tax relief. See *CWG2 Employers Further Guide to PAYE and NICs* for more information.
Final tax code	Fill in boxes from the left-hand side.
	Always show the last tax code you were using at the 5 April date.
Payment in week 53	Use only if Week 53 is included in the Pay and Tax totals, and then put one of the following in this box:
	'53' if 53 weekly pay days were in the year
	'54' if 27 fortnightly pay days were in the year
	'56' if 14 four-weekly pay days were in the year.

Book IV

Keeping On Top of the Books

HM Revenue & Customs ask that you submit your P14 forms in alphabetical order.

The last part of form P14 is the P60, but the form is blue (instead of orange). You don't send this to HM Revenue & Customs. Instead, you give each employee her own copy, which summarises pay, tax, NIC deductions and so on made during the year.

Don't give a P60 to employees who were no longer with the business at the end of the tax year.

Detailing benefits on forms P9D, P11D and P11D (b)

Fortunately, you don't need these forms for the majority of your employees in the typical small business. Basically, these forms are used to report back to HM Revenue & Customs the various benefits in kind that employees received during the year.

The forms and the circumstances they address are as follows:

- ✔ Use the fairly simple form P9D if the employee in question earned at the rate of £8,500 per annum or less. Earnings includes all bonuses, tips and benefits.

- ✔ Use the significantly more complicated form P11D for employees who earned at the rate of £8,500 or more, and for all directors, regardless of earnings.

- ✔ Use form P11D(b) to:

    - Confirm that by 6 July all forms P11D have been completed and sent to your HM Revenue & Customs office.

    - Declare the total amount of Class 1A NICs you are due to pay. *Class 1A* contributions are the extra NICs that may be due on taxable benefits that you provide to your employees.

HM Revenue & Customs produces a series of guides to help you get this area of reporting right. Look for the publication for the current tax year:

- ✔ *480 Expenses and Benefits – A Tax Guide:* This guide runs to some 100 pages and is the definitive guide.

- ✔ *CWG2 Employers' Further Guide to PAYE and NICs.*

- ✔ *CWG5 Class 1A NICs on benefits in kind.*

- ✔ *P11D Guide*: This guide is a four-page overview, which makes reference to the *480* guide for more detail.

Within the confines of this book, we can't possibly hope to do justice to the whole detail of benefit-in-kind reporting. However, the following list gives you a brief outline of the kind of things that are deemed to be benefits in kind and need to be included on the P9D or P11D:

- ✔ Assets transferred (cars, property, goods or other assets)
- ✔ Payments made on behalf of the employee
- ✔ Vouchers and credit cards
- ✔ Living accommodation
- ✔ Mileage allowance payments/passenger miles
- ✔ Cars, vans and car fuel
- ✔ Interest-free, low interest and notional loans
- ✔ Private medical treatment or insurance
- ✔ Qualifying relocation expenses payments and benefits
- ✔ Services supplied
- ✔ Assets placed at employees' disposal
- ✔ Computer equipment
- ✔ Other items – subscriptions, educational assistance, non-qualifying relocation benefits and expenses payments, incidental overnight expenses
- ✔ Employer-provided child care
- ✔ Expenses payments made to, or on behalf of, the director or employee – general expenses for business travel, travel and subsistence, entertainment, home telephone, other non-qualifying relocation expenses

The list seems to go on and on.

Reporting PAYE-free earnings on forms P38, P38A and P38 (S)

Forms P38 and P38A ask you to report payments made to employees from whom you haven't deducted PAYE – such as part-time casual staff. Form P38 (S) applies to students. The following subsections show the type of payments that you need to include or omit on forms P38 or P38A.

Section A

In this section, you:

- ✔ Include payments above the PAYE threshold.
- ✔ Include payments to employees who haven't produced a P45 and were engaged for more than one week, if both of the following conditions are met:
    - The rate of pay was above £95 per week or £412 per month.
    - The employee failed to complete certificate A or B on form P46.
- ✔ Exclude payments included on form P14.

Section B

In this section, you:

- ✔ Include payments that total over £100 made to any employee including casuals during this tax year.
- ✔ Exclude those included on forms P14, those in section A (above), those payments to employees with completed P46 certificates A and B, and payments returned on forms P38(S).

P38(S)

P38(S) is the appropriate return for students who work for you solely during a holiday. You don't need to deduct tax from a student as long as:

- ✔ They fill in the student's declaration, *and*
- ✔ The student's pay in your employment doesn't exceed £6,475 during the tax year.

    If a student's pay in your employment exceeds this figure, you must deduct tax using code 'OT week 1/month 1' in accordance with paragraphs 110 and 111 of the booklet *CWG2 Employers' Further Guide to PAYE and NICs*.

Submitting Summary Information on Form P35

Form P35 is part of the Employers' Annual Return. In essence it lists every employee, including directors (who must be shown first with an asterisk by their names), NIC amounts and income tax you deducted from their pay. If you have more than ten employees, you need one or more continuation sheets (form P35CS).

Also, as per the P14, you need to list employees in alphabetical order.

✔ Page 1 tells you what your obligations are and where to get further help: nothing to complete here.

✔ Pages 2 and 3 require you to list the details of your employees and summarise your payments of NICs, PAYE tax, SSP, SMP and SAP for the year.

✔ Page 4 contains several tick-box questions for you to complete before signing and dating the form.

Figure 2-2 shows an example of completed pages 2 and 3 of form P35.

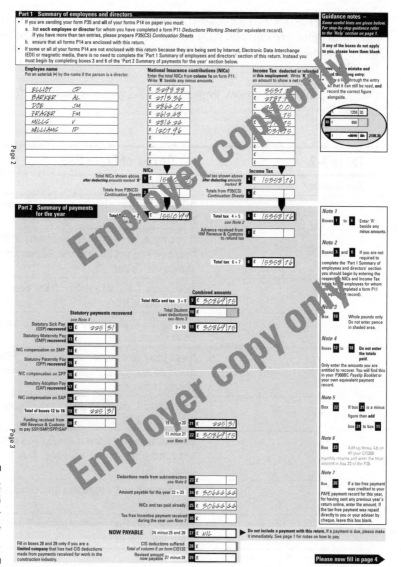

Figure 2-2:
Sample P35
End of Year
Summary
for 2009/10.

Book IV

**Keeping On
Top of the
Books**

Boxing out Parts 1 and 2

You can get much of the information you need for Parts 1 and 2 of form P35 from the P11 forms you have for each person to whom you pay money:

- ✔ The total of each employee's and the employer's NICs are in column 1e of the P14 End of Year Summary.
- ✔ The total tax deducted or refunded is in the 'In this employment' box in the Pay and Income Tax section towards the bottom of the page.

Completing Parts 1 and 2 makes you check that your payments to the accounts office are correct. If this form shows that you should have paid over more to HM Revenue & Customs during the year, you need to make an additional payment.

Okay, we can't put it off any longer; Table 2-2 ploughs through the 29 boxes of form P35.

Table 2-2	Boxes of Form P35
Box Number	**What to Do**
1	Add up all the entries from the NICs columns on the form.
2	If you have any continuation sheets (P35CS), add these up and put the total for all continuation sheets in this box.
3	Add boxes 1 and 2 together. If the figure is a refund, mark 'R'.
4	Add up the entries from the income tax column on the form.
5	If you have any continuation sheets (P35CS), add these up and put the total for all continuation sheets in this box.
6	Add boxes 4 and 5 together. If the figure is a refund, mark 'R'.
7	Use this box only if the business has asked your accounts office for an advance; if so, enter that amount here.
8	Add boxes 6 and 7 together and enter the total here.
9	Add NIC and Tax together (boxes 3 and 8) and enter the total here.

Box Number	What to Do
10	Fill in this box only if you made student loan deductions this year. Pick up the total of all the boxes at the bottom of column 1k on each of the form P11s and enter the total here (whole pounds only).
11	Add box 9 to box 10 and enter the total here.
12	If you've paid any Statutory Sick Pay (SSP) to employees, enter the amount you're entitled to recover under the Percentage Threshold Scheme (PTS) in this box. Include any payments you received directly from your accounts office to cover recovery of SSP, which you show in box 20. For further details see the *Employer Helpbook E14, What to do if your employee is sick.*
13	If you paid any SMP (Statutory Maternity Pay) to employees, enter in this box the amount you're entitled to. Include any payments you received directly from your accounts office to cover recovery of SMP, which you show in box 20. For further details see the *Employer Helpbook E15, Pay and time off work for parents.*
14	Enter here any compensation you're entitled to claim in addition to the SMP recovered. For further details see the *Employer Helpbook E15, Pay and time off work for parents.*
15	Enter here any SPP (Statutory Paternity Pay) you've paid to employees and are entitled to recover. For further details see the *Employer Helpbook E15, Pay and time off work for parents.*
16	Enter here any compensation you're entitled to claim in addition to the SPP recovered. For further details see the *Employer Helpbook E15, Pay and time off work for parents.*

(continued)

Table 2-2 *(continued)*

Box Number	What to Do
17	Enter here any SAP (Statutory Adoption Pay) paid to employees that you're entitled to recover. Include any payments received directly from your accounts office to cover the recovery of SAP, also shown in box 20.
	For further details see the *Employer Helpbook E16, Pay and time off work for adoptive parents*.
18	Enter here any compensation you're entitled to claim in addition to the SAP recovered.
	For further details see the *Employer Helpbook E16, Pay and time off work for adoptive parents*.
19	Add all boxes from 12 to 18 and enter the total in box 19.
20	Use this box only if you received funding from your accounts office to pay SSP/SMP/SPP/SAP. Enter here the amount you received in funding.
21	Calculate box 19 minus box 20 and enter the total here.
22	Calculate box 11 minus box 21 and enter the total here.
23	Use this box for deductions made from sub-contractors. Add up boxes 4.6 on your CIS300 monthly returns and enter the total amount here.
24	Calculate box 22 plus box 23 and enter the total here.
25	Enter here the total of NICs and tax paid over so far for the tax year.
26	Enter here any amount credited to the business's PAYE payment record for tax-free incentives for sending in its return electronically the previous year.
27	Calculate box 24 minus boxes 25 and 26.
The following boxes are only for limited companies that deducted CIS (Construction Industry Scheme) deductions from payments	CIS deductions suffered. Refer to form CIS132 (which summarises all employees), column E, for the total deductions suffered and copy this amount here.
28	
29	Calculate box 27 minus box 28.

Ticking off the Part 3 checklist

Page 4 of the form has three sections – Parts 3, 4 and 5. Part 3 has no numbers, just a checklist of questions to answer:

✔ **Question 1:** If you had any employees for whom you didn't complete a form P14 or P38(S), tick 'No'.

These employees are likely to be part-time or casual staff. If you tick 'No' you must complete a *P38A, Employer's Supplementary Return.*

✔ **Question 2:** Did you make any 'free-of-tax' payments to an employee? A free-of-tax payment is one where the employer bears any tax due.

✔ **Question 3:** Has anyone other than the employer paid expenses or provided benefits to any of your employees during the year as part of their employment with you?

✔ **Question 4:** This question is in two parts. If the answer to the first part is 'Yes', you have to complete a form P14 for each employee concerned.

✔ **Question 5:** This question asks if you've paid any part of an employee's pay direct to anyone else, for example, paying school fees direct to a school. If you did, you need to report whether the payment was included in the employee's pay for tax and NICs purposes and in the pay shown on form P14. This question doesn't include attachment of earnings orders or payments to the Child Support Agency.

✔ **Question 6:** This question covers IR35 under which HM Revenue & Customs has restricted workers' ability to form services companies or partnerships through which they sell their services. Your best bet is to find out about IR35 at www.hmrc.gov.uk/ir35 to make sure that you comply. If, for example, you don't deduct tax and NICs when you need to, you may become liable for any non-payment of tax and NICs by the person employed.

If you included PAYE and NICs from workers who you deemed to be employees, tick the second box 'Yes'. If you tick the second box 'Yes' but the amount of the deemed payment is provisional, confirm on a separate sheet and send it with the form P35.

Pensioning out Part 4

If you have a company pension scheme that was contracted-out of the State Second pension, enter your business's contracted-out number here (you can find this on your contracting-out certificate).

Certifying your employer status in Part 5

This part is the check-up part, where you ensure that you've included all the necessary forms and sign on the dotted line. Tick to confirm that you enclose all forms P14, P38A, P11D and P11D(b) and confirm that P38A (see question 1 in the checklist of Part 3) is enclosed or not due. Sign and print the name and capacity of the person signing and the date. Phew! Everything's done!

Computerised systems

If you use a computerised payroll system, you can save a lot of grief because most of the year-end reports (certainly P14, P35 and P60) are done automatically. If you use the HM Revenue & Customs payroll CD-ROM that comes with the New Employer Pack, you can enjoy the same benefits of a computerised payroll system and all the online HM Revenue & Customs guides.

Chapter 3

Getting Down to Bookkeeping Basics

*A*ll businesses need to keep track of their financial transactions, which is why bookkeeping and bookkeepers are so important. Without accurate records, how can you tell if your business is making a profit or taking a loss?

In this chapter, we cover the key aspects of bookkeeping: we introduce you to the language of bookkeeping, familiarise you with how bookkeepers manage the accounting cycle and show you how to understand the more complex type of bookkeeping – double-entry bookkeeping.

Bookkeeping: The Record-Keeping of the Business World

Bookkeeping, the methodical way in which businesses track their financial transactions, is rooted in accounting. *Accounting* is the total structure of records and procedures used to record, classify and report information about a business's financial transactions. Bookkeeping involves the recording of that financial information into the accounting system while maintaining adherence to solid accounting principles.

The bookkeeper's job is to work day in and day out to ensure that transactions are accurately recorded. Bookkeepers need to be very detail-oriented and love working with numbers, because numbers and the accounts the numbers go into are what these people deal with all day long.

Bookkeepers aren't required to belong to any recognised professional body, such as the Institute of Chartered Accountants of England and Wales. You can recognise a chartered accountant by the letters *ACA* after the name, which indicates that he is an Associate of the Institute of Chartered Accountants. If he's been qualified much longer, he may use the letters *FCA*, which indicate that the accountant is a Fellow of the Institute of Chartered Accountants.

Of course, both Scotland and Ireland have their own chartered accountant bodies with their own designations. Other accounting qualifications exist, offered by the Institute of Chartered Management Accountants (ACMA and FCMA), the Institute of Chartered Certified Accountants (ACCA and FCMA) and the Chartered Institute of Public Finance Accountants (CIPFA).

The Association of Accounting Technicians offers a bookkeeping certificate (ABC) programme, which provides a good grounding in this subject. In reality, most bookkeepers tend to be qualified by experience.

If you're after an accountant to help your business, use the appropriate chartered accountants or a chartered certified accountant as they have the most relevant experience.

On starting up their businesses, many small-business people serve as their own bookkeepers until the business is large enough to hire a dedicated person to keep the books. Few small businesses have accountants on the payroll to check the books and prepare official financial reports; instead, they have bookkeepers (either on the payroll or hired on a self-employed basis) who serve as the outside accountants' eyes and ears. Most businesses do seek out an accountant, usually a chartered accountant (ACA or FCA), but this is typically to submit annual accounts to the Inland Revenue, which is now part of HM Revenue & Customs.

In many small businesses today, a bookkeeper enters the business transactions on a daily basis while working inside the business. At the end of each month or quarter, the bookkeeper sends summary reports to the accountant who then checks the transactions for accuracy and prepares financial statements such as the profit and loss statements.

In most cases, the accounting system is initially set up with the help of an accountant. The aim is to ensure that the system uses solid accounting principles and that the analysis it provides is in line with that required by the business, the accountant and HM Revenue & Customs. That accountant periodically reviews the system's use to make sure that transactions are being handled properly.

Accurate financial reports are the only way to ensure that you know how your business is doing. These reports are developed using the information you, as the bookkeeper, enter into your accounting system. If that information isn't accurate, your financial reports are meaningless: remember, 'Garbage in, garbage out'.

Wading through Basic Bookkeeping Lingo

Before you can take on bookkeeping and start keeping the books, you first need to get a handle on the key accounting terms. This section describes the main terms that all bookkeepers use on a daily basis.

Accounts for the balance sheet

Here are a few terms you need to know:

- **Balance sheet:** The financial statement that presents a snapshot of the business's financial position (assets, liabilities and capital) as of a particular date in time. The balance sheet is so-called because the things owned by the business (assets) must equal the claims against those assets (liabilities and capital).

  On an ideal balance sheet, the total assets need to equal the total liabilities plus the total capital. If your numbers fit this formula, the business's books are in balance. (We discuss the balance sheet in greater detail in Chapter 6 of Book IV.)

- **Assets:** All the items a business owns in order to run successfully, such as cash, stock, buildings, land, tools, equipment, vehicles and furniture.

- **Liabilities:** All the debts the business owes, such as mortgages, loans and unpaid bills.

- **Capital:** All the money the business owners invest in the business. When one person (sole trader) or a group of people (partnership) own a small business, the owners' capital is shown in a Capital account. In an incorporated business (limited company), the owners' capital is shown as shares.

  Another key Capital account is *Retained Earnings,* which shows all business profits that have been reinvested in the business rather than paid out to the owners by way of dividends. Unincorporated businesses show money paid out to the owners in a Drawings account (or individual drawings accounts in the case of a partnership), whereas incorporated businesses distribute money to the owners by paying *dividends* (a portion of the business's profits paid out to the ordinary shareholders, typically for the year).

Accounts for the profit and loss statement

Following are a few terms related to the profit and loss statement that you need to know:

- **Profit and loss statement:** The financial statement that presents a summary of the business's financial activity over a certain period of time, such as a month, quarter or year. The statement starts with Sales made, subtracts out the Costs of Goods Sold and the Expenses, and ends with the bottom line – Net Profit or Loss. (We show you how to develop a profit and loss statement in Chapter 5 in Book IV.)

- **Income:** All sales made in the process of selling the business's goods and services. Some businesses also generate income through other means, such as selling assets the business no longer needs or earning interest from investments. (We discuss how to track income in Chapter 5 in Book IV.)

- **Cost of Goods Sold:** All costs incurred in purchasing or making the products or services a business plans to sell to its customers. (We talk about purchasing goods for sale to customers in Chapter 5 in Book IV.)

- **Expenses:** All costs incurred to operate the business that aren't directly related to the sale of individual goods or services. (We review common types of expenses in Chapter 5 in Book IV.)

Other common terms

Some other common terms include the following:

- **Accounting period:** The time for which financial information is being prepared. Most businesses monitor their financial results on a monthly basis, so each accounting period equals one month. Some businesses choose to do financial reports on a quarterly basis, so the accounting period is three months. Other businesses only look at their results on a yearly basis, so their accounting period is 12 months. Businesses that track their financial activities monthly usually also create quarterly and *annual reports* (a year-end summary of the business's activities and financial results) based on the information they gather.

- **Accounting year-end:** In most cases a business accounting year is 12 months long and ends 12 months on from when the business started or at some traditional point in the trading cycle for that business. Many businesses have year-ends of 31 March (to tie in with the tax year) and 31 December (to tie in with the calendar year). You're allowed to change your business year-end to suit your business.

  For example, if you started your business on July 1, your year-end will be 30 June (12 months later). If, however, it is traditional for your industry to have 31 December as the year-end, it is quite in order to change to this date. For example, most retailers have 31 December as their year-end. You of course have to let HM Revenue & Customs know and get their formal acceptance.

✓ **Trade Debtors (also known as Accounts Receivable):** The account used to track all customer sales made on credit. *Credit* refers not to credit-card sales, but to sales in which the business gives a customer credit directly, and which the business needs to collect from the customer at a later date.

✓ **Trade Creditors (also known as Accounts Payable):** The account used to track all outstanding bills from suppliers, contractors, consultants and any other businesses or individuals from whom the business buys goods or services.

✓ **Depreciation:** An accounting method used to account for the ageing and use of assets. For example, if you own a car, you know that the value of the car decreases each year (unless you own one of those classic cars that goes up in value). Every major asset a business owns ages and eventually needs replacement, including buildings, factories, equipment and other key assets.

✓ **Nominal (or General) Ledger:** Where all the business's accounts are summarised. The Nominal Ledger is the master summary of the bookkeeping system.

✓ **Interest:** The money a business needs to pay when it borrows money from anybody. For example, when you buy a car using a car loan, you must pay not only the amount you borrowed (capital or principal), but also additional money, or interest, based on a percentage of the amount you borrowed.

✓ **Stock (or Inventory):** The account that tracks all products sold to customers.

✓ **Journals:** Where bookkeepers keep records (in chronological order) of daily business transactions. Each of the most active accounts, including cash, Trade Creditors and Trade Debtors, has its own journal.

✓ **Payroll:** The way a business pays its employees. Managing payroll is a key bookkeeping function and involves reporting many aspects of payroll to HM Revenue & Customs, including Pay As You Earn (PAYE) taxes to be paid on behalf of the employee and employer, and National Insurance Contributions (NICs). In addition, a range of other payments such as Statutory Sick Pay (SSP) and maternity/paternity pay may be part of the payroll function. (We discuss employee payroll in Book IV, Chapter 2.)

✓ **Trial balance:** How you test to ensure that the books are in balance before pulling together information for the financial reports and closing the books for the accounting period.

Book IV

Keeping On Top of the Books

Pedalling through the Accounting Cycle

As a bookkeeper, you complete your work by completing the tasks of the accounting cycle, so-called because the workflow is circular: entering transactions, manipulating the transactions through the accounting cycle, closing the books at the end of the accounting period and then starting the entire cycle again for the next accounting period.

The accounting cycle has eight basic steps, shown in Figure 3-1.

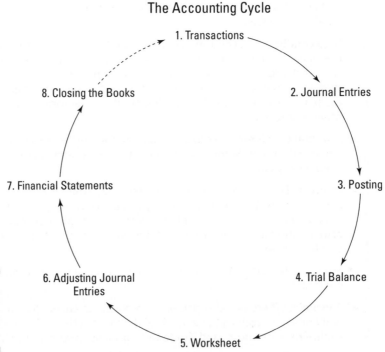

The Accounting Cycle

1. Transactions
2. Journal Entries
3. Posting
4. Trial Balance
5. Worksheet
6. Adjusting Journal Entries
7. Financial Statements
8. Closing the Books

Figure 3-1: The Accounting Cycle.

1. **Transactions:** Financial transactions start the process. Transactions can include the sale or return of a product, the purchase of supplies for business activities or any other financial activity that involves the exchange of the business's assets, the establishment or payoff of a debt or the deposit from or payout of money to the business's owners. All sales and expenses are transactions that must be recorded. We cover transactions in greater detail throughout the book as we discuss how to record the basics of business activities – recording sales, purchases, asset acquisition or disposal, taking on new debt or paying off debt.

2. **Journal entries:** The transaction is listed in the appropriate journal, maintaining the journal's chronological order of transactions. (The journal is also known as the *book of original entry* and is the first place a transaction is listed.)

3. **Posting:** The transactions are posted to the relevant account. These accounts are part of the Nominal Ledger, where you can find a summary of all the business's accounts.

4. **Trial balance:** At the end of the accounting period (which may be a month, quarter or year depending on your business's practices), you prepare a trial balance.

5. **Worksheet:** Unfortunately, often your first trial balance shows that the books aren't in balance. In this case, you look for errors and make corrections called *adjustments,* which are tracked on a worksheet. Adjustments are also made to account for the depreciation of assets and to adjust for one-time payments (such as insurance) that need to be allocated on a monthly basis to match monthly expenses with monthly revenues more accurately. After you make and record adjustments, you take another trial balance to be sure that the accounts are now in balance.

6. **Adjusting journal entries:** You post any necessary corrections to the relevant accounts when your trial balance shows that the accounts balance (after the necessary adjustments are made to the accounts). You don't need to make adjusting entries until the trial balance process is completed and all needed corrections and adjustments have been identified.

7. **Financial statements:** You prepare the balance sheet and profit and loss statement using the corrected account balances.

8. **Closing the books:** You close the books for the Revenue and Expense accounts and begin the entire cycle again.

At the end of the accounting year (year-end) all the accounting ledgers are closed off. This situation means that Revenue and Expense accounts must start with a zero balance at the beginning of each new accounting year. In contrast, you carry over Asset, Liability and Capital account balances from year to year, because the business doesn't start each cycle by getting rid of old assets and buying new assets, paying off and then taking on new debt, or paying out all claims to owners and then collecting the money again.

Book IV

Keeping On Top of the Books

Understanding Accounting Methods

Many not-for-profit organisations, such as sports clubs, have very simple accounting needs. These organisations aren't responsible to shareholders to account for their financial performance, though they are responsible to their members for the safe custody of their subscriptions and other funds. Consequently, the accounting focus isn't on measuring profit but more on accounting for receipts and payments. In these cases, a simple cash-based accounting system may well suffice, which allows only for cash transactions – no provisions are made for giving or receiving credit. However, complications may arise when members don't pay their subscriptions during the current accounting year, and the organisation needs to reflect this situation in its accounts. In this case, the accrual accounting method is best.

A few businesses operate on a cash basis, and their owners can put forward a good case for using this method. However most accountants and HM Customs & Revenue don't accept this method as it doesn't give a very accurate measure of profit (or loss) for accounting periods.

In the next sections, we explain how cash-based accounting works before dismissing it in favour of the more accepted and acceptable accrual method.

Realising the limitations of cash-based accounting

With *cash-based accounting,* you record all transactions in the books when cash actually changes hands, which means when the business receives cash payment from customers or pays out cash for purchases or other services. Cash receipt or payment can be in the form of cash, cheque, credit card, electronic transfer or other means used to pay for an item.

Cash-based accounting can't be used when a business sells products on credit and collects the money from the customer at a later date. No provision exists in the cash-based accounting method to record and track money due from customers at some point in the future.

This situation also applies for purchases. With cash-based accounting, the business only records the purchase of supplies or goods that are to be sold later when it actually pays cash. When the business buys goods on credit to be paid later, it doesn't record the transaction until the cash is actually paid out.

Depending on the size of your business, you may want to start out with cash-based accounting. Many small businesses run by a sole proprietor or a small group of partners use the easier cash-based accounting system. When your business model is simple – you carry no stock, start and finish each job within a single accounting period, and pay and get paid within this period – the cash-based accounting method can work for you. But as your business grows, you may find it necessary to switch to accrual accounting in order to track revenues and expenses more accurately and to satisfy the requirements of the external accountant and HM Revenue & Customs. The same basic argument also applies to not-for-profit organisations.

Cash-based accounting does a good job of tracking cash flow but a poor job of matching revenues earned with money laid out for expenses. This deficiency is a problem particularly when, as often happens, a business buys products in one month and sells those products in the next. For example, you buy products in June paying £1,000 cash, with the intent to sell them that same month. You don't sell the products until July, which is when you receive cash for the sales. When you close the books at the end of June, you have to show the £1,000 expense with no revenue to offset it, meaning you have a loss that month. When you sell the products for £1,500 in July, you have a £1,500 profit. So, your monthly report for June shows a £1,000 loss, and your monthly report for July shows a £1,500 profit, when in reality you had revenues of £500 over the two months. Using cash-based accounting, you can never be sure that you have an accurate measure of profit or loss, but as cash-based accounting is for not-for-profit organisations, this isn't surprising.

Because accrual accounting is the only accounting method acceptable to accountants and HM Revenue & Customs, we concentrate on this method. If you choose to use cash-based accounting because you have a cash-only business and a simple trading model, don't panic: most of the bookkeeping information here is still useful, but you don't need to maintain some of the accounts, such as Trade Debtors and Trade Creditors, because you aren't recording transactions until cash actually changes hands. When you're using a cash-based accounting system and you start to sell things on credit, though, you need to have a way to track what people owe you.

Our advice is to use the accrual accounting method right from the beginning. When your business grows and your business model changes, you need the more sophisticated and legally required accrual accounting.

Book IV

Keeping On Top of the Books

Recording right away with accrual accounting

With *accrual accounting,* you record all transactions in the books when they occur, even when no cash changes hands. For example, when you sell on credit, you record the transaction immediately and enter it into a Trade Debtors account until you receive payment. When you buy goods on credit, you immediately enter the transaction into a Trade Creditors account until you pay out cash.

Like cash-based accounting, accrual accounting has drawbacks; it does a good job of matching revenues and expenses, but a poor job of tracking cash. Because you record income when the transaction occurs and not when you collect the cash, your profit and loss statement can look great even when you don't have cash in the bank. For example, suppose you're running a contracting business and completing jobs on a daily basis. You can record the revenue upon completion of the job even when you haven't yet collected the cash. When your customers are slow to pay, you may end up with lots of income but little cash. Remember – *never* confuse profit and cash. In the short term, cash flow is often more important than profit, but in the long term profit becomes more important.

Many businesses that use the accrual accounting method monitor cash flow on a weekly basis to be sure that they have enough cash on hand to operate the business. If your business is seasonal, such as a landscaping business with little to do during the winter months, you can establish short-term lines of credit through your bank to maintain cash flow through the lean times.

Seeing Double with Double-Entry Bookkeeping

All businesses use *double-entry bookkeeping,* whether they use the cash-based accounting method or the accrual accounting method. Double-entry bookkeeping – so-called because you enter all transactions twice – helps minimise errors and increase the chance that your books balance.

When it comes to double-entry bookkeeping, the key formula for the balance sheet (Assets = Liabilities + Capital) plays a major role.

In the bookkeeping world, you use a combination of debits and credits to adjust the balance of accounts. You may think of a debit as a subtraction, because debits usually mean a decrease in your bank balance. On the other hand, you probably like finding unexpected credits in your bank account or on your credit card, because they mean more money has been added to the account in your favour. Now forget everything you know about debits or credits. In the world of bookkeeping, their meanings aren't so simple.

The only definite thing when it comes to debits and credits in the bookkeeping world is that a debit is on the left side of a transaction and a credit is on the right side of a transaction. Everything beyond that can get very muddled. We show you the basics of debits and credits in this chapter, but don't worry if you find these concepts difficult to grasp. You get plenty of practice using these concepts throughout this book.

Before we get into all the technical mumbo-jumbo of double-entry bookkeeping, here's an example of the practice in action. Suppose you purchase a new desk for your office that costs £1,500. This transaction actually has two parts: you spend an asset – cash – to buy another asset, furniture. So, you must adjust two accounts in your business's books: the Cash account and the Furniture account. The transaction in a bookkeeping entry is as follows:

Account	*Debit*	*Credit*
Furniture	£1,500	
Cash		£1,500

To purchase a new desk for the office.

In this transaction, you record the accounts impacted by the transaction. The debit increases the value of the Furniture account, and the credit decreases the value of the Cash account. For this transaction, both accounts impacted are Asset accounts, so, looking at how the balance sheet is affected, you can see that the only changes are to the asset side of the balance sheet equation:

Assets = Liabilities + Capital

Furniture increase = No change to this side of the equation

Cash decrease

In this case, the books stay in balance because the exact pounds sterling amount that increases the value of your Furniture account decreases the value of your Cash account. At the bottom of any journal entry, include a brief explanation of the purpose of the entry. In the first example, we indicate this entry was 'To purchase a new desk for the office'.

To show you how you record a transaction that impacts both sides of the balance sheet equation, here's an example that records the purchase of stock. Suppose that you purchase £5,000 worth of widgets on credit. (Have you always wondered what widgets were? Can't help you. They're just commonly used in accounting examples to represent something purchased where what is purchased is of no real significance.) These new widgets add value to your Stock Asset account and also add value to your Trade Creditors account. (Remember, the Trade Creditors account is a Liability account where you track bills that need to be paid at some point in the future.) The bookkeeping transaction for your widget purchase looks as follows:

Account	*Debit*	*Credit*
Stock	£5,000	
Trade Creditors		£5,000

To purchase widgets for sale to customers.

This transaction affects the balance sheet equation as follows:

Assets = Liabilities + Capital

Stock increases = Creditor increases + No change

In this case, the books stay in balance because both sides of the equation increase by £5,000.

You can see from the two example transactions how double-entry bookkeeping helps to keep your books in balance – as long as you make sure that each entry into the books is balanced. Balancing your entries may look simple here, but sometimes bookkeeping entries can get very complex when the transaction impacts more than two accounts.

Don't worry, you don't have to understand double-entry bookkeeping totally now. Throughout the book, we show you how to enter transactions, depending upon the type of transaction being recorded. We're just giving you a quick overview to introduce the subject right now.

Double-entry bookkeeping goes way back

No one's really sure who invented double-entry bookkeeping. The first person to put the practice on paper was Benedetto Cotrugli in 1458, but mathematician and Franciscan monk Luca Pacioli is most often credited with developing double-entry bookkeeping. Although Pacioli is called the Father of Accounting, accounting actually occupies only one of five sections of his book, *Everything About Arithmetic, Geometry and Proportions,* which was published in 1494.

Pacioli didn't actually *invent* double-entry bookkeeping; he just described the method used by merchants in Venice during the Italian Renaissance period. He's most famous for his warning to bookkeepers: 'A person should not go to sleep at night until the debits equal the credits!'

Sharing a secret

Don't feel embarrassed if you forget which side the debits go on and which side the credits go on. One often-told story is of a young clerk in an accounts office plucking up courage to ask the chief accountant, who was retiring that day, why for 30 years he had opened his drawer and read the contents of a piece of paper before starting work. The chief accountant at first was reluctant to spill the beans, but ultimately decided he had to pass on his secret – and to who better than an up-and-coming clerk? Swearing the young clerk to secrecy, he took out the piece of paper and showed it to him. The paper read: 'Debit on the left and Credit on the right.'

Differentiating Debits and Credits

Because bookkeeping's debits and credits are different from the ones you're used to encountering, you're probably wondering how you're supposed to know whether a debit or credit increases or decreases an account.

Believe it or not, identifying the difference becomes second nature as you start making regular entries in your bookkeeping system. But to make things easier for you, Table 3-1 is a chart that bookkeepers and accountants commonly use. Yep, everyone needs help sometimes.

Table 3-1	How Credits and Debits Impact Your Accounts	
Account Type	*Debits*	*Credits*
Assets	Increase	Decrease
Liabilities	Decrease	Increase
Income	Decrease	Increase
Expenses	Increase	Decrease

Copy Table 3-1 and post it at your desk when you start keeping your own books (a bit like the chief accountant in the nearby 'Sharing a secret' sidebar). We guarantee that the table helps to keep your debits and credits straight.

Book IV

Keeping On Top of the Books

Chapter 4

Controlling Your Books, Your Records and Your Money

Cash is an extremely important asset in any business, and it must be accurately recorded and monitored. Every business takes in cash in some form or another: notes and coins, cheques, and credit card and electronic payments are all eventually deposited as cash into the business's accounts. Before you take in that first penny, your initial concern must be controlling that cash and making sure that none of it walks out the door improperly.

Finding the right level of cash control, while at the same time allowing your employees the flexibility to sell your products or services and provide ongoing customer service, can be a monumental task. If you don't have enough controls, you risk theft or embezzlement. Yet if you have too many controls, employees may miss sales or anger customers.

In this chapter, we explain the basic protections you need to put in place to be sure that all cash coming into or going out of your business is clearly documented and controlled. We also review the type of paperwork you need to document the use of cash and other business assets. Finally, we tell you how to organise your staff to control the flow of your assets properly and insure yourself against possible misappropriation of those assets.

Putting Controls on Your Business's Cash

Think about how careful you are with your personal cash. You find various ways to protect the cash you carry around, you dole it out carefully to your family members and you may even hide cash in a safe place in the house just in case you need it for unexpected purposes.

You're very protective of your cash when you're the only one who handles it, but consider the vulnerability of your business cash. After all, you aren't the only one handling that cash. You have some employees encountering incoming cash at cash registers, others opening the post and finding cheques for orders to purchase products or pay bills, as well as cheques from other sources. And don't forget that employees may need petty cash to pay for postage and other small items that the business requires.

If you watch over every transaction in which cash enters your business, you have no time to do the things you need to do to grow your business. When the business is small, you can sign all cheques and maintain control of cash going out, but as soon as the business grows, you just may not have the time.

The good news is that just putting in place the proper controls for your cash can help protect it. Cash flows through your business in four key ways:

- ✔ Deposits and payments into and out of your current accounts
- ✔ Deposits and payments into and out of your savings accounts
- ✔ Petty cash funds in critical locations where quick access to cash may be needed
- ✔ Transactions made in your cash registers

The following sections cover some key controls for each of these cash-flow points.

The high cost of employee versus customer theft

According to the Centre for Retail Research, internal theft by employees cost UK retailers £3,000 million in 2010 (see www.retail research.org/grtb_globaltrends. php). You don't hear much about it, though, because many businesses choose to keep quiet. Four key situations in the workplace provide opportunities for theft and embezzlement: poor internal controls, too much control given to certain individuals, lax management and failure to pre-screen employees adequately.

Current accounts

Almost every penny that comes into your business flows through your business's current account (at least that *should* happen). Whether the cash is collected at your cash registers, payments received in the post, cash used to fill the cash registers or petty cash accounts, payments sent out to pay business obligations or any other cash need, this cash enters and exits your current account. Thus, your current account is your main tool for protecting your cash flow.

Choosing the right bank

Finding the right bank to help you set up your current account and the controls that limit access to that account is crucial. When evaluating your banking options, ask yourself the following questions:

- ✔ Does this bank have a branch conveniently located for my business?
- ✔ Does this bank operate at times when I need it most?
- ✔ Does this bank offer secure ways to deposit cash even when the bank is closed?

    Most banks have secure deposit boxes for cash so that you can pay in cash receipts as quickly as possible at the end of the business day rather than secure the cash overnight yourself. You don't have to wait in a queue to deposit cash at the counter: simply fill out a paying-in slip, put it and the money into an envelope supplied by the bank and post the envelope into a special deposit box within the bank.

Visit local bank branches yourself and check out the type of business services each bank offers. Pay particular attention to:

- ✔ The type of personal attention you receive
- ✔ How questions are handled
- ✔ What type of charges may be tacked on for personalised attention

Some banks require business account holders to call a centralised line for assistance rather than depend on local branches. Most banks charge if you use a cashier rather than an ATM (automatic teller machine). Other banks charge for every transaction, whether a deposit, withdrawal or cheque. Many banks have charges that differ for business accounts. If you plan to accept credit cards, compare the services offered for that as well.

The general rule is that banks charge businesses for everything they do. However, they charge less for tasks that can be automated and thus involve less manual effort. So, you save money when you use electronic payment and receipt processes. In other words, pay your suppliers electronically and get your customers to pay you the same way to reduce your banking costs.

Deciding on types of cheques

After you choose your bank, you need to consider what type of cheques you want to use in your business. For example, you need different cheques depending upon whether you handwrite each cheque or print cheques from your computerised accounting system.

Writing cheques manually

If you plan to write your cheques, you're most likely to use a business cheque book, which in its simplest form is exactly the same as a personal cheque book, with a counterfoil (or cheque stub) on the left and a cheque on the right. This arrangement provides the best control for manual cheques because each cheque and counterfoil is numbered. When you write a cheque, you fill out the counterfoil with details such as the date, the cheque's recipient and the purpose of the cheque. The counterfoil also has a space to keep a running total of your balance in the account.

Printing computer-generated cheques

If you plan to print cheques from your computerised accounting system, you need to order cheques that match that system's programming. Each computer software program has a unique template for printing cheques, and some provide bespoke stationery for their accounting software. The key information is exactly what you expect to see on any cheque – payee details, date and amount in both words and numbers.

Unlike a manual cheque, you don't have a counterfoil to fill in, which isn't a problem because your computerised accounting system records this information for you: it keeps an internal record of all cheques issued. If you need to check that you issued a cheque correctly, you can always run a report or make an on-screen enquiry on your computerised accounting system.

Initially, when the business is small, you can sign each cheque and keep control of the outflow of money. But as the business grows, you may find that you need to delegate cheque-signing responsibilities to someone else, especially if you travel frequently. Many small business owners set up cheque-signing procedures that allow one or two of their staff to sign cheques up to a designated amount, such as £5,000. Any cheques above that designated amount require the owner's signature, or the signature of an employee and a second designated person, such as an officer of the business.

Making deposits in the current account

Of course, you aren't just withdrawing from your business's current account (that would be a big problem). You also need to deposit money into that account, and you want to be sure that your paying-in slips contain all the necessary detail as well as documentation to back up the deposit information. Most banks provide printed paying-in slips with all the necessary detail to be sure that the money is deposited into the appropriate account, together with who wrote each cheque, the value and the date received.

A good practice is to record cheques immediately as part of a daily morning routine. Enter the details onto the paying-in slip and update your computerised or manual accounting system at the same time. Make sure that you pay in any money received before 3.30 p.m. on the same day, to ensure that your bank account gets credit that day rather than the next. (We talk more about controls for incoming cash in the 'Dividing staff responsibilities' section, later in this chapter.) If you get both personal and business cheques sent to the same address, instruct the person opening the post about how to differentiate the types of cheques and how each type of cheque needs to be handled to best protect your incoming cash, whether for business or personal purposes.

You may think that making bank deposits is as easy as 1-2-3, but when it comes to business deposits and multiple cheques, things get a bit more complicated. To make deposits to your business's current account properly, follow these steps:

1. **Record on the paying-in slip the full details of all cheques being deposited as well as the total cash being deposited. Also make a note of how many cheques you're paying into the bank on that paying-in slip.**

2. **Record the details regarding the source of the deposited cash before you make the deposit. If you're operating a manual system, you can write the entries in your Cash Receipts book, or if using a computerised system, you can enter the details from the paying-in slip directly into the computer.** (We talk more about filing in the section 'Keeping the Right Paperwork', later in this chapter.)

3. **Make sure that the cashier at the bank stamps the paying-in slip as confirmation that the bank has received all the cheques and cash.**

   If you're paying in cheques via the ATM, treat it exactly as if you were paying in via the cashier. Still prepare your own paying-in slip and make sure that you pick up the receipt that the ATM gives you. This doesn't ensure that things won't go wrong, but it means you have a paper trail if they do. Note on your paying-in slip counterfoil that you have paid via the deposit box or ATM.

Savings accounts

Some businesses find that they have more cash than they need to meet their immediate plans. Rather than keep that extra cash in a non-interest-bearing account, many businesses open a savings account to store the extra cash.

If you're a small business owner with few employees, you probably control the flow of money into and out of your savings account yourself. As you grow and find that you need to delegate the responsibility for the business's savings, ensure that you think carefully about who gets access and how you can document the flow of funds into and out of the savings account. Treat a savings account like a current account and use paying-in slips to record deposits and cheque-book stubs to record payments. Alternatively, you can arrange for the bank to automatically transfer surplus funds from your current account across to your savings account when the current account reaches a specified amount.

Petty cash accounts

Every business needs cash on almost a weekly basis. Businesses need to keep some cash on hand, called *petty cash,* for unexpected expenses such as money to pay for letters and packages delivered COD, money to buy a few emergency stamps to send the post or money for some office supplies needed before the next delivery.

You certainly don't want to have a lot of cash sitting around in the office, but try to keep £50 to £100 in a petty cash box. If you subsequently find that you're faced with more or less cash expenses than you expected, you can always adjust the amount kept in petty cash accordingly.

No matter how much you keep in petty cash, make sure that you set up a good control system that requires anyone who uses the cash to write a petty cash voucher specifying how much was used and why. Also ask that a cash receipt, for example from the shop or post office, is attached to the voucher in order to justify the cash withdrawal whenever possible. In most cases, a member of staff buys something for the business and then gets reimbursed for that expense. If the expense is small enough, you can reimburse through the petty cash fund. If the expense is more than a few pounds, ask the person to fill out an expense account form and get reimbursed by cheque. Petty cash is usually used for minor expenses of £10 or less.

The best way to control petty cash is to pick one person in the office to manage the use of all petty cash. Before giving that person more cash, she should be able to prove the absence of cash used and why it was used.

Poor control of the petty cash box can lead to small but significant losses of cash. Quite often you can find it difficult or impossible to identify or prove who took the cash. The best solution is to make it slightly more difficult for employees to obtain petty cash; a locked box in a cupboard works very well.

For the ultimate control of cash, use the imprest system in which a fixed amount is drawn from the bank and paid into petty cash (the float). After that, cash is issued only against a petty cash voucher. This system means that, at any point, cash, or cash plus vouchers, should be equal to the total of the petty cash float. At the end of the week (or month) the vouchers are removed and the cash made up to the original amount.

Cash registers

Have you ever gone into a business and tried to pay with a large note only to find out that the cashier has no change? This frustrating experience happens in many businesses, especially those that don't carefully monitor the money in their cash registers. Most businesses empty cash registers each night and put any cash not being deposited at the bank that night into a safe. However, many businesses instruct their cashiers to deposit their cash in a business safe periodically throughout the day and get a paper voucher to show the cash deposited. These daytime deposits minimise the cash held in case the store is the victim of a robbery.

All these types of controls are necessary parts of modern business operations, but they can have consequences that make customers angry. Most customers just walk out the door and don't come back when they can't buy what they want using the notes they have to hand.

At the beginning of the day, cashiers usually start out with a set amount of cash in the register. As they collect money and give out change, the register records the transactions. At the end of the day, the cashier must count out the amount of change left in the register, run a copy of all transactions that passed through that register and total the cash collected. Then the cashier must prove that the amount of cash remaining in that register totals the amount of cash the register started with plus the amount of cash collected during the day. After the cashier balances the register, the person in charge of cash deposits (usually the shop manager or someone on the accounting or bookkeeping staff) takes all the cash out, except the amount needed for the next day, and deposits it in the bank. (We talk more about separation of staff duties in the section 'Dividing staff responsibilities', later in this chapter.)

In addition to having the proper amount of cash in the register necessary to give customers the change they need, you also must make sure that your cashiers are giving the right amount of change and actually recording all sales on their cash registers. Keeping an eye on cashier activities is good business practice in any case, but you can also protect against cash theft by your employees in this way. Three ways exist in which cashiers can pocket some extra cash:

✔ **They don't record the sale in the cash register and instead pocket the cash.** The best deterrent to this type of theft is supervision. You can decrease the likelihood of theft through unrecorded sales by printing up sales tickets that the cashier must use to enter a sale in the cash register and open the cash drawer. If cash register transactions don't match sales receipts, the cashier must show a voided transaction for the missing ticket or explain why the cash drawer was opened without a ticket.

✔ **They don't provide a sales receipt and instead pocket the cash.** In this scenario the cashier neglects to give a sales receipt to one customer in the queue. The cashier gives the next customer the unused sales receipt but doesn't actually record the second transaction in the cash register. Instead, she just pockets the cash. In the business's books, the second sale never took place. The customer whose sale wasn't recorded has a valid receipt though it may not match exactly what was bought. Therefore, the customer is unlikely to notice any problem unless something needs to be returned later. Your best defence against this type of deception is to post a sign reminding all customers that they must get a receipt for all purchases and that the receipt is required to get a refund or exchange. Providing numbered sales receipts that include a duplicate copy can also help prevent this problem; cashiers need to produce the duplicates at the end of the day when proving the amount of cash flow that passed through their registers.

In addition to protection from theft by cashiers, the printed sales receipt system can be used to monitor shoplifters and prevent them from getting money for merchandise they never bought. For example, suppose a shoplifter takes a blouse out of a store, as well as some blank sales receipts. The next day the shoplifter comes back with the blouse and one of the stolen sales receipts filled out as though the blouse had actually been purchased the day before. You can spot the fraud because that sales receipt is part of a numbered batch of sales receipts that you've already identified as missing or stolen. You can quickly identify that the customer never paid for the merchandise and call the police.

✔ **They record a false credit voucher and keep the cash for themselves.** In this case the cashier writes up a credit voucher for a nonexistent customer and then pockets the cash refund. Most shops use a numbered credit voucher system to control this problem, so each credit can be carefully monitored with some detail that proves its connection to a previous customer purchase, such as a sales receipt. Customers are often asked to provide an address and telephone number before receiving a refund. Although this may not put off the determined fraudster, the opportunist thief is likely to be deterred. Also, shops usually require that a manager review the reason for the credit voucher, whether a return or exchange, and approve the transaction before cash or credit is given. When the bookkeeper records the sales return in the books, the number for the credit voucher is recorded with the transaction so that the detail about that credit voucher is easy to find if a question is raised later about the transaction.

Even if cashiers don't deliberately pocket cash, they can inadvertently give the wrong change. If you run a retail outlet, training and supervising your cashiers is a critical task that you must handle yourself or hand over to a trusted employee.

Keeping the Right Paperwork

When handling cash, you can see that a lot of paper changes hands, whether from the cash register, deposits into your current accounts or petty cash withdrawals. Therefore, careful documentation is paramount to control the movement of cash into and out of your business properly. And don't forget about organisation; you need to be able to find that documentation if questions about cash flow arise later.

Monitoring cash flow isn't the only reason why you need to keep loads of paperwork. In order to do your taxes and write off business expenses, you need receipts for those expenses. You also need details about the money you pay to employees, and tax and National Insurance contributions collected for your employees, in order to file the proper reports with HM Revenue & Customs. Setting up a good filing system and knowing what to keep and for how long is very important for any small-business person.

Creating a filing system

To get started setting up your filing system, you need the following supplies:

- **Filing cabinets:** Pretty self-explanatory – you can't have a filing system with nothing to keep the files in.

- **File folders:** Set up separate files for each of your suppliers, employees and customers who buy on credit, as well as files for backup information on each of your transactions. Many bookkeepers file transaction information using the date the transaction was added to their journal. If the transaction relates to a customer, supplier or employee, they add a duplicate copy of the transaction to the individual files as well.

  Even if you have a computerised accounting system, you need to file paperwork related to the transactions you enter into your computer system. You still need to maintain employee, supplier and customer files in hard copy just in case something goes wrong – for example, if your computer system crashes, you need the originals to restore the data. Back up your computerised accounting system's data regularly to minimise the effects of such a crisis. Daily backups are best; one week is the longest you should ever go without a backup.

- **Ring binders:** These binders are great for things you add to regularly and the binders make adding additional pages easy. Make sure that you number the pages as you add them to the binder, so that you can quickly spot a missing page. How many binders you need depends on how many financial transactions you have each accounting period. You can keep everything in one binder, or you may want to set up a binder for the Chart of Accounts and Nominal Ledger and then a separate binder for each of your active journals. The decision is based on what makes your job easier.

Book IV

Keeping On Top of the Books

✔ **Expandable files:** These files are the best way to keep track of current supplier activity and any bills that may be due. Make sure that you have:

- **An alphabetical file:** Use this file to track all your outstanding purchase orders by supplier. After you fill the order, you can file all details about that order in the supplier's individual file in case questions about the order arise later.

- **A 12-month file:** Use this file to keep track of bills that you need to pay. Simply place the bill in the slot for the month payment is due. Many businesses also use a 30-day expandable file. At the beginning of the month, the bills are placed in the 30-day expandable file based on the dates that they need to be paid. This approach provides a quick and organised visual reminder for bills that are due.

If you're using a computerised accounting system, you don't need the expandable files because your accounting system can remind you when bills are due. You can also print an Aged Debtor report, which shows you who owes you money, and an Aged Creditor report, which shows you how much money you owe your suppliers and how many days overdue your invoices are.

✔ **Rewritable CDs** can be used to backup your computerised system on a daily basis. Keep the backup discs in a fire safe or somewhere unaffected if a fire destroys the business. (A fire safe is the best way to keep critical financial data safe, and is therefore a must for any business.) If you don't have a fire safe, use two different CDs for backup on alternate days. Take the most recent backup off-site each night and leave the other CD at the office. In the event that disaster strikes, you are only ever one day behind with your backup data.

Working out what to keep and for how long

As you can probably imagine, the pile of paperwork you need to hold on to can get very large very quickly. As they see their files getting thicker and thicker, most businesspeople wonder what they can toss, what they really need to keep and how long they need to keep it.

Generally, keep most transaction-related paperwork for as long as HM Revenue & Customs can come and audit your books. For most types of audits, that means six years. But if you fail to file your tax return or file it fraudulently (and we hope this doesn't apply to you), HM Revenue & Customs may question you about it any time, because no time limitations exist in these cases.

HM Revenue & Customs isn't the only reason to keep records around for longer than one year. You may need proof-of-purchase information for your insurance company if an asset is lost, stolen or destroyed by fire or other accident. Also, you need to hang on to information regarding any business loan until paid off, just in case the bank questions how much you paid. After the loan's paid off, ensure that you keep proof of payment indefinitely in case a question about the loan ever arises. Information about property and other asset holdings needs to be kept around for as long as you hold the asset and for at least six years after the asset is sold. You're legally required to keep information about employees for at least three years after the employee leaves.

Keep the current year's files easily accessible in a designated filing area and keep the most recent past year's files in accessible filing cabinets if you have room. Box up records when they hit the two-year-old mark and put them in storage. Make sure that you date your boxed records with information about what they are, when they were put into storage and when you can destroy them. Many people forget that last detail, and boxes pile up until total desperation sets in and no more room is left. Then someone must take the time to sort through the boxes and figure out what needs to be kept and what can be destroyed – not a fun job.

It's a legal requirement to keep information about all transactions for six years. After that, make a list of things you want to hold on to for longer for other reasons, such as asset holdings and loan information. Check with your solicitor and accountant to get their recommendations on what to keep and for how long.

Protecting Your Business Against Internal Fraud

Many businesspeople start their operations by carefully hiring people they can trust, thinking: 'We're a family – they'd never steal from me.'

Often a business owner finds out too late that even the most loyal employee may steal from the business if the opportunity arises and the temptation becomes too great – or if the employee gets caught up in a serious personal financial dilemma and needs fast cash. In this section, we talk about the steps you can take to prevent people stealing from your business.

Facing the reality of financial fraud

The four basic types of financial fraud are:

- **Embezzlement,** which is the illegal use of funds by a person who controls those funds. For example, a bookkeeper may use business money for her own personal needs. Many times, embezzlement stories don't appear in the newspapers because businesspeople are so embarrassed that they choose to keep the affair quiet. They usually settle privately with the embezzler rather than face public scrutiny.

- **Internal theft,** which is the stealing of business assets by employees, such as taking office supplies or products the business sells without paying for them. Internal theft is often the culprit behind stock shrinkage.

- **Payoffs and kickbacks,** which are situations in which employees accept cash or other benefits in exchange for access to the business, often creating a scenario where the business that the employee works for pays more for the goods or products than necessary. That extra money finds its way into the pocket of the employee who helped facilitate the access. For example, say Business A wants to sell its products to Business B. An employee in Business B helps Business A get in the door. Business A prices its product a bit higher and gives the employee of Business B the extra profit in the form of a kickback for helping it out. A payoff is paid before the sale is made, essentially saying 'please'. A kickback is paid after the sale is made, essentially saying 'thank you'. In reality, payoffs and kickbacks are a form of bribery, but few businesses report or litigate this problem (although employees are fired when deals are uncovered).

- **Skimming,** which occurs when employees take money from receipts and don't record the revenue in the books.

Although any of these financial crimes can happen in a small business, the one that hits small businesses the hardest is embezzlement. This crime happens most frequently when one person has access or control over most of the business's financial activities. For example, a single bookkeeper may write cheques, make deposits and balance the monthly bank statement – talk about having your fingers in a very big till.

Dividing staff responsibilities

Your primary protection against financial crime is properly separating staff responsibilities when the flow of business cash is involved. Basically, never have one person handling more than one of the following tasks:

✔ **Bookkeeping:** Involves reviewing and entering all transactions into the business's books. The bookkeeper makes sure that transactions are accurate, valid, appropriate and have the proper authorisation. For example, if a transaction requires paying a supplier, the bookkeeper makes sure that the charges are accurate and someone with proper authority has approved the payment. The bookkeeper can review documentation of cash receipts and the overnight deposits taken to the bank, but shouldn't actually make the deposit. Also, if the bookkeeper is responsible for handling payments from external parties, such as customers or suppliers, she shouldn't enter those transactions in the books.

✔ **Authorisation:** Involves being the manager or managers delegated to authorise expenditures for their departments. You may decide that transactions over a certain amount must have two or more authorisations before cheques can be sent to pay a bill. Spell out authorisation levels clearly and make sure that everyone follows them, even the owner or managing director of the business. (Remember, as owner, you set the tone for how the rest of the office operates; when you take shortcuts, you set a bad example and undermine the system you put in place.)

✔ **Money-handling:** Involves direct contact with incoming cash or revenue, whether cheque, credit card or credit transactions, as well as outgoing cash flow. People who handle money directly, such as cashiers, shouldn't also prepare and make bank deposits. Likewise, the person writing cheques to pay business bills shouldn't be authorised to sign those cheques; to be safe, have one person prepare the cheques based on authorised documentation and a second person sign those cheques, after reviewing the authorised documentation.

When setting up your cash-handling systems, try to think like an embezzler to figure out how someone can take advantage of a system.

✔ **Financial report preparation and analysis:** Involves the actual preparation of the financial reports and any analysis of those reports. Someone who's not involved in the day-to-day entering of transactions in the books needs to prepare the financial reports. For most small businesses, the bookkeeper turns over the raw reports from the computerised accounting system to an outside accountant who reviews the materials and prepares the financial reports. In addition, the accountant does a financial analysis of the business activity results for the previous accounting period.

Book IV

Keeping On Top of the Books

Caught with fingers in the till

Alice is a bookkeeper who's been with Business A for a long time. She was promoted to office manager after being with the business for 20 years. She's like a family member to the business owner, who trusts her implicitly. Because he's so busy with other aspects of running the business, he gives her control of the daily grind of cash flow. The beloved office manager handles or supervises all incoming and outgoing cash, reconciles the bank statements, handles payroll, signs all the cheques and files the business's tax returns.

All that control gives her the opportunity, credibility and access to embezzle a lot of money. At first, the trust is well founded, and Alice handles her new responsibilities very well. But after about three years in the role as office manager, she develops a gambling habit and the debts mount up.

Alice decides to pay herself more money. She adds her husband to the payroll and documents the cheques for him as consulting expenses. She draws large cash cheques to buy non-existent office supplies and equipment, and then, worst of all, she files the business's tax returns and pockets the money that should go to paying the tax due. The business owner doesn't find out about the problem until HM Revenue & Customs comes calling, and by then, the office manager has retired and moved away.

This story may sound far-fetched, but you can read about similar embezzlement schemes in the national newspapers.

We realise that you may be just starting up a small business and therefore not have enough staff to separate all these duties. Until you do have that capability, make sure that you stay heavily involved in the inflow and outflow of cash in your business. The following tips tell you how:

- ✔ **Periodically (once a month) open your business's bank statements and review the transactions.** Someone else can be given the responsibility of reconciling the statement, but you still need to keep an eye on the transactions listed.

- ✔ **Periodically look at your business cheque book counterfoils to ensure that no cheques are missing.** A bookkeeper who knows that you periodically check the books is less likely to find an opportunity for theft or embezzlement. If you find that a cheque or page of cheques is missing, act quickly to find out if the cheques were used legitimately. If you can't find the answer, call your bank and put a stop on the missing cheque numbers.

- ✔ **Periodically observe your cashiers and managers handling cash to make sure that they're following the rules you've established.** This practice is known as *management by walking around* – the more often you're out there, the less likely you are to be a victim of employee theft and fraud.

Balancing control costs

As a small-business person, you're always trying to balance the cost of protecting your cash and assets with the cost of adequately separating those duties. Putting in place too many controls, which end up costing you money, can be a big mistake. For example, you may create stock controls that require salespeople to contact one particular person who has the key to your product warehouse. This kind of control may prevent employee theft, but can also result in lost sales, because salespeople can't find the key-holder while dealing with an interested customer. In the end, the customer gets mad, and you lose the sale.

When you put controls in place, talk to your staff both before and after instituting the controls to see how they're working and to check for any unforeseen problems. Be willing and able to adjust your controls to balance the business needs of selling your products, managing the cash flow and keeping your eye on making a profit. Talk to other businesspeople to see what they do and pick up tips from established best practice. Your external accountant can be a good source of valuable information.

Generally, as you make rules for your internal controls, make sure that the cost of protecting an asset is no more than the asset you're trying to protect. For example, don't go overboard to protect office supplies by forcing your staff to wait around for hours to access needed supplies while you and a manager are at a meeting away from the office.

Ask yourself these four questions as you design your internal controls:

- What exactly do I want to prevent or detect – errors, sloppiness, theft, fraud or embezzlement?
- Do I face the problem frequently?
- What do I estimate the loss to be?
- What is the cost to me of implementing the change in procedures to prevent or detect the problem?

You can't answer all these questions yourself, so consult with your managers and the staff the changes are likely to impact. Get their answers to these questions and listen to their feedback.

When you finish putting together the new internal control rule, ensure that you document why you decided to implement the rule and the information you collected in developing it. After the rule's been in place for a while, test your assumptions. Make sure that you are in fact detecting the errors, theft, fraud or embezzlement that you hoped and expected to detect. Check the costs of keeping the rule in place by looking at cash outlay, employee time and morale, and the impact on customer service. If you find any problems with your internal controls, take the time to fix them and change the rule, again documenting the process. Detailed documentation ensures that, if two or three years down the road someone questions why she is doing something, you have the answers and are able to determine whether the problem is still valid, as well as whether the rule is still necessary or needs to be changed.

Insuring Your Cash through Fidelity Bonds

Employers can insure themselves against the loss of money through embezzlement by employees. A *fidelity bond* is a form of insurance that companies can take out to protect themselves against financial loss caused by employee theft or dishonesty. If an employee steals from you or one of your customers, the insurance covers the loss.

This type of insurance is a specialist one and can be packaged up with your normal business insurance. The cost varies greatly depending on the type of business you operate and the amount of cash or other assets that are handled by the employees you want to bond. Ask your insurance broker to get an accurate quotation for your business.

Chapter 5

Producing a Profit and Loss Statement

*W*ithout one very important financial report tool, you can never know for sure whether or not your business is making a profit. This tool is called the *profit and loss statement,* and most businesses prepare this statement on a monthly basis, as well as quarterly and annually, in order to get periodic pictures of how well the business is doing financially.

Analysing the profit and loss statement and the details behind it can reveal lots of useful information to help you make decisions for improving your profits and business overall. This chapter covers the various parts of a profit and loss statement, and how you develop one, and examples of how you can use it to make business decisions.

Lining Up the Profit and Loss Statement

Did your business make any profit? You can find the answer in your *profit and loss statement,* the financial report that summarises all the sales activities, costs of producing or buying the products or services sold and expenses incurred in order to run the business.

Profit and loss statements summarise the financial activities of a business during a particular accounting period (which can be a month, quarter, year or some other period of time that makes sense for a business's needs).

Normal practice is to include two accounting periods on a profit and loss statement: the current period plus the year to date. The five key lines that make up a profit and loss statement are:

- ✔ **Sales or Revenue:** The total amount of invoiced sales taken in from selling the business's products or services. You calculate this amount by totalling all the sales or revenue accounts. The top line of the profit and loss statement is sales or revenues; either is okay.

- ✔ **Cost of Goods Sold:** How much was spent in order to buy or make the goods or services that were sold during the accounting period under review. The section 'Finding Cost of Goods Sold' below shows you how to calculate Cost of Goods Sold.

- ✔ **Gross Profit:** How much a business made before taking into account operations expenses; calculated by subtracting the Cost of Goods Sold from the Sales or Revenue.

- ✔ **Operating Expenses:** How much was spent on operating the business; these expenses include administrative fees, salaries, advertising, utilities and other operations expenses. You add all your expenses accounts on your profit and loss statement to get this total.

- ✔ **Net Profit or Loss:** Whether or not the business made a profit or loss during the accounting period in review; calculated by subtracting total expenses from Gross Profit.

Formatting the Profit and Loss Statement

Before you actually create your business's profit and loss statement, you have to pick a format in which to organise your financial information. You have two options to choose from: the single-step format or the multi-step format. They contain the same information but present it in slightly different ways.

The *single-step format* groups all data into two categories: revenue and expenses. The *multi-step format* divides the profit and loss statement into several sections and offers some key subtotals to make analysing the data easier.

You can calculate the same subtotals from the single-step format in the multi-step format, although it means more work. Therefore, most businesses choose the multi-step format to simplify profit and loss statement analysis for those who read their external financial reports.

The following is an example of a basic profit and loss statement prepared in the single-step format:

Revenues

Net Sales	£1,000
Interest Income	£100
Total Revenue	£1,100

Expenses

Cost of Goods Sold	£500
Depreciation	£50
Advertising	£50
Salaries	£100
Supplies	£100
Interest Expenses	£50
Total Expenses	£850
Net Profit	£250

Using the same numbers, the following is an example of a basic profit and loss statement prepared in the multi-step format.

Revenues

Sales	£1,000
Cost of Goods Sold	£500
Gross Profit	£500

Operating Expenses

Depreciation	£50
Advertising	£50
Salaries	£100

Supplies	£100
Interest Expenses	£50
Total Operating Expenses	£350
Operating Profit	£150
Other Income	
Interest Income	£100
Total Profit	£250

Of course, in both examples you end up with the same profit, but the second profit and loss statement provides the reader with a better analysis of what happened in the business.

Preparing the Profit and Loss Statement

Before you can prepare your profit and loss statement, you have to calculate Net Sales and Cost of Goods Sold.

Finding Net Sales

Net Sales is a total of all your sales minus any discounts. In order to calculate Net Sales, you look at the line items regarding sales, discounts and any sales fees on your worksheet. For example, suppose that your worksheet lists Total Sales at £20,000 and discounts given to customers at £1,000. Also, according to your worksheet, your business paid £125 in credit card fees on sales. To find your Net Sales, you subtract the discounts and credit card fees from your Total Sales amount, leaving you with £18,875.

Finding Cost of Goods Sold

Cost of Goods Sold is the total amount your business spent to buy or make the goods or services that you sold. To calculate this amount for a business that buys its finished products from another business in order to sell them to customers, you start with the value of the business's Opening Stock (the amount in the Stock account at the beginning of the accounting period), add all purchases of new stock and then subtract any Closing Stock (stock that's still on the shelves or in the warehouse; it appears on the balance sheet, which is covered in Chapter 6 in Book IV).

The following is a basic Cost of Goods Sold calculation:

Opening Stock + Purchases = Goods Available for Sale

£100 + £1,000 = £1,100

Goods Available for Sale – Closing Stock = Cost of Goods Sold

£1,100 – £200 = £900

To simplify the example for calculating Cost of Goods Sold, these numbers assume the Opening Stock (the value of the stock at the beginning of the accounting period) and Closing Stock (the value of the stock at the end of the accounting period) values are the same. So to calculate Cost of Goods Sold you need just two key lines: the purchases made and the discounts received to lower the purchase cost, as in the following example.

Purchases – Purchases Discounts = Cost of Goods Sold

£8,000 – £1,500 = £6,500

Drawing remaining amounts from your worksheet

After you've calculated Net Sales and Cost of Goods Sold (see the preceding sections), you can use the rest of the numbers from your worksheet to prepare your business's profit and loss statement. Figure 5-1 shows a sample profit and loss statement.

You and anyone else in-house are likely to want to see the type of detail shown in the example in Figure 5-1, but most business owners prefer not to show all their operating detail to outsiders: they like to keep the detail private. Fortunately, if you operate as a sole trader or partnership, only HM Revenue & Customs needs to see your detailed profit and loss figures. If your turnover is less than around £70,000 per annum, HM Revenue & Customs allow you to file an abbreviated set of accounts for the purpose of completing your Self Assessment Tax return, only requesting the following headings:

- Turnover
- Other Income
- Cost of Goods Sold
- Car, Van and Travel Expenses (after private-use deduction)
- Wages, Salaries and Other Staff Costs
- Rent, Rates, Power and Insurance Costs
- Repairs and Renewals of Property and Equipment

✔ Accountancy, Legal and Other Professional Fees

✔ Interest, Bank and Credit Card Financial Charges

✔ Phone, Fax, Stationery and Other Office Costs

✔ Other Allowable Business Expenses

Also, if you are a small limited company, when you file your accounts at Companies House you can file abbreviated accounts, which means that you can keep your detailed profit and loss figures secret. Speak with your external accountant about whether you qualify as a small company because the exemption levels do change from time to time.

Profit and Loss Statement

May 2010

Month Ended	May
Revenues:	
Net Sales	£ 18,875
Cost of Goods Sold	(£ 6,500)
Gross Profit	£ 12,375
Operating Expenses:	
Advertising	£ 1,500
Bank Service Charges	£ 120
Insurance Expenses	£ 100
Interest Expenses	£ 125
Legal & Accounting Fees	£ 300
Office Expenses	£ 250
Payroll Taxes Expenses	£ 350
Postage Expenses	£ 75
Rent Expenses	£ 800
Salaries	£ 3,500
Supplies	£ 300
Telephone Expenses	£ 200
Utilities	£ 255
Total Operating Expenses	£ 7,875
Net Profit	£ 4,500

Figure 5-1: A sample profit and loss statement.

Gauging your Cost of Goods Sold

Businesses that make their own products rather than buy them for future sale must record stock at three different levels:

- ✔ **Raw materials:** This line item includes purchases of all items used to make your business's products. For example, a fudge shop buys all the ingredients to make the fudge it sells, so the value of any stock on hand that hasn't been used to make fudge yet needs to appear in the raw materials line item.

- ✔ **Work-in-progress stock:** This line item shows the value of any products being made that aren't yet ready for sale. A fudge shop is unlikely to have anything in this line item because fudge doesn't take more than a few hours to make. However, many manufacturing businesses take weeks or months to produce products and therefore usually have some portion of the stock value in this line item.

  Valuing work in progress can be very complex. As well as the raw material content, you need to add in direct wages and production overheads consumed to produce the products to the stage they're at. In reality most small businesses don't attempt to value work in progress.

- ✔ **Finished-goods stock:** This line item lists the value of stock that's ready for sale. (For a business that doesn't make its own products, finished-goods stock is the same as the stock line item.)

If you keep the books for a business that manufactures its own products, you can use a computerised accounting system to record the various stock accounts described here. However, your basic accounting system software won't cut it – you need a more advanced package in order to record multiple stock types. One such system is Sage 50 Accounts.

Deciphering Gross Profit

Business owners must carefully watch their Gross Profit trends on monthly profit and loss statements. Gross Profit trends that appear lower from one month to the next can mean one of two things: sales revenue is down, or Cost of Goods Sold is up.

If revenue is down month to month, you may need to find out quickly why and fix the problem in order to meet your sales goals for the year. Or, by examining sales figures for the same month in previous years, you may determine that the drop is just a normal sales slowdown given the time of year and isn't cause to hit the panic button.

If the downward trend isn't normal, it may be a sign that a competitor's successfully drawing customers away from your business, or it may indicate that customers are dissatisfied with some aspect of the products or services you supply. Whatever the reason, preparing a monthly profit and loss statement gives you the ammunition you need to find and fix a problem quickly, thereby minimising any negative hit to your yearly profits.

The other key element of Gross Profit, Cost of Goods Sold, can also be a big factor in a downward profit trend. For example, if the amount you spend to purchase products that you sell goes up, your Gross Profit goes down. As a business owner, you need to do one of five things if the Cost of Goods Sold is reducing your Gross Profit:

✔ Find a new supplier who can provide the goods more cheaply.

✔ Increase your prices, as long as you don't lose sales because of the increase.

✔ Find a way to increase your volume of sales so that you can sell more products and meet your annual profit goals.

✔ Find a way to reduce other expenses to offset the additional product costs.

✔ Accept the fact that your annual profit is going to be lower than expected.

The sooner you find out that you have a problem with costs, the faster you can find a solution and minimise any reduction in your annual profit goals.

Monitoring Expenses

The Expenses section of your profit and loss statement gives you a good summary of how much you spent to keep your business operating that wasn't directly related to the sale of an individual product or service. For example, businesses usually use advertising both to bring customers in and with the hopes of selling many different types of products. That's why you need to list advertising as an Expense rather than a Cost of Goods Sold. After all, rarely can you link an advertisement to the sale of an individual product. The same is true of all the administrative expenses that go into running a business, such as rent, wages and salaries, office costs and so on.

Business owners watch their expense trends closely to be sure that they don't creep upwards and lower the business's bottom lines. Any cost-cutting you can do on the expense side is guaranteed to increase your bottom-line profit.

Using the Profit and Loss Statement to Make Business Decisions

Many business owners find it easier to compare their profit and loss statement trends using percentages rather than the actual numbers. Calculating these percentages is easy enough – you simply divide each line item by Net Sales. Figure 5-2 shows a business's percentage breakdown for one month.

Profit and Loss Statement

May 2010

Month Ended	May	
Net Sales	£ 18,875	100.0%
Cost of Goods Sold	(£ 6,500)	34.4%
Gross Profit	£ 12,375	65.6%
Operating Expenses:		
Advertising	£ 1,500	7.9%
Bank Service Charges	£ 120	0.6%
Insurance Expenses	£ 100	0.5%
Interest Expenses	£ 125	0.7%
Legal & Accounting Fees	£ 300	1.6%
Office Expenses	£ 250	1.3%
Payroll Taxes Expenses	£ 350	1.9%
Postage Expenses	£ 75	0.4%
Rent Expenses	£ 800	4.2%
Salaries	£ 3,500	18.5%
Supplies	£ 300	1.6%
Telephone Expenses	£ 200	1.1%
Utilities	£ 255	1.4%
Total Operating Expenses	£ 7,875	41.7%
Net Profit	£ 4,500	23.8%

Figure 5-2: Percentage breakdown of a profit and loss statement.

Looking at this percentage breakdown, you can see that the business had a gross profit of 65.6 per cent, and its Cost of Goods Sold, at 34.4 per cent, accounted for just over one third of the revenue. If the prior month's Cost of Goods Sold was only 32 per cent, the business owner needs to find out why the cost of the goods used to make this product seems to have increased. If this trend of increased Cost of Goods Sold continues through the year without some kind of fix, the business makes at least 2.2 per cent less net profit.

You may find it helpful to see how your profit and loss statement results compare to industry trends for similar businesses with similar revenues, a process called *benchmarking*. By comparing results, you can find out if your costs and expenses are reasonable for the type of business you operate, and you can identify areas with room to improve your profitability. You also may spot some red flags for line items upon which you spend much more than the national average.

To find industry trends for businesses similar to yours with similar revenues, visit www.bvdinfo.com. The FAME database contains full financial data on approximately two million companies in the UK and Ireland that file their accounts at Companies House. A word of warning though: small companies are required to file very little financial information – typically just a balance sheet. This means that if you want to see detailed profit and loss information you have to look at the big businesses with turnover above £5.6 million and a balance sheet greater than £2.8 million.

However, the information available for all the companies on this database is useful and can be searched in a number of ways. For example, you can compile industry-average statistics, which can be a useful way to see how your business compares with others in the same line of business. You can take this a stage farther and compare your business to other businesses that you already know or have found on this database.

You can also find out how your business looks to the outside world if you use FAME to dig out the financials for your business. A credit rating, details of any court judgements and other interesting information are all included in the reports.

FAME is available by subscription, which may make it expensive for the occasional user. You may find that a regional library has FAME available to the public on a free basis or through a per-session cost. Most of the UK universities have FAME, so if you can access one of their library services you can also use this facility. This service may be available through an annual library subscription.

Another source of financial information is your local Business Link (www.businesslink.gov.uk). Business Link acts as a signpost to help small and medium-sized businesses. They can help you access your trade association and other business support agencies and consultancies that run benchmarking.

Testing Profits

With a completed profit and loss statement, you can do a number of quick ratio tests of your business's profitability. You certainly want to know how well your business did compared to other similar businesses. You also want to be able to measure your *return* (the percentage you made) on your business.

Three common tests are Return on Sales, Return on Assets and Return on Shareholders' Capital. These ratios have much more meaning if you can find industry averages for your particular type of business, so that you can compare your results. Check with your local Chamber of Commerce to see whether it has figures for local businesses or order a report for your industry online from FAME.

Return on Sales

The Return on Sales (ROS) ratio tells you how efficiently your business runs its operations. Using the information on your profit and loss statement, you can measure how much profit your business produced per pound of sales and how much extra cash you brought in per sale.

You calculate ROS by dividing net profit before taxes by sales. For example, suppose your business had a net profit of £4,500 and sales of £18,875. The following shows your calculation of ROS.

Net profit before taxes ÷ Sales = Return on Sales

£4,500 ÷ £18,875 = 23.8%

As you can see, your business made 23.8 per cent on each pound of sales. To determine whether that amount calls for celebration, you need to find the ROS ratios for similar businesses. You may be able to get such information from your local Chamber of Commerce, or you can order an industry report online from FAME.

Return on Assets

The Return on Assets (ROA) ratio tests how well you're using your business's assets to generate profits. If your business's ROA is the same or higher than other similar companies, you're doing a good job of managing your assets.

To calculate ROA, you divide net profit by total assets. You find total assets on your balance sheet, which you can read more about in Chapter 6, Book IV. Suppose that your business's net profit was £4,500 and total assets were £40,050. The following shows your calculation of ROA.

Net profit ÷ Total assets = Return on Assets

£4,500 ÷ £40,050 = 11.2%

Your calculation shows that your business made 11.2 per cent on each pound of assets it held.

ROA can vary significantly depending on the type of industry in which you operate. For example, if your business requires you to maintain lots of expensive equipment, as a manufacturing firm does, your ROA is much lower than a service business that doesn't need as many assets. ROA can range from below 5 per cent, for manufacturing businesses that require a large investment in machinery and factories, to as high as 20 per cent or even higher for service businesses with few assets.

Return on Shareholders' Capital

To measure how successfully your business earned money for the owners or investors, calculate the Return on Shareholders' Capital (ROSC) ratio. This ratio often looks better than Return on Assets (see the preceding section) because ROSC doesn't take debt into consideration.

You calculate ROSC by dividing net profit by shareholders' or owners' capital. Suppose your business's net profit was £4,500 and the owners' capital was £9,500. Here is the formula:

Net profit ÷ Shareholders' or owners' capital = Return on Shareholders' Capital

£4,500 ÷ £9,500 = 47.3%

Most business owners put in a lot of cash upfront to get a business started, so seeing a business whose liabilities and capital are split close to 50 per cent each is fairly common.

Branching Out with Profit and Loss Statement Data

The profit and loss statement you produce for external use – financial institutions and investors – may be very different from the one you produce for in-house use by your managers. Most business owners prefer to provide the minimum amount of detail necessary to satisfy external users of their financial statements, such as summaries of expenses instead of line-by-line expense details, a Net Sales figure without reporting all the detail about discounts and fees, and a cost of goods number without reporting all the detail about how that was calculated.

Internally, the contents of the profit and loss statement are a very different story. With more detail, your managers are better able to make accurate business decisions. Most businesses develop detailed reports based on the data collected to develop the profit and loss statement. Items such as discounts, returns and allowances are commonly pulled out of profit and loss statements and broken down into more detail:

✔ **Discounts** are reductions on the selling price as part of a special sale. They may also be in the form of volume discounts provided to customers who buy large amounts of the business's products. For example, a business may offer a 10 per cent discount to customers who buy 20 or more of the same item at one time. In order to put their Net Sales numbers in perspective, business owners and managers must monitor how much they reduce their revenues to attract sales.

✔ **Returns** are transactions in which the buyer returns items for any reason – not the right size, damaged, defective and so on. If a business's number of returns increases dramatically, a larger problem may be the cause; therefore business owners need to monitor these numbers carefully in order to identify and resolve any problems with the items they sell.

✔ **Allowances** cover gifts cards and other accounts that customers pay for upfront without taking any merchandise. Allowances are actually a liability for a business because the customer (or the person who was given the gift card) eventually comes back to get merchandise and doesn't have to pay any cash in return.

Another section of the profit and loss statement that you're likely to break down into more detail for internal use is the Cost of Goods Sold. Basically, you take the detail collected to calculate that line item, including Opening Stock, Closing Stock, purchases and purchase discounts, and present it in a separate report. (We explain how to calculate Cost of Goods Sold in the section 'Finding Cost of Goods Sold', earlier in this chapter.)

No limit exists to the number of internal reports you can generate from the detail that goes into your profit and loss statement and other financial statements. For example, many businesses design a report that looks at month-to-month trends in revenue, Cost of Goods Sold and profit. In fact, you can set up your computerised accounting system (if you use one) to generate this and other custom-designed reports automatically. Using your computerised system, you can produce these reports at any time during the month if you want to see how close you are to meeting your month-end, quarter-end or year-end goal.

Many businesses also design a report that compares actual spending to the budget. On this report, each of the profit and loss statement line items appear with their accompanying planned budget figures and the actual figures. When reviewing this report, you flag any line item that's considerably higher or lower than expected and then research them to find a reason for the difference.

Chapter 6

Developing a Balance Sheet

In This Chapter

▶ Tackling the balance sheet

▶ Pulling together your balance sheet accounts

▶ Choosing a format

▶ Drawing conclusions from your balance sheet

▶ Polishing electronically produced balance sheets

*P*eriodically, you want to know how well your business is doing. Therefore, at the end of each accounting period, you draw up a balance sheet – a snapshot of your business's condition. This snapshot gives you a picture of where your business stands – its assets, its liabilities and how much the owners have invested in the business at a particular point in time.

This chapter explains the key ingredients of a balance sheet and tells you how to pull them all together. You also find out how to use some analytical tools called ratios to see how well your business is doing.

Breaking Down the Balance Sheet

Basically, creating a balance sheet is like taking a picture of the financial aspects of your business.

The business name appears at the top of the balance sheet along with the ending date for the accounting period being reported. The rest of the report summarises:

  ✔ **The business's assets,** which include everything the business owns in order to stay in operation

  ✔ **The business's debts,** which include any outstanding bills and loans that must be paid

  ✔ **The owners' capital,** which is basically how much the business owners have invested in the business

Assets, liabilities and capital probably sound familiar – they're the key elements that show whether or not your books are in balance. If your liabilities plus capital equal assets, your books are in balance. All your bookkeeping efforts are an attempt to keep the books in balance based on this formula, which we talk more about in Chapter 3 in Book IV.

Gathering Balance Sheet Ingredients

You can find most of the information you need to prepare a balance sheet on your trial balance worksheet, the details of which are drawn from your final adjusted trial balance.

To keep this example simple, we assume that the fictitious business has no adjustments for the balance sheet as of 31 May 2010. In the real world, every business needs to adjust something (usually stock levels at the very least) every month.

To prepare the example trial balances in this chapter, we use the key accounts listed in Table 6-1; these accounts and numbers come from the fictitious business's trial balance worksheet.

Table 6-1	Balance Sheet Accounts	
Account Name	*Balance in Account*	
	Debit	Credit
Cash	£2,500	
Petty Cash	£500	
Trade Debtors (Accounts Receivable)	£1,000	
Stock	£1,200	
Equipment	£5,050	
Vehicles	£25,000	
Furniture	£5,600	
Drawings	£14,500	
Trade Creditors (Accounts Payable)		£2,200
Loans Payable		£29,150
Capital	£5,000	
Net Profit for the Year	£14,500	
Total	£50,850	£50,850

Dividing and listing your assets

The first part of the balance sheet is the Assets section. The first step in developing this section is dividing your assets into two categories: current assets and fixed assets.

Current assets

Current assets are things your business owns that you can easily convert to cash and expect to use in the next 12 months to pay your bills and your employees. Current assets include cash, Trade Debtors (money due from customers), marketable securities (including shares, bonds and other types of securities) and stock.

When you see cash as the first line item on a balance sheet, that account includes what you have on hand in the tills and what you have in the bank, including current accounts, savings accounts, money market accounts and certificates of deposit. In most cases, you simply list all these accounts as one item, Cash, on the balance sheet.

The current assets for the fictional business are:

Cash	£2,500
Petty Cash	£500
Trade Debtors	£1,000
Stock	£1,200

You total the Cash and Petty Cash accounts, giving you £3,000, and list that amount on the balance sheet as a line item called Cash.

Fixed assets

Fixed assets are things your business owns that you expect to have for more than 12 months. Fixed assets include land, buildings, equipment, furniture, vehicles and anything else that you expect to have for longer than a year.

The fixed assets for the fictional business are:

Equipment	£5,050
Vehicles	£25,000
Furniture	£5,600

Book IV

Keeping On Top of the Books

Most businesses have more items in the fixed assets section of a balance sheet than the few fixed assets we show here for the fictional business. For example:

- A manufacturing business that has a lot of tools, dies or moulds created specifically for its manufacturing processes needs to have a line item called Tools, Dies and Moulds.

- A business that owns one or more buildings needs to have a line item labelled Land and Buildings.

- A business that leases a building with an option to purchase it at some later date considers that *capitalised lease* to be a fixed asset, and lists it on the balance sheet as a Capitalised Lease. An example of a capitalised lease is where you pay a premium for a lease and regard that premium as a fixed asset rather than an expense. The premium becomes a capitalised lease and set against profits over the life of the lease.

- A business may lease its business space and then spend lots of money doing it up. For example, a restaurant may rent a large space and then furnish it according to a desired theme. Money spent on doing up the space becomes a fixed asset called Leasehold Improvements and is listed on the balance sheet in the fixed assets section.

Everything mentioned so far in this section – land, buildings, capitalised leases, leasehold improvements and so on – is a *tangible asset*. These items are ones that you can actually touch or hold. Another type of fixed asset is the *intangible asset*. Intangible assets aren't physical objects; common examples are patents, copyrights and trademarks:

- A **patent** gives a business the right to dominate the markets for the patented product. When a patent expires (usually after 20 years), competitors can enter the marketplace for the product that was patented, and the competition helps to lower the price to consumers. For example, pharmaceutical businesses patent all their new drugs and therefore are protected as the sole providers of those drugs. When your doctor prescribes a brand-name drug, you're getting a patented product. Generic drugs are products whose patents have run out, meaning that any pharmaceutical business can produce and sell its own version of the same product.

- A **copyright** protects original works, including books, magazines, articles, newspapers, television shows, movies, music, poetry and plays, from being copied by anyone other than the creator(s). For example, this book is copyrighted, so no one can make a copy of any of its contents without the permission of the publisher, John Wiley & Sons, Ltd.

- A **trademark** gives a business ownership of distinguishing words, phrases, symbols or designs. For example, check out this book's cover to see the registered trademark, *For Dummies*, for this brand. Trademarks can last forever, as long as a business continues to use the trademark and file the proper paperwork periodically.

In order to show in financial statements that their values are being used up, all fixed assets are depreciated or amortised. Intangible assets such as patents and copyrights are amortised (amortisation is very similar to depreciation). Each intangible asset has a lifespan based on the number of years for which the rights are granted. After setting an initial value for the intangible asset, a business then divides that value by the number of years it has protection, and the resulting amount is then written off each year as an Amortisation Expense, which is shown on the profit and loss statement. You can find the total amortisation or depreciation expenses that have been written off during the life of the asset on the balance sheet in a line item called Accumulated Depreciation or Accumulated Amortisation, whichever is appropriate for the type of asset.

Acknowledging your debts

The Liabilities section of the balance sheet comes after the Assets section and shows all the money that your business owes to others, including banks, suppliers, contractors, financial institutions and individuals. Like assets, you divide your liabilities into two categories on the balance sheet:

- ✔ **Current liabilities:** All bills and debts that you plan to pay within the next 12 months. Accounts appearing in this section include Trade Creditors (bills due to suppliers, contractors and others), Credit Cards Payable and the current portion of a long-term debt (for example, if you have a mortgage on your premises, the payments due in the next 12 months appear in the Current Liabilities section).

- ✔ **Long-term liabilities:** All debts you owe to lenders that are to be paid over a period longer than 12 months. Mortgages Payable and Loans Payable are common accounts in the long-term liabilities section of the balance sheet.

Most businesses try to minimise their current liabilities because the interest rates on short-term loans, such as credit cards, are usually much higher than those on loans with longer terms. As you manage your business's liabilities, always look for ways to minimise your interest payments by seeking longer-term loans with lower interest rates than you can get on a credit card or short-term loan.

The fictional business used for the example balance sheets in this chapter has only one account in each liabilities section:

Current liabilities:

Trade Creditors   £2,200

Long-term liabilities:

Loans Payable   £29,150

Naming your investments

Every business has investors. Even a small family business requires money upfront to get the business on its feet. Investments are reflected on the balance sheet as *capital.* The line items that appear in a balance sheet's Capital section vary depending upon whether or not the business is incorporated.

If you're preparing the books for a business that isn't incorporated, the Capital section of your balance sheet contains these accounts:

- ✔ **Capital:** All money invested by the owners to start up the business as well as any additional contributions made after the start-up phase. If the business has more than one owner, the balance sheet usually has a Capital account for each owner so that individual stakes in the business can be recorded.

- ✔ **Drawings:** All money taken out of the business by the business's owners. Balance sheets usually have a Drawing account for each owner in order to record individual withdrawal amounts.

- ✔ **Retained Earnings:** All profits left in the business.

For an incorporated business, the Capital section of the balance sheet contains the following accounts:

- ✔ **Shares:** Portions of ownership in the business, purchased as investments by business owners.

- ✔ **Retained Earnings:** All profits that have been reinvested in the business.

Sorting out share investments

You're probably most familiar with the sale of shares on the open market through the various stock market exchanges, such as the London Stock Exchange (LSE) and the Alternative Investment Market (AIM). However, not all companies sell their shares through public exchanges; in fact, most companies aren't public companies but rather remain private operations.

Whether public or private, ownership in a business is obtained by buying shares. If the business isn't publicly traded, shares are bought and sold privately. In most small businesses, these exchanges are made among family members, close friends and occasionally outside investors who have been approached individually as a means to raise additional money to build the business.

The value of each share is set at the time the share is sold. Many businesses set the initial share value at £1 to £10.

Because the fictional business isn't incorporated, the accounts appearing in the Capital section of its balance sheet are:

Capital	£5,000
Retained Earnings	£4,500

Pulling Together the Final Balance Sheet

After you've grouped together all your accounts (see the preceding section 'Gathering Balance Sheet Ingredients'), you're ready to produce a balance sheet. Businesses in the United Kingdom usually choose between two common formats for their balance sheets: the Horizontal format or the Vertical format, with the Vertical format preferred. The actual line items appearing in both formats are the same; the only difference is the way in which you lay out the information on the page.

Horizontal format

The Horizontal format is a two-column layout with assets on one side and liabilities and capital on the other side.

Figure 6-1 shows the elements of a sample balance sheet in the Horizontal format.

Balance Sheet
As of 31 May 2010

Fixed Assets			Capital	
Equipment	£ 5,050		Opening balance	£ 5,000
Furniture	£ 5,600		Net Profit for year	£ 14,500
Vehicles	£ 25,000			£ 19,500
		£ 35,650	Less Drawings	£ 10,000
				£ 9,500
			Long-term Liabilities	
			Loans Payable	£ 29,150
Current Assets			**Current Liabilities**	
Stock	£ 1,200		Trade Creditors	£ 2,200
Trade Debtors	£ 1,000			
Cash	£ 3,000			
		£ 5,200		
		£ 40,850		£ 40,850

Figure 6-1: A sample balance sheet using the Horizontal format.

Vertical format

The Vertical format is a one-column layout showing assets first, followed by liabilities and then capital.

Using the Vertical Format, Figure 6-2 shows the balance sheet for a fictional business.

Balance Sheet
As of 31 May 2010

Fixed Assets		
Equipment	£ 5,050	
Furniture	£ 5,600	
Vehicles	£ 25,000	
		£ 35,650
Current Assets		
Stock	£ 1,200	
Trade Debtors	£ 1,000	
Cash	£ 3,000	
	£ 5,200	
Less: Current Liabilities		
Trade Creditors	£ 2,200	
Net Current Assets		£ 3,000
Total Assets Less Current Liabilities		£ 38,650
Long-term Liabilities		
Loans Payable		£ 29,150
		£ 9,500
Capital		
Opening Balance		£ 5,000
Net Profit for Year		£ 14,500
		£ 19,500
Less Drawings		£ 10,000
		£ 9,500

Figure 6-2: A sample balance sheet using the Vertical format.

Whether you prepare your balance sheet as per Figure 6-1 or Figure 6-2, remember that Assets = Liabilities + Capital, so both sides of the balance sheet must balance to reflect this.

The Vertical format includes:

✔ **Net current assets:** Calculated by subtracting current assets from current liabilities – a quick test to see whether or not a business has the money on hand to pay bills. Net current assets is sometimes referred to as *working capital.*

✔ **Total assets less current liabilities:** What's left over for a business's owners after all liabilities have been subtracted from total assets. Total assets less current liabilities is sometimes referred to as *net assets.*

Putting Your Balance Sheet to Work

With a complete balance sheet in your hands, you can analyse the numbers through a series of ratio tests to check your cash status and monitor your debt. These tests are the type of tests that financial institutions and potential investors use to determine whether or not to lend money to or invest in your business. Therefore, a good idea is to run these tests yourself before seeking loans or investors. Ultimately, the ratio tests in this section can help you determine whether or not your business is in a strong cash position.

Testing your cash

When you approach a bank or other financial institution for a loan, you can expect the lender to use one of two ratios to test your cash flow: the *current ratio* and the *acid test ratio* (also known as the *quick ratio*).

Current ratio

This ratio compares your current assets to your current liabilities and provides a quick glimpse of your business's ability to pay its bills in the short term.

The formula for calculating the current ratio is:

Current assets ÷ Current liabilities = Current ratio

The following is an example of a current ratio calculation:

£5,200 ÷ £2,200 = 2.36 (current ratio)

Lenders usually look for current ratios of 1.2 to 2, so any financial institution considers a current ratio of 2.36 a good sign. A current ratio under 1 is considered a danger sign because it indicates the business doesn't have enough cash to pay its current bills. This rule is only a rough guide and some business sectors may require a higher or lower current ratio figure. Get some advice to see what the norm is for your business sector.

A current ratio over 2.0 may indicate that your business isn't investing its assets well and may be able to make better use of its current assets. For example, if your business is holding a lot of cash, you may want to invest that money in some long-term assets, such as additional equipment, that you can use to help grow the business.

Acid test (quick) ratio

The acid test ratio uses only the financial figures in your business's Cash account, Trade Debtors and Marketable Securities – otherwise known as *liquid assets*. Although similar to the current ratio in that it examines current assets and liabilities, the acid test ratio is a stricter test of a business's ability to pay bills. The assets part of this calculation doesn't take stock into account because it can't always be converted to cash as quickly as other current assets and because, in a slow market, selling your stock may take a while.

Many lenders prefer the acid test ratio when determining whether or not to give a business a loan because of its strictness.

Calculating the acid test ratio is a two-step process:

1. **Determine your quick assets.**

   Cash + Trade Debtors + Marketable securities = Quick assets

2. **Calculate your quick ratio.**

   Quick assets ÷ Current liabilities = Quick ratio

The following is an example of an acid test ratio calculation:

£2,000 + £1,000 + £1,000 = £4,000 (quick assets)

£4,000 ÷ £2,200 = 1.8 (acid test ratio)

Lenders consider that a business with an acid test ratio around 1 is in good condition. An acid test ratio less than 1 indicates that the business may have to sell some of its marketable securities or take on additional debt until it can sell more of its stock.

Assessing your debt

Before you even consider whether or not to take on additional debt, always check out your debt condition. One common ratio that you can use to assess your business's debt position is the *gearing ratio*. This ratio compares what your business owes – *external borrowing* – to what your business owners have invested in the business – *internal funds.*

Calculating your debt to capital ratio is a two-step process:

1. **Calculate your total debt.**

   Current liabilities + Long-term liabilities = Total debt

2. **Calculate your gearing ratio.**

   Total debt ÷ Capital = Gearing ratio

The following is an example of a debt to capital ratio calculation:

£2,200 + £29,150 = £31,350 (total debt)

£31,350 ÷ £9,500 = 3.3 (gearing ratio)

Lenders like to see a gearing ratio close to 1 because it indicates that the amount of debt is equal to the amount of capital. Most banks probably wouldn't lend any more money to a business with a debt to capital ratio of 3.3 until its debt levels were lowered or the owners put more money into the business. The reason for this lack of confidence may be one of two:

✔ They don't want to have more money invested in the business than the owner.

✔ They are concerned about the business's ability to service the debt.

Generating Balance Sheets Electronically

If you use a computerised accounting system, you can take advantage of its report function to generate your balance sheets automatically. These balance sheets give you quick snapshots of the business's financial position but may require adjustments before you prepare your financial reports for external use.

One key adjustment you're likely to make involves the value of your stock. Most computerised accounting systems use the averaging method to value stock. This method totals all the stock purchased and then calculates an average price for the stock. However, your accountant may recommend a different valuation method that works better for your business. Therefore, if you use a method other than the default averaging method to value your stock, you need to adjust the stock value that appears on the balance sheet generated from your computerised accounting system.

Book V

Marketing and Advertising Your Wares

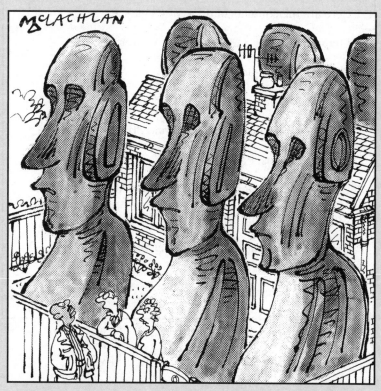

'When we bid for these half dozen garden ornaments from an exotic island, they looked a lot smaller on the screen.'

In this book . . .

You know what you want to be selling or what service you're providing . . . so let this book lead you through the best methods of getting your customers to buy from you. Covering a whole swathe of marketing styles and advertising ideas, we help you to work out who to sell to and how to do so.

Here are the contents of Book V at a glance:

Chapter 1

Taking a Closer Look at Customers

The most crucial part of business planning involves taking a long, hard look at customers – those you enjoy having, those you would love to land, and those you would just as soon give away to some unsuspecting competitor. The stakes are high. How well you know your customers ultimately determines how successful you are. But figuring out what makes customers tick can be downright frustrating. If you've tried it before, you may be tempted to throw up your hands and leave the entire mess to the so-called experts – marketing gurus, consultants or perhaps astrologers. Don't. This chapter shows you how to better acquaint yourself with your customers so that you can offer them more value and serve them more profitably than anyone else out there.

In this chapter, we take a closer look at why customers buy your products and services in the first place by exploring their needs and motives. And we investigate how they make choices in the marketplace by examining customer perceptions and their decision-making process. Finally, we take a quick look at your customers that are actually other businesses.

Checking Out Who Your Customers Are

A fresh look at customers starts with the ones you enjoy seeing – those who regularly purchase goods or services from you. But sometimes, knowing what something is *not* can be just as important as knowing what it *is*. You can discover as much about your own business and best customers by observing the other kinds of customers out there – the customers who are difficult, the customers who are gone, and the customers whom you never had.

The good customer

Good customers are the ones who bring a smile to your face, the ones you like serving, the ones who appreciate you, the ones who keep you in business. They are the customers you want to keep coming back time and again. To keep all those good customers happy, however, you may need to know more than the fact that Tom likes Chinese food, Mary has a weakness for chocolates and Harry loves red ties.

Why? Isn't simply knowing individual customers on some personal basis enough? Well, not quite. What happens if you have hundreds or even thousands of small customers, as a shop does, or if your staff turnover is high as in most parts of the catering industry?

In such cases there's no substitute for a good database sytem for tracking your relationship with clients and then making appropriate product or service offers. For example supermarkets now analyse customer purchases and make targeted special offers based on their understanding of the customer profile. This all helps to make customers feel special and loved. Your business can measure and describe its customers in several ways:

- ✔ Track *where* your customers are, breaking them down by country, region, city or postcode.

- ✔ Figure out *who* your customers are, including their age, gender, occupation, income and ethnic origin.

- ✔ Find out more about *how* they live – their hobbies, favourite sports teams, restaurant choices and holiday destinations, for example.

You're probably a step ahead of us here and have already noticed that many of these criteria result in groups of customers that look alike. When marketing gurus divide customers into specific groups, they call them *market segments*.

When it comes to understanding customers, one good strategy is to find out what other businesses try to find out about their customers. Keep track of the questions that other companies ask you. Richer Sounds stores (a chain of hi-fi and home cinema retailers), for example, routinely ask for your postcode when you step up to the till. And you often find a list of personal questions on product registration forms, warranty cards and customer service mailings. Some companies even offer a small reward if you tell them something – anything – about yourself. But go easy here. Radio Shack, an American electronics retailer, began to lose a lot of goodwill when customers grew suspicious about – or just annoyed by – all the questions that their shop assistants were asking.

The bad customer

'A bad customer? Isn't that a contradiction in terms?' you ask. 'How can there be such a thing as a bad customer, especially for a customer-oriented company?' Keep in mind that your initial reaction doesn't always tell the whole story. Remember that *you* don't really define the business that you're in, your *customers* do. They place a series of demands on your company and then evaluate how well it performs against those demands.

Good customers do the following:

✔ Ask you to do things that you do well

✔ Place value on the things that you do and are willing to pay for them

✔ Challenge you to improve your skills, expand your knowledge, and focus your resources

✔ Take you in new directions that are consistent with your strategy and planning

Bad customers represent the flip side. They do the following:

✔ Ask you to do things that you aren't equipped to do well

✔ Distract you, causing you to veer away from your strategy and your business plan

✔ Purchase in such small quantities that the cost of doing business with them far outweighs any revenue that they generate

✔ Require so much service and attention that you can't focus your efforts on more valuable (and profitable) customers

✔ Remain dissatisfied with what you do, despite all your best efforts

✔ Fail to pay on time – or to pay at all!

The pundits have come up with a principle that we can apply here: the *80/20 principle*. In this case, the rule says that if you survey all your customers, 20 per cent of them account for about 80 per cent of your business. These 20 per cent are your good customers. You obviously want to keep them – and keep them happy! But look at the other 80 per cent your customers, and you may discover a few whom you'd rather hand over to the competition.

When you analyse what you do for that 80 per cent of customers and what they do for you, these customers are often more trouble than they're worth. Their shoe styles are never in stock, and their special orders are always returned. Maybe their finances are a mess, which makes them late in paying. Still, the lure of additional revenue and more customers – or the belief that you should never say no to any customer – often keeps you involved with this group. You would be better off without these customers, though, and leaving your competitors to handle such bad business impairs their ability to compete with you for good business.

To handle bad customers, follow these steps:

1. **Figure out who they are, by establishing if you can make a profit out of doing business with them.**

2. **Convert them into good customers, by exploring ways of turning loss-making customers into profitable ones. For example, by putting up prices, introducing minimum order sizes or minimum drop quantities or by encouraging them to order online.**

3. **Alternatively, hand them over to someone else. If they don't accept the changes to your service that you introduce to ensure they make you money, they'll soon move on to other suppliers.**

A note of caution: some of this year's bad customers may become next year's good customers. Ensure you only divest yourself of *permanently* bad customers.

The other guy's customer

You may think that focusing on customers whom you've never had points to another sort of failure on your part, but actually, these people present an opportunity. The fact that you haven't been able to serve this group gives you a challenge: to find out what your market really thinks is important. Your competitors' customers are telling you what you are not. This information is extremely useful, especially when you're working on the big picture in the early stages of business planning, defining who you are and who you want to serve.

Unfortunately, getting information out of your competitors' customers is often an expensive proposition. You don't know them, and you don't have an ongoing relationship with them. Market research firms, of course, are always eager to work with you. These companies are willing to bring together focus groups and talk to consumers about all sorts of things that relate to your products in comparison to the competition. The catch, of course, is that their services don't come cheap.

Fortunately, you don't have to be quite this formal about the information-gathering process, at least in the initial stages. As long as you can get selected people to provide sincere answers, you probably can approximate the results of a focus-group study on your own.

Getting to know your competitors' customers is often difficult, but not impossible.

✔ Spend some time where customers gather. Use trade shows, user groups and industry conferences to make informal contacts and begin a dialogue with your non-customers.

✔ Ask pointed questions of people who choose competing products. Did they take the time to see what was available on the market? Have they even heard of your product or service? If they have, did they actually take the time to look at it? If not, why not? If so, what were their impressions?

✔ Really listen to what they have to say, no matter how painful it is. Don't get defensive when people say negative things about your company or your products.

Information about your customers is valuable, if not priceless. A consultant will charge you thousands of pounds for the same information.

✔ To plan effectively, discover as much about your customers as you can.

✔ Of all your customers, 20 per cent are likely to account for 80 per cent of your business.

✔ Some of your customers may actually cost you money.

✔ Your competitors' customers can tip you off to new opportunities.

Discovering Why Your Customers Buy

Perhaps the most difficult – and useful – question that you can answer about your customers is why they buy what they buy. What actually compels them to seek out your products or services in the marketplace? What's important to them? What are they really looking for?

Understanding needs

Why do people buy things in the first place? Psychologist types tell us that *needs fulfilment* is really at the heart of all consumer behaviour (see Figure 1-1, based on the social psychologist Abraham Maslow's famous 'Hierarchy of Needs' model). Everybody has needs and wants. When a need is discovered, it creates the motivation that drives human activity.

- ✔ Survival, at the most basic level, results in the universal need for grocery shops, carpenters and tailors.
- ✔ The urge for safety, security and stability generates the need for bank accounts, disability health insurance and home alarm systems.
- ✔ The desire for belonging and acceptance creates the need for designer-label polo shirts, members-only clubs and participation in expensive diet programmes.
- ✔ The urge to be recognised and held in esteem establishes the need for company banquets, fast cars and award plaques.
- ✔ The desire for self-achievement and fulfilment results in the need for adventure holidays, quiz shows and correspondence courses.

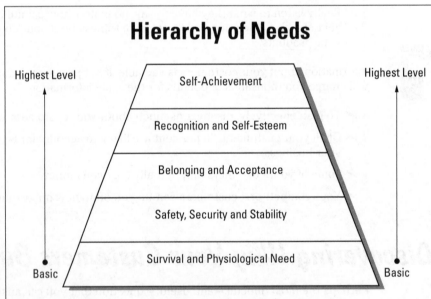

Figure 1-1:
A basic overview of people's needs.

DHL, for example, is really in the reliability business. Many of its customers are businesses that want the assurance – absolutely, positively – that their precious shipments will be delivered early the next day or even the same day. These customers are so motivated by this need that they are willing to pay a substantial premium over other alternatives, simply for absolute reliability and their own peace of mind.

Determining motives

Motives are needs that have been awakened and activated, so to speak. Motives send people scurrying into the marketplace, searching for products or services that can fulfil a particular need. Motives aren't always what they seem to be.

✔ Greetings card companies, for example, don't just sell cute little jingles printed on glossy paper at exorbitant prices. The prices are justified because the companies are actually selling small insurance policies against their customers' fear of feeling guilty. Perhaps fear of guilt (over a missed birthday or a forgotten anniversary) is really what propels the buyer into the greetings card market.

✔ Recent MBA graduates have been asked to rank the things that are most important to them when they decide among various job offers. When asked point-blank, a substantial majority rank quality of life, community and schools at the top of the list and place starting salary somewhere in the middle. A more careful survey and analysis of the MBA selection criteria, however, usually settles upon compensation as being the single most important variable in accepting a new position fresh out of university.

✔ Most of us have a need to be accepted and liked by other people. This powerful motivation creates great market opportunities for the likes of beauty salons, gyms and breath-mint companies.

Although motives obviously apply to individual consumers, they work equally well in the context of business or corporate behaviour. When a particular manufacturing company contracts with a private health and medical insurance company, such as BUPA, for example, is the company motivated to improve the health of its employees? Or is it motivated to reduce the cost of its health insurance premiums so that it can better compete with foreign companies (fulfilling its own need to survive)? If you run BUPA, how you answer this question has a major impact on your internal management of costs versus the overall quality of the health care that you provide.

Your job, of course, is to dig beneath the obvious customer responses and consumption patterns to determine what the buyers' real motives are in purchasing goods and services in your own market. When you understand what's actually driving customer behaviour, you're in a much better position to talk about your own product in terms that customers will respond to.

✔ The most important question to ask about your customers is why they buy what they buy.

✔ Customer needs range from basic survival and security to the urge for self-improvement.

✔ Motives such as vanity, status-seeking and guilt are the hot buttons that can *really* get customers to buy.

Finding Out How Your Customers Make Choices

How do customers make choices in the marketplace? The most important thing to remember is that customers decide to buy things based on their own view of the world – their own perceptions of reality. Few customers buy without thinking. Instead, they bring their perceptions of the world into a decision-making process that (ideally) leads them to purchase your product or service instead of other options.

Perceptions are reality

Customer perceptions represent the market's world view and include not only what your customers think of your products and services, but also how they see your company and view your competitors.

As customers turn to the marketplace, they confront a mind-boggling array of competing products. Many variables influence your customers as they evaluate their choices: advertising, endorsements, reviews and salesmanship, not to mention their own gut reactions. You need to know how customers respond to all these stimuli if you ultimately want to earn and keep their business.

Have you ever wondered, for example, why so few yellow jumpers are available in the men's departments of clothing shops? Market research consistently shows that a majority of men believe that the colour yellow suggests weakness. Subconsciously, men feel that they may be perceived as being wimps if they have anything to do with the colour. So the yellow-jumper option isn't too popular.

Or have you noticed that Madonna doesn't do many endorsements? Okay, it's not as though she needs the extra income. But companies may feel that her image is just too controversial, resulting in negative perceptions and the risk that potential buyers will be driven away.

Never lose sight of the marketer's motto:

Customer perceptions are the market reality.

People buy goods and services based on what they perceive to be true, not necessarily on what you know to be the facts. To be successful in the marketplace, you have to develop a clear insight into customers' perceptions, understanding how buyers react to products and services in your market before you complete your own business plans.

The five steps to adoption

Marketing gurus often refer to the customer's *decision-making process* as the *DMP* (the acronym makes the term sound more official). In many markets, the DMP involves a series of well-defined steps that are dubbed the *consumer adoption process*. (Okay, we'll call it the *CAP.*) In this case, of course, *adoption* refers to a newly formed relationship with a product, not a child.

By understanding the steps that consumers often go through, you're better able to take advantage of customers' behaviour and build strategies that help them complete the adoption process. The process involves five major steps, which are described in Table 1-1.

Suppose that you're in a start-up firm with a top-notch consumer-software title. You're afraid, however, that customers are reluctant to give the program a try, for fear the software will be difficult to learn or incompatible with their computers. (Keep in mind that people act on their perceptions of reality rather than on the reality itself!) To move potential customers past the evaluation and into the trial step of the adoption process, you may want to consider setting up a free new-user hotline and offering a money-back, no-questions-asked guarantee.

Table 1-1	The Consumer's Five-Step Adoption Process	
Primary Steps	*Description of Consumer*	*Your Task*
Awareness	Aware of a product or service but lacking detailed knowledge	Develop a strategy that educates and excites potential customers
Interest	Curious because of publicity and seeking more information	Provide more detailed product information and continue to build momentum
Evaluation	Deciding whether to test the product or service	Make the product-evaluation process as easy and rewarding as possible
Trial	Using the product or service on a test basis	Make the trial as simple and risk-free as you can
Adoption	Deciding to become a regular user	Develop strategies to retain good customers

- Customers make choices based on their perceptions, not necessarily on the facts.

- Before they buy, customers go through a distinct decision-making process.

- The five steps in making a purchase are awareness, interest, evaluation, trial and adoption.

- If you understand how customers make choices, you have a better chance of getting their business.

Remembering the Big Picture

Remember that old saying about not seeing the wood for the trees? Well, when you first start to think about your customers, you don't want to fall into a similar trap. Seeing only the small number of individual customers whom you know, and focusing on their personal habits, likes and dislikes, is tempting sometimes. Even when you begin to look at more general customer trends, including why your customers buy and how they make choices, getting buried in the details still is awfully easy.

Don't take the bait! Don't view your customers and your own business activities too narrowly. Look instead at the larger wood – those general customer behaviours and basic needs that define your market.

If you think about your business only in terms of your existing products, for example, you risk losing sight of customer needs that you've overlooked – needs that a competitor is no doubt going to satisfy at some point. You also create a short-sighted view of your own strategic choices that can result in missed market opportunities and woefully inadequate business plans.

Unfortunately, companies (and even entire industries) still lose sight of the big picture all the time. Markets are viewed too narrowly, and customer needs are neglected – a classic management blunder. Check out these examples:

- Companies that make home-improvement tools often view their business in terms of product components – the making and selling of 6mm drill bits, for example. But when you think about it, nobody really wants or needs 6mm drill bits (not even your dentist). What customers are *really* looking for are 6mm holes. That basic need creates the potential opportunity for any number of possible solutions.

- Glasses manufacturers – the companies that make the frames and lenses – continue to see themselves as being in the glasses-fashion business. But the customers, frustrated by not being able to read a menu closer than three feet away when they've forgotten their glasses, simply want to see better. The manufacturers are now learning a hard lesson with the advent of laser technologies that promise to improve vision by reshaping the cornea – no vision problems, no need for glasses, no more business.

Politics and the marketplace

Bill Clinton had a little sign tacked up on the back wall of his 1992 US presidential campaign headquarters that read 'It's the economy, Stupid!'.

Campaign manager James Carville posted the sign because he wanted everyone to focus not so much on the product – Mr Clinton – as on the marketplace and customer needs.

In this case, of course, the marketplace was the election itself, and the customers were the voting public. At the time, workers in the United States were suffering through a steep recession, worried about foreign competition and petrified about the 'new world economy'. As a shrewd campaign strategist, Carville knew that the road to success lay in getting beyond the candidates themselves and appealing to the voters' innermost needs – those universal, underlying issues that would ultimately sway decision making in the polling booth.

As a business planner, you have to do the same thing: focus on being market-driven when you approach your customers.

Charles Revson revolutionised the cosmetics industry when he quipped, 'In the factory, we make cosmetics; in the store, we sell hope.' As the founder of Revlon, he understood that he was offering his customers something far more important than chemistry: the prospect of youth, beauty and sex appeal.

The key point here is simple: if you don't know what your customers really want, you can't possibly fulfil their needs in an effective way.

Put yourself in your customer's shoes:

- ✔ Take a hard look at one of your own products or services, and honestly ask yourself, 'Why would *I* need this thing?'
- ✔ Ask the same question of several people who use your product or service.
- ✔ Try to imagine a world without your product or service. What would you substitute for it?

Answering questions such as these goes a long way towards fostering creativity, generating new strategies and providing expanded market opportunities.

Dealing with Business Customers

Although we've mentioned companies that sell principally to other companies (as opposed to those that sell primarily to individual consumers), some of you in this so-called *business-to-business market* may think that we're ignoring you.

We aren't – honest! In this section, you find details on how companies, institutions and government agencies act when they themselves are the customers. What makes the business buyer different? Many things.

Secondhand demand

Demand for goods and services in business-to-business markets is almost always *derived demand*. In other words, businesses purchase only those goods and services that they can use to better serve their own customers.

Steel, for example, is a product that no end-user buys. When was the last time you had the urge to go out and get your hands on some flat-rolled sheeting? Steel purchasers tend to be car manufacturers, construction firms, appliance companies and the like. After these businesses have used the steel to make their own products (cars, office blocks and refrigerators), we come into the picture as potential customers.

What are the implications for the steel sellers? If a steelmaker cuts its prices across the board, for example, should it expect a huge increase in orders? Not necessarily. Steel buyers will increase their purchases only if they think that they can sell more of the things that *they* make, and their own sales may be affected by many factors beyond the underlying steel price. How many of us went out to buy a car the last time steel prices were reduced by 10 per cent?

Inelastic demand is a term that number crunchers use when they talk about demand for a particular product that doesn't stretch or change automatically when the price of the product changes.

If you offer products or services in the business-to-business market, make sure that you take the time to think through what your planning decisions mean to your business buyers. And that means thinking about your customers' customers as well.

- ✔ Will a price reduction on your part result in increased sales for your customers – and your company?

- ✔ Will your customers (and their customers) benefit if you offer them additional bells and whistles while raising their costs?

- ✔ Are your customers looking for continuity and price stability?

Decision making as a formal affair

Purchase decisions in the business-to-business marketplace tend to be more formal, rational and professional than in most consumer markets. Many people from different parts of the target company are often involved in the decision-making process (DMP). One division in the company may recommend your product or service, another may acquire it, yet another may pay for it, and all of them do the work for a separate customer centre that actually uses that product. Taken together, these divisions form the *decision-making unit* (or DMU) – another marketing term foisted off on us nice folks by marketing gurus.

Table 1-2 describes three ways in which a business DMU may behave when it's thinking about buying a product or service.

Table 1-2	How Businesses Behave When They Buy
Buying Behaviour	*Description of the Customer's DMP*
Business as usual	Continues to order more of the product or service, perhaps even automating the process so that inventories don't fall below certain levels.
Yes, but . . .	Asks for changes in the existing sales arrangement, modifying one or more purchase terms (such as pricing, financing, quantities and options) and including various people who are part of the DMU.
Opportunity knocks	Purchases a product or service for the first time, perhaps after putting out a request for proposal (RFP) to several possible suppliers and making a deliberate, complete decision involving all parties in the DMU.

Forces to be reckoned with

In working with business customers, you most likely have to deal with several powerful customer forces that you rarely encounter in consumer markets. If your business-to-business strategies are going to succeed over time, you must factor these forces into your business plans. Consider the following questions:

- What's the state of the customer's business?
  - Is it booming, mature or dying?
  - Is it facing increased competition or enjoying record profits?
  - Is it outsourcing business, creating new opportunities?
  - Does it threaten to become a competitor?

✔ How does the customer's company operate?

- Does the customer purchase centrally, or does it have buyers scattered around the company?

- Does it require several levels of approval before a decision is made?

- Do senior executives (who may or may not know a lot about the product) make the ultimate purchase decisions?

✔ Who's important to whom?

- Do the customer's key decision-makers tend to be engineers or marketing people?

- Does the customer use both small and large suppliers?

- Does it have a policy of requiring more than one supplier in critical areas?

As you begin to develop strategies for your business customers, take the time to investigate the forces that are unique in business-to-business markets.

✔ Get out into the field and talk to potential business buyers.

✔ Read about customers' organisations and their industries.

✔ Attend the conferences and conventions that your customers attend, and find out about the critical events and forces that shape their thinking.

All these activities take time and resources, of course, but your investment will be rewarded many times over when you incorporate what you find out into your business-to-business planning.

✔ Some of your customers may be other businesses, and the way in which they buy is different from the way that individuals buy.

✔ Several people may be involved in making the decision to buy from you.

✔ Sometimes your business customers aren't the end users, so you need to understand your customers' customers as well.

Chapter 2

Marketing Your Wares

- -

In This Chapter

▶ Understanding the marketing mix and how to use it

▶ Deciding the advertising message

▶ Choosing the media

▶ Reviewing selling options

- -

*E*ntering the market with your product or service involves deciding on what mix of marketing ingredients to use. In cooking, the same ingredients used in different ways can result in very different products. The same is true in business, where the 'ingredients' are product (or service), price, place and promotion. A change in the way you put these elements together can produce an offering tailored to meet the needs of a specific market. For example, a hardback book isn't much more expensive to produce than a paperback. However, with a bit of clever publicity, bringing the hardback out a few months before the paperback edition, and a higher price tag, the publisher can create an air of exclusivity that satisfies a particular group of customers.

Making Up the Marketing Mix

The key to successful promotion lies in knowing exactly what you want people to do. A few elements can make or break the successful marketing of your business. The elements you need to consider that go to make up the marketing mix are:

✔ *Place* is a general term to cover everything from where you locate your business to how you get your product or service to market. Poor distribution often explains sluggish sales growth. If your type of product gets to market through several channels but you only use one of them, then no amount of price changes or extra promotion makes much difference.

✔ *Pricing* strategies can range from charging what the market may bear, right through to *marginal cost* (just enough to cover direct costs and a small contribution to overheads). Knowing your costs is important, but this is only one element in the pricing decision. You also have to take account of the marketplace, your competition and your product position (for example, if you offer a luxury item, your place in the market is different to that of someone who sells necessities).

✔ The *product or service* is what people use, but what they buy are the underlying benefits it confers on them. For example, when someone buys a camera she's not really considering whether it's SLR or digital, what lens it has, even what film it takes in the case of more traditional snappers – these end products aren't what customers want, what she's looking for is good pictures.

✔ *Promotion* is the means by which you tell your market(s) about your products or services. This includes such elements as your website, leaflets, advertising and even basic items such as business cards and letterheads.

Defining Your Product or Service Parameters

To be successful in any marketplace, you need to have a clear picture of exactly what you want to do and for whom you're doing it. In other words, you need a vision and a mission. (Chapter 4 in Book I offers advice on developing your mission statement.)

To market your product effectively, you have to make decisions about factors such as product range and depth before you're ready to enter the market. Having decided to open a corner shop, for example, you still have to decide whether to focus on food only, or to carry household items and perhaps newspapers and flowers too. You also need to decide whether to carry more than one brand and size of each product.

If the key advantages of your corner shop are its location, opening hours, delivery service and friendly staff, all at competitive prices, then perhaps you don't need a wide or deep product range.

Using Advertising to Tell Your Story

You can't be confident that your customers share your zeal for your business proposition, so you need to convince them that they need what you're offering.

The way to do this is to tell potential customers about what you're selling by advertising your wares.

The skill of advertising lies in reducing the global population to your target audience and reaching as many of them as you can at an economic cost. You first analyse the benefits or virtues of your product, isolate the features and translate these into customer benefits. Who has a need for your product? Define exactly who your potential customers are.

Question all the time. Then the advertising process is to set objectives for your campaign, decide on a budget, design the message, pick the medium to reach your target audience and determine how you're going to evaluate the success of your advertising.

When you understand the basics, which we go through in the following sections, you should also be able to analyse advertisements better, break them down into their elements and avoid the all too common mistakes that advertisers make every day.

Advertising by itself doesn't sell. It doesn't shift a bad product (or at least not more than once) or create new markets. Sales literature, order forms, a sales force, stocks, distributors and a strategy must back up your advertising.

Considering the customer's point of view

People buy a product or service for what it can do for them. Customers look for the benefits. As the seller, your mission is to answer the question 'What's in it for me?' from your potential customer's point of view.

Every time you compose a sales letter, write an advertisement or plan a trade show, you must get to the heart of the matter. Why should customers purchase your product or service? What benefit may it bring them?

You need to view all your marketing efforts from the prospect's point of view, not just your own. When you know what you're selling and to whom, you can match the features of the product (or service) to the benefits the customers can get when they purchase. A *feature* is what a product has or is, and *benefits* are what the product does for the customer. Finally, include proof that the product or service can deliver these benefits. Table 2-1 shows an analysis of features, benefits and proofs.

Table 2-1	Listing Features and Benefits	
Feature	*Benefit*	*Proof*
We use a unique hardening process for our machine.	Our tools last longer and that saves you money.	We have a patent on the process; independent tests carried out by the Cambridge Institute of Technology show our product lasts longest.
Our shops stay open later than others in the area.	You get more choice when to shop.	Come and see.
Our computer system is fault-tolerant using parallel processing.	You have no downtime for either defects or system expansion.	Our written specification guarantees this – come and talk to satisfied customers operating in your field.

You can employ this format to examine the features, benefits and proofs for your own products or services and use the information to devise your ads. Remember, the customer pays for the benefits and the seller for the features. So the benefits provide the copy for most of your future advertising and promotional efforts.

Try this out on your business idea. Keep at it until you really have a good handle on what makes your customers tick. To make the process work best, you need to talk to some real prospective customers in your target market.

Making an exhibition of yourself

One way to gather useful ideas on how to market your wares is to attend exhibitions and see how your competitors set out their stalls. This is also a useful way of seeing whether a demand for what you have to offer is likely to exist, because hundreds of key decision makers are gathered in one place for you to make a pitch to.

You can find out when exhibitions relevant to your business take place in the UK by searching Exhibitions UK (www.exhibitions.co.uk), the official website for the British exhibition industry, sponsored by UK Trade & Investment, the government organisation responsible for all trade promotion and development work. If you want to exhibit or attend a show overseas, TSNN (www.tsnn.com), which calls itself 'The Ultimate Trade Show Resource', operates a widely consulted event database containing data on more than 15,000 trade shows, exhibitions, public events and conferences worldwide. You need to register (free) for full access to the database.

Business Link, the British government's help agency for small businesses, has a comprehensive guide to getting the best out of exhibitions (go to `www.businesslink.gov.uk`, then select Sales and Marketing, Marketing, and finally Trade Shows and Exhibitions).

Setting advertising objectives

You're wasting your time advertising your product or service unless it leads to the opportunity for a sale in a significant number of instances. Ask yourself what potential customers have to do to enable you to make these sales. Do you want them to visit your showroom, phone you, write to your office, return a card or send an order in the post? Do you expect them to order now, or to remember you at some future date when they have a need for your services?

The more specifically you identify the response you want, the better you can tailor your promotional effort to achieve your objective, and the more clearly you can assess the effectiveness of your promotion.

The more general your advertising objective is – for example to 'improve your image' or 'to keep your name in front of the public' – the more likely it is to be an ineffective way of spending your money.

Deciding the budget

People commonly use two methods to calculate advertising budget numbers:

- ✔ **What can we afford?** This approach accepts that cash is usually a scarce commodity and advertising has to take its place alongside a range of competing demands.

- ✔ **Cost/benefit:** This approach comes into its own when you have clear and specific promotional goals. If you have spare capacity in your factory or want to sell more out of your shop, you can work out how much it costs you to increase your production and sales, and how much you may benefit from those extra sales. You then figure out how much advertising money it takes to get you the extra business.

Suppose you expect a £1,000 advertisement to generate 100 enquiries for your product. If your experience tells you that on average 10 per cent of enquiries result in orders, and your profit margin is £200 per product, then you can expect an extra £2,000 profit. That benefit is much greater than the £1,000 cost of the advertisement, so it seems a worthwhile investment.

In practice, you use both these methods to decide how much to spend on promoting your products.

Defining the message

To define your message, you must look at your business and its products from the customer's standpoint and be able to answer the question 'Why should I buy your product?'. The best way is to consider the answer in two stages:

1. **'Why should I buy your *product or service?'***

   The answer comes naturally when you look carefully at customers' motives for buying and the benefits they get from the product.

2. **'Why should I buy *your* product or service?'**

   The only logical and satisfactory answer is: 'Because it's better and so it's different.'

   The difference can arise in two ways:

   - You, the seller, are different. To achieve this, you establish a particular niche for your business.

   - Your product or service is different. Each product or service should have a unique selling point, based on fact.

Your promotional message must be built around the strength(s) of your product or service and must consist of facts about the company and about the product or service.

The stress here is on the word *fact*. Although many types of fact may surround you and your products, your customers are only interested in two – the facts that influence their buying decisions, and the facts of how your business and its products stand out from the competition.

The assumption is that everyone buys for obvious, logical reasons only, but of course innumerable examples show that this isn't so. Does a woman buy a new dress only when an old one is worn out? Do bosses have desks that are bigger than their subordinates' because they have more papers to put on them?

Choosing the media

Broadly, your advertising choices are *above-the-line* media, which is jargon for the Internet, newspapers and magazines, television, radio and other broadcast media, and *below-the-line* activities such as distributing brochures, leaflets and visiting cards, stationery, your letterhead and the way you answer the phone.

The printed word (the Internet, newspapers and magazines) probably takes most of your above-the-line advertising budget. It's the accepted medium to reach the majority of customers. Most people read a newspaper, especially on Sunday, and magazines cater for every imaginable interest and range from parish magazines to Sunday supplements. News and articles are also increasingly available on the Internet, either as online versions of conventional papers or via blogs.

You must advertise where your buyers and consumers are likely to see your message. Your market research (which we talk about in Chapter 1 in Book I) tells you where your likely prospects lie. Before making your decision about which paper or journal to advertise in, you need to get readership and circulation numbers and the publication's reader profile.

You can get this information directly from the journal or paper or from *BRAD* (British Rate and Data), www.brad.co.uk, which has a monthly classified directory of all UK and Republic of Ireland media. You should be able to access this through your local business library. The Audit Bureau of Circulations Electronic (www.abce.org.uk) audits website traffic, among other media, and Rajar (Radio Joint Audience Research) independently compiles radio audience statistics every quarter, providing an industry benchmark (www.rajar.co.uk). Newsgator (www.newsgator.com) and Blog Catalogue (www.blogcatalog.com) operate blog indexing services that can help you filter through the millions of blogs to let you home in on the ones that operate in your business sector.

When considering below-the-line advertising, identify what business gurus call *moments of truth* – contact points between you, your product or service and your customer. Those moments offer you a chance to shine and make a great impression. You can spot the difference at once when you get a really helpful person on the phone or serving you in a shop. The same is true of product literature that's actually helpful, a fairly rare event in itself.

Some of the most effective promotional ideas are the simplest, for example a business card with a map on the reverse showing how to find you, or thank-you cards instead of letters on which you can show your company's recently completed designs.

Choosing the frequency

Think carefully about the timing of your advertising in relation to the kind of media you're considering. The copy dates of some monthly publications are two months before publication; trade exhibitions often only occur once or twice a year. This poses problems if you're waiting on a shipment or uncertain about a product change. Daily or weekly publications allow much prompter changes. The ultimate are probably the Internet, which can be updated minute by minute, and radio, where messages can be slotted in on the same day. Yearbooks, diaries and phone directories require long forward notice.

Using the Internet for viral marketing

The Internet is now central to the marketing process for most businesses. Even where customers don't buy online, most consumers and all business buyers check out products and services using the Internet to check price, quality and competitive offers. Increasingly, products that once had a physical presence are disappearing from the shelf. Music, software, film and now even books are available in 'soft' form to try or buy and download online.

Nine out of every ten visitors to a website arrive there via a search engine and your chances of being found depend on how your website is constructed, what words you use and where they're positioned on the page.

Viral marketing is a term that describes the ability of the Internet to accelerate interest and awareness in a product by rapid word-of-mouth communications. To understand the mathematical power behind this phenomena, take a look at the nearby sidebar 'How viral marketing works'.

How viral marketing works

Take a look at recent communications networks and how they work.

The simplest are the 'one-to-one' broadcast systems such as television and radio. In such systems the overall value of the network rises in a simple relationship to the size of the audience. The bigger the audience, the more valuable your network. Mathematically, the value rises with N, where N represents the size of the audience. This relationship is known as Sarnoff's Law, after a pioneer of radio and television broadcasting.

Next in order of value comes the telephone network, a 'many-to-many' system where everyone can get in touch with anyone else. Here the mathematics are subtly different. With N people connected, every individual has the opportunity to connect with N–1 other people (you exclude yourself). So the total number of possible connections for N individuals $= N(N-1)$. Or N^2-N. This relationship is known as Metcalf's Law,

after Bob Metcalf, an inventor of computer networking. The size of a network under Metcalf's Law rises sharply as the value of N rises, much more so than with simple one-to-one networks.

The Internet, however, has added a further twist. As well as talking to each other, Internet users have the opportunity to form groups in a way they can't easily do on the telephone. Any Internet user can join discussion groups, auction groups, community sites and so on. The mathematics now becomes interesting. As David Reed, formerly of Lotus Development Corporation demonstrated, if you have N people in a network they can in theory form 2^n-N-1 different groups. You can check this formula by considering a small N, of say three people, A, B and C. They can form three different groups of two people, AB, AC and CB, and one group of three people, ABC, making a total of four groups as predicted by the formula. As the value of N increases the size of the network explodes.

The birth of viral marketing, using the power of Reed's Law to the full (see the sidebar 'How viral marketing works' for details of this law), has been attributed to the founder of Hotmail, who insisted that every email sent by a Hotmail user should incorporate the message: 'Get your free web-based email at Hotmail.' By clicking on this line of text, the recipient would be transported to the Hotmail home page. Although this email sent by the company itself wouldn't have had much effect, at the foot of an email sent by a business colleague or friend it made a powerful impact. The very act of sending a Hotmail message constituted an endorsement of the product and so the current customer was selling to future customers on the company's behalf just by communicating with them. The recipient of a Hotmail message discovered that the product works, but also that someone she respected or liked was a user.

You only have to see how quickly a harmful computer virus can spread in hours and days, to cover the whole world, to see the potential of viral marketing. For a small firm this technique has the added advantage of being inexpensive and easy to execute. Just look at some major sites on the Internet to get ideas. Book e-tailors all have links for you to email a friend about a book you've 'stumbled' across on their site. Travel sites encourage you to email any of their special offers that you don't plan to take up to a friend. However, the beauty and limitation of viral marketing is that it only works when you're talking about a good product. People don't recommend something they don't like using themselves.

Providing opportunities to see

The more opportunities you give potential customers to see your name or your product, the greater the chance of them remembering you. This is why direct mail letters usually involve more than one piece of literature. The theory is that the recipient looks at each piece before discarding it. The recipient may only give a brief scan, but it gives the seller another chance to hook a customer. So rather than using different advertising messages, try getting the same or a similar message to one customer group several times.

One claimed benefit of breakfast television is that it can get your message out before the shops open. In business-to-business sales, trade buyers are deluged with calendars, diaries, pen sets and message pads in the hope that when the buyer is making a decision, the promotional materials are still close at hand and have an influence on that decision.

Figuring your bang-for-the-buck ratio

Only undertake advertising where you can realistically measure the results. Everything else is self-indulgent. The formula to keep in mind is:

Effectiveness = Total cost of the advertising activity concerned ÷ Results (in measurable units such as customers, new orders or enquiries)

A glance at the advertising analysis in Table 2-2 shows how one organisation went about measuring and comparing the effectiveness of different advertising methods. Table 2-2 shows the advertising results for a small business course run in London. At first glance the Sunday paper produced the most enquiries. Although it cost the most, £340, the cost per enquiry was only slightly more than the other media used. But the objective of this advertising wasn't simply to create interest; it was intended to sell places on the course. In fact, only 10 of the 75 enquiries were converted into orders – an advertising cost of £34 per head. On this basis the Sunday paper was between 2.5 and 3.5 times more expensive than any other medium.

Table 2-2		**Measuring Advertising Effect**			
Media Used	*Enquiries*	*Cost of Advertising*	*Cost per Enquiry*	*No. of Customers*	*Advertising Cost per Customer*
Sunday paper	75	£340	£4.50	10	£34
Daily paper	55	234	4.25	17	14
Posters	30	125	4.20	10	12
Local weekly paper	10	40	4.00	4	10
Personal recommendation	20	N/A	N/A	19	N/A

Selling and Salesmanship

More direct than advertising or publicity, selling is at the heart of every business. Whatever kind of selling your business involves, from moving goods over a counter to negotiating complex contracts, you need to understand the whole selling process and be involved with every aspect of it.

Telling the difference between selling and marketing

Marketing involves the whole process of deciding what to sell, who to sell it to and how. The theory is that a brilliant marketing strategy should all but eliminate the need for selling. After all, selling is mostly concerned with shoe-horning customers into products that they don't really want, isn't it? Absolutely not! Although the more effort you put into targeting the right product or service to the right market, the less arduous the selling process is, you still have a selling job to do.

The primary job of the sales operation is to act as a bridge or conduit between the product and the customer. Across that gulf flows information as well as products and services. You need to tell customers about your great new ideas and how your product or service performs better than anything they've seen to date.

Most businesses need selling and marketing activities in equal measure to get their message across effectively and get goods and services into their markets.

Selling yourself

One of the most important operational issues to address is your personal selling style. If you've sold products or services before, you may have developed a successful selling style already. If not, you need to develop one that's appropriate for your customers and comfortable for you. Regardless of your experience, assessing your selling style helps define and reinforce your business goals.

Check that you and your salespeople always see things from the customer's point of view. Review the sales styles of your salespeople to see how they can improve. Consider whether your own and your salespeople's selling styles are *consultative*, where you win the customer over to your point of view, or *hard*, where you try forcing the customer to take your product or service.

In assessing your selling style, consider the following:

- ✔ Always have a specific objective for any selling activity, together with a fall-back position. For example, your aim may be to get an order, but you may settle for the chance to tender for a customer's business. If you don't have objectives, much of your sales activity may be wasted on courtesy calls that never reach the asking-for-an-order stage.

- ✔ The right person to sell to is the one who makes the buying decision. You may have to start further down the chain, but you always need to know whom you finally have to convince.

- ✔ Set up the situation so you can listen to the customer. You can best do this by asking open questions that look for long answers as opposed to closed questions that solicit a 'yes or no' response. When the customer has revealed what her needs really are, confirm these back to her.

- ✔ Explain your product or service in terms of the customer's needs and requirements.

✔ Deal with objections without hostility or irritation. Objections are a sign that the customer is interested enough in what you have to say at least to discuss your proposition. After you've overcome the customer's objections and established a broad body of agreement, you can try to close the deal.

✔ Your approach to closing can be one of a number of ways. The *assumptive close* takes the tack that because you and the customer are so much in agreement, an order is the next logical step. If the position is less clear you can go for the *balance sheet close*, which involves going through the pros and cons, arriving at a larger number of pros. So once again, the most logical way forward is for the customer to order. If circumstances allow, you can use the *special situation* closing technique. This may be appropriate if a product is in scarce supply or on special offer for a limited period.

✔ If you're unsuccessful, start the selling process again using your fall-back objective as the goal.

Outsourcing selling

Hiring sales people can prove to be too costly for a new or small business. A lower-cost and perhaps less risky sales route is via agents. Good agents should have existing contacts in your field, know buyers personally and have detailed knowledge of your product's market. Unlike someone you recruit, a hired agent should be off to a flying start from day one.

The big difference is that agents are paid purely on commission – if they don't sell they don't earn. The commission amount varies, but is rarely less than 7 per cent of the selling price and 25 per cent isn't unknown.

You can find an agent by advertising in your specialist trade press or newspapers such as the *Daily Telegraph* and *Exchange and Mart*. You can also try the Manufacturers' Agents' Association (MAA; website: www.themaa.co.uk; tel: 01582-767618), whose membership consists entirely of commission agents selling in all fields of business. The website has a search facility that can help you find a sales agent by geographical area, industry sector or types of customer served. You have to pay £150 plus £26.25 VAT by credit card for an MAA Net Search, allowing you to contact up to 20 agents in one search. Alternatively, trade directories list other agents' associations. However, the most reliable method is to approach outlets where you wish to sell. They know the honest, competent and regular agents who call on them. Draw up a shortlist and invite those agents to apply to you.

The International Union of Commercial Agents and Brokers (www.iucab.org/nl) has details on some 470,000 commercial agents in Europe and North and South America.

When interviewing potential sales agents, find out:

Book V

Marketing and Advertising Your Wares

- ✔ What other companies and products do they already sell? You want them to sell related, but not competing, products or services to yours.

- ✔ What's their knowledge of the trade and geographical area that you cover? Sound them out for specific knowledge of your target market.

- ✔ Who are their contacts?

- ✔ What's their proven selling record? Find out who their biggest customers are and talk to these directly.

- ✔ Do they appear honest, reliable and fit to represent your business? Take up references and talk to their customers.

Finding professional representation is a challenge, so your product has to be first-class and your growth prospects good, with plenty of promotional material and back-up support.

When you do find someone to represent your product, draw up an agreement to cover the main points, including geographical area, commission rates, when commission is payable, customers you want to continue dealing with yourself, training and support given, prohibited competing agencies and periods of notice required to terminate. Also build in an initial trial period after which both parties can agree to part amicably.

Measuring results

Sales results can take time to appear. In the meantime you need to make sure you or your agent are doing things that eventually lead to successful sales. You need to measure the following:

Activities

- ✔ Sales appointments made
- ✔ Sales calls made per day, per week, per month. Monitor trends, because last quarter's sales calls give you a good feel for this quarter's sales results
- ✔ Quotations given

Results

- ✔ New accounts opened
- ✔ Old accounts lost
- ✔ Average order size

Pricing for Profit

Pricing is another element of the marketing mix and represents the biggest decision you have to make about your business and the one that has the biggest impact on company profitability. You need to keep pricing constantly under review.

To get a better appreciation of the factors that may have an influence on what you charge, every business should keep these factors in mind.

Caring about business conditions

Obviously, the overall conditions in the marketplace have a bearing on your pricing policy. In boom conditions, where products are so popular that they're virtually being rationed, you can expect the overall level of prices for some products to rise disproportionately. And conditions can vary so much from place to place that they have a major impact on pricing. For example, one business starter produced her beauty treatment price list based on prices near to her home in Surrey. However, she planned to move to Cornwall to start her business, where prices were 50 per cent lower, reflecting lower rates of pay in the county. So although she got a boost by selling her Surrey home for much more than she paid for a house in Cornwall, that gain was offset by having to charge much lower prices for her services.

Seasonal factors can also contribute to changes in the general level of prices. A turkey, for example, costs less on the afternoon of Christmas Eve than it does at the start of Christmas week.

Working to your capacity

Your capacity to produce your product or service, bearing in mind market conditions, influences the price you set. Typically, a new venture has limited capacity at the start. A valid entry strategy may be to price high enough to just fill your capacity, rather than so low as to swamp you.

A housewife started a home ironing service at £5.50 per hour's ironing, in line with competition, but because she only had 20 hours a week to work in, she rapidly ran out of time. It took six months to get her price up to £7 an hour and her demand down to 20 hours per week. Then she was able to recruit some assistance and had a high enough margin to pay some outworkers and make some profit herself.

Understanding consumer perceptions

A major consideration when setting your prices is customers' perception of the value of your product or service. Their opinion of value may have little or no relation to its cost, and they may be ignorant of the price that the competition charges, especially if your product or service is a new one.

Skimming versus penetrating

The overall image that you want to portray in the marketplace influences the prices you charge. A high-quality image calls for higher pricing, naturally. However, within that pricing policy you have the option of either setting a high price, which just *skims* the market by only being attractive to a small population of wealthier customers; or going for a low price to *penetrate* the market, appealing to the mass of customers.

Skim pricing is often adopted with new products with little or no competition that are aimed at affluent buyers who are willing to pay more to be the trend-setters for a new product. After the innovators have been creamed off the market, you can drop the price to penetrate to lower layers of demand.

The danger with this strategy is that high prices attract the interest of new competitors. If you have a product that's easy to copy and impossible to patent, you may be better off setting the price low to discourage competitors and to spread your product throughout the market quickly.

Avoiding setting prices too low

The most frequent mistake that companies make when setting a selling price for the first time is to pitch it too low. Either through failing to understand all the costs associated with making and marketing your product or through yielding to the temptation to undercut the competition at the outset, you set your price so low that you risk killing your company.

Pondering Place and Distribution

Place is the fourth 'p' in the marketing mix. Place makes you review exactly how you get your products or service to your customers.

If you're a retailer, restaurateur or garage proprietor, for example, then your customers come to you. Your physical location probably is the key to success. If your business is in the manufacturing field, you're more likely to go out and find customers. In this case, your channels of distribution are the vital link.

Even if you're already in business and plan to stay in the same location, you may find benefit in taking the opportunity to review that decision. If you're looking for additional funds to expand your business, your location is undoubtedly an area that prospective financiers want to explore.

Choosing a location

From your market research data you should be able to come up with a list of criteria that are important to your choice of location. Some of the factors you need to weigh up when deciding where to locate are:

- ✔ If you need skilled or specialist labour, is it readily available?

- ✔ Are the necessary back-up services available, such as computer support, equipment repairs and maintenance?

- ✔ How readily available are raw materials, components and other supplies?

- ✔ How does the cost of premises, rates and utilities compare with other areas?

- ✔ How accessible is the site by road, rail and air?

- ✔ Are there any changes in the pipeline that may adversely affect trade? Examples include a new motorway bypassing the town, changes in transport services and the closure of a large factory.

- ✔ Are there competing businesses in the immediate neighbourhood? Are these likely to have a beneficial or detrimental effect?

- ✔ Is the location conducive to the creation of a favourable market image? For instance, a high-fashion designer may lack credibility trading from an area famous for its heavy industry and infamous for its dirt and pollution.

- ✔ Is the area generally regarded as low or high growth? Is the area favourable to businesses?

- ✔ Can you and your key employees get to the area easily and quickly?

You may even have spotted a role model – a successful competitor, perhaps in another town, who appears to have got the location spot on. You can use its location criteria as a guide to developing your own.

Using these criteria you can quickly screen out most unsuitable areas. You may have to visit other locations several times, at different hours of the day and on different days of the week, before screening these out too.

Selecting a distribution channel

When you know where you want to locate, selecting a distribution channel involves researching methods and deciding on the best way to get your product to your customers.

Moving a product through a distribution channel calls for two sorts of selling activity. *Push* is the name given to selling your product in, for example, a shop. *Pull* is the effort that you carry out on the shop's behalf to help it sell your product. Your advertising strategy or a merchandising activity may cause the pull. You need to know how much push and pull are needed for the channel you're considering. If you aren't geared up to help retailers sell your product, and they need that help, then this may be a poor channel for you.

The way in which you have to move your product to your end customers is an important factor to weigh up when choosing a channel. As well as such factors as the cost of carriage, you also have to decide about packaging materials. As a rough rule, the more stages in the distribution channel, the more robust and expensive your packaging has to be.

Not all channels of distribution settle their bills promptly. For example, mail-order customers pay in advance, but retailers can take up to 90 days or more to pay. You need to take account of this settlement period in your cash-flow forecast.

Consider these factors when choosing channels of distribution for your particular business:

- *Does the channel meet your customers' needs?* You have to find out how your customers expect their product or service to be delivered to them and whether they need that particular route.

- *Will the product itself survive?* Fresh vegetables, for example, need to be moved quickly from where they're grown to where they're consumed.

- *Can you sell enough this way?* 'Enough' is how much you want to sell.

- *Is the channel compatible with your image?* If you're selling a luxury product, then door-to-door selling may spoil the impression you're trying to create in the rest of your marketing effort.

- *How do your competitors distribute?* If they've been around for a while and are obviously successful, you may benefit from looking at how your competitors distribute and using that knowledge to your advantage.

- *Is the channel cost-effective?* A small manufacturer may not find it cost-effective to supply retailers in a particular area because the direct 'drop' size – that is, the load per order – is too small to be worthwhile.

- *Is the mark-up enough?* If your product can't bear at least a 100 per cent mark-up, then it's unlikely that you can sell it through department stores. Your distribution channel has to be able to make a profit from selling your product too.

Working from home

If you plan to work from home, have you checked that you aren't prohibited from doing so by the house deeds, or whether your type of activity is likely to irritate the neighbours? This route into business is much in favour with sources of debt finance, because it lowers the risks during the vulnerable start-up period. Venture capitalists, on the other hand, may well see it as a sign of 'thinking too small' and steer clear of the proposition. Nevertheless, working from home can make sound sense.

You also have to consider whether working from home suits you and your partner's domestic arrangements. For instance, if you have young children you may find difficulty in explaining to them that you're really at work, when everything looks much the same all the time.

If you're the type of person who needs the physical separation of work and home to give a structure to your life, then working from home may not be right for you.

Looking at Legal Issues in Marketing

Nothing in business escapes the legal eye of the law and marketing is no exception. If anything, marketing is likely to produce more grey areas from a legal point of view than most others. You have patent and copyright issues to consider.

There are a number of vitally important aspects of your business that distinguish it from other similar firms operating in or near to your area of operations. Having invested time, energy and money in acquiring some distinction you need to take steps to preserve any benefits accruing from those distinctions. Intellectual property, often known as IP, is the generic title that covers the area of law that allows people to own their creativity and innovation in the same way that they can own physical property. The owner of IP can control and be rewarded for its use, and this encourages further innovation and creativity.

The following three organisations can help direct you to most sources of help and advice across the entire intellectual property field. They also have helpful literature and explanatory leaflets and guidance notes on applying for intellectual property protection:

- UK Patent Office (www.patent.gov.uk)
- European Patent Office (www.european-patent-office.org)
- US Patent and Trade Mark Office (www.uspto.gov)

We cover the most common types of intellectual property in the following sections.

Naming your business

You're reasonably free to use your last name for the name of your business. The main consideration in choosing a business name, however, is its commercial usefulness. You want one that lets people know as much as possible about what you do. It's therefore important to choose a name that will convey the right image and message.

Whichever business name you choose, it will have to be legally acceptable and abide by the rules of the Business Names Act 1985. Detailed information on this subject is available from the Business Names section at the Companies House website. Go to www.companieshouse.gov.uk and click on 'Guidance Booklets & FAQ' and then 'Business Names'.

Looking at logos

It isn't mandatory to have a logo for your business, but it can build greater customer awareness. A logo may be a word, a typeface, a colour or a shape. The McDonald's name is a logo because of its distinct and stylistic writing. Choose your logo carefully. It should be one that is easily recognisable, fairly simple in design and one that can be reproduced on everything associated with your business. As far as the law is concerned a logo is a form of trademark.

Registering a domain name

A domain name is your own web address, which you register so that your business will have the exclusive right of use. It identifies your business or organisation on the Internet, and it enables people to find you by directly entering your name into their browser address box. You can check whether your choice of name is available by using a free domain search service available at websites that register domain names such as www.yourname.com.

If your company name is registered as a trademark (see below), you may (as current case law develops) be able to prevent another business from using it as a domain name. Once you have decided on a selection of domain names, you can choose several different registration options:

✔ Use Nominet UK (www.nic.uk), which is the Registry for UK Internet domain names. Just as Companies House holds authoritative records for company names, Nominet maintains the database of UK registered Internet names. They charge £80 plus VAT for two years' registration.

✔ Most countries have a central registry to store these unique domain names. Two sites that maintain world directories of Internet domain registries are www.internic.net and www.norid.no/domreg.html, who between them cover pretty well every registration authority in the world.

In order to be eligible to register direct you must provide the Internet Protocol addresses of two named servers that are permanently connected to the Internet.

- ✔ Use Internet service providers (ISPs) which act as agents for their customers and will submit a domain name application for registration.

- ✔ Register online. Hundreds of websites now offer domain-name registration online; it's a good idea to search the Internet for these sites, as they often sell domain names as loss-leaders. Most of these providers also offer a search facility so you can see if your selected name has already been registered.

- ✔ Obtain free domain names along with free web space by registering with an Internet community. These organisations offer you web pages within their community space as well as a free domain name, but most communities only offer free domain names that have their own community domain tagged on the end – this can make your domain name rather long and hard to remember.

Once your domain name has been registered and paid for, you'll receive a registration certificate, either directly or through your ISP. This is an important document as it confirms you as the legal registrant of a domain name. If any amendments need to be made at any point during the registration period, the registry and your ISP must be informed.

Protecting patents

The patent system in its current form was introduced over 100 years ago, although some type of protection has been around for about 350 years, as an incentive to get inventors to disclose their ideas to the general public and so promote technical advancement in general.

A patent can be regarded as a contract between an inventor and the state. The state agrees with the inventor that if she is prepared to publish details of her invention in a set form and if it appears that she has made a real advance, the state will then grant her a monopoly on her invention for 20 years: 'protection in return for disclosure'. The inventor uses the monopoly period to manufacture and sell the innovation; competitors can read the published specifications and glean ideas for their research, or they can approach the inventor and offer to help to develop the idea under licence.

The granting of a patent doesn't mean the proprietor is automatically free to make, use or sell the invention herself since to do so may involve infringing an earlier patent which has not yet expired. A patent really only allows the inventor to stop another person using the particular device which forms the subject of the patent. The state doesn't guarantee validity of a patent either, so it's not uncommon for patents to be challenged through the courts.

If you want to apply for a patent it's essential not to disclose your idea in non-confidential circumstances. If you do, your invention is already 'published' in the eyes of the law, and this may well invalidate your application. Ideally, the confidentiality of the disclosure you make should be written down in a confidentiality agreement and signed by the person to whom you're making the disclosure. This is particularly important if you're talking to a commercial contact or potential business colleague. The other way is to get your patent application on file before you start talking to anyone about your idea. You can talk to a Chartered Patent Agent in complete confidence as they work under strict rules of confidentiality.

The patenting process has two distinct stages:

- From filing an application up to publication of the patent
- From publication to grant of the patent

Two fees are payable for the first part of the process and a further fee for the second part. The Patent Office Search and Advisory Service will give some estimate of the costs associated with a specific investigation. They suggest, for example, that subject matter searches will cost upwards of £500, validity searches from £1000, and infringement searches from £1,500. And these are just the costs for the very start of the procedure.

The whole process takes some two and a half years. Relevant forms and details of how to patent are available free of charge from the Patent Office at `www.patent.gov.uk`. You can also write to them: The Patent Office, Concept House, Cardiff Road, Newport, NP10 8QQ.

Registering a trademark

A *trademark* is the symbol by which the goods of a particular manufacturer or trader can be identified. It can be a word, a signature, a monogram, a picture, a logo, or a combination of these.

To qualify for registration the trademark must be distinctive, must not be deceptive and must not be capable of confusion with marks already registered. Excluded are national flags, royal crests, and insignia of the armed forces. A trademark can only apply to tangible goods, not services (although pressure is mounting for this to be changed).

The Trade Mark Act 1994 offers protection of great commercial value since, unlike other forms of protection, your sole rights to use the trademark continue indefinitely.

To register a trademark you or your agent needs to first conduct preliminary searches at the Trade Marks Branch of the Patent Office to check there are no conflicting marks already in existence. You then apply for registration on the official trademark form and pay a fee (currently £200). Your application is then advertised in the weekly *Trade Marks Journal* to allow any objections to be raised. If there are none, your trademark will be officially registered and you pay a further fee (currently £200).

Registration is initially for ten years. After this, it can be renewed for further periods of ten years at a time, with no upper time limit. It's mandatory to register a trademark.

If an unregistered trademark has been used for some time and could be construed as closely associated with the product by customers, it will have acquired a 'reputation' which will give it some protection legally, but registration makes it much simpler for the owner to have recourse against any person who infringes the mark.

Detailing your design

You can register the shape, design or decorative features of a commercial product if it's new, original, never published before or – if already known – never before applied to the product you have in mind. Protection is intended to apply to industrial articles to be produced in quantities of more than 50. The Design Registry can be accessed at the Patent Office website www. patent.gov.uk.

Design registration only applies to features that appeal to the eye – not to the way the article functions.

To register a design, apply to the Design Registry and send a specimen or photograph of the design plus a registration fee (currently about £100).

There's no such thing as an all-embracing international registration for designs. If you want protection of your design outside the UK, you generally have to make separate applications for registration in each country in which you want protection.

You can handle the design registration yourself but it may be preferable to let a specialist do it for you.

Controlling a copyright

Copyright gives protection against the unlicensed copying of original artistic and creative works – articles, books, paintings, films, plays, songs, music, engineering drawings. To claim copyright the item in question should carry this symbol © with the author's name and date.

No other action is required to take out copyright. The Copyright service is accessed through the Patent Office website (www.patent.gov.uk).

Copyright doesn't last forever. The duration is dependant on the type of copyright involved and can be anything from 25 to 70 years after the creator's death.

Setting terms of trade

All business is governed by terms of trade, which are in turn affected by *contractual* relationships. Almost everything done in business, whether it's the supply of raw materials, the sale of goods and services, or the hire of a fax machine is executed under contract law. This is true whether the contract is in writing or whether it's verbal – or even merely implied.

Only contracts for the sale of land, hire-purchase, and some insurance contracts have to be in writing to be enforceable.

To make life even more complicated, a contract can be part written and part oral. So statements made at the time of signing a written contract can legally form part of that contract. For a contract to exist three events must take place:

- ✔ There must be an offer.
- ✔ There must be an acceptance.
- ✔ There must be a consideration – some form of payment.

When selling via the Internet or mail order the contract starts when the supplier 'posts' an acceptance letter, a confirmation, or the goods themselves – whichever comes first.

Under the Distance Selling Regulations brought into effect in October 2001, customers have seven working days after they've received the goods to change their minds and return them. They don't need a reason and can get a full refund.

Consumers must also be given:

- ✔ Information about the company they are dealing with, such as the business name, registered and trading addresses, and directors
- ✔ Written confirmation of the order – by fax, letter or email
- ✔ A full refund if their goods don't arrive by the date agreed in the original order; if no date was agreed they must be delivered within 30 days
- ✔ Information about cancellation rights
- ✔ Protection against credit card fraud

Certain standards have to be met by law for the supply of goods and services. Over and above these you need your own terms and conditions if you're not to enter into 'contracts' you didn't intend. You need help to devise these terms. The following four basic propositions will govern your conditions:

- ✔ The conditions must be brought to the other party's attention before he or she makes the contract.

- ✔ The last terms and conditions specified before acceptance of an offer apply.

- ✔ If any ambiguity or uncertainty exists in the contract terms they'll be interpreted against the person who inserted them.

- ✔ The terms may be interpreted as unreasonably unenforceable, being in breach of various Acts of Parliament.

The Office of Fair Trading (www.oft.gov.uk) and the Trading Standards Institute (www.tradingstandards.gov.uk) and Trading Standards Service (www.tradingstandards.gov.uk) can provide useful information on most aspects of trading relationships.

Describing your goods

You can't make any claim you like for the performance of your goods or services. If you state or imply a certain standard of performance for what you're selling, your customers have a legally enforceable right to expect it. So if you state your new slimming method will not only make people lose weight, but make them happier, richer and more successful, then you had better deliver on all those promises.

The Trades Descriptions Acts and related legislation make it an offence for a trader to describe their goods falsely. The Acts cover everything from the declared mileage of second-hand cars to the country of manufacture of a pair of jeans.

The Trading Standards Service is operated at county level throughout the country to ensure trading laws are met. Contact your council by phone or via their website (www.tradingstandards.gov.uk).

Abiding by fair business rules

The whole way in which businesses and markets operate is the subject of keen government interest. It isn't a good idea, for example, to gang up with others in your market to create a *cartel,* in which you all agree not to lower your prices or compete with each other too vigorously.

Any such action may be brought to the attention of the Office of Fair Trading (OFT). The OFT's (www.oft.gov.uk) job is to make markets work well for consumers. Markets work well when businesses are in open, fair and vigorous competition with each other for the consumer's custom. As an independent organisation, the OFT have three main operational areas which make up three divisions – Competition Enforcement, Consumer Regulation Enforcement, Markets and Policies Initiatives.

The OFT's Consumer Regulation Enforcement department

✔ Ensures that consumer legislation and regulations are properly enforced

✔ Takes action against unfair traders

✔ Encourages codes of practice and standards

✔ Offers a range of information to help consumers understand their rights and make good choices

✔ Liaises closely with other regulatory bodies that also have enforcement powers

Dealing with payment problems

Getting paid isn't always as simple a process as sending out a bill and waiting for the cheque. Customers may dispute the bill, fairly or unfairly.

A businessperson can use the Small Claims Court to collect bills, to obtain a judgement for breach of contract, or to seek money for minor property damage claims – for example, suing someone who broke a fence around your property or parking area. The Small Claims Court offers you an opportunity to collect money that would otherwise be lost as it would be too expensive to sue in regular court. True, for very small cases, it's not always cost-effective, and occasionally you have problems collecting your judgement. But the Small Claims Court should still be part of the collection strategies of your business.

The Small Claims Court aims to provide a speedy, inexpensive resolution of disputes that involve relatively small amounts of money. The advantage of the Small Claims Court is that if you can't afford a solicitor and you aren't entitled to Legal Aid you can still bring your case to the court yourself. Even if you can afford a solicitor, her fees may be more than the amount you're claiming. If you don't manage to get your opponent to pay your costs then you won't be any better off.

The *jurisdictional limits* (the amount for which you can sue) in these courts are rising fairly quickly. In the UK if the amount of money claimed is under £5,000, it's likely to come under the jurisdiction of the Small Claims Court. However, if your claim is for personal injury it will only be heard in the Small Claims Court if the claim for the injury itself is not more than £1,000.

Before you start legal proceedings, investigate alternatives. If your case involves a written contract, check to see if the contract requires mediation or arbitration of disputes. If so, this may limit or cut off your right to go to any court, including the Small Claims Court. Second, consider other cost-effective options, such as free or low-cost publicly operated mediation programmes. If you're in a dispute with a customer, or perhaps another business, and you still have hopes of preserving some aspect of the relationship, mediation – even if not provided for in a contract – is often a better alternative than going to court. Any litigation tends to sour people's feelings.

Since January 2002 anyone claiming up to £100,000 can sue through the Internet at any time, day or night. If the claim is undefended, the money can be recovered without anyone having to go to court. The service, called Money Claim Online, can be reached at www.courtservice.gov.uk

Chapter 3

Writing a Marketing Plan

• •

• •

*Y*ou don't have to write a marketing plan to use this book or even to ben-efit from this chapter. But you may want to, because doing so isn't as hard as you may think, and, most important, a good plan increases the odds of success. In fact, most of the really successful businesses we know – small or large, new or old – write a careful marketing plan at least once a year.

Marketing combines lots of activities and expenditures in the hope of gen-erating or increasing sales and maintaining or increasing market share. You won't see those sales numbers rise without a coherent plan linking a strategy, based on the strengths of your position, to your sales and marketing activi-ties that can convince targeted customers to purchase. Marketing can get out of control or confused in a hurry unless you have a plan. Every successful business needs a marketing plan. (Yes, even if you're in a small or start-up business. In fact, especially if you are; you don't have the resources to waste on unplanned or ineffective marketing.)

Identifying Planning Rules and Tips

Marketing plans vary significantly in format and outline from company to company, but all have core components covering:

- ✔ **Your current position** in terms of your product, customers, competition and broader trends in your market.

- ✔ **For established businesses, what results you achieved in the previous period** in terms of sales, market share and possibly also in terms of profits, customer satisfaction or other measures of customer attitude and perception. You may want to include measures of customer retention, size, frequency of purchase or other indicators of customer behaviour, if you think them important to your new plan.

- ✔ **Your strategy** – the big picture that will help you get improved results.

- ✔ **The details of your marketing activities**, including all your company's specific activities, grouped by area or type, with explanations of how these activities fit the company strategy and reflect the current situation.

- ✔ **The numbers**, including sales projections and costs. Consider whether knowing these additional numbers would help your business: market share projections, sales to your biggest customers or distributors, costs and returns from any special offers you plan to use, sales projections and commissions by territory or whatever help you quantify your specific marketing activities.

- ✔ **Your learning plans.** You may want to test the waters or experiment on a small scale if you have a new business or new product or if you're experimenting with a new or risky marketing activity. You need to determine what positive results you want to see before committing to a higher level. Wisdom is knowing what you don't know – and planning how to work it out.

The more unfamiliar the waters, the more flexibility and caution your plan needs. If you're a start-up, for example, consider a step-wise plan with a timeline and alternatives or options in case of problems. Especially if you're writing a marketing plan for the first time, make flexibility your first objective. Avoid large advance purchases of media space or time, use short runs of marketing materials at the copy shop instead of cheaper off-set printing of large inventories and so on. Optimising your plan for flexibility means preserving your choice and avoiding commitments of resources. Spending in small increments allows you to change the plan as you go.

If your business has done this all before, however, and your plan builds on years of experience, you can more safely favour *economies of scale* over flexibility. (Advertising, for example, is cheaper and more efficient if you do it on a large scale, because you get bigger discounts on design of ads and purchase of media space or airtime.) If you know a media investment is likely to produce leads or sales, go ahead and buy media in larger chunks to get good rates. You don't have to be as cautious about testing mailing lists with small-scale mailings of a few hundred pieces. A good in-house list supplemented by 20 per cent or fewer newly purchased names probably warrants a major mailing without as much emphasis on advance testing. Adjust your plan to favour economies of scale if you feel confident that you can make sound judgements in advance, but always leave yourself at least a *little* wiggle room. Reality never reflects plans and projections 100 per cent of the time. Aim for an 80 per cent match in marketing, and plan accordingly.

The following sections share a few other suggestions to follow if you want to increase your marketing plan's chances of success.

Avoiding common mistakes

Marketing campaigns end up like leaky boats very easily, so be sure to total up your costs fully and carefully. Each activity seems worthy at the time, but too many of them fail to produce a positive return – ending up like holes in the bottom of your boat. To avoid the costly but all-too-common mistakes that many marketers make, follow these suggestions:

- ✔ **Don't ignore the details.** You build good plans from details like customer-by-customer, item-by-item or territory-by-territory sales projections. Generalising about an entire market is hard. Your sales and cost projections are easier to get right if you break them down to their smallest natural units (like individual territory sales or customer orders), do estimates for each of these small units, and then add those estimates up to get your totals.

- ✔ **Don't imitate the competitors.** Even though everyone seems to market their products in a certain way, you don't have to imitate them. High-performing plans clearly point out what aspects of the marketing are conventional and why – and these plans also include some original, innovative or unique elements to help differentiate your company from and outperform the competition. Your business is unique, so make your plan reflect your special talents or advantages.

- ✔ **Don't feel confined by last period's budget and plan.** Repeat or improve the best-performing elements of the past plans, but cut back on elements that didn't produce high returns. Every plan includes some activities and spending that aren't necessary and can be cut (or reworked) when you do it again next year. Be ruthless with any under-performing elements of last year's plan! (If you're starting a new business, at least this is one problem you don't have to worry about. Yet.)

- ✔ **Don't engage in unnecessary spending.** Always think your plan through and run the numbers before signing a contract or writing a cheque. Many of the people and businesses you deal with to execute your marketing activities are salespeople themselves. These people's goal is to get *you* to buy their ad space or time, to use their design or printing services or spend money on fancy websites. They want your marketing money and they don't care as much as you do whether you get a good return or not. You have to keep these salespeople on a tight financial rein.

Breaking your plan into simple sub-plans

If all your marketing activities are consistent and clearly of one kind, a single plan is fine. But what if you sell services (like consulting or repairs) and also products? You may find that you need to work up one plan for selling products (perhaps this strategy aims to find new customers) and another plan for convincing product buyers to also use your services. Follow the general rule that if the plan seems too complicated, divide and conquer! Then total everything up to get the big picture with its overall projections and budgets.

If you have 50 products in five different product categories, writing your plan becomes easier if you come up with 50 sales projections for each product and five separate promotional plans for each category of product. (This method sounds tricky but will make life much simpler.) We've included some methods to break down your planning, making it easier and simpler to do:

- ✔ Analyse, plan and budget sales activities by sales territory and region (or by major customer if you're a business-to-business (B2B) marketer with a handful of dominant companies as your clients).

- ✔ Project revenues and promotions by individual product and by industry (if you sell into more than one).

- ✔ Plan your advertising and other promotions by product line or other broad product category, as promotions often have a generalised effect on the products within the category.

- ✔ Plan and budget publicity for your company as a whole. Only budget and plan publicity for an individual product if you introduce it or modify it in some way that may attract media attention.

- ✔ Plan and budget for brochures, websites and other informational materials. Remain focused in your subject choices: one brochure per topic. Multipurpose brochures or sites never work well. If a website sells cleaning products to building maintenance professionals, don't plan for it to broker gardening and lawn-mowing services to suburban homeowners as well. Different products and customers need separate plans.

Remember that every type of marketing activity in your plan has a natural and appropriate level of breakdown. Find the right level, and your planning will be simpler and easier to do.

Writing a Powerful Executive Summary

An executive summary is a one-page plan. This wonderful document conveys essential information about your company's planned year of activities in a couple of hundred well-chosen words or less. If you ever get confused or disoriented in the rough-and-tumble play of sales and marketing, this clear, concise summary can guide you back to the correct strategic path. A good executive summary should be a powerful advertisement for your marketing, communicating the purpose and essential activities of your plan in such a compelling manner that everyone who reads it eagerly leaps into action and does the right things to make your vision come true.

Draft the executive summary early in the year as a guide to your thinking and planning. But revise this document often, and finish it only after finishing all the other sections, because it needs to summarise them.

Help yourself (and your readers, if others in your company are going to be involved in approving or implementing the plan) by giving an overview of what's the same and what's different in this plan, compared with the previous period's plan. Draft a short paragraph covering these two topics.

Summarise the main points of your plan and make clear whether the plan is:

- ✔ **Efficiency-oriented:** For example, your plan introduces a large number of specific improvements in how you market your product.

- ✔ **Effectiveness-oriented:** For example, your plan identifies a major opportunity or problem and adopts a new strategy to respond to it.

Summarise the bottom-line results – what your projected revenues will be (by product or product line, unless you have too many to list on one page) and what the costs are – and show how these figures differ from last year's figures. Keep the whole summary under one page in length if you can.

If you have too many products to keep the summary under a page list them by product line or do more than one plan. If a plan can't be neatly summarised in a page, it probably needs more thought. We've worked with many businesses in which marketing prepares a separate plan for each product.

Divide and conquer.

Clarifying and Quantifying Your Objectives

Objectives are the quantified, measurable versions of your strategies. For example, if your strategy involves raising the quality of service and opening a new territory in order to grow your sales and market share, you need to think through how you'll do that and set a percentage increase goal for sales and a new, higher goal for market share. These numbers become your objectives. The objectives flow from your thinking about strategies and tactics, but put them near the front of your plan to help others understand what you're saying.

What objectives do you want your plan to help you accomplish? Will the plan increase sales by 25 per cent, reposition a product to make it more appealing to upmarket buyers, introduce a direct marketing function via the Internet or launch a new product? Maybe the plan will combine several products into a single family brand and build awareness of this brand through print and radio advertising. This approach could gain market share from several competitors and cut the costs of marketing by eliminating inefficiencies in coupon processing, media buying and sales force management. Address these sorts of topics in the objectives section of the plan. These points give the plan focus.

If you write clear, compelling objectives, you never get too confused about what to write in other sections. When in doubt, you can look back at these objectives and remind yourself what you're trying to accomplish, and why.

Try to write this part of the plan early, but keep in mind that you'll rewrite it often as you gather more information and do more thinking. Objectives are such a key foundation for the rest of the plan that you can't ever stop thinking about them. However, for all their importance, objectives don't need a lot of words – half a page to two pages, at most. (Paradoxically, we have to tell you more about these short upfront sections than about the longer, detail-oriented sections in the back because planners find the short sections more conceptually challenging.)

Preparing a Situation Analysis

The context is different for every marketing plan. A *situation analysis* examines the context, looking at trends, customer preferences, competitor strengths and weaknesses and anything else that may impact sales. The question your situation analysis must answer is, 'What's happening?' The answer to this question can take many forms, so we can't give you an easy formula for preparing the situation analysis. You need to analyse the most important market changes to your company – these changes can be the sources of problems but also potential opportunities. (See Book I Chapter 6 for formal research techniques and sources.)

What are the most important changes that have occurred since you last examined the situation? The answer depends on the situation. See the difficulty? Yet somehow you have to gain enough insight into what's happening to see the problems and opportunities clearly.

Seeing trends more clearly than others do

Your goal is to see the changes more clearly than the competition. Why? Because if your situation analysis isn't as accurate as the competition's, you'll lose market share to them. If your analysis is about the same as your

Chapter 3: Writing a Marketing Plan *435*

Book V

Marketing
and
Advertising
Your Wares

competition's, then you may hold even. Only if your situation analysis is better than your rivals' can you gain market share on the competition.

What you want from your situation analysis is:

- ✔ **Information parity:** When you know as much as your leading competitors. If you don't do enough research and analysis, your competitors have an information advantage, so you need to gain enough insight to put you on a level playing field with your rivals. (That includes knowing about any major plans they may have. Collect rumours about new products, new people and so on. At a minimum, do a weekly search on a web-based search engine for news about them. You can customise web pages such as Google News to highlight stories about specific brands or businesses and have them delivered to your email inbox.)

- ✔ **Information advantage in specific areas:** This is insight into the market that your competitors don't have. Information advantage puts you on the uphill side of an uneven playing field and that's a good place from which to design and launch a marketing campaign. Look for new fashions, new technologies, new ways to segment the market – anything that you can use to change the rules of the game even slightly in your favour.

Most marketing plans and planners don't think about their situation analysis in this way. We're telling you one of our best-kept secrets because we don't want you to waste time on the typical *pro forma* situation analysis, in which the marketer rounds up the usual suspects and parades dull information in front of them without gaining an advantage from it. That approach, although common, does nothing to make the plan a winner.

Using a structured approach to competitor analysis

What kinds of information can you collect about your competitors? You can gather and analyse examples of competitors' marketing communications. You may have (or be able to gather) some customer opinions from surveys or informal chats. You can group the information you get from customers into useful lists, such as discovering the three most appealing and least appealing things about each competitor. You can also probably get some information about how your competitors distribute and sell, where they are (and aren't) located or distributed, who their key decision-makers are, who their biggest and/or most loyal customers are, and even (perhaps) how much they sell. Gather any available data on all-important competitors and organise the information into a table for easy analysis.

Building a competitor analysis table

Develop a format for a generic competitor analysis table. Make entries on the following rows in columns labelled for Competitor No. 1, Competitor No. 2, Competitor No. 3 and so on:

- ✔ **Company.** Describe how the market perceives it and its key product.

- ✔ **Key personnel.** Who are the managers, and how many employees do they have in total?

- ✔ **Financial.** Who owns it, how strong is its *cash position* (does it have spending power or is it struggling to pay its bills?), what were its sales in the last two years?

- ✔ **Sales, distribution and pricing.** Describe its primary sales channel, discount/pricing structure and market share estimate.

- ✔ **Product/service analysis.** What are the strengths and weaknesses of its product or service?

- ✔ **Scaled assessment of product/service.** Explore relevant subjects such as market acceptance, quality of packaging, ads and so on. Assign a score of between 1 and 5 (with 5 being the strongest) for each characteristic you evaluate. Then add the scores for each competitor's row to see which seems strongest, overall.

- ✔ **Comparing yourself to competitor ratings.** If you rate yourself on these attributes, too, how do you compare? Are you stronger? If not, you can include increasing your competitive strength as one of your plan's strategic objectives.

Explaining Your Marketing Strategy

Many plans use this section to get specific about the objectives by explaining how your company will accomplish them. Some writers find this task easy, but others keep getting confused about the distinction between an objective and a strategy. The objective simply states something your business hopes to accomplish in the next year. The strategy emphasises the big-picture approach to accomplishing that objective, giving some good pointers as to what road you'll take.

An objective sounds like this: to solidify our leadership of the home PC market by increasing market share by 2 points.

A strategy sounds like this: to introduce hot new products and promote our brand name with an emphasis on high-quality components, in order to increase our market share by 2 points.

Combining strategies and objectives

Some people view the difference between objectives and strategies as a pretty fine line. If you're comfortable with the distinction, write a separate *Strategy* section. If you're not sure about the difference, combine this section with the objectives section and title it *Objectives and Strategies*; what you call the points doesn't matter, as long as they're good.

Your strategies accomplish your objectives through the tactical use of the elements of the marketing mix. The plan explains how your tactics use your strategies to accomplish your objectives.

Giving your strategy common sense

This advice isn't easy to follow and make concrete. Unlike a mathematical formula or a spreadsheet column, no simple method exists to check a marketing strategy to make sure that it really adds up. But you can subject a marketing strategy to common sense and make sure that it has no obvious flaws – as outlined in the following sections.

Strategy fails to reflect limitations in your resources

Don't pull a Napoleon. If you're currently the tenth-largest competitor, don't write a plan to become the largest by the end of the year simply based on designing all your ads and mailings to claim you're the best. Make sure that your strategy is achievable. Would the average person agree that your strategy sounds attainable with a little hard work? (If you're not sure, find some average people and ask them.) And do you have enough resources to execute the strategy in the available time?

Strategy demands huge changes in customer behaviour

You can move people and businesses only so far with marketing. If you plan to get employers to give their employees every other Friday off so those employees can attend special workshops that your firm sponsors, well, we hope you have a back-up plan. Employers don't give employees a lot of extra time off, no matter how compelling your sales pitch or brochure may be. The same is true of consumer marketing. You simply cannot change strongly held public attitudes without awfully good new evidence.

A competitor is already doing the strategy

This assumption is a surprisingly common error. To avoid this mistake, include a summary of each competitor's strategy in the *Strategy* section of your plan. Add a note explaining how your strategy differs from each of them. If you're marketing a computer installation and repair service in the Liverpool area, you really need to know how your strategy differs from the multiple competitors also trying to secure big corporate contracts in that area. Do you specialise in certain types of equipment that others don't? Do you emphasise speed of repair service? Are you the only vendor who distributes and supports CAD/CAM equipment from a leading maker? You need a distinctive strategy to power your plan. You don't want to be a 'me-too' competitor.

Strategy requires you to know too much that you don't already know

You can't use some brilliant strategies for your business because they'd require you to do too many things you don't know anything about. For example, a growing need exists for computer skills training, but if your business is in selling and servicing computer equipment, that doesn't automatically give you experience in developing, selling or delivering computer courses. Strategies that involve doing a lot of things you have little or no expertise in are really start-up strategies, not marketing strategies. If you want to put a minority of your resources into trying to start a new business unit, go ahead. But don't put your entire marketing plan at risk by basing it on a strategy that takes you into unfamiliar waters.

Is your strategy flaky?

What do you do if you're the leading producer of breakfast cereals, but the total market for breakfast cereals is declining? Find new and exciting ways for people to consume breakfast cereals, obviously. When Kellogg decided to launch its Cereal Mates product, it thought it was following changes in customer behaviour rather than asking people to radically change their ways. The pattern of breakfast consumption had changed, with fewer people having the time or inclination for a sit-down breakfast at home. The trend was for breakfast on the go, so Kellogg created cereal to go.

Cereal Mates was an all-in-one single serve version of Kellogg's most popular breakfast cereals. It came with its own spoon and was sealed in such a way that the milk didn't need refrigerating. Mistake number one – consumers didn't want warm milk on their cereal. So Kellogg changed tactic and situated Cereal Mates in supermarket chill cabinets. Mistake number two – who looks in the chill cabinets for breakfast cereal?

Consumers were even more confused by the advertising, which showed kids helping themselves at home while their parents slept. Finally, the price was prohibitive (certainly too high to encourage trial) at around 65p. At the time, you could buy a family-sized box of cereal for not much more than that.

Cereal Mates was eventually killed off when Kellogg finally realised they had confused a change in consumer eating habits with a change in the way people wanted to consume breakfast cereal – not the same thing at all. The company got the strategy right when it eventually launched a product that could be eaten on the go but was only dimly related to cereal – its NutriGrain bars. You have to sense-check your strategy, especially when you're asking your customers to try something radically different.

Summarising Your Marketing Mix

Your *marketing mix* is the combination of marketing activities you use to influence a targeted group of customers to purchase a specific product or line of products. Creating an integrated and coherent marketing mix starts, in our view, with an analysis of your *touchpoints* (see below) – in other words, how your organisation can influence customer purchases. And the creative process ends with some decisions about how to use these touchpoints. Usually you can come up with tactics in all areas of the marketing - product, price, place (or distribution), promotion, people, process and physical presence.

Prioritising your touchpoints and determining cost

Prioritise by picking a few primary touchpoints – ones that will dominate your marketing for the coming planning period. This approach concentrates your resources, giving you more leverage with certain components of the mix. Make the choice carefully; try to pick no more than three main activities to take the lead. Use the other touchpoints in secondary roles to support your primary points. Now begin to develop specific plans for each, consulting later chapters in this book as needed to clarify how to use your various marketing components.

Say that you're considering using print ads in trade magazines to let retail store buyers know about your hot new line of products and the in-store display options you have for them. That's great, but now you need to get specific. You need to pick some magazines. (Call their ad departments for details on their demographics and their prices.) You also need to decide how many of what sort of ads you'll run, and then price out this advertising campaign.

Do the same analysis for each of the items on your list of marketing components. Work your way through the details until you have an initial cost figure for what you want to do with each component. Total these costs and see if the end result seems realistic. Is the total cost too big a share of your projected sales? Or (if you're in a larger business), is your estimate higher than the boss says the budget can go? If so, adjust and try again. After a while, you get a budget that looks acceptable on the bottom line and also makes sense from a practical perspective.

A spreadsheet greatly helps this process. Just build formulas that add the costs to reach subtotals and a grand total, and then subtract the grand total from the projected sales figure to get a bottom line for your campaign. Figure 3-1 shows the format for a very simple spreadsheet that gives a quick and accurate marketing campaign overview for a small business. In this figure, you can see what a campaign looks like for a company that wholesales products to gift shops around the UK. This company uses personal selling, telemarketing and print advertising as its primary marketing components. The company also budgets some money in this period to finish developing and begin introducing a new line of products.

Overview of Campaign to Target Retail Store Buyers	
Components	**Direct Marketing Costs (£)**
Primary influence points:	
– Sales calls	£265,100
– Telemarketing	162,300
– Ads in trade magazines	650,000
– New product line development	100,000
	Subtotal: £1,177,400
Secondary influence points:	
– Quantity discounts	£45,000
– Point-of-purchase displays	73,500
– New Web page with online catalogue	15,000
– Printed catalogue	30,500
– PR	22,000
– Packaging redesign	9,200
	Subtotal: £195,200
Projected Sales from This Programme	£13,676,470
Minus Campaign Costs	– 1,372,600
Net Sales from This Marketing Campaign	**£12,303,870**

Figure 3-1:
A campaign budget, prepared on a spreadsheet.

This company's secondary influence points don't use much of the marketing budget when compared with the primary influence points. But the secondary influence points are important too. A new web page is expected to handle a majority of customer enquiries and act as a virtual catalogue, permitting the company to cut back on its catalogue printing and postage costs. Also, the company plans to introduce a new line of floor displays for use at point of purchase by selected retailers. Marketers expect this display unit, combined with improved see-through packaging, to increase turnover of the company's products in retail stores.

Marketing plans for multiple groups

If your marketing plan covers multiple groups of customers, you need to include multiple spreadsheets (such as the one in Figure 3-1) because each group of customers will need a different marketing mix.

For example, the company whose wholesale marketing campaign you see in Figure 3-1 sells to gift shops. But the company also does some business with stationery shops. And even though the same salespeople call on both, each of these customers has different products and promotions. They buy from different catalogues. They don't use the same kinds of displays. They read different trade magazines. Consequently, the company has to develop a separate marketing campaign for each customer, allocating any overlapping expenses appropriately. (For example, if you make two-thirds of your sales calls to gift shops, then the sales-calls expense for the gift shop campaign should be two-thirds of the total sales budget.)

Exploring Your Marketing Components

In this part of your plan, you need to explain the details of how you aim to use each component of your marketing mix. Devote a section to each component – this part of your plan may be lengthy (give it as many pages as you need to lay out the facts). At a minimum, this part of the plan should have sections covering the product, pricing, place (or distribution), promotion, people, process and physical presence. But more likely, you want to break these categories down into more specific areas.

The more of your thinking you get on paper, the easier implementing the plan will be later, as will rewriting the plan next year.

Don't bother going into detail on components that you can't alter. Sometimes, the person writing the marketing plan can't change pricing policy, order up a new product line or dictate a shift in distribution strategy. Explore your boundaries and try to stretch them, but you need to admit they exist or your plan can't be practical. If you can only control promotion, then this section of the plan should concentrate on the ways that you'll promote the product – in which case, never mind the other Ps. Acknowledge in writing any issues or challenges you have to cope with, given that you can't change other factors. Now write a plan that does everything you can reasonably do given your constraints. (A section called *Constraints* ought to go into the *Situation analysis*, if your company or department has such constraints.)

Managing Your Marketing

The management section of the plan's main purpose is simply to make sure that enough warm bodies are in the right places at the right times to get the work done. This section summarises the main activities that you, your employees or your employer must perform in order to implement the components of your marketing mix. The section then assigns these activities to individuals, justifying the assignments by considering issues such as an individual's capabilities and capacities, and how the company will supervise and control that individual.

Sometimes this section gets more sophisticated by addressing management issues, such as how to make the sales force more productive or whether to decentralise the marketing function. If you have salespeople or distributors, develop plans for organising, motivating, tracking and controlling them. Also create a plan for them to use in generating, allocating and tracking sales leads. Start these subsections by describing the current approach, and do a strengths/weaknesses analysis of that approach, using input from the salespeople, reps or distributors in question. End by describing any incremental changes/improvements you can think to make.

Make sure that you've run your ideas by the people in question *first* and received their input. Don't surprise your salespeople, sales reps or distributors with new systems or methods. If you do, these people will probably resist the changes, and sales will slow down. So schmooze and share, persuade and propose, and enable them to feel involved in the planning process. People execute sales plans well only if they understand and believe in those plans.

Projecting Expenses and Revenues

Now you need to put on your accounting and project management hats. (Perhaps neither hat fits very well but try to bear them for a day or two.) You need these hats to:

- ✓ Estimate future sales, in units and by value, for each product in your plan.
- ✓ Justify these estimates and, if they're hard to justify, create worst-case versions, too.
- ✓ Draw a timeline showing when your marketing incurs costs and when each component begins and ends. (Doing so helps with the preceding section and also prepares you for the unpleasant task of designing a monthly marketing budget.)
- ✓ Write a monthly marketing budget that lists all the estimated costs of your activity for each month of the coming year and breaks down sales by product, territory and month.

If you're a start-up or small business, we highly recommend doing all your projections on a *cash basis*. In other words, put the payment for your year's supply of brochures in the month in which the printer wants the money, instead of allocating that cost across 12 months. Also factor in the wait time for collecting your sales revenues. If collections take 30 days, show money coming in during December from November's sales, and don't count any December sales for this year's plan. A cash basis may upset accountants, who like to do things on an accrual basis – see *Accounting For Dummies*, 4th Edition, by John A. Tracy (Wiley) if you don't know what that means; cash-based accounting keeps small businesses alive. You want a positive cash balance (or at least to break even) on the bottom line during every month of your plan.

If your cash-based projection shows a loss in some months, fiddle with the plan to eliminate that loss (or arrange to borrow money to cover the gap). Sometimes a careful cash-flow analysis of a plan leads to changes in underlying strategy. One B2B company made its primary marketing objective the goal of getting more customers to pay with credit cards instead of on invoices. The company's business customers co-operated, and average collection time shortened from 45 days to under 10, greatly improving the cash flow and thus the spending power and profitability of the business.

Several helpful techniques are available for projecting sales, such as build-up forecasts, indicator forecasts and time-period forecasts. Choose the most appropriate technique for your business based on the reviews in this section. If you're feeling nervous, just use the technique that gives you the most conservative projection. Here's a common way to play it safe: use several of the techniques and average their results.

Build-up forecasts

These predictions go from the specific to the general, or from the bottom up. If you have sales reps or salespeople, ask each one to project the next period's sales for their territories and justify their projections based on what changes in the situation they anticipate. Then aggregate all the sales force's forecasts to obtain an overall figure.

If you have few enough customers that you can project per-customer purchases, build up your forecast this way. You may want to work from reasonable estimates of the amount of sales you can expect from each shop carrying your products or from each thousand catalogues sent out. Whatever the basic building blocks of your marketing, start with an estimate for each element and then add these estimates up.

Indicator forecasts

This method links your forecast to economic indicators that ought to vary with sales. For example, if you're in the construction business, you find that past sales for your industry correlate with *gross domestic product* (known as *GDP* or national output) growth. So you can adjust your sales forecast up or down depending upon whether experts expect the economy to grow rapidly or slowly in the next year.

Multiple scenario forecasts

You base these forecasts on what-if stories. They start with a straight-line forecast in which you assume that your sales will grow by the same percentage next year as they did last year. Then you make up what-if stories and project their impact on your plan to create various alternative projections.

You may try the following scenarios if they're relevant to your situation:

- ✔ What if a competitor introduces a technological breakthrough?
- ✔ What if your company acquires a competitor?
- ✔ What if the government deregulates/regulates your industry?
- ✔ What if a leading competitor fails?
- ✔ What if your company has financial problems and has to lay off some of its sales and marketing people?
- ✔ What if your company doubles its ad spending?

For each scenario, think about how customer demand may change. Also consider how your marketing would need to change in order to best suit the situation. Then make an appropriate sales projection. For example, if a competitor introduced a technological breakthrough, you might guess that your sales would fall 25 per cent short of your straight-line projection.

The trouble with multiple scenario analysis is that . . . well, it gives you multiple scenarios. Your boss (if you have one) wants a single sales projection, a one-liner at the top of your marketing budget. One way to turn all those options into one number or series of numbers is to just pick the option that seems most likely to you. That's not a very satisfying method if you aren't at all sure which option, if any, will come true. So another method involves taking all the options that seem even remotely possible, assigning each a probability of occurring in the next year, multiplying each by its probability and then averaging them all to get a single number.

For example, the 'cautious scenario' projection estimates £5 million, and the 'optimistic scenario' projection estimates £10 million. The probability of the cautious scenario occurring is 15 per cent, and the probability of the optimistic scenario occurring is 85 per cent. So you find the sales projection with this formula: [(£5,000,000 × 0.15) + (£10,000,000 × 0.85)] ÷ 2 = £4,630,000.

Time-period projections

To use this method, work by week or month, estimating the size of sales in each time period and then add up these estimates for the entire year. This approach helps you when your marketing activity or the market isn't constant across the entire year. Ski resorts use this method because they get certain types of revenue only at certain times of the year. Marketers who plan to introduce new products during the year or to use heavy advertising in one or two *pulses* (concentrated time periods) also use this method because their sales go up significantly during those periods. Entrepreneurs, small businesses and any others on a tight cash-flow lead need to use this method because it provides a good idea of what cash will be flowing in by week or month. An annual sales figure doesn't tell you enough about when the money comes in to know whether you'll be short of cash in specific periods during the year.

Creating Your Controls

This section is the last and shortest of your plan but in many ways, is the most important. This section allows you and others to track performance.

Identify some performance benchmarks and state them clearly in the plan. For example:

- All sales territories should be using the new catalogues and sales scripts by 1 June.

- Revenues should grow to £75,000 per month by the end of the first quarter if the promotional campaign works according to plan.

These statements give you (and, unfortunately, your employers or investors) easy ways to monitor performance as you implement the marketing plan. Without these targets, nobody has control over the plan; nobody can tell whether or how well the plan is working. With these statements, you can identify unexpected results or delays quickly – in time for appropriate responses if you've designed these controls properly.

A good marketing plan gives you focus and a sense of direction, and increases your likelihood to succeed, but writing a good one takes time and many businesses don't have a lot of that to spare. A sensible rule is to spend time on your marketing plan, but not so much that you don't have a chance to look up and see whether the market has changed since you started writing it. If the plan you wrote at the start of the year is no longer relevant because business conditions have changed quickly, tear it up and start again – don't stick rigidly to something that's no longer relevant just because it's there.

Using Planning Templates and Aids

Referring to model plans can help you in this process. Unfortunately, most companies don't release their plans; they rightly view them as trade secrets. Fortunately, a few authors have compiled plans or portions of them, and you can find some good published materials to work from.

Several books provide sample marketing plans and templates. These texts show you alternative outlines for plans and include budgets and revenue projections in many formats, one of which may suit your needs pretty closely:

- *The Marketing Kit For Dummies*, by Greg Brooks, Ruth Mortimer and Alex Hiam (Wiley), includes a five-minute marketing plan worksheet if you're the impatient sort

- *The Marketing Plan*, by William Cohen (Wiley), is a practical step-by-step guide that features sample plans from real businesses

- *The Marketing Planning Tool* is available online free to both members and non-members through the 'Marketing Shop' section of the Chartered Institute of Marketing's website (www.cim.co.uk)

Chapter 4

Brochures, Press Ads and Print

- -

In This Chapter

▶ Recognising the elements of printed advertising

▶ Understanding design and layout issues

▶ Designing with type

▶ Designing the simplest print product of all – brochures

▶ Placing and testing your print ad

- -

Most marketers budget more for print advertising than any other type – the exception being the major national or multinational brands that market largely on television. But for most local and regional advertising, print probably provides the most flexible and effective all-around marketing medium, although Internet advertising is fast eating into this lead.

Print advertising also integrates well with many other marketing media. You can use written brochures and other sales support materials (which have many design elements in common with print advertising) to support personal selling. Similarly a print ad in a magazine can generate leads for direct marketing. Print ads also work well to announce sales promotions or distribute coupons.

Anyone with a basic computer and inkjet printer can now set up shop and create her own fliers, brochures, business cards and ad layouts. In fact, Microsoft Office includes a number of excellent templates that simplify layout and allow you to bang out a new brochure or other printed marketing piece in as little as an hour. Print advertising and print-based marketing are the backbone of most marketing campaigns, even in today's high-tech world.

Designing Printed Marketing Materials

Many marketers start with their printed marketing materials (such as ads, brochures or downloadable PDF product literature on their websites) and then work outwards from there to incorporate the appeal and design concepts from their printed materials or ads into other forms of marketing. (A common look and feel should unite your print ads, brochures and website.)

Brochures, *tear sheets* (one-page, catalogue-style descriptions of products), posters for outdoor advertising, direct mail letters and catalogues all share the basic elements of good print advertising: good copy and visuals alongside eye-catching headlines. All good marketers thus need mastery of print advertising as an essential part of their knowledge base. This section covers the essentials.

When designing anything in print, remember this: your ad's purpose is to stimulate a sale. Think ahead to that goal. What will people see when they make that purchase? If your product sells in shops, create signs, packaging, displays or coupons that echo the ad's theme and remind the buyer of it. If you're selling online, make sure you provide a web address on your print ads that helps the consumer to find the product you're advertising. If you make the sale in person, supply the salespeople or distributors with catalogues, order forms, PowerPoint presentations or brochures (see the 'Producing Brochures, Fliers and More' section later in this chapter) that are consistent with your design, to remind them of the ad that began the sales process. If you intend contacting the customer after the sale, ensure that any mailings continue the look and feel of the ad that began the sales process.

Dissecting printed materials

Before you can create great printed marketing materials, you need to dissect an ad, brochure, tear sheet or similar printed marketing matter and identify its parts. Inside most printed marketing materials, you'll find parts and each part has a special name:

- ✔ **Headline:** The large-print words that first attract the eye, usually at the top of the page.
- ✔ **Subhead:** The optional addition to the headline to provide more detail, also in large (but not quite as large) print.
- ✔ **Copy or body copy:** The main text, set in a readable size.
- ✔ **Visual:** An illustration that makes a visual statement. This image may be the main focus of the ad or other printed material (especially when you've designed an ad to show readers your product), or it may be secondary to the copy. Such an image is also optional. After all, most

classified ads use no visuals at all, yet classifieds are effective for the simple reason that people make a point of looking for them (instead of making a point to avoid them, as many people do with other types of ads!).

✔ **Caption:** Copy attached to the visual to explain or discuss that picture. You usually place a caption beneath the visual, but you can put it on any side or even within or on the image.

✔ **Logo:** A unique design that represents the brand or company (like Nike's swoosh). Register logos as trademarks.

✔ **Signature:** The company's trademarked version of its name. Often, advertisers use a logo design that features a brand name in a distinctive font and style. The signature is a written equivalent to the logo's visual identity. Here's how a furniture maker called Heritage Colonial Furniture may do it:

HERITAGE

Colonial Furniture®

✔ **Slogan:** An optional element consisting of a (hopefully) short phrase evoking the spirit or personality of the brand. For example, when you think of sportswear company Nike, you immediately conjure up its famous slogan summing up the brand in three short words: 'Just Do It.' The creation of this slogan, voted one of the top five ad slogans of the twentieth century by *Advertising Age* magazine, is designed to emphasise the characteristics of the brand – Nike represents achievement, whether that means winning, taking part or just enjoying yourself. The slogan is broad enough to work in tandem with the theme of any advert – such as athletes running their hardest or footballers attempting to score a goal. The furniture maker Heritage Colonial, used earlier, could use 'Bringing the elegance and quality of early antiques to the modern home' as its slogan.

The shorter and snappier the slogan, the more likely it is to be recalled by the consumer.

Figure 4-1 shows each of these elements in a rough design for a print ad (a brochure's layout is a bit more complicated and is covered later in this chapter). We use generic terms in place of actual parts of an ad ('headline' for the headline, for example) so that you can easily see all the elements in action. This fairly simple palette for a print ad design allows you endless variation and creativity. You can say or show anything, and you can do so in many different ways. (And you can use this layout for a one-page marketing sheet to include in folders or as handouts at trade shows even if you aren't buying space to run the ad in a magazine or newspaper.)

Figure 4-1:
The
elements of
a print ad.

Putting the parts together: Design and layout

Design refers to the look, feel and style of your ad or other printed marketing materials. Design is an aesthetic concept and, thus, putting it into precise terms is difficult. But design is vitally important: it has to take the basic appeal of your product and make that appeal work visually on paper.

Book V

Marketing
and
Advertising
Your
Wares

Specifically, the design needs to overcome the marketer's constant problem: nobody cares about your advertising. So the design must somehow reach out to readers, grab their attention, hold it long enough to communicate the appeal of the product you're advertising and attach that appeal to the brand name in the readers' memories.

A memorable photograph is often the easiest way to grab attention. Depending on your brand or product, you could choose options such as an interesting face, a photo of a child or a beautiful scene, as long as you can make the image relevant in some way to your product; pretty much anything that grabs attention goes.

Great advertising has to rise off the page, reach out and grab you by the eyeballs. In the cluttered world of modern print-based marketing, this design goal is the only one that really works. So we want you to tape up a selection of ads from the same publication(s) that yours will go in (or use samples of competitor brochures or catalogue sheets or whatever exactly it is you'll be designing in print). Put a draft of your design up along with these bench-marks. Step back – a long way back. Now, does your ad grab the eye more than all the others? If not . . . back to the drawing board!

Understanding the stages in design

Designers often experiment with numerous layouts for their print ads or other printed materials before selecting one for formal development. We strongly recommend that you do the same or insist that your designer or agency does the same. The more layouts you look at, the more likely you are to get an original idea that has eye-grabbing power. But whether you design your own print materials or have experts do the work for you, you want to be familiar with the design stages.

✔ **Step 1. Thumbnails:** The rough sketches designers use to describe layout concepts are called *thumbnails*. They're usually small, quick sketches in pen or pencil. You can also use professional design and layout packages like Quark XPress or InDesign to create thumbnails.

✔ **Step 2. Roughs:** Designers then develop thumbnails with promise into *roughs* – full-size sketches with headlines and subheads drawn carefully enough to give the feel of a particular font and *style* (the appearance of the printed letters). Roughs also have sketches for the illustrations. The designers suggest body copy using lines (or nonsense characters, if the designer does the rough using a computer).

Are you using an ad agency or design firm to develop your print ads or other printed marketing materials? Sometimes clients of ad agencies insist on seeing designs in the rough stage, to avoid the expense of having those designs developed more fully before presentation. We recommend that you ask to see rough versions of your designs, too, even if your agency hesitates to show you its work in unfinished form. When the agency realises that you appreciate the design process and don't criticise the roughs simply because they're unfinished, you can give the agency more guidance and help during the design process.

✔ **Step 3. Comprehensive layout:** Designers then develop chosen roughs into a *comp* (short for *comprehensive layout*). A comp should look pretty much like a final version of the design, although designers produce a comp on a one-time basis, so the comp may use paste-ups in place of the intended photos, colour photocopies, typeset copy and headlines. Designers used to assemble comps by hand, but now most designers and agencies do their comps on computer. A high-end PC and colour printer can produce something that looks almost like the final printed version of a four-colour ad or other printed marketing material. Designers refer to a computer-made comp as a *full-colour proof*.

✔ **Step 4. Dummy:** A *dummy* is a form of comp that simulates the feel – as well as the look – of the final design. (Every design should have a feel or personality of its own, just as products should have a personality. Often you can create the best personality for your ad simply by carrying over the brand identity you've created for the product. Consistency helps.) Dummies are especially important for brochures or special inserts to magazines, where the designer often specifies special paper and folds. By doing a dummy comp, you can evaluate the feel of the design while you're evaluating its appearance.

Designing and submitting your ads the old-fashioned way

The traditional way to submit a design to a printing firm was to generate what printers call *camera-ready artwork*, a version of the design suitable for the printer to photograph with a large-scale production camera in order to generate *colour keys* (to convert colours to specific inks) and *films*, clear sheets for each layer of colour to be printed. You (or the designer) would produce this camera-ready art by making a *mechanical* or *paste-up*, in which typeset copy, visuals and all the other elements of the design go onto a foam-core board, using a hot wax machine.

The hot wax machine heated wax and spread it on a roller so that you could roll a thin layer of warm wax onto the back of each element. The wax stuck each piece neatly to the board, allowing those pieces to be peeled off easily, in case you wanted to reposition anything. When you had everything the way you wanted it, this was the point when you would send the artwork off to your printer.

Designing and submitting your ads on a computer

If you're quick and able on a computer and like to work in design and layout programs (such as Adobe InDesign or Quark XPress), you can do the same kind of creative rough designing simply by searching for images on the Web. (To find an image, try specifying an image search in Google, but remember not to use copyrighted images in your final design without permission or payment. Plenty of royalty-free image websites are available, or consider budding photographers who won't charge too much for using their pictures.) Copy the chosen images onto your computer and you can click and drag them into different programs and pages.

Invest a bit of time and effort in honing these computer-based design techniques. Look up the latest *For Dummies* books on how to use Quark Xpress, Adobe InDesign or any other design and layout program of your choice, or just work in Microsoft Word, which is pretty impressive in its latest incarnations as a basic design program itself. Also, take a look at the growing number of great-looking ad templates you can purchase online and then adapt them in any of the common graphic design programs. As an example, see many options at www.stocklayouts.com or www.mycreativeshop.com.

When your preliminary design is ready for the printer, you (or the ad agency) can send the design over the Web using desktop publishing software. You can even do the colour separations for four-colour work on your PC and send those colour separations too. (Ask the printer for instructions to make sure that you submit the design in a format that their system can use.) The printer then makes plates for printing the design straight from the file that you've emailed to them. (*Plates* are metal or plastic sheets with your design on them – the printer applies the ink to the plates when the printing press does its thing.)

Until recently, electronic submission to printing firms generally had to be done from a professional software package like Quark XPress, but increasingly, printers are accepting Word files or PDF files generated by Acrobat (lots of people prefer this route because it reduces the chances of incompatibility problems). And if you're designing in a recent version of Word, you'll find that creating a PDF file can be done from your program because Acrobat is now built in.

Finding your font

A *font* is a particular design's attributes for the *characters* (letters, numbers and symbols) used in printing your design. *Typeface* refers only to the distinctive design of the letters (Times New Roman, for example). Font, on the other hand, actually refers to one particular size and style of a typeface design (such as 10-point, bold, Times New Roman).

The right font for any job is the one that makes your text easily readable and harmonises with the overall design most effectively. For a headline, the font also needs to grab the reader's attention. The body copy doesn't have to grab attention in the same way – in fact, if it does, the copy often loses readability. For example, a *reverse font* (light or white type on dark paper) may be just the thing for a bold headline, but if you use it in the body copy, too, nobody reads your copy because doing so's just too hard on the eye.

Choosing a typeface

What sort of typeface do you want? You have an amazing number of choices because designers have been developing typefaces for as long as printing presses have existed. (Just click on the font toolbar in Microsoft Word to see an assortment of the more popular typefaces.)

A clean, sparse design, with a lot of white space on the page and stark contrasts in the artwork, deserves the clean lines of a *sans serif typeface* – meaning one that doesn't have any decorative *serifs* (those little bars or flourishes at the ends of the main lines in a character). The most popular body-copy fonts without serifs are Helvetica, Arial, Univers and Avant Garde. Figure 4-2 shows some fonts with and without serifs.

Figure 4-2: Fonts with and without serifs.

A richly decorative, old-fashioned sort of design, in contrast, needs a more decorative and traditional serif typeface, such as Century or Times New Roman. The most popular body-copy fonts with serifs include Garamond, Melior, Century, Times New Roman and Caledonia.

Table 4-1 shows an assortment of typeface choices, in which you can compare the clean lines of Helvetica, Avant Garde and Arial with the more decorative designs of Century, Garamond and Times New Roman.

Table 4-1	**Popular Fonts for Ads**
Sans Serif	*Serif*
Helvetica	Century
Arial	Garamond
Univers	Melior
Avant Garde	Times New Roman

In tests, Helvetica and Century generally top the lists as most readable, so start with one of these typefaces for your body copy; only change the font if it doesn't seem to work. Also, research shows that people read lowercase letters about 13 per cent faster than uppercase letters, so avoid long stretches of copy set in all capital letters. People also read most easily when letters are dark and contrast strongly with their background. Thus, black 14-point Helvetica on white is probably the most readable font specification for the body copy of an ad (or other printed marketing materials), even if the combination does seem dull to a sophisticated designer.

Generalising about the best kind of headline typeface is no easy task because designers play around with headlines to a greater extent than they do with body copy. But, as a general rule, you can use Helvetica for the headline when you use Century for the body, and the other way round. Or you can just use a bolder, larger version of the body copy font for your headline. You can also reverse a larger, bold version of your type onto a black background for the headline. Use anything to make the headline grab the reader's attention, stand out from the body copy and ultimately lead her vision and curiosity into the body copy's text. (Remember to keep the headline readable – nothing too fancy, please.)

Sometimes the designer combines body copy of a decorative typeface, one with serifs, like Times New Roman, with headers of a sans serif typeface, like Helvetica. The contrast between the clean lines of the large-sized header and the more decorative characters of the smaller body copy pleases the eye and tends to draw the reader from header to body copy. This book uses that technique. Compare the sans serif bold characters of this chapter's title with the more delicate and decorative characters in which the publishers set the text for a good example of this design concept in action.

Making style choices within the typeface

Any typeface gives the user many choices and so selecting the typeface is just the beginning of the project when you design your print. Other questions include: how big should the characters be? Do you want to use the standard version of the typeface, a lighter version, a **bold** (or darker) version or an *italic* version (one that leans to the right)? The process is easier than it sounds. Just look at samples of some standard point sizes (12- and 14-point text for the body copy, for example, with 24-, 36- and 48-point for the headlines). Many designers make their choice by eye, looking for an easy-to-read size that isn't so large that it causes the words or sentences to break up into too many fragments across the page – but not so small that it gives the reader too many words per line. Keep readability in mind as the goal.

Figure 4-3 shows a variety of size and style choices for the Helvetica typeface. As you can see, you have access to a wonderful range of options, even within this one popular design.

Helvetica Light 14 point

Helvetica Italic 14 point

Helvetica Bold 14 point

Helvetica Regular 14 point

Helvetica Regular 24 point

Helvetica Regular Condensed 14 point

Helvetica Bold Outline 24 point

Figure 4-3: Some of the many choices that the Helvetica typeface offers designers.

Keep in mind that you can change just about any aspect of type. You can alter the distance between lines – called the *leading* – or you can squeeze characters together or stretch them apart to make a word fit a space. Assume that anything is possible. Ask your printer or consult the manual of your desktop publishing or word-processing software to find out how to make a change.

While anything is possible, be warned that your customers' eyes read type quite conservatively. Although most of us know little about the design of typefaces, we find traditional designs instinctively appealing. The spacing of characters and lines, the balance and flow of individual characters – all these familiar typeface considerations please the eye and make reading easy and pleasurable. So, although you should know that you can change anything and everything, you must also know that too many changes may reduce your design's readability. Figure 4-4 shows the same ad laid out twice – once in an eye-pleasing way and once in a disastrous way.

Don't just play with type for the sake of playing (as the designer did in the left-hand version of the classified ad in Figure 4-4). Stick with popular fonts, in popular sizes, except where you have to solve a problem or you want to make a special point. The advent of desktop publishing has led to a horrifying generation of advertisements in which dozens of fonts dance across the page, bolds and italics fight each other for attention and the design of the words becomes a barrier to reading, rather than an aid.

WHEN LIFE GIVES YOU LEMONS...

What should you do? Juggle them? Make lemonade? Open a farm stand? Or give up and go home to Momma?

WHO KNOWS? It's often hard to come to grips with pressing personal or career problems. Sometimes it's hardest to see your *own* problems clearly. Fortunately, JEN KNOWS. Jen Fredrics has twenty years of counseling experience, a master's in social work, and a busy practice in personal problem solving. Call her today to find out how to turn your problems into opportunities.

And next time, when life gives you lemons, you'll know just what to make. An appointment.

WHEN LIFE GIVES YOU LEMONS...

What should you do? Juggle them? Make lemonade? Open a farm stand? Or give up and go home to Momma?

WHO KNOWS? It's often hard to come to grips with pressing personal or career problems. Sometimes it's hardest to see your own problems clearly. Fortunately, JEN KNOWS. Jen Fredrics has twenty years of counseling experience, a master's in social work, and a busy practice in personal problem solving. Call her today to find out how to turn your problems into opportunities.

And next time, when life gives you lemons, you'll know just what to make. An appointment.

Figure 4-4:
Which copy would you rather read?

Choosing a point size

When designers and printers talk about *point sizes*, they're referring to a traditional measure of the height of the letters (based on the highest and lowest parts of the biggest letters). One *point* equals about $\frac{1}{72}$ of an inch, so a 10-point type is $\frac{10}{72}$ of an inch high, at the most.

Personally, we don't really care – we've never measured a character with a ruler. We just know that if the letters seem too small for easy reading, then we need to bump the typeface up a couple of points. Ten-point type is too small for most body copy but you may want to use that size if you have to squeeze several words into a small space. (But why do that? You're usually better off editing your body copy and then bumping up the font size to make it more readable!) Your eye can't distinguish easily between fonts that are only one or two sizes apart, so specify a larger jump than that to distinguish between body copy and subhead or between subhead and headline.

Producing Brochures, Fliers and More

You can get your print design out to the public in an easy and inexpensive way, using brochures, fliers, posters and many other forms – your imagination is the only limit to what you can do with a good design for all your printed materials. Your word-processing or graphics software, a good inkjet or laser printer, and the help of your local photocopy or print shop (which should also have folding machines) allow you to design and produce brochures quite easily and also come up with many other forms of printed marketing materials. In this section, however, we focus largely on a basic brochure, because this form's easy, a business staple and effective at marketing your company.

You can also do small runs (100 or less) straight from a colour printer. Buy matte or glossy brochure paper designed for your brand of printer and simply select the appropriate paper type in the print dialog box. Today's inexpensive inkjet printers can produce stunning brochures. But you have to fold these brochures yourself and the ink cartridges aren't cheap. So print as needed or try contacting your local copy shop. Kall Kwik and many other copy shops now accept emailed copies of files and can produce short runs of your brochures, pamphlets, catalogue sheets or other printed materials on their colour copiers directly from your file.

Many brochures foolishly waste money because they don't accomplish any specific marketing goals; they just look pretty, at best. To avoid creating an attractive, but pointless, brochure that doesn't achieve a sales goal, make sure that you know:

- ✔ Who will read the brochure.
- ✔ How they will get the brochure.
- ✔ What they should discover from and do after reading the brochure.

These three questions focus your brochure design and make it useful to your marketing.

Marketers often order a brochure without a clear idea of what purpose the brochure should serve. They just think a brochure is a good idea: 'Oh, we need them to, you know, put in the envelope along with a letter, or, um, for our salespeople to keep in the boots of their cars; maybe we'll send some out to our mailing list or give them away at the next trade show.'

With this many possibilities, the brochure can't be properly suited to any single use. It becomes a dull, vague scrap of paper that just talks about the company or product but doesn't hit readers over the head with any particular appeal and call to action – something that's become increasingly important, as consumers can look up information about your company online at any time.

Book V

Marketing
and
Advertising
Your
Wares

Listing your top three uses

Define up to three specific uses for the brochure. No more than three, though, because your design can't accomplish more than three purposes effectively. The most common and appropriate uses for a brochure are:

- ✔ To act as a reference on the product, or technical details of the product, for sales prospects.

- ✔ To support a personal selling effort by lending credibility and helping overcome objections.

- ✔ To generate leads through a direct-mail campaign.

Say you want to design a brochure that does all three of these tasks well. Start by designing the contents. What product and technical information must be included? Write the information down and collect necessary illustrations, so that you have the *fact base* (the essential information to communicate) in front of you.

Writing about strengths and weaknesses

After you've created your fact base (see the preceding section), organise these points in such a way that they highlight your product's (or service's) greatest strengths and overcome its biggest challenges. Don't know what your product's strengths and weaknesses are? List the following, as they relate to sales:

- ✔ The common sales objections or reasons prospects give for not wanting to buy your product.

- ✔ Customers' favourite reasons for buying, or the aspects of your product and business that customers like most.

With your fact base organised accordingly, you're ready to begin writing. Your copy needs to read as if you're listening to customers' concerns and answering each concern with an appropriate response. You can write subheads in the format: 'Our Product Doesn't Need XXX' and 'Our Product Brings You XXX' so that salespeople or prospects can easily see how your facts (in copy and/or illustrations) overcome each specific objection and highlight all the major benefits.

Incorporating a clear, compelling appeal

Add some basic appeal communicated in a punchy headline and a few dozen words of copy, along with an appropriate and eye-catching illustration. You need to include this appeal to help the brochure stand on its own as a marketing tool when it's sent out to leads by post or passed on from a prospect or customer to one of her professional contacts.

The appeal needs to project a winning personality. Your brochure can be fun or serious, emotional or factual – but it must be appealing. The appeal is the bait that draws the prospect to your hook, so make sure your hook is well baited!

Putting it all together

When you have all the parts – the appeal, the fact base and the design – you're ready to put your brochure together. The appeal, with its enticing headline and compelling copy and visual, goes on the front of the brochure – or the outside when you fold it for mailing, or the central panel out of three if you fold a sheet twice. The subheads that structure the main copy respond to objections and highlight strengths on the inside pages. You then organise the fact base, for reference use, in the copy and illustrations beneath these subheads.

Although you can design a brochure in many ways, we often prefer the format (along with dimensions for text blocks or illustrations) in Figure 4-5. This format is simple and inexpensive because you print the brochure on a single sheet of 490mm × 210mm paper that you then fold three times. The brochure fits in a standard DL (110mm × 220mm) envelope or you can tape it together along the open fold and mail it on its own. This layout allows for some detail, but not enough to get you into any real trouble. (Larger formats and multi-page pieces tend to fill up with the worst, wordiest copy, and nobody ever reads those pieces.)

You can use the design shown in Figure 4-5 for direct mailings to generate sales leads and you can also hand the brochure out or use it for reference in direct-selling situations. You can produce this brochure, using any popular desktop publishing software and you can print and fold it at the local copy shop (if you don't need the thousands of copies that make offset printing cost-effective). To convert this design to a simpler, cheaper format, use A4 paper and eliminate the *return mailer* (the left-hand page on the front, the right-hand on the back, which can be returned with the blanks filled in to request information or accept a special offer). If you do remove the return mailer, include follow-up instructions and contact information on an inside page!

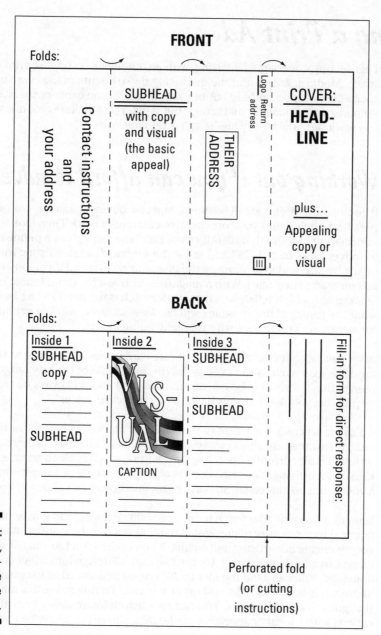

Figure 4-5:
A simple, multi-purpose brochure layout.

Placing a Print Ad

This section covers *media buying*, with an emphasis on buying print ad space. Media agencies and the marketing departments of big companies have specialists who do nothing but buy media, and some brokers specialise in it for mid-sized or smaller marketers. But if you're a smaller-scale marketer, you can work out how to buy media space on your own.

Working out if you can afford to advertise

If you're marketing a small business, start by buying magazines or newspapers that you're sure your prospective customers read. Then look for the information in them that identifies the publisher and gives a phone number for advertisers to call. Call and request a *rate card* (a table listing the prices of ads by size and also showing the discount rate per ad if you buy multiple ads instead of just one). With a magazine, also ask for the *schedule* or *forward features list*, which tells you when ads for each issue need to be placed and what the topics of future issues will be. Alternatively, you can get information for advertisers on the websites of many publications.

After you've collected a selection of rate cards, take a hard look at the pricing. How expensive is the average ad (in the middle of the size range for each publication)? This may be a broad number and should always be treated as negotiable: you don't always have to pay rate card prices!

If a single ad costs 5 per cent or more of your marketing budget for the entire year, throw the rate sheets away and forget about advertising there. Your business isn't currently operating on a large enough scale to be able to do this kind of advertising. You need dozens of ad placements at a minimum to make a good print ad campaign, so don't begin unless you can afford to keep going.

Instead of blowing that much money on a single ad, spread it over more economical forms of advertising and marketing, such as brochures, mailings, search engine advertising and emails. If you operate on too small a scale or budget to afford advertising, try turning that ad design into a flier and mailing it instead. You can send the flier to 200 names and see what happens. This approach is a lot less risky and expensive than buying space in a magazine that goes to 200,000 names. You can also search for smaller-circulation publications with a local or specialist readership, where rates may be cheaper.

Finding inexpensive places to advertise

Many local businesses buy ad space in theatre programmes. What does this cost? About £550 for a quarter page colour ad for three months in one theatre in a small town. Compare that price to a full-colour ad in a national newspaper, which can cost £50,000. That's a big difference! If buying ads in the best publications to reach your market is too expensive, you can always find smaller-circulation publications that charge less.

One great way to advertise for less is to take advantage of the tens of thousands of newsletters published by professional groups and interest groups. You can buy ad space in 10 or 20 such newsletters for far less money than buying one ad insertion in a national daily newspaper. But you may have to be creative and persistent, because opportunities to advertise in newsletters aren't as obvious as with larger and more professional publications.

Professional associations' monthly newsletters provide an excellent opportunity for small-budget advertising. Professionals are people who have buying power, so even if you don't sell a product aimed at the people the newsletter is written for, they may still respond to your ad. Some insurance agents have advertised successfully in newsletters that go to doctors, for example. Increasingly, newsletters are published in web versions in addition to – or even instead of – print versions. With a web publication, you can take advantage of the larger reach of the Internet to reach more people while paying the lower price of a small publication.

Also explore local newspapers. You can find hundreds of newspapers and weeklies with *circulation* (readership) in the tens of thousands, which means their rates for ads are one-fifth to one-tenth the price of a national newspaper. Of course, you don't reach as many people, either – advertising tends to be priced on a *cost per thousand readers* basis (the cost of buying that ad divided by the number of readers who read the publication, then multiplied by 1,000). You generally get as much exposure as you're willing to pay for. But by buying ads in small-circulation publications, you avoid taking huge risks and you minimise your investment. If an ad pays off, you can try running it in additional publications. But if the ad doesn't produce the results you want, you can afford to write off the cost without feeling too much pain.

Keep the scale of your print advertising (and indeed any advertising) at a level you're comfortable with, even if your ad doesn't produce any sales. Although that outcome's certainly not your goal, zero sales are always a possibility and you want to base your buying decision on that possibility.

Selecting the ad size

What size ad should you buy? The answer depends in part on the design of your ad. Does the ad have a strong, simple visual or headline that catches the eye, even if it only takes up a third of a page? Or does the ad need to be displayed in a larger format to work well? In addition to your (or your designer's) judgement about the specifics of your ad, take into account some general statistics on what percentage of readers *notice* an ad, based on its size. As you may expect, the rate goes up with size – bigger ads get more notice (all other things being equal), according to a study by US research company, Media Dynamics (see Table 4-2).

Table 4-2	Selecting the Right Size
Size of Ad	*Index (Recall Scores)*
Page, colour	100
2-page spread, colour	130
⅔-page vertical, colour	81
½-page horizontal, colour	72

Remember: the bigger the ad, the bigger the impact. But the percentage of readers noticing your ad doesn't go up *in proportion* to the increase in size. Doubling the size of an ad gives you about a quarter more readers, not twice as many, which is partly a full-page ad isn't twice the cost of a half-page ad.

If you're watching your pennies, a full-page ad is often your best choice. Even though a large ad costs more, it's sufficiently more noticeable than smaller sizes, which means you'll reach more readers and, thus, bring the cost per exposure down a bit. However, remember that while a full-page ad is more economical, it's also more risky, because you'll have blown more money if it doesn't work. You may want to test a new design with a quarter-page, inexpensive ad and, if that pays off, buy a full-page ad next time.

Testing and improving your print ad

Is anybody actually reading your ad? A *direct-response ad*, one that asks readers to take a measurable action such as calling, texting a mobile phone number or going to a shop, gives you a quick, clear indication of that ad's effectiveness. Say you expect to receive a lot of enquiries and orders over the telephone during the week the issue with your ad goes on sale. If you don't receive those calls, you know you have a problem. Now what?

Book V

Marketing
and
Advertising
Your
Wares

Troubleshooting your ad

What if you want to know more about why that direct-response ad didn't get the desired level of response? Or what if you want to study an *indirect-response ad* – one that creates or strengthens an image or position in order to encourage sales? Much brand advertising is indirect, leaving it to the retailer or local office to close the sale. No phones ring, whether consumers liked the ad or not, so how do you know whether the ad worked?

To get this sort of information, you can go to a market research firm and have your ad tested for effectiveness. If you plan to spend more than £100,000 on print ads, you can probably consider the £1300 or so needed to hire a research firm to pre-test the ad money well spent. *Pre-testing* means exposing people to the ad in a controlled setting and measuring their reactions to it.

To test an ad's effectiveness, use one of the free techniques in 'Getting ad analysis for free' later in this chapter: you can assemble your own panel of customers and ask them to rate your ad and give you feedback about why they do or don't find that ad appealing. This feedback can give you ideas for an improved version next time. You can also tap into the large-scale studies of ad readership done by research firms. Just subscribe to the study, and the firm feeds you detailed data about how well each ad you publish works.

Commercial media research services can give you information such as what your competitors are up to in terms of advertising and how much they're spending. TNS Media Intelligence (www.tns-mi.com) and Nielsen (www.nielsen.com) are the best known companies. Using their services, you can find out exactly what your competitors are up to, where they're spending their advertising money and how much they're spending, enabling you to plan your own campaigns accordingly. Other services such as GfK NOP Media (www.gfknop.com) can help you to find out to what extent consumers notice or read an ad and to measure the level of interest an ad generated.

Say that GfK NOP data shows that readership of your ad falls lower than average and that, although many people note the ad, few read enough to get the point or the brand name. Should you kill this ad and start again? The answer depends on what's wrong with the ad. Sometimes using the data provided by these research companies can help you to identify a fixable problem. Maybe your headline and photo work well, but the body copy doesn't work with consumers. You can try rewriting and shortening the copy, or changing the layout or fonts. Perhaps the body copy is in reverse font, which consumers find hard to read. Often, switching the text to dark letters on a white or light background can help, without the need for any other changes!

Or maybe you need to switch from a black-and-white or two-colour visual to a four-colour one. You have to pay more, but the resulting ad may yield a better return. Studies show that consumers recall full-colour ads better than two-colour ads, which in turn outperform mono ads. So, as with size, more is better in relation to colours. However, you need to run the numbers to see how the extra costs and extra readers affect your cost-per-thousand figure. As with all print ad decisions, you can reduce the options to reasonable estimates of costs and returns and then pick the highest-yielding option.

Getting ad analysis for free

Maybe you don't really need to spend good money on a research service to find out if your ads are working. Here are some alternatives:

- ✔ Run three variations on the ad and see which one generates the most calls or website visits (offering a discount based on a code number or using different phone numbers on different ads tells you which responses come from which ad and which media work best).

- ✔ Ask people to look at your ads for 20 seconds, and quiz them about what they remember. If they missed much of the ad, you probably need to rewrite it.

- ✔ Run the same ad (or very similar ones) in large and small formats and see which pulls in the largest number of consumers.

Any experiments you can run as you do your marketing give you useful feedback about what is and isn't working. Always think of ways to compare different options and see how those options perform when you advertise, giving you useful insight into ad effectiveness.

Considering some brilliant examples

Marketers generally assume that they have to work hard with colours and text to make their ads noticeable and persuasive. Statistically, they're right. But don't discount the power of imaginative design to simplify the task. A simple two-colour ad can actually work better than other, more elaborate ads.

Two famous press campaigns prove that simple can be best. One from *The Economist* uses the same white and red design that the magazine has been using in its poster advertising for the past few years. The press ad consists of a black-and-white Albert Einstein mask with a dotted line around it – the idea being that readers can cut out and wear the mask to look intelligent, or they can buy the magazine. Only two colours and two words are on the page – '*The Economist*'.

An ad from Volkswagen uses more words but even less colour. Their full-page 'Word Search' ad plays on the simple puzzle idea but with a twist. The design is the shape of a car (the Golf) created from black letters on the white page, while in the top left-hand corner is a list of phrases, such as 'power-assisted steering' and 'engine immobiliser'. The strapline says, 'Full of hidden extras', inviting the reader to look for the hidden words inside the car. Great print advertising doesn't have to be expensive; it just has to be clever.

Chapter 5

Signs, Posters and More

· ·

In This Chapter

▶ Finding successful signs for your business

▶ Using flags, banners and awnings

▶ Designing billboards and other large signs

▶ Utilising transport advertising

▶ Opting for bumper stickers, umbrellas and shopping bags

· ·

*O*utdoor advertising refers to a wide variety of advertising. The most obvious types (but not necessarily most important for you) are large (to very large!) signs and posters, including roadside billboards, but we also include signs, flags and banners in this medium. Outdoor advertising also includes what the experts call *ambient advertising*, which means putting an ad in an unexpected place to catch people by surprise.

All these methods try to communicate your message through public display of a poster, sign or something of similar design requirements. For this reason we incorporate signs, flags, banners, bumper stickers, transport advertising and even T-shirts in this chapter, along with the traditional poster formats. These media are more powerful than many marketers realise and some businesses succeed by using no other advertising. In this chapter, you find out how to design for and use outdoor advertising (the term we use to indicate outdoor signs and banners, plus related displays like posters and signs, which, just to keep you on your toes, can be displayed indoors as well as out).

Whenever you review your marketing, do an audit of your signs, posters, T-shirts and other outdoor ads. How many do you have displayed? Are they visible, clear and appealing? In good repair? And then ask if you can find an easy way to increase the number and impact of these signs. You can never do too much to make your brand identity and marketing messages visible.

Introducing the Essential Sign

Signs (small, informational outdoor ads or notices) don't show up in the index or table of contents of most books on marketing. *Signs* are displays with brand or company names on them and sometimes a short marketing message or useful information for the customer, too. In our experience, every marketer needs to make good use of signs.

Signs are all over the place; if you're in an office right now, look out of the nearest window and you can probably see a handful with ease. Signs are undeniably important. Even if they serve only to locate a shop or office, signs do a job that marketers need done. If your customers can't find you, you're out of business. So why do marketers – those marketing experts who write the books – tend to ignore signs so completely?

The Outdoor Advertising Association (www.oaa.org.uk) provides information on how to buy outdoor advertising space, relevant regulations and standard sizes. While the Outdoor Advertising Association can help with some general guidance, when evaluating signs, we can't send you to the experts as easily as we can with radio, TV, print or other outdoor media. You may end up working with a local sign manufacturer, and you and your designer will have to specify size, materials, copy and art. Fortunately, you're not all on your own; you can find some guidance and help. You need to remember a few things:

✔ The Outdoor Advertising Association has a good round-up of information and regulations. The 'Planning Regulations' section on its website (under 'General Information') can help you out. Most basic signs are normally permitted, while others will require planning application consent from your local authority.

✔ If you rent retail or office space, your landlord may have put some restrictions regarding signs into your lease. Research these possible constraints, and talk to those who feel they have authority over your sign and seek their approval based on a sketch and plan before you spend any money having signs made or installed.

✔ Consult your local or regional business telephone listings when you need to have a sign made. You should find several options. You may want to talk to a good design firm or experienced designer for a personal reference, too. Modern high-street copy shops also now provide cheap high-tech solutions for smaller or temporary signs.

✔ To stand out next to those shiny, high-tech signs and project a quality image, have your sign designed and painted by an artist or consider hiring a cabinet-maker, stained glass artist or oil painter. Most signs have little real art about them so unusual and beautiful ones tell the world that your company's special. A really special sign, well displayed in a high-traffic area, can have more power to build an image or pull in prospects than any other form of local advertising.

Appreciating what your sign can do

Signs have limited ability to accomplish marketing goals but perhaps not as limited as you think. As well as displaying the name of your business, you can include a phone number, website address or email contact details so that, even when your premises are closed, potential customers know how to get in touch with you. And you can say what your business does – a butcher doesn't have to be just a 'butcher', he can be a 'family-owned, free-range butcher'. With signs, as with all marketing communications, the way you say it is what counts!

Every morning on our way to work, we pass Munson's coffee shop. We couldn't begin to tell you how many other shops we must pass or what they're called, but we remember Munson's (and go in occasionally) because of the chalk board they put on the pavement outside the shop. No matter how early we are, a new piece of homespun philosophy is always written on the board – for example 'We are here to clear the path for the children behind' – intriguing people and enticing customers in for a drink or snack. This board offers cheap, easy and effective marketing – it's a sign (literally!).

Aside from their practical value (letting people know where you are), signs can and should promote your image and brand name. An attractive sign on your building or vehicle can spread the good word about your business or brand to all who pass by. Don't miss this brilliant opportunity to put your best foot forward in public.

Many commercial signs are in poor condition. Signs sit out in the weather, and when they fade, peel or fall over, they act as negative advertising for your business. Don't let your signs give the public the impression that you don't care enough to maintain them (they may even think you're going out of business!). Renew and religiously maintain your signs to get the maximum benefit from them.

Writing good signs

As a marketer, you need to master the strange art of writing for signs. Too often, the language marketers use on signs is ambiguous. The sign doesn't say anything with enough precision to make its point clear. Keep in mind the suggestions outlined in the following sections.

Make sure your sign says what you want it to

One of our favourite stories about how to easily turn a bad sign into a good one comes from the marketing consultant Doug Hall. A friend of his put up a sign that read 'Seasons in Thyme – Epicurean Food & Wine'. Do you have any idea what that company does? Doug changed his friend's sign to 'Seasons in Thyme RESTAURANT. Casual, Elegant, Island Dining'. For the first time in all his years in business, the owner received some customers who said they came in because they'd seen the sign.

Before you approve any design, review the copy to make sure that the writing provides a model of clarity. Try misinterpreting the wording. Can you read the sign in a way that makes it seem to mean something you don't intend to say? And try thinking of questions the sign doesn't answer that seem obvious to you – remember that the consumer may not know the answers. For example, some people have a terrible sense of direction, so a sign on the side of a shop leaves them confused about how to enter the premises. Solution? Put an arrow and the instructions 'Enter from Front' on the sign.

Use a header to catch your customer's eye

Marketers design some signs to convey substantial information – directions, for example, or details of a shop's merchandise mix. Information-heavy signs are often too brief or too lengthy. Divide the copy and design into two sections, each with a separate purpose, as follows:

- **Have a header.** The first section resembles the header in a print ad, and you design it to catch attention from afar and draw people to the sign. Given this purpose, brevity is key – and don't forget the essential large, catchy type and/or visuals.

- **Communicate essential information.** The second section of the sign needs to communicate the essential information accurately and in full. If the first section does its job, viewers walk right up to the sign to read the part with all the important information, so you don't need to make that type as large and catchy. The consumer should be able to easily read and interpret the wording and type used for the information, and this section needs to answer all likely viewer questions.

Most signs don't have these two distinct sections, and so they fail to accomplish either purpose very well – they neither attract people very strongly nor inform them fully. Unfortunately, most sign-makers have a strong urge to make all the copy the same size. When pressed, the sign-makers sometimes make the header twice as big as the rest of the copy, but going further than that seems to upset them. Well, to get a good sign, you may have to upset some people. As in many aspects of marketing, if you want above-average performance, you have to swim against the current.

You may have to make your sign bigger to fit the necessary words on it in a readable font. So be it. The form of the sign must follow its function.

Be creative!

Consider adding a beautiful photograph to your sign to give it more of the eye-catching appeal of a good print ad. Most sign-makers and printers can include photos now, but few marketers take advantage of this option.

Book V

Marketing
and
Advertising
Your
Wares

Another problem is that marketers write the copy on most signs in the most tired and obvious manner. Tradition says that a sign, unlike any other marketing communication, must simply state the facts in a direct, unimaginative way. One reason for this lack of creativity is that most marketers assume people *read* signs. The conventional wisdom is that your customers and prospects automatically find and read your signs.

Try walking down an average high street and later listing all the signs you remember seeing. Some stand out, but most go unseen. And we bet you can't re-create the text of the majority of those signs your eye bothered to linger on long enough to read. To avoid having yours being lost in this sea of similar signs, you have to make it stand out!

 Whenever you find other marketers making silly mistakes, you can turn their errors into your opportunities. Signs permit innovation in two interesting areas. You can be innovative with the copy and artwork, just as you can in any print medium, from a magazine ad to a roadside billboard. But you can also innovate in the form of the sign itself. Experiment with materials, shapes, lighting, location and ways of displaying signs to come up with some novel ideas that help your sign grab attention. Signs should be creative and fun. (So should all marketing, for that matter.)

Here are some of the many variations in form that you can take advantage of when designing a creative sign:

- Vinyl graphics and lettering (quick and inexpensive but accurate to your design)

- Hand-painted (personal look and feel)

- Wood (traditional look; routing or hand carving enhances the appeal)

- Metal (durable and accurate depictions of art and copy, but not very pretty)

- Window lettering (hand-painted or with vinyl letters/graphics)

- Light boxes (in which lettering is back-lit; highly visible at night)

- Neon signs (high impact)

- Magnetic signs (for your vehicles)

- Electronic displays (also known as *electronic message repeaters*; movement and longer messages, plus a high-tech feel, make these displays appropriate in some situations)

- Flat-panel TV screens (with shifting sign content and images or video; the price of these TVs has been coming down in recent years)

- Pavement projection (a unit in the shop window moves and spins a logo or message at the feet of passers-by at night)

Discovering Flags, Banners and Awnings

Movement is eye-catching, so think of flags as more dynamic kinds of sign, and try to find ways to use them to build brand awareness, to make your location(s) more visible or to get a marketing message displayed in more forms and places than you can otherwise. Cloth-based forms of advertising can be surprisingly reasonable, which is why outdoor messages on canvas or synthetic cloth make up an important part of many marketing campaigns.

Flagging down your customers

Did you know that Shakespeare used flags to advertise? In Elizabethan times the Globe Theatre in London had a small tower with a flagpole for advertising the next play to be shown – they were even colour coded, black for a tragedy and white for a comedy. Today theatres, galleries and museums are still some of the biggest users of flags and banners because they can adorn their buildings with colourful displays that promote forthcoming performances – the temporary nature of the medium suits the rotation of the plays and exhibitions. Do you have a similar short-term message that you can get across on a flag or banner?

A number of companies specialise in making custom-designed flags and banners. Of course, you see tacky paper banners – often produced by the local copy shop – hanging in the windows of shops on occasion. But we're not talking about those banners (because they probably don't help your image). We mean a huge, beautiful cloth flag flapping in the breeze. Or a bold 3-x-5-foot screen-printed flag suspended like a banner on an office or trade-show wall. Or a nylon table banner that turns the front and sides of a table into space for your marketing message.

Consider using a flag or banner as a sign for your shop or business. Doing so will help you stand out because so few marketers take advantage of this way to use a banner. A flag or banner is less static and dull than the typical metal or wood sign. Cloth moves, and even when it isn't moving, you know it has the potential for movement. This gives the banner a bit of excitement and helps it seem decorative and festive. People associate flags and banners with special events because these decorations are traditionally used in that context, instead of for permanent display.

Flag companies give you all these options and more. These businesses regularly sew and screen large pieces of fabric, and they can also supply you with all the necessary fittings you need to display flags and banners. In recent years, silk-screening technology and strong synthetic fibres have made flags and banners brighter and more permanent, expanding their uses in marketing.

Book V

Marketing
and
Advertising
Your
Wares

It's a wrap

Only the size of the building you can hang it from and your budget limit how big or imaginative you can get with a banner. Many big organisations commission temporary *building wraps* nowadays, which cover the whole or a large part of their premises. When London was bidding to win the 2012 Olympics, the group leading the bid revealed the biggest building wrap in Europe – two banners covering the roof of what was then the Millennium Dome, which could be seen from planes as they flew into London. Thanks to its innovative thinking (including this stunt), London won the 2012 Olympic Games. You may not be able to do anything on this scale, but this example does show that sticking to stock formats isn't necessary.

You can find suppliers of a full line of stock and custom products by searching online, looking in your local *Yellow Pages* or in the directory sections of trade magazines such as *Marketing Week*. Whoever you contact, ask to see their custom flag and banner price list, which includes a lot of design ideas and specs, and photos of effective banners made for previous clients.

Utilising canopies and awnings

If appropriate for your business, consider using an awning and canopy. For retailers, awnings and canopies often provide the boldest and most attractive form of roadside sign. Office sites may also find them valuable.

Awnings combine structural value with marketing value by shading the interior and can even extend the floor space of your shop by capturing some of the pavement as transition space. An awning can perform all the functions of a sign in a highly visible but not intrusive way. Conveniently, a row of awnings doesn't look as crass and commercial as huge signs because your eye accepts them as a structural part of the building. So a row of awnings provides you with the same amount of advertising as a big sign but without looking pushy.

Putting Up Posters: Why Size Matters

If you're planning to use posters to advertise, one of the first things to think about is how much time customers will have to read your ad and how far away they'll be. This information will help you decide how much you can say in your ad and how to say it.

Here's a simple exercise to help you understand the design requirements for a large-format poster. Draw a rectangular box on a sheet of blank paper, using a ruler as your guide. Make the box 12 cm wide and 6 cm high – the proportion of a standard *48-sheet* poster (we talk more about poster formats later in this section). Although a poster is large (over 6 metres wide in this instance), from a distance it will look as small as that box on your sheet (see Figure 5-1). Now hold your paper (or Figure 5-1) at arm's length and think about what copy and artwork can fit in this space while remaining readable to passers-by at this distance. Not much, right? Now imagine they're driving past it in a car. Next imagine them staring at it for minutes while waiting for the 8.30am train from Dorking to Waterloo. Sometimes you need to limit your message to a few, bold words and images to avoid your poster becoming a mess that no one can read. At other times you can afford to include more detail. The people waiting for that train may even be grateful for the distraction!

Figure 5-1:
From a
distance,
a large
roadside
poster looks
no bigger
than this
image.

CANYOUREADTHIS
CANYOUREADTHIS
CANYOUREADTHIS
CANYOUREADTHIS
CANYOUREADTHIS

The problem with outdoor advertising in general is that viewers have to read the ad in a hurry, and often from a considerable distance. So the ad has to be simple. Yet people who walk or drive the same route view the same ad daily. So that ad has to combine lasting interest with great simplicity.

With all these constraints, you see the difficulty of designing effective outdoor ads. Make your message fun, beautiful or at least important and clear, so that people don't resent having to see it often.

Deciding on outdoor ad formats

The Outdoor Advertising Association (www.oaa.org.uk) describes three different sectors in the outdoor market – roadside, transport and retail/point-of-sale/leisure:

✔ **Roadside.** You can choose anything from phone booths to 96-sheet ads, which at 40-feet wide by 10-feet high are the largest of the standard poster formats. Special versions, such as a real car stuck to a billboard, and banners count as roadside ads, too. The OAA claims that this method is particularly good for reaching young male audiences.

✔ **Transport.** While it includes standard poster sites in stations, airports and on trains and tubes, transport is a wide-ranging outdoor sector that also covers (literally) bus-sides, taxis and trucks. For that reason, this medium has its own lexicon of jargon, from *L-Sides* to *T-Sides* and the enticingly named *Super Rears*. All that really matters is that these terms describe ways of advertising on the outside of buses, which we cover later in this chapter. The OAA claims that this method is effective for reaching people 'dwelling' longer in front of ads.

✔ **Retail/point-of-sale/leisure.** If you sell your products through retailers, outdoor ads near those outlets can make a lot of sense. As well as poster sites at supermarkets, the retail sector includes shopping centres, cinemas, gyms and petrol stations, and can include ads on trolleys and screens. The OAA claims that these types of ad are good for reaching those people with their minds already in 'shopping' mode.

✔ **Non-traditional formats and ambient** is also a sector, but no one's come up with a straightforward name for it, which just proves its diversity. Think petrol pump nozzles, takeaway lids, ticket backs, beer mats, floor stickers – in fact, think anything at all. We talk about some of the more popular ambient formats, as well as the truly outlandish, later in the chapter.

Figure 5-2 shows the proportions and relative sizes of the standard *roadside* outdoor formats.

You can also explore the growing number of variations on these standards. Do you want your message displayed on a lobby floor, on a shopping trolley or alongside the notice boards at leisure centres? Or how about on signs surrounding the arenas and courts hosting athletic events? You can use all of these options and more, by directly contacting the businesses that control such spaces or using one of a host of ad agencies and poster contractors that can give you larger-scale access.

Maximising your returns

Outdoor advertising costs vary widely. As an example, a 48-sheet roadside poster in the North West region (Manchester and Liverpool) will cost you around £320–350 per panel for a two-week period – the standard time for an outdoor campaign. You're unlikely to buy just one poster site, and even more unlikely to find an outdoor advertising company that will sell you one. Poster space is typically sold by a pre-determined group of panels in one area, or a national campaign. So, if you want to advertise on 25 of the best 48-sheet sites in Manchester and Liverpool for two weeks, you'll pay approximately £11,250–14,300. Seventy sites, giving coverage across the whole North West region, will cost £24,000–34,500 (including a back-lit element).

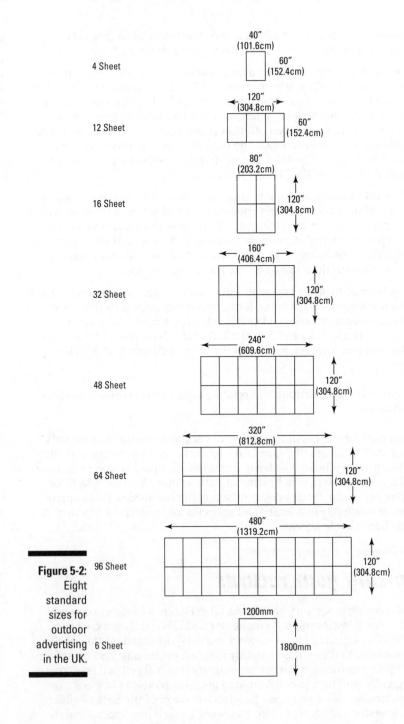

Figure 5-2:
Eight
standard
sizes for
outdoor
advertising
in the UK.

Book V

Marketing
and
Advertising
Your
Wares

The money is one thing, but who's seeing your posters is quite another. Poster campaign audiences are measured in several ways; broadly, how many people in the local or national population will see it, how often and how clearly. For example, you can buy 100 48-sheet posters in London for £55,000, which will be seen by 2 million Londoners over a two-week period. That figure's around 26 per cent of the area's population, so you achieve a *cover* of 26 per cent. Your *frequency* is the number of times a person sees your ad over the period, in this case 8.1 times. And your *Visibility Adjusted Contacts* (*VACs*) for each panel is a score telling you who actually looks at each panel. VAC isn't a measure of the quality or location of your panels but it does tell you broadly how many 'eyes' have seen your sites. Basically, the higher the score, the more effective the campaign is believed to be (but also the higher the cost). Your 100 48-sheets in London have a VAC of 105, but if you were to splash out £105,000 on the 50 best 96-sheets in the capital you'd get a VAC of 180.

Postar (www.postar.co.uk) offers data on outdoor advertising effectiveness, but as you have to pay a subscription fee, we suggest going direct to the outdoor advertising companies for rate cards and data. You can find the main poster companies through the Outdoor Advertising Association website (www.oaa.org.uk).

Delivering Messages on the Move: Transport Advertising

Transport advertising is any advertising in or on railway or underground systems, airports, buses, taxis, on the sides of vans or lorries, and more. Although transport advertising is a form of outdoor advertising, this term is misleading because you set up some transport ads indoors: ads at airport terminals, ads displayed within tube carriages and so on.

Transport ads work well if you get the people in transit to take an interest in your product, from consumer items to business services. We've seen transport ads generate sales leads for local estate agents and for international consulting firms. Yet few marketers make use of them. Consider being an innovator and trying transit ads, even if your competitors don't.

Standard options – the ones most easily available through media buying firms and ad agencies – include bus shelter panels, bus and taxi exterior signs, posters and back-lit signs in airports.

Transport advertising offers one definite advantage: it typically delivers high frequency of viewer impacts in a short period of time. Public transport vehicles generally travel the same routes over and over again, and so almost everyone along the route sees an ad multiple times.

Bus advertising

Shelter panels are 6-sheet (120 cm x 180 cm) posters, which appear on bus shelters. You can mount them behind a Lucite sheet to minimise graffiti problems. In many cities, the site owners have back-lit some of the shelter panels for night-time display. A two-week showing typically costs anywhere from £70 to £350, depending upon the area, or up to £900 per panel for the busiest London sites.

Well-accepted standards exist for *bus advertising* in the UK, largely due to the fixed available space on any single- or double-decker bus – although some companies now also offer the option of full-bus branding. Figure 5-3 shows the standard bus ad sizes, but do contact a contractor who specialises in this kind of advertising (such as CBS Outdoor; www.cbsoutdoor.co.uk) before producing any posters.

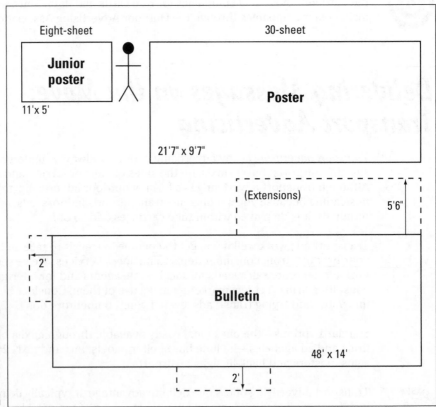

Figure 5-3:
Standard sizes for bus advertising in the UK.

Sometimes advertisers combine an L-Side with rear panels to maximise impact on pedestrians and drivers as they watch the bus go by. Add a shelter poster to the mix, and you achieve incredibly good coverage! Such combinations can be effective, especially if you think your ad may be challenging to read or you want to display two or three complementary ads to the same viewer. You can brand a double-decker London bus in this way for around £3000 per a month, while a single side costs around £300.

Taxi advertising

Taxi advertising provides you with a route to target local customers and high-value businesspeople. You can advertise on the outside, inside, covering the whole cab, or on the back of receipts. A company called Cabvision even sells ads on its in-taxi TV channel! You can expect to pay £5000 for 40 side panels for a month in a city like Bristol or Newcastle or up to £75,000 for 600 panels in London. Liveried taxis, where the vehicle is wrapped in your ad or identity for maximum standout, costs around £38,500 for ten over six months in cities such as Liverpool, Leeds and Glasgow. Contact a company that specialises in this form of advertising, such as Taxi Media (www.taxi-media.co.uk).

Airport advertising

Airport advertising is a fairly new option but is taking off fast. If you want a relatively well-to-do audience with a rich mix of tourists and professional travellers, enquire about airport advertising with international site owners and domestic specialists such as JCDecaux (www.jcdecauxairport.co.uk) or Airport Partners Advertising (www.airportpartners.co.uk).

A note about your own vehicles

Does your company have its own vehicles on the road? If so, are you using them for outdoor advertising? Most marketers say either 'no' or 'sort of' when we ask them this question. Small, cheap, magnetic signs on the doors don't count; nor does a painted name on the door or side panel of a van or lorry. If you pay for as much display space as even a standard-sized van offers, you'd probably hire a designer or agency and put great care into your message. In fact, you're paying for the exterior space on your vehicles; the cost just doesn't show up in the marketing budget. So why not cash in on this investment more fully by treating that lorry or van as a serious advertising medium? Mount frames for bus-sized posters and display a professionally designed ad that you change monthly or weekly. Or hire a competent airbrush painter to do a more permanent, custom job on each vehicle.

Freight company, Eddie Stobart, uses branded vehicles to great effect. You have seen the dark green lorries with yellow and red lettering on the motorway, but did you know that each one carries a different woman's name. Its branding is so good that an Eddie Stobart fan club exists, with more than 25,000 members, and many more people are secret 'Eddie Spotters'. A different company, coincidentally using similar colours, is the Foxtons chain of estate agents. Since 2001, Foxtons has branded its entire fleet of company cars in striking limited edition liveries, from 'Italian Job' to 'Urban Graffiti'. You can use your vehicles as more than just a form of transport too; all you require is a little imagination.

Being Innovative with Ambient Media – Your Ad in Unusual Places

Ambient or *non-traditional advertising* does exactly what it says on the tin (or takeaway lid, egg, or petrol pump nozzle.) In fact, we can't really tell you what ambient media is, as the concept covers so much and changes so rapidly. We can tell you what it isn't, which is any of the traditional outdoor advertising opportunities. Ambient is one of the fastest-growing sectors within outdoor advertising because you can create a lot of impact for relatively little outlay. The nature of ambient advertising also means it can offer you precise targeting by area or by audience type.

We like to divide ambient advertising into two parts: the uncontroversial and the unconventional. *Uncontroversial* includes all forms of outdoor advertising that are really just poster ads in disguise, and which are in almost constant use by fairly major advertisers. These ads appear on petrol pump nozzles, floor stickers in supermarkets and train stations, and posters in public conveniences. *Unconventional* includes everything else. We've heard of ads that appear on pretty much everything you can imagine, and a lot of what you probably can't. These unconventional places include tube maps and tickets, tattoos, urinal stickers and even on cows standing by the sides of major roads.

Just because the concept's different doesn't mean ambient advertising is a great idea for your product or service. Only use ambient advertising when you know that the idea is a good fit for your brand or you're prepared to take a gamble with the investment (most of the wilder ideas have poor audience measurement, so the choice is based more on whether it feels right to you).

Here are some of the most interesting ambient media ideas we've encountered and some of the companies that have used them effectively:

Book V

Marketing
and
Advertising
Your
Wares

✔ **Rubbish skips.** Directory enquiries service 118-118 used skips to get across the idea of people throwing away their old telephone directories.

✔ **Petrol pump nozzles.** Good for targeting drivers with impulse buys, and used by food and drink brands such as Polo and Red Bull.

✔ **Takeaway lids.** Full-colour Adlids have been used by a host of organisations, from Blockbuster video ('Here's just four of our new takeaways', plus a money-off coupon) to the Inland Revenue.

✔ **Chalk ads.** Sometimes known as vandaltising, chalk-drawn ads on pavements have been used by companies such as Gossard to advertise a new range of underwear. Be careful, though: this idea is less popular with local councils, despite the fact that the ads eventually wash away.

✔ **Car park tickets.** A great way to reach people just before they go shopping, used by retailers such as Sainsbury's and Specsavers.

✔ **Shopping trolleys and floor posters.** We group these together as they offer the same great benefits to you if your products are found on supermarket shelves. Did you know that 75 per cent of purchasing decisions are made in-store and over 90 per cent of advertising budget is spent out of store? Trolleys and floor posters are reminders to shoppers that your product exists, and can even direct them to the right shelf.

✔ **Adwalker wearable ads.** These modern 'sandwich boards' involve people wearing interactive screens. They can be used not only to advertise your services but also to get potential customer information. Brands such as Nivea, Yahoo! and Sony have used this approach to engage customers on the street and at airports.

✔ **ForeheADS.** Why use your head when you can use someone else's? This wacky idea involves renting out the foreheads of cash-strapped students, who must be seen out in public for at least three hours a day to earn their fee. Companies including *FHM* magazine and CNX have used ForeheADS to carry their logos in the form of temporary tattoos.

Advertising on T-shirts to Shopping Bags

Broadly defined, a sign may include any public display of your brand or marketing message. To us, a message on a T-shirt is just as legitimate as one on a poster. And a T-shirt ad is often a lot easier and cheaper to make. The following sections share simple, small-scale ways to get your message across.

Embellishing T-shirts, umbrellas and bumper stickers

Sometimes you can get people to advertise your company on their vehicles or bodies for free (see 'Praising T-shirts' in the nearby sidebar.) Your customers may think of a nice T-shirt as a premium item or gift for them, but you can see that T-shirt as a body billboard! Similarly, umbrellas can broadcast your logo and name and a short slogan or headline. Isn't it nice that people are willing to go around with your advertising messages on their clothes (or even on their bodies – temporary tattoos are also a marketing option)? Don't overlook this concept as a form of outdoor advertising. In fact, use it as much as you can. People happily display marketing messages if they like them.

Don't overlook bumper and car-window stickers. If you make them clever or unique enough, people eagerly seek those stickers out. Don't ask me why. But because people do, and because producing bumper stickers is cheap, why not come up with an appealing design and make stickers available in target markets as giveaways on shop counters or at outdoor events?

Commercial or brand-oriented bumper stickers are used by people who think the brand is so cool that it enhances the car. Achieving coolness and desirability is very difficult for most marketers however. An alternative is to keep your brand identity small, and use an appealing message instead. A clever joke, an inspiring quote or something similar is appealing enough to get your message displayed. And for mugs, window stickers and other premium items, the secret is to have a great visual design or other picture that people enjoy, or to offer a humorous cartoon.

You can even include a nice sticker in a direct-mail piece, where that sticker can do double duty by both acting as an incentive to get people to retain and read the mailing and giving you cheap outdoor advertising when they display the sticker on their vehicles. (Contact local print shops, sign-makers or T-shirt silk-screeners; any of these businesses may also produce bumper stickers.)

Bagging it up

Big stores believe in the importance of shopping bags as an advertising medium. But many other businesses fail to take advantage of the fact that shoppers carry bags around busy shopping centres and high streets, and also on trains and buses, giving any messages on the bags high exposure.

To use bags effectively, you need to make them easier to read and more interesting than the average brown paper or white plastic bag. Remember, you're not just designing a bag – you're designing a form of outdoor advertising. So apply the same design principles. Come up with a *hook*: a striking image or attention-getting word or phrase that gets everyone looking at that bag. Try alternative colours or shapes. (By the way, most bag suppliers can customise their bags – check with suppliers in your local area. If no suppliers near you can do so, contact printers and silk-screeners instead.)

If you offer the biggest, strongest bag in a shopping area, shoppers will stuff everyone else's bags into yours, giving your advertising message maximum exposure. Bigger, stronger bags do cost more, but these days, with environmental concerns relating to plastic bags, you may win more customers with a heavy-duty plastic bag for multiple uses or better still you can invest in a cotton or recyclable version and broadcast your green credentials into the bargain. After all, if you have an ad message you can get across with a bag, compare the cost of a better bag to other media. Pretty cheap, right?

If you aren't in the retail business, you may think that this idea doesn't apply to you. Wrong! Plenty of store managers view bags as an irritating expense rather than a marketing medium. Offer to supply them with better bags – or more environmentally friendly ones – for free, in exchange for the right to print your message on the bags. Result: a new marketing medium for your campaign. A specialist such as Bag Media (www.bagmedia.co.uk) can design and distribute bags for you to pre-selected groups of retailers, from veterinary practices to garden centres and sandwich bags to pizza boxes.

Praising T-shirts

Sometimes you just need a cheap T-shirt. We have drawers stuffed full of them, and many of those shirts feature artwork promoting a company or brand name. If you can make a T-shirt appropriate to your brand, by all means use T-shirts as a premium item!

Even a good-quality T-shirt is pretty cheap, so you can easily implement a quality premium strategy with this medium. You achieve quality by using a heavy, all-cotton fabric and sporting a compelling design developed by a real designer. Oh, and you need to use an experienced, quality-conscious silk-screener to put that fine design on those good T-shirts.

T-shirt buyers are frustrated by the poor selection of shirts available in the shops. A lack of exciting new designs, not a lack of drawer space, holds these customers back. So you just need to put a cool design on your T-shirt to get your target audience to want it. Customers can't get enough of this premium item as long as your design is fresh and good. No, we don't really want another cheap pen with some company's name on it. But we're happy to get another good T-shirt or two. We may even pay you for it – if it's good enough.

To find companies providing customised T-shirts, try searching online, your local *Yellow Pages* for listings of silk-screening businesses near you (generally listed under 'Printing'), or take a look at the back of a trade magazine such as *Marketing Week*.

Considering a Few Common-Sense Rules for Outdoor Advertising

Depending on whether you're advertising on roadside or transport sites, follow these common-sense rules when designing your poster to make sure that it catches and holds customers' attention:

✔ If your poster site is by the side of a main road, people will have just a few seconds to see and understand your ad. Keep the image simple and use as few, large words as possible. Make sure that you use colours that contrast, so they can be seen from a good distance.

✔ Think like a bored passenger. When you advertise on interior tube panels, inside taxis or on train platform posters, you can afford to use more complex visuals and a greater number of words.

✔ Consider layering the message so that you provide a clear, large-scale, simple message for first-time viewers, but also a more detailed design and message for repeat viewers to find within the poster.

✔ Humour and word play work well for posters. Try to use them in your ad to build viewer involvement.

✔ Show your logo. Whether you're just using posters or are including other media in your marketing campaign, don't forget the logo! Using your logo consistently on everything you do will improve recognition of your business and achieve better results from your advertising.

Chapter 6

Public Relations and Word of Mouth

In This Chapter

▶ Generating positive publicity about products and organisations

▶ Writing an effective press release

▶ Harnessing the power of customer word of mouth

. . . .

*W*hen people bump into reminders of your company name, brand, product or service, they're more likely to buy. And if those exposures to your identity create a strongly positive impression, they can have a big impact on sales. So far, so simple.

But while advertising does work, most people who are affected by it don't like to admit to it. Plenty of people will deny ever having bought anything as a result of seeing an ad for it. However, we bet you've never come across anyone who says the same about a magazine article or something a relative or friend recommends to them.

Independent endorsements for your product or service can be so much more powerful than 'pure' advertising, for the simple reason that consumers are more sceptical about a message that's been paid for and is self-serving.

In this chapter, we discuss the two key ways of gaining independent endorsement for your business: *public relations* (when exposure to or mention of your company, service or product becomes part of the news or an editorial feature) and *word of mouth* (what people say about you to others). Each endorsement can make a positive impression in a low-key, polite manner and can do so – if managed well – for surprisingly low cost.

Public relations and word of mouth have traditionally been vastly under-rated techniques for communicating with your customers but, these days, companies are realising their power. The ease with which information can be passed between people on the Internet means that your messages can be spread further and more quickly than ever before. These endorsements belong in the front lines of your marketing plan because of their ease of use, simplicity, low cost and potential.

Using Publicity to Your Advantage

Publicity is coverage of your product or business in the editorial portion of any news medium. Why would journalists cover a product as a story? One reason is that the product is better or worse than expected. If, for example, *Which?* magazine runs an article praising your product as best in a particular category, that's publicity. Good publicity. If, in contrast, the evening television news programmes run a story saying that experts suspect your product caused numerous accidents, that's publicity, too. Bad publicity.

Obviously, any marketer aims for good publicity. But if you do find yourself facing bad publicity, don't despair. Good public relations (PR) can be turned to an organisation's advantage. For example, when someone claimed to have poisoned Snickers and Mars bars in Australia, the confectionary company made a big show of recalling all the bars and creating a hotline for concerned consumers. The company then launched a campaign giving away free bars, running ads and reminding everyone how much they'd miss the brands if they weren't around. The bad publicity cost the confectionary business some money in the short term but overall the response improved its image in the country. Compare this outcome to when Perrier found benzene in its water in 1990. The company had little choice but to withdraw the water from shop shelves but didn't back up doing so with enough information. Consumers were confused and worried, and the brand suffered. Perrier did set up a customer care line in the UK to try to deal with the anxious public but it failed to realise that the issue had become global. Its market share never fully recovered.

Product quality was the key factor to both stories reaching the news in the first place. Keep this fact in mind.

When you use publicity, remember the all-important factor – the quality of your product innovation and production/delivery. You can gain positive publicity simply by designing and making a truly superior product. If you want to generate negative publicity, just make your product shoddy or carry out your service poorly. *Good publicity starts with a pursuit of quality in your own business!*

Waitrose is a great example of PR and word of mouth working together in harmony, but how do you go about getting the PR machine started in the first place? The following sections list ways that you can take advantage of good publicity (and, if the need arises, neutralise bad publicity) in your marketing materials.

Tackling public relations

Book V

Marketing
and
Advertising
Your
Wares

Public relations (PR) is the active pursuit of publicity for marketing purposes. You use PR to generate good publicity and try to minimise bad publicity. Generally, marketers have the responsibility of generating good publicity. If marketers create good stories and communicate them to the media effectively (see the following two sections), the media pick them up and turn them into news or entertainment content. Good publicity.

Although marketers or general managers wear the PR hat in smaller organisations, large companies generally have a PR person or department whose sole job is to manage its reputation – generating good news but also reacting promptly and effectively to publicity crises. Also, many businesses hire *PR consultancies* – agencies that can work for a number of clients, planning and delivering messages to the press or reacting to incoming enquiries.

If you need help writing a good press release and placing the story, enlisting this professional help is worthwhile – you may not get any coverage without it.

PR consultancies vary in size from international groups employing thousands to single owner-operator PR professionals. You can also find specialists, who have expertise in industry sectors such as IT or healthcare. Around 3000 PR consultancies operate in the UK, so you need help narrowing down your search. If you're serious about hiring one, the Public Relations Consultants Association offers a free online service called PReview (www.prca.org.uk), which identifies the member consultancies that most closely match your needs.

Creating a good story

To a journalist, a *good story* is anything that has enough public interest to attract readers, viewers or listeners and hold their attention. For example, a good story for a journalist covering the plastics industry must hold the attention of people in that industry.

We're sorry to say that most of what you want to communicate to your market doesn't fall into the category of a good story. For that reason, you need to develop your story (by collecting the right facts and quotes and writing them down clearly and well) to a level that may qualify as good editorial content. And when you think of good editorial content, think like a journalist would.

Finding the hook

The *hook* is what it sounds like: the compelling bit of information that snags your reader's interest and draws her to the story.

Here's a simple exercise to help you understand how hooks work. Scan today's newspaper (whichever one you like to read) and rank the top five stories based on your interest in them. Now analyse each one in turn to identify the one thing that made that story interesting enough to hold your attention. The hooks, the things that made each story interesting to you, differ. But every story has a hook, and all hooks have certain elements in common:

- ✔ Hooks often give you new information (information you didn't know or weren't sure of).

- ✔ Hooks make that new information relevant to your activities or interests.

- ✔ Hooks catch your attention, often by surprising you with something you hadn't expected.

- ✔ Hooks promise some benefit to you – although the benefit may be indirect – by helping you understand your world better, avoid something undesirable or simply enjoy yourself as you read the paper.

Combining the hook with your marketing message

You need to design hooks to make your marketing message into stories that appeal to journalists. Your hooks need to be just like the ones that attracted your attention to those newspaper stories, with one exception: *you need to somehow tie them to your marketing information*. You have to make sure that at least a thin line exists connecting the hook to your brand identity, the news that you've just introduced a new product or whatever else you want the public to know. That way, when journalists use your hook in their own work, they end up including some of your marketing information in their stories as an almost accidental side effect.

Journalists don't want to help you communicate with your target market but they'll happily use any good stories that you're willing to write for them. If your product gets mentioned or you get quoted as a result, they don't have a problem giving you the reference. So what's the secret, the key or the essence of good publicity? Develop stories with effective hooks and give those stories to overworked journalists with empty pages to fill.

Communicating your story to the media: Press releases

For communicating a news story the most basic format is the press release. Unfortunately, journalists don't like press releases. We know this because we are journalists. We get hundreds of press releases emailed and posted to us every day. Most of them are rubbish, which is exactly where they end up. At the head of every magazine, covering every imaginable professional or consumer interest, is the equivalent of us – a stressed-out editor with the next deadline looming. So look on your challenge as getting past us, or at least the equivalent of us.

When we say that journalists don't like press releases, what we mean is that we don't like admitting to being influenced by them – a bit like consumers with advertising, really. Now we're not going to attempt to hold back the tide of press releases that flood into our inbox, but we shall give some insider advice about how to get on the right side of journalists by giving them what they need and not troubling them with what they don't.

A list of do's

Here's a list of ways that you can get a positive response from the journalists you contact:

✔ **Do offer exclusives.** Offering the news as an *exclusive* is the best way to make a journalist feel better about a press release (but remember, it still has to be a relevant story). An exclusive means that the journalist you're dealing with gets the story before it appears anywhere else, the story gets a more prominent position in the newspaper or magazine and the journalist scores points with her editor. Everybody's happy.

You, or your PR consultancy, need to get close to the journalists that are most relevant to your business – this usually means calling them with the story first to discuss it and then sending the press release if they've shown an interest. Most companies do it the other way round, or worse, simply blanket email to every journalist on their database.

✔ **Do make it relevant and timely.** Target the right media and contacts. The food critic doesn't need a release about a new robotics manufacturing facility. And the business correspondent doesn't either, if the facility opened two months ago, because now that story's old news.

You need to have read the paper or magazine and be familiar with its content before making contact with its journalists. Don't pitch a story without having knowledge of the media you're targeting or you risk making a fool of yourself.

✔ **Do build up a list of media contacts.** You need to create an accurate database of journalists with all contact details so you can get in touch with them quickly. Emailing your release can be sensible because journalists work on tight deadlines, so include fields for email addresses in your database. Think about developing a list identifying which journalists write articles that may be similar to stories related to your business. Now you have a smaller list that's a much tighter match with your content and target audience. You can get commercial lists and information on journalists from PR directories and list-sellers. You can find these through any search engine or PR agency.

✔ **Do think creatively.** Journalists need stories; you need some positive PR – so think up a story idea that serves both needs. A common but effective PR tactic is to carry out a piece of consumer research that's relevant to your business and let a newspaper publish the results. For example, a DVD rental company may research a list of people's favourite films.

Include something helpful, such as tips, rules or principles, which the media can quote. (An osteopath's practice may send out a release that includes five tips for a healthier back. A management consultant may offer five tips for avoiding cash-flow crises. A home inspection firm may offer five tips to avoid costly surprises when buying a home.)

✔ **Do offer yourself as an expert commentator on industry-related matters, in case they need a quote for another article.** A journalist may just include one sentence from you, but if she mentions your company name, you just got some good publicity. For example, an article on how to shop for a used car in the Sunday magazine of a newspaper may quote the owner of a large car dealership as saying, 'If you don't have an independent mechanic evaluate a used car before buying it, I guarantee you'll be in for some unpleasant surprises.' The article may also mention that this dealership's repair department does free evaluations for car buyers. The combination of a quote and a bit of information about the free service is going to attract many new customers, some of whom will become steady users of the dealership's repair service, and some of whom will become buyers of new or used cars from the dealership.

✔ **Do keep it brief.** Journalists are quick on the uptake and work fast, so let them call or email if they need more information.

✔ **Do post your press releases on your website.** Even if you've given your story as an 'exclusive', your press releases can do double duty on the Web, providing information for journalists to follow up once the exclusive story becomes public. Remember to provide a phone number too in case reporters want more information on a story.

✔ **Do send releases to every local editor in your area, no matter how small their publication or station.** You can get local coverage more easily than regional or national coverage and that local coverage can be surprisingly helpful.

And a few don'ts

The do's must be balanced by a few helpful don'ts that will help your information stand out from the junk that flies into every journalist's inbox:

✔ **Don't make a nuisance of yourself.** One of the worst pieces of advice that is seemingly given to every aspiring PR practitioner is to make a follow-up call. If your media contacts database is accurate, the journalist will have received your press release: if it's a good story she'll use it; if not, she won't. You can't do anything to change your press release after the event, so make sure that what you send is as carefully crafted as it can be.

✔ **Don't ask for clippings.** Journalists don't want to send you clippings of the articles they write, so don't bother asking. Nor do they care to discuss with you why they didn't run a story, or why they cut off part of a quote when they did run a story. They're busy with the next story. Forget about it. You focus on the next story too. If you want a clipping, most publications keep an online database of all their published stories.

✔ **Don't make any errors.** Typos throw the facts into question. Don't include any inaccurate facts, either. You want the journalist to have trust in the information you're providing. Prove that you're worthy of that confidence.

✔ **Don't give incomplete contact information.** Make sure you include up-to-date names, postal and email addresses and phone numbers on the press release. Let the contacts know when they should be available if reporters need to speak to them and brief them properly about what they should say so that the journalist finds them helpful and co-operative.

✔ **Don't ignore the journalists' research needs.** The more support you give a journalist, the easier she finds it to cover your story. Remember to send over a high-resolution photograph of your product or a quoted expert with your press release. Some story slots in magazines or news-papers require images; if you send one over, you're a little bit closer to being chosen, with very little effort. Don't overload emails with lots of pictures, though – you don't want to make reporters' inboxes crash – but do offer in the release to provide more images, if they're wanted. Also consider offering tours of any venues mentioned, interview times, sample products or whatever else may help journalists cover your story.

✔ **Don't forget that journalists work on a faster clock than you do.** When a journalist calls about your release, return the call (or make sure that somebody else does) in minutes or hours, not days. If you handle media requests slowly, a journalist will just find another source or write another story by the time you've returned the call.

Considering video and electronic releases

You can get a story out to the media in ways other than press releases. Consider generating a video release, with useful footage that a television producer may decide to run as part of a news story. Or put a written press release on the PR Newswire (see below) or any other such service that distributes hard copy or electronic releases to its media clients – for a fee from the source of the release, of course. You can also pitch your stories to the Associated Press, Reuters and other newswires (but we recommend hiring a major PR firm before trying to contact a newswire).

TIP

prnewswire.co.uk and businesswire.co.uk

For easy access to a cheap way of distributing releases, check out www.prnewswire.co.uk, where you can click on 'Our Services' and then 'Small Business Toolkit' to access information on prices charged for distributing press releases. At time of writing, the site offers to create and send a release to all the media in the UK, plus consumer and trade publications, thousands of news-oriented websites, and online services and databases, for prices from £220. Not bad, but we recommend using this service alongside making key journalistic contacts because you can't beat the personal touch. A similar service is offered at www.businesswire.co.uk.

Being interviewed for TV and radio

So now you've got a hook or a reputation for expertise within your sector (see earlier sections in this chapter), the requests for interviews will come flooding in. Okay, usually the process isn't that simple but you need to be prepared for when a broadcast interview does come your way. A few people are naturally confident and gifted when speaking publicly or on radio or TV – but they're not normal! You will feel nervous the first time you're in an unusual interview situation. Professional media training is available, where you're put into mock interviews in front of real cameras and microphones and put through your paces by professional journalists. Or you can prepare yourself by simply following these basic (and much cheaper) tips:

- ✔ **Give no more than three key messages.** If you're tempted to blurt out everything you know about your subject, your main messages will get lost and people won't remember anything. Prepare in advance what you want to say and then say it.

- ✔ **Know your audience.** Find out as much as you can about the interview, the programme and its audience. Is it live or prerecorded? Light-hearted chat or serious comment? For business experts or housewives?

- ✔ **Be positive.** State your main messages in positive terms, and provide examples rather than go on the defensive. Whatever you do, don't say 'no comment' – the interviewer and audience will assume you've got something to hide. Watch how politicians manage this scenario when they're being interviewed. They repeat their key message and studiously ignore the question.

✔ **Know what not to wear.** Avoid patterns when on TV, as sometimes the cameras can't cope and viewers get a disturbing strobe effect. Small checks and herringbone are obviously out, but also avoid bold patterns as they'll distract attention from what you're trying to say. Keep your attire simple and light – dark clothes can drain colour from your face.

✔ **Speak like a normal human being.** After all, normal people are watching or listening, so thinking about what they may or may not know about the subject and tailoring your message to them pays. Imagine you're speaking to someone who's bright, but knows nothing about the topic. Don't patronise, but definitely don't overwhelm them with jargon and abbreviations.

Making the Most of Word of Mouth

Word of mouth (WOM) gives a consumer (or a marketer) the most credible source of information about products, aside from actual personal experience with those products. What consumers tell each other about your products has a huge impact on your efforts to recruit new customers. WOM also has a secondary, but still significant, impact on your efforts to retain old customers.

If you survey customers to identify the source of positive attitudes towards new products, you generally find that answers such as 'my friend told me about it' outnumber answers like 'I saw an ad' by ten to one. WOM communications about your product don't actually outnumber advertising messages; but when customers talk, other customers listen.

How can you control what people say about your product? You can't very effectively encourage customers to say nice things about and prevent them from criticising your product. But you can influence WOM – and you have to try. Making your product special is the most obvious way to influence WOM. A product that surprises people because of its unexpectedly good quality or service is special enough to talk about. A good product or a well-delivered service wins fans and turns your customers into your sales force. Other tactics for managing WOM about your business or product may not be so obvious. Fortunately, we discuss them in the following sections.

Doing good deeds

If no aspect of your product is itself particularly wonderful or surprising, do some attention-grabbing activity and associate that with your product. Consider these strategies for generating positive publicity and word of mouth:

✔ Get involved with a charity or not-for-profit organisation that operates in your area.

✔ Stage a fun event for kids.

✔ Let your employees take short sabbaticals to volunteer in community services.

Get creative. You can think of something worthwhile, some way of helping improve your world that surprises people and makes them take notice of the good you're doing in the name of your product. But bear in mind that any positive deeds you do are much more credible, memorable and impressive if they have some association with what your organisation does. For example, a washing powder business may offer to wash a football team's kit free for a year. Or a sports company could get its employees to do a fun run for charity.

Spicing up your sales promotions

A 20p-off coupon isn't worth talking about. But a competition in which the winners get to spend a day with the celebrity of their choice can get consumers excited – and can be cheaper, too. You can generate positive PR and a lot of word of mouth with such a premium.

You can use special offers and competitions to get people to recommend a friend. For example, the mobile phone company T-Mobile has run offers giving subscribers £20 credit if they recommend the service to a friend who then signs up. The friend also gets £20 credit. Everyone wins and even those people who don't want to sign up immediately may remember this 'generosity' when considering a new mobile deal later on. You see, you can influence word of mouth.

Identifying and cultivating decision influencers

In many markets, some people's opinions matter a lot more than others. These people are *decision influencers,* and if you (hypothetically) trace back the flow of opinions in your industry, you may find that many of them originate with these people. In business-to-business (B2B) marketing, the decision influencers are often obvious. A handful of prominent executives, a few editors working for trade magazines and some of the staff at trade associations probably exert a strong influence over everybody else's opinions. You can find identifiable decision influencers in consumer markets, as well. Just think about chat show host Oprah Winfrey, in the US. If she recommends a book on her TV show, the author sees an immediate spike in sales. She's so important to the publishing market that now any titles that Oprah picks for her special 'book club' are often marketed more heavily on that detail than their plot or author. The same has happened in the UK with Richard and Judy's Book Club and sales of certain products named by celebrity chefs – such as the lift in sales of any product featured by Delia Smith or Jamie Oliver.

To take advantage of decision influencers, develop a list of who falls into that category for your product or service and then make a plan for cultivating them. Match these people with appropriate managers or salespeople who can take them to events or out to lunch, just for fun. You just need to make sure that people associated with your business are in the personal networks of these decision influencers. Consider developing a series of giveaways and mailshots to send to these decision influencers. If we wanted to sell a football boot to youth players, we'd send free samples of a new shoe to youth coaches. When you know who's talking and who's listening, you can easily focus your efforts on influencing the talkers.

Seizing control of the Internet

Okay, you can't actually take over the Internet, but you need to be aware of what people are saying about your product or service online. Weblogs, or blogs as they're commonly known, are one of the latest phenomena of the Internet age. What are blogs? The term *blogs* refers to personal web publishing based on a topic or topics that attract a like-minded community of online participants. In other words, blogging is word of mouth on the Web. Blogs exist dedicated to pretty much every subject you can imagine, from cars to politics to chocolate. You need to know about blogs because you can use them to your advantage in two key ways:

- ✔ **Get in on the discussion.** If a website dedicated to your market exists, try to get your product mentioned or even establish a link between your site and the blog (blogs make extensive use of links to other sites). A survey among more than 600 blog publishers found that two thirds would be happy to consider a direct public relations approach. Microsoft has sent out new laptop models to key bloggers before they become available to the public in order to generate some buzz about them.

- ✔ **Create your own blog.** Blogs are cheap and easy to set up, which is why they're blossoming on the Web. You can use free blog sites such as www.wordpress.com or www.blogger.com and start publishing within the day. You can use your blog to promote your products and services and elicit feedback (bad as well as good) from potential and existing customers. Make sure you can moderate any feedback before it goes live to avoid libellous information but don't be tempted to ditch any negative comments – people won't use your service to give their views if they think you ignore anything but good news.

Not all blogs or their users are business-friendly, and you need to remember this when making approaches or setting up your own blog. Blogs are run by enthusiasts and are usually independent of corporate ties: that's their point, as well as their appeal. While Microsoft attracted a lot of attention for its laptops by sending them to bloggers, it also received criticism as some people considered it too close to paying for publicity.

Controlling what people say about you on blogs is also difficult. You can't, so don't try to. If a comment about your product or service is incorrect, identifying yourself and responding is the best approach. Or just leave it be: you need to accept that not everyone will like what you do but that situation's all right.

Regulations now exist to control corporate blogging. These regulations ensure that consumers aren't fooled into thinking that corporate remarks are those made by ordinary people.

In 2005, people working on behalf of household cleaning product Cillit Bang made the mistake of commenting on some blogs in the guise of the brand's fictional spokesperson Barry Scott. This deceit was uncovered by a blogger and the clumsy marketing attempt made online headlines around the world.

Now posting on blogs on behalf of businesses without revealing your identity as representing that organisation is banned. The Consumer Protection from Unfair Trading 2008 regulation aims to stamp out this practice. Read up on this regulation if you plan to comment on other people's blogs or start your own. Visit the Office of Fair Trading's website (www.oft.gov.uk), where you can find the relevant information under 'Advice for Businesses' in the 'Competing Fairly' section.

In addition to blogs, Facebook, Foursquare, Twitter and a host of other social networks are now an important way and in some cases – such as when marketing to the under 25s – the only way to get your message across. Often more systematic processes are in place; TripAdvisor for information on hotel users' experiences is a good example, where different aspects of a hotel experience – accommodation, service, value for money – are rated on a points scale. This allows potential customers to see if the particular aspect or aspects they are looking for in a hotel are likely to be delivered.

So you need to build these social network routes into your marketing plans. Shiv Singh's *Social Media Marketing For Dummies* (published by Wiley) contains everything you need to know about this vital topic.

Chapter 7

Planning Your Business Website

. . . .

In This Chapter

▶ Creating a simple and effective business website

▶ Deciding on your site's contents

▶ Designing a look and feel for your site

▶ Having someone else create your site

. . . .

Amarketing-oriented business website is the meat and drink of the online marketing world: not too exciting, but satisfying and extremely sustaining. By creating and maintaining a straightforward business website, you can easily provide customers, press and analysts with vital information about your company and products. If the initial effort is successful, your site can lay the groundwork for a larger online marketing effort, possibly including your first move into online sales.

You've probably seen a lot of advanced web technology used in high-profile websites – technologies such as Flash and Dynamic HTML. These innovations are all good, if used properly, but they have little place in a marketing-oriented business website. You can create a basic business website without too much planning. You can even begin to construct the site while you're in the midst of the planning process. The idea here is to jump-start your online presence by getting a competent representation of your company up and running – fast.

In this chapter, we describe how to create the initial site yourself or by working with a few colleagues or consultants.

Although some companies and consultants advertise that they'll create a basic business website for you for as little as £200, many of these ads are teasers designed to get you to pick up the phone and begin a process that can lead to you spending big money. Although you can and should use consultants or specialist suppliers for larger web efforts, developing and publishing the initial site yourself is sensible. After you get some hands-on experience, you can know what you're paying for when you hire a web-design agency to expand your website later. If you do hire help for the initial website effort, use this chapter to do as much of the work as you can on your own, and to double-check the outsiders' advice so that you can make sure that you're getting your money's worth.

Guiding Principles for Business Sites

A basic business website is like a simple, glossy brochure that briefly describes your company and is a showcase for your products. It reassures people that you're a competent player who'll be around for a while and from whom they can buy with confidence. Your website also lets users move easily from picking up basic information to more active steps such as contacting you by writing to you, or sending you an email. But watch this last option, because it can backfire; you can receive so many emails that you have trouble responding to all of them. See Chapter 9 in this Book for more on emails.

These underlying principles should guide your effort to create a basic business website:

- **Harmlessness:** The first words of the doctors' Hippocratic Oath are 'First, do no harm', and this dictum should be honoured by people doing marketing as well. Misspellings, poor grammar and basic errors in your site's text harm your company's image of competence. Web pages with large graphics that download slowly, or that have been developed using advanced technologies that not everyone can use, irritate potential customers. Allowing people to send you email that goes unanswered can cause lost sales. Be cautious and avoid problems.

- **Fast build:** Your initial website effort should develop quickly from the initial idea to a live site. If you can do all the work yourself and don't need anyone's approval, you may get the site up and running in two weeks. If you need to discuss certain aspects of your site in advance and you need approval of the final product at the end, you may need a month or two to complete the site. Keep the project time as short as possible. However, make sure that you have a long-term plan in mind of what the site will look like once launched and evolved. Think about content and other sections you may want to add so that when you do, you don't have to completely rebuild your website!

- **Cheap:** A basic website can be created in-house, with perhaps some outside help on the look and feel, and published on a web server by your Internet Service Provider (ISP) or web-hosting service for very little cost. Expect to spend a few weeks on creating the site, possibly £1,000 on a consultant for graphics and navigation help, and around £20 a month for an ISP to host the site on its server.

- **Effective:** Any marketing effort needs to support moving a prospective customer along the sales cycle. A basic website helps potential customers consider you as a possible supplier and encourages them to contact you in order to go further. (A website gets press, analysts and investors to take you seriously, as well.)

✔ **Widely usable:** A basic website needs to be usable by anyone with an Internet connection and a web browser; it mustn't contain any advanced web technology that isn't supported by almost every available browser. That means no frames, no Flash, no Dynamic HTML – so no complicated animations or clever graphics. Keeping it simple makes your website easier to design and use.

✔ **Fits in on the Net:** Because of its origins among academics and scientists, the Internet has certain standards and practices that you ignore at your peril. (Until early in the 1990s, any commercial use of the Internet was forbidden, and even now, although it's dying out, some resistance to online commerce remains.) Respect the history of the medium by avoiding hype, overstatement, alarming layouts and graphics, and so on. A conservative or formulaic approach will serve you well until you develop a good feel for where you can have some fun.

Specifying Your Site Content

A basic business website isn't something you should advertise or market heavily. The site is there for people to find when they're looking for information on the Web. Therefore the site's contents need to be simple and easy to access, attractive but not exuberant. In footballing terms, the idea is that it's early in the match, and you want to start things on a positive note by not being too gung ho in attack for the first quarter of the game.

A basic website will help you fulfil the first marketing-related function that any website must fulfil, that of a validator. 'Valid' means 'worthy', and a website functions as a validator by showing that you're worthy of doing business with. Validators do much of their work on a subconscious level, so the absence of key validators makes people feel uncomfortable, in ways that they find difficult to define but that operate very effectively in steering them clear of you. The powerful role of validators is why, as we mention in the 'Guiding Principles for Business Sites' section earlier in this chapter, ensuring your website is free of errors, technical barriers and other irritants is important. (Would you send out salespeople who were poorly trained, ignorant of your products and unable to speak the same language as your customers? Apply similar considerations to your website.)

A basic website has to meet fundamental information needs, but not much more than that. In fact, putting more information on it than is absolutely necessary is more likely to make your site difficult to navigate than to make it more useful. Avoid piling on a lot of content until you can also devote some time and energy to making your website easy to navigate.

If some of your planned material seems like a good idea but not strictly necessary, drop it (or, better still, put it on a list for later). Your final list of contents will vary depending on your company, your industry and the available information resources you have at hand that can readily be re-purposed for the Web. But most sites include the following:

- **About Us and Contact information:** This information is vital, and many sites – even big ones that cost a lot to create and maintain – either don't include it at all or bury it. Remember your customers may well be looking on your website to find out what your company does/how it does it. Also make sure that you provide your company, address, main phone number and fax number. (Don't include your email address until after you read Chapter 9 in Book V.) Make your contact information easily accessible, one link away from your homepage.

- **Where you do business:** If your geographic range is limited, make this fact clear upfront. Be subtle and positive. On your homepage or contact information page, include a phrase like 'London's leading supplier of electrical services to business' or 'Western Europe's most innovative maker of widgets'. Help people who don't need to spend time on your website find that fact out quickly and in a positive context so that they leave happy, rather than annoyed.

- **Key people:** A brief list of key people, with a paragraph or so of descriptive information about each, can go far to make people comfortable with your company. (Some companies are reluctant to include this kind of information because they're afraid of attracting executive recruiters, but the benefits to your site's visitors outweigh this risk.) Don't include spouse-hobbies-and-kids stuff – just name, title, and a brief biography.

- **Key clients:** Though some companies are reluctant to include it for fear of attracting competitors, a list of key clients is a very strong validator of your success. List their names and a sentence or two about how they use your product or what you did for them. (Make sure that you ask your customers whether they mind this inclusion and whether they want you to include a link to their websites.) But don't include this kind of list until your customer list is at least a little bit impressive.

- **Products and services:** Include simple, brief descriptions of your products and services. You can also link to more detailed information, but put the simple descriptions in one place and make them easy to access; that way, prospects can scan descriptions quickly to decide whether to explore your site further.

- **Price:** Include specific price information if you can. Price can vary by sales channel, by location, by options or by many other factors, so including specific prices can be difficult, but at least find some way to communicate the rough price range of your product. Describing the price paid in a few specific instances does nicely. People hate to 'turn off'

Book V

Marketing
and
Advertising
Your
Wares

customers, which may happen when you indicate your pricing structure, but encouraging people who can't afford your product to contact you (by not letting them know your price range) isn't in anyone's interest.

- **Where and how to buy:** Tell people who visit your website where and how to buy your products and services. This kind of information is hidden or absent on all too many websites. If you have several sales channels, list each of them, along with a brief description of each channel that highlights its unique advantages. One excellent method is to set up an interactive area of a web page that lets people enter their locations and then receive information about nearby sales outlets. If this feature involves too much work to handle right now, consider getting and publicising an 0800 number as a stand-by until you can design and implement an interactive web capability.

- **Company, product and service validators:** You put information that validates specific products and services, employees or the company as a whole here. List positive descriptions of your company, people, products and services from any reputable source, including analyst reports, the general press, the trade press and individual customers from well-known companies or other organisations. Include any awards you've won. Like your company website itself, these validators let people know that your company is worth doing business with.

- **Company news:** People visit your website when they hear about your company in connection with offline events such as trade shows, product launches and so on. You look clueless if you don't list a few basics: trade-show appearances, product launches, press releases, article mentions of your company and so on. (Oh, you don't do many press releases? Now's the time to start! Read Chapter 6 in Book V.) Figure 7-1 shows the news section of a well-designed website. Construct this section after you've cut your teeth on the others and then put some real time and energy into getting it right.

- **Industry news:** This detail is optional, but important. A great way to position your company as an industry leader is to put industry news on your site. The goals of such an area include educating customers about your industry, validating your place in the industry and getting repeat visitors by creating a 'must-read' news area for customers, analysts and press. (You think your competitors won't be annoyed when everyone in your industry goes to your site for news? Especially when they find themselves doing it too!) Don't hold up your site launch in order to get this detail in, but consider creating such an area as soon as you can.

If you don't want to develop your own news area, you can even link to a blog through one of the mainstream blogging tools like www.blogger.com. These self-publishing sites can be updated as regularly as you want and can be easily linked to your business website.

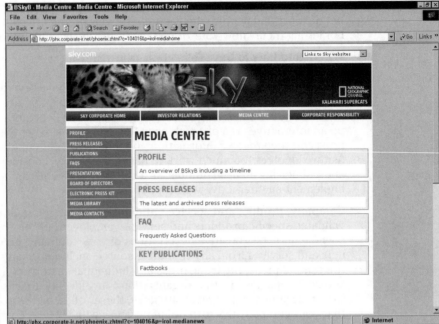

Figure 7-1:
Sky gets the
message
across
through
Sky.com.

Creating a Look and Feel for Your Site

Most marketers that we know are very good with words – either in writing, public speaking or both – and can create vivid pictures in listeners' minds. However, most of them lack graphic-design skills.

Graphic design is the art of using visual elements to create a pleasing impression in the viewer's mind, and is a very important element in website design – to some of your website visitors, the most important element of all. Having a good design, or look and feel as it's called within the industry, is crucial to getting the right message across. Making a snap decision on the design of your site is wrong as it's probably one of the most vital decisions you may make when building your website.

Graphic design for the Web is a specialised art. Users view a company web page in different-sized windows, using different-sized screens, with different colour capabilities, in all sorts of lighting conditions. Some users have custom settings to override the designer's choice of font, size and text colours. Large graphics may make a page look strikingly attractive, yet take such a long time to download that they annoy and drive away users.

Using colour correctly on the Web is an art in and of itself. Colours and colour combinations that look attractive on one computer can look awful on another. In fact, out of the millions of shades of colour that a higher-end computer system can display, only 216 'browser-safe' colours exist that work well across most people's web setups. If you use other colours, your site is likely to look awful to at least some of your visitors.

All these complexities and opportunities for error add up to a simple rule: unless you have graphic-design experience and know, or are willing to learn, the details of web-specific design, you need specialist help in designing the look and feel of your site. Here are a few possible sources of help:

- **Existing resources:** Your company may already have brand guidelines or a style guide based on its logo and marketing collateral, such as annual reports. Consider adapting this look for the Web, giving people who are familiar with your company in an offline context a comfortable feeling when they encounter your firm online.

- **Other well-designed sites:** Stealing the designs of other sites just isn't on. Looking at other sites, finding ones you like, and using the same *principles* as they do, however, is fine. (You're also free to avoid the practices of the sites that irritate you!)

- **Online advice:** Many sources of online advice on all aspects of web page creation, including graphics, are available. Two places to start are the World Wide Web Consortium at www.w3.org and www.webreview.com.

- **CD-ROM resources:** CD-ROMs with 'clip art' – professionally designed, non-copyrighted graphics optimised for online use – are available. You can pick up a few thousand buttons, backgrounds, icons and other graphical elements for under £50 in many cases. An average person can achieve amazing effects with a little time and a good CD-ROM art collection.

- **Printed advice:** Many good books and articles describe how to create and deploy online graphics. Visit online bookshops such as Amazon.com (www.amazon.co.uk).

Outside help is an available resource and a good idea when creating your first site. Consider hiring a graphic designer to assist with the look of your website. Graphic designers who advertise on the Web are likely to have designed several sites they can refer you to as examples of their work. An example of one designer's web presence is shown in Figure 7-2. If you need help finding a designer consider using a graphic design student; increasing numbers are available as the number of courses offering web design grows. One of the best known is the University of Brighton (www.brighton.ac.uk).

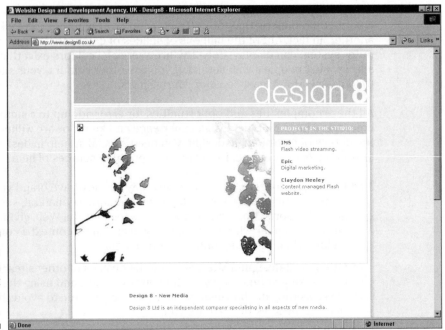

Figure 7-2:
Design8 has
a simple but
effective
website.

Hiring a graphic designer is different from hiring a web-design company. A web-design company will construct your entire site for you; a graphic designer will just work on the look. For a basic site, which you want to do quickly and cheaply while finding out as much as possible yourself, a graphic designer is preferable. You can get him involved early in the process, late, or even after your initial site is live.

Tell the designer who your expected visitors are, share any existing design elements that you have and then let the designer work. Unlike a web-design company, a graphic designer needs clear instructions on everything else about the site, including content and navigation. Expect to get a couple of alternatives and a quote for updating your site to include the design. (The designer may even offer to update your printed materials as well, improving consistency.)

At the end of the job, you should own the designer's work. This arrangement is called *work for hire* and is looked down upon by top professionals doing large jobs but is a fact of life for smaller jobs and for designers who haven't yet made a name for themselves. Avoid complicated intellectual property arrangements in which the designer retains rights to the design.

Having Your Site Done for You

Creating your initial site yourself is a good idea, but if you feel that you don't have the time or the expertise to do so, get outside help. The good news is that many individual consultants and web-design agencies have sprung up to help companies create and maintain their websites. The bad news is that many ways exist to go wrong in hiring a digital agency.

But wait, we have more bad news! Having an external supplier or an individual do your website will probably save only a small amount of your time. A website is such an important reflection of your business that you must expect to be heavily involved with the project from start to finish.

The important steps in working with an outside supplier are setting up the engagement, managing the work, and following through when the work is done. Although these steps are the same for any general project, some specifics exist for a web project that may surprise you.

Many of these steps apply to managing an internal web project as well. Check these steps out even if you're doing the work yourself.

Getting engaged

Hiring an agency is often referred to as an 'engagement', and starting one may require more forethought than some marriages! Here are some simple rules that will help you get good results from a web agency:

✔ **Find a site that has the elements you need.** Surf websites both inside and outside your own industry to find a site that has most of the pieces you need. A clean and attractive front page, easy-to-find contact info, simple navigation, and brief, clear product descriptions are some of the elements you may be looking for. Figure 7-3 is a good example of a site with these elements.

✔ **Decide how many pages you want in your site.** Remember those sites you surfed? See what the major areas are in sites you like and count how many pages are in each area. Come up with a rough estimate of the number of pages in your site. *Hint:* The lower the number, the lower the cost and the greater the odds that your project will be a success.

✔ **Find several local agencies or consultants.** Even in this wired age, being able to meet someone in person is a real benefit – especially for your initial project. Look at local business sites that you like and find out who created them. Talk to friends and colleagues to find specialists in your local area who have done good work. Check the *Yellow Pages* or the trade press for any local suppliers.

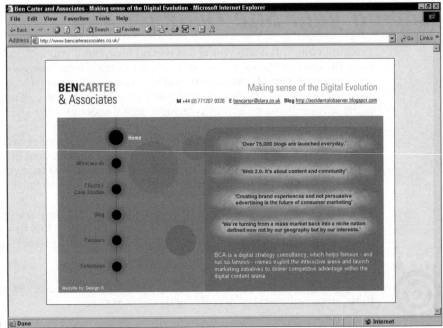

Figure 7-3:
BCA is an
uncompli-
cated
website
with clear
aims.

✔ **Set a budget.** Now that you have some idea of what you want and what other sites have cost in your area, set an upper limit for your budget. Ensure the figure you come up with is in line with the benefits you expect to get from your site. As a test, consider the impact that spending the same amount of money on radio advertising may have for you.

✔ **Hold a pitch.** Talk to the agencies you identified. (Talking to more than one really helps, so don't rush this stage.) Get their ideas of what they think you need. Tell them what you're looking for and get a ballpark estimate as to timeframe and budget. *Hint:* Consider going to a marketing services intermediary like the AAR (www.aargroup.co.uk) or Haystack (www.thehaystackgroup.com) to help you find your agency.

✔ **Choose an agency.** Make an initial choice. Don't throw away the others' business cards until your first choice has shown good initial results!

Picking someone you believe you can trust is the most important part of engaging a specialist. You can always have your website made larger or flashier later, but the initial site simply needs to look good, be complete within a limited initial scope, and be delivered on time and on budget.

Ensure that you understand before engaging a firm whether it considers itself primarily a web-programming company, a web-design company, or a balance of both. Some agencies are excellent at creating the technical infrastructure of a site and making it work well but aren't adept at doing the graphics and copywriting. Others are excellent at look-and-feel but have little understanding of good website navigation or making things work 'under the bonnet'. The ideal firm has a good grasp of both aspects or admits what its expertise isn't, allowing you to hire a freelancer to fill the gap.

As the focus moves away from building websites to what customers expect from websites, a need exists for more strategic thinking. Agencies often can't provide this strategy overview, so working with digital consultants (such as the authors of this book, say) to get the bigger picture of where your website will fit, what it will do and how it will develop is useful.

Projecting your management style

Project management for websites has a lot in common with other projects, but a few Web-specific techniques exist that you need to be aware of in addition to your usual tactics. The main problem with a web project is that people react strongly to the look of a website – and if you wait until the end, an influential person may send the whole project back to the beginning. So clear up process hurdles early on to avoid hassle later.

- ✔ **Identify approvers.** Before you start, identify everyone who'll need to approve the site before it can go live and be publicised. This list should be short – and the people on it given status reports and updates at every major step.

- ✔ **Image is everything!** People are likely to react first and foremost to the look and feel of your website – the way background colours, images, navigation elements and layout work together. Get a mock-up early on, and have all your approvers look at it and, when they find it acceptable, initial it. Better still, get two or three mock-ups that you can live with, and let the approvers make their choice on which should go forward to the next step.

- ✔ **Make a first impression.** Have your agency create a working version of the first page of your website hosted on a development site. At this point, get everyone's final okay on the basic look of the site. Figure 7-4 shows the first page of a website we like.

  The first page of a website commonly gets 20–25 per cent of all the page views for the site, so getting it right is important. Also, if the first page meets with everyone's approval, the rest of the site is likely to receive only minor comments.

- ✔ **Get skeleton text ready.** Next, fill out the site by creating a dummy page for each and every page on the site. Each dummy page should have the agreed-upon look and feel for the site plus a one-paragraph description of what will be on that specific page. You can use the skeleton to test overall navigation. Have people review the dummy pages too – providing a last chance for 'shouldn't we have a page about our company history?' type comments.

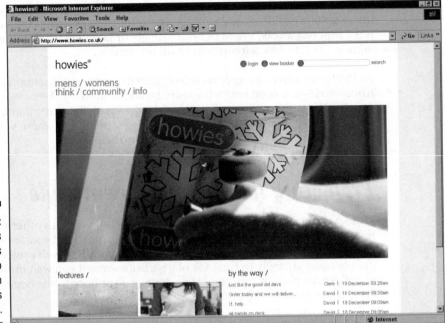

Figure 7-4:
Howies
uses its
website to
get its green
credentials
across.

✔ **Fill in the blanks.** Now fill in the content of each page. (This task can often be spread among several people, who can 'borrow' content from your business plan and any brochures or other marketing materials you have.) If your site has several sections (news, products and so on), each written by several people, make sure that each content section has a content 'lead' who is responsible for ensuring that the writing style and tone match across all of that section's pages.

If you don't already have an in-house copywriter then you need to consider hiring one who can rewrite your draft copy. Again, choosing the right copywriter is vital as the content of your site is imperative to getting the right message across to your customers!

✔ **Make time for the testing.** After the site's dummy pages are filled in, set aside some time to test it. Have one person read through all the pages to make sure that they're consistent in how they present your company and its products. If there's a danger that your customers may stumble across it then consider hosting it on a development or a test server to iron out the tweaks. Also make sure that the website works with all the different browsers like Internet Explorer, Mozilla Firefox and Safari. When you're happy, do a 'soft launch' – put the site up on the Web, but don't publicise its existence until everyone who needs to approve of the site has had a chance to do so.

Book V

Marketing
and
Advertising
Your
Wares

✔ **Go, go, go!** After the site's up and you're happy with it, get the word out. Put the URL on business cards, stationery, advertisements and more. Ask for feedback from people you know and from site visitors as well.

This process crucially has many checkpoints, making it difficult for the project to get too far off-track without your knowing about it – and having a chance to fix the problem.

Beating the wrap-up

Plan now for future updating of your website. The basic structure you've created should last for a long time. Work with your agency now to identify procedures for the following important tasks:

✔ **Updating content:** You want to be able to update the site's content without the agency's help and to do this you need to have access to a content management system, unless you want them involved as a checkpoint. Specify how content within a page will be updated.

Content Management Systems (CMS) are important if you want to be able to update your website and if you're going to have a lot of text that will need changing regularly. Having CMS built in from the start will save you a lot of hassle and will mean that you can access/change your site very easily. There are lots of different CMS options but if you're a complete web novice then you need the simplest one. Known as *WYSIWYG* CMS (standing for 'What you see is what you get'), such a system will enable you to cut and paste copy into text boxes via a simple web interface. You don't need to understand HTML to operate this, which is why it appeals to those who aren't web wizards.

✔ **Adding pages:** Identify likely areas in which you may want to add a new page; the product area will need to be extended, for instance, if you launch a new product. Work out how long it should take to add a page from initial idea to launch, and who needs to be involved.

✔ **Revising the whole site:** At some point, you'll want to revise the whole site. Work out what may trigger that revision, and set up regular meetings with your agency – say, quarterly – to identify needed changes and to start the next major overhaul.

Don't be afraid to tell your agency that you may get other people involved for some or all of the work ahead; for your first agency to play a lesser role as the project develops or to have no role at all is common. Do let them know about expectations that weren't met as well as the things you were happy about, and whether they can expect a good reference from you for future clients.

A caution about copyright

Getting wrapped up in the gorgeous graphics and clean navigation that a website consultant develops for you is easy. But before making the new site live, ask the agency the difficult question, 'You do have the right to use all those design elements, don't you?'

A few inexperienced, rushed or simply unscrupulous web agencies have been known to copy graphic elements they like from existing websites and reuse them in sites they're creating, without permission. Doing so can violate the copyright of whoever created or owns the original site – and cause legal problems for you later, so play it safe. Make sure that you get assurance from your agency, in writing, that all its design elements and text are either original or properly licensed.

Making your site accessible

Make your site as accessible to as many people as possible. Avoid being in a situation where some of your customers can't use your site when they find it – you're committing corporate suicide.

Lots of agencies will offer you an *analytics* service as part of the web build project, in which they monitor how a test-base of users use and navigate the site. These 'test sessions' are crucial for you to identify any problems or pitfalls in the way the site has been designed and built. Better to spot flaws now rather than when the site goes live: bad websites result in lost custom. Also, make sure that your site can be accessed and used by disabled people. Since 1999, the Disability Discrimination Act has put the onus on web publishers to ensure that their sites have a basic level of accessibility. Ignore this advice at your peril: you may be breaking the law!

More information on accessibility guidelines and standards, which are endorsed by the UK government, can be found at the World Wide Web Consortium: www.w3.org.

Chapter 8

Choosing and Equipping Your New Online Business

Starting your online business is like refurbishing an old house. Both projects involve a series of recognisable phases:

✔ **The idea phase:** First, you tell people about your great idea. They hear the enthusiasm in your voice, nod their heads and say something like, 'Good luck'. They've seen you in this condition before and know how it usually turns out.

✔ **The decision phase:** Undaunted, you begin honing your plan. You read books (like this one), ask questions and shop around until you find just the right tools and materials to get you on your way. Of course, when you're up to your neck in work, you may start to panic, asking yourself whether you're really up for the task.

✔ **The assembly phase:** Undeterred, you forge ahead. You plug in your tools and go to work. Drills spin and sparks fly as your idea becomes reality.

✔ **The test-drive phase:** One fine day, out of the dust and fumes, your masterpiece emerges. You invite everyone over to enjoy the fruits of your labour. All those who were sceptical before are now awestruck and full of admiration. Satisfied with the result, you enjoy your project for years to come.

If refurbishing a house doesn't work for you, think about restoring an antique car, planning an anniversary party or devising a mountain-climbing excursion in Tibet. The point is that starting an online business is a project like any other – one that you can construct and accomplish in stages. Right now, you're at the first stage of launching your new business. Your creativity is working overtime. You may even have some rough sketches that only a mother could love.

This chapter helps you get from concept to reality. Your first step is to imagine how you want your business to look and feel. Then you can begin to develop and implement strategies for achieving your dream. You've got a big advantage over those who started new businesses a few years ago: you've got thousands of predecessors to show you what works and what doesn't.

Starting Off on the Right Foot

As you travel along the path from idea to reality, you must also consider equipping your online business properly – just like you'd have to equip a traditional, bricks-and-mortar business. One of the many exciting aspects of launching a business online, however, is the absence of many *overheads* (that is, operating expenses). Many real world businesses resort to taking out loans to pay the rent, and design their shop fronts, pay fees and purchase shop furniture. In contrast, the primary overhead for an online business is computer gadgetry. It's great if you can afford top-of-the-line equipment, but you'll be happy to know that the latest bells and whistles aren't absolutely necessary in order to build a business online and maintain it effectively. But in order to streamline the technical aspects of connecting to the Internet and creating a business website, some investment is always necessary.

Don't rush into a contract with a web designer or hosting company without researching the market and finding out exactly what you're getting for your money. Dan once made the mistake of paying upfront for a hosting and design package; he now believes that after they've got your money, they sit back and don't work hard for your business. You need to demand an invoice for work done and make them tell you what they'll actually do for your business in the real world. A search engine optimisation package, for example, may be a waste of money as you can do it yourself (see Chapter 9 in Book V for more on search engines). Most importantly, make the company spell out a timeline of progress so that you have a rough idea of when you'll be ready to launch.

Mapping Out Your Online Business

How do you get off square one? Start by imagining the kind of business that's your ultimate goal. This step is the time to indulge in some brainstorming. Envisioning your business is a creative way of asking yourself the all-important questions: Why do I want to go into business online? What are my goals? Table 8-1 illustrates possible objectives and suggests how to achieve them. By envisioning the final result you want to achieve, you can determine the steps you need to take to get there.

Table 8-1		Online Business Models
Goal	**Type of Website**	**What to Do**
Make big bucks	Sales	Sell items or get lots of paying advertisers
Gain credibility and attention	Marketing	Put your CV and samples of your work online
Turn an interest into a source of income	Hobby/special interest	Invite like-minded people to share your passion, participate in your site and generate traffic so that you can gain advertisers or customers

Getting inspired

You don't need to feel like you have to reinvent the wheel. A great idea doesn't necessarily mean something completely fresh that's never been done before (although if you have a great new idea, then good for you!). Sometimes, spending just half an hour surfing the Net can stimulate your mental network. Find sites with qualities you want to emulate. Throughout this book, we suggest good business sites you can visit to find good models to follow.

Many people start up online selling to people just like themselves. For example, a motorbike enthusiast may start up a parts business or an informative site about the best bikes and where to buy them. If you're a hobby geek, then your own likes and dislikes have a lot of value. As you search the Web for inspiration, make a list as you go of what you find appealing and jot down notes on logos, designs, text and *functionality* (how the site lets you access its features). That way, you have plenty of data to draw upon as you begin to refine what you yourself want to do.

Standing out from the crowd

The online world has undergone a population explosion. According to Internet Systems Consortium's Domain Survey (www.isc.org), in July 2010, 768.9 million computers that hosted websites were connected to the Internet, compared with 439.2 million in 2006 and 171.6 million in 2002. As an online entrepreneur, your goal is to make your mark – or to 'position yourself in the marketplace', as business consultants like to say. Consider the following tried-and-tested suggestions if you want your website to be a popular corner of the Internet:

- **Do something you know all about.** Experience adds value to the information you provide. Doing something that you have experience of also keeps you interested throughout the roller-coaster ride that is starting a business. Most importantly, in the online world, expertise sells.

- **Make a statement.** On your website, include a mission statement that clearly identifies what you do, the customers you hope to reach and how you're different from your competitors. Depending on what you plan to set up, this statement may be on the home page (in the form of a concise About Us statement) or in a frequently asked questions (FAQ) section of the site.

- **Include contact details.** We may be in a digital age, but people still crave the personal touch. You must prove that you're not a machine by keeping the language you use friendly, and including a phone number and email address is best practice. People are also very suspicious of websites that don't declare their address. (In addition, the legal requirements for a business website include putting your company name, registration number, registered office and VAT number on the site.)

- **Give something away for free.** We really can't stress this tip enough. Giveaways and promotions are proven ways to gain attention and develop a loyal customer base. You don't have to give away an actual product; you can offer words of wisdom based on your training and experience. Take a look at the hugely popular Money Saving Expert website at www.moneysavingexpert.com, which has allowed countless consumers to get great deals or learn about consumer rights without them forking out a penny.

- **Be obvious.** Money Saving Expert, which we list in the preceding bullet, does what it says on the tin. It helps if your website tells people what it does before they even get to the home page.

- **Find your niche.** Web space is a great place to pursue *niche marketing*. In fact, it often seems that the quirkier the item, the better it sells. Don't be afraid to target a narrow audience and direct all your sales efforts to a small group of devoted followers.

✔ **Do something you love.** The more you love your business, the more time and effort you're apt to put into it and, therefore, the more likely it is to be successful. Such businesses take advantage of the Internet's worldwide reach, which makes it easy for people with the same interests to gather at the same virtual location.

The top new economy millionaires have followed many, if not all, of the aforementioned strategies. Take Rightmove.co.uk. It was already making £8.9 million profit back in 2005, because its founders saw a trend towards people looking for property online. The founders built a simple and functional website and quickly cornered the burgeoning market. In March 2006, the company floated on the stock market and by 2007, 90 per cent of all UK real estate agents were Rightmove.co.uk members, advertising their properties via the website. In 2009, its profit had grown to a whopping £41.9 million!

Nick Robertson's ASOS.com (formally known as As Seen On Screen) jumped on people's insatiable appetite for the lifestyles of the rich and famous. The premise was simple: dress like the stars you worship. The website's meteoric success has allowed it to expand beyond its TV-based roots, and now it boasts a huge array of celebrity-inspired fashion. Oh, and the profitable company made £233 million in sales the year ending March 2010 – up 35 per cent on the previous year – and a profit of £14.6 million after tax. Not bad considering the economic climate!

Evaluating commercial websites

Is your website similar to others? How does it differ? (Or to put it another way: how is it better?) Your customers will be asking these questions, so you may as well start out by asking them as well.

Commercial websites – those whose Internet addresses usually end with `.co.uk`, `.com` or `.biz` – are the fastest-growing segment of the Net and this is the area you'll be entering. The trick is to be comfortable with the size and level of complexity of a business that's right for you. In general, your options are

✔ **A big commercial website:** The Web means big business, and plenty of big companies create websites with the primary goal of supplementing a product or service that's already well known and well established. Just a few examples are the Ribena website (`www.ribena.co.uk`), the Pepsi World website (`www.pepsiworld.com`) and the Toyota website (`www.toyota.com`). True, these commercial websites were created by corporations with many millions of pounds to throw around, but you can still look at them to get ideas for your own site.

✔ **A mid-sized site:** You can look at mid-sized companies too, which use the Web as an extension of their brand. Brilliant examples of mid-sized companies are Ben & Jerry's ice cream (www.benjerry.co.uk) and Innocent Drinks (www.innocentdrinks.co.uk). Stephen Fry is famous for being a prolific Twitter user, but he writes far lengthier observations on his website, www.stephenfry.com. Sites such as CD Wow (www.cdwow.co.uk) and Play.com (www.play.com) are mid-sized companies, but their websites are as good as any blue chip you're likely to come across.

✔ **A site that's just right:** No prerequisites for prior business experience guarantee success on the Web. Starting out as a single person, couple or family is also fine. In fact, we devote the rest of this book to helping you produce a top-notch, home-grown entrepreneurial business with the minimum of assistance. This chapter gets you off to a good start by examining the different kinds of business you can launch online and some business goals you need to be setting yourself.

Checking Out Flavours of Online Businesses You Can Taste Test

If you're an excitable character, you may have to curb your enthusiasm as you comb the Internet for ideas. Use the following examples to create a picture of your business and then zero in on the kind of sites that can help you formulate its look and feel.

Selling consumer products

The Web has always attracted those looking for unique items or something customised just for them. Consider taking your wares online if one or both of the following applies to you:

✔ You're a creative person who creates as a hobby the type of stuff people may want to buy (think artists, designers, model makers, calligraphers and so on).

✔ You have access to the sort of products or services that big companies simply can't replicate. Those items may mean regional foods, hand-made souvenirs or items for car enthusiasts; the list is truly endless – you just have to find your niche.

Innocent Drinks (www.innocentdrinks.co.uk) has never lost its 'community' feel, despite becoming bigger and bigger and moving on from simply selling smoothies to producing vegetable pots and fruit purees. Their website talks to you as if you're an old friend, and it even offers you fun things to do when you're bored such as browsing a gallery of past adverts or knitting tiny hats for their bottles in aid of charity. They even suggest calling their headquarters, Fruit Towers, on the Banana Phone. If that's not enough, you can contact any member of staff simply by clicking on his or her 'embarrassing' headshot. Their branding is brilliant and rare – try to match it (without copying), but remember that you must reflect your own business style and the people you want to sell to.

Punting what you're good at

Either through a website or through listings in indexes and directories, offering your professional services online can expand your client base dramatically. It also gives existing clients a new way to contact you or just see what's new with your business. Here are just a few examples of professionals who are offering their services online:

- ✔ **Solicitors:** John Pickering and Partners are personal injury solicitors (aren't they all nowadays) who specialise in severe diseases and critical injuries sustained at work. The firm is based in Manchester, but its website gives it a national and even global reach (www.johnpickering. co.uk). To give it a professional feel, something which is vital in this profession, the website features relevant news updates, information about claims and even information on how to choose a solicitor.

- ✔ **Nutritionists:** Registered nutritionist Jackie Farr has a simple, uncomplicated website (www.truenutrition.co.uk) that has easy-to-access sections defining nutritional therapy and describing a typical consultation (see Figure 8-1). Yet even before clicking through to these areas, the home page outlines who Jackie is, what nutritional therapy can do for you and how bad nutrition may be responsible for frequent infections, bad skin and lethargy.

- ✔ **Architects:** When the first edition of this book came out, we pointed out that the website of Robertson Francis Partnership, a chartered architect based in Cardiff, was under construction (www.rfparchitects. co.uk). Guess what? In 2011, the site *still* hadn't been built (ironic, eh?). Plenty of professional websites take an age to get up and running because people are too busy running their businesses. At least the architects put up their contact details on their holding page. If you're too busy running your business, at the very least do what these guys did and get something up there – even if it's just your name and address.

✔ **Music teachers:** Do a search on Gumtree (`www.gumtree.com`) or Google local (`local.google.co.uk`) and you see just how many music teachers are plying their wares online. Many don't have a website themselves, but are savvy enough to know that people will be searching for their services online.

We're busy people who don't always have the time to pore over the small print. Short and snappy nuggets of information draw customers to your site and make them feel as though they're getting something for free. One way you can put forth this professional expertise is by starting your own online newsletter. You get to be editor, writer and mailing-list manager. Plus, you get to talk as much as you want, network with tons of people who subscribe to your publication and put your name and your business before lots of people. Writer Sean McManus puts out a monthly newsletter that supplements his site (`www.sean.co.uk`), as do many other online businesspeople.

Figure 8-1:
A Kent nutritionist provides her contact information and fields of expertise on this simple, yet informative, web page.

Website designed by Scott Parker Consultancy (`www.scottparker.co.uk`)

Making money from your expertise

The original purpose of the Internet was to share knowledge via computers, and information is the commodity that has fuelled cyberspace's rapid growth. As the Internet and commercial online networks continue to expand, information remains key.

Collecting and disseminating data can be a profitable pastime. Think of all the websites where information is the chief commodity rather than clothes or music. The fact is, people love to get knowledge they trust from the comfort of their own homes.

Apart from the obvious online newspapers and blogs, here are just a few examples of the types of business that feed on our love of knowledge:

✔ **Search engines:** Some businesses succeed by connecting web surfers with companies, organisations and individuals that specialise in a given area. Yahoo! (www.yahoo.co.uk) is an obvious example. Originally started by two college students, Yahoo! has become an Internet behemoth by gathering information in one index so that people can easily find things online.

✔ **Links pages:** The Prize Finder (www.theprizefinder.com) lists thousands of current UK competitions and is updated daily. The site's been up and running for a decade and makes its money through *affiliate links* to other contest websites who advertise on the site. In the US, a similar site is Grandma Jam (www.grandmajam.com) run by Janet Marchbanks Aulenta. 'The key to succeeding at this type of site is to build up a regular base of users that return each day to find new contests – the daily upkeep is very important,' Janet says.

✔ **Personal recommendations:** The personal touch sells. Just look at Web 2.0 site Digg.com. This guide to the online world provides web surfers with a central location where they can track down popular news stories. Despite various controversial redesigns, the site's premise remains the same: it works because real people submit the stories, and only the most popular stories make it to the top of page one. The users themselves are who 'digg' stories – the most popular ones rise up the rankings. Digg now has a My News page that delivers a personalised newspaper that's based on actions performed on Digg profiles you follow: if they 'digg' a story, it'll probably appear on your My News page.

Resource sites can transform information into money in several ways. In some cases, individuals pay to become members (such as *Which?'s* independent product tests at www.which.co.uk). Sometimes, businesses pay to be listed on a site. Other times, a site attracts so many visitors on a regular basis that other companies pay to post advertising on the site. Big successes – such as Facebook (www.facebook.com) and Digg (www.digg.com) – carry a healthy share of ads and strike lucrative partnerships with big companies as well.

Don't panic if you've never heard of Web 2.0. For geeks it's the greatest thing since sliced bread. The term describes websites populated largely by 'User-generated' content – examples include bookmarks, comments, ideas, links, ratings, reviews, opinions and much more. Big beasts in the Web 2.0 jungle include YouTube, FaceBook, Wikipedia, LinkedIn, Technorati, Trip Advisor and StumbleUpon. Sir Tim Berners-Lee, the man credited with inventing the World Wide Web reckons the term 'Web 2.0' is just a piece of jargon. His vision for the Web was a place where people in different locations could share knowledge. An early name he coined was the 'Read/Write Web'. Well, bolt on a picture or two and the basic idea still holds.

Creating opportunities with technology

What could be more natural than using the Web to sell what you need to get and stay online? The online world itself, by the very fact that it exists, has spawned all kinds of business opportunities for entrepreneurs:

✔ **Computers:** Some discount computer houses have made a killing by going online and offering equipment for less than conventional high street shops. Being on the Internet means that they save on overheads and then pass on those savings to their customers.

✔ **Web hosts:** These businesses house your website – your virtual home. Many, such as 1&1 (www.1and1.co.uk), are big concerns. Medium-sized companies, such as Positive Internet (www.positiveinternet.com), offer hosting services and similar levels of service too.

✔ **Software:** Matt Wright is well known on the Web for providing free computer scripts that add important functionality to websites, such as processing information that visitors submit via online forms. Matt's Script Archive site (www.scriptarchive.com) receives 300,000 unique visitors a month and several prominent advertisements appear on his site, as well as an invitation for businesses to advertise on it.

Being a starving artist without starving

Being creative no longer means you have to live out of your flower-covered VW van, driving from art fairs to craft shows (unless you want to, of course). If you're simply looking for exposure and feedback on your creations, you can put samples of your work online. Consider the following suggestions for virtual creative venues (and revenues):

✔ **Display your artwork.** Thanks to tools that make it easy to display online galleries, you can showcase your work in a matter of minutes. Photographers, for example, can use sites like Shutterchance (www.shutterchance.com) and Flickr (www.flickr.com) to display their images. Through Flickr, Kim has sold several hundred pounds' worth of photographs after receiving enquiries from interested companies and publishers. One photograph, of a snow-covered taxi, has even been featured on two Christmas cards published by two separate card-making businesses. Meanwhile, Deviant Art (www.deviantart.com) displays all manner of creations and lets visitors purchase prints of the artwork and related merchandise such as hoodies and T-shirts, which generates income for the young artists who frequent the site. The personal website created by artist Alban Low (www.albanlow.com; see Figure 8-2) has received worldwide attention. (The upcoming sidebar, 'Painting a new business scenario', profiles Alban's site.)

✔ **Publish your writing.** These days every man and his dog seem to create *blogs* (web logs, or online diaries). The problem is that absolutely millions exist, and most aren't worth your time. However, the most successful are generating ad revenue. To find out how to create one yourself, check out Blogger (www.blogger.com). For inspiration, check out a successful independent blog, such as Seth Godin's (sethgodin.typepad.com) or a blog attached to an online newspaper.

Figure 8-2: A British artist created a website to gain recognition and sell his creative work. It's quite basic – but it lets the artwork shine.

- ✔ **Sell your music.** Singer-songwriter Sam Roberts sells his own CDs, videos and posters through his online shop (`www.samrobertsband.com`), and you can sell your tracks if you don't have your own website by listing them with Apple iTunes, Spotify (`www.spotify.com`) or independent digital music sites like Indmill (`www.indmill.com`).

- ✔ **Be a video star.** Once in a while, someone creates a funny or genuinely useful video on YouTube, and the entire world notices. Take South Shields mum Lauren Luke, who started uploading makeup tutorials from her bedroom on YouTube as a way to sell her eye-shadow products. Her videos have now notched up 100 million views and she's written for numerous publications such as the *Guardian* and *Glamour* magazine. Eventually, her success culminated in a book deal and she continues to upload videos. Check out her YouTube channel at `www.youtube.com/panacea81`.

Marketing One to One with Your Customers

After you've reviewed websites that conduct the sorts of business ventures that interest you, you can put your goals into action. First you develop a marketing strategy that expresses your unique talents and services. People need encouragement if they're going to flock to your website, so try to come up with a cunning plan. One marketing ploy may be enough; we suggest coming up with five individual means to bring the customers in. For example, you can blog about your website, answer questions in forums, do a competition, go to networking events, start up a Facebook page and so on.

The fact is that online communities are often close-knit, long-standing groups of people who are good friends. The Web, newsgroups and email allow you to communicate with these communities in ways that other media can't match.

Focusing on a customer segment

Old-fashioned business practices, such as getting to know your customers as individuals and providing personal service, are alive and well in cyberspace. Your No. 1 business strategy when it comes to starting your business online sounds simple: know your market.

But who is your market? On the Internet, it takes some work to get to know exactly who your customers are. Web surfers don't leave their names, addresses or even email addresses when they visit your site. Instead, when you check the raw, unformatted records (or *logs*) of the visitors who've connected to you, you see pages and pages of what appears to be computer gobbledygook. Special tools, such as Google Analytics, interpret the information and present it to you in easy-to-understand pie charts and bullet points.

How do you develop relationships with your customers?

✔ **Get your visitors to identify themselves.** Encourage them to send you emails, place orders, enter contests or provide you with feedback.

✔ **Become an online researcher.** Find existing users who already purchase goods and services online that are similar to what you offer. Visit sites that are relevant to what you sell, and participate in discussions so that people can find out more about you.

✔ **Keep track of your visitors.** Count the visitors who come to your site and, more importantly, the ones who make purchases or seek out your services. Manage your customer profiles so that you can sell your existing clientele the items they're likely to buy.

✔ **Help your visitors get to know you.** Web space is virtually unlimited. Feel free to tell people about aspects of your life that don't relate directly to your business or to how you plan to make money. Consider Sean McManus, a technology author and journalist. His website (www.sean.co.uk), shown in Figure 8-3, includes the usual links to his serious books and articles, but also travel photos, a 3D version of his site you can view while wearing 3D glasses, games you can play on the site and even a 'Virtual Sean' you can 'chat' to, all of which show off Sean's fun and outgoing personality. He advises: 'The Web is quite a sterile and unfriendly environment, compared to doing business in person. Use real photos of you and your team to make your business seem friendlier. It's okay to tell people about your hobbies and interests and to convey a bit of personality too, as long as you don't go too far and include a gallery of cat photos. Don't forget a headshot of yourself too, so people don't forget you're a real person!'

Figure 8-3:
What you put on your website about yourself and your interests encourages visitors to tell you about themselves.

After getting to know your audience, job No. 2 in your marketing strategy is to catch their attention. You have two ways to do this:

✔ **Make yourself visible.** In web space, your primary task is simply making people aware that your site exists at all. You do so by getting yourself included in as many reputable and relevant indexes, search sites and business listings as possible. Never use automated services that try to get you listed on any old website because this can have a negative effect on your search result ranking – search engines may suspect you of manipulating the system and they may even ban your site from being indexed.

As Google itself explains in its tips for webmasters, 'The best way to get other sites to create relevant links to yours is to create unique, relevant content that can quickly gain popularity in the Internet community. The more useful content you have, the greater the chances someone else will find that content valuable to their readers and link to it. Before making any single decision, ask yourself the question: is this going to be beneficial for my page's visitors?'

✔ **Make your site an eye-catcher.** Getting people to come to you is only half the battle. The other half is getting them to shop when they get there. Combine striking images with promotions, offer useful information and provide ways for customers to interact with you.

Getting involved in social media

Social media is just a fancy way of describing the current generation of socially focused websites that let people share content among themselves – be it a 140-character message on Twitter or a six-minute video on YouTube – with other like-minded individuals. Rather than conventional media like magazines, television and newspapers, the emphasis is on user-generated content.

Social media tools easily let you broadcast messages to all your friends or followers. From a commercial perspective, this means you can communicate bursts of information about your business, such as a clearance sale, to tens of thousands (or possibly even millions) of people in an instant. Because the content is only broadcast to people with an active interest in your business, they're more likely to engage with it rather than ignore it.

Many multinational companies such as Microsoft employ social media editors full time to help attract followers to their brand and keep fans informed about the latest products, competitions and other events. Social media's interactive nature means that people can comment on anything you post, such as pictures or important announcements, so you have to keep an eye on what's being said – good and bad – about your business.

Painting a new business scenario

British artist Alban Low spent several years living in the peaceful French village of Cambieure, where he says his painting first 'came alive'. As he describes on his website, 'I used to love the daily comings and goings of the tractors and farmers . . . I often left the studio to paint the landscape around me. Sheltering in the shade was a necessity during July and August; the fig trees offered ample coverage with their huge leaves. The complex shapes, cool colours, abundant fruit and scenes beyond inspired me.' Alban returned to London in 2003 with the ability to see things in a completely new light. 'For so often I'd hurried past rivers, buildings, even railways, without a second thought. I began to notice their hidden beauty, arching bridges and competing colours.' He now uses his website as well as social media tools like Facebook, YouTube and blogs to showcase his work and drum up business.

Q. Why did you decide to set up a website to display your work?

A. Initially, as an online portfolio and because other people pressurised me to do so. My brother broke his leg and wanted a project to keep him sane. Also, he's very nice. He taught himself how to [design my site] then taught me how to keep it up to date and in order.

Q. Has your website raised your profile as an artist?

A. At first, it was useful as an online archive and I could mention it when I met people at exhibitions. Now it helps when other people talk about my work. To start with, I had a selling section, which just wasn't realistic. It has now helped gain commissions and exhibitions through its presence. I can refer to its content quickly and I can talk on the phone with a client while we both look through the pictures. I have approached many galleries over the past couple of years and having a website must have helped.

Q. How else do you use the Web to gain interest in your work?

A. This is the most interesting question for me. I have started to use many different aspects of the Web to fuel or help my professional practice. Last month, I got my first commission from New Zealand via Facebook. We used it for everything: checking details and showing the initial sketch and the final painting before it was packed off. And in this last year, I've used three different blogs to showcase and organise exhibitions. They're free to set up, nimble and easy to update. I've also had a Picasa account to hold images, which I've used to show galleries.

Lastly, I secured some television work on the strength of work I'm posting on YouTube (`www.youtube.com/user/albanlow`) to publicise my work. A director at TennisTV.com saw one of my animations and commissioned me to make an animation for their coverage. This was subsequently used by the BBC.

Q. What advice would you give an artist wanting to go online?

A. Start posting your work on Facebook as low-resolution images; involve friends as much as possible.

If you don't have much money to outlay, start with a blog. They're free and easier to update and adapt. If you involve other people in your work, they will also promote the sites and help you reach an audience outside your inner circle.

(continued)

(continued)

If your work is good and interesting, people will want to find out about you. The artwork is the initial point of contact for me and the Web is a great support and a great tool.	My website was made for free and is hosted by my kind family. The cost of my domain name is nominal. I have no marketing budget and make headway through hard work and getting out into the real world too!
Q. How much does your website cost to run?	

Boosting your credibility

You need to transfer your confidence and sense of authority about what you do to anyone who visits you online. Convince people that you're an expert and a trustworthy person with whom they can do business.

Customers may have fewer reasons to be wary about using the Internet nowadays. But remember that the Web as you know it has been around only a short time, and a large minority of people are still wary of surfing online, let alone shopping. Here, too, you can do a quick two-step in order to market your expertise.

Documenting your credentials

Feature any honours, awards or professional affiliations you have that relate to your online work. If you're providing professional or consulting services online, you may even make a link to your online CV. If you feel it's relevant, give details about how long you've been in your field and how you got to know what you know about your business.

If these forms of verification don't apply to you, all isn't lost. Just move to the all-important technique that we describe in the next section.

Convincing with must-have information

Providing useful, practical information about a topic is one of the best ways to market yourself online. One of the great things about starting an online business is that you don't have to incur the design and printing charges to get a brochure or flyer printed. You have plenty of space on your online business site to talk about your sales items or services in as much detail as you want. Try not to bore people though, will you?!

What, exactly, can you talk about on your site? Here are some ideas:

✔ Provide detailed descriptions and photos of your sale items.

✔ Include a full list of clients you've worked for previously.

✔ Publish a page of testimonials from satisfied customers.

✔ Give your visitors a list of links to web pages and other sites where people can find out more about your area of business.

✔ Toot your own horn: explain why you love what you do and why you're so good at it.

Ask satisfied customers to give you a good testimonial. All you need is a sentence or two that you can use on your website. We mentioned The Prize Finder website earlier; it has success stories from previous prizewinners as well as testimonials from advertisers listed on its site.

A site that contains compelling, entertaining content will become a resource that online visitors bookmark and return to on a regular basis. Be sure to update it regularly, and you'll have fulfilled the dream of any online business owner.

When using social media, it's crucial not to go overboard with the communication updates because you want to maintain that trust in your brand. You don't want people to think you're out to make a quick buck and are relentlessly pushing your products.

Creating customer-to-customer contact: Everybody wins

A 16-year-old cartoonist named Gabe Martin (www.gabemartin.com) put his cartoons on his website, called The Borderline. Virtually nothing happened. But when his dad put up some money for a contest, young Gabe started getting hundreds of visits and enquiries. He went on to create 11 mirror sites around the world, develop a base of devoted fans and sell his own cartoon book.

People regularly take advantage of freebies online by, for example, downloading *shareware* or *freeware* programs (programs that people develop and distribute for free). They get free advice from the Web, and they find free companionship from chat rooms and discussion forums. Having already paid for network access and computer equipment, they actually *expect* to get something for free.

Your customers will keep coming back if you devise as many promotions, giveaways or sales as possible. You can also get people to interact through online forums or other tools, as we describe in later in this chapter.

In online business terms, anything that gets your visitors to click links and enter your site is good. Provide as many links to the rest of your site as you can on your home page. Many interactions that don't seem like sales do lead to sales, and your goal is always to keep people on your site for as long as possible.

For more about creating websites, check out *Creating Web Pages For Dummies,* 9th Edition, by Bud E. Smith and Arthur Bebak (Wiley).

Being a player in online communities

You may wait until the kids go off to school to tap away at your keyboard in your home office, but that doesn't mean that you're alone. Thousands of home-office workers and entrepreneurs just like you connect to the Net every day and share many of the same concerns, challenges and ups and downs as you.

Starting an online business isn't only a matter of creating web pages, scanning photos and taking orders. Marketing and networking are essential to making sure that you meet your goals. Participate in groups that are related either to your particular business or to online business in general. Here are some ways that you can make the right connections and get support and encouragement at the same time.

Becoming a forum fanatic

Businesspeople tend to overlook online discussion boards, forums and other groups because of admonitions about *spam* (pesky emails sent without permission by people trying to make money dishonestly) and other violations of *Netiquette* (the set of rules that govern online communications). However, when they join an online community and play an active role in helping others by answering questions and participating in discussions, online groups can be a wonderful resource for businesspeople. They attract knowledgeable consumers who are strongly interested in a topic – just the sort of people who make great customers.

A few forums especially intend to discuss small business issues and sales. Here are a few suggestions:

- ✔ www.uksmallbizworld.co.uk
- ✔ www.startups.co.uk/Forums
- ✔ www.ukbusinessforums.co.uk

You can also participate in discussion boards called *newsgroups*. The easiest way to access newsgroups is to use Google's web-based directory (`groups.google.com`).

Book V

Marketing and Advertising Your Wares

Be sure to read a group or forum's FAQ page before you start posting. It's a good idea to *lurk before you post* – that is, simply read messages being posted to the group in order to find out about members' concerns. Stay away from groups that seem to consist only of get-rich-quick schemes or other scams. When you do post a message, be sure to keep your comments relevant to the conversation and give as much helpful advice as you can.

Some of the UK's most influential websites have a huge community of members participating in forums. Mumsnet (`www.mumsnet.com`) is a place for parents to discuss parenting-related issues; participate in live chats with prime ministers, opposition leaders and other top-ranking politicians; and make new friends. Parents are always online at all hours of the night chatting away in the wee hours as their little ones wake up for a feed. *The Times* calls it 'the most popular meeting point for parents'.

Being signature savvy

The most important business technique in communicating by either email or newsgroup postings is to include a signature file at the end of your message. A *signature file* is a simple message that newsgroup and mail software programs automatically add to your messages (just like corporate emails). In the early days of the free web-based email service Hotmail, an automatic signature message was added to the bottom of every email that got sent out inviting recipients to try Hotmail for free. This led to an enormous spike in take-up, and the term *viral marketing* was born. By the time Microsoft purchased the then two-year-old company for £248 million at the end of 1997, the site had 9 million subscribers. Fourteen years on, it now boasts 364 million users, according to comScore.

Figure 8-4 shows an example of author Sean McManus's signature file, which clearly lists the books he's written and a call to action for people to get 'FREE' chapters and bonus book content via his website.

Exchanging emails

Email discussion groups or *discussion lists* work by exchanging email messages between members who share a common interest. They've become a little outdated now that online forums and tools such as Facebook make it so easy to exchange messages with more than one person at a time, but they're still around.

Each email message sent to the list is distributed to all the list's members. Any of those members can, in turn, respond by sending email replies. The series of back-and-forth messages develops into discussions.

Figure 8-4: A descriptive signature file on your messages serves as an instant business advertisement.

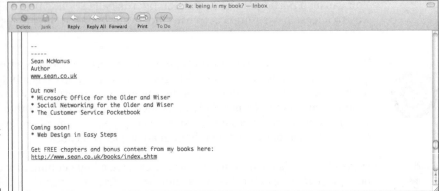

The nice thing about a discussion list is that it consists only of people who've subscribed to the list or group, which means that they really want to be involved and participate.

Yahoo! Groups lets people start up their own online discussion groups, and members may receive new messages as emails as they happen or as a daily digest. They can post messages to a group via email too. The non-profit Freecycle network (www.freecycle.org), which lets people give away unwanted stuff for free, is a good example and is administered using Yahoo! Groups.

Adding ways to sell and multiply your profits

Many successful online businesses combine more than one concept of what constitutes electronic commerce. Chapter 9 of this Book discusses ways to sell your goods and services on your website, but the Internet offers other venues for promoting and selling your wares.

Selling through online classifieds

If you're looking for a quick and simple way to sell products or promote your services online without having to pay high overhead costs, consider taking out a classified ad in an online publication or a popular site like Craigslist (www.craigslist.org) or the online version of the Loot newspaper at www.loot.com.

The classifieds work the same way online as they do in print publications: you pay a fee and write a short description along with contact information, and the publisher makes the ad available to potential customers. However, online classifieds have a number of big advantages over their print equivalents:

- ✔ **Audience:** Rather than hundreds or thousands who may view your ad in print, tens of thousands – or perhaps even millions – can see it online.

- ✔ **Searchability:** Online classifieds are often indexed so that customers can search for particular items with their web browser. This index makes it easier for shoppers to find exactly what they want, whether it's a Hello Kitty figurine or a Martin guitar.

- ✔ **Time:** On the Net, ads are often online for a month or more.

- ✔ **Cost:** Some sites, such as Gumtree (www.gumtree.com) and Friday-Ad (www.friday-ad.co.uk), let you post classified ads for free.

On the downside, classifieds are often buried at the back of online magazines or websites, just as they are in print, so they're hardly well-travelled areas. Also, most classifieds don't make use of the graphics that help sell and promote goods and services so effectively throughout the Web.

Classifieds are an option if you're short on time or money. But don't forget that on your own online business site you can provide more details and not have to spend a penny.

Selling via online auctions

Many small businesses, such as antique dealerships or jewellery shops, sell individual merchandise through online auctions. eBay.co.uk and other popular auction sites provide effective ways to target sales items at collectors who are likely to pay top dollar for desirable goodies. If you come up with a system for finding things to sell and for turning around a large number of transactions on a regular basis, you can even turn selling on eBay into a full-time source of income.

Looking at Easyware (Not Hardware) for Your Business

Becoming an information provider on the Internet places an additional burden on your computer and peripheral equipment, such as your phone, printer/scanner and so on. When you're 'in it for the money', you may very well start to go online every day, perhaps for hours at a time, especially if you buy and sell on eBay.co.uk. The better your computer setup, the more photos, email messages and catalogue items you can store, and so on. In this section, we introduce you to many upgrades you may need to make to your existing technology.

Some general principles apply when assembling equipment (which we discuss in this section) and programs (which we discuss in a subsequent section, 'Considering Essential Software and Services for Your Online Business') for an online business:

- ✔ **Look on the Internet for what you need.** You can find just about everything you want to get you started.

- ✔ **Be sure to pry before you buy!** Don't pull out that credit card until you get the facts on what warranty and technical support your hardware or software vendor provides. Look for online reviews from ordinary customers: Amazon.co.uk has tons of customer reviews for hardware and software. Make sure that your vendor provides phone support 24 hours a day, 7 days a week. Also ask how long the typical turnaround time is in case your equipment needs to be serviced.

If you purchase lots of new hardware and software, remember to update your insurance by sending your insurer a list of your new equipment. Also consider purchasing insurance specifically for your computer-related items from a company such as Insure and Go (www.insureandgo.com) or Hiscox (business.hiscox.co.uk).

Choosing the right computer for your online business

You may very well already have an existing computer setup that's adequate to get your business online and start the ball rolling. Or you may be starting from scratch and looking to purchase a computer for personal and/or business use. In either case, it pays to know what all the technical terms and specifications mean. Here are some general terms you need to understand:

- ✔ **Processor speed:** A processor's speed measure indicates how quickly it can perform functions. The central processing unit (CPU) of a computer is where the computing work gets done. Traditionally, processor speeds were measured in gigahertz (GHz) and megahertz (MHz), but today major manufacturers like Intel have ditched the technical jargon, choosing to use terms like Intel Pentium Dual Core. A faster processor is great, but you don't need the biggest and best processor out there for typical online business tasks. (For more on choosing the right processor, see the next section.)

- ✔ **Random access memory (RAM):** This is the memory that your computer uses to temporarily store information it needs to operate programs. RAM is usually expressed in millions of bytes, or megabytes (MB). The more RAM you have, the more programs you can run simultaneously. We recommend buying as much RAM as you can afford. Different types of RAM exist; DDR (double data rate) and the newer standard, DDR2, are the major types and they can dramatically improve the clock rate of a CPU.

✔ **Virtual memory:** This is a type of memory on your hard drive that your computer can 'borrow' to serve as extra RAM.

✔ **Network interface card (NIC):** You need this hardware add-on if you have a cable or DSL modem or if you expect to connect your computer to others on a network. Having an NIC usually provides you with Ethernet data transfer to the other computers. (*Ethernet* is a network technology that permits you to send and receive data at very fast speeds.) If you want to wirelessly network your desktop computer to a wireless router, you can buy a wireless networking dongle that plugs into your USB port without requiring an NIC. Modern laptops should already have built-in wireless access.

The Internet is teeming with places where you can find good deals on hardware. A great place to start is a review site, such as Ciao (www.ciao.co.uk) or Review Centre (www.reviewcentre.com), which allows customers to express their views about the equipment they've bought. Visit a few of these sites and select the most popular items.

Processor speed and memory

Computer processors are getting faster all the time; by the time you get it home another, faster, chip will already have hit the streets. In years past, a computer's processing speed was measured in megahertz or gigahertz but these numbers have become less and less relevant.

Now categories of chips such as Intel's dual-core and quad-core processors are better able to handle multiple tasks simultaneously. These are more efficient because they're essentially two processors in one, working in tandem so that the computer can process information faster. A handy decision-making tool on Intel's website at www.intel.com helps you decide on the type of processor you should be using for your computer, based on your business requirements.

Having as much memory as you can afford (RAM) is what we recommend. Memory acts like a 'buffer', allowing programs and large files to load and run quickly. Take a look at the memory required to run the types of applications listed in Table 8-2. Compared with earlier editions of this book, the amount of recommended RAM has increased several times over for applications such as Internet Explorer because they've become larger and more complex – but at the same time the price of memory has significantly decreased. (Note that these numbers are only estimates, based on the Windows versions of these products that were available at the time of writing.)

Table 8-2	Memory Requirements	
Type of Application	*Example*	*Amount of RAM Recommended*
Web browser	Internet Explorer	512MB
Word processor	Microsoft Word 2010	256MB (512MB recommended for advanced functionality)
Graphics program	Corel Paint Shop Pro Photo X2	512MB (768MB recommended)
Accounting software	Microsoft Excel	256MB (512MB recommended for advanced functionality)
Animation/presentation	Adobe Flash Player	128MB

We'd say that at least 4GB of RAM is necessary if you plan to work – in the last edition of this book we were only recommending at least 512MB of RAM, yet many computers now require this amount to run just one application! Memory is cheap so the more you can swing, the better it is in the long run.

Hard drive storage

Random access memory is only one type of memory your computer uses; the other kind, *hard drive*, stores information, such as text files, audio files, programs and the many essential files that your computer's operating system needs. Most of the new computers on the market come with hard drives that store hundreds of gigabytes of data. Even if you aren't doing a lot of graphics work, those of you using your computer for other tasks such as storing photographs will find your hard drive space being slowly eaten up. Applications, too, can take up a lot of storage space.

Most new computers come with hard drives that are around 500GB in size. Again, the more you can afford, the better.

DVD±RW or Blu-Ray drive

Having a recordable drive in your computer may not seem essential at first, but it can be unbelievably useful for storing backups of files. The DVD drive also performs essential installation, storage and data communications functions, such as installing software and saving and sharing data.

Recordable DVD drives should come as standard on modern computers. More and more computers now include higher capacity Blu-Ray drives that also let you watch or record high definition (HD) movies. You can fit 4.7GB (or more) of data on a conventional DVD±RW, and at least 25GB on Blu-Ray drives. DVD and Blu-Ray drives are backwards-compatible, meaning you can still read and write older CDs.

Be sure to protect your equipment against electrical problems that can result in loss of data or substantial repair bills. You can limit the damage caused by power outages or surges, or just by glitches in your computer programs, simply by saving your data. You can buy separate hard drives, as well as disks and data sticks on which you can store your most precious data. Keep backup data away from your workstation so that in the event of a fire or flood you still have a surviving copy.

Monitor

In terms of your online business, the quality or thinness of your monitor doesn't affect the quality of your website directly. Even if you have a poor-quality monitor, you can create a website that looks great to those who visit you. The problem is that you won't know how good your site really looks to customers who have high-quality monitors.

Flat-panel LCD (liquid crystal display) monitors are standard now, and the sizes available keep getting bigger and bigger. Back in 2003, Kim was reviewing 15-inch LCD monitors. Just a year later you could get 17-inch models for the same price, and by 2007, 19-inch and 21-inch monitors were hot items. Now you can get 25-inch (and bigger) LCDs and widescreen models too that are all perfectly affordable – and for the same price the 15-inch monitors were back in the old days! (Current HD televisions are also computer friendly, allowing you to plug right into the display.) The main things you need to look out for when buying an LCD monitor have remained the same, however, and include:

- ✔ **Resolution:** The resolution of a computer monitor refers to the number of pixels (the tiny dots that you see on screen) it can display horizontally and vertically. A resolution of 640 x 480 means that the monitor can display 640 pixels across the screen and 480 pixels down the screen. Higher resolutions, such as 1,024 x 768, make images look sharper but require more RAM in your computer. Anything less than 640 x 480 is unusable these days.

- ✔ **Size:** Monitor size is measured diagonally, as with TVs. Big sizes are snazzy and may be in your budget, but may not be practical for a small home office.

You can even consider working from *two* monitors to extend your workspace. The setup is simple: just plug both monitors into your computer and use the display settings under the Windows Control Panel to get monitor one and monitor two established. Your mouse pointer simply flows between two monitors. If you have an old monitor lying around the place, then this is a great option. Having two monitors gives you more 'real estate' to play with. You can use one screen for email and dealing with customer and administrative tasks, and the other for graphics work and website maintenance.

✔ **Response time:** Monitors need to react quickly in order to effectively display what's going on. Particularly for moving images, a slow response time (measured in milliseconds) means you get a shadowy effect known as 'ghosting' on screen. The lower the response time, the better. LCDs should suit your business just fine, but the emerging market is now in LED (light emitting diode) technology, which uses less energy than LCDs and can produce thinner and longer-lasting displays.

Keep in mind that lots of web pages seem to have been designed with 19-inch or 21-inch monitors in mind. The problem isn't just that some users (especially those with laptops) have 15-inch monitors, but you can never control how wide the viewer's browser window will be. And they may not even have their web browser window open to its maximum size when viewing your page. The problem is illustrated in the Yale Style Manual (`www.webstyleguide.com`), one of the classic references of website design.

Computer monitors display graphic information that consists of little units called *pixels*. Each pixel appears on-screen as a small dot – so small that it's hard to perceive with the naked eye, unless you magnify an image to look at details close up. Together, the patterns of pixels create different intensities of light in an image, as well as ranges of colour. A pixel can contain one or more bytes of binary information. The more pixels per inch (ppi), the higher a monitor's potential resolution. The higher the resolution, the closer the image appears to a continuous-tone image such as a photo. When you see a monitor's resolution described as 1,280 x 1,024, for example, that refers to the number of pixels that the monitor can display.

If you're one of the three people reading this who still regularly use a fax machine, you don't want it tying up your phone line and causing your customers to hear busy signals. Fax machines are virtually obsolete. Faxes themselves are still used in certain types of businesses, but you can sign up to electronic services that let you send faxes via your computer, or receive your faxes and email them to you as attachments. Alternatively, if you must use a machine, then get a second dedicated phone line.

Book V

Marketing
and
Advertising
Your
Wares

Image capture devices

When you're ready to move beyond the basic hardware and on to some jazzy value-adding add-ons, think about obtaining a tool for capturing photographic images. (By *capturing*, we mean *digitising* an image or, in other words, saving it in digital format.) Photos are often essential elements of business web pages: they attract a customer's attention, they illustrate items for sale in a catalogue and they can provide before-and-after samples of your work. If you're an artist or designer, having photographic representations of your work is vital.

Including a clear, sharp image on your website greatly increases your chances of selling your product or service. You have two choices for digitising: a scanner or digital camera.

Digital camera

Not so long ago, digital cameras cost thousands of pounds. These days, you can find a decent digital camera made by a reputable manufacturer, such as Nikon, Fuji, Canon, Olympus, Panasonic or Kodak, for £100 to £200. You have to make an investment up front, but this particular tool can pay off for you in the long run. With the addition of a photo printer, you can even print your own photos. For mass production (such as flyers) you can use online printing services from companies like VistaPrint (www.vistaprint.co.uk) because these may be more cost-effective than printing from a typical inkjet printer.

Don't hesitate to fork out the extra dough to get a camera that's easy to use and gives you good resolution (*resolution* is the measure of detail in a photograph).

You actually don't need a camera with top-notch resolution because online material is primarily intended to be displayed on computer monitors (which have limited resolution), and hundreds of low-cost devices out there have brilliant features. Anything 6 megapixels (Mp) and above will suffice, which is actually more than good enough to print a clear 10 x 8 sized photograph.

Megapixels are calculated by multiplying the number of pixels in an image – for example, when actually multiplied, 1,984 x 1,488 = 2,952,192 pixels or 2.9 megapixels. The higher the resolution, the fewer photos your camera can store at any one time because each image file requires more memory, but you can always reduce the resolution using your camera settings or buy a memory card with bigger capacity to solve the problem.

Before being displayed by web browsers, you need to compress photographs (usually in a format called JPEG). Your camera can take images in JPEG format.

Also, smaller and simpler images (as opposed to large, high-resolution graphics) generally appear more quickly on the viewer's screen. You can often reduce the file size of images in your photo editing software quite dramatically without seeing any discernible loss in quality. If you make your customers wait too long to see an image, they're well within their rights to go to someone else's online shop.

When shopping for a digital camera, look for the following features:

- Easy to use, with accessible buttons
- Bundled image-processing software
- The ability to download image files directly to a memory card that you can easily transport to a computer's memory card reader
- A large, clear LCD screen that lets you see your images immediately
- Minimal *shutter lag* (the delay between pressing the shutter and the camera taking the image)

Digital photography is a fascinating and technical process, and you'll do well to read more about it in other books. Look out for *Digital Photography For the Older and Wiser* by Kim Gilmour (Wiley; 2010). And you don't have to be old (or wise) to read it!

Scanners and multifunction devices

Scanning is the process of turning the colours and shapes contained in a photographic print or slide into digital information that a computer can understand. You place the image in a position where the scanner's camera can pass over it, and the scanner turns the image into a computer document that consists of tiny dots called *pixels* (short for picture elements; 1 million pixels equals 1 megapixel) that make up an image. With flatbed scanners, you place the photo or other image on a flat glass bed, just like you find on a photocopier. An optical device moves under the glass and scans the photo.

The best news about scanners is that they've been around for a while, which, in the world of computing, means that prices are going down all the time. Scanners are not a fast-moving market either, so you don't need to worry about getting one that's outdated. The bargain models are well under £50, and you can pick one up for around £30 if you use cost comparison websites, such as Pricerunner (www.pricerunner.co.uk) or Kelkoo (www.kelkoo.co.uk).

A type of scanner that has lots of benefits for small or home-based businesses is a multifunction device. You can find these units, along with conventional printers and scanners, at computer outlets or at Pricerunner and Kelkoo. Multifunction devices save you a lot of desk space and are designed for home offices like yours. The average multifunction device can photocopy, scan and print photographs; you can also buy ones that combine a phone, fax and answering machine.

When choosing a printer or multifunction device, always remember that the cost of the device isn't its true cost. Printing costs can notch up – paper and ink can be expensive, particularly because manufacturers recommend you use their own brand of ink for best results. Ink cartridges often have a computer chip on them to deter third-party manufacturers from selling compatible inks; and photo paper is supposedly optimised for use with certain ink. Also, when buying a printer, try to choose one that uses separate ink cartridges for the printer colours (blue, magenta, cyan and black) rather than one containing all colours in the one unit. This is so you only need to replace the cartridge for the ink colour you're running low on.

Scan and deliver

Getting your photos online is so easy nowadays – by 2013, it's estimated that 124 billion photos will be hosted on Facebook (in 2009, the number stood at 15 billion). So the process is far from a technical minefield – it's very likely that you've shared photos on Facebook, and the latest smartphones also let you post your photos online to Facebook and Flickr from virtually wherever you are.

But your website isn't all about photographs from your digital camera. Scanners still play their part if, say, you're an artist and just want to scan in a few drawings for your website without having to go through the hassle of learning how to optimise them for the Web. Or perhaps you have some old print photographs or negatives that you want to use for your site? Your local photo shop or copy centre can help. Many high street photographic shops, like Jessops and Snappy Snaps, for example, provide computer services that include scanning photos. You can also have the images placed online or on a CD when you develop your snaps.

Tell the technician that you want the image to appear on the Web, so it should be optimised in JPEG format. Also, if you have an idea of how big you want the final image to be when it appears online, tell that to the technician too. Jargon corner: the screen resolution your images need to be for online use should be around 72 pixels per inch; note that this is smaller than the print resolution they need to be for printing (300 dots per inch). The shop can save the image in the size that you want so you don't have to resize it later in a graphics program. However, getting images scanned at the biggest size you're willing to display or print it at is best, then you can scale down later – any image program will let you do this.

If you don't even want to buy a camera, you can always try Flickr (www.flickr.com), the online photo album that anyone can add to. People who post their pics can choose to allow others to use them for free through an open licensing scheme called Creative Commons. Usually, all you need to do is credit the author. Flickr allows you to contact photographers when you need to obtain their permission or download a higher-quality image.

Getting Online: Connection Options

Now you can get a broadband connection from a reputable company for £15 a month. You can also bundle Internet access up with your phone connection and even digital TV to save a bit more cash.

Dial-up is simply pointless. Broadband speeds in the UK are now exceptionally fast – BT has even been testing 1 gigabit broadband connections (which translates to practically lightning speed). The communications regulator, Ofcom, estimates that 70 per cent of UK households have a fixed broadband connection with more than a quarter able to achieve up to 10 megabit speeds.

Although on a typical home broadband connection it's slower to upload information to the Web (such as your web pages) than it is to download, it's still much faster than dial-up. A broadband connection can save you an hour a day, which you can spend on planning, on stock checks or taking well-earned rests.

Broadband is a generic term describing the bandwidth of your Internet connection. It's broad, so more information can pass through it in a shorter space of time. *Asymmetrical Digital Subscriber Line* (ADSL) is the predominant form of broadband in the UK and transmits information via your phone line at different speeds depending on whether you're sending (uploading) or receiving (downloading) data. *Symmetrical Digital Subscriber Line* (SDSL) transmits information at the same speed in both directions.

Considering Essential Software and Services for Your Online Business

One of the great things about starting an Internet business is that you get to use software. As you probably know, the programs you use online are inexpensive (sometimes free), easy to use and install, and continually updated.

Like your website itself, you don't even need to install a lot of programs on your computer any more, and you needn't cram all your data onto your hard drive, either. All you need is a web browser and a broadband connection to conduct a raft of activities. This shift to moving services to the Internet is known as *cloud computing* (*cloud* describes the Internet). It's revolutionising the way people buy and sell, consume entertainment, communicate and create.

Book V

Marketing
and
Advertising
Your
Wares

You're probably already using the cloud on a consumer level. If you use a web-based email service with one of the major providers like Google, Yahoo! or Microsoft, then you know how all your messages reside on their servers, ready for you to access at any time. You don't have to worry about your computer running out of storage space. Many of the leading providers also let you use your accounts with them to do things such as edit Word documents and spreadsheets, view PDF files, share photos and videos with friends, and manage your website files and statistics.

And if you have a blog, then you know that all you need to do is log in to your website (or the blog host's) and start creating posts or redesigning the look and feel of your site – all from within the comfort of your web browser.

There's still a place for good old software that you download and install on your computer; particularly because it works in tandem with your online activities. For the rest of this section, we describe some programs you may not have as yet and that will come in handy when you create your online business.

Don't forget to update your insurance by sending your insurer a list of new software (and hardware) or even by purchasing insurance specifically for your computer-related items.

Anyone who uses firewall or antivirus software will tell you how essential these pieces of software are, for home or business use.

Web browser

A *web browser* is software that serves as a window to the images, colours, links and other content contained on the Web. The most popular such program is still Microsoft Internet Explorer. But its market share has been eroded in recent years, making way for increasingly popular browsers such as Mozilla Firefox, Safari, Chrome and Opera, all of which are gaining new fans every day. See which one you like the best.

Your web browser is your primary tool for conducting business online, just as it is for everyday personal use. When it comes to running a virtual shop or consulting business, though, you have to run your software through a few more paces than usual. You need your browser to

- ✔ Preview the web pages you create

- ✔ Display animations, movie clips and other goodies you plan to add online

- ✔ Support some level of Internet security, such as Secure Sockets Layer (SSL), if you plan to conduct secure transactions on your site

In addition to having an up-to-date browser with the latest features, installing a few major browsers on your computer is a good idea. For example, if you use Microsoft Internet Explorer, be sure to download the latest copy of Firefox as well. That way, you can test your site to make sure that it looks good to all your visitors. Remember, too, that people use Apple Macs as well as PCs, laptops, palmtops and smartphones – and they also view web pages at different resolutions, depending on their monitor size and viewing preferences. Your website has to look good on all of them. Tools such as Browser Cam (www.browsercam.com) can help you see what your site looks like in several browsers.

Web page editor or content management platform

HyperText Markup Language (HTML) is a set of instructions used to format text, images and other web page elements so that web browsers can correctly display them. Meanwhile, keeping a site's font, body font, font sizes, page width, background images and other formatting consistent throughout an entire website relies on code called Cascading Style Sheets (CSS). The CSS attributes are usually contained in files ending in .css; in order to reflect changes across your entire website, you just edit the CSS files rather than painstakingly change every single HTML page.

You don't have to master HTML or CSS to create your own web pages. Tools including *web page editors* and *content management systems* are available to help you format text, add images, make hyperlinks and do all the assembly steps necessary to make your website a winner. Content management systems like Joomla! (www.joomla.com) and Drupal (www.drupal.com) make it easy to slot in the elements you need for a seemingly complex page. Web page editors are a little outdated, but if you have a simple-to-manage site that doesn't sell products and will generally remain static (apart from say a blog or a news page), then a web page editor should still fit the bill.

Taking email a step higher

You're probably very familiar with sending and receiving email messages or attaching files to them. But when you start an online business, make sure that your email software has some advanced features:

Book V

Marketing
and
Advertising
Your
Wares

✔ **Autoresponders:** Some programs automatically respond to email requests with a form letter or document of your choice.

✔ **Mailing lists:** With a well-organised address book, you can collect the email addresses of visitors or subscribers and send them a regular update of your business activities or, better yet, an email newsletter (so long as they're happy to receive it). As your customer base grows, you may consider a plug-in that helps you manage the list more effectively.

✔ **Signature files:** Your email software should automatically include a simple electronic signature at the end. Use this space to list your company name, your title and your website URL.

✔ **Anti-spam and security software:** Your security software may come with tools to filter out junk email (known as spam). It should also scan incoming emails for viruses.

✔ **Email marketing tools:** Services for small businesses like VerticalResponse (`www.verticalresponse.com`), which Sean McManus (see the earlier section 'Focusing on a customer segment') uses to send his monthly newsletter out to subscribers, let you create an email message to send to your customers in mere minutes.

In some cases, you can install software that works in conjunction with your existing email program (known as a plug-in). Because these functions are all essential aspects of providing good customer service, we discuss them in more detail in Chapter 9 of Book V.

Discussion forum software

When your business site is up and running, consider taking it a step farther by creating your own discussion area, or _forum_, right on your website. This is a web-based discussion area where your visitors can compare notes and share their passion for the products you sell or the area of service you provide.

It does take a lot of effort and time to maintain a forum though, and not all websites are suited to one. As web consultant Scott Parker says, 'They are really hard to manage and get off the ground. Start off with a blog that allows feedback.' If you go for the forum route, popular forum software includes vBulletin (`www.vbulletin.com`) and the free phpBB (`www.phpBB.com`).

FTP software

FTP (File Transfer Protocol) is one of those acronyms you see time and time again around the Internet. When you create your own web pages, a simple, no-nonsense FTP program is the easiest way to transfer them from your computer at home to your web host. If you need to correct and update your web pages quickly (and you will), you'll benefit by having your FTP software ready and set up with your website address, username and password so that you can transfer files right away.

Image editors

You need a graphics-editing program either to create original artwork for your web pages or to crop and adjust your scanned images and digital photographs. In the case of adjusting or cropping photographic image files, the software you need almost always comes bundled with the scanner or digital camera, but you may need to upgrade to a more advanced program if you want to adjust the colours, clone out unwanted elements, remove red eyes and so on.

Plenty of free image-editing tools do great jobs. Google's Picasa (http://picasa.google.com) is highly functional, as is Microsoft's Windows Live Photo Gallery (www.live.com). Pay a little and you can get even more creative with your graphics, if that's what you want. Two programs we like are Adobe Photoshop Elements (www.adobe.co.uk) and Corel Paint Shop Pro. These are available off the shelf in boxed form from computer outlets, but you can download both these programs from the Web to use on a trial basis. After the trial period is over, you need to pay to upgrade and keep the program.

Many programs are available as *shareware*. The ability to download and use free (and almost free) software from shareware archives and many other sites is one of the nicest things about the Internet. Keep the system working by remembering to pay the shareware fees to the nice folks who make their software available to individuals like you and me.

Instant messaging

You may think that MSN Messenger, AOL Instant Messenger, Google Talk and Yahoo Messenger are just for chatting online, but instant messaging has its business applications too. Here are a few suggestions:

- ✔ If individuals you work with all the time are hard to reach, you can use a messaging program to tell you whether those people are logged on to their computers. The program allows you to contact them the moment they sit down to work.

- ✔ With a microphone, sound card and speakers, you can carry on voice conversations through your messaging software.

MSN Messenger enables users to do file transfers without having to use FTP software or attaching files to email messages.

The Internet phone service Skype (www.skype.com) means you can make video and phone calls for free to other people with Skype accounts, as well as low cost calls to landlines. Skype also has an instant messaging system.

Backup software

Losing your personal documents is one thing, but losing business files can hit you hard in the pocket. That makes it even more important to make backups of your online business computer files. External hard drives are manufactured by companies including Iomega, Seagate, Freecom, Western Digital and more. These typically come with software that lets you automatically make backups of your files, but backup tools are also built into the latest Windows and Mac systems. Make sure that *all* your files are backed up, not just elements of your drive and, if you can afford it, back up onto *two* drives!

Chapter 9

E-marketing

. . . .

In This Chapter

▶ Choosing a web address that has maximum impact

▶ Creating a compelling website

▶ Designing and placing banner ads

▶ Utilising affiliate marketing

▶ Blogging for business

▶ Connecting to customers by mobile phone

▶ Budgeting your e-marketing plan

. . . .

*W*hat does e-marketing make you think of? Websites and the Internet, yes. But e-marketing includes online advertising, email and also using text, pictures or even video to reach customers through their mobile phones. These digital tools have opened up lots of new ways to help you sell your products or services. Even better, a lot of these tools are cheaper and certainly more cost-effective than traditional advertising using press or TV.

Nearly every month it seems a new way to communicate with customers using digital media emerges. The market is indeed rapidly evolving but for most marketers, waiting a while before jumping in to the newest techniques is safest, as they can be untried and possibly aggravating to the very people you're trying to win over if you don't execute them well. However, if used properly, many of these new techniques can prove immensely valuable and have been particularly effective in opening up markets for smaller businesses.

According to the communications regulator Ofcom, nearly two thirds of UK homes are now online using broadband and 15.5 million 3G (or Internet-capable) mobile phone connections exist, representing more than a quarter of total mobile connections in the UK. These figures mean that, however much or little you spend on e-marketing, you have to find a space for it in your marketing budget. For that reason, this chapter covers just what you need to know to begin your digital adventures.

Reaching Out with a Website

E-marketing changes fast and often, and changing with it is essential. To be a part of the revolution, you need to create a website for your business.

Consider this fact: people spend more time using the Internet than they do any other media apart from TV. In fact, a recent report from the European Interactive Advertising Association found that 16–24 year olds are now accessing the Internet more frequently than they're watching TV – 82 per cent of this younger demographic use the Internet between five and seven days each week, while just 77 per cent watch TV as regularly. The same report found that three quarters (75 per cent) of all Internet users go online between five and seven days per week, an increase from 61 per cent in 2004. However, the number that watches TV has remained stable at 86 per cent for the last three years. You would certainly advertise on TV if your budget stretched to it (and few people use the TV to do their shopping), so you need to have a presence on the other most-used medium. Importantly, advertising online is something you can afford to do. In fact, you can't afford not to!

Gaining a web presence is relatively easy. Sometimes doing so can be as simple as getting a listing on an online business directory covering your area, so that when consumers key in your company name or look for the type of services you offer using a search engine such as Google or MSN, they can find your address and phone number. We strongly believe that every business – including yours – needs a website, even if all it does is provide your contact details and opening hours. You can think of your website as a shop window, where potential customers from all over the world can look at the products or services you offer. You can even turn this site into an actual shop. Having a transactional website can be one of the lowest-cost ways to expand geographically without having to move out of your neighbourhood (it's not called the World Wide Web for nothing, you know!).

A good website can bring in customers who would never find your product or service were it not for the Internet. So spending some time and money creating a decent website to attract them is worthwhile.

You need a unique and memorable website address and an easy to use and appealing design (doubly so, if you intend creating a *transactional site* where customers can buy products or services using a credit or debit card). The following sections cover what you need to know.

Choosing a web address

First you need to find and register a web address (also known as a *domain name* or *URL*). Unless you're starting a business from scratch, you probably already have a web address in mind that you want to use. Your web address should be as close as you can possibly get to the name of your business, or, if you need a site for each of your products and services, it should relate closely to them. You may think this detail sounds obvious, but we see too many web addresses falling into the trap of having little to do with the parent business (usually because the most obvious name is being used by someone else; see 'Checking your name's availability' later in this chapter).

Totally Thomas is a small independent toy shop based in a small town in West Yorkshire. We live at the opposite end of the country and would never have found it if the owners hadn't picked a good name (and made sure it could be found through the Google search engine). Buying a suitable toy for a small boy can be tricky, but most love Thomas the Tank Engine and this shop is dedicated to Thomas products. The web address is `www.totallythomas.net`, although the owner also uses `www.totallythomas.co.uk` to redirect users to the website. The owner has made a good choice of web address because he hasn't been put off by the fact that `www.totallythomas.com` belongs to a company in San Diego that also sells Thomas merchandise. Instead of going for a unique but obscure name, the owner has registered both the `.net` and `.co.uk` extensions to make sure any UK customers are likely to end up at his online store.

As you search for potential web addresses, keep the following points in mind to ensure you end up with the best name for your site:

- ✔ **A good address relates to your business or product.** The web address `www.streetspavedwithgold.com` is available to register, along with all of the other main name extensions. The address is catchy and amusing. Should you rush off and register it? Not if it fails this first test: does the name relate to your product or service? Remember, being relevant is better than being clever.

- ✔ **A good name is memorable.** Customers should be able to remember your web address easily. That doesn't mean you have to register anything stunningly cool or clever – and besides, if the web address is obscure, people are less likely to remember it. Using your company name makes the site memorable to anyone who knows the name of your business. You can easily remember that IKEA's global web address is `www.ikea.com` and for the UK is `www.ikea.co.uk`. But you can just as easily combine two or three easy words and make a string into a memorable address. An online competitor to IKEA in the UK is the very simply named `www.thisisfurniture.com`.

- ✔ **A good name isn't easily confused with other addresses.** If consumers can easily mix up your site with similar addresses, some will go to the wrong site by accident. If your company name is a common word or is similar to others, add an extra term or word to your web address to distinguish it. For example, Triumph is a brand name that the lingerie maker and the motorcycle manufacturer have equal claim to. Although customers are unlikely to mistake one brand for the other, they could easily find themselves on the wrong website. As a result, the motorbike brand trades from `www.triumphmotorcycles.com` while Triumph International uses `www.triumph.com`.

✔ **A good name doesn't violate trademarks.** You don't want to bump into someone's trademark by accident. Legal rights now favour the trademark holder rather than the domain-name holder – putting an end to the ugly practice of 'cyber-squatting' that existed a few years ago. To be sure that you don't inadvertently step on someone else's toes, check any web address against a database of trademarks. The Intellectual Property Office provides a searchable database at `www.ipo.gov.uk` but if you think you may run into a problem, ask a lawyer to do a more detailed analysis. We cover trademark law in Chapter 2 in Book I.

Checking your name's availability

Picking a name is the easy part. The tricky part is finding out whether that name's available and then getting creative if you find out it's not.

Check a domain name's availability by typing it into the web browser to see if someone already has it. If you want to check out if a domain name's available in a number of extensions, sites exist to help you.

Any good provider of web services will have its own site that allows you to check on the availability of a web address. One such provider is `www.network solutions.com`, the administrator of the `.com` domain name extension, but you can just type in 'domain names' and pick any of the companies that offer registration services. The service you need will be on the homepage of any of these sites; just remember to check your preferred address against all of the main *extensions* – `.com`, `.co.uk`, `.net` or `.org` are among the most desirable, as people remember them first.

Interestingly, `www.networksolutions.com/whois/index.jsp` gives you information on who owns a domain name, so if a URL fits your business perfectly, you can always offer that person some money to hand it over!

In the best of all possible worlds, your web name search will reveal that your name is free. If that's the case, thank your lucky stars, jump up and down and make a few happy noises. Then register your name. The section 'Registering your site name' tells you how. But, as few of us live in the best of all possible worlds, you're more likely to find that your name is already taken. In that case, don't despair. You still have options and, depending on which avenue you take, you may still get to use your name.

If someone has registered the name you want with one or most of the main extensions, but left the more obscure .biz, .org.uk or even .me.uk extensions, seeking another name is wisest because customers could forget your extension and go to someone else's site instead. If the other businesses using the extensions are selling similar products to yours, in the same country, people may be confused, so choosing another name is crucial.

When the Web's an important sales route for your business, aim to own most or all of the possible extensions and versions of your web address.

If the person who owns the rights to your web address isn't willing to sell it, consider going back to the drawing board and finding another name that isn't being held hostage. Many online operators are looking to make easy money by buying up web addresses for the purpose of selling them at a profit.

Other routes can help you secure the name you want. Many sites that were registered in the frenzy of the dotcom boom eventually come back on to the open market because they were never used or because the original registrar forgot to re-register. When this happens, the web address becomes *detagged*. Alternatively, if you believe you have a stronger or more legitimate claim to a web address than someone else, you can use a disputes resolution service, or even legal action, to make them give the name up. For information on detagging and disputes, visit Nominet at www.nominet.org.uk, which is officially recognised as the .uk name registry by the industry and government.

Registering your site name

After ensuring that your web address is available, you're ready to register your name. Doing so is inexpensive, and the process is simple. The example we give here is based on the provider easily.co.uk, which charges £25 to register a .com, .org or .net address for two years, or £8.99 to register a .uk address. All you need to do is type in the domain name you want, and the site tells you which extensions are available (if any aren't, you can also see who owns them). Highlight all the extensions you want and then get out your credit card. The process is as easy as that – and easily.co.uk will even email you a reminder when the address needs to be renewed.

You can use any provider to register your web address and some are half as cheap as the example we give here. The only thing to stop you going for the cheapest price is to consider whether you also want the provider to *host* the site (meaning to provide the server space where your site resides on the web). You can transfer web addresses to another provider after the event, but it is simpler (and sometimes cheaper) to find the right provider for your needs in the first place.

If consumers may get confused by alternative spellings or misspellings of your domain name, register them too. Registering a name is cheap, so don't lose a prospective customer just because they can't spell your name. You can always redirect them from a misspelt URL to your website – if you don't, your competitors may view this mistake as an easy way to steal potential customers from you.

Creating a Compelling Website

Designing good web pages is a key marketing skill, because your website is at the centre of all you do to market online. Also, increasingly, websites are at the heart of companies' marketing – businesses put their Internet addresses on every marketing communication, from premium items (like company pens) to letterheads and business cards, and in ads, brochures and catalogues. Serious shoppers will visit your website to find out more about what you offer, so make sure your site is ready to close the sale. Include excellent, clear design, along with plenty of information to answer likely questions and move visitors towards a purchase. Websites have earned their place in the core of any marketing activity. If you're a consumer-oriented marketer, you want your website to be friendly and easily navigated, as well as to do the following:

- ✔ Engage existing customers, giving them reasons to feel good about their past purchases and connect with your company and other consumers (at least to connect emotionally, if not in actual fact).

- ✔ Share interesting and frequently updated information about your products or services, industry and organisation on the site, so the consumer can gain useful knowledge by visiting it.

- ✔ Maintain a section of the site or a dedicated site for business-to-business (B2B) relationships that matter to your marketing (such as distributors, stores and sales reps). Almost all consumer marketers also work as B2B marketers and the advice we gave on B2B at the beginning of this section also applies to this aspect of consumer marketing.

Finding resources to help with design

You can easily create a basic website – one that includes your contact details plus a few pages showing what your business does – on your own. Doing so is the simplest and cheapest route to create a web presence, if all you need is to let customers know where to find you and why they should get in touch. If your needs are more advanced and you want customers to be able to buy direct from your site, for example, skip down to the section on 'Hiring a professional designer'. This section doesn't cover how to use authoring languages or do any of the programming. That information would fill an entire book, not a chapter, let alone a section. If you decide to create a sophisticated website yourself, you can find excellent books that do go into all the details.

If you want to create your own web pages, we recommend, in particular, *Creating Web Pages All-in-One Desk Reference For Dummies* by Richard Mansfield and Richard Wagner (Wiley). It goes a bit deeper than the also good *Creating Web Pages For Dummies* by Bud E. Smith and Arthur Bebak (also by Wiley). These two titles cover the range in both price and detail, so take your pick. If you like tinkering, you can certainly build your own web pages using web authoring software such as FrontPage or Dreamweaver and contract with a web provider to put them up.

You can find a provider to host your site quite easily – and searching the Web is the best place to start. Just pick one that offers the fee structure, services and flexibility you want at the right price – and change providers if they don't satisfy.

Consider using your domain name and provider to create your own email addresses, too. An example is jane@janesmithflowers.com if your website is www.janesmithflowers.com. Having your email reflecting your own website URL looks so much more professional than going through a public domain does. An email like jane@janesmithflowers.com looks much better than using janesmithflowers@yahoo.co.uk.

Hiring a professional designer

If you aren't a do-it-yourselfer, a very easy way to create good web pages is available: find an expert who can do it for you under contract.

Good website design is harder than it looks and going to a reputable design firm and asking them to do it for you is probably best. We recommend a business relationship (spelled out on paper in advance) that specifies that you, not they, own all content at the end (so that you can switch to another vendor if it doesn't work out or they go bust) and also specifies an hourly rate and an estimate of the site's size and complexity, with a cap on the number of billable hours needed to design it.

You can expect to pay anything from £750 for a basic brochure-style website of ten pages to upwards of £10,000 for a Flash-animated fully transactional (or e-commerce) one. That's quite a range, even for custom-designed pages, so here's a basic list of what you can expect to get, and for what price:

- ✔ If you have no budget at all – not even £25 – you can always use a free blog site service such as Wordpress or Blogger to make a very basic updatable site. This option allows you to post stories and makes your contact details available for Internet users. But bear in mind that this site will look very home-made and amateur, so is probably only an option if you really have no other alternatives and are prepared to update it regularly.

✔ You can get a simple template-style website for as little as £50 from some of the web providers that register domain names and host websites, or with web authoring software programs like FrontPage and Dreamweaver. Some programs are quite good, but people often recognise these one-size-fits-all designs, which may lower their opinion of your site design.

✔ For a basic, custom-designed site (around five to ten pages), where the client provides a company logo, images and copy, plan to spend around £750 to £1500. A dedicated *Content Management System* (*CMS*) costs around £2000 to £2500. You can get a web designer to arrange the web hosting set-up, too. A basic hosting plan costs around £50 to £100 per year, which includes domain name registration.

✔ A more advanced site of up to 20 pages with a custom look built around your logo, and which contains navigation suited to the service or product that you're offering, costs between £1500 and £3500 (although here the price starts climbing depending on what bells and whistles you want to add on). The customised graphics and stock photography necessary for these sites can also drive up your costs, but if your online presence needs this unique, professional look to set you apart from your competitors, then the money may well be worth it.

Beyond the cost of the site, you also need to be aware of additional costs that you may incur – or that you need to budget for – in order to enhance the professional appearance and functionality of your website:

✔ Consider an online shopping trolley, for an extra £300 to £500 on top of your bespoke site design. Many basic hosting plans include a shopping trolley, so you can implement this feature fairly easily by using theirs (but you lose out on the custom-look website). Assume that you'll be adding products over time, so select a shopping trolley that gives you room to grow.

✔ Consider streaming video, animation and database management. You can use these technologies as important delivery methods, like showing a speaker in action, demonstrating a new product or providing services, and supporting the consumer online.

✔ Build some room for stock photography into your budget because sites with relevant images – especially of real people – are graphically more appealing and hold the visitor's attention longer. We highly recommend using photographs in most sites. If you use high-resolution files of the photos, they may be slow to load, which means you may lose some impatient viewers or the few who are still on low-speed phone lines. But stock photography houses sell (at a lower price) low-resolution images that are optimal for the Web and load quickly. These won't slow your site down.

✔ Get your contractor to update your site monthly (web designers charge around ₤70 per hour) because these updates give customers good reasons to keep coming back to the site. Special promotions or some other monthly feature will add to this evolving appeal.

✔ Plan to spend more for search engine submission, a service which automatically submits your website to all the major search engines so that traffic goes up. This service costs around ₤100 per year for monthly submissions.

Developing a registration service

Many sites used to have a registration system for consumers to complete to gain access to the website. Now most sites give free access to everyone and, in the case of sites with content such as stories or video, they make their money through advertising instead.

Don't create a site that needs the user to register to gain access to basic information – after all, you want to sell something to them, so why stop them from looking at the product? We know that creating a free registration hurdle in order to collect their information for future marketing purposes is tempting, but in the long run, this tactic is the wrong way to go about getting hold of this valuable information.

Instead, a handy trick is to offer some extra content – the latest product updates, exclusive content or behind-the-scenes photos – in order to get your customers to sign up with their details. All online businesses want to find out who their customers are because this information allows them to target them more effectively with products and services; these days, however, accessing customer details is more likely to put off Internet users than bring you any benefit unless you're offering something extra.

Driving traffic with content

Most websites are really just huge, interactive advertisements or sales promotions. After a while, even the most cleverly designed ad gets boring. To increase the length of time users spend with your materials and to ensure high involvement and return visits, you need to think like a publisher and not just an advertiser. For this reason, we consider web content to be the hidden factor for increasing site traffic. Unless you have valuable and appealing content, you may have difficulty building up traffic on your site.

Make sure you offer information and entertainment. People like to use the Web for research. Often, that research relates to a purchase decision. To be part of that research and purchase process, put useful, non-commercial information on your site. B&Q, the home improvement retailer, strikes a nice balance between online sales and DIY adviser. Its site, at www.diy.com, lists all its major product lines as you'd expect, but also offers a useful 'Knowledge Centre' area that provides step-by-step instructions on everything from building a barbecue to tiling a wall. Professional services firms can get in on the act, too. If you're a law firm, why not offer some simple, downloadable legal guides for the public? Keep these updated so that people always have a reason to visit.

Tracking Your Site's Traffic

The web offers an unmatched ability to evaluate how effectively your online marketing is working and to capture information on the people who are visiting your site. Compared with other media, digital marketing is entirely transparent – meaning you can see how many visitors you get and, if they register for more information on your site, who they are. Make the most of this rare opportunity to measure the impact of your expenditure.

Interpreting click statistics

You may find click-through statistics a useful and easy-to-get indicator of how well an ad or search-engine placement is performing. If you get a lot of people clicking through to your site from an ad or placement, that ad is clearly doing its job of attracting traffic for you. So, all else being equal, more clicks are better. However, all else isn't equal all the time. Here are a few wrinkles to keep in mind when interpreting click rates:

✔ When a pop-up ad appears, the companies you buy the ad space from usually report it as a click. But don't believe the numbers because you have no indication that someone actually read or acted on that pop-up – they may have just closed it without looking. Dig deeper into the statistics from whoever sold you that pop-up ad to find out how it actually performed. You can probably get some more detailed data if you ask, but you need more than the simple click count.

✔ Some ads have multiple elements that load in sequence, creating a countable click with each loading, so that one ad may generate several click-through counts. This counting method may lead you to think that the more complex ad is better, but the higher number can be an artefact of the way those who sell ad space on the web count the clicks. (Ask your provider if it can sell web ad space to you, or visit a really popular site and look for the section offering ad space to advertisers.)

✔ Quality is more important than quantity. Who are these people who clicked to your site? That information is harder to obtain but more important. Getting 10,000 clicks in a week is nice – but do they include relevant and active prospects? Only by digging into detailed reports on who goes where and looks at what on your website, plus information on what types of emailed questions you receive and the average order size per week, can you really begin to evaluate the quality of those clicks. See the following section 'Paying attention to your site's visitors' for details on how to find out who's visiting your site.

If you're generating poor quality traffic, experiment with putting ads in other places or redesign your ads to specifically focus on your desired target. Keep working on it until you achieve the best click-through rates, regardless of numbers.

You can evaluate performance of web advertising every day or week, and get statistics on each and every ad that you run. So use this data intelligently to experiment and adjust your approach. Aim to increase both the quantity and the quality of clicks week by week throughout your marketing campaign and track the impact on enquiries and sales.

Paying attention to your site's visitors

Each time someone visits your website, he's exhibiting interest in you and your products (or he's lost, which is less likely if your site is aptly named and clearly designed so that no one can confuse it with unrelated types of business). And someone exhibiting interest makes him interesting to you. So whatever you do, however you go about setting up a site, make sure that you capture information about your visitors in a useful form that gets sent to you regularly.

Ask your web provider what kinds of reports they can offer you – probably more than you imagined possible. With these reports in hand, you can track traffic to your site. You probably notice that you, unlike the giants of the Web, don't have as much traffic as you may want. Sure, millions of people use Google to do searches or go to eBay to bid on auctioned products. But the average website only has a few dozen visitors a day. For an effective site, you need to build up this traffic at least into thousands of visitors per day. How? By making sure it gets noticed in search engines. Free, easy to use analytics packages are now available, which can provide you with interesting information about people visiting your site. They can tell you where visitors come from and where they go to. Check out `www.google.com/analytics` for more information.

Designing and Placing a Banner Ad

A lot has changed in just a few years in Internet advertising. You can see how quickly things have moved on just by looking at what's happened to the most common form of online advertising – the *banner ad*. A banner used to be the only format for online advertising. That traditional format still exists, but for many marketers 'banner' has become a generic term for a whole host of different online ad formats.

We've jumped from one-size-fits-all banners, through as many different types of ad formats as you could wish for, and have come out at the other end with a selection of standard sizes that fit the needs of most advertisers (see Figure 9-1). The *Universal Advertising Package* (*UAP*), as its creators at the Internet Advertising Bureau (IAB) call it, comprises a banner (running across the top of a web page), skyscraper, large rectangle and regular rectangle. You can find out all about the technical specifications for UAP formats at the IAB's website (www.iabuk.net).

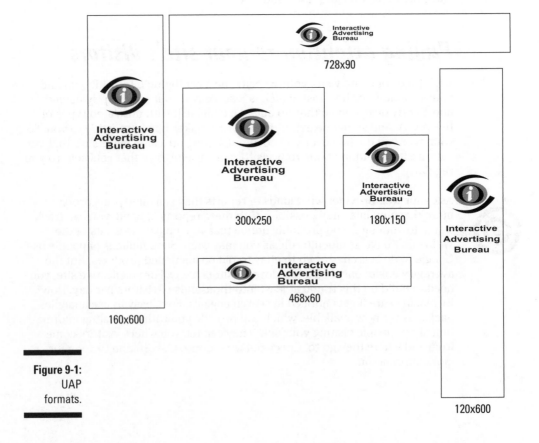

Figure 9-1:
UAP
formats.

UAP formats make the whole process of buying online advertising much more cost-effective. You should pay less for the production of an online campaign if you don't have to re-create your ad for each website you advertise on, and you can compare costs of online ad space more easily if you're comparing like with like – rather than apples with oranges, as was the case before.

Hiring a web media service

Companies providing *web media services* (meaning web page design) can also design and place banner ads and pop-up ads for you. Searching for agencies or individuals to do this work for you can be a long and random process, however. If you're lucky enough to know a competent web designer or programmer, seriously consider using their services – they can create custom banners to your specification quite easily because they're such a small ad format.

If you have more ambitious plans for rich media online ads, however, you need to study the extensive field. We recommend you go straight to the Internet Advertising Bureau website (www.iabuk.net) and visit the membership directory section. In this section, you find companies offering every kind of web media service, from ad server and counting providers (online campaign analysis) to website design. Listed under 'creative agencies' alone are 50 suppliers, from Advertising.com to Zenith Optimedia.

While the larger (and more expensive) agencies are well represented in the IAB membership, finding cheaper, local assistance is possible if you're prepared to put in the leg work.

Creating your own banner ad

Creating your own banner ads is a relatively easy process, particularly if you've designed your own website and are familiar with HTML coding. Basic banner ads can be created using off-the-shelf design software such as Photoshop or Paint Shop Pro. Not surprisingly, the web is a good starting point for finding templates for banner ads. Because the format is now so common, a lot of sites allow you to use their standard designs for free. One of the best known is AdDesigner.com (you can guess the web address), which makes designing a professional looking animated banner ad within minutes easy. We can't see why any marketer planning a small-scale online campaign would take anything other than the DIY route, given the high standards of these templates, but if you're really not keen on having a go, searching for one of the many factory-oriented banner ad designers that can make you an ad quickly and for less than £50 is just as simple.

Focusing on a simple design

The best design for starters is a banner that flashes a simple one-line offer or headline statement, shows an image of your logo or product and then switches to a couple more lines of text explaining what to do and why to do it ('Click here to take advantage of our introductory offer for small business owners and get 20% off your first order of . . . ').

You want your ad to be simple and bold – able to attract the viewer's attention from desired information elsewhere on the screen for long enough to make a simple point.

This ad style delivers a clear marketing message using both print and illustration. Make sure that if prospects click on the banner, they go directly to a page on your website that supports the product or service with more information and with several easy purchase options.

Being positively creative with your ad

Online advertising, done well, can do many more tasks for you than a TV ad, press ad or poster. For a start, users who click on your ad can be delivered directly to your transactional website. Job done (well, almost – see 'Creating a Compelling Website' earlier in this chapter). An online ad can be tactical, by alerting customers to a special offer, or it can help with brand-building, by raising awareness of your product or service without a clear call to action. Unlike TV or press ads, you (or the size of your budget) control how intrusive your ad becomes.

Why would you want any web user to miss an ad you're paying good money for? Obviously, you wouldn't. So be careful about the gimmicks your ad uses. Case in point: bells-and-whistles online advertising gimmickry (or *rich media*, as the experts call it). With this type of media, you can buy an ad that totally obscures a page someone's trying to view, that chases his cursor around the screen, and basically forces him either to pay attention or close it. That technology runs contrary to every other trend in the advertiser– customer relationship, which is why this tactic has fallen out of favour in recent years. Instead, create some eye-catching online ad designs that integrate with the web page they appear on and don't irritate potential customers.

Placing your banner ads

Designing the banner is just the beginning because you then have to buy space to display it from publishers. If you poke around on large sites like Yahoo! or Google, you can find sections devoted to advertisers like you, where you can explore ad buying options and rates and ask for help from a salesperson. Alternatively, you can go to an online media-buying agency and hire them to do the placement. These agencies take a small commission but probably more than make up for this loss by knowing where to place the ads to target your core customer base, negotiating better rates, and avoiding some of the inflation of exposure numbers that can happen when you have to rely on the publisher's accounting.

Placing a banner ad typically costs between £1 and £5 per thousand viewers, depending on where it's placed – not bad if you have an ad that actually generates some responses. But watch the banner ad closely and pull or modify it, or try running it elsewhere, if the click rate is too low to justify the cost. You may have to try a few versions to get it right, but with the rapid feedback possible on the Web, this experimentation can take place fairly quickly and inexpensively.

Getting Others to Do the Work: Affiliate Marketing

Affiliate marketing is another term for 'finder's fees' or 'lead fees'.

Affiliate marketing programmes work by rewarding websites that deliver users to other websites. Affiliate programmes are usually used by online retailers who pay the referring website a fee for every consumer that completes a certain function, such as purchasing or signing up for something. Although early affiliate deals rewarded on a click basis, so that every click that went through to the destination was paid for, this system has changed in recent years and nearly always uses a performance-based remuneration model – so, as an advertiser, you only pay if you make money. Brilliant!

Carried out correctly, affiliate marketing can be a remarkably effective method for advertisers to get people to their site to buy things. Its payment by results nature also means that you needn't be afraid to get involved.

Getting started

Unless you're a big company with lots of time and resources to spare to develop your own programme, seek to join an existing affiliate network. A number of these networks exist in the UK and all have different affiliate member websites and focuses, so matching your business to the network that can deliver you the best results is important.

To begin with, here's a list – in no particular order – of the bigger networks active in the UK today:

- ✔ www.tradedoubler.co.uk
- ✔ www.affiliatefuture.co.uk
- ✔ www.dgmaffiliates.com
- ✔ www.affiliatewindow.com
- ✔ www.buy.at
- ✔ www.paidonresults.com
- ✔ www.webgains.com
- ✔ www.linkshare.com/uk
- ✔ www.uk.cj.com

We won't go through every option that every affiliate network offers you or you'll be reading forever. But as an example of how different networks can deliver a variety of results, the DGM affiliate network covers the travel, finance, shopping, telecoms and automotive sectors and the Trade Doubler network is used by companies including Dell and Domino's Pizza. As you can see, you have a lot of scope for shopping around, although almost all networks will have strengths and weaknesses in different areas.

Every network will also most likely show you the three arms of its business on its homepage: merchants (advertisers), affiliates (publishers) and agencies. In this case, you're the advertiser, so check out what the network has to offer for you. You never know, you may even want to join a programme yourself as a publisher and make some extra money!

Choosing a network

Picking your way through the different affiliate network offerings can be a bit of a minefield, but when you're engaging any agency for outsourced work, try to get as much information about them as possible.

Use the checklist below to help you select an affiliate partner:

- ✔ Ask the network about their expertise in your chosen sector and ask them to back it up with examples and case studies, if possible.
- ✔ Get them to show you a client list and any testimonials that they have.
- ✔ Ask them about the size and breadth of their network. Is it only UK based? What are the demographics?

✔ Check out the top ranking affiliate networks from a search engine results page, using the search term 'affiliate marketing'. Search is a key part of affiliate marketing and the result may say a lot about the network.

✔ Have an immediate conversation about pricing and costs. You're better off knowing what you're dealing with at the outset.

✔ Come into the process with your eyes wide open. These people want to sell you the affiliate marketing dream, so don't get carried away with the hype. If their claims sound too good to be true, they may well be.

✔ Ask them what support and services they offer to advertisers.

✔ Find out which networks your competitors use. Being in the same network as a competitor can drive up the price of your affiliate marketing as your rival may offer a better commission deal to publishers than you do. Publishers will then try harder on behalf of your competition than for you and force you into a bidding war.

✔ Find out what measurement technology the network uses to track clicks to your site.

✔ Discover the publishers' payment basis.

Going through this checklist means you've applied due diligence to the process and will thus know less chance exists of anything going wrong when you begin using affiliate marketing.

Entering the Blogosphere

You have your website and have set up an online advertising programme and also maybe an affiliate programme; now you're ready to enter the Blogosphere! We don't mean outer space but the online world of blogs.

At its most basic, blogging is a way of recording thoughts, collecting links and sharing ideas with other people via a very simple website. In effect, blogs are online journals for individuals or organisations. A blogging craze is currently sweeping the world, with millions of people writing them on a daily basis. Statistics industry site Technorati shows that over 133 million blogs have been created since 2002.

Although still behind the US, blogging has become massively popular in the UK. Some are political in nature, such as Guido Fawkes (http://5thnovember.blogspot.com), and some detail intimate details of people's lives.

Anyone who's anyone is blogging – from David Cameron to London Underground tube drivers. Some blogs have also turned their authors into mini-celebrities. 'Perez Hilton' is the world's most famous celebrity blogger, reporting on the underbelly of Hollywood, and is now a media mogul in his own right with everything from a clothing range to a TV show.

If you want people to keep coming back to look at your blog you need to keep it up to date, interesting and relevant. Boring blogs are a turn-off!

Blogger and Wordpress are free blogging tools but many others charge you a monthly or annual subscription. Moving your blog from one tool to another isn't easy, so make your decision carefully.

A number of the biggest companies, such as Guinness, Honda and BT, are now using blogs to communicate with their customers with varying degrees of success. These are known as corporate blogs and yours will fall into this category (albeit on a smaller scale). The Guinness blog (www.guinness blog.com) is perhaps the most engaging of the corporate offerings as the black stuff's marketing team write it and it gives Guinness fans a behind the scenes look into how the drink's produced and how the company goes about making its ads. Companies are increasingly starting to view blogging as a crucial communications tool, and you need to follow the guidelines below to ensure that your company gets the most out of this medium:

✔ Be open and honest. Hiding the truth on the Internet is impossible and if you try to mislead consumers via your blog you'll get burnt (or 'flamed' in blog jargon).

✔ Keep your blog up to date, relevant and interesting. No one wants to read a blog from two years ago; it looks like your company gives up on things when they become too much trouble.

✔ Be clear about the aims of your blog from the outset and stick to them.

✔ Do let bloggers comment on what you write and make sure you don't overreact if or when they post anything negative about your company. If you really want a conversation with customers, be prepared for people to tell you their truth, not just yours.

✔ If negative posts do appear, react in an open and honest way. Blogs are a very useful way of developing your product or service to better meet the needs of your customers.

✔ Avoid 'corporate speak'. Blogs are about presenting a side to the business not encompassed in the official website, so don't weigh them down with jargon.

✔ Don't try to sell to your audience. That's a job for an official website; if you make your blog a sales pitch, people simply won't visit it.

✔ Make sure that if more than one person is blogging on behalf of the company, everyone is clear on what are acceptable topics for discussion, and what are the right tone and style so it remains consistent rather than appearing confused.

Bloggers hate being sold to and react badly to companies that try to do so. Using subversive means is particularly frowned upon.

Using Email for Marketing

Email is a powerful digital marketing tool. This medium may seem a bit old hat in a world of Facebook and MySpace, but you can create yourself, or hire a designer to create, a professional email that looks like a well-designed web page, with animation and clickable buttons linking to your site. Now, all you have to do is blast out your message to millions of email addresses and surely you can make millions overnight!

Not so fast! Okay, so you have this great marketing message or sales pitch, and you want to send it to everyone in the world who has an email address. You can actually do that, but we don't advise doing so. The more specific and narrow your use of email for marketing, the better. In fact, since the introduction of legislation in the UK, Europe and the US, marketers must be careful to avoid violating all sorts of restrictions on *spam*, or junk emails. We help you stay on the sunny side of the law in this section.

Sending only good emails

The best email is a personal communication with a customer you know (and who wants to hear from you), sent individually from you with an accurate email return address as well as your name, title, company name, full mailing address and phone number. The email may read as follows:

Dear So-and-so

I wanted to follow up after your purchase of (your product) on (date) to see how it's working out for you and to thank you for your continuing business. If you have any concerns or questions, please let me know by return email, or feel free to call me directly on 0123 123 1234.

Best wishes

Your Name

Your customer is going to receive, open, read and appreciate an email like this one. He may even respond to it, especially if the customer has any current concerns or questions or has another order on its way. Even if he doesn't reply to it, he still appreciates that email. And that message doesn't irritate anyone or look like spam.

Use email as much as you can for legitimate, helpful, one-to-one contact and support of customers or prospects. Sometimes you can offer services or content online that requires a registration. As part of that registration process, consider asking your customers if they want to receive more information on any of your products. If they opt in, you can be sure that they'll value your follow-up emails.

Sending out an email to a list rather than an individual is also possible, but ensure that you have a clear purpose that benefits those people on the list. Also make sure that your list only includes people who've indicated they're happy to be communicated with so you stay within the law and don't anger people. Never attempt to contact people who've opted out of contact with you.

Understanding email etiquette

Goodwill is a valuable asset, so don't destroy it with your emails! The following list provides some additional rules for good mass emailing. Our inspiration for these rules comes from the Direct Marketing Association's guidelines for responsible use of email. We also bear the legal restrictions in mind.

- ✔ **Send emails only to those people who ask for them.** Your bulk emails should go only to those people who give you permission to contact them. The law (the Privacy and Electronic Communications Regulations) requires that no emails are sent without prior consent. What does that mean? It means that everyone you send an email to should have 'opted in' to receive emails from you, and each time you contact them, you must give them an option to reply and be taken off the list.

  If you have a 'prior relationship' with that contact (such as them being a previous customer or requesting information from you) the rules are slightly softer. Consider asking visitors to your website to register for extra information; you can then get these requests by creating a useful e-newsletter and advertising it on the Web as a free subscription. Those people who sign up really want it, and they're happy to see the next issue arrive.

- ✔ **Remove addresses from your list immediately when people ask for them to be removed.** Remember that refusing to allow people to opt out is illegal. Also, people have such widespread distrust of web marketers that you may consider writing the person a brief, individual email from you (identify yourself and your title for credibility), letting him know that you've eliminated him from the list and are sorry if you've inconvenienced him. You don't need to say any more in the email. Don't try to make a sale – you just irritate the person even more. You generally make a positive impression by being so responsive to the person's complaint, so don't be surprised if your special attention to his request leads him to initiate a sale later on.

✔ **If you insist on buying email lists, test them before using them.** We're assuming that the list you buy in is legal (check first that the people on it have agreed to being contacted by third-party advertisers, like yourself). Then try sending a very simple, short, non-irritating message to people on the list, such as an offer to send them a catalogue or free sample, and ask for a few pieces of qualifying information in return. See what happens. Cull all the many bounce-backs and irritated people from the list. Now your list is a bit better quality than the raw original. Save those replies in a separate list – they're significantly better and more qualified and deserve a more elaborate email, mailing or (if the numbers aren't too high) personal contact.

✔ **Respect privacy.** People don't want to feel like someone's spying on them. Never send to a list if you'd be embarrassed to admit where you got the names from. You can develop an email list in plenty of legitimate ways (from customer data, from web ads, from enquiries at trade shows, from return postcards included in mailings, and so on), so don't do anything that your neighbours would consider irritating or sleazy.

✔ **Send out your bulk emails just like you send an individual one.** Use a real, live, reply-able email address. We hate it when we can't reply to an email – it makes us angry!

✔ **Make sure that the subject line isn't deceptive.** Good practice and good sense dictate that you make the subject line straightforward. In marketing, you want to know straight away if someone isn't a good prospect, instead of wasting your time or his when he has no interest in your offer. A whole other book could be written about creating snappy lines that ensure emails get opened, but just consider what makes you do so. Opening with a deception such as 'Free money for you!' just looks like spam and will be deleted.

✔ **Keep your email address lists up to date.** When you get a *hard bounce-back* (notice that a message was undeliverable) from an address, remove it immediately and update your email list for the next mailing.

A *soft bounce-back* is an undeliverable message resulting from some kind of temporary problem. Track it to see if the email eventually goes through. If not, eliminate this address from your list, too.

People change their email addresses and switch servers. You can have bounce-backs on your list who may still be good customers or prospects. At least once a year, check these inactive names and try to contact them by phone or post to update their email addresses. Some of these people are still interested and don't need to be cut from your list; they just need their email addresses updated.

If you're emailing to an in-house list of people who've bought from you, gone to your seminar or asked for information in the past, remind them of your relationship in the email – they may have forgotten.

We hate *spam* – junk emails that clog up our mailboxes. We bet you feel the same way. So don't let your web marketing make you part of this problem. Use good quality lists, be polite and respectful, and integrate email into your broader web strategy so that you don't have to rely too heavily on email. Real people live at the end of those email addresses. Treat them as such!

Getting Mobile with Your Marketing

A staggering 6.5 billion text messages were sent in the UK during May 2008. According to the Mobile Data Association, 16.43 million mobile Internet (WAP) users were evident in the UK in the same month, and the latest Ofcom Communications Market Report showed that 12.5 million 3G (the fastest mobile speed) connections existed in the UK in August 2008.

Mobile marketing is held up as being one of the most important mediums of the future but, as you can see from the numbers, the possibilities for now aren't half bad either. We emphasise that things are constantly changing in mobile marketing, so the technologies of today will certainly be superseded some time soon.

The most basic, and therefore most developed, method of mobile marketing is by Short Message Service, or SMS – which most people simply call texting. You can send a personal, targeted message by text in the same way as you send an email (and subject to the same laws on privacy; see 'Understanding email etiquette' earlier in this section), and you can reach your customers 24 hours a day.

Of course, you can also use a mobile phone as the launch pad for a whole host of marketing wonderment. MMS, WAP, Bluetooth, 3G – the terminology is almost as impenetrable as the average marketer's ability to take advantage of it. For the time being we suggest that, if you're interested in trying out mobile marketing, stick to the tried and tested methods (or at least as tried and tested as a less than ten-year-old method can be). The following list gives some pointers and ideas on how to use mobile marketing:

- ✔ **Keep it short and to the point.** An SMS message can only be 160 characters long – so your message has to be quick and clear. That's enough, however, to provide customers with a money-off message or coupon, for example.

- ✔ **Know who's using the mobile.** People of all ages use mobile phones, so try to fit the message to your knowledge of who owns the number.

✔ **Be prepared for a good response.** If you do plan to offer a mobile token or other giveaway, be aware that response rates can be as much as 15 per cent higher than direct marketing – and a large chunk of that response will be immediate.

✔ **Respect privacy at all times.** Mobile marketing is subject to the same laws as email marketing, covered earlier in this section. You must have the permission of the person you're texting. Respecting the principles of permission-based marketing makes good sense.

✔ **Get help (you'll need it).** You can build your own database of mobile numbers and send messages directly to them, but doing so is time-consuming and, for all but the smallest databases, uneconomical. Consider buying in a list of numbers from a database company and then getting an SMS broadcast provider to send the messages for you. Like a mailing house or call centre, these companies can give you feedback on the campaign and manage the customer response.

For now, we suggest leaving the development of Apple iPhone applications or Google Phone services to the larger brands, as new advertising eco-systems like these have multiple pitfalls. Letting someone else discover them before you take on this type of sophisticated mobile advertising is probably best.

Knowing How Much to Budget

If you're in a business-to-business (B2B) marketing situation, we strongly urge you to put at least 15 per cent of your marketing budget into the Web, both for maintaining a strong website and for doing some web advertising and search-engine placement purchases. If you add an e-newsletter, web distribution of press releases and occasional announcements to your email list, you may need to set aside as much as 20 per cent of your budget. These figures are only a guide, however, and if the Web is your main sales channel, dedicating more budget to the medium is probably worthwhile.

Online advertising looks set to overhaul TV advertising in the UK. Online media is ahead of press classified advertising and direct mail and more than radio, outdoor and cinema advertising put together. The money follows the eyeballs in the advertising industry and, as such, digital advertising is becoming even more important as more people spend more time online.

We believe that digital marketing is great because you can turn it up or down depending on its performance. If you book a big outdoor campaign, you won't find out you've wasted your money until you've already paid for it. Online, you can see how things are going on a minute-by-minute basis and adjust your spend accordingly. If you find that your web ads, search engine listings or emails are pulling well for you and making a profit, try doubling your effort and spending on them and seeing what happens. Still working well? Double again. You may find that the Web can do a lot more of your basic marketing work than you think. Many marketers hold web spending down to a small minority of their budget for no good reason other than tradition and fear of all things new. Why not dive in and reap the rewards?

One Final, Important Thought

The single most important point to remember about websites and e-marketing in general is that investing in it routinely is crucial so that you're always changing and improving your presence. Whether you're a do-it-yourself online marketer or are willing to hire a professional online agency, your e-marketing needs to be a living thing. Don't let parts of your site get old and stale. Don't continue to run a *banner ad* (an ad that appears on a major website or service) or bid on a *keyword or phrase* (a word or phrase people use in searching for websites, which you can pay to have your message linked to) if you aren't getting results in clicks and sales. Do adapt and change all the time. The Web is a dynamic marketing medium. Be dynamic!

Book VI

Growing and Improving Your Business

'I like a young man who knows where he's going.
If you'll just go through that door while
my directors & I discuss your promotion
application . . .'

In this book . . .

If all goes according to plan, or your business is already booming, we take this opportunity to suggest ways to grow your business. From expanding your own skills as a manager to improving your company's overall performance, this book contains some great ideas for helping your business to grow and grow and grow.

Here are the contents of Book VI at a glance:

Chapter 1

Thinking Strategically

. . . .

In This Chapter

▶ Discovering why strategy can make a difference

▶ Exploring the low-cost leadership strategy

▶ Applying differentiation strategies

▶ Focusing on a focus strategy

▶ Examining other strategic alternatives

▶ Coming up with your own strategy

. . . .

In this chapter, we help you formulate a strategy for your company that's in keeping with its basic mission. First, we explore why strategy is so important to the business-planning process. We examine what it means to have a strategy and when that strategy works best, and introduce several basic strategies that you can apply across many industries. These off-the-shelf strategies include efforts

✔ To be the low-cost provider

✔ To differentiate your products

✔ To focus on specific market and product areas

We talk about several other general strategic alternatives as well, answering questions such as 'What does it mean to become more vertically integrated as a company?' and 'How should you act when you're the market leader or a market follower?' We also give you some pointers about creating a strategic blueprint for your own company.

Making Strategy Make a Difference

Some companies think that *strategy* and *planning* are four-letter words. Those companies would never think of using either term in the context of their own organisations. It isn't that these companies don't move forward; it's just that they don't talk much about it ahead of time. So why do the two terms have such bad reputations in certain quarters? More than likely, it's because they've been misunderstood or applied incorrectly. *Strategy* and *planning* have become such buzzwords in today's business world that their real meanings are easily lost in all the muddle surrounding them.

The colourful and outspoken Wall Street trader Alan 'Ace' Greenberg, head of the Bear Stearns brokerage house, is no fan of strategic planning. He has even gone so far as to suggest that because strategic plans have such poor track records, he should establish a Backward Planning Committee to guarantee his company's success. What a card. Still, although Greenberg won't give business planners the time of day, it's clear that he has a strong personal vision, strategy and plan to make Bear Stearns successful over the long haul.

At the opposite end of the playing field from Ace Greenberg is a fictional character named Joe Clueless, who doesn't give a hoot about the future. Joe doesn't have a personal vision or a strategy. He doesn't have his own plan, because he's an opportunist. Maybe he's in the right place at the right time, right now. But no one can consistently survive on short-term breaks alone. As the old saying goes:

> *Luck sometimes visits a fool, but it never sits down with him for long.*

The process of strategic planning creates a framework and a discipline to guide those of us who find ourselves somewhere in between Ace, who has built-in business radar, and Joe, who can't be bothered. We know that strategic planning works, because we've seen it with our own eyes. We've also seen where a lack of strategic planning can lead. A 2000 survey of close to 500 small companies backs us up; it found that companies that have strategic plans have 50 per cent more revenue and profit growth than companies that fail to plan. It's that simple.

What strategy means

The word *strategy* comes to us from the ancient Greeks and translates literally as *the art of generalship*. When you compete, you probably feel that you're suiting up for battle, jousting with your competitors for the hearts and minds of customers.

Modern definitions of the word are even less precise, so we're proposing our own standard definition of *strategy* in the business arena. A strategy does the following things:

✔ Describes how to reach the goals and objectives that you set for the company

✔ Takes into account the personal and social values that surround your company

✔ Guides the way that you allocate and deploy your human and financial resources

✔ Creates an advantage in the marketplace that you can sustain, despite intense and determined competition

Putting together a strategic business plan requires you to gather data, analyse the information, and then do something with it – something more than just reformatting it, printing it and packaging it in a tidy report titled 'The Five-Year Plan'. In most cases, that kind of report begins and ends with numbers – revenue projections, cash flows, expense allocations and the like, which are things that don't help you figure out what to do next. Reports like this are sure to fall victim to the dreaded SPOTS (Strategic Plans on Top Shelves) syndrome: they gather dust and little else. These reports don't represent strategy or planning; they represent a waste of time.

What can you do to make sure that this doesn't happen to your business plan? For one thing, a healthy dose of plain old common sense works wonders as you pull all the pieces together to create your strategy. Experience in your industry and some nous are advantages, too. Unfortunately, we can't give you any of these gifts. But we can offer you some solid advice about laying out your strategy, including some hints that make you look like a planning pro.

Keep the following questions in mind as you begin to formulate your strategic plan:

✔ What markets and segments does your company plan to compete in?

✔ Which products and services will your company develop and support?

✔ Where is your company's competitive advantage in these markets and products?

✔ How will your company sustain that competitive advantage over time?

The answers that you come up with go a long way towards keeping your strategy focused and on target, so you want to return to them from time to time at each phase of the planning process.

When strategy works

Strategy works when you have a process to ensure that planning is consistently tied to the ongoing operations of your business. If strategic plans fail, it's usually because they don't seem to be relevant to the issues and problems at hand. Strategy and planning get linked with committee meetings, bureaucracy, overheads and all those other barriers that are thrown up to ensure that results aren't achieved. As a result, strategy and planning are seen by some companies as a part of the problem, not a solution.

Strategy works best when strategic planning is integrated into every aspect of your business, every day of the week and every week of the year. An ongoing strategic-planning process means that you do the following things:

- ✔ Always question what makes your company successful.
- ✔ Continually observe customers and markets, tracking their wants and needs.
- ✔ Relentlessly examine the competition and what it's up to.
- ✔ Steadily work at maintaining your competitive advantage.
- ✔ Continually search for ways to leverage your core competence.

Some managers may do all these things automatically and intuitively. But if you want to make sure that strategy and planning are carried out in all parts of your company, you have to create a framework to ensure that it happens. When you make strategic planning a basic responsibility, you get the added benefit of including all levels of employees in the planning process. Employees often have different and equally valuable viewpoints about shaping strategy, and a strategic-planning framework ensures that their voices are heard.

To start the ball rolling in your own company, pull together a group of employees who represent different functions and various levels in your organisation. Meet on a regular basis to talk about strategy and planning. Concentrate on how to set up a framework to promote strategic thinking, and focus on problems associated with the strategic-planning process itself. Then group members can take what they learn back to their own areas and begin to integrate strategic planning into the way that they do business.

- ✔ Strategy is the art and science of creating a business plan that meets your company's goals and objectives. See Chapter 4 in Book I for more on creating a business plan.
- ✔ Strategy works best when strategic planning is integrated into every aspect of your business.

> ✔ Don't fall victim to the SPOTS (Strategic Plans on Top Shelves) syndrome.
>
> ✔ On average, small companies that have strategic plans have 50 per cent higher revenue and profit growth than companies that fail to plan.

Applying Off-the-Shelf Strategies

Maybe you think your company's situation is absolutely unique and the issues you face are one of a kind. Does this mean that your strategy and business plan have to be unique as well? Not entirely. If you look through a microscope, every snowflake is different. But snowflakes have a great deal in common when you stand back and watch them pile up outside. Companies are like snowflakes. Although all the details give companies their individual profiles, companies and industries in general display remarkable similarities when you step back and concentrate on their basic shapes.

Book VI

Growing and Improving Your Business

Master business strategist and Harvard University professor Michael Porter was one of the first to recognise, and take an inventory of, standard business profiles. Based on what he saw, he came up with three generic approaches to strategy and business planning. These *generic strategies* are important because they offer off-the-shelf answers to a basic question: 'What does it take to be successful in a business over the long haul?' And the answers work across all markets and industries.

Generic strategies boil down to the following standard approaches (highlighted in Figure 1-1):

> ✔ **Cut costs to the bone.** Become the low-cost leader in your industry. Do everything that you can to reduce your own costs while delivering a product or service that measures up well against the competition.
>
> ✔ **Offer something unique.** Figure out how to provide customers with something that's both unique and of real value, and deliver your product or service at a price that customers are willing to pay.
>
> ✔ **Focus on one customer group.** Decide to focus on the precise needs and requirements of a narrow market, using either low cost or a unique product to woo your target customers away from the general competition.

It's not surprising that cutting costs and offering something unique represent two generic strategies that work almost universally. After all, business, industry and competition are all driven by customers who base their purchase decisions on the value equation – an equation that weighs the benefits of any product or service against its price tag. Generic strategies merely concentrate your efforts on influencing one side of the value equation or the other.

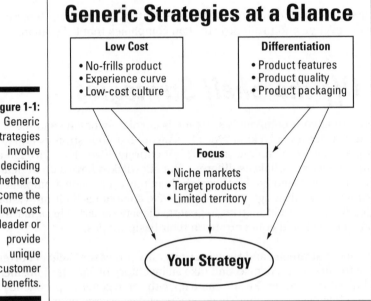

Figure 1-1:
Generic
strategies
involve
deciding
whether to
become the
low-cost
leader or
provide
unique
customer
benefits.

Low-cost leadership

Becoming the low-cost leader in your industry requires the commitment and co-ordination of every aspect of your company, from product development to marketing, from manufacturing to distribution, from raw materials to wages and benefits. Every day and in every way, you track down and exterminate unnecessary costs. Find a new technology that simplifies manufacturing? Install it. Find a region or country that has a more productive labour force? Move there. Find suppliers to provide cheaper raw materials? Sign 'em up.

A cost-leadership strategy is often worth the effort because it gives you a powerful competitive position. When you're the low-cost leader, you call the shots and challenge every one of your competitors to find other ways to compete. Although the strategy is universal, it works best in markets and industries in which price tends to drive customer behaviour – the bulk- or commodity-products business, for example, or low-end, price-sensitive market segments.

The following sections describe the ways in which you can carry out a cost-leadership strategy.

No-frills product

The most obvious and straightforward way to keep costs down is to invoke the well-known KISS (Keep It Simple, Stupid!) principle. When you cut out all the extras and eliminate the options, your product is bound to be cheaper to put together. A no-frills product can be particularly successful if you're able to match it with a market that doesn't see any benefit in (or is even annoyed by) other products' bells and whistles – the couch potatoes whose video recorders sport a flashing 12:00, for example, or famous-writers-to-be who are baffled by their word processors.

In addition to removing all the extras, you can sometimes take advantage of a simple product redesign to gain an even greater cost advantage. Home developers have replaced plywood with pressed board, for example, to lower the costs of construction. Camera makers have replaced metal components with plastic. And, of course, there's always the Pizza Express solution; the company reduced costs at one point simply by making its pizzas a wee bit smaller.

Stripped-down products and services eventually appear in almost every industry. The most obvious examples today are:

- ✔ No-frills airlines such as easyJet and Ryanair
- ✔ Warehouse stores such as Aldi, Costco and Lidl, which offer a wide selection, low prices and no help
- ✔ Bare-bones brokerage houses such as Hargraves Lansdown and TD Waterhouse, which charge low commissions on trades without any hand-holding or personal investment advice

Experience curve

Cost leadership is often won or lost based on the power of the *experience curve,* which traces the declining unit costs of putting together and selling a product or service over time (see Figure 1-2).

The curve measures the real cost per unit of various general business expenses: plant construction, machinery, labour, office space, administration, advertising, distribution, sales – everything but the raw materials that make up the product in the first place. All these costs combined tend to go down over time when they're averaged out over all the products that you make or services that you provide.

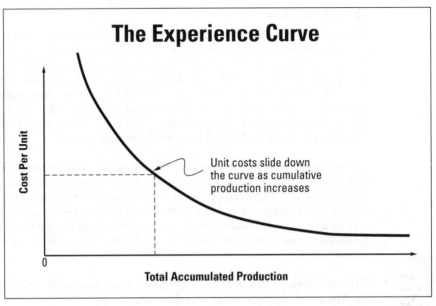

Figure 1-2:
The
experience
curve
traces the
declining
unit costs
of putting
together
and selling
a product
as total
accumu-
lated
production
increases.

The underlying causes of the experience curve include the following:

✔ **Scale.** *Scale* refers to the fact that you have fixed business costs, which are fixed in the sense that they're not affected by how much of your product you make and sell. (Fixed costs usually include such things as your rent, the equipment that you buy, and some of your utility bills.) The more products you produce, the more you gain an immediate scale advantage, because the fixed costs associated with each unit go down automatically.

Think about widgets for a moment. Suppose that you rent a building at £1,000 a month to house widget production. So as not to lose money, you have to add that rental expense into the cost of the widgets that you make. Perhaps the first month, you turn out only ten widgets. No matter what else they cost, you have to add £100 rent (£1,000 divided by ten units) to the price of each widget. But if you can boost production to 100 units the next month, you have to add only £10 in rent (£1,000 divided by 100 units) to the price of each widget, and you reduce your rental costs per unit by a whopping 90 per cent. Scale is good for business and your bottom line.

✔ **Scope.** *Scope* works a little like the scale effect, but scope refers to the underlying cost benefit that you get by serving larger markets or by offering multiple products that share overhead expenses associated with such things as advertising, product service and distribution. These expenses aren't exactly fixed, but you do gain an automatic scope advantage if the ad that you decide to run reaches a larger market or if your delivery trucks deliver two or three products to each of your sales outlets instead of one.

✔ **Learning.** Remember the first time you tried to tie your shoelaces? Big job. A lot of work. Now you can do it in your sleep. What happened? The more you tied your shoes, the better you got at it. The same is true whether you're on a factory floor, at a computer workstation or in a conference room. You (and your employees) get better at something the more you do it. As you learn, the overall cost of doing business goes down.

A general rule suggests that all these underlying causes result in what's known as an 80 per cent experience curve. Every time you double the total number of products produced, unit costs go down by about 20 per cent – to 80 per cent of what they were before.

The cost benefit that you actually get out of your own company's experience is bound to vary and depends partly on your industry. A few industries don't benefit from experience effects at all. In industries in which the basic costs of raw materials are high, for example, there's not much room for gaining a big advantage through experience. Many service industries may not get much of an advantage from experience, either. It doesn't matter how good hairstylists become at what they do; it still takes them about an hour to wash and style each customer's hair, so the company's costs don't change.

Low-cost culture

You can sustain low-cost leadership only if every part of your company is committed to keeping costs under control, reducing or eliminating expenses and unnecessary spending. This kind of commitment doesn't occur without leadership and the example set by the owners themselves.

Perhaps more than any other strategy and business plan that you can pursue, the push to be the low-cost leader in your industry succeeds or fails based on how well you actually carry it out. Knowing where and when to bring in cost-saving technology may be one important aspect of your drive, for example. But at the heart of your plan, it's absolutely critical that you figure out how to structure the company, reward your employees and create the spirit of a 'lean, mean fighting machine'. In the end, your employees determine just how efficient your company really is. This may mean that you don't drive a company car or that you never, ever make personal long-distance calls from work. You can bet that your employees will follow your lead.

Low-cost leadership means exactly what it says. It's just not good enough to be first, second or third runner-up; it's not even all right to be first among equals. If you can't assume the cost-leadership position, you run the risk of playing a part in your own worst nightmare: a high-stakes, cut-throat industry in which price-war shoot-'em-outs threaten to destroy all the players. After all, if no one's a clear leader, everyone's a challenger, and when low-cost challengers decide to battle for market-share advantage, they use price as their favourite weapon. If you happen to find yourself in such a Wild West industry, take action. Look for new and different ways to compete – alternative strategies that are more likely to reward you in the end.

Standing out in a crowd

Not every company can be the low-cost leader in an industry, and many companies don't even want to be. Instead, they prefer to compete in the marketplace by creating products and services that are unique, offering customers things that they just have to have – things that they're willing to pay a little extra for. The strategy is known as *differentiation*.

Differentiation has a great deal going for it, because companies can be different in many ways, which means that there are many ways to be successful. Although the low-cost strategy that we talked about in the preceding sections can easily produce a win-lose situation for many companies, differentiation often creates room for more players, each of which competes successfully in its own special ways. That's not to say that competition isn't fierce, even when companies offer distinctly different products or services.

Companies that can make themselves distinct from their competitors often enjoy enviable profits, and they frequently use those extra pounds to reinforce their unique positions in the marketplace. A premium winery, for example, earns its reputation based on the quality of grapes and expertise of the winemaker, but it goes on to polish that reputation through expensive packaging and promotional campaigns. All these added investments make it more difficult for competitors to join in, but they also raise the cost of doing business. Although a maker of house wine has trouble competing in premium markets, a premium winery really can't afford to compete on price alone. No company can ignore cost, of course, even if it offers something that no one else does. Wine-lovers may be willing to spend £15 for a special bottle of Chardonnay but may baulk at a £30 price tag.

Chances are that you can make your company unique in a number of ways. You can set your product or service apart based on what it can do, how well it works, or the way it is packaged and distributed. Then you can go on to develop any of these aspects into a successful differentiation strategy, creating a loyal set of customers along the way.

Because a differentiation strategy hinges completely on your relationship with customers, however, stop and ask yourself several questions before you move ahead:

✔ Who are your customers?

✔ How would you best describe them?

✔ What are their basic wants and needs?

✔ How do they make choices?

✔ What motivates them to buy things?

Check out Chapter 6 in Book I for insight on customers. The following sections describe ways that you can set yourself apart from the competition.

Product features

You can often find the basic outlines of a successful differentiation strategy in what your product can and can't do for customers. After all, a product's features are frequently among the first things that a potential buyer considers. How do your products stack up? Are you particularly strong in product design and development? If so, you probably want to consider how to leverage your strength in developing new features to make your company's product stand out.

Unfortunately, product features represent a big target for your competitors to aim at, and trying to be different based on major product attributes alone is sometimes hard to sustain over the long haul. Technology-driven companies such as Sony, 3M and Intel have managed to stay one step ahead of the competition for many years by always offering the latest and greatest products. But it's not easy (or inexpensive) to be chased all the time.

Rather than always take the lead in product development, you can make your company stand out by enhancing a product in more subtle ways, offering customers unique and tailored options that are appreciated all the more because they're often unexpected. Examples include an insurance policy that makes it easy to keep track of what you own and then automatically updates your coverage and software that actually helps you remove every bit of itself from your hard drive when you want to get rid of it.

Product quality

When you offer a product or service that's known for its quality, you take a big step towards standing out in the marketplace. In some sense, quality captures what differentiation is all about. Quality of one sort or another is what everybody seems to be looking for, and it's often in the eyes of the beholder. Although customers can't always tell you exactly what quality is, they know it when they see it, and when they see it, they like it – and may even pay a little extra for it.

Book VI

Growing and Improving Your Business

Customers are likely to perceive quality in your product a bit differently from how they do quality in a service that you may offer. The differences between product and service quality are big enough, in fact, that we treat the two separately in Table 1-1.

Table 1-1	Product and Service Quality Examples
Product Quality	*Example*
Performance	Do pots and pans get clean in the dishwasher?
Consistency	Is the restaurant's pasta special always tasty?
Durability	How long will the hiking boots last?
Reliability	Will the answering machine save all the messages?
Appearance	Does the watch have that special look and feel?
Brand name	Which stereo system is known for its quality?
Service quality	*Example*
Capability	Does the brain surgeon know what she's doing?
Dependability	Will the newspaper be delivered in the morning?
Responsiveness	Can the 999 emergency team arrive in time?
Integrity	How much should the lawyer be trusted?
Attentiveness	Does the bank clerk smile and say hello?
Tangibles	Which airline has the cleanest onboard toilets?

The different quality dimensions depend on the industry that you're in and on the customers you're serving. Even in a particular industry, companies create successful differentiation strategies for distinct dimensions. The car industry is a prime example. When you think of Porsche, for example, you think of performance; Volvo means safety; and Toyota and Honda are reliable choices. These differences allow competitors to prosper in the same industry, each in its own way.

Things are a bit different in service industries. For one thing, you can't help but face the importance of customers' impressions when you're dealing with services. By definition, a service is something that can't be held; you can't really touch it, feel it or kick its tyres. So customers are in a bit of a quandary when it comes to making well-informed decisions. Figuring out what is and isn't a quality service is harder. How do you really know whether your doctor's a genius or a quack, for example? Is the pilot of today's flight an ace or just so-so? Is your dentist a saint or a sadist?

That's why perceptions come into play. When customers don't have all the data, they go with what they see. No matter what other dimensions are important, the tangibles – equipment, facilities and personnel – play a significant part in customers' perceptions of service quality. As an airline executive said:

> *Filthy toilets and dirty trays are bound to lead to engine failure.*

Because customers have no way of evaluating the quality of an airline's engine-maintenance programme, they look at the things that they *can* judge, and they form their opinions accordingly.

Product packaging

Customers often look beyond the basics in making the final decision on what to buy. In fact, your customers may be influenced as much by the packaging as by the standard set of features that your product or service has to offer. Accordingly, you can develop an effective differentiation strategy based on product packaging – how it's advertised, when it's serviced, and where it's sold.

Given creative advertising, attentive service and sophisticated distribution, almost anything can be made unique in one way or another. If you don't believe us, check out the produce section in a classy supermarket. Fruit and vegetables are routinely identified by country, county or even farm of origin. Signs tell customers whether the produce was grown with or without chemicals and even specify the harvest date. Each combination represents a differentiated product to be advertised, displayed and priced based on the unique benefits that it offers.

It's all in how it's packaged

- Calvin Klein underwear costs more than the Jockey brand, but Calvin Klein boxers and briefs are big sellers because they capture the imagination of men who want to look like Calvin Klein models in nothing but their undies.

- Avon products look a great deal like cosmetics that you can buy almost anywhere, but the Avon Lady still gets the attention of women across the country who want to be pampered on their own sofas with their favourite skin-care products.

- Local gift shops may not offer the lowest prices, but by serving up homemade cakes and jams when you come in the door, they provide a unique shopping experience that keeps many customers coming back.

A special kind of Cat

Caterpillar, Inc. is the giant company that builds those giant yellow machines that build motorways, bridges, dams and airports around the globe. Caterpillar makes some of the best heavy-construction machines in the world, but its customers are impressed by much more than just equipment specs. What really sets this company apart is its unmatched capability to deliver service and spare parts at short notice. Caterpillar makes this commitment to each of its customers: no matter where you are in the world, no matter what replacement part you need, they'll see that you have it to hand within 24 hours.

It's a big and expensive promise. Caterpillar has spent a fortune creating a global service network with distribution depots that can fulfil its pledge, which of course means higher prices for Cat equipment. But customers don't mind paying those extra pounds, because they know how much they stand to lose if they have to shut down huge construction projects for want of a spark plug or fan belt. So Caterpillar sells peace of mind along with its machinery.

A focus on focus

The two generic strategies that we've talked about so far concentrate on one side of the customer value equation or the other. A cost-leadership strategy points out the price tag, whereas differentiation emphasises the unique benefits that a product or service has to offer. The final generic strategy plays off the first two strategies. A *focus strategy* still aims at either price or uniqueness, but it concentrates on a smaller piece of the action.

A focus strategy works because you concentrate on a specific customer group. As a result, you do a better job of meeting those customers' particular needs than do any of your competition, many of whom are trying to serve larger markets. The following sections discuss several ways to concentrate your efforts.

Niche markets

Small, well-defined market segments provide an opportunity not only to meet customers' needs, but also to exceed their expectations. If these market segments happen to be at the high end, you're likely to be well rewarded for your attentions as the money keeps rolling in. Small, upmarket hotels, for example, pamper their well-heeled customers with valets, butlers and even a chauffeured service to restaurants and the airport. A new breed of takeaway food services treats customers to mix-and-match offerings from the best restaurants in town, well-dressed delivery people and even sit-down catering, complete with china, crystal and kitchen staff.

Customers are willing to pay a premium for this kind of service, and that means big profits. Niche markets don't have to be upmarket, of course; factory outlet stores are thriving by serving cost-conscious customers who have high-end tastes.

Targeted products

Companies that are driven by volume sales in large markets often ignore so-called speciality products and services – all those non-standard items and services that have limited appeal and not much market potential. If these companies do get into a speciality business, they're usually fairly inefficient at it; size and overhead costs simply work against them. Speciality products and services spell potential opportunity for a focused strategy to be successful.

Speciality hardware manufacturers, for example, have found a ready market for their new lines of old hardware. As it turns out, antique screws, hinges, doorknobs and hundreds of other hard-to-find items are absolute necessities for turning rundown terraced houses back into elegant period dwellings.

Limited territory

Sometimes, a focus on geography results in cost advantages, better-served markets or both. Where local tastes are strong, for example, or service and distribution costs are particularly high, a regional business can flourish. Independent restaurants and grocery shops, TV stations and newspapers all attract a community of customers who want local news, buy regional products and like to patronise neighbourhood shops. Commuter airlines focus on regional service, offering frequent flights and the best schedules to out-of-the-way destinations, and they keep costs down by flying smaller planes, limiting facilities and running bare-bones operations.

A focus strategy works especially well if you're the new kid on the block, trying to establish a foothold in an industry in which the big guys have already staked out their claims. Rather than go after those fat, juicy markets (and get beaten up right away), you can sometimes avoid head-on competition by focusing on smaller markets, which may be less attractive to existing players. Once you're established in a niche market, you may decide that it's time to challenge the market leaders on their own turf. Morrisons, the supermarket chain, for example, started out as a small local chain offering bargain prices and a limited range. The company became a major regional player, and with its acquisition of Safeway, is now the third most successful supermarket nationally.

For small established companies in a market, a focus strategy may be the only ticket to survival when the big guys decide to come to town. If your company has few assets and limited options, concentration on a specific customer segment at least gives you a fighting chance to leverage the capabilities and resources that you do have.

Customer loyalty can prove to be a potent weapon, even against much larger companies. Tesco, for example, finds moving their superstores into small rural towns to be increasingly difficult, because the neighbours rally around local businesses and merchants that have made them satisfied customers over the years, despite the fact that Tesco probably has a wider selection of products at lower prices.

Unfortunately, a focus strategy is one of the most difficult to defend over time. Dangers lurk both inside and outside the company. If the market segment that you're in suddenly takes off, you can pretty much count on intense competition down the road from much bigger players with much deeper pockets.

If your market niche stays small, you face a powerful urge to spread your wings and expand into new and different markets, knowing full well that you may lose many of your original strengths and advantages. Your best bet is to stay focused. Small companies have the best chance of sticking around over the long haul if they stick to a strategy and business plan that concentrate their resources and capabilities, focusing their energies on serving a specific market segment better than anyone else out there.

✔ Planning pundits highlight three generic strategies that can jump-start your planning efforts: cutting costs, offering unique products or services, and focusing on one customer group.

✔ To be a low-cost leader, track down and exterminate unnecessary costs.

✔ To set your company apart, offer something new and different – faster, stronger, tastier, longer-lasting or more reliable.

✔ To adopt a focus strategy, zero in on a specific group of customers, and serve them better than anyone else does.

Checking Out Strategic Alternatives

A successful strategy and plan depend on your business circumstances – what's happening in the industry and marketplace, and what your competitors are up to. In particular, consider a couple of common business situations that you may find yourself in.

Up, down or sideways

The range of activities that define your industry – called *vertical integration* – measure how many phases of the business you and your competitors are involved in. Vertically integrated companies are involved in many parts of an industry, from supplying raw materials to selling products and services to customers. Companies that are not vertically integrated tend to focus on one or two major aspects of the business. Some breweries, for example, concentrate on one central activity: the brewing of beer. Other breweries also get involved in growing the barley and hops; in making the beer bottles, labels and cans; in trucking the beer around; and even in running the pubs that sell the beer to all those loyal customers.

Book VI

Growing and Improving Your Business

Exactly where does your company stand in terms of vertical integration in your own industry? The question's important, because it affects your decision about whether to become more or less vertically integrated over time. Several terms have been coined by business gurus to describe the strategic moves that you may decide to make:

- **Backward integration.** *Backward integration* means extending your business activities in a direction that gets you closer to the raw materials, resources and expertise that go into creating and producing your company's products.

- **Forward integration.** *Forward integration* means extending your business activities in a direction that gets you closer to the marketplace by involving the company in packaging, marketing, distribution and customer sales.

- **Outsourcing.** *Outsourcing* means concentrating on your core business activities by farming out other parts of your company's operations to outside contractors and vendors that specialise in those particular areas.

- **Divesting.** *Divesting* means reducing your company's activities to focus on specific aspects of your business by spinning off or selling other pieces of the company.

Tables 1-2 and 1-3 describe some of the pros and cons of vertical integration.

Table 1-2	Pros of Vertical Integration
Pro	**Reason**
Efficiencies	If you're in charge, it's sometimes easier to co-ordinate activities at the various business stages along the way, combining related functions or getting rid of overlapping areas to streamline your overall operations.
Resources	If you have a hand in the upstream (early-stage) activities of a business, you can guarantee that your company has access to the raw materials and resources that it needs to stay in business.
Customers	If your company is involved in downstream (late-stage) activities, you not only get to know a great deal about customers, but also create lasting relationships and secure your own long-term access to the market.

Table 1-3	Cons of Vertical Integration
Con	**Reason**
Overhead	If your company tries to control all stages of its industry, it can run into all sorts of extra expenses because of mismatched operations, idle resources, and added co-ordination costs.
Mediocrity	If your company is involved in a wide range of activities, it's much tougher to be the best at any of them, and the company risks becoming average in everything that it does.
Size and slowness	If your company is vertically integrated, its size often makes it difficult to quickly respond to change, and commitments to various parts of the industry leave it little room to be flexible.

There's both good news and bad news in terms of deciding just how much vertical integration is best. Over the years, there have been swings in the popularity of vertically integrated companies: a rush towards control of all aspects of an industry is followed by the race to break up companies and concentrate on specific business activities. Then the cycle repeats itself.

Today's wisdom seems to come down on the side of breaking companies apart. Worldwide competition in all industries over the past decade has made it more cost-effective to go out and buy what you need rather than to try to build up resources and expertise inside the company. That practice has resulted in a wave of downsizing and restructuring as companies struggle to remain competitive at what they do best.

And the future? One thing seems to hold true across the swings and cycles: the most successful and profitable businesses most often do business at one of the two extremes of integration. Companies that are heavily integrated reap all the real benefits of vertical integration; those that concentrate on a single activity eliminate all the costs and inefficiencies. Whatever you do, try not to get stuck in the middle, with few of the benefits and too many of the costs.

Leading and following

No matter what industry you're in, you can divide your competition into two major groups: the market leaders and all the market followers nipping at their heels. *Market leaders* are those top-tier companies that set the agenda for the industry and make things happen; they're the ones in the driver's seat. The *market followers,* well, they follow along. But in this second group, you find the companies that work hard, think big and keep the market leaders on their toes.

Depending on the market situation, companies in both groups behave very differently. Whether you're already a part of an industry or are thinking of joining it as a new business owner, it's important that you understand what motivates both the market leaders and the rest of the pack. The following sections explore some market strategies.

Market-leader strategies

Market leadership comes in various forms, from the absolute dominance of one company to shared control of the industry by several leading players. If you're a market leader, here are some possible strategic approaches for you:

- ✔ **Full speed ahead.** In this situation, your company is the clear market leader. Even so, you always try to break further away from the pack. You're always the first to make a move, whether in implementing new technology and introducing innovative products or in promoting new uses and setting aggressively low prices. You not only intend to stay on top, but also want to expand your lead.

- ✔ **Hold the line.** Your company's certainly in the top tier in the market, but it doesn't have a commanding position of strength in the industry, so your goals centre on hanging on to what you've already got. Those goals may involve locking distributors into long-term contracts, making it more difficult for customers to switch to competing brands or going after new market segments and product areas to block competitors from doing the same thing.

✔ **Steady as she goes.** In this case, your company is one of several power-ful companies in the market. As one among equals, your company takes on part of the responsibility of policing the industry to see that nothing upsets the boat. If an upstart challenger tries to cut prices, for example, you're there to quickly match those lower prices. You're always scan-ning the horizon for new competitors, and you work hard to discourage distributors, vendors and retailers from adding new companies and brands to their lists.

Market-follower strategies

Market followers are often forced to take their cues and develop strategies based on the strength and behaviour of the market leaders. An aggressive challenger, for example, may not do well in an industry that has a powerful, assertive company on top. Fortunately, you can choose among several strate-gic alternatives if you find yourself in a market-follower position:

✔ **Make some waves.** In this case, your company has every intention of growing bigger by increasing its presence in the industry, and you're quite willing to challenge the market leadership head-on to do it. Perhaps your strategy includes an aggressive price-cutting campaign to gain as much market share as you can. Maybe you back up this campaign with a rapid expansion of distribution outlets and a forceful marketing effort. The strategy requires deep pockets, will and the skill to force a market leader to blink, but in the end, it could make you the leader of the pack.

✔ **Turn a few heads.** In this situation, your company is certainly not one of the market leaders, but it's successful in its own market niche, and you want it to stay that way. So although you're careful not to challenge the market leadership directly, you're fierce about defending your turf. You have strengths and advantages in your own market segment because of the uniqueness of your product and customer loyalty. To maintain this position, you focus on customer benefits and the value that you bring to the market.

✔ **Just tag along.** It's easy to point out companies that have settled into complacency. Frankly, they're usually in rather boring industries in which not much ever happens. These companies are quite happy to remain towards the end of the pack, tagging along without a worry. Don't count on them to do anything new or different in the marketplace. (If you find yourself in a company like this, you may want to think about making a change while you're still awake.)

Remember the following when checking out strategic alternatives.

- A successful strategy must take into account what your competitors are up to.

- Vertically integrated companies control many aspects of their business and can streamline their operations.

- Companies that concentrate on one or two activities are more flexible and can focus on what they do best.

- Market leaders set the agenda for the industry and shape the competitive landscape.

- Market followers aren't in the driver's seat, but they work hard, think big and sometimes become leaders of the pack.

Book VI

Growing and Improving Your Business

Coming Up with Your Own Strategy

If you feel a bit overwhelmed by all the possibilities for devising a strategy for your own company, stop and take a deep breath. Remember one important thing: strategy isn't a test that you take once and have to get a perfect score the first time. Instead, it's the way that you decide to do business over the long haul. Strategy is an ongoing process, so don't be alarmed if you can't see how all the pieces fit together all at once.

Coming up with the right strategy is something that you have the chance to work on over and over again – rethinking, revising, reformulating. If you approach strategy in the wrong way, you probably won't ever finish the task.

As you begin to shape your own strategy, the following pointers can guide you:

- Never develop a strategy without first doing your homework.

- Always have a clear set of goals and objectives in front of you.

- Remember what assumptions you make, and make sure that they hold up.

- Build in flexibility, and always have an alternative.

- Understand the needs, desires and nature of your customers.

- Know your competitors and don't underestimate them.

- Leverage your strengths and minimise your weaknesses.

- Emphasise core competence to sustain a competitive advantage.

- Make your strategy clear, concise, consistent and attainable.

- Trumpet the strategy so that you don't leave the organisation guessing.

These guidelines are not only helpful for creating a strategy, but also useful for reviewing and revising one as well. Make sure that you return to them on a regular basis as part of your ongoing commitment to the strategy and planning process.

Companies that take strategy and business planning seriously know that to reach a target, it's 'ready, aim, fire' – not 'ready, fire, aim'. It's that simple. In other words, almost any strategy is better than no strategy at all. Companies that have clear strategies don't hit the bull's-eye every time; no strategy can promise that. But these companies succeed in the end because they subscribe to a strategic process that forces them to ask the right questions and come up with good answers – answers that are often better than their competitors' answers.

Chapter 2

Managing More than One Product

*W*atching over a product or service as it makes its way through the cold, cruel marketplace is an awesome responsibility. It requires a major commitment of time and resources, as well as a great deal of careful planning. First, you have to understand what's required for the product to be successful. Which attributes and aspects should you stress? How do you make sure that people take notice (and like what they see)? What must you do to support and guide your product or service along the way, getting it into the right hands? You want to take advantage of opportunities as they appear. At the same time, you have to worry about the threats and competitive pressures that are lurking out there.

Does this sound a lot like rearing a child? Well, your product's your baby, and as any parent will tell you, there's going to be one blessed thing after another. Think how many times you've heard a parent say, 'You think they're difficult now? Just wait!'

Products and kids have a great deal in common; both of their worlds are continually changing, yet they eventually manage to grow up. For decades, the Dr Spocks of the business world have poked, probed, pinched and studied products at all ages, and they've come up with a useful description of the common stages that almost all products go through. When you create a business plan, you have to plan for the changes in your own product's life cycle.

In this chapter, we explain the product life cycle and what it means for your company. We talk about ways to keep your company growing. We show you how to expand into new markets with existing products, as well as how to extend your product line to better serve current customers. We explore the opportunities and pitfalls of trying to diversify. We talk about strategic business units (SBUs) and introduce several portfolio tools to help you plan and manage a family of products.

Facing the Product/Service Life Cycle

If you could use only one word to describe what it feels like to be in business and to compete in a marketplace, that word probably would be *change*. The forces of change are everywhere, ranging from major trends in your business environment to the shifting tastes and demands of your customers and the unpredictable behaviour of your competitors.

You may think that all these factors, stirred together, create a world filled with chaos and uncertainty. Not so. The experts have stumbled onto some basic patterns, and the cycles that they've created do a good job of describing what happens in the face of all the market turmoil and confusion.

One of these patterns – the *product life cycle* – illustrates what happens to a new kind of product or service after you launch it in the market. The product life cycle describes four major stages that your product is likely to go through:

- ✔ An introduction period
- ✔ A growth period
- ✔ Maturity
- ✔ A period of decline

Most product life cycles look something like Figure 2-1.

The curve traces your product sales volume over time. You can think about the sales volume in terms of the revenue that you take in or the number of units that you sell, and you may end up measuring the time scale in weeks, months, years or even decades.

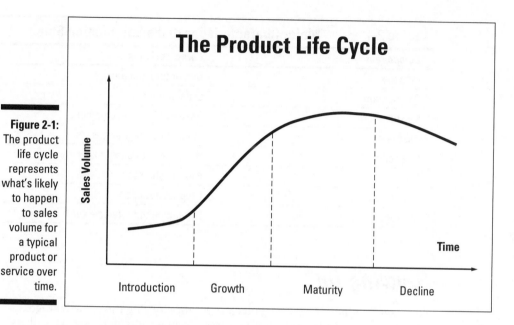

Every stage of your product's life cycle presents a unique set of market conditions and a series of planning challenges. The different stages require different management objectives, strategies and skills. The following sections discuss what you need to think about at each stage.

Starting out

You introduce a new kind of product or service in the market, and it begins to generate revenue. Because costs are relatively high at this stage, you usually don't find too many competitors around. Growth is limited instead by your company's ability to make the product, generate market awareness, and get customers to accept and adopt the new product.

At this stage in the product life cycle, efforts focus on getting your product out the door, or on rolling out the new service and ensuring that everything works the way that it's supposed to. At the same time, you have to drum up lots of interest and struggle to create a brand-new market. Table 2-1 points out many characteristics of the introduction stage.

Table 2-1	Major Characteristics of the Introduction Stage
Component	**Characteristics**
Industry	One or two companies
Competition	Little or none
Key function	Research and development
Customers	Innovators and risk-takers
Finances	High prices and expenses
Profits	Non-existent to negative
Objectives	Product adoption
Strategy	Expanding the total market

Growing up

Your new product or service gains a reputation during the growth stage. Demand rises rapidly, and sales increase. Competition increases as well, as competing products jump into the fray to take advantage of an expanding market. Customers begin to develop brand loyalties, and companies tweak their product features to better serve customer needs – needs that are now easier to recognise.

As the growth stage kicks in, your priorities turn towards meeting growing product demand, improving your product or service, and targeting specific groups of customers. Along the way, you have to fend off a growing crop of competitors. Table 2-2 highlights characteristics of the growth stage.

Table 2-2	Major Characteristics of the Growth Stage
Component	**Characteristics**
Industry	Many companies
Competition	Growing strength and numbers
Key function	Marketing
Customers	Eager to try products
Finances	Variable prices and costs
Profits	Growing rapidly
Objectives	Sales growth and market share
Strategy	Establishing and defending position

Middle age

The growth of your product or service begins to slow in the maturity stage, as market demand levels off and new customers become harder to find. New competitors are also harder to find, and the competition stabilises. Profits keep on growing, however, as costs continue to fall. Changes in market share reflect changes in product value and often come at the expense of competing products.

As maturity sets in, your attention turns towards reducing costs and finally reaping the benefits of stable profits. Although it's easy to feel comfortable at this stage, you need to think about what's going to happen next. Table 2-3 identifies the characteristics of the maturity stage.

Book VI

Growing and Improving Your Business

Table 2-3	Major Characteristics of the Maturity Stage
Component	*Characteristics*
Industry	Not as many companies
Competition	Stronger, but stable
Key function	Operations
Customers	The majority of buyers
Finances	Competitive prices and lower costs
Profits	At or near peak
Objectives	Cash flow and profit
Strategy	Maintaining competitive position

Senior stretch

At some point in your product's life cycle, sales start to fall off, and revenue begins to decline. Competitors drop out of the market as profits all but disappear. The decline stage may be triggered by large-scale changes in the economy or technology, or it may simply reflect changing customer needs and behaviour. Products still on the market in this stage are either redesigned, repositioned or replaced.

As the decline stage looms, you have to get back into the business trenches. Your work shifts to redesigning your product or redefining its market, or maybe coming up with new uses or different kinds of customers. If all these attempts fail, you have to concentrate on ways to get out of the market and not lose too much money. Table 2-4 shows various characteristics of the decline stage.

Table 2-4	Major Characteristics of the Decline Stage
Component	*Characteristics*
Industry	Few companies
Competition	Declining in number
Key function	Finance and planning
Customers	Loyal, conservative buyers
Finances	Falling prices and low costs
Profits	Much reduced
Objectives	Residual profits
Strategy	Getting out alive

Where you are now

Take your own product or service and see whether you can come up with its estimated position on the product life cycle curve (refer to Figure 2-1 earlier in this chapter). If you're stumped, ask yourself the following kinds of questions:

- ✔ How long has the product been on the market?
- ✔ How rapidly is the market growing?
- ✔ Is the growth rate increasing, decreasing or flat?
- ✔ Is the product profitable?
- ✔ Are profits heading up or down?
- ✔ How many competitors does the product have?
- ✔ How fast are product features changing?
- ✔ Are there more or fewer competing products than there were a year ago?

Perhaps you feel confident about where your product is in its life cycle. That's good. Just make sure, though, that you take the time to confirm your analysis. Chances are that you're going to get mixed signals from the marketplace, and the clues may even contradict one another. No two products ever behave the same way when it comes to the product life cycle. Unfortunately, acting prematurely on the evidence at hand can lead to hasty planning and a self-fulfilling prophecy.

Suppose that the widget manager at Global Gizmos Company detects a slow-down in widget sales. As a faithful believer in the absolute law of the product life cycle, she comes to the obvious conclusion that the growth stage for widgets is finally coming to an end. What does she do? For one thing, she begins to think about ways to reduce costs. Maybe she cuts the advertising budget and begins to phase out incentives for the sales force. What happens? Sales of widgets decline even further, just as she predicted. So she pats herself on the back for being the first to recognise the early stages of a worldwide widget decline.

But what if the sales slump is actually reversible, simply caused by a bit of bad weather, some delivery problems, or any number of other reasons? By substituting blind faith in a business textbook for her own good judgement and careful analysis, the widget manager actually caused the outcome that she so confidently predicted in the first place.

What good is a business concept if you can't really count on it? Well, don't get us wrong here. The product life cycle is a powerful planning tool if you use it to support – not replace – your own solid skills. When it's deployed as an early warning system, the product life cycle alerts you to potential changes, allowing you time to plan for a different business environment and to respond quickly when your product finally enters a new stage in its life cycle.

Book VI

Growing and Improving Your Business

- ✔ Your product or service goes through a life cycle that includes introduction, growth, maturity and (alas) decline.

- ✔ When you introduce a new kind of product, costs are high but competitors are few.

- ✔ During your product's growth stage, demand increases fast, but so does competition.

- ✔ At maturity, competition stabilises, and as your costs continue to decline, profits grow.

- ✔ When decline sets in (as new technologies come along or customers' habits change), sales, revenue and profits head south.

Milking cash cows

Products in decline aren't all bad news. Often at that stage the full costs of developing and launching them have been recovered, they no longer warrant much advertising or support and as a consequence are major cash generators. By contrast, new products need bags of cash, so why not marry them up. Cash cows, as products in decline can be, can be used to support tomorrow's stars.

See more on this process later in this chapter when we cover the Boston Matrix.

Finding Ways to Grow

Let's face it – your product simply isn't going to be the same tomorrow as it is today. You may not plan to do anything to it at all, but everything around your product is going to change. The world will take another step ahead. The economy, technology, your industry and the competition will all change a bit. As a result, your customers will think about your company and your product a bit differently, even if you see yourself as being exactly the same.

How does your company find ways to grow and prosper in the face of almost certain product mortality? You probably have every intention of creating a new business plan (beyond turning off the lights and locking all the doors) as your product begins to age. But which way do you turn? Mark Twain had a bit of tongue-in-cheek advice for people who prefer to keep things just as they are:

> Put all your eggs in one basket . . . and watch that basket!

Trouble is, the eggs are going to hatch, and the chicks will probably run away. So doing nothing except watching and waiting isn't really an option. But what are your alternatives?

Fortunately, you don't have to invent the alternatives yourself; planning for long-term growth has been a philosophical favourite of management gurus for decades. One of the pioneers of business-growth techniques was a man named Igor Ansoff, who came up with a simple matrix to represent the possible directions of growth (see Figure 2-2).

Figure 2-2:
The Growth Directions Matrix describes different ways in which your company can grow, based on a combination of products and markets.

The Growth Directions Matrix really captures nothing more than basic common sense: it says that if you want to make your business grow, you have to start somewhere. The logical place to begin is to take advantage of where you are today and what you have to work with. How fast you grow in any of these directions has everything to do with your own capabilities and resources, as well as the rate of change in your industry. Consider the following ways in which you can move your company ahead:

- ✔ **You are here (existing product and market).** Continue to grow by doing what you're already doing, but do it a little bit better, so that customers use more of your product or service more often and in more ways than before. Encourage people to use more toothpaste, for example, by brushing their teeth (or even their dog's teeth) more often.

- ✔ **New market, existing product.** Grow in the near term by finding a fresh market for your existing product, either by expanding geographically or by reaching out to completely different kinds of customers. If you make baking soda, for example, get people to put baking soda in their refrigerators to keep them odour-free.

- ✔ **New product, existing market.** Grow by developing additional product features, options or even a related product family with the intention of enticing your existing customers. Think of the array of apple drinks that are available these days – everything from Appletiser to apple-flavoured water.

- ✔ **New market, new product.** Grow over the long term by going after new and unfamiliar markets with new and different products. Ford Motor Company, for example, used to make and sell prefabricated homes.

Book VI

Growing and Improving Your Business

Without getting bogged down in a lot of details, try to come up with a dozen different ways to grow your company. Get yourself into the right frame of mind by first reviewing your company's mission and vision statements. (Don't have 'em? Flip to Chapter 4 in Book I for everything that you need to know.) Then complete the following steps:

1. **Identify three things that you can do right away to stimulate demand for your existing product in your current markets.**

   These things may include cutting costs, offering rebates or maybe coming up with some new product uses.

2. **List three steps that you can take in the next six months to capture new markets for your existing product.**

   Some ideas include radio or television ads that target new customers, direct-mail campaigns and stepped-up appearances at trade shows.

3. **Specify three development efforts that you can launch over the coming year to extend your current product line.**

   These efforts may include enhancing product features or adding options.

4. **Describe three directions that you can take over the next three to five years that will move you into new products and markets.**

More than one or two experts believe that any talk about brand-new products for completely new markets is really none of your business as a manager. These financial gurus think that managers are simply too biased to be objective when it comes to assessing totally new opportunities. They argue that you should return all your extra profits to investors and let them decide where to place their bets on the future. You probably don't agree with them; after all, investors have made monumental mistakes in the past. But they do have a good point. It's probably worth remembering that growth in new directions is a tricky business, no matter how it's done or who ends up doing it.

Same product/service, same market

Many successful big-name companies have become as big and successful as they are by relentlessly pursing a single business, a single market or even an individual product decade after decade. When you hear the name BT, for example, you think of picking up a telephone. When you see a Coca-Cola sign, you imagine drinking a Coke. And when you pass a McDonald's, you probably picture a Big Mac. But these companies haven't turned into billion-pound corporations simply by launching their flagship products and letting the marketplace take care of the rest. Companies that largely depend on a single product spend enormous amounts of time and effort to continually rejuvenate and revitalise their core markets.

If you glance back at the Growth Directions Matrix shown in Figure 2-2 earlier in this chapter, you notice that these companies invest heavily in the top-left box. How do they manage to do that successfully? They use the four main strategies described in the following sections.

✔ **Encourage greater product use.** A company increases demand by encouraging its customers to consume more of a product or service every time they use it. Maybe that means getting customers to feel good about buying more or giving them a better deal when they do. Customers may do the following things:

   • Buy larger bottles of cola because they can save some money.

   • Apply for more insurance coverage because you carefully show them that it's the prudent thing to do.

- Stay on the phone longer because the rates are lower.

- Opt for a packaged computer or stereo system with all the components because it's simpler to assemble.

✔ **Generate more-frequent product use.** A company stimulates sales by getting customers to use its product or service more often. That may mean making the product more convenient, introducing it as part of customers' regular routine or offering incentives to frequent customers. Customers may do the following things:

- Use toothpaste after every meal because they think it's hygienic.

- Regularly drink wine at dinner because they think it's healthy.

- Join a frequent-flyer programme and take an extra trip just to build more miles.

✔ **Devise new uses.** A company expands its market by coming up with new ways for customers to use its product or service. That may include getting customers to use the product at different times, in different places, on novel occasions or in unconventional ways. All of a sudden, customers may do the following things:

- Snack on breakfast cereal during the day because it's handy and tastes good.

- Put a radio in the shower and a TV in the car because they're convenient.

- Make videos of every imaginable event from childbirth to pet funerals.

✔ **Woo customers away from competitors.** A company can also increase demand for its product or service the old-fashioned way: by taking customers away from the competition. Although the result is sometimes a fierce and unwanted response from competitors, companies can do the following things:

- Create incentives to switch from competing products and give rewards for staying put.

- Concentrate on becoming a low-cost provider with the best prices around.

- Package a product so that it's distinctive and stands out in the marketplace.

- Focus on meeting or exceeding the needs of specific customer groups.

Companies that manage to grow in the same old market with the same old product do so by continually generating new demand as well as maintaining or even increasing their market share. Often, these companies succeed in slowing the product life cycle, extending its maturity stage almost indefinitely. In some cases, they even manage to reset the life cycle, pulling the product back into the growth stage by inventing new and creative product uses. But steady and sustained market penetration based on a single product doesn't always work forever, and companies sometimes have to look in new directions for growth.

New market or new product

At some point in the life of your company, a single product or service may not be enough to sustain an attractive level of growth in your business. Where do you turn? The Growth Directions Matrix (refer to Figure 2-2, earlier in this chapter) suggests that the most reliable and productive paths point to market expansion in the near term, as well as to extending your product line. These two directions for growth have the distinct advantage of building on capabilities and resources that you already have. Market expansion leverages your current product expertise, and product extension builds on your experience and knowledge of current customers and the marketplace.

Successful big-name companies such as BT, Coca-Cola and McDonald's usually are much bigger than just the flagship products that we associate with them, and if you look closely at the ways in which they grow, they almost always do so through a combination of expanding into new markets and extending their product lines. BT looks for new customers in both local and foreign markets, and it also offers a range of calling services (including direct-dial, reverse-charge and third-party calling; messaging; paging; and now Internet access service). Coca-Cola enters new markets throughout the developing world by offering a family of cola beverages that includes Classic Coke, Diet Coke and Caffeine-free Coke. And McDonald's is open for breakfast, lunch and dinner with Egg McMuffins, Big Macs and Chicken McNuggets, whilst at the same time making subtle variations to its products to fit in with local market needs: salads and wine in France, and even English language tuition for children in Japan, using the menu as the vocabulary.

New market

Expanding into a new market is something that your company can do rather quickly, because it can take advantage of its current business model, copying many of the activities that it's already engaged in – producing, assembling and distributing products, for example.

You can expand your market in two basic ways: move into new geographical areas or go after new market segments.

✔ **Geography.** The most obvious way to grow beyond your core product and market is to expand geographically, picking up new customers based solely on where they live and work. This kind of expansion has many advantages. You not only do business in the same way as before, but you also have a head start in understanding many of your new customers, even with their regional differences. Because geographic expansion may require you to do business in unfamiliar areas or even new countries, however, you have to pay special attention to how your company must change to accommodate the specific demands of your expanded market.

✔ **New market segments.** Sometimes you can expand the market for your product or service by finding new kinds of customers. If you're creative, maybe you can identify a group of customers that you've neglected in the past. Look carefully at your product's features and packaging, how it's priced and delivered, who's buying and why they buy. Also, reassess the customer benefits that you provide. Then ask yourself how attractive a new market segment is in terms of its size and potential to grow. What strengths do you bring to the market? What competitors are already there? How do you plan to gain an advantage over the long haul?

New product

Extending the number of products or types of services that you offer is something that you need to plan for well ahead of time. All too often, companies develop new product features, options and major product enhancements without giving much thought to the implications for the company's future direction and growth. Instead, a customer asks for this or that special feature, or a distributor requests a particular option or accessory, and before you know it, you have additional products to support.

The good news, of course, is that you already have customers. But you also have to be sure that those customers represent a larger market that benefits from your product extension and that the additional products make sense in terms of your own business strategy and plan.

You can extend your product or service in two basic ways: offer new features and options or create related families of products.

✔ **New features and options.** The most common way to extend a product line involves adding bells and whistles to your product and giving customers the chance to choose which bells and whistles they want. The advantages are easy to tick off: you work from your existing strengths in product design and development, and you use real live customers to help you decide which incremental changes to make. It sounds like the perfect game plan.

The danger comes from losing track of the bigger picture – where you want your company to end up. Individual customers, no matter how good they are, don't always reflect the direction of larger markets. So avoid creating a bunch of marginal products that you can't really sell or support. Instead, plan to develop a smaller number of products with features and options that are designed to meet the needs of specific market segments.

✔ **Related product groups.** You may create a group of products based on a common element of some sort. You can develop a product family to use the same core technology, to meet a series of related customer needs or to serve as accessories for your primary product.

You want the product group to look stronger in the market than the individual products do separately. That way, the risks inherent in product development are reduced, and the rewards are potentially greater. Take time to understand just how products in the group actually work together. Also, make sure that you address the separate challenges that each product poses in terms of customers, the competition and your own company's assets and capabilities.

Before you put your plans for growth into action, make sure that they draw on your company's strengths, reflect the capabilities and resources that you have available, and help maintain your competitive advantage. Ask yourself the following questions:

✔ How well are you doing in the markets that you're already in?

✔ In what ways is the expanded market different from your current market?

✔ What parts of your business can you leverage in the expanded market?

✔ What functions and activities have to change to accommodate more products?

✔ How well will your extended product line meet specific customer needs?

✔ Is your extended product family stronger than each product by itself?

✔ How easy is it to scale up your business to meet the expected growth?

✔ How will your competitive environment change?

New product and new market

Has your company hit a midlife crisis? Do you find yourself searching for attractive new customers, sexy technologies and aggressive competition? Well, it's not unusual for a company to think about rejuvenating itself from time to time. A plan to move in new directions often involves diversifying the company, moving down into the bottom-right corner of the Growth

Directions Matrix (refer to Figure 2-2 earlier in this chapter). That corner, after all, is where the grass always looks much greener – and the profits look greener, too.

But you have to balance the potential rewards against the challenges and risks that go along with diversification. Too many companies end up looking foolish as they try to learn new tricks in unfamiliar businesses without much time to practise – and they often face the financial consequences.

To better your odds of success, start by doing your homework, which means researching all the new issues and new players. If this task sounds daunting, it's meant to. The stakes couldn't be much higher.

Your chances of success improve substantially when you identify the ways that a potential new business is related to what your company already does. But even without the benefit of any existing product or market expertise, you can often discover aspects of a new business opportunity that play right into your company's core competence. Here's what to look for:

- ✔ **Name recognition.** If your company has worked hard to create a name for itself, you can sometimes make use of its brand identity in a new business situation. Name recognition is particularly powerful when the associations are positive, clearly defined and can be carried over to the new product and market. Luxury-car companies such as BMW, for example, now give their names to expensive, upmarket lines of touring and mountain bikes.

- ✔ **Technical operations.** The resources and skills required to design, develop or manufacture products in your own industry – or perhaps the technical services that you offer – may be extended to support additional product areas. Japanese electronics giants such as Sony and Mitsubishi, for example, are experts in miniaturisation, automation and quality control. Given those skills, they can acquire original technology or experimental products and then go on to create product lines based on their expertise.

- ✔ **Marketing experience.** If your company has a great deal of marketing expertise available, you can often put that expertise to good use to expand the awareness and strengthen the positioning of a new product. Examples include the creative software products that small, independent developers produce and then sell to larger companies such as Symantec or Netscape – companies that have the marketing muscle to successfully advertise, promote and distribute those products.

- ✔ **Capacity and scale.** Sometimes you can take the excess capacity that your company has in production, sales or distribution and apply that capacity directly to a new business area. That way, you reap the benefits of a larger scale of operations and use your resources more efficiently. Many car dealerships around the UK, for example, reached out in the 1980s to show, sell and service Toyotas and Hondas, permanently adding them to their British car lines. Now, of course, that's all that UK motor dealerships have to offer, so their new products eventually became their main and only products.

✔ **Financial considerations.** Persistent demands on your company's revenue, cash flow or profits may inevitably point you in a new business direction. Although a financial opportunity by itself offers a fairly flimsy link to your existing products and markets, a new business may – just may – be justified on the basis of financial considerations alone. Large tobacco companies, for example, use their huge cash reserves to diversify into unrelated business areas that have brighter, smoke-free futures.

The temptation to set off in new directions and diversify into new businesses, creating brand-new products for brand-new markets, has bewitched and bothered business planners for decades. Unfortunately, the failure rate for new products can be as high as 75 per cent. And the most perplexing part of the puzzle is the fact that in the beginning, everything looks so good on paper. Here are some examples:

✔ Campbell Soup Company thought that it had a winner when it decided to launch a family of juice drinks for kids. But its Juice Works brand had trouble, in part because so many competitors had better brand-name recognition in the juice business.

✔ Federal Express set out to create the future of immediate document delivery by introducing a new computer network-based product. But customers turned to FedEx to send hard copy, not email, and the company got zapped by its Zap Mail service.

✔ Laura Ashley, co-founder with her husband Bernard of the firm of the same name, never liked the concept of fashion, insisting instead that her clothes and furnishings were designed to endure. In the 1960s, the company's fresh cotton print dresses offered a clear alternative to the miniskirts of Mary Quant. In the late 1980s, following Laura Ashley's tragic death, the company made the mistake of trying too hard to get with it, downplaying its heritage, neglecting its long print tea-dresses and Viyella checks. The flirtation with fashion was a disaster, heralding a decade or so of revolving doors at management level, and strategic twists and turns that make fascinating, if depressing, case study material for MBA classes the world over.

A few companies, however, manage to succeed with new products and markets time and time again. Think Tesco, and you could be forgiven for thinking of value food in the UK. But the company has successfully introduced thousands of non-food products in the past decade – everything from fashion clothing to microwaves; they even have a substantial personal finance business, and perhaps the world's only profitable Internet home delivery service. Tesco's stated goal is to bring value, choice and convenience to customers – notice that food isn't mentioned here. It's a goal it pursues with vigour in Asia, Central and Eastern Europe, and the US.

- ✔ One way to grow is to encourage customers to use more of your existing product more often and in more ways.

- ✔ To grow in new directions, your company has to look to new products, new markets or entirely new businesses.

- ✔ When you expand into a new market, you can take advantage of expertise in creating and delivering your existing product.

- ✔ When you extend your product line, you can take advantage of your knowledge of customers and the marketplace.

- ✔ When you go after a totally new business (new product, new market), the stakes are high, so do your homework.

Understanding the adoption cycle

Customers are usually not hanging around hoping for new products or services to arrive so they can rush out to buy them. Word spreads slowly as the message is diffused throughout the various customer groups. Even then you notice that generally the more adventurous types first buy into new ideas. Only after these more adventurous customers have given their seal of approval do the 'followers' come along. Research shows that this *adoption process*, as it's known, moves through five distinct customer characteristics, from Innovators to Laggards, with the overall population being different for each group.

Suppose you've identified the market for your Internet gift service. Initially your market has been confined to affluent professionals within five miles of your home to keep delivery costs low. So if market research shows that there are 100,000 people that meet the profile of your ideal customer and they have regular access to the Internet, the market open for exploitation at the outset may be as low as 2,500, which is the 2.5 per cent of innovators.

This adoption process, from the 2.5 per cent of innovators who make up a new business's first customers, through to the laggards who won't buy from anyone until they've been in business for 20 years, is most noticeable with truly innovative and relatively costly goods and services. The general trend, though, is true for all businesses. Until you've sold to the innovators, you can't achieve significant sales. So, an important first task is to identify these innovative customers. The moral is: the more you know about your potential customers at the outset, the better your chances of success.

One further issue to keep in mind when shaping your marketing strategy is that innovators, early adopters and all the other sub segments don't necessarily use the same media, websites, magazines or newspapers, or respond to the same images and messages. So you need to market to them in very different ways.

Managing Your Product Portfolio

When you decide that it's time to branch out into new products and markets or to diversify into new businesses, you're going to have to learn how to juggle. You no longer have the luxury of doting on a single product or service; now you have more than one product and market to deal with. You have to figure out how to keep every one of your products in the air, providing each one with the special attention and resources that it needs, depending on which part of the product life cycle it's in.

Strategic business units

Juggling usually requires a bit of preparation, of course, and the first thing that you want to find out is how many oranges and clubs – or products and services, in this case – you have to keep in the air at one time. It's easy to count oranges, and counting clubs isn't tough, either. For products and services, though, the following questions tend to pop up. Often, these questions have no right answer, but just taking time to think through the issues helps you better understand what you offer.

- ✔ Just how many products or services does your company have?
- ✔ When you add another feature or an option to your product, does the addition essentially create a new product that requires a separate business plan?
- ✔ When you have two separate sets of customers using your service in different ways, do you really have two services, each with its own business plan?
- ✔ When you offer two different products to the same set of customers, each of which is manufactured, marketed and distributed in much the same way, are you really dealing with one larger product area and a single business plan?

General Electric struggled with these questions in the late 1960s. The company had grown well beyond the original inventions of its founder, Thomas Edison; it wasn't just in the electric light bulb business any more. In fact, it was a diversified giant, with businesses ranging from appliances and aircraft engines to television sets and computers. The company had to decide the best way to divide itself up so that each piece was a manageable size and could be juggled with all the other pieces.

The managers at General Electric hit on the clever idea of organising the company around what they called strategic business units. A *strategic business unit* (SBU) is a piece of your company that's big enough to have its own well-defined markets, attract its own set of competitors, and demand tangible resources and capabilities from you. Yet an SBU is small enough that you can craft a strategy with goals and objectives designed to reflect its special business environment. By using the SBU concept, General Electric transformed nearly 200 separate, independent product departments into fewer than 50 strategic business units, each with its own well-defined strategy and business plan.

Book VI

Growing and Improving Your Business

Consider ways to reorganise your own company around strategic business units. Each time you outline a separate business plan, you identify a potential SBU. How do you get started? Because strategic business units often refer to particular product and market areas taken together, begin with the following steps:

1. **Break your company into as many separate product and market combinations as you can think of.**

2. **Fit these building blocks back together in various ways, trying all sorts of creative associations of products and markets on different levels and scales.**

   Think about how each combination may work in terms of creating a viable business unit.

3. **Keep only those combinations of products and markets that make sense in terms of strategy, business planning, customers, the competition and your company's structure.**

4. **Step back to determine how well these new SBUs mesh together and account for your overall business.**

   If you don't like what you see, try the process again. Don't make the changes for real until you're satisfied with your new organisation.

Aiming for the stars

Rather than juggle a set of who knows how many ill-defined products, practise your juggling technique on the Strategic Business Units (SBUs) that you identify instead.

Start by dividing your SBUs into two basic groups, depending on the direction of their cash flow: put the ones that bring money into your company on one side and the ones that take money out on the other side. Maybe you're surprised that you have two sides here. Because every product goes through a life cycle that's likely to include an introduction stage, growth, maturity and then decline, different SBUs naturally have different cash-flow requirements. You must invest in products during their introduction and growth phases, and your mature products end up paying all the bills. So as a successful juggler, you always need at least one mature SBU aloft to support the SBUs that are coming along behind.

Some of this juggling stuff may sound familiar if you've ever tried to manage your own personal savings or retirement accounts. Every financial adviser tells you the same thing: spread your investments out to create a more stable and predictable set of holdings. Ideally, financial advisers want to help you balance your portfolio based on how much money you need to earn right away and what sort of nest egg you expect to have in the future. Given your financial needs and goals, planners may suggest buying blue-chip stocks and bonds that generate dividends right away, and also investing in more speculative companies that pay off well down the road.

Your company's strategic business units have a great deal in common with a portfolio of stocks and bonds – so much, in fact, that the SBU juggling that we're talking about is called *portfolio management*. To manage your own SBU portfolio as professionally as financial experts track stocks and bonds, you need some guidance, which is where portfolio analysis comes in. *Portfolio analysis* helps you look at the roles of the SBUs in your company and determine how well the SBUs balance one another so that the company grows and remains profitable. In addition, portfolio analysis offers a new way to think about strategy and business planning when you have more than one strategic business unit to worry about.

You can make your first attempt at simple portfolio analysis with two SBU categories: those that make money and those that take money. Then all you have to do is make sure that the first category is always bigger than the second. But the two categories don't give you much help in figuring out what's going to happen next. Fortunately, the people at the Boston Consulting Group came up with an easy-to-use portfolio-analysis tool that provides some useful planning direction.

The Boston Consulting Group's Growth-Share Grid (see Figure 2-3) directs you to divide your SBUs into four groups.

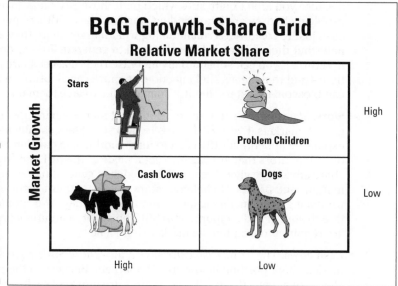

BCG Growth-Share Grid
Relative Market Share

Stars

Problem Children

Cash Cows

Dogs

Market Growth

High

Low

High

Low

Figure 2-3:
The Growth-
Share Grid
divides your
company's
SBUs into
four major
groups.

Book VI

Growing
and
Improving
Your
Business

You base your portfolio analysis on two major factors: market growth and market share.

✔ **Market growth.** Is the SBU part of a rapidly expanding market or does it fall somewhere in a slow- or no-growth area? You use market growth to define your portfolio because it forces you to think about just how attractive the SBU may be over the long haul. The exact point that separates high-growth and low-growth markets is rather arbitrary; start by using a 10 per cent annual growth rate as the midpoint.

✔ **Relative market share.** Does your SBU command a market-share advantage over its nearest competitors, or does its market share place it down the list relative to the competition? You use relative market share as a major characteristic to define your SBU portfolio because all sorts of evidence suggests that a strong market-share position is closely tied to the profitability of the SBU. Separate your SBUs into those where you have the highest market share and those where you don't.

Here's a review of the types of SBUs:

✔ **Problem children.** *Problem children* are SBUs that have relatively low market share in high-growth markets. Problem children often represent newer businesses and are sometimes referred to as *question marks*, because you aren't quite sure which path these SBUs may take. Because problem children are in expanding markets, these SBUs require lots of cash just to tread water, maintaining what market share they already have, but their relatively low sales tend to generate little or no revenue in return. If you can substantially increase their market share over time – and that means shelling out even more cash – problem children can blossom into stars. If not, you may have to give them up.

✔ **Stars.** *Stars* are SBUs that have a dominant market-share position in high-growth markets. Every SBU wants to be a star. Stars usually have an expensive appetite for the cash to fund continual expansion and to fend off competitors that are eager to get a piece of the turf. But their market-share advantage gives these SBUs an edge in generating revenue, high margins and profits. On balance, stars usually support themselves, both producing and consuming large amounts of money. You shouldn't hesitate to step in and support a star SBU, however, if additional resources are required to maintain its market-share lead.

✔ **Cash cows.** The name *cash cows* says it all – these SBUs have a major market-share position in low-growth markets. Because of their market-share advantage, these SBUs generate a great deal of cash, and the best part is the fact that they don't require much in return. Their low-growth markets usually are mature, and the products are already well established. The bottom line: you can milk cash cows to produce a cash surplus and then redirect that cash to fund promising SBUs in other quadrants.

✔ **Dogs.** *Dogs* are SBUs that deliver low market share in low-growth markets – and little else. Although many of us are dog lovers, it's hard to love this particular breed. Revenue and profits usually are small or non-existent, and the SBUs are often net users of cash. Although they require periodic investments, these marginal businesses usually never amount to much, so it may be best to turn your attention to more-promising SBU candidates.

It's time to put all the pieces together so that you can construct a Growth-Share Grid to represent your own portfolio of strategic business units. Ideally, of course, you see mostly stars and cash cows, with enough problem children (the question marks) to ensure your company's future. Ideally, you have few dogs to contend with.

But the world isn't always ideal. Fortunately, you can also use the Growth-Share Grid as a tablet to sketch out what you plan to do with your SBUs to balance them in the future. Here's what you do:

1. **Sort through your company's SBUs, and get ready to put them in a blank Growth-Share Grid.**

    To see the grid format, refer to Figure 2-3 earlier in this chapter.

2. **Place each SBU in its proper quadrant, given what you know about market growth and the SBU's relative market share.**

3. **Draw a circle around each SBU to represent how big it is in relation to your other SBUs.**

   Base the size of your SBUs on revenue, profits, sales or whatever measure is most convenient.

4. **For each SBU in the grid, forecast its movement in terms of overall market growth and market-share position.**

   Use a time frame that's appropriate for your industry and its rate of change.

5. **To capture this forecast, draw arrows indicating the direction of movement and where you plan to have each SBU end up in the future.**

   Arrows that point outside the grid indicate that you plan to get rid of the SBUs in question.

The BCG Growth-Share Grid, with its quirky cast of characters and its black-and-white view of the world, is hard to resist, because it makes the complex, difficult job of juggling several businesses seem to be almost effortless. After it first caught on nearly 30 years ago, however, the model became so widely overused and misapplied that the entire business of understanding business portfolios went out of fashion. Today, of course, we understand that portfolio-analysis tools have their place, but they have to be used sensibly. As the saying goes, if something looks too easy to be true, it probably is.

Before you start moving your SBUs around the Growth-Share Grid like pieces on a chessboard, remind yourself that the following strings are attached:

- ✔ Market growth is singled out as the only way to measure how attractive a market is and to determine whether or not you'd like to be in business there. But growth isn't the only interesting variable. Markets may turn out to be attractive because of advances in technology, changes in regulation, profits – you name it.

- ✔ Relative market share alone is used to describe how competitive you are and how profitable your company is likely to be. But market share is really relevant only when you're competing on the basis of size and sales volume. There are other ways to compete, including making your product unique in some way, focusing on a particular group of customers, or concentrating on service.

- ✔ The SBUs in the Growth-Share Grid are linked only by the flow of cash in and out of the different businesses. But there are many other ways to think about how strategic business units may relate to one another and function together, including views that stress the competition or focus on market risk factors.

✔ The differences between a star and a cash cow (or a problem child and a dog) are arbitrary and subject to all sorts of definition and measurement problems, so without careful analysis and a dose of good judgement, it's easy to cast your SBUs in the wrong roles. You may end up abandoning a problem child too soon, for example, because you think that the SBU is a dog, or you may neglect and hurt a star SBU by assuming that it's a cash cow that you can milk for money.

Extending Your E-Penetration

The online world has come a long way since eBay and a handful of other brave souls blazed the trail. Today, a visible place in cyberspace is all but essential if you want to make any impact on the wider business world. Alongside the greater use of the Internet, just as with computers, the price of getting online is dropping sharply and the power and quality of what those fewer bucks will buy is immeasurably improved. Everything from books and DVDs, through computers, medicines and financial services, on to vehicles and property is being sold or having a major part of its selling process transacted online. Holidays, airline tickets, software, training and even university degrees are bundled in with the mass of conventional retailers such as Tesco, who fight for a share of the ever-growing online market. The online gaming market alone has over 217 million users.

Not all business sectors are penetrated to the same extent by the Internet; according to Forrester (www.forrester.com), the Internet research company, although sales of clothing and footwear online is a multi-billion pound business it only accounts for 8 per cent of total sales. Contrast that with computers where 41 per cent of sales occur online.

According to eMarketer (www.emarketer.com) 88 per cent of shoppers prefer online to conventional shopping because they can shop at any time; 66 per cent like being able to shop for more than one product and in many outlets at the same time; 54 per cent claim to be able to get products they can only find online; 53 per cent like not having to deal with sales people; 44 per cent reckon product information is better online; and perhaps the most revealing statistic of all, only 40 per cent preferred online to offline because they expected to find lower prices.

All this is to say the Internet is important – but it's also different, and even selling the same product or service online represents a different product or market competitive environment. So, for example, Tesco sells wine in its stores on the shelf with nothing more than the labels to explain the product on offer. Online, the website is full of information on wine, tasting notes, a magazine and a wine club. Online, Tesco competes with companies such as Laithwaites who don't have a retail presence at all.

So you need to run through all of this chapter twice. Once for your bricks (your real-world business) and once more for the clicks (your online activities); the dynamics are different.

Buying Out Competitors

One strategy that encompasses all of those discussed earlier in the chapter is an acquisition. When economic growth is virtually static, or if you want to achieve really dramatic growth, then buying someone else's business can be a very attractive option. Each year about 2,000 private companies change hands in the UK alone. The average size, in turnover terms, of the companies bought and sold was under £7 million per annum, with many having sales below £0.5 million. Forty-five per cent of the acquisitions were viewed as wholly amicable. There was a willing buyer and a willing seller, and no other parties were involved. Another 45 per cent were classified as partly contested, either because there were several interested buyers, or because there was resistance within the vendor to being taken over.

Even when acquisitions took place under friendly or fairly friendly conditions, only 55 per cent were eventually rated as successful or very successful by both buyers and sellers. So buying a company is certainly not always a sure-fire winning strategy.

Use a seven-point plan – based on issues we cover in the following sections – to make sure that you end up with the most successful acquisition, merger or joint venture you can.

Knowing why you want to buy

Big companies end up on the takeover trail for matters of management ego as much as corporate strategy. Over 40 per cent of big companies listed 'sending signals to the City' as their principal reason for buying. A further 35 per cent put it down to the 'chairman's insistence'. Not surprisingly, many acquisitions are financially unrewarding or worse. Sound reasons for acquisitions include:

- ✔ To increase market share and eliminate a troublesome competitor.

- ✔ To broaden your product range or give you access to new markets.

- ✔ To diversify into new markets, acquiring the necessary management, marketing or technical skills to enable you to capture a reasonable slice of the market relatively quickly.

✔ To get into another country or region.

✔ To protect an important source of supply which may be under threat from a competitor.

✔ To acquire additional staff, factory space, warehousing and distribution channels, or to get access to additional major customers more quickly than by starting up yourself.

Produce a written statement explaining the rationale behind your reason to buy – before you start looking for companies to buy – or otherwise you may end up pursuing a 'bargain' that has absolutely nothing to do with your previously defined commercial goals just because it seems cheap. It's also worth remembering that companies available at knockdown prices are likely to need drastic surgery. So unless you fancy your chances as a company doctor, stay well away.

Understanding what you want to buy

It takes over one man-year of work, on average, to find and buy a company. The more accurately you describe your ideal purchase the simpler, quicker and cheaper your search will be. Just imagine trying to buy a house without any idea where you wanted to live, how much you wanted to spend, how many bedrooms were needed, whether you wanted a new house or a listed building or if you wanted a garden. The search would be near impossible to organise, it could take forever, and the resulting purchase would almost certainly please no one. The same problem is present when buying a company. The definition of what you want to buy should explain:

✔ The business area/products/service the company is in.

✔ The location of the target company.

✔ The price range and the cash you have available.

✔ The management depth and the management style you're looking for in the company.

✔ The minimum profitability and return on capital employed you can accept. Remember that if the company you plan to buy only makes 1 per cent net profit after tax whilst you make 5 per cent, and you are of equal size, the resultant profit margin will be 3 per cent $[(5 + 1) \div 2]$. This may make the combined business look worse rather than better.

✔ The image compatibility between your company and any target.

✔ The scope for integration and cost saving.

Starting to look

Once you have a profile of the sort of company you would like to buy, you can begin to assemble your shopping list. Three sources are of particular use:

✔ **FAME (Financial Analysis Made Easy)** is a powerful database that contains information on 3.4 million companies in the UK and Ireland. Typically the following information is included: contact information including phone, email and web addresses plus main and other trading addresses, activity details, 29 profit and loss account and 63 balance sheet items, cash flow and ratios, credit score and rating, security and price information (listed companies only), names of bankers, auditors, previous auditors and advisers, details of holdings and subsidiaries (including foreign holdings and subsidiaries), names of current and previous directors with home addresses and shareholder indicator, heads of department, and shareholders. You can compare each company with detailed financials with its peer group based on its activity codes, and the software lets you search for companies that comply with your own criteria, combining as many conditions as you like. FAME is available in business libraries and on CD from the publishers, who also offer a free trial (`http://fame2.bvdep.com/version-2009727/Home.serv?product=fameneo`).

✔ **Companies House** (`www.companieshouse.gov.uk`) is the official repository of all company information in the UK. Their WebCheck service offers a free-of-charge searchable company names and address index which covers 2 million companies. You can use it to search for a company either by its name or its unique company registration number. You can use WebCheck to purchase a company's latest accounts, giving details of sales, profits, margins, directors, shareholders and bank borrowings at a cost of £1 per company.

✔ **BusinessesforSale.com** (`www.businessesforsale.com`) has a database of over 50,000 businesses for sale, searchable by country, county, size, business sector and price.

Investigate and approach

Once you have your shopping list of prospective purchases you need to arm yourself with everything you can find out about them. Visit their website, get their literature, samples, copies of their advertising, press comment and, of course, their accounts. Then get out and see their premises and as much of their operation as you're able to. If you can't get in, get one of your salespeople in to look the business over for you. This investigation will help you to both shorten your shopping list, and put it into order of priority. Now you're ready for the approach.

Although you're technically *buying*, psychologically you would be well advised to think of acquiring a company as a *selling* job. As such you cannot afford to have any approach rejected either too early or without a determined effort. You have three options as to how to make the initial approach and each has its merits. You can

- ✔ Telephone, giving only the broadest reason for your approach – saying perhaps you wish to discuss areas of common interest.

- ✔ Write and be a little more specific on your purpose, following that up with a phone call to arrange a meeting, perhaps over lunch.

- ✔ Use a third party such as an accountant, merchant bank or consultant. Reasons of secrecy may make this method desirable. If executive time is at a premium there may be no other practicable way.

The first meeting is crucial and you need to achieve two objectives. First, you must establish mutual respect, trust and rapport. Nothing worthwhile will follow without these. Then you need to establish in principle that both parties are seriously interested. Time scale, price, methods of integration and other matters can all be side-stepped until later, except in the most general sense.

Valuing the business

Once you've found a business that you want to buy, and that's probably for sale, you now need your accountants to investigate the business in depth to see exactly what's on offer. This can take several weeks, and is a little like having a house surveyed. You need to remember that accounts are normally prepared on the *going concern* basis, which implies the company is going to continue trading much as before. This means that the historical cost of fixed assets such as buildings, land, machinery and so on can appear in the balance sheet, rather than the market worth. After all, until you came along they hadn't planned to sell their fixed assets, but now the figures will have to be recast using different principles.

Ultimately, what you're buying is either extra profit or, perhaps, lower costs in your own business. You have to decide how much that is worth. Public companies usually have general rules for each sector. For example, much of the retail sector is valued on a price/earnings ratio (P/E) of 12, which means retailers are seen as being worth 12 times last year's net profit. A private company in the same sector would only be worth two thirds that figure, as their shares are less easily bought and sold. The worth of the assets in the business would also be important, and whatever the nature of the business you're usually buying people – their knowledge and skills – unless of course you're simply *asset stripping* (buying a business primarily to sell its assets rather than to continue to run it).

Prices paid for private companies are monitored in a three-monthly index prepared by accountancy firm BDO Stoy Hayward. (www.bdo.uk.com/publications/private-company-price-index.html). Based on completed acquisitions the index tracks the ratio between the purchase price of private companies sold during a three-month period and their historical earnings.

The P/E ratio of the index of private companies is usually about 20 per cent lower than the trading P/E multiple of companies in the FT Index for the same period. This reflects the value placed on liquidity. Valuing business is no great science, just a rather messy art. At the end of the day you can always work out if it would be cheaper to start up from scratch yourself. That will give you an outer figure for your negotiations. Any higher purchase price wouldn't represent good value, as you could start up yourself for less money.

Limiting the risks

Buying a business is always risky. If you've done your homework and got the price right, with any luck the risks will be less. Some other things you can do to lessen the risks include the following.

- ✔ **Set conditional terms:** For example, you can make part of the price conditional upon a certain level of profit being achieved.

- ✔ **Handcuff key employees:** Not literally, you understand, but if most of the assets you're buying are on two legs, then get service contracts or consultancy arrangements, either of which will get a degree of commitment in place before the deal is signed, so you can be sure they'll be around for a while at least.

- ✔ **Insert non-competition clauses:** Make sure that neither the seller nor her key employees can set up in competition, taking all the goodwill you've just bought.

- ✔ **Get tax clearances:** Obviously you want to make sure any tax losses you're buying, or any tax implications in the purchase price, are approved by Her Majesty's Revenue and Customs, before committing yourself.

- ✔ **Insist on warranties and indemnities:** If, after you've bought, you find there is a compulsory purchase order on the vendor's premises and the patent on her new product is invalid, you would quite rightly be rather miffed. Warranties and indemnities set out those circumstances in which the seller will make good the buyer's financial loss. So anything crucial that looks worrying, you can try to include under this heading. Not unnaturally, the seller will resist, but you need to be firm on key points.

Managing the acquisition

However well-negotiated the deal, most acquisitions that go wrong do so because of the human factor, particularly in the first few weeks after the deal is made public. Some important rules to follow are:

- ✔ Have an outline plan for how to handle the 'merger', and be prepared to be flexible. Interestingly enough, only one buyer in five has a detailed operational plan of how to manage their acquisition, but 67 per cent of those being bought believe the buyer has such a plan so it's psychologically important.

- ✔ Let business go on as usual for a few weeks, as you find out more about the internal workings of the company. Then you can make informed judgments on who or what should go and who should remain in post. Ninety per cent of successful acquisitions follow this rule.

- ✔ Hold management and staff meetings on the first day after the takeover to clear as much misunderstanding as you can. Do as much of this yourself as you possibly can.

- ✔ Never announce takeovers on a Friday. Staff will have all weekend to spread rumours. Wednesdays are best – just enough time to clear up misunderstandings, followed by a useful weekend breathing space.

- ✔ Make cuts/redundancies a once-only affair. Cut deep, and then get on with running the business. Continuous sackings sap morale, and all the best people will leave before it's their turn.

- ✔ Set limits of authority and reporting relationships and put all banking relationships in the hands of your own accounts department, as quickly as possible.

Chapter 3

Improving Performance

An unpleasant truism in business, and in much else, is that after resources are allocated they become misallocated over time. Another way of looking at this problem is to say that just because something 'ain't broke', it doesn't mean you can't make it perform better still. To get your business to grow and keep growing needs a continuous effort to improve every aspect of that business.

In this chapter we tell you how to boost your business by keeping your customers happy, improving your efficiency and effectiveness, and increasing and expanding your business.

Checking Your Internal Systems

In order to improve performance you have to have systems in operation that help you measure performance in the first place.

A good test of whether you're allocating enough time to the task of improving performance is to keep a track of how you spend your time, say, over a month. As well as recording the work you do and the time you spend on each major task, put the letter R for routine, S for strategic or I for improving performance next to the task.

A routine task is something like meeting a customer or the bank manager, delivering a product or service, or taking on a new employee. Strategic tasks include considering a major shift of activities, say from making a product to just marketing it, forming a joint venture or buying out a competitor. Improvement activities include all the elements we talk about in this chapter – activities focused on getting more mileage, lower costs or higher yields out of the existing business.

Most owner-managers spend 95 per cent of their day on routine tasks and only tackle improvement and strategic issues when they hit the buffers. For example, most entrepreneurs don't worry too much about cash until it runs out. Then they pick up the phone and press customers into paying up. What they should have done, however, is introduce new procedures for collecting cash *before* the crunch.

If you're not spending at least 30 per cent of your time on improving your business and strategic issues, then you're probably heading for the buffers.

A good way to test whether you're doing enough to keep on top of your markets is to conduct a SWOT analysis. See Book 1, Chapter 5 for more on this.

Retaining Customers

Businesses spend an awful lot of time and money on winning customers and nothing like enough time and money on keeping them. This behaviour is as pointless as pouring water, or perhaps molten gold would be a better material to keep in mind, into a bucket with a big hole in the bottom. You need most if not all of the flow to keep the bucket partly full. However fast the flow in, the flow out is just as fast.

Virtually all managers agree that customer care is important. A recent survey of major British companies showed that 75 per cent had recently instituted customer care quality schemes. Sadly, another survey, conducted by American consultancy company Bain, also revealed that less than a third of those companies saw any payback for their efforts in terms of improved market share or profitability.

Bain suggests that the reason companies are disappointed with their attempts to improve customer care is that they don't have anything tangible to measure. To help overcome that problem, it suggests that managers focus on the Customer Retention Ratio, a Bain invention. For example, if you have 100 customers in January and 110 in December, but only 85 of the original customers are still with you, then your retention rate is 85 per cent. Bain's study demonstrated that a 5 per cent improvement in retention had a fairly dramatic effect on clients. For a credit card client it boosted profits by 125 per cent; for an insurance broker a 5 per cent increase in profits occurred; and a software house benefited from a 35 per cent improvement in profits. Bain claims that the longer customers stay with you, the more profitable they become. The next section explains why.

Realising why retaining customers matters

Studies and common sense indicate several principal reasons for retaining customers being so vital:

- Acquiring new customers costs more than retaining the ones you have. What with market research, prospecting, selling time and so on, acquiring a new customer costs between three and seven times as much as retaining an old one.

  This is nothing more than the old military maxim applied by Montgomery, that attacking forces need several times the strength of the defenders to guarantee success.

- The longer you retain a customer, the more years you have to allocate the costs of acquiring that customer to. By spreading the costs of acquiring new customers over ten years, instead of one or two, the annual profit per customer is higher. Suppose it costs you £500 to get a new customer, and that customer makes you £1,000 profit each year you keep him. If you keep the customer one year, your annual profit is £500 (£1,000 minus £500). However, if you keep the customer ten years, your annual profit is £950 (£1,000 minus £500 ÷ 10). Customers who stay tend, over time, to spend more.

- Regular customers cost less to serve than new customers. Insurance and underwriting costs as a percentage of sales fall by 40 per cent for renewal policies, for example. You don't incur up-front costs again.

- Long-term customers are often willing to pay a premium for service. They're also less prone to check your competitors because they know and like you.

Book VI

Growing and Improving Your Business

Avoiding the consequences of losing customers is a powerful motivator for keeping in your customers' good graces. Some of those consequences are:

- Dissatisfied customers tell between 8 and 15 others about their experience. Just avoiding this negative publicity has a value.

- Your former customers are fertile ground for your competitors. If you keep your customers, your competitors have to offer inducements to dislodge those customers and this is expensive and time-consuming.

Working to retain customers

Use these five rules to make sure that you retain customers and so improve your profit growth:

✔ Make customer care and retention a specific goal, and reward people for keeping customers, not just for getting them in the first place.

✔ Find out why you lose customers. Don't just let them go – either send them a follow-up questionnaire or get someone other than the salesperson concerned to visit former customers to find out why they changed supplier. You may be surprised how pleased people are to tell you why they didn't stay with you, if you explain that it may help you serve them better the next time. QuestionPro, a web-based service for conducting online surveys, has a number of customer satisfaction survey templates that you can download for free (go to www.questionpro.com/akira/showArticle.do). Also see 'Chapter 6 in Book I for more ideas.

✔ Research your competitors' service levels as well as their products. If practical, buy from them on a regular basis. If you can't buy from competitors, keep close to people who do.

✔ If one part of your organisation is good at caring for customers, get people there to teach everyone else what they do.

✔ Recognise that the best people to provide customer care are those who work directly with customers. But this means that you have to train them and give them the authority to make decisions on the spot. Aloof or indifferent employees don't convince customers that you really want to keep their business.

Retaining customers isn't the passive activity it sounds. The next sections offer concrete ways to keep your customers happy.

Monitoring complaints

One terrifying statistic is that 98 per cent of complaints never happen. People just don't get round to making the complaint, or worse still, they can find no one to complain to. You'd have to be a hermit never to have experienced something to complain about, but just try finding someone to complain to at 8 p.m. on a Sunday at Paddington Station and you get a fair impression of how being in the Gobi Desert feels.

You can never be confident that just because you're not hearing complaints your customers and clients aren't dissatisfied and about to defect. Not making complaints also doesn't mean that they may not run around badmouthing you and your business. Remember that on average people share their complaint with a score of others, who in turn are equally eager to share the bad experience. The viral effect of email has the potential to make any particularly juicy story run around the world in days if not hours.

Set up a system to ensure that your customers have ample opportunity to let you know what they think about your product or service. This may involve a short questionnaire, a follow-up phone call or an area on your website devoted to customer feedback. As a bonus you may find you get some great ideas on how to improve your business.

Giving customers opportunities to complain

One entrepreneur who's more than aware of the problems (and incidentally opportunities) presented by complaints is Julian Richer, founder of the retail hi-fi chain Richer Sounds. His maxim is that his staff should maximise customers' opportunities to complain. The operative word in that sentence is *opportunities*, which you shouldn't confuse with *reasons*. In order to put this policy into effect, Richer uses a range of techniques. The whole customer satisfaction monitoring process starts from the moment customers enter one of his retail outlets. A sign near the door invites people to ring a bell if they've had particularly good service or help while in the shop. That help may be simply getting some great advice, or finding a product they want to buy at a very competitive price.

Customers find that when they get their hi-fi equipment home it contains a short questionnaire on a postcard asking them for their immediate post-purchase feelings. Does the product work as specified, is it damaged in any way, were they delighted with the service they received? The postcard is addressed to 'Julian Richer, Founder' and not, as is the case with so many other big businesses, to 'Customer Services, Department 126754, PO Box, blah blah blah'.

Richer does surveys on customer satisfaction and encourages his staff to come up with their own ideas for monitoring customer reactions. In fact, he insists that they hit minimum targets for getting customer feedback. Silence on the customer satisfaction front isn't an option for management in his business.

Ninety-eight per cent of customers who have a complaint are prepared to buy from you again if you handle their complaint effectively and promptly. Not only do they buy from you again, but also they spread the gospel about how clever they were in getting you to respond to their complaint. Nothing makes people happier than having something to complain about that ends up costing them next to nothing.

Setting customer service standards

Customer service is all those activities that support a customer's purchase, from the time they become aware that you can supply them with a particular product or service, to the point at which they own that product or service and are able to enjoy all the benefits they were led to believe were on offer.

The largest part of the value of many products and services lies in how the company delivers customer service. This is also the area most likely to influence whether customers come back again or recommend you to others. Customer service works best when:

- Customers are encouraged to tell you about any problems.

- Customers know their rights and responsibilities from the beginning.

- Customers know the circumstances under which they're entitled to get their money back and how to take advantage of other rights.

✔ Customers feel in control. You're far better advised to provide a full refund if the customer is dissatisfied than to demand that the customer come up with a good reason for the refund. A refund, or any other recourse you offer, needs to be prompt.

Repeat business is another key profit maker. Repeat business comes from ensuring that customers are completely satisfied with and ideally pleasantly surprised by the quality of your product. Repeat sales save unnecessary expenditure on advertising and promotion to attract new customers.

As standards of living rise, quality, convenience and service are going to become even more important relative to price. An investment in a strategy of quality customer service now is an investment in greater future profitability. You need to have a model to follow for effective customer service and consider using mystery shopping as a way to keep tabs on your customer service standards – both issues are covered in the next sections.

Customer service is often the difference between keeping customers for life and losing customers in droves. You and your staff have to deliver outstanding customer service at all times. In order to do this everyone has to know what the important elements of good customer service are and everyone needs to incorporate those elements into their everyday customer interactions.

The key elements of your customer service plan should include:

✔ **Initial contact:** The customer's first contact with staff creates a lasting impression and can win and sustain customers. All your staff need to be aware of how to handle enquiries quickly and competently. They should know how to leave potential customers feeling confident that their requirements can be met.

✔ **Information flow:** Keeping customers informed of where their orders are in the process influences their feelings about the way you do business. Your action plan needs to specify each step of your process – quotation; order confirmation; delivery notification; installation instructions. A regular flow of information throughout this period makes your customers feel that they matter to you.

✔ **Delivery:** Delivering the goods or service is a key part of customer service. Your product needs to be available in a timely manner, delivery lead times must be reasonable and the delivery itself must be in a way that meets the customer's requirements.

✔ **After-sales support:** Good coverage in areas such as maintenance, repairs, help lines, upgrade notification, instruction manuals, returns policy and fault tracing helps customers feel that you care about their total experience with your products and business.

✔ **Problem solving:** Often the acid test of customer service, your staff need to be able to recognise when a customer has a real crisis and what your procedure is for helping them.

High customer service standards enable many firms to charge a premium for their products. Yet in many ways, good customer service can be a nil-cost item. After all, answering the phone politely takes as much effort as doing so with a surly and off-putting tone. So improved customer service is one route to increased profitability.

Rewarding loyalty

The reasons that loyalty improves profitability are:

✔ Retaining customers costs less than finding and capturing new ones.

✔ Loyal customers tend to place larger orders.

✔ Loyal customers don't always place price first, but new ones usually do.

So what works and what doesn't when it comes to keeping customers loyal? One idea that hasn't lived up to its promise is customer loyalty cards. When they were launched, retailers made big claims about how they were going to gather tons of invaluable data about customers. But mostly they possess just huge virtual warehouses of information that hasn't been used. Analysing the buying habits of millions of shoppers as their cards are swiped at the till can be prohibitively expensive and few companies have used much of the data gathered to make their customers feel special and hence want to stay loyal.

Asked to give reasons for loyalty, the top five elements consumers list are:

✔ Convenience

✔ Price

✔ Range

✔ Customer service

✔ Quality

What this means is that you have to get your basic marketing strategy right and understand what your customers want and how much they're prepared to pay. If that's wrong, no loyalty scheme is going to keep them on board. Customer service and quality are about getting things right first time, every time. So always under-promise and over-deliver.

Care and help lines, where customers are encouraged to call for advice, information or help with problems, help keep customers loyal and make them more likely to buy from you in the future. If the line is a freephone service it's even more effective. Keeping in touch with customers can also bind them more securely. Questionnaires, newsletters, magazines, letters about incentives, customer service calls, invitations to sales events and 'member get member' schemes are all ways of achieving this result.

Book VI

Growing and Improving Your Business

Improving Productivity

Improving productivity is a constant requirement for a growth-minded business, not simply an activity during periods of economic recession (when it is still, nonetheless, important). You need to improve productivity by acting on both your costs and your margins.

You can increase margins by changing the mix of products and services you sell to focus on those yielding the best return, or by raising your selling price. Cutting costs has the merit of showing quick and certain returns.

Trimming expenses

You need continually to keep expenses under tight control and balance them against the requirements for good quality and good service. In particular, you need to separate and act on your variable and fixed costs.

Variable cost cutting is always in evidence in a recession; witness the automotive and banking staff cuts in the early 1990s, in 2002–2003 and with a vengeance in 2009–2010. Cutting variable costs includes such things as wages and materials that are directly related to the volume of sales.

Cutting fixed costs such as cars, computers and equipment – costs that don't change directly with the volume of sales – shouldn't include scrapping investments that may bring economies and extra nimbleness in the future (like flexible-manufacturing facilities, where, for example, Peugeot has invested in product lines that can turn out two models of vehicle at once). Equally, alliances between firms, aiming to reduce fixed-cost investments, can be advantageous. In the soft drinks industry, Perrier provides distribution for Pepsi in France and Bulmers reciprocates for Perrier in England, avoiding the need for extra investment in warehousing and transport.

Focusing attention on the 20 per cent of items that make up 80 per cent of your costs probably yields your biggest savings. The 80/20 rule is helpful in getting costs back into line, but what if the line was wrong in the first place?

Increasing margins

To achieve increased *profit margins*, which is the difference between the costs associated with the product or service you sell and the price you get in the market, you need first to review your sales. This requires accurate costs and gross margins for each of your products or services. Armed with that information, you can select particular product groups or market segments that are less price-sensitive and potentially more profitable.

No one rushes out to buy expensive, overpriced products when cheaper alternatives that are just as good are readily available. The chances are that your most profitable products are also the ones that your customers value the most. Start your efforts to increase margins by concentrating on trying to sell the products and services that make you the most money.

Pricing is the biggest decision your business has to make, and one it needs to keep constantly under review. Your decision on pricing is the one that has the biggest impact on company profitability. Try the consultants' favourite exercise of computing and comparing the impact on profits of a 5 per cent

- ✔ Cut in your overheads
- ✔ Increase in volume sales
- ✔ Cut in materials purchased
- ✔ Price increase

Book VI

Growing and Improving Your Business

All these actions are usually considered to be within an owner-manager's normal reach. Almost invariably, the 5 per cent price increase scores the highest, because it passes straight to the net profit, the bottom line. Even if volume falls, because of the effect that price has on growth margin, you usually gain more profit from selling fewer items at a higher price. For example, at a constant gross margin of 30 per cent with a 5 per cent price increase, profits are unchanged even if sales decline 14 per cent. Yet if prices are cut 5 per cent, an extra 21 per cent increase in sales is needed to make the same amount of profit.

Frequently, resistance to increasing prices, even in the face of inflationary cost rises, can come from your own team members, eager to apportion blame for performance lapses. In these instances making detailed price comparisons with competitors is important.

Working smarter

Making more money doesn't always have to mean working longer hours. You can just work smarter – and who knows, you may even end up working fewer hours than you do now and still make more money.

One way to get everyone's grey matter working overtime is to create 'smart circles', comprising people working in different areas of your business who you challenge to come up with ideas to make the business better (and smart rewards, which include extra resources, holidays and recognition for their achievements, rather than cash). You can formalise the process of encouraging employees to rethink the way they work and reward them in a way that makes their working environment better still.

Rewarding results

If you can get the people who work for you to increase their output, you can improve productivity. The maxim 'What gets measured gets done and what gets rewarded gets done again' is the guiding principle behind rewards, and setting objectives is the starting point in the process.

The objectives you want people to achieve in order to reward them beyond their basic pay need to be challenging but achievable too, which is something of a contradiction in terms. Problems start to arise as soon as professional managers and supervisors come on board with experience of working in big companies. They, and probably you, tend to take objectives and the ensuing budgets very seriously. You have to hit the budgets, so it makes sense to pitch them on the conservative side.

But in a small business, growth and improvement percentages have the potential to be much greater than in larger firms. A big business with a third of its market can only grow very quickly by acquisition or if the market itself is growing very fast. A small firm, on the other hand, can grow by very large amounts very quickly. Moving from 0.01 per cent of a market to 0.02 per cent is hardly likely to upset many other players, but it can represent a doubling in size for a small firm. However, exceptional performance, even in a small firm, is only attainable with breakthrough thinking and performance. The question may not be how to grow the business by 20 per cent a year, but how to grow it by 20 per cent a month.

Nevertheless, if you set goals too aggressively people may leave. Even, perhaps especially, great performers balk if the hurdle is put too high.

Rewarding excellent results

Nick White's Ecotravel company sends people to off-the-beaten-track exotic locations and to conservation areas where money goes into research projects. Ecotourists who book with Ecotravel pay to see animals in conservation areas and a proportion of the money they spend on the holiday goes directly to conservation projects.

White expanded the business slowly, until two years ago when he introduced a 'rewarding excellence' initiative and sales shot up by 40 per cent in just six months. The basis of the reward is an accelerating bonus. If the company hits its sales targets, staff share in a 5 per cent bonus. If it exceeds targets, the bonus rates rise too. For every 20 per cent of achievement above target, the bonus rate goes up 1 per cent. Targets are reset each year using a similar formula, but starting from a new and higher base level.

One way to get the best of both worlds is to have a performance band rather than just one number. The reward for achieving a really great result should be massive, but if the employee misses this high goal slightly, you reward him as if the goal had been set at the level he reached. The reward is proportionately smaller, so your rewards budget still balances. This technique can get an 'inspiration dividend'. You can persuade teams to set higher goals than they may otherwise have set, and even if they miss them, the year-on-year improvements can be stunning.

Budgeting for Beginners

One sure-fire way to get poor performance back on track or, better still, to turn satisfactory results into exceptional ones is to set specific goals to make that happen. Sure, you have a long-term business plan that looks out to the distant horizon (we cover this in Chapter 4 in Book I). But you also need something with a bit more immediacy and a whole lot of bite. In the business world this process is known as *budgeting*. Budgets set goals in terms of revenues and expenses for the year ahead and are usually reviewed at least halfway through the year and often quarterly. At that review you can add a further quarter or half-year to the budget to maintain a one-year budget horizon. This is known in the trade as a *rolling quarterly (half-yearly) budget*.

You can think of a budget as doing much the same as a coach does with an athlete in setting improvement targets to be achieved by some specific date in the future. Then the coach gets a stopwatch out, checks on performance and cheers or cajoles as the situation warrants.

Setting the guidelines

Budgets should adhere to the following general principles:

✔ Budgets should be based on realistic but challenging goals. Those goals combine both a top-down aspiration of the boss (you) and a bottom-up forecast of what the employees or departments concerned see as possible.

✔ It should be prepared by those responsible for delivering the results – the salespeople should prepare the sales budget, and the production people the production budget.

✔ Agreement to the budget should be explicit. During budgeting, several versions of a particular budget should be discussed. For example, the boss wants a sales figure of £20,000 but the sales team's initial forecast is for £15,000. After some debate, £18,000 is the figure agreed upon.

After a figure is agreed, a virtual contract exists that declares a commitment from employees to achieve the target and commitments from the employer to be satisfied with the target and to supply resources in order to achieve it. It makes sense for this contract to be in writing.

✔ The budget needs to be finalised at least a month before the start of the year and not weeks or months into the year.

✔ The budget should undergo fundamental reviews periodically throughout the year to make sure all the basic assumptions that underpin it still hold good.

✔ Accurate information reviewing performance against budgets should be available seven to ten working days after the month's end.

Analysing the variances

Understanding variances is a key task, so as the boss you need to carefully monitor and compare performance against the budget as the year proceeds, taking corrective action where necessary. You do this on a monthly basis (or using shorter time intervals if required), showing both the company's performance during the month in question and throughout the year so far.

Looking at Table 3-1, you can see that the business is behind on sales for this month, but ahead on the yearly target. The convention is to put unfavourable variations in brackets. Hence, a higher-than-budgeted sales figure doesn't have brackets, but a higher materials cost does. You can also see that although profit is running ahead of budget, the profit margin is slightly behind (–0.30 per cent). This is partly because other direct costs, such as labour and distribution in this example, are running well ahead of budget.

Table 3-1	The Fixed Budget in £'000s					
	Month			Year to Date		
	Budget	*Actual*	*Variance*	*Budget*	*Actual*	*Variance*
Sales	805	753	(52)	6,358	7,314	965
Materials	627 (78%)	567	60	4,942	5,704	(762)
Less Cost of Materials	178 (22%)	186	8	1,416	1,610	194
Direct Costs	74	79	(5)	595	689	(94)
Gross Profit	104	107	3	820	921	101
Percentage	12.92	14.21	1.29	12.90	12.60	(0.30)

Flexing the figures

A budget is based on a particular set of sales goals, few of which are likely to be exactly met in practice. Table 3-1 shows a company that's used £762,000 more materials than budgeted (see variance column under Year to Date). Because more has been sold than was budgeted for, this is hardly surprising. The way to manage this situation is to flex the budget to show what, given the sales that actually occurred, would be expected to happen to expenses. Applying the budget ratios to the actual data does this. For example, materials were planned to be 78 per cent of sales in the budget. Applying that to the actual month's sales you arrive at a materials cost of £587,000 (78% of £753).

Looking at the flexed budget in Table 3-2 , you can see that the company has spent £19,000 more than expected on the material given the level of sales actually achieved, rather than the £762,000 overspend shown in the fixed budget.

The same principle holds for other direct costs, which appear to be running £94,000 over budget for the year. When you take into account the extra sales shown in the flexed budget, you can see that the company has actually spent £4,000 over budget on direct costs. Although this is serious, it's not as serious as the fixed budget suggests.

The flexed budget allows you to concentrate your efforts on dealing with true variances in performance.

Book VI

Growing and Improving Your Business

Table 3-2	The Flexed Budget in £'000s					
	Month			Year to Date		
	Budget	*Actual*	*Variance*	*Budget*	*Actual*	*Variance*
Sales	753	753	–	7,314	7,314	–
Materials	587	567	20	5,685	5,704	(19)
Less Cost of Materials	166	186	20	1,629	1,610	(19)
Direct Costs	69	79	(10)	685	689	(4)
Gross Profit	97	107	10	944	921	(23)
Percentage	12.92	14.21	1.29	12.90	12.60	(0.30)

The SCORE website has a downloadable Excel spreadsheet from which you can make sales and cost projections on a trial and error basis (www.score.org; go to Business Tools, Template Gallery and Sales Forecast). When you're satisfied with your projection, use the profit and loss projection (Template Gallery, then Profit and Loss Projection [3 Years]) to complete your budget.

The figures shown for each period of the budget aren't the same. For example, a sales budget of £1.2 million for the year doesn't translate to £100,000 a month. The exact figure depends on two factors:

✔ The projected trend may forecast that sales at the start of the year may be £80,000 a month and will change to £120,000 a month by the end of the year. The average would be £100,000, but month by month the budget figure against which performance should be measured is going up.

✔ By virtue of seasonal factors, each month may also be adjusted up or down from the underlying trend. For example, you could expect the sales of heating oil to peak in the autumn and tail off in the late spring.

Budgeting from zero

When a team discusses budgets, arguments always revolve around how much more each section needs next year. The starting point is usually this year's costs, which are taken as the only facts on which to build. So, for example, if you spent £25,000 on advertising last year and achieved sales of £1 million, your advertising expense was 2.5 per cent of sales. If the sales budget for next year is £1.5 million, it seems logical to spend £37,500 next year on advertising. That, however, presupposes that you spent last year's sum wisely and effectively in the first place, which you almost certainly did not.

Zero-based budgeting turns the cost argument on its head. It assumes that each year every cost centre starts from zero spending and, based on the goals of the business and the resources available, presents arguments for every pound you're planning to spend, *not just for the increase*. So each year starts out with a blank sheet of paper rather than last year's figures.

Chapter 4

Franchising for Growth

If your business concept looks as though it can be replicated in several other places, you have a number of choices. The most obvious is to open up more branches. But you can consider a faster, and in some ways safer, route by franchising your business for others to roll out and share the risk.

Franchising is a great way into business, as a start-up, and a great way to grow a business, too – as a model to follow later when you're looking for some serious growth opportunities. Over 700 different types of franchise are on offer somewhere in the world, so you can almost certainly find one that suits your needs and aspirations.

Defining a Franchise

Franchising is a marketing technique used to improve and expand the distribution of a product or service. The franchiser supplies the product or teaches the service to you, the franchisee, who in turn sells it to the public. In return for this, you pay a fee and a continuing royalty, based usually on turnover. The franchiser may also require you to buy materials or ingredients from it, which gives it an additional income stream. The advantage to you is a relatively safe and quick way of getting into business for yourself, but with the support and advice of an experienced organisation close to hand.

A *franchise agreement* is just like any business contract, in that it sets out what each party is expected to do and what can happen if he doesn't.

The main ingredients of a franchise agreement are:

✔ Permission to use a business name and so be associated with that bigger enterprise

✔ The right for the franchiser to set and enforce business and product standards, such as the use of ingredients, cooking processes, opening times, staff uniforms and so forth

✔ An obligation for the franchiser to provide help, training and guidance in all aspects of operating the business

✔ A definition of the way in which the rights to operate the franchise are to be paid for, for example royalties on sales, initial purchase fee, marketing levy, mark-up on goods and services provided and so forth

A standard franchise agreement is available from the British Franchise Association (BFA). Their standard agreement, though helpful, doesn't cover everything you need to know to make a sound decision. For example, though running a pilot scheme is a condition of membership of the BFA, that in itself is no guarantee that the business model is fully tried and tested. Nor does the BFA standard contract mention that the business, when set up, is the property of the franchisee, or warn the franchisee of the degree of control the franchiser may subject her to. Further, it gives no indication of the extent of the back-up services that the franchisee may reasonably expect to get for her money. In other words, the BFA definition isn't a sufficient standard against which to check the franchise contract.

The British Franchise Association expects its members to follow its code of practice, and you can find out more on its website: www.thebfa.org.

You have two possible strategies for harnessing the power of franchising to your business. You can consider taking on a franchise or master franchise that's complementary to your existing business, or you can franchise your own business concept, taking on self-employed franchisees instead of hired-in managers to run your new branches or outlets.

Bolting On a Franchise

Adding a franchise to your own business is a safer way to grow than franchising your own business idea. After all, after a franchise is up and running you can see how well it works. You can assess the franchise's track record, and though no guarantee of success exists, at least the franchise has ironed out many of the unknowns associated with any new venture. The following sections outline the two routes to deploying this growth strategy.

Adding a franchise

A few years back Harrods, London's up-market department store, opened the first British outlet of Krispy Kreme Doughnuts. For Harrods the sale of doughnuts is complementary to its other food and beverage sales, so the addition represents pure extra revenue. For Krispy Kreme, the venture represents a chance to enter the British market, which it believes is ripe for development with no dominant doughnut brand in the market.

The aim in adding a franchise to your existing business is to leverage, as the business gurus say, your customer or resource base, in order to get more sales per customer or square metre of space.

So if your customers are buying chocolate, sweets and stationery from you, adding a freezer with ice cream is no big deal. Chances are that the ice cream supplier is so keen to extend its distribution that it throws in the freezer cabinet for free. You're taking someone else's business model, product and support systems and bolting them on to your business to add turnover and profits.

Taking out a master franchise

Instead of just adding a franchise to complement your business, you can consider rolling out a chain of franchises. That involves taking a master franchise for a country or region. You can also look on this as a strategy for rapidly expanding your own business, if you can put it into a franchise format. We cover that aspect of expansion in 'Rolling out the franchise', later in this chapter.

You can find out more about taking on a master franchise from Master Franchises for Sale (www.masterfranchisesforsale.com), Franchise Solutions (http://uk.franchisesolutions.com) and Franchise Direct (www.franchisedirect.co.uk).

Weighing the Advantages and Disadvantages

From the franchiser's point of view, one huge financial advantage is that you don't have any direct investment in any of your franchises. The franchisee owns the inventory and equipment.

Because of the shortage of prime sites, one growing trend is for franchisers to acquire leases on behalf of franchisees, or at any rate to stand as guarantors. Nevertheless, the effect on the liquidity of the franchiser, in contrast to expansion by opening branches, is enormous.

However, you do face heavy start-up costs in piloting the franchise and in setting up and maintaining training if you do the job properly. Thereafter you incur further costs in providing a continuing service to franchisees in such matters as research and development, promotion, administrative back-up, and feedback and communication within the network.

As a franchiser, you're dependent on the willingness of the franchisee to observe the rules and play the game, and any failure of the franchisee to do so is equally and perhaps more damaging to you and to other franchisees than it is to the wayward franchisee.

Doing the Pilot

After you've developed a franchise concept, you need to run a pilot operation for at least a year. Someone as similar to the intended typical franchisee for the chain as is practical should run the pilot. The aim isn't just to test the business concept, but to see whether you've described the operating systems well enough for people outside the founding business organisation to run them.

Take as an example a fast-food outlet offering slimmers' lunches. You already own a couple of outlets for which you've found a catchy name, Calorie Counter. You've established a standard image in terms of decor, layout, tableware, menus and graphics, and your staff members have a stylish uniform. Your gimmick is that on the menu every dish has a calorie rating and a breakdown of the fibre and salt content, and along with their bill customers get a calorie and fibre count for what they've bought. You also have some recipes that you've pioneered.

In the year since you opened you've ironed out most of the start-up bugs and discovered a lot about the catering, accounting and staffing problems in running a business of this kind.

The indication is that demand exists for more restaurants like yours, but you have neither the capital nor the inclination to take on restaurant managers. Being a thorough sort of person, you've documented every aspect of running your restaurant, covering everything from recipes, ingredients and cooking times, to opening hours, wages, incentives and dress code. You've also standardised your accounting system and linked the electronic till to your raw material and stock systems, so that you can order key ingredients automatically. From your experience in opening two of your own restaurants you know how and where to advertise, how much to spend and how sales demand is likely to grow in the early weeks and months. You've captured all this knowledge in a sort of manual, which you propose to use as a guide for whoever you select to open your next outlet.

You're now ready to run your first pilot franchise. This involves using your manual and procedures with a real live franchisee. True, you may have to give the franchisee some incentive to join you in the risk. But whatever you end up negotiating, as long as it gives you the benefits of franchising that we list in 'Weighing the advantages and disadvantages', earlier in this chapter, you're ahead of the game.

When your pilot franchisee gets under way you have the opportunity to test your manual in action. You, after all, invented the business, so you should know what to do in every situation – but seeing whether a green franchisee straight off the street can follow your 'map' and get a result is the acid test.

Put what you find out from the pilot into a revised franchise manual, sort out your charging and support systems, and you're ready to start to roll the franchise out.

Book VI

Growing and Improving Your Business

Finding Franchisees

Sorry, but the last sentence in the previous section was a bit misleading. Despite having a great business, a robust and proven business manual and a couple of pilot runs under your belt, you aren't quite ready to roll the franchise out around the world, or even around your neighbourhood. The most recent NatWest/British Franchise Association survey (they do one every year and have done for the last 20) asked franchisers what they consider to be the biggest barrier to the growth of the number of franchises they operate. By far the greatest number of respondents – 41 per cent – said that it was the lack of suitable franchisees.

Visit any franchise exhibition – and you visit many if you're serious about growing in this way – and the thousands of people milling around the stands and in the seminar rooms may convince you that no lack of interest exists among the general public to taking up a franchise.

Finding potential franchisees isn't a problem. You can meet franchisees at any of the dozen or so franchise exhibitions held around the country each year. The BFA Diary page (www.thebfa.org/diary.asp) gives details of dates and venues. Attend as many of these exhibitions as you can and you should have applicants coming out of your ears.

Yet turning that latent demand into done deals isn't so easy. One international franchise chain only offers franchises to 30 per cent of the people it interviews, and it only interviews a small fraction of the number of people it sees at exhibitions.

This begs the obvious question: what sort of person makes the ideal franchisee? Well, looking at past career patterns may not be much help. Les Gray, chairperson of Chemical Express, a 104-outlet cleaning products franchise chain, lists a postman, a sales manager, a buyer, a farmer and a shipping agent as the occupations of his most successful franchisees.

Franchisers say that they have the most success with franchisees who are motivated, able to work hard, have some management aptitude, good communication and people skills and are *not* too entrepreneurial. They aren't looking for people with relevant industry skills and experience, because they want to inculcate candidates into their own formula.

Look at Chapter 2 in Book III for some tips on how to recruit and select great people.

Rolling Out the Franchise

So now you have a proven formula and a steady stream of candidates, you really are ready for the big roll out. Carefully select locations and areas that most closely fit your business model. For example, the Hard Rock Café model is known as a capital city business. In other words, room only exists for one in each major international city. ProntaPrint, on the other hand, can accommodate an outlet in each major business area within a city, or a single outlet in any major town with a population over around 30,000 people.

Your equation depends on your customer profile. A fast-print outlet may find the going tough in a seaside town with 20,000 pensioners and 10,000 holidaymakers.

Chapter 5

TV and Radio Ads (Or Your Own Show!)

*R*adio and television are well-established, extremely powerful market-ing media, while video (especially if shot in digital format) is a hot new item for streaming-video messages on your website. Video can also offer marketing messages on television screens and computers on your stand at a trade show.

The problem with radio and TV is that the costs associated with producing and broadcasting ads have traditionally been quite high, making these media too expensive for smaller marketers. We want to encourage you to be open-minded about radio, video and TV because new and easier ways to produce in these media are emerging all the time, along with a growing number of low-cost ways to broadcast your ads. Every year brings more radio and television stations, including those appearing online, on mobile phones, and on cable and satellite TV channels. Digital radio is also available that you can listen to through a digital set, digital TV or your PC.

Even if you don't use these commercial media, you can possibly find more modest ways in which to share your ads with prospects. In fact, increas-ingly marketers use CDs or websites that communicate using digital video, PowerPoint or radio-style voice-overs. Modern technology is making these media more flexible and affordable for all marketers.

Creating Ads for Radio

Conventional wisdom says you have only three elements to work with when you design for radio: words, sound effects and music. In a literal sense that wisdom's true, but you can't create a great radio ad unless you remember that you want to use those elements to generate *mental images* for the listener. And that means you can often perform the same basic plot on radio as on TV. Radio isn't really as limited as people think but is now rarely used to its full advantage. Society's love affair with radio has been eclipsed by its love of TV and films.

When creating radio ads, favour direct action goals over indirect ones. Sometimes you may want to use radio just to create brand awareness (*indirect-action advertising*) but in general the most effective radio ads call for direct action. Give out a web address (if the listener can remember that address easily) or a freephone number in the ad.

Put your brand name into your radio ad early and often, regardless of the story line. If you fail to generate the desired direct action, at least you build awareness and interest for the brand, which supports other points of contact in your marketing campaign. Radio is a great support medium and not enough marketers use it that way. You may as well fill the vacuum with *your* marketing message!

Here's a simple rule that can help you avoid confusion in your radio ad: ensure that your script identifies all sound effects. Sound effects are wonderful and evocative, but in truth, many sound very similar. Without context, rain on the roof can sound like bacon sizzling in a pan, a blowtorch cutting through the metal door of a bank vault or even an alien spaceship starting up. So the script must identify that sound, either through direct reference or through context. You can provide context with the script, the plot or simply by other sound effects. The sounds of eggs cracking and hitting a hot pan, coffee percolating and someone yawning, all help to identify that sizzle as the breakfast bacon, rather than rain on the roof or a blowtorch.

Buying airtime on radio

We often find ourselves urging marketers to try radio in place of their standard media choices. Why? Because, although local retailers frequently use radio to pull people into stores for sales or special offer periods, many other marketers overlook radio as a viable medium. Those advertisers don't realise how powerful radio can be and may not be aware of its incredible reach. In the UK, around 45.1 million people (74 per cent of the population) tune into digital and non-digital radio every week. We bet your target audience is in there somewhere! (Also consider radio not just for advertising but for editorial publicity. Many radio talk shows will be willing to invite you on as a guest if you pitch your expertise well and have a unique angle to discuss.)

RAJAR (Radio Joint Audience Research) is the UK's audience measurement system for commercial radio stations and the BBC. Every quarter, RAJAR releases detailed listening figures for all the UK's national and local radio stations, which you can access for free at www.rajar.co.uk. You can also get in touch with the Radio Advertising Bureau (RAB), which does a good job of promoting radio as an advertising medium and is a great source of campaign data and ideas for creative radio advertising (www.rab.co.uk).

Experts often talk about how the traditional media environment is fragmenting, with fewer people watching TV and more people accessing entertainment online and through their mobile phones. While radio will be affected by this development, in many ways it will also benefit. Radio fits with people's increasingly mobile lives. It allows people to listen to it while doing other things – like cleaning, driving, sitting on the bus or getting stuck in a traffic jam! Those people can only welcome the distraction of your well-crafted radio ad.

You can also target radio advertising quite narrowly – both by type of audience and by geographic area. This fact helps make radio a very good buy. The general lack of appreciation for this medium also helps by keeping ad prices artificially low.

Radio airtime is cheaper and more cost-effective than TV airtime, but the biggest advertisers can reach a larger total audience by using TV, so this medium's not ideal for everyone. For some younger audiences, web advertising may be even more suitable. But some radio bodies claim that studies have shown that radio airtime is a seventh of the price of TV and that radio offers three fifths of the advertising awareness effect of TV. If you divide effectiveness by cost, you can see that radio is around four times as cost-effective as TV.

Targeting advertising via radio

We like the fact that radio stations make a real effort to target specific audiences – after all, most advertisers try to do the same thing. You can get good data, both demographic and lifestyle- or attitude-oriented information, on radio audiences. And you can often find radio stations (or specific programmes on those stations) that reach a well-defined audience, rich in those people you want to target, making radio an even better buy.

You can get details of radio station formats and audience characteristics for all UK commercial radio stations from the communications regulator Ofcom, just by going to the Radio Broadcast Licensing section of its website, at www.ofcom.org.uk.

And here's another option for radio advertising that you may not have considered. How about running ads over the internal broadcasting systems used in many shops? This opportunity gives you another great way to target a particular audience going about a particular task – for instance, you can advertise your brand of tiles to DIY shoppers using Tiles FM. *In-store radio* is an entirely different medium from a buying perspective because the shop, or more usually a specialist media owner, develops and controls the programming. As a result, most marketers don't know how to use in-store radio. But an ad agency may be able to help you gain access and some media-buying firms handle this kind of advertising, too.

So remember: don't overlook radio! It can give you better reach, better focus on your target market and greater cost-effectiveness than other media. Like TV, radio can *show* as well as tell – you just have to use the listener's imagination to create visual images. And if you manage to create a really good script, we guarantee you can catch and hold audience attention.

If you're planning to make radio a big part of your marketing plan, we can recommend a book dedicated to telling you how to do it better – *An Advertiser's Guide to Better Radio Advertising*, by Andrew Ingram and Mark Barber from the RAB, also published by Wiley.

Finding Cheaper Ways to Use the Power of Video

If you're thinking of skipping this section, consider this: video can cost £1000 per minute to produce – or even £10,000 if you're making a sophisticated national TV ad – not including the cost of the airtime to actually air the ad! But video can also cost £50 a minute or even less.

Do you have access to a high-quality, handheld digital video camera? Well, that camera (when combined with a good microphone) is actually capable of producing effective video for your marketing, especially for use on the Web, where low-resolution video files are usually used, making camera quality less important. Just think of all those videos getting millions of viewers on YouTube; the quality isn't great but people keep watching because they're interested in the content.

Many marketers don't realise that the limiting factor in inexpensive or home-made video is usually the sound quality, not the picture quality. So as long as you plug in a remote microphone and put it near anyone who's speaking, you can probably make usable video yourself.

Here are some tips if you decide to shoot video yourself:

✔ Write a simple, clear script and time it before you bother to shoot any video.

✔ Clean up the background. Most amateur efforts to shoot video presentations or ads for marketing are plagued by stuff that shows up in the background. Eliminate rubbish bins, competitors' signs and anything else unsightly.

✔ Use enough light and try to have multiple light sources. A digital video camera is just a fancy camera and it needs light to work. Normal indoor lighting is too dim for quality video. Instead, add more lights, including bright floodlights and open windows. And make sure light shines from both sides so that you fill the shadows. (Shadowed areas get darker in the video.)

✔ Shoot everything more than once. Editing is easy (well, easier) as a result of the many software programs you can use on your own computer to edit video. But editing is much easier if you have lots of footage to select from. Always repeat each short section several times, then, in editing, choose the version that came out best. That approach is how they make films stars look good and it can work well for you, too! If you have more than one camera, you can even edit shots from different angles.

✔ You can produce radio ads or sound-only messages for your website using the same digital recording and editing capabilities as you use for home-made digital video. The key is a quiet environment and a good microphone for recording. Or you can go into a production studio's sound booth and let the technicians there worry about the technical aspects.

✔ If you want actors, consider recruiting them locally and even asking people to volunteer. We hate to promote this idea, but if you're still a small organisation, avoiding paying Equity rates for your actors makes things considerably cheaper. Paying union rates and residuals is appropriate for major or national campaigns but can be prohibitive for small marketers. However, employees can make great brand ambassadors too – just look at the popularity of Howard in the Halifax adverts!

For information on editing and production, check out the many *For Dummies* books that can help you better understand what's involved or hire a media production firm that can do high-quality work at moderate rates. With plenty of smaller production firms around, try interviewing some in your area and getting samples of their work plus price quotes – you may find that by the time you master the software and come up to speed, you're spending as much doing your own work!

Book VI

Growing and Improving Your Business

Designing Ads for TV

Television is much like theatre. TV combines visual and verbal channels in real-time action, making it a remarkably rich medium. Yes, you have to make the writing as tight and compelling as good print copy, but the words must also sound good and flow with the visuals to create drama or comedy.

TV ads must use great drama (whether funny or serious), condensed to a few seconds of memorable action. These few seconds of drama must etch themselves into the memory of anyone who watches your ad.

You can't reduce a great film to a formula. You must have a good script with just the right touch of just the right emotion. Great acting. Consistent camera work and an appropriate set. The suspense of a developing relationship between two interesting characters. Achieving this level of artistry isn't necessary to make a good TV ad, but to stand out yours certainly needs to be higher than average, and if you can create truly great TV, your ad pays off in gold.

TV looks simple when you see it, but don't be fooled – it's not simple at all. Hire an experienced production company to help you do the ad or do what many marketers do and hire a big ad agency (at big ad agency prices) to design and supervise its production. This choice costs you, but at least you get quality work. Just remember that *you* ultimately decide whether the script has that star potential or is just another forgettable ad. Don't let the production company shoot until they have something as memorable as a classic film (or at least close).

If you work for a smaller business and are used to shoestring marketing budgets, you may be shaking your head at our advice. You think you can do it yourself. But why waste even a little money on ads that don't work? If you're going to do TV, do it right. Either become expert yourself or hire an expert. Without high-quality production, even the best design doesn't work. Why? Because people watch so much TV that they know the difference between good and bad ads and they don't bother to watch anything but the best.

If you're on a shoestring budget and can't afford to hire an expert or don't have the time to become one yourself, consider the following bits of advice:

✔ **Forgo TV ads and put your video to work in more forgiving venues.** Simple video can look great in other contexts, like your website or a stand at a trade show, even if it would look out of place on television. (See the 'Finding Cheaper Ways to Use the Power of Video' section earlier in this chapter.)

✔ **Consider doing a self-made *spoof ad*.** Make fun of one of the silly TV ad genres, such as the one where a man dressed in black scales mountain peaks and jumps over waterfalls to deliver a box of chocolates to a beautiful woman. Because the whole point is to make a campy spoof, you don't want high production values. You can follow this strategy on your own pretty easily, but you still need help from someone with experience in setting up shots and handling cameras and lights.

✔ **Find a film student at a nearby college who's eager to help you produce your ad.** To budding film-makers, your video is an opportunity to show they can do professional work. For you, using a student may be an opportunity to get near-professional work at a very low price. But make sure the terms are clear upfront. Both the student and his tutor need to clarify (in writing) that you'll own the resulting work and use it in your marketing.

Getting emotional

TV differs from other media in the obvious way – by combining action, audio and video – but these features make TV different in less obvious ways as well. Evoking emotions in TV and video is especially easy, just like in traditional theatre. When planning to use TV as your marketing tool, always think about what emotion you want your audience to feel.

Select an emotional state that fits best with your appeal and the creative concept behind your ad. Then use the power of imagery to evoke that emotion. This strategy works whether your appeal is emotional or rational. Always use the emotional power of TV to prepare your audience to receive that appeal. Surprise, excitement, empathy, anxiety, scepticism, thirst, hunger or the protective instincts of the parent – you can create all of these emotional states and more in your audience with a few seconds of TV. A good ad creates the right emotion for your appeal. The classic Hamlet cigar ad, which no longer appears on TV, always aimed for a strictly emotional appeal ('Happiness is a cigar called Hamlet'). Even though that ad hasn't been on the box for years, we bet you can still hear the music as you read that line.

Some marketers measure their TV ads based on warmth. Research firms generally define warmth as the good feelings generated from thinking about love, family or friendship. Although you may not need to go into the details of how researchers measure warmth, noting *why* people measure it can help you. Emotions, especially positive ones, make TV ad messages far more memorable. Many marketers don't realise the strength of this emotional effect because you can't pick it up in the standard measures of ad recall. In day-after recall tests, viewers recall emotional-appeal TV ads about as easily as rational-appeal ads. But in-depth studies of the effectiveness of each kind of ad tend to show that the more emotionally charged ads do a better job of etching the message and branding identity in viewers' minds.

So when you think TV advertising, think emotion. Evoking emotion is what TV can do – often better than any other media, because it can showcase the expressiveness of actors and faces – and emotion makes for highly effective advertising.

Showing your message

Be sure to take full advantage of TV's other great strength: its ability to show. You can demonstrate a product feature, show a product in use and do a thousand other things just with your visuals.

Actually, in any ad medium, you want to show as well as tell. (Even in radio, you can create mental images to show the audience what you want them to see, see 'Creating Ads for Radio' earlier in this chapter.) The visual and verbal modes reinforce each other. And some people in your audience think visually while others favour a verbal message, so you have to cover both bases by using words and images in your advertising. But in TV, you have to adapt this rule: the TV ad should *show* and tell (note the emphasis on showing). Compare this scenario with radio, where you show by telling; or print, where the two modes balance each other out, so the rule becomes simply to show and tell.

Because of this emphasis on showing, TV ad designers rough out their ideas in a visually-oriented script, using quick sketches to indicate how the ad will look. You – or preferably the competent agency or scriptwriter you hire – need to prepare rough storyboards as you think through and discuss various ad concepts. A *storyboard* is an easy way to show the key visual images of film, using pictures in sequence. The sketches run down the centre of a sheet of paper or poster board in most standard storyboard layouts. On the left, you write notes about how to shoot each image, how to use music and sound effects, and whether to superimpose text on the screen. On the right, you include a rough version of the *script* (the words actors in the scenes or in a voice-over say). See Figure 5-1 for an example storyboard.

Considering style

You can use a great variety of styles in TV advertising. A celebrity can endorse the product. Fruit modelled from clay (claymation) can sing and dance about it. Animated animals can chase a user through the jungle in a fanciful exaggeration of a real-life situation. Imagination and videotape know no limits, especially with the growing availability of high-quality computerised animation and special effects at a reasonable cost. But some of the common styles work better – on average – than others in tests of ad effectiveness. Table 5-1 shows styles that are more and less effective.

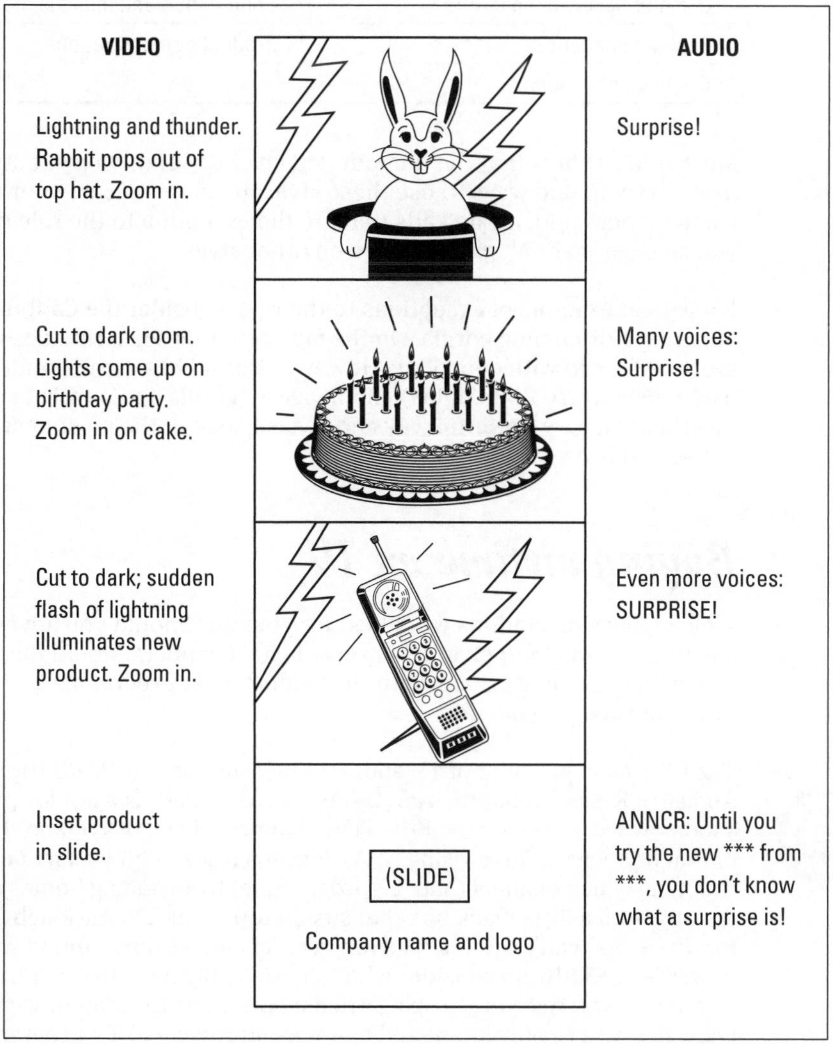

VIDEO		AUDIO
Lightning and thunder. Rabbit pops out of top hat. Zoom in.		Surprise!
Cut to dark room. Lights come up on birthday party. Zoom in on cake.		Many voices: Surprise!
Cut to dark; sudden flash of lightning illuminates new product. Zoom in.		Even more voices: SURPRISE!
Inset product in slide.	(SLIDE) Company name and logo	ANNCR: Until you try the new *** from ***, you don't know what a surprise is!

Figure 5-1: Roughing out a TV ad on a storyboard.

Table 5-1	It Don't Mean a Thing If It Ain't Got That Swing
More Effective Styles	*Less Effective Styles*
Humorous commercials	Candid-camera style testimonials
Celebrity spokespeople	Expert endorsements
Commercials with children	Song/dance and musical themes
Real-life scenarios	Product demonstrations
Brand comparisons	

Most studies show that the humour and celebrity endorsement styles work best. So try to find ways to use these styles to communicate your message. On the other hand, making ads that are the exception to the rule may give you an edge, so don't give up hope on other styles.

For a great example of exceptions to the rule, consider the Cadbury's ad featuring a drumming gorilla. On the face of it, this scenario doesn't have a great deal to do with chocolate. However, this ad has great standout value, uses music (retro Phil Collins) and imagery (gorilla and purple background) together in a very powerful way and is easily one of the most memorable ads of the past few years.

Buying airtime on TV

Which television stations work best for your ad? Should you advertise on a national (*terrestrial*) channel or on a digital channel? Should the ad run in prime time, evening or late night-time slots? What programmes provide the best audience for your ad?

The UK's main provider of TV audience measurement is BARB (Broadcasters' Audience Research Board; www.barb.co.uk). BARB is a not-for-profit organisation owned jointly by the BBC, ITV, Channel 4, Five, BSkyB and the Institute of Practitioners in Advertising (IPA). It keeps track of how many people are watching which channel (and TV programme) by installing homes around the country with a little black box that sits on top of the TV. Although BARB is not for profit, you can't get this data for free. An annual subscription will cost you upwards of £5,910, so consider whether you really need that depth of data. For instance, if you're trying to sell gardening products to amateur gardeners and know that you're only interested in home-improvement TV programmes, the channels themselves can give you the viewing figures you need.

Some of BARB's biggest customers are the ad and media-buying agencies, so if you're using an agency to buy your airtime or create your ad, asking them for media data before getting out your own credit card is worthwhile.

Working out the cost of a TV ad

Several different factors affect how much you pay for a TV advertising campaign.

The first, and most important, bit of jargon you need to know is *TVRs*, which means television ratings. Audience delivery is measured in TVRs, which can be confusing but has the merit of giving you an idea of how many people in a particular target audience will see your ad. Knowledge of target audiences is important to avoid wasting money advertising to people who're unlikely to buy your product. A TVR is defined as the percentage of a particular audience that has seen a piece of TV content (although they may have spent an ad break talking to their partner or making the tea, so this figure is always an approximation). So, for example, if *Coronation Street* achieved a Housewives TVR of 20 in Yorkshire, this means that 20 per cent of all housewives in the Yorkshire region watched the soap opera.

You can actually get a TVR for your ad that's higher than 100 per cent, which means that a viewer may see your ad more than once and this is counted separately each time. The actual number of times viewers are exposed to a commercial break is called *impacts*. If you think that repeat viewing is important to your campaign, these can be useful programmes or times of the day to target.

Identifying your target audience

You can choose any of the target audiences, shown in the following list, that are commonly sold by broadcasters. Heavy TV viewers such as housewives or general audiences are usually cheaper to buy because they're easier to reach than audiences such as upmarket men.

Adults

16- to 34-year-old adults

ABC1 (upmarket) adults

Men

16- to 34-year-old men

ABC1 men

Women

16- to 34-year-old women

ABC1 women

Housewives

Housewives and children

ABC1 housewives

Children

Timing your broadcast

The size and type of audience likely to see your ad is governed by the time of day it appears – so that factor will also affect how much you pay. Broadcasters call these *dayparts*, and they're timed as follows:

Daytime: 6am–5.29pm

Early peak: 5.30–7.29pm

Late peak: 7.30–11pm

Night-time: 11.01pm–5.59am

Some broadcasters may break down these dayparts even further, adding in such elements as 'breakfast time' during the day. The highest price you usually pay is for the highest audience – in peak time, between 5.30pm and 11pm, although again this timing can vary.

Remembering other factors

You also need to factor in a few other variables to the cost of your ad:

- ✔ **The length of your commercial.** Airtime is sold in multiples of 10 seconds, with 30 seconds being the most common ad length.

- ✔ **What time of year you need to advertise.** If you're in the business of selling Christmas gifts, you pay considerably more for airtime than if you can advertise in the cheaper months of January, February, March and August.

- ✔ **Size of the region you advertise in.** Prices also vary by *macro region*, which reflects the size of the local population and relative demand. The highest advertiser demand is for London, which makes it the most expensive. If you operate outside London, however, targeting the precise areas where you're based, such as Yorkshire or Tyne-Tees, may be more cost-effective. Some TV macro regions can even be split into *micro regions*. So if your business is in the East Anglia area, for instance, you can buy just that small part of the larger Anglia macro region, giving you tighter targeting and better value for money. You can find a good explanation of how the regions are broken down on the website of TV marketing body, Thinkbox (www.thinkbox.tv). Look under 'Planning', then 'Targeting', then 'Regional TV'.

Because of the complexity of some of these calculations, think hard about using a media agency to plan and buy the airtime. You can let a media agency know what you're trying to achieve with your ad and what type of people you need to target and then let their experts do the rest. Many of these agencies buy up chunks of airtime in advance, so you benefit from an agency-wide deal and don't have to negotiate individually with the TV sales houses. Media agencies can also advise you on TV opportunities you may not have previously considered.

Making your own TV (or radio) programme

A lot of TV and radio ads exist out there and yours is in constant danger of becoming just one of the many that people are exposed to and increasingly, trying to avoid. You don't want your ad to be the one that makes the viewer leave the room to make the tea. The following sections give you a few alternative strategies to consider.

Using advertiser-funded programming (AFP)

The experts have come up with a new term, *branded content*, to describe something that isn't quite an ad but which can be used to communicate a commercial message. In TV and radio, branded content means creating your own show (or at least, segment of a show) – the official term for which is *advertiser-funded programming* or *AFP*. This type of communication is becoming increasingly frequent, although many restrictions are still in place about what you can or cannot say about your product. But asking your agency, or the radio stations and channels themselves, about these opportunities is worthwhile because they allow your message to stand out from the clutter of all the other ads.

Book VI

Growing and Improving Your Business

Vodafone TBA and *Transmission With T-Mobile* are just two examples of AFP. Both of these shows have been screened on Channel 4. *Vodafone TBA* involves the telecoms company organising 'secret' gigs by stars, including rapper Kanye West. The gigs are then shown on TV. *Transmission With T-Mobile* is a Friday night TV music show, which includes street gigs hosted by the mobile phone company. This type of communication is generating a lot of excitement because it allows advertisers to give viewers something they want (entertainment) rather than something many of them don't (ads).

Now look at those programme names again. The real benefit of AFP is that you can give viewers *relevant content* or information that's close to your product or service. Vodafone and T-Mobile use these shows to promote their growing music services. Don't get too close, though. Heinz nearly got fined by the TV regulators for showing recipes that used baked beans and spaghetti hoops when it ran a show called *Dinner Doctors* on Five in 2003. This area is still in development, but AFP will become a popular route for advertisers and you need to look out for likely opportunities.

The social networks, such as Bebo, are also creating programme placement and branded content opportunities for brands (see Chapter 2 of Book V for more on social marketing). As yet, the regulations relating to brands and content online aren't as restrictive as those for TV. Online soap operas such as *Sofia's Diary*, which showed on Bebo in 2008, attract millions of young viewers. *Sofia's Diary* gathered 5 million viewers in its first month and featured Unilever's Sure deodorant brand and Pearl Drops toothpaste as part of the storyline. As a result of its popularity, this soap opera later went on to appear on a digital channel, Fiver, moving from the computer screen to the TV screen.

Sponsoring a TV or radio programme

If AFP is still waiting in the wings, then sponsorship must be centre stage. All right, you don't quite get your own TV or radio programme, but if you find a show that's a good fit with your product, this route's almost as good (and a lot less risky).

TV and radio sponsorship is growing fast in the UK as advertisers try to avoid the dual issues of ad clutter and digital personal video recorders (PVRs) such as Sky+, BT Vision and TiVo, which allow viewers to skip through the ad break. You don't need us to tell you that TV and radio sponsorship is growing – you'll have seen it for yourself. TV sponsorship was worth around £190 million last year; *Loose Women* and Maltesers, *Wrigley's* and Hollyoaks and Bombardier English Bitter and *Al Murray's Happy Hour* are all good examples of current sponsorship deals because you can see how the brands are relevant to the programmes.

You don't need to pay anything like the £10 million that Cadbury paid to sponsor *Coronation Street* for three years. You can find relevant programmes at less popular times of the day, or on digital channels, for a sponsorship price of around £150,000.

Advertising on interactive TV

Interactive TV advertising has more in common with traditional spot TV advertising, but we include it here because, if you can get viewers to press the red button on their remote control, you can take them away from the mainstream TV environment and into your own dedicated space. This ability represents both the opportunity and the main problem with this medium.

Interactive TV advertising gives you a lot of opportunities to do things a traditional 30-second spot won't. You can give additional product information, issue a call to action (such as requesting a brochure) or capture your prospective customers' data. You can even fulfil a transaction entirely using interactive TV ads. An additional cost for constructing the microsite and capturing the data (upwards of £100,000) is entailed, though, on top of the cost of the airtime for the ad itself. The benefit of interactive TV ads is that you get real, measurable customer transactions from your investment – something that traditional TV advertising can't always deliver.

The drawback is that the viewer is actually watching TV to see a certain programme and so may not want to be distracted by going off into an advertiser controlled environment during the ad break in case they miss the start of the next part of the show. This market is still developing and trials of 'red button' advertising that loads information 'behind' the viewed show, to be watched later, seem promising.

Advertising online

Television is no longer confined to the box in the corner of the living room; it also appears on your computer. You may think the computer is a relatively small market but nearly a third of all Internet users watched video clips and webcasts in 2007, according to a report by the UK communications regulator, Ofcom. This figure is 50 per cent higher than the previous year.

Multiple TV streaming and download channels are now available for all the main broadcasters on terrestrial television, and also web-only channels such as Babelgum and Joost. As these are still relatively new media channels, you may find opportunities to get involved with sponsorship or advertising at a lower cost than with normal TV. And if you're targeting young people who use the web a lot, this medium may be the best place to promote your products or services.

Even if you don't have the budget or know how to appear on an online TV channel, why not consider using video site YouTube? You can post a version of your ad on the site, create a little trailer to promote your product or even just come up with a humorous spot to generate interest. If your product needs some explaining or assembling, why not create a 'how-to' video? You may be surprised by how many people find a demonstration useful and how offering one may bring publicity to your company through sites such as YouTube and `www.videojug.com`.

Even huge brands use YouTube to generate interest in their products and marketing. The American Super Bowl, during which the biggest and most expensive ads are shown each year, even has its own branded channel on YouTube! People can see the ads, post their own spoofs and leave comments. YouTube offers a tool for research, feedback and promotion all in one. Just make sure that you monitor any responses to your promotional work carefully!

Chapter 6

Becoming a Great Manager

. . . .

In This Chapter

▶ Seeing why you need a team and how to build one

▶ Planning for your own successor

▶ Delegating effectively

▶ Developing the right leadership style

▶ Preparing for change

. . . .

*I*n business, one of the simplest profit calculations is profit per employee. Until you become a massive company with more than 500 employees, each employee you add increases your profit. Still, you needn't worry too much about what happens when you have 500 employees on your hands. Well, not in this book, anyway.

But employees aren't a trouble-free resource. To maximise the employee–profit ratio, you have to manage your employees so that they produce quality work for you. You have to build them into teams, and lead and manage them to prepare them for the roller-coaster life of change that is the inevitable lot of a small, growing business.

In this chapter, we give you the tools you need to become a successful and effective manager.

Building a Team

Teams are a powerful way to get superb results out of even the most average individual employees. With effective teamwork, a small firm can raise its efficiency levels to world-class standards. Some small firms have built their entire success around teams.

Identifying a successful team

A group of people working together isn't necessarily a team. A successful sports team has the right number of players for the game, each with a clearly defined role. The team has a coach, to train and improve players' performances, and measurable goals to achieve in the shape of obvious competitors to beat. Contrast that with the situation that usually prevails in a typical small firm. The number of players is the number who turn up on a particular day, and few have specific roles to play. Some are trained and properly equipped and some aren't. For the most part the business's objectives aren't clearly explained to employees, nor are any performance-measuring tools disclosed. Most of the players in the home team are highly likely not even to know the name or characteristics of the enemy against whom they're competing.

Clearly, a successful sports team and an unorganised group of co-workers have little in common, but you can clearly see what you need to do to weld people at work into a team.

Successful teams have certain features in common. They all have:

- ✔ Strong and effective leadership
- ✔ Clear objectives
- ✔ Appropriate resources
- ✔ The ability to communicate freely throughout the organisation
- ✔ The authority to act quickly on decisions
- ✔ A good balance of team members, with complementary skills and talents
- ✔ The ability to work collectively
- ✔ A size appropriate to the task

However talented the soloists are in a small business, in the end orchestras are what make enough noise to wake up slumbering customers and make them aware of your virtues as a supplier. But teams don't just happen. However neat the curricula vitae and however convincing the organisational chart, you can't just turn out a team-in-a-box. The presumption that people are naturally going to work together is usually a mistake. Chaos is more likely than teamwork.

Founding principles

Successful teams share common principles, outlined in the following list.

✔ **Balanced team roles:** Every team member must have a valuable team role. Experts in team behaviour such as R Meredith Belbin have identified the key team profiles that are essential if a team is to function well (you can find full details on Belbin's widely used team role evaluation system at www.belbin.com or by calling 01223-264975). Any one person may perform more than one of these roles. But if too many people are competing to perform one of the roles, or if one or more of these roles is neglected, the team is unbalanced. Its members then perform in much the same way as a car does when a cylinder misfires. The key roles that Belbin describes are:

- **Chairperson/team leader:** Stable, dominant, extrovert. Concentrates on objectives. Does not originate ideas. Focuses people on what they do best.

- **Plant:** Dominant, high IQ, introvert. A 'scatterer of seeds' who originates ideas. Misses out on detail. Thrusting but easily offended.

- **Resource investigator:** Stable, dominant, extrovert and sociable. Lots of contacts with the outside world. Strong on networks. Salesperson/diplomat/liaison officer. Not an original thinker.

- **Shaper:** Anxious, dominant, extrovert. Emotional and impulsive. Quick to challenge and to respond to a challenge. Unites ideas, objectives and possibilities. Competitive. Intolerant of woolliness and vagueness.

- **Company worker:** Stable, controlled. A practical organiser. Can be inflexible but likely to adapt to established systems. Not an innovator.

- **Monitor evaluator:** High IQ, stable, introvert. Goes in for measured analysis not innovation. Unambiguous and often lacking enthusiasm, but solid and dependable.

- **Team worker:** Stable, extrovert, but not really dominant. Much concerned with individuals' needs. Builds on others' ideas. Cools things down when tempers fray.

- **Finisher:** Anxious introvert. Worries over what may go wrong. Permanent sense of urgency. Preoccupied with order. Concerned with 'following through'.

✔ **Shared vision and goal:** The team members must have ownership of their own measurable and clearly defined goals. This means involving the team in business planning. It also means keeping the communication channels open as the business grows. Those in the founding team knew clearly what they were trying to achieve and because they probably shared an office they shared information as they worked. But as the group gets larger and new people join, you have to help the informal communication systems work better. Briefing meetings, social events and bulletin boards are all ways to get teams together and keep them facing the right way.

✔ **Shared language:** To be a member of a business team, people have to have a reasonable grasp of the language of business. Extolling people to improve return on capital employed or reduce debtor days isn't much use if they have only the haziest notion of what those terms mean, why they matter or how they can influence the business's results. So you need to develop rounded business skills across all the core team members through continuous training, development and coaching.

✔ **Compatible personalities:** Although having different team profiles is important, having a team who can get on with one another is equally vital. Team members have to be able to listen to and respect the others' ideas and views. They need to support and trust one another. They need to be able to accept conflict as a healthy reality and work through it to a successful outcome.

✔ **Good leadership:** First-class leadership is perhaps the most important characteristic that distinguishes winning teams from the also-rans. However good the constituent parts, without leadership a team rapidly disintegrates into a rabble bound by little but a pay cheque.

You can't just pick people and put them into teams because of their particular professional or job skills. If the team is to function effectively, its balance of behavioural styles has to mesh too.

Coaching and Training

Coaching and training are two ways to help individuals and teams improve their performance.

A *coach* is a skilled and experienced person who watches an individual or small group performing a task. The coach shows them individually how they can improve their performance. The emphasis is on personalised instruction. *Training* is usually a more formal process, where the trainer has a set agenda for the event based on the knowledge required by the trainees. Everyone being trained goes through much the same process, at the same time.

Small firms are notoriously bad at recognising the need for training of any type. Over 40 per cent of small firms devote only one day or less to staff training each year. Only 13 per cent invest five days or more in training. Amateur football teams spend more time in training than the average small firm, so the fact that few teams in that firm ever realise their true potential, or come anywhere near becoming professionals, is hardly surprising.

And yet all the evidence is that training pays a handsome and quick return.

The choices a small firm has for training are:

- ✔ **On-the-job coaching:** This is where people learn from someone more experienced about how a job should be done. The advantages are that this kind of coaching is free and involves no time away from work. It should also directly relate to an individual's training needs. However, the coaching is only as good as the coach, and if the coach is untrained you may end up simply replicating poor working standards.

- ✔ **In-house classroom training:** This is the most traditional and familiar form of training. Some, or all, of your employees gather in a 'classroom', either on your premises or in a local hotel. You hire in a trainer or use one of your own experienced staff. This method provides plenty of opportunity for group interaction and the instructor can motivate the class and pay some attention to individual needs. The disadvantages, particularly if you hold the training away from your premises, are that you incur large costs that are more to do with hospitality than training, and for a small firm, releasing a number of employees at the same time is time-consuming and difficult.

- ✔ **Public courses:** These are less expensive than running a training programme in a hotel. You can also select different courses for different employees and so tailor the training more precisely to their needs. However, most public courses are generic and the other attendees are more likely to come from big business or even the public sector, so much of what is covered may be of little direct relevance to your business. Quality can be patchy.

- ✔ **Interactive distance learning:** This kind of training can be delivered by a combination of traditional training materials, teleconferencing and the Internet and email discussions. You miss out on the personal contact, but the costs are much lower than traditional training. Most of the learning programmes are aimed at larger firms, so some material may not be so relevant.

- ✔ **Off-the-shelf training programmes:** These come in packaged kits, which may consist of a training manual, video and/or a CD-ROM. Once again, the cost is lower than for face-to-face training, but you miss out on a professional trainer's input.

- ✔ **College courses:** Many universities and business schools now offer programmes tailored to the needs of small firms. Professional instructors who understand the needs of small firms deliver these courses. They're relatively expensive, but can often be very effective.

- ✔ **Government initiatives:** Governments have an interest in encouraging training in small firms. As well as providing information on where their training schemes are being run, governments often provide training grants to help with the costs.

Book VI

Growing and Improving Your Business

To make sure that you get the best out of your training, follow these guidelines.

- ✔ Introduce a routine that ensures that all employees attending training are briefed at least a week beforehand on what to expect and what you expect of them.

- ✔ Ensure that all employees discuss with you or their manager or supervisor what they got out of the training programme – in particular, did it meet both their expectations? This should take place no later than a week after the programme.

- ✔ You or the manager need to check within a month, and then again at regular intervals, to see whether their skills have improved, and that they're putting those skills into practice.

Evaluate the costs and financial benefits of your training and development plans, and use this information to help set next year's training budget.

You can find a training course or programme for yourself and anyone you employ from Business Link (go to www.businesslink.gov.uk, then click on Employment and skills followed by Find and fund training, How to find a Provider/Course.) The Massachusetts Institute of Technology (http://ocw.mit.edu/index.htm) makes virtually all its courses freely available on the World Wide Web for non-commercial use, as part of its long-standing objective to focus the contributions of both its faculty and its new technologies on broad, societal benefits.

Appraising Performance

Appraising the performance of both teams and individuals isn't primarily concerned with blame, reward or praise. Its purpose is to develop people and help them perform better and be able to achieve their career goals. The result of an appraisal is a personal development plan.

Appraisal lies at the heart of assessing, improving and developing people's performance for the future of the business. However, for it to be an effective tool, everyone involved needs to approach appraisal seriously and professionally. The appraisal has to be a discussion between people who work together rather than simply a boss dictating to a subordinate. It should be an open, two-way discussion for which both the appraiser and appraisee prepare in advance.

The ground rules for successful appraisals are:

✔ It should be results-oriented. The appraisal interview starts with a review against objectives and finishes by setting objectives for the year to come.

Set intermediate goals and objectives for new staff even if you can't realistically set final goals. For example, challenge new salespeople to acquire product knowledge and visit all the key customers, leaving actual sales achievement objectives until later in the year.

✔ The appraisal discussion should be separate from salary review. A discussion about salary is unlikely to encourage people to be open and frank, but an appraisal must be both those things. The salary review and the appraisal must be seen as different events and if possible carried out at different times of the year.

✔ The appraisal format is a narrative rather than consisting of tick boxes and ratings schedules. It covers a discussion of achievements, areas for improvement, overall performance, training and development, and career expectations.

Allow plenty of time for each appraisal interview (one and a half hours on average). The setting should be free from interruptions and unthreatening.

Carry out appraisals at least once a year, with more regular quarterly reviews – you need to review new staff after three months. Some owner-managers question the necessity of a formal annual appraisal when they feel that they're already appraising their team informally on a day-to-day basis. That approach is rather like trying to assess a business by its daily trading figures rather than its annual profit and loss account. The changes in behaviour and performance you're trying to assess happen over a longer time span and may not be easy to see on a day-to-day basis. Also, your daily assessments are likely to be influenced by pressures and feelings on the day and may not reflect the true longer-term picture.

Use appraisals to identify training needs and incorporate any deficiencies into a personal or company-wide training plan.

EPIC Training and Consulting Services has a free Workforce Development Toolkit on its website, including a guide on carrying out appraisals and templates for both appraiser and appraisee (`http://workforce.epicltd.com`).

Developing a Leadership Style

Most large organisations have grown up according to basic management principles. If you started your business career working for a bigger firm, or your present managers worked in such enterprises, you know the scenario.

Managers in these organisations plan, organise and control in a way that produces consistent if unexciting results. The formula worked remarkably well for much of the 20th century, when all a successful company had to do to prosper was more of the same. But management that's all about maintaining order and predictability is ill-equipped to deal with change, which is the order of the day in the 21st century. To cope with change effectively you need to be a leader as well as a competent manager – and young businesses are in greater need of leaders than they are of managers, at the outset at least.

Understanding leadership

Leadership and management aren't the same, although many businesspeople fail to make the distinction. The late management professor Peter Drucker summed up the difference between leaders and managers thus: 'A leader challenges the status quo; a manager accepts it.'

In a world where product lifecycles are shrinking, new technologies have an ever shorter shelf life and customers demand faster delivery and higher quality, the leader's job increasingly means defining and inspiring change within a company. By setting a company's direction, communicating this to its workforce, motivating employees and taking a long-range perspective, a leader adapts the firm to whatever volatile environment it does business in. In short, leaders become the change masters in their own firms.

Delegating

Overwork is a common complaint of those running their own business. They never have enough time to think or plan. But if you don't make time to plan you can never move forward.

Delegating some tasks eases the stress. *Delegation* is the art of getting things done your way by other people. Or as one entrepreneur succinctly put it, 'making other people happy to make you rich'.

Many owner-managers are unable to delegate, either because they draw comfort from sticking to routine tasks such as sending out invoices, rather than tackling new and unfamiliar ones such as keeping up on developments in the industry, or because they just don't know how to delegate. Either way, neither the business nor those in it can grow until delegation becomes the normal way to operate.

Delegating brings benefits to everyone involved in the process.

Benefits for the boss include:

- ✔ **More time to achieve more today and to plan for the future:** In this way you can free up time to tackle high-value-added tasks such as recruitment and selection, or motivation.

- ✔ **Back-up for emergencies and day-to-day tasks:** By delegating, you have a reserve of skilled people who can keep the business running profitably if you're not there. This can also give customers and financial backers the comfort of knowing that they aren't dealing with a one-person operation that would fall apart without you.

Benefits for employees include:

- ✔ **The opportunity to develop new skills:** Failing to delegate deprives employees of the opportunity to learn new skills and to grow themselves, and drives good employees, just the ones a growing organisation desperately needs, away in search of greater challenges. Employees who have assumed the responsibility for new tasks train their staff in the same way. Then the organisation can grow and have in-depth management.

- ✔ **Greater involvement:** Research consistently shows that employees rank job satisfaction to be of equal or greater value than pay. Delegation encourages people to take ownership of their decisions and increases their enthusiasm and initiative for their work, so they get more satisfaction from their work.

Benefits for the business are:

- ✔ **Efficiency improves** by allowing those closest to the problems and issues being faced to take the decisions in a timely manner.

- ✔ **Flexibility of operations increases** because several people are able to perform key tasks. In this way you can rotate and expand or contract teams and tasks to meet changing circumstances. Delegation also results in more people being prepared for promotion.

Delegation is a management process that you shouldn't confuse with 'dumping', in which unpopular, difficult or tedious tasks are unceremoniously shoved onto the shoulders of the first person who comes to hand. To make delegation work successfully, adopt the following five-point plan.

Book VI

Growing and Improving Your Business

1. **Decide what and what not to delegate.**

   The general questions for deciding what should be delegated are:

   - Can anyone else do or be trained to do the work to a satisfactory standard?

   - Is all the information necessary to carry out the task available to the person(s) to whom you're planning to delegate the task?

   - Is the task largely operational rather than strategic?

   - Would delegating the task save you a reasonable amount of time?

   - Would some initial teething problems while the new person settles into the task cause undue problems? Delegation itself is a form of risk taking, so if you can't deal with a few mistakes then delegation proves difficult.

   - Can someone other than you properly exercise direct control over the task?

   You can usually readily delegate any routine jobs, information gathering or assignments involving extensive detail or calculations. Tasks that are less easy to delegate include all confidential work, discipline, staff evaluation and complex or sensitive issues.

2. **Decide to whom to delegate.**

   The factors to consider here are:

   - Who has the necessary skills?

   - Who could or should be groomed for future promotion?

   - Who's most likely to respond well to the challenge?

   - Who's most likely to be or continue to be a loyal employee?

   - Whose workload allows her to take on the task(s)?

3. **Communicate your decision.**

   Approaches to consider here are:

   - Discuss the task you propose to delegate one to one with the individual concerned.

   - Confirm that she feels up to the task or agree any necessary training, back-up or extra resources.

   - Set out clearly in writing the task broken down into its main components, the measurable outcomes, the timescales and any other important factors.

   - Allow time for the implications to sink in and then discuss with the person concerned how she proposes going about the task.

   - Let others in the business know of your decision.

4. **Manage and evaluate.**

From the beginning, clearly establish set times to meet the person delegated to and review her performance. Make the intervals between these reviews short at first, lengthening the period when the person's performance is satisfactory. The secret of successful delegation is to follow up.

5. **Reward results.**

Things that get measured get done and those that are rewarded get done over again. The reward need not be financial. Recognition or praise for a job well done is often more valuable to an ambitious person than money.

Evolving leadership styles for growth

All businesses require leadership, but they don't require the same type or amount of leadership all the time. As with children, businesses don't grow seamlessly from being babies to adulthood. They pass through phases – infancy, adolescence, teenage years and so on. Businesses also move through phases if they're to grow successfully. Each of these phases is punctuated by a *crisis*, used in this sense to signify a dangerous opportunity.

Researchers have identified several distinctive phases in a firm's growth pattern, which provide an insight into the changes in organisational structure, strategy and behaviour that you need to move successfully on to the next phase of growth. The inability to recognise the phases of growth and to manage the transition through them is probably the single most important reason for most owner-managed firms failing to achieve their true potential, let alone their founder's dreams.

Typically, a business starts out taking on any customers it can get, operating informally, with little management and few controls. The founder – who usually provides all the ideas, brings all the drive, makes all the decisions and signs the cheques – becomes overloaded with administrative detail and operational problems. Unless the founder can change the organisational structure, any further growth leaves the business more vulnerable. The crises of leadership, autonomy and control loom large.

Over time, the successful owner-manager tackles these crises and finds a clear focus, builds a first-class team, delegates key tasks, appraises performance, institutes control and reporting systems, and ensures that progress towards objectives is monitored and rewarded. The firm itself consistently delivers good results. There's no set time that each of these phases should last. A firm may take anything from three to ten years to reach the third phase of growth.

Each phase of growth calls for a different approach to leading the business. At times strong leadership is required; at others a more consultative approach is appropriate. Some phases call for more systems and procedures, some for more co-operation between staff. Unfortunately, as the business gets bigger most founders try to run their business in much the same way as they did when it was small. They end up with a big small company, rather than the small big company that they require if they're to achieve successful growth. They believe that taking on another salesperson, a few hundred square metres of space or another bank loan can solve the problems of growth. This approach is rather like suggesting that the transition from infancy to adulthood can be accomplished by nothing more significant than providing larger clothes.

Managing change

The late professor Peter Drucker claimed that the first task of a leader is to define the company's mission. In a world in which product and service lifecycles are shrinking, new technologies have ever shorter shelf lives and customers demand ever higher levels of both quality and innovation. Entrepreneurial leadership means inspiring change.

Being flexible enough to change

In adapting the business to an increasingly volatile and competitive environment, the boss must become the change master in the firm. Small firms are usually better at handling change than big firms. A speedboat can always alter course faster than a supertanker. However, small firms often have to adapt to much more change than big established firms. Big firms usually define the standards in an industry and the small firms have to scramble to keep up.

The turbulence created by changes in the economy can also create a wash that can sink small firms unless they can adapt and change quickly. Those small firms most able to adapt and change, and of course those who are most prepared, are most likely to survive and prosper during turbulent times.

But recognising the need for change falls a long way short of being able to implement it successfully. Few people like change and even fewer can adapt to new circumstances quickly and without missing a heartbeat.

By definition, a small business seeking growth must be able to manage a fast rate of change. Entrepreneurs must see change as the norm and not as a temporary and unexpected disruption that goes away when conditions improve.

Planning for change

Change management is a business process, like any other business process. Following a tried and proven procedure can improve your chances of getting it right more often.

These four steps show how you can break down change management into its elements.

1. **Tell staff why change is necessary (or better still, help them to find out for themselves).**

   The benefits of change aren't always obvious. So spell them out in much the same way as you explain the benefits of your product or service to a prospective customer.

   Explaining the background to the changes you want to make helps people see the changes as an opportunity to be competitive rather than a threat to existing work practices.

   Better than just explaining is to encourage staff to look outside the business for themselves, identify potential problems and suggest their own solutions. Not only may they have great ideas for change – perhaps better than yours – but they may be more willing to take responsibility for making the changes succeed.

2. **Make the change manageable.**

   Even when people are dissatisfied with the present position and know exactly what needs to be done to improve things, the change may still not happen. The change may be just too big for anyone to handle. But if you break the change down into manageable bits, you can make it happen.

3. **Take a shared approach.**

   Involve people early on. Asking them to join you in managing change only at the implementation stage is too late to get their full co-operation. Give your key participants some say in shaping the change right from the start. This means that nobody feels that you're imposing the change and more brains are brought to bear on the problem.

   Individual resistance to change is a normal reaction. By understanding why people are resisting you can help them overcome their doubts and embrace the change. Try to anticipate the impact of the change on the people involved:

   • Get an overview of the forces at work, both in favour of and against the change.

- Make a list of those most affected by the change. Put each person into one of four categories – no commitment; will let it happen if others want it; will help it happen; will make it happen.

  Examine how each person is likely to be affected by the change. Look at career prospects, working hours and conditions, team membership and so forth.

  - Anticipate retraining. Often a fear of failing is the principal reason for people not trying something new.

Open, face-to-face communication is the backbone of successful change. It gets across the 'why' of change and allows people to face up to problems openly. It also builds confidence and clears up misunderstandings.

Open communication is vital, but announcing intended changes before you have some committed participants alongside you is risky.

4. **Reinforce individual and team identity.**

   People are more willing to accept change and to move from the known to the unknown if they have confidence in themselves and their boss. Confidence is most likely to exist where people have a high degree of self-esteem. Building up self-esteem involves laying stress on the positive rather than the negative aspects of each person's contribution. Exhortations such as 'you guys have had it too easy for too long' are unlikely to do much for people when you're faced with major competitive pressure.

   You need to emphasise the importance to the change project of each person, both as an individual and, where appropriate, as a team member. A positive, confident climate for change needs lots of reinforcement, such as the following ideas:

   - Reward achievement of new goals and achieving them quickly.

   - Highlight success stories and create as many winners as possible.

   - Hold social events to celebrate milestones.

   - Pay personal attention to those most affected by the change.

Change takes longer than you think. Most major changes make things worse before they make them better. More often than not, the immediate impact of change is a decrease in productivity, as people struggle to cope with new ways of working while they move up their own learning curve.

The doubters can gloat and even the change champions may waver. But the greatest danger now is pulling the plug on the plan and either adopting a new plan or reverting to the status quo.

To prevent this 'disappointment', you have to set realistic goals for the change period and anticipate and plan how to handle the time lag between change and results.

Measuring Morale

How your employees feel about their jobs, their co-workers, the company, and you and other bosses has a direct effect on how well or poorly they do their jobs. You need to stay on top of morale issues to keep your business running smoothly.

The most reliable way to measure morale at work is to carry out an attitude survey. In a big company, one-to-one interviews and focus groups may accompany such surveys. But in a small firm that's not really an option.

In much the same way as you may survey customers to find out how happy they are with your products and services, survey your employees to find out what they feel about their employment conditions. Attitude surveys provide an objective measure to counterbalance the more descriptive view that you can obtain from discussions and gossip. They also provide a useful way to see whether morale is getting better or worse over time.

Book VI

Growing and Improving Your Business

You may decide to introduce attitude surveys because of a particular event, such as a number of key staff leaving at the same time or some other obvious problem. Change can upset morale and that can have a knock-on effect on business performance. But after you've started, keeping the practice up makes sense. At the very least surveying your employees demonstrates your concern, and at the best it gives you valuable pointers to raising morale, output and profits.

A word of warning: your attitude surveys are inevitably going to reveal two basic facts. The first is that everyone believes that they're underpaid. The second is that everyone believes that communication is awful. Both these feelings are fairly normal and you can at least draw comfort from that.

Most people believe that they're underpaid both by market standards and in relation to the effort they put in. They also believe that the gap between levels in the company is too great. This belief that they're poorly rewarded exists irrespective of how much people are actually paid, or indeed how hard they work. If you ask them why they don't leave, they tell you about loyalty to a small firm or perhaps, more flatteringly, loyalty to you.

Nearly all employees also believe that their boss knows a secret that directly affects them and that the boss isn't willing to divulge. This may be about restructuring, moving, merging or outsourcing. This phenomenon happens at all levels. The shop floor believes that supervisors have secrets; supervisors believe that managers withhold crucial information on plans that involve them; and the remaining managers know that the directors are planning their future in secret. So they become convinced that a communication problem exists in the organisation because no one tells them what is *really* going on.

You have to take all the information from your employees into consideration when sizing up the situation, and not just the results of one attitude survey.

HR-Survey (www.hr-survey.com) and Custom Insight (www.custom insight.com) provide fast, simple and easy-to-use software to carry out and analyse human resources surveys. They both have a range of sample surveys that you can see and try before you buy, which may just be enough to stimulate your thinking.

Introducing attitude surveys

John Huggett, a young and abrasive entrepreneur, moved south from Yorkshire and bought up a small but seriously troubled engineering factory. The company employed 22 people and had shrunk over the years from more than 50. The business had suffered losses for over a year. But Huggett succeeded brilliantly in solving the problems that had built up over the years.

In the process, by his own admission, he came close to committing murder – telephone directories and occasionally the telephone itself flew through the air. Those in the organisation perceived John – not unnaturally given his style and the rescue job he was attempting – as a fire-eating monster. No one saw the human behind the gruff exterior.

At that time this didn't matter. However, as the factory moved into a period of growth and expansion, John recognised that he and the management team needed to make a conscious effort to change towards a more consensual style of management. People didn't feel empowered and they weren't about to stick their necks out when the blood still ran from the walls. John stood up in front of the workforce and said, 'We're going to have a different management style, and we're going to change.' He introduced an attitude survey to take the temperature of the water and committed himself, in advance of the survey, to live by its results.

He and the management team have done just that, introducing exceptionally effective team briefings, management walkabouts and other consultative mechanisms. The work force took time to be convinced, but they came greatly to respect John's integrity and open style.

Index

Notes

Notes

Notes

FOR DUMMIES®

Making Everything Easier!™

UK editions

BUSINESS

978-0-470-97626-5

978-0-470-97211-3

978-0-470-71119-4

REFERENCE

978-0-470-68637-9

978-0-470-97450-6

978-0-470-74535-9

HOBBIES

978-0-470-69960-7

978-0-470-68641-6

978-0-470-68178-7

Asperger's Syndrome For Dummies
978-0-470-66087-4

Boosting Self-Esteem For Dummies
978-0-470-74193-1

British Sign Language
For Dummies
978-0-470-69477-0

Coaching with NLP For Dummies
978-0-470-97226-7

Cricket For Dummies
978-0-470-03454-5

Diabetes For Dummies, 3rd Edition
978-0-470-97711-8

English Grammar For Dummies
978-0-470-05752-0

Flirting For Dummies
978-0-470-74259-4

Football For Dummies
978-0-470-68837-3

IBS For Dummies
978-0-470-51737-6

Improving Your Relationship
For Dummies
978-0-470-68472-6

Lean Six Sigma For Dummies
978-0-470-75626-3

Life Coaching For Dummies,
2nd Edition
978-0-470-66554-1

Management For Dummies,
2nd Edition
978-0-470-97769-9

Nutrition For Dummies, 2nd Edition
978-0-470-97276-2

FOR DUMMIES®

A world of resources to help you grow

UK editions

SELF–HELP

Cognitive Behavioural Therapy For Dummies
978-0-470-66541-1

Neuro-linguistic Programming For Dummies
978-0-470-66543-5

Mindfulness For Dummies
978-0-470-66086-7

STUDENTS

Philosophy For Dummies
978-0-470-68820-5

Student Cookbook For Dummies
978-0-470-74711-7

Sociology For Dummies
978-1-119-99134-2

HISTORY

The Tudors For Dummies
978-0-470-68792-5

Medieval History For Dummies
978-0-470-74783-4

British History For Dummies
978-0-470-97819-1

Origami Kit For Dummies
978-0-470-75857-1

Overcoming Depression For Dummies
978-0-470-69430-5

Positive Psychology For Dummies
978-0-470-72136-0

PRINCE2 For Dummies, 2009 Edition
978-0-470-71025-8

Psychometric Tests For Dummies
978-0-470-75366-8

Reading the Financial Pages For Dummies
978-0-470-71432-4

Rugby Union For Dummies, 3rd Edition
978-1-119-99092-5

Sage 50 Accounts For Dummies
978-0-470-71558-1

Self-Hypnosis For Dummies
978-0-470-66073-7

Starting a Business For Dummies, 2nd Edition
978-0-470-51806-9

Study Skills For Dummies
978-0-470-74047-7

Teaching English as a Foreign Language For Dummies
978-0-470-74576-2

Time Management For Dummies
978-0-470-77765-7

Training Your Brain For Dummies
978-0-470-97449-0

Work-Life Balance For Dummies
978-0-470-71380-8

Writing a Dissertation For Dummies
978-0-470-74270-9

FOR DUMMIES®

The easy way to get more done and have more fun

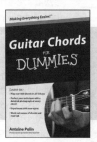

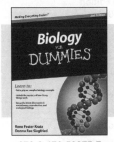
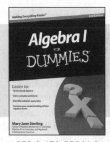

FOR DUMMIES®

Helping you expand your horizons and achieve your potential

COMPUTER BASICS

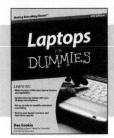

978-0-470-57829-2

978-0-470-46542-4

978-0-470-49743-2

DIGITAL PHOTOGRAPHY

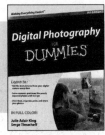

978-0-470-25074-7

978-0-470-76878-5

978-0-470-59591-6

MICROSOFT OFFICE 2010

978-0-470-48998-7

978-0-470-58302-9

978-0-470-48953-6

Access 2010 For Dummies
978-0-470-49747-0

Android Application Development
For Dummies
978-0-470-77018-4

AutoCAD 2011 For Dummies
978-0-470-59539-8

C++ For Dummies, 6th Edition
978-0-470-31726-6

Computers For Seniors For Dummies,
2nd Edition
978-0-470-53483-0

Dreamweaver CS5 For Dummies
978-0-470-61076-3

Green IT For Dummies
978-0-470-38688-0

iPad All-in-One For Dummies
978-0-470-92867-7

Macs For Dummies, 11th Edition
978-0-470-87868-2

Mac OS X Snow Leopard For Dummies
978-0-470-43543-4

Photoshop CS5 For Dummies
978-0-470-61078-7

Photoshop Elements 9 For Dummies
978-0-470-87872-9

Search Engine Optimization
For Dummies, 4th Edition
978-0-470-88104-0

The Internet For Dummies,
12th Edition
978-0-470-56095-2

Visual Studio 2010 All-In-One
For Dummies
978-0-470-53943-9

Web Analytics For Dummies
978-0-470-09824-0

Word 2010 For Dummies
978-0-470-48772-3